W9-DAS-053

THE
NEW
AMERICAN
NATION
1775–1820

*A Twelve-Volume
Collection of Articles
on the Development
of the Early American
Republic*

Edited by

PETER S. ONUF
UNIVERSITY OF VIRGINIA

A GARLAND SERIES

THE NEW AMERICAN NATION
1775–1820

Volume
12
★

AMERICAN CULTURE 1776–1815

Edited with an
Introduction by

PETER S. ONUF

GARLAND PUBLISHING, INC.
NEW YORK & LONDON
1991

Introduction © 1991 by Peter S. Onuf

Library of Congress Cataloging-in-Publication Data

American culture, 1776–1815 / edited with an introduction by Peter S. Onuf.
   p.   cm. — (New American nation, 1776–1815 ; v. 12)
   Includes bibliographical references.
   ISBN 0-8153-0447-1 (alk. paper) : $49.99
   1. United States—Civilization—1783–1848. 2. United States—Civilization—To 1783. I. Onuf, Peter S. II. Series.
   E164.N45   1991 vol. 12
   973—dc20   91-15465
             CIP

Printed on acid-free, 250-year-life paper.
Manufactured in the United States of America

THE NEW AMERICAN NATION, 1775–1820

EDITOR'S INTRODUCTION

This series includes a representative selection of the most interesting and influential journal articles on revolutionary and early national America. My goal is to introduce readers to the wide range of topics that now engage scholarly attention. The essays in these volumes show that the revolutionary era was an extraordinarily complex "moment" when the broad outlines of national history first emerged. Yet if the "common cause" brought Americans together, it also drove them apart: the Revolution, historians agree, was as much a civil war as a war of national liberation. And, given the distinctive colonial histories of the original members of the American Union, it is not surprising that the war had profoundly different effects in different parts of the country. This series has been designed to reveal the multiplicity of these experiences in a period of radical political and social change.

Most of the essays collected here were first published within the last twenty years. This series therefore does *not* recapitulate the development of the historiography of the Revolution. Many of the questions asked by earlier generations of scholars now seem misconceived and simplistic. Constitutional historians wanted to know if the Patriots had legitimate grounds to revolt: was the Revolution "legal"? Economic historians sought to assess the costs of the navigation system for American farmers and merchants and to identify the interest groups that promoted resistance. Comparative historians wondered how "revolutionary" the Revolution really was. By and large, the best recent work has ignored these classic questions. Contemporary scholarship instead draws its inspiration from other sources, most notable of which is the far-ranging reconception and reconstruction of prerevolutionary America by a brilliant generation of colonial historians.

Bernard Bailyn's *Ideological Origins of the American Revolution* (1967) was a landmark in the new historical writing on colonial politics. As his title suggests, Bailyn was less interested in constitutional and legal arguments as such than in the "ideology" or political language that shaped colonists' perception of and responses to British imperial policy. Bailyn's great contribution was to focus attention on colonial political culture; disciples and critics alike followed his lead as they explored the impact—and limits—of "republicanism" in specific colonial settings. Meanwhile, the social historians who had played a leading role in the transformation of colonial historiography were extending their work into the late colonial period and were increasingly interested in the questions of value, meaning, and behavior that were raised by the new political history. The resulting convergence points to some of the unifying themes in recent work on the revolutionary period presented in this series.

A thorough grounding in the new scholarship on colonial British America is the best introduction to the history and historiography of the Revolution. These volumes therefore can be seen as a complement and extension of Peter Charles Hoffer's eighteen-volume set, *Early American History*, published by Garland in 1987. Hoffer's collection includes numerous important essays essential for understanding developments in independent America. Indeed, only a generation ago—when the Revolution generally was defined in terms of its colonial origins—it would have been hard to justify a separate series on the "new American nation." But exciting recent work—for instance, on wartime mobilization and social change, or on the Americanization of republican ideology during the great era of state making and constitution writing—has opened up new vistas. Historians now generally agree that the revolutionary period saw far-reaching and profound changes, that is, a "great transformation," toward a more recognizably modern America. If the connections between this transformation and the actual unfolding of events often remain elusive, the historiographical quest for the larger meaning of the war and its aftermath has yielded impressive results.

To an important extent, the revitalization of scholarship on revolutionary and early national America is a tribute to the efforts and expertise of scholars working in other professional disciplines. Students of early American literature have made key contributions to the history of rhetoric, ideology, and culture; political scientists and legal scholars have brought new clarity and sophistication to the study of political and constitutional thought and practice in the founding period. Kermit L. Hall's superb Garland series, *United States Constitutional and Legal History* (20 volumes, 1985), is another fine resource for students and scholars interested in the founding. The sampling of recent work in various disciplines offered in these volumes gives a sense of the interpretative possibilities of a crucial period in American history that is now getting the kind of attention it has long deserved.

Peter S. Onuf

INTRODUCTION

Independent America long remained in the cultural thrall of the British metropolis. Though cultural nationalists asserted the need for a new American literature and proclaimed the distinctive virtues of American English, Americans continued to read English books and ape English fashions. The absence of a leisured aristocracy deprived aspiring artists and writers of the audiences and patronage that sustained high culture in Britain. And despite—or perhaps because of—their cultural subservience, provincial Americans righteously resisted the corrupting influence of novel reading, theaters, and other manifestations of Old World decadence.

Literary historians traditionally have moved quickly through the Revolutionary and early national periods, with condescending nods at the Connecticut Wits and novelist Charles Brockden Brown, and with an expectant eye toward the achievements of Hawthorne, Melville, Emerson, and other writers of the American Renaissance. More recently, however, historians have given up the futile search for great writers to study the conditions of artistic production and consumption in the new nation. Their challenge has been to illuminate American culture before the advent of a literary marketplace provided a substitute for aristocratic patronage.

The influence of Bernard Bailyn, whose *The Ideological Origins of the American Revolution* (1967) established the importance of a popular pamphlet literature in the radical transformation of colonial political thought, is again noteworthy. Patriot polemicists may have produced crude imitations of Augustan literary forms, but they successfully engaged a growing readership in a widely literate society. For Bailyn the adaptation of borrowed forms and themes to local conditions—and the way readers responded to them—revolutionized American political culture. If the Revolution was, in some sense, a literary event, then new governments at the state and federal levels were constructed and legitimated by acts of writing and reading. Written constitutions, as Michael Warner and Robert Ferguson suggest, were distinctively American "literary texts."

From the perspective of the new literary history, Revolutionary and early national culture no longer looks like the provincial wasteland described by earlier scholars—or by ambitious and frustrated contemporaries. Important ideological work was in progress on various fronts. Feminist scholars such as Ruth Bloch and Jan Lewis have shown how the constitution of new governments was accompanied by the republican reconstitution of gender and family relations. Just as Patriot pamphleteers appropriated and transformed British political writing, American writers and readers sought to make sense of rapid social change through fiction, belles lettres, and didactic literature. Jay Fliegelman's *Prodigals and Pilgrims* (1982) offers an excellent analysis of this fascinating literature, demonstrating the many ways in which these often ephemeral cultural expressions addressed prevalent social anxieties.

Revolutionary Americans may have been the "pragmatists" depicted by Daniel Boorstin in *The Americans: The National Experience* (1965), with little interest in abstract ideas or esthetics. But the more visionary Revolutionaries believed that their republican society would transcend the conventional, aristocratic distinction between the arts and sciences and the business of everyday life. A well-informed, enterprising citizenry would construct a better, "improved," and therefore more beautiful world. If such pretensions seemed ludicrously exaggerated to genteel Britons—and Americans—they inspired a proliferation of new institutions and associations for scientific, educational, and philanthropic purposes. Because state governments failed to take a leading role in these enterprises, most notably in supporting public education, this new republican culture was by necessity the creation of a multitude of private initiatives.

The vitality of early American culture was apparent in the democratization of religious life, a boisterous partisan press, and the uninhibited pursuit of personal and social "improvement." From a traditional perspective, such developments signified the decline of authority and incipient anarchy. But as Alexis de Tocqueville would later argue in *Democracy in America,* centrifugal tendencies in this new society were countered by powerful countervailing and homogenizing forces. The principle of equality and an ethos of conformism provided alternative sources of social order and stability to the hierarchical authority of the old regime. And racism, as de Tocqueville noted, established the new democracy's outer limits.

The master institution of the emerging social order was the marketplace. A culture dedicated to the pursuit of private profit was enormously liberating for the free white male property owners who could reap its benefits. But liberal culture exacted a toll, not only from the oppressed and excluded but also from the

chronically anxious and aspiring who dreamed of great wealth—
or who feared losing what they had.

Peter S. Onuf

ADDITIONAL READING

Bernard Bailyn. *The Ideological Origins of the American Revolution.*
Cambridge: Harvard University Press, 1967.
Daniel J. Boorstin. *The Americans: The National Experience.* New York:
Random House, 1965.
Richard D. Brown. *Knowledge Is Power: The Diffusion of Information in
Early America, 1700–1865.* New York: Oxford University Press, 1989.
Emory Elliott. *Revolutionary Writers: Literature and Authority in the New
Republic, 1725–1810.* New York: Oxford University Press, 1982.
Robert A. Ferguson. *Law and Letters in American Culture.* Cambridge:
Harvard University Press, 1984.
Jay Fliegelman. *Prodigals and Pilgrims: The American Revolution Against
Patriarchal Authority, 1750–1800.* New York: Cambridge University
Press, 1982.
John C. Greene. *American Science in the Age of Jefferson.* Ames: Iowa State
University Press, 1984.
Karl F. Kaestle. *Pillars of the Republic: Common Schools and American
Society, 1780–1860.* New York: Hill and Wang, 1983.
Kenneth Silverman. *A Cultural History of the American Revolution: Paint-
ing, Music, Literature, and the Theatre in the Colonies and the United
States from the Treaty of Paris to the Inauguration of George Washing-
ton, 1763–1789.* New York: T. Y. Crowell, 1976.
Alexis de Tocqueville. *Democracy in America.* 2 vols. Phillips Bradley,
trans. New York: Alfred A. Knopf, 1945.
Michael Warner. *The Letters of the Republic: Publication and the Public
Sphere in Eighteenth-Century America.* Cambridge: Harvard University Press, 1990.

CONTENTS

Volume 12—American Culture, 1776–1815

Lee I. Schreiber, "The Changing Social Climate, 1790–1810 and the Pennsylvania Academy of the Fine Arts," *Journal of American Culture*, 1979, 2(3): 361–375.

Sidney Hart and David C. Ward, "The Waning of an Enlightenment Ideal: Charles Willson Peale's Philadelphia Museum, 1790–1820," *Journal of the Early Republic*, 1988, 8:389–418.

David W. Robson, "College Founding in the New Republic, 1776–1800," *History of Education Quarterly*, 1983, 23:323–341.

Neil McDowell Shawen, "Thomas Jefferson and a 'National' University: The Hidden Agenda for Virginia," *Virginia Magazine of History and Biography*, 1984, 92(3):309–335.

M. J. Heale, "Humanitarianism in the Early Republic: The Moral Reformers of New York, 1776–1825," *Journal of American Studies*, 1968, 2(2):161–175.

Shane White, "A Question of Style: Blacks in and around New York City in the Late 18th Century," *Journal of American Folklore*, 1989, 102:23–44.

Nathan O. Hatch, "The Christian Movement and the Demand for a Theology of the People," *Journal of American History* , 1980, 67(3):545–567.

Shomer S. Zwelling, "Robert Carter's Journey: From Colonial Patriarch to New Nation Mystic," *American Quarterly*, 1986, 38(4):613–636.

Alan Taylor, "The Early Republic's Supernatural Economy: Treasure Seeking in the American Northeast, 1780–1830," *American Quarterly*, 1986, 38(1):6–34.

ACKNOWLEDGMENTS

Volume 12—American Culture, 1776–1815

David Lundberg and Henry F. May, "The Enlightened Reader in America," *American Quarterly*, 1976, 28(2):262–293. Reprinted with the permission of the author, and the American Studies Association as publisher. Courtesy of Yale University Sterling Memorial Library.

Lester H. Cohen, "Eden's Constitution: The Paradisiacal Dream and Enlightenment Values in Late–Eighteenth–Century Literature on the American Frontier," *Prospects*, 1977, 3:83–109. Reprinted with the permission of the Cambridge University Press. Courtesy of Yale University Sterling Memorial Library.

Michael T. Gilmore, "Eulogy as Symbolic Biography: The Iconography of Revolutionary Leadership, 1776–1826," *Harvard English Studies*, 1978, 8:131–157. Reprinted with the permission of the Harvard University Press, by the President and Fellows of Harvard College. Courtesy of Yale University Sterling Memorial Library.

Robert Ferguson, "'Mysterious Obligation': Jefferson's Notes on the State of Virginia," *American Literature*, 1980, 52:381–406. Reprinted with the permission of Duke University Press. Courtesy of Duke University Press.

Harold Hellenbrand, "Roads to Happiness: Rhetorical and Philosophical Design in Jefferson's Notes on the State of Virginia," *Early American Literature*, 1985, 20(1):3–23. Reprinted with the permission of North Carolina Press. Courtesy of Yale University Sterling Memorial Library.

Cathy N. Davidson, "Female Authorship and Authority: The Case of Sukey Vickery," *Early American Literature*, 1986, 21(1):4–28. Reprinted with the permission of North Carolina Press. Courtesy of Yale University Sterling Memorial Library.

Jan Lewis, "The Republican Wife: Virtue and Seduction in the Early Republic," *William and Mary Quarterly*, 1987, 44(4) (Third Series):689–721. Originally appeared in *William and Mary Quarterly*. Courtesy of Yale University Sterling Memorial Library.

Ruth H. Bloch, "American Feminine Ideals in Transition: The Rise of the Moral Mother, 1785–1815," *Feminist Studies*, 1978, 4:101–126. Reprinted with the permission of the publisher, Feminist Studies, Inc., c/o Women's Studies Program, University of Maryland, College Par, MD 20742. Courtesy of Feminist Studies.

Richard M. Rollins, "Words as Social Control: Noah Webster and the Creation of the *American Dictionary*," *American Quarterly*, 1976, 28(4):415–430. Reprinted with the permission of the author, and the American Studies Association as publisher. Courtesy of Yale University Sterling Memorial Library.

Patricia Cline Cohen, "Statistics and the State: Changing Social Thought and the Emergence of a Quantitative Mentality in America, 1790 to 1820," *William and Mary Quarterly*, 1981, 38(1) (Third Series):35–55. Originally appeared in the *William and Mary Quarterly*. Courtesy of Yale University Sterling Memorial Library.

Darwin H. Stapleton and Edward C. Carter II, "'I Have the Itch of Botany, of Chemistry, of Mathematics . . . Strong upon Me': The Science of Benjamin Henry Latrobe," *Proceedings of the American Philosophical Society*, 1984, 128(3):173–192. Reprinted with the permission of the American Philosophical Society. Courtesy of the American Philosophical Society.

Lee I. Schreiber, "The Changing Social Climate, 1790–1810 and the Pennsylvania Academy of the Fine Arts," *Journal of American Culture*, 1979, 2(3):361–375. Reprinted with the permission of the The Popular Press. Courtesy of the *Journal of American Culture*.

Sidney Hart and David C. Ward, "The Waning of an Enlightenment Ideal: Charles Willson Peale's Philadelphia Museum, 1790–1820," *Journal of the Early Republic*, 1988, 8:389–418. Reprinted with the permission of Indiana University, Department of History. Courtesy of Yale University Sterling Memorial Library.

David W. Robson, "College Founding in the New Republic, 1776–1800," *History of Education Quarterly*, 1983, 23:323–341. Previously published in the *History of Education Quarterly*. Courtesy of Yale University Sterling Memorial Library.

Neil McDowell Shawen, "Thomas Jefferson and a 'National' University: The Hidden Agenda for Virginia," *Virginia Magazine of History and Biography*, 1984, 92(3):309–335. Reprinted with the permission of the Virginia Historical Society. Courtesy of Yale University Sterling Memorial Library.

M. J. Heale, "Humanitarianism in the Early Republic: The Moral Reformers of New York, 1776–1825," *Journal of American Studies*, 1968, 2(2):161–175. Reprinted with the permission of Cambridge University Press. Courtesy of Yale University Sterling Memorial Library.

Shane White, "A Question of Style: Blacks in and around New York City in the Late 18th Century," *Journal of American Folklore*, 1989, 102:23–44. Reproduced by permission of the American Folklore Society. Not for further reproduction. Courtesy of Yale University Sterling Memorial Library.

Nathan O. Hatch, "The Christian Movement and the Demand for a Theology of the People," *Journal of American History*, 1980, 67(3):545–567. Reprinted with the permission of the *Journal of American History*. Courtesy of Yale University Sterling Memorial Library.

Shomer S. Zwelling, "Robert Carter's Journey: From Colonial Patriarch to New Nation Mystic," *American Quarterly*, 1986, 38(4):613–636. Reprinted with the permission of the author, and the American Studies Association as publisher. Courtesy of Yale University Sterling Memorial Library.

Alan Taylor, "The Early Republic's Supernatural Economy: Treasure Seeking in the American Northeast, 1780–1830," *American Quarterly*,

1986, 38(1):6–34. Reprinted with the permission of the author, and the American Studies Association as publisher. Courtesy of Yale University Sterling Memorial Library.

THE ENLIGHTENED READER
IN AMERICA

DAVID LUNDBERG AND HENRY F. MAY
University of California, Berkeley

THIS ARTICLE IS A BRIEF PRELIMINARY REPORT ON THE AUTHORS' ATTEMPT
to develop statistical information on the reception in America of certain
major authors of the European Enlightenment. We hope that what we have
to say, both here and later in fuller form, may serve to refine and criticize
some generalizations about the transmission of enlightened ideas. We hope
also that other historians may be interested in developing further, and using
for their own purposes, some of the data we have accumulated.

The categories used emerged directly from Henry May's work on the
Enlightenment in America. Historians of this subject have made a great
many statements about the spread of enlightened ideas, many simply assuming that these were very widely accepted and others concluding from their
studies that they did not spread beyond a few especially well read people. It
seemed that some study of the actual availability of European books might
help, along with many other kinds of evidence, to give some substance to a
discussion of this problem. It also became apparent that the same people,
and the same kinds of people, seemed unlikely to have been attracted by
cautious spokesmen of moderation like Locke, politically conservative sceptics like Gibbon, and prophets of utopian change like Godwin. What seemed
necessary was to develop a method of finding out, as nearly as possible,
which books were most often read, when, and where.

At the time we began working, a number of monographs of varying quality
had dealt with the popularity of various authors. Articles on the contents of
particular libraries existed, as well as a few studies of libraries in single
colonies or states. Yet no general quantitative survey of the whole country
had been attempted. At present it is clear that the history of eighteenth-
century books, publishing, and popular taste is much more highly developed
among historians of Europe than among Americanists.[1] Yet in some ways,

---

[1] Useful summaries in English of these French developments can be found in two articles by
Robert Darnton, "In Search of the Enlightenment: Recent Attempts to Create a Social History
of Ideas," *Journal of Modern History*, 43 (1971), 113–132; and "Reading, Writing, and Publishing in Eighteenth-Century France: A Case Study in the Sociology of Literature," *Daedalus*, 100
(1971–2), 214–256.

for research into reading habits as for other kinds of quantitative research, early America offers great advantages. Unlike France, eighteenth-century America presents no major problems arising from literary censorship or clandestinity. The scale is much smaller than for the major European countries, and most known libraries are public rather than private.

David Lundberg suggested starting with the very considerable number of booksellers' lists, sales catalogues, etc., which are available in that great mainstay of early American historians, Charles Evans' *American Bibliography*.[2] For the period after 1800, the sequel to Evans, Ralph R. Shaw and Richard H. Shoemaker, *American Bibliography*, was similarly used. Shaw and Shoemaker's listings are less complete than Evans'. They are at present mostly available on microcard up to the year 1813. To supplement these two basic collections, a number of other sources have been used, especially in an effort to give due representation to the South. Because the great bulk of bookselling, as of publishing, took place from Philadelphia northward, this last effort has not been completely successful. Of our 291 libraries, 36 are in the South. Of this number, 20 were in private hands.

The collections checked include booksellers' auction or sale catalogues, college or other institutional libraries, circulating libraries, library companies or societies, and private libraries. (We hereafter use the word "libraries" to include all these.) It should be noted that our total does not represent 291 separate libraries, but rather, in some 44 instances, revised library catalogues (usually those put out by colleges or library companies) to which new books were added. The New York Society Library, for example, issued 9 catalogues between 1758 and 1813, each greatly expanded over the one which preceded it. In such cases we avoided duplication by recording only the initial appearance of a title. The libraries show great diversity. Some are large and comprehensive, like the Philadelphia Library Company. Others, such as the Friends Library or the Pennsylvania Hospital Library, are small or specialized. Thus the listings do not have equal weight. Obviously the presence of a book in a private library may reflect only an eccentric individual taste, while its presence in a college library may mean that it was available to a considerable number of students over a long time. Booksellers' catalogues, by far our most numerous category, suggest the kinds of books which enterprising businessmen thought most likely to be in demand. Of all our libraries, more than two-thirds were open to the public.[3]

When published in full, our data will make it easy for the reader to see how many copies of a given book were to be found in each sort of library, and in each colony, state, or region. For the present article, for reasons of space,

[2]Clifford K. Shipton and James E. Mooney, eds., *The Short-Title Evans* (2 vols; Worcester, Mass.: American Antiquarian Society, 1969) proved a useful supplement to Evans' original work.

[3]The numerical breakdown is as follows: 150 booksellers' catalogues; 35 institutional libraries; 13 circulating libraries; 69 library companies; 24 private libraries.

we are limiting ourselves to presenting national percentages. We have noted the numbers of editions published in America, and it will be evident that in certain instances (Pope's *Essay on Man*, works by Paine, tracts by Philip Doddridge or Hannah More) editions far outrun copies in libraries. We think that this usually indicates that an item was published in pamphlet form. Such pamphlets were not attractive to booksellers or collectors, but were probably sold by peddlers or spread in other informal ways. Thus in the cases of these special items, American editions may indicate even greater popularity than library copies, and the two taken together will surely give us more information than either alone.

We are not attempting to determine which were absolutely the most popular books in America, but rather to find out which were the most popular among a selected list. We have not dealt, for instance, with the extremely popular works of novelists like Samuel Richardson, Laurence Sterne, or Tobias Smollett. The list of books to be checked, the intellectual categories in which they are arranged, and the chronological periods are those which seemed to be the most relevant for a study of the spread of the European Enlightenment in America.

The number of libraries we have found is different for each chronological period. (The small number of libraries we were able to find for the revolutionary period makes our conclusions for that period less valuable than they are for the periods before and after.) For each of the other three periods, we have a reasonable sample, but differences in the total numbers of libraries should constantly be borne in mind.[4] To make this easier, our graphs show percentages of the total number of libraries in each period in which each book appeared. Absolute numbers of appearances are also given.

Finally, we have not attempted to include the books published serially or excerpted in newspapers. This method of publication undoubtedly accounted for the spread of many enlightened works—particularly political works—in America. Still less does this data tell us what sort of ideas spread orally, in unpublished sermons or speeches, or simply by hearsay. Even among the books listed, we may assume that some, by their nature, were read more intensively than others and had a deeper and more lasting effect.

Despite all these limitations, we think this comparative examination of all the libraries of all kinds that we could find will say something about the *relative* popularity and availability of various authors and types of authors within each of four periods. Provided one makes due allowances for the varying length of these periods and the different numbers of libraries examined in each period, we think one can gather from our data some interesting sugges-

[4] We have eliminated twenty libraries of those which we have located on the ground that they contained none of the books we were checking. Most of these collections were highly specialized.

tions about the rise and fall over time in the popularity of particular authors and types of authors. One can also see how much time elapsed, usually very little, between the publication of particular authors in Europe and their availability in America. With all due caution, we think the data allow some valid inferences about what kind of books Americans did and did not like, and (perhaps more clearly) what kinds of books enterprising booksellers thought would or would not sell. Moreover, the inferences we make are usually confirmed by other and more fragmentary kinds of evidence, for instance contemporary statements about the vogue of particular authors, or statements suggesting that a reference to a given author is taken for granted in different sorts of discourse.

The categories used are, like all such categories, both arguable and overlapping. Some authors belong almost equally to more than one category. The first grouping, "The First Enlightenment," includes those authors who, following the Glorious Revolution and the Newtonian triumph, emphasized balance and moderation in all things, often balancing reason against revelation as a source of knowledge, reason against passion in their account of human nature, monarchy against aristocracy and democracy in their theory of government. Of these, that cautious part-way empiricist John Locke is obviously the great starting-point. The other philosophers we have included are Shaftesbury, Berkeley, Hutcheson and Hartley, all of whom were conciliatory and moderate in dealing with religion and morals. Of literary works we have selected Pope's *Essay on Man,* the most familiar and eloquent of all works written in defense of the balanced view, and several sample works of Addison, the great essayist of moderation. Of moderate divines we have selected Archbishop Tillotson, the major spokesman of latitudinarianism, and Samuel Clarke, the principal theologian of moderate Arianism. Most of the works in this category are by Englishmen, but we have also included the eclectic and judicious Montesquieu and also Vattel and Burlamaqui, two continental theorists of natural law who kept religion and reason in balance in their dealings with that subject.

The second category, "English Deists," consists mainly of those deists who took part in the celebrated polemical argument with Christianity in the early part of the century. We have added Hobbes, the early prophet of English materialism, and Mandeville, the foremost assailant of conventional morality. These last two seem to be part of the first major British challenge to Christian orthodoxy, and in this way related to the Deist offensive. Wollaston is a figure on the borderline between Deism and liberal Christianity.

The third category, "Commonwealth and Radical Whigs," draws on the list that has been made familiar to historians by the works of Caroline Robbins, Bernard Bailyn, and others. These include seventeenth-century republican theorists like Sidney and Harrington, and also those who later kept Radical Whiggery alive like Trenchard and Gordon, Burgh, or Catharine Macaulay.[5] We have placed Richard Price and Joseph Priestley here, since both were Dissenters who strongly sympathized with the American and French Revolutions. Rapin, the pro-Whig French historian of the Glorious Revolution, seems a reasonable addition. The very popular Charles Rollin is more doubtful. A French Jansenist who lost his chair for his views, he inculcated the moralistic and Protestant view of antiquity which forms part of the radical Whig theory of history.

The fourth category, "The Second Enlightenment," refers to the new varieties of scepticism and materialism, related to English Deism but going well beyond it, that developed on the Continent and primarily in Paris during the second half of the century, receiving their first major expression in the *Encyclopédie*. That work itself is not listed, since both expense and language precluded wide American circulation. For this category, and also for some of the others, translation is a crucial matter. Of the 291 libraries we have surveyed in all periods, only 26 include any books in French. Of these 26, 4 are specialized collections of French books for sale by immigrants from France. Of the borderline figures in this category, Bayle seems an obvious forerunner. Hume clearly belongs here rather than in the earlier English group, and we have placed Ferguson here because of the strong relativist and somewhat materialist drift of his works. Chesterfield, of course no theorist, is listed here because of the cynical and morally iconoclastic tenor of his writings.

"The Third Enlightenment" consists of those authors who looked for a sweeping and fundamental change in institutions, on the basis of a new and radical conception of human nature. Members of this group are different from the Commonwealthmen in being more secular and more future-oriented. They are also very different from men of the First or Second Enlightenment because of their idealistic and emotional idea of humanity. Obviously the great progenitor of this school, despite all his contradictions, is Rousseau. In addition to French theoretical radicals of the prerevolutionary and early revolutionary epoch like Mably or Condorcet, we have included the chief English radicals of the period during and after the upheaval in France. We have put Paine here, listing only his *Rights of Man* and *Age of Reason*. (Of his other major works, *Common Sense* and the *Crisis* papers seem to us rather American political works than specimens of the European

[5] John Toland, regarded by Franco Venturi as a prominent representative of Whig radicalism influential in England and America, seems rather to have been known in the colonies as a Deist, and for that reason seldom cited among radical authorities. He is listed here in category two. Cf. Venturi, *Utopia and Reform in the Enlightenment* (Cambridge: Cambridge Univ. Press, 1971).

Enlightenment.) Godwin and Wollstonecraft, on the other hand, clearly carry on from the work of radical theorists like Condorcet.

The fifth category consists entirely of the major spokesmen of Scottish Common Sense philosophy and closely related views. This variety of thought, similar in its moderation to the First Enlightenment, was formulated as a defense of the reliability of moral and rational judgment against Humean scepticism. Pressed into service in America in the battle against enlightened scepticism and radicalism, the Common Sense philosophy was forced into a more conservative mold than had been intended by any of its Scottish spokesmen except James Beattie.

Our sixth category consists of a few devotional writers and Christian apologists, selected from a larger number on whom we have data, for the purpose of serving as a control and suggesting the limits of enlightened thought. We have added one further category, "Romanticism," to indicate the beginning of that post-Enlightenment current of thought.

For our first period, eighteenth-century America before the Revolution, we have examined 92 libraries. Since only 18 of these are from the period before 1750, this really represents mid-century taste. During this period the First Enlightenment was obviously very strong, especially in the persons of Tillotson, Addison, and Locke. As much recent research has suggested, Locke's epistemological *Essay* was then and remained through all the periods surveyed far more widely read than his political *Two Treatises*. Important secondary figures of the First Enlightenment were Shaftesbury, Pope, Hutcheson and (if one takes all his works together) Clarke. The idealist Berkeley, the Christian quasi-materialist Hartley, and the two natural lawyers appear less often.

The Deists, who appear relatively seldom in this or any period, were apparently known more through anti-Deist tracts and sermons than directly. The most popular works are those which belong in this category barely if at all—the political writings of Bolingbroke, two of the more cautious works of Middleton, and Wollaston's moderate *Religion of Nature*.

Of the central figures of the Commonwealth school, Sidney is the most popular of the older works and Trenchard and Gordon of the newer, and only these come close in popularity to the best-liked authors of the Moderate Enlightenment. Harrington, despite John Adams' well-known admiration of him, figures in only six libraries. The two moralistic French historians, Rapin and Rollin, are far more popular than any of the political pamphleteers.

Of the representatives of the sceptical Second Enlightenment, Voltaire was and continued to be the most popular, but mainly for his relatively uncontroversial histories. His *English Letters* (ostensibly in praise of English moderation but really going beyond it in tendency) had considerable popu-

larity; his more obviously sceptical *Philosophical Dictionary* was only beginning to be read. Bayle, rather surprisingly, appears in 13 collections, well
distributed through the colonies. Hume's *History* and (mostly political and
economic) *Essays* are beginning their long popularity. His philosophical *Inquiry*, which Hume himself called the best and least noticed of his writings,
appears in only four libraries.

Of the idealistic and radical Third Enlightenment, the popularity of
Rousseau was only beginning, with his enticing *Émile* and *Héloïse* well ahead
of his political works. Many writers of this school had not yet appeared in
Europe. The long American popularity of the Scots in America was also only
beginning before the Revolution, despite the efforts of John Witherspoon. Of
this school, the most popular book was Adam Smith's work on moral
philosophy. Devotional and apologetic writers appear to have had a steady
rather than an overwhelming popularity except for the liberal Dissenter
Philip Doddridge, whose many sermons and tracts made him one of the most
popular writers of colonial (and also of revolutionary) America. Burke's
romantic or pre-romantic esthetic work appears in only six collections.

As a whole the taste of colonial America appears from our data to be standard and unexciting, with such moderates of various categories as Locke,
Tillotson, and Doddridge most prominent. Colonial preference was probably
pretty similar to English, except for the more prominent position accorded
to works representing Commonwealth and Dissenting authors.

Our second period, Revolutionary and postwar America, represents for
obvious reasons something of a hiatus in colonial importation, sale, and
collection of European books. This period is represented by only 29 libraries,
less than a third of those used for the long previous period. With this
difference borne in mind, a few trends can be noticed. Of the First Enlightenment authors, Locke is found in proportionately more libraries, with his
Essay still more than twice as common as his *Two Treatises* despite the connection between the *Second Treatise* and the Declaration of Independence.
Montesquieu gains in popularity, and Pope's *Essay* is reprinted eleven times.
The popularity of the Deists, never great, shows minor fluctuations for individual authors with no significant change for the group as a whole.

Our data show little increase—in fact a slight proportional loss—in the
popularity of most of the older Commonwealth writers. Rollin remains
popular. Of the later Radical Whigs Price, Priestley, Burgh, and Catharine
Macaulay all make some impact but none of these seems spectacularly
popular according to our limited data. One of Price's works is much reprinted.

Of the sceptical Enlightenment Voltaire holds his popularity. Hume's *History*, despite its alleged Tory tendencies, is far more popular than the
radically Whig histories by Rapin and Macaulay (one remembers Jefferson's
distress at this fact). Two newcomers make a considerable impact despite

wartime conditions. Gibbon's *Decline and Fall* finds its way into 11 American libraries despite its author's Toryism and scepticism, and Chesterfield's works are an immediate and major hit despite his aristocratic cynicism. Of the idealistic and radical Enlightenment, Rousseau's novels continue to be read and his *Confessions* appears in six libraries. Beccaria gains sharply and Raynal, a very readable writer who deals with American subjects, begins his very considerable American popularity. There is a sharp growth in the popularity of the Scots, especially Kames, Reid, Smith (for the new *Wealth of Nations* as well as the *Moral Sentiments*). A new writer, Hugh Blair, achieves immediate and striking popularity. Of devotional writers, Doddridge holds firm and two new apologists, William Paley and (especially) Hannah More are read and reprinted.

The most striking fact about this period seems to be the small extent to which American taste for *European* reading seems to have been affected by the struggle over the Revolution and the Constitution. Among new works Gibbon, Chesterfield, and Blair run well ahead of Burgh and Macaulay. Older staples of various non-political kinds—Locke's *Essay*, Rollin's and Hume's histories—retain their popularity. Pope's *Essay* is the most frequently reprinted work on our list. Of political works, the moderate Montesquieu and the idealistic Beccaria appear most often in our libraries. Of course one must remember here the immense part played in the revolutionary argument by American propaganda, which undoubtedly drew many Americans away from reading European books. Perhaps those Americans who bought or collected European works during these years of intense struggle wanted either solid and traditional works for reassurance, or entertaining new authors for escape.

With our third period, the 1790s, it is not surprising to find both the burgeoning of libraries (119 recorded) and the overwhelmingly clear impact of ideological struggle. Of the authors of the First Enlightenment, Locke and Pope remain popular; Addison, Montesquieu, and Hutcheson decline only slightly, and Burlamaqui scores very sharp gains. The Deists are read proportionately even less than before the Revolution, their places having been taken by newer kinds of iconoclasts. In an analogous fashion, Commonwealth radicalism seems to have given place to the more up-to-date radicalism associated with the French Revolution. Sidney, Rapin, Hoadley, Trenchard and Gordon, and Macaulay decline. Burgh gains sharply, and Price and Priestley come into wide popularity, but it should be noted that each of these authors is represented on our lists for this period mainly by his least political or controversial works (Burgh's *Human Nature,* Price's *Sermons,* and Priestley's moralistic and conventional *Lectures on History*). Of the sceptical writers, Voltaire is very popular and his outspoken *Philosophical Dictionary* makes a noticeable gain. Hume's *History* and *Essays* are very much in demand, and his daringly anti-religious *Dialogues* now oc-

9

cur in 15 libraries and are once reprinted in America. Gibbon and Chesterfield continue their immense popularity, and the severely materialist Helvétius makes a surprising showing. Diderot, d'Alembert, and Holbach seem
to be almost unknown.

The most startling fact about this period is the sweeping gains scored by
two opposite groups of authors, the writers of the radical Third Enlightenment and the conservative Common Sense Scots. Rousseau is much more
popular than before the Revolution. In comparison with the revolutionary
period itself, in the 1790s his *Social Contract* gains, while *Émile* loses. His
Confessions (surely disturbing to morally conservative Americans) occurs in
33 libraries and is reprinted once. Beccaria, Raynal, Volney and Condorcet
are all major successes and Paine of course very often reprinted. Perhaps
more surprisingly, Godwin and especially Wollstonecraft become very familiar entries.

The Scots, drawn on by anti-sceptical and anti-radical Americans in this
period, appear in libraries in enormous volume, especially Kames, Smith,
Beattie, and Blair. Reid, whose views were conquering American college
teaching, appears often for a demanding and unsensational philosopher. Of
the Christian apologists, also heavily used by the opponents of the more
radical forms of Enlightenment, Butler, Doddridge, and Paley are very
prominent, and Hannah More's tracts are frequently reprinted. Burke is
read both as an anti-revolutionary and an esthetician. Between the most
popular radicals and the most popular conservatives there seems to have
been something like a standoff battle for popularity, with the latter obtaining
a slight edge. Perhaps more surprising is the showing made by some
genuinely sceptical and radical authors, including Helvétius, Wollstonecraft,
and Godwin as well as Paine.

We regret greatly that our sample of our fourth period, the beginning of
the nineteenth century, is again a much smaller one (51 collections). This
does not mean that fewer booksellers or collectors existed. It reflects rather
the deficiencies of the major compilation available, Shaw and Shoemaker, as
against Evans. A few tentative comparisons can be made, taking account of
the very sharply smaller sample available. Of the by now old-fashioned First
Enlightenment, Locke's *Essay* is much reprinted (probably for college use)
and such writers as Shaftesbury, Clarke, Addison, and Pope hold their own.
Of the Commonwealth school, Sidney, Burgh, and Macaulay increase or
hold their own. Priestley's *Lectures* continue popular, while his controversial
religious works are sold and reprinted much less often than in the previous
period. Of the sceptics Voltaire, Hume, Ferguson, Gibbon, and Chesterfield
continue to be read; d'Alembert, Diderot, and Holbach continue almost unknown.

The writers of the radical Enlightenment continue to be read more than
one might have guessed. Most of Rousseau, as well as Beccaria, Condorcet,

Raynal, Paine, and Godwin more or less hold their own, and Volney gains sharply. On the other hand, Rousseau's *Confessions* disappears, and Wollstonecraft's *Rights of Women* declines relatively. It seems that the anti-radical crusade of Jedidiah Morse and others failed to halt the reading of most radicals. It may, like the anti-Deist tracts of the mid-eighteenth century, have given publicity to the authors being attacked.

The real triumph of moral and religious conservatism is shown by the great popularity of the Scottish moralists (used in America for conservative purposes) and the Christian apologists. The Scots, the staple of American education in this period, hold onto their sharp gains of the previous period and some crucial books, including Reid's *Enquiry* and Smith's *Wealth of Nations*, reach new heights. Of the religious apologists in this period of religious revival, Butler and Doddridge hold their popularity in libraries while that of Paley, More, and Wilberforce gain very strikingly. Doddridge, More, and Paley are constantly reprinted. Booksellers' lists demonstrate the well-known fact that the romantic poets attracted American readers very slowly, though Scott is frequently reprinted.

* * *

From this brief survey a few tentative conclusions may be ventured. First, it seems clear that Americans were exposed to all the major currents of the eighteenth-century French and British Enlightenment except perhaps for the extremes of French materialism, though Helvétius was not unknown. Second, our data corroborate the dramatic story of the sharp rise of enlightened radicalism—or at least of interest in enlightened radicalism—in the period of the French Revolution, of the countervailing power of the Scottish Common Sense realists and of Christian apologists through that period, and of the relative triumph of these last two groups over their radical opponents after 1800. One notices also the continuing hold in America, throughout the century and after, of such traditional, sedate, and respectable works as Locke's *Essay,* Rollin's *Ancient History,* and the critical works of Lord Kames. It is more surprising to discover the great popularity among American republicans and Protestants of such monarchical historians as Hume and Voltaire, and of such religious and moral sceptics as Gibbon and Chesterfield. This suggests that in the eighteenth century a "correct and graceful style" could weigh heavily even in conjunction with deplorable opinions.*

*Thanks are due to the Social Science Research Fund and the Margaret Byrne Chair Funds of the University of California, Berkeley, which have supported research by David Lundberg on which this article is based.

11

THE ENLIGHTENED READER IN AMERICA: 1700 to 1813

The first four bars show the percentages of libraries in each period in which each book appeared in each time period. The fifth bar indicates the percentage of the total number of libraries, in all periods, in which each book appears. Absolute numbers of appearances in each period are listed, in chronological order, below each title. After a colon, following the titles, are the dates of initial publication and of any English translations.

Graph Code

FIRST PERIOD, 1700 to 1776: 92 Libraries

SECOND PERIOD, 1777 to 1790: 29 Libraries

THIRD PERIOD, 1791 to 1800: 119 Libraries

FOURTH PERIOD, 1801 to 1813: 51 Libraries

CUMULATIVE TOTAL FOR ALL FOUR PERIODS: 291 Libraries

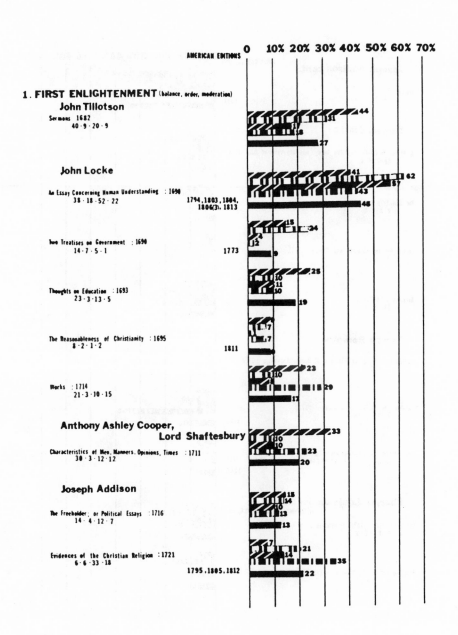

1. FIRST ENLIGHTENMENT (balance, order, moderation)

John Tillotson
Sermons 1682
40 · 9 · 20 · 9

John Locke

An Essay Concerning Human Understanding : 1690
38 · 18 · 52 · 22
1794, 1803, 1804, 1806(3), 1813

Two Treatises on Government : 1690
14 · 7 · 5 · 1
1773

Thoughts on Education : 1693
23 · 3 · 13 · 5

The Reasonableness of Christianity : 1695
8 · 2 · 1 · 2
1811

Works : 1714
21 · 3 · 10 · 15

**Anthony Ashley Cooper,
Lord Shaftesbury**
Characteristics of Men, Manners, Opinions, Times : 1711
30 · 3 · 12 · 12

Joseph Addison

The Freeholder; or Political Essays : 1716
14 · 4 · 12 · 7

Evidences of the Christian Religion : 1721
6 · 6 · 33 · 18
1795, 1805, 1812

13

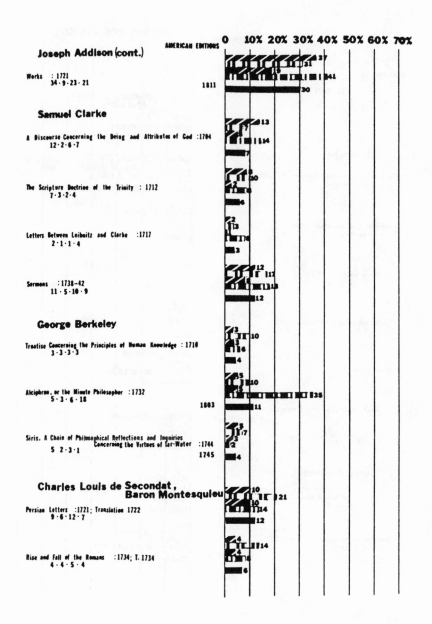

Joseph Addison (cont.)

Works : 1721
34 · 9 · 23 · 21
1811

Samuel Clarke

A Discourse Concerning the Being and Attributes of God : 1704
12 · 2 · 6 · 7

The Scripture Doctrine of the Trinity : 1712
7 · 3 · 2 · 4

Letters Between Leibnitz and Clarke : 1717
2 · 1 · 1 · 4

Sermons : 1738–42
11 · 5 · 10 · 9

George Berkeley

Treatise Concerning the Principles of Human Knowledge : 1710
3 · 3 · 3 · 3

Alciphron, or the Minute Philosopher : 1732
5 · 3 · 6 · 18
1803

Siris, A Chain of Philosophical Reflections and Inquiries
Concerning the Virtues of Tar-Water : 1744
5 2 · 3 · 1
1745

Charles Louis de Secondat,
Baron Montesquieu

Persian Letters : 1721; Translation 1722
9 · 6 · 12 · 7

Rise and Fall of the Romans : 1734; T. 1734
4 · 4 · 5 · 4

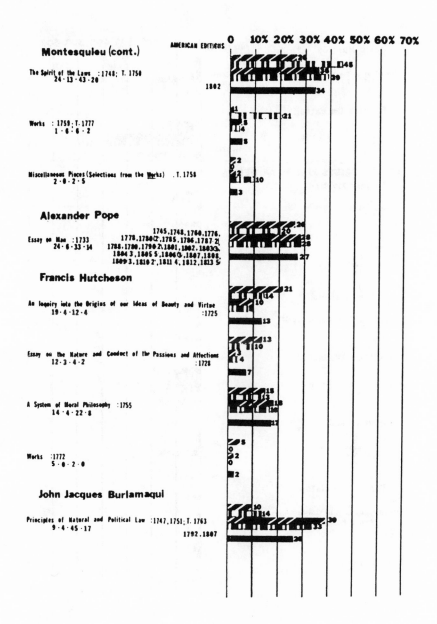

Montesquieu (cont.)

AMERICAN EDITIONS

0 10% 20% 30% 40% 50% 60% 70%

The Spirit of the Laws : 1748; T. 1750
24 · 13 · 43 · 20

Works : 1759; T. 1777
1 · 6 · 6 · 2

Miscellaneous Pieces (Selections from the Works) . T. 1759
2 · 0 · 2 · 5

Alexander Pope

Essay on Man : 1733
24 · 6 · 33 · 14

1745, 1748, 1760, 1776,
1778, 1780 (2), 1785, 1786, 1787 2,
1788, 1789, 1790 2, 1801, 1802, 1803 3,
1804 3, 1805 5, 1806 6, 1807, 1808,
1809 3, 1810 2', 1811 4, 1812, 1813 5'

Francis Hutcheson

An Inquiry into the Origins of our Ideas of Beauty and Virtue
19 · 4 · 12 · 4
: 1725

Essay on the Nature and Conduct of the Passions and Affections
12 · 3 · 4 · 2
: 1728

A System of Moral Philosophy : 1755
14 · 4 · 22 · 8

Works : 1772
5 · 0 · 2 · 0

John Jacques Burlamaqui

Principles of Natural and Political Law : 1747, 1751; T. 1763
9 · 4 · 45 · 17

1792, 1807

15

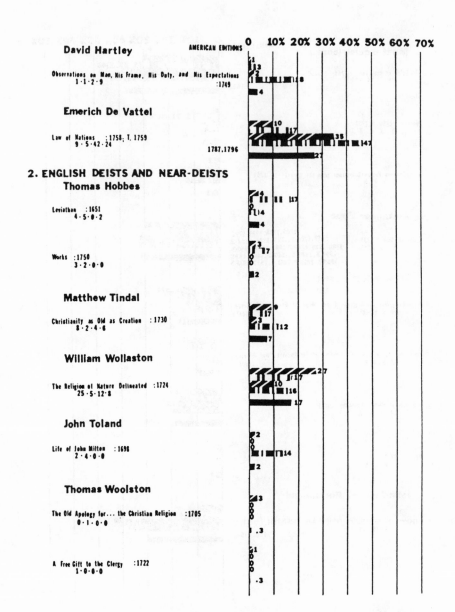

David Hartley

AMERICAN EDITIONS

Observations on Man, His Frame, His Duty, and His Expectations
1·1·2·9
:1749

Emerich De Vattel

Law of Nations : 1758; T. 1759
9·5·42·24

1787,1796

2. ENGLISH DEISTS AND NEAR-DEISTS
Thomas Hobbes

Leviathan : 1651
4·5·0·2

Works : 1750
3·2·0·0

Matthew Tindal

Christianity as Old as Creation : 1730
8·2·4·6

William Wollaston

The Religion of Nature Delineated : 1724
25·5·12·8

John Toland

Life of John Milton : 1698
2·4·0·0

Thomas Woolston

The Old Apology for... the Christian Religion : 1705
0·1·0·0

A Free Gift to the Clergy : 1722
1·0·0·0

16

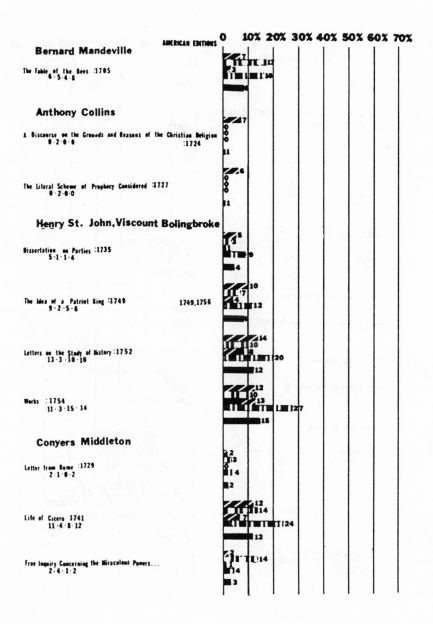

Bernard Mandeville

The Fable of the Bees :1705
6·5·4·8

Anthony Collins

A Discourse on the Grounds and Reasons of the Christian Religion
:1724

The Literal Scheme of Prophecy Considered :1727
0·2·0·0

Henry St. John,Viscount Bolingbroke

Dissertation on Parties :1735
5·1·1·4

The Idea of a Patriot King :1749
9·2·5·6

1749,1756

Letters on the Study of History :1752
13·3·10·10

Works :1754
11·3·15·14

Conyers Middleton

Letter from Rome :1729
2·1·0·2

Life of Cicero 1741
11·4·8·12

Free Inquiry Concerning the Miraculous Powers...
2·4·1·2

AMERICAN EDITIONS

0   10% 20% 30% 40% 50% 60% 70%

17

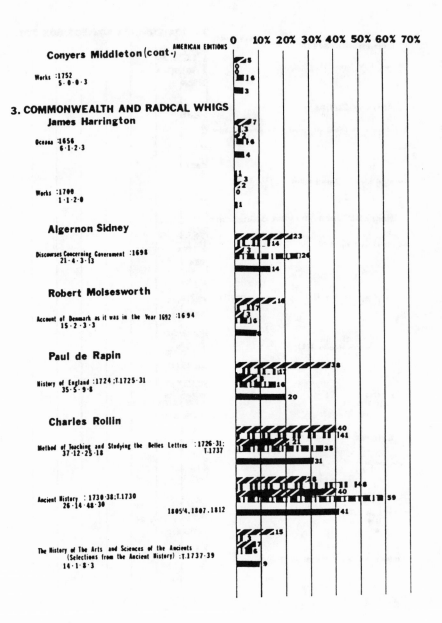

Conyers Middleton (cont.) AMERICAN EDITIONS

Works :1752
5 · 0 · 0 · 3

3. COMMONWEALTH AND RADICAL WHIGS
James Harrington

Oceana :1656
6 · 1 · 2 · 3

Works :1700
1 · 1 · 2 · 0

Algernon Sidney

Discourses Concerning Government :1698
21 · 4 · 3 · 13

Robert Molsesworth

Account of Denmark as it was in the Year 1692 :1694
15 · 2 · 3 · 3

Paul de Rapin

History of England :1724 ;T.1725-31
35 · 5 · 9 · 8

Charles Rollin

Method of Teaching and Studying the Belles Lettres :1726-31;
37 · 12 · 25 · 18   T.1737

Ancient History : 1730-38;T.1730
26 · 14 · 48 · 30

1805'4, 1807 . 1812

The History of The Arts and Sciences of the Ancients
(Selections from the Ancient History) :T.1737-39
14 · 1 · 8 · 3

18

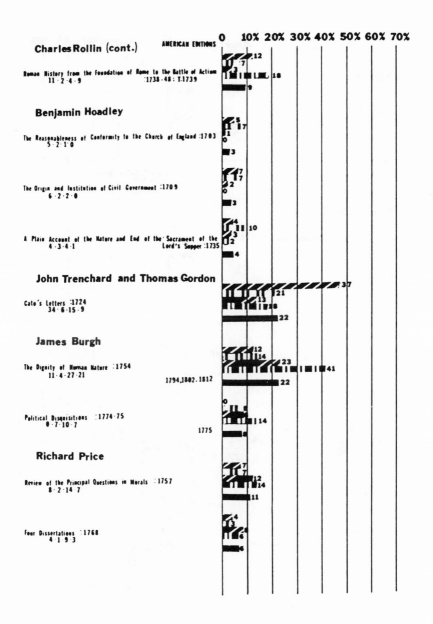

Charles Rollin (cont.)

AMERICAN EDITIONS

0 10% 20% 30% 40% 50% 60% 70%

Roman History from the Foundation of Rome to the Battle of Actium
11 · 2 · 4 · 9   :1738 · 48 : T.1739

Benjamin Hoadley

The Reasonableness of Conformity to the Church of England :1703
5 · 2 · 1 · 0

The Origin and Institution of Civil Government :1709
6 · 2 · 2 · 0

A Plain Account of the Nature and End of the Sacrament of the
4 · 3 · 4 · 1   Lord's Supper :1735

John Trenchard and Thomas Gordon

Cato's Letters :1724
34 · 6 · 15 · 9

James Burgh

The Dignity of Human Nature :1754
11 · 4 · 27 · 21   1794,1802 · 1812

Political Disquisitions :1774 · 75
0 · 7 · 10 · 7   1775

Richard Price

Review of the Principal Questions in Morals :1757
8 · 2 · 14 · 7

Four Dissertations :1768
4 · 1 · 9 · 3

19

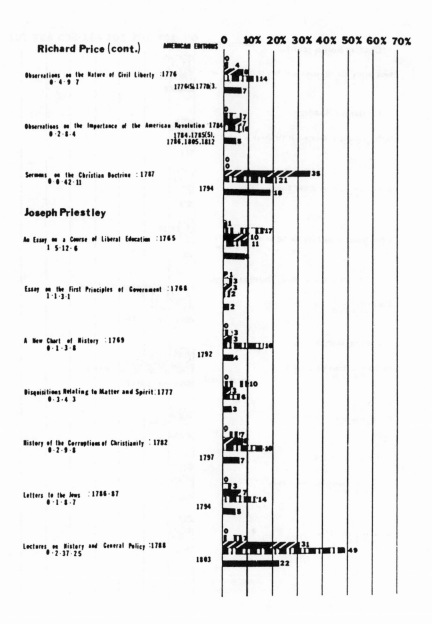

Richard Price (cont.)

Observations on the Nature of Civil Liberty :1776
0 · 4 · 9 · 7

Observations on the Importance of the American Revolution :1784
0 · 2 · 8 · 4

Sermons on the Christian Doctrine : 1787
0 · 0 · 42 · 11

Joseph Priestley

An Essay on a Course of Liberal Education : 1765
1 · 5 · 12 · 6

Essay on the First Principles of Government : 1768
1 · 1 · 3 · 1

A New Chart of History : 1769
0 · 1 · 3 · 8

Disquisitions Relating to Matter and Spirit : 1777
0 · 3 · 4 · 3

History of the Corruptions of Christianity : 1782
0 · 2 · 9 · 8

Letters to the Jews : 1786 · 87
0 · 1 · 8 · 7

Lectures on History and General Policy :1788
0 · 2 · 37 · 25

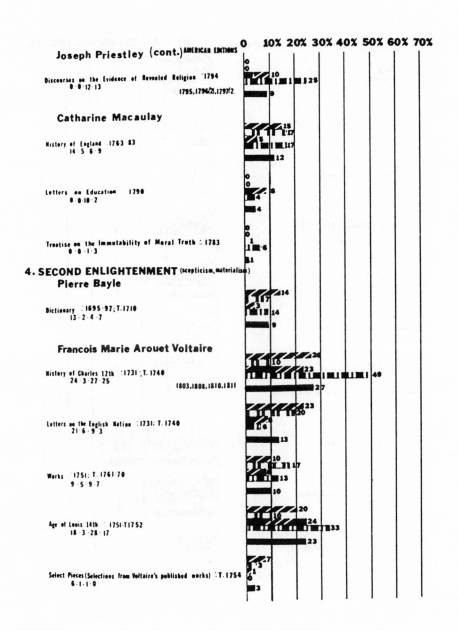

Joseph Priestley (cont.) AMERICAN EDITIONS

0   10% 20% 30% 40% 50% 60% 70%

Discourses on the Evidence of Revealed Religion : 1794
0 · 0 · 12 · 13
1795,1796/2,1797/2.

Catharine Macaulay

History of England : 1763-83
14 · 5 · 6 · 9

Letters on Education   1790
0 · 0 · 10 · 2

Treatise on the Immutability of Moral Truth : 1783
0 · 0 · 1 · 3

4. SECOND ENLIGHTENMENT (scepticism, materialism)
Pierre Bayle

Dictionary   : 1695-97; T.1710
13 · 2 · 4 · 7

Francois Marie Arouet Voltaire

History of Charles 12th   :1731 ; T.1740
24 · 3 · 27 · 25
1803,1808,1810,1811

Letters on the English Nation   :1731; T.1740
21 · 6 · 9 · 3

Works   :1751; T.1761-70
9 · 5 · 9 · 7

Age of Louis 14th   : 1751-T.1752
18 · 3 · 28 · 17

Select Pieces (Selections from Voltaire's published works) :T.1754
6 · 1 · 1 · 0

21

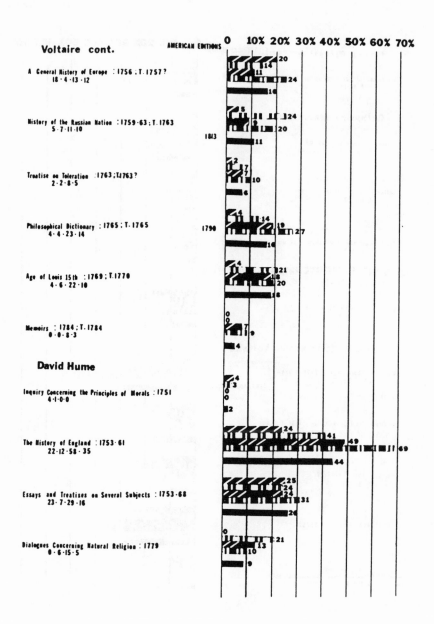

Voltaire cont.

A General History of Europe : 1756 ; T. 1757 ?
18 · 4 · 13 · 12

History of the Russian Nation : 1759-63 ; T. 1763
5 · 7 · 11 · 10

Treatise on Toleration : 1763 ; T. 1763 ?
2 · 2 · 8 · 5

Philosophical Dictionary : 1765 ; T. 1765
4 · 4 · 23 · 14

Age of Louis 15th : 1769 ; T. 1770
4 · 6 · 22 · 10

Memoirs : 1784 ; T. 1784
0 · 0 · 8 · 3

David Hume

Inquiry Concerning the Principles of Morals : 1751
4 · 1 · 0 · 0

The History of England : 1753-61
22 · 12 · 58 · 35

Essays and Treatises on Several Subjects : 1753-68
23 · 7 · 29 · 16

Dialogues Concerning Natural Religion : 1779
0 · 6 · 15 · 5

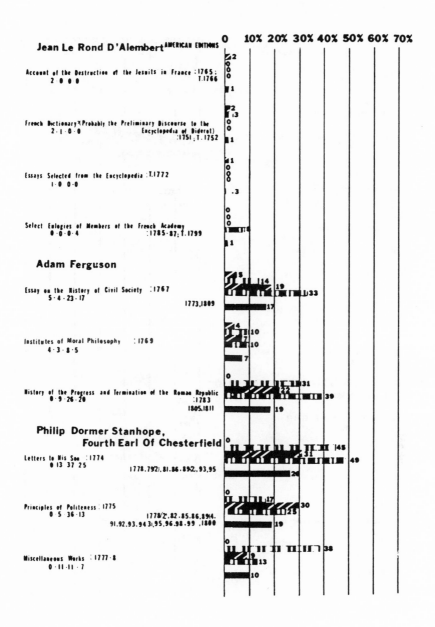

Jean Le Rond D'Alembert AMERICAN EDITIONS

Account of the Destruction of the Jesuits in France :1765;
2 · 0 · 0 · 0   T.1766

French Dictionary X Probably the Preliminary Discourse to the
2 · 1 · 0 · 0   Encyclopedia of Diderot)
                                  :1751 ; T .1752

Essays Selected from the Encyclopedia :T.1772
1 · 0 0 · 0

Select Eulogies of Members of the French Academy
0 · 0 · 0 · 4   :1785 · 87; T.1799

Adam Ferguson

Essay on the History of Civil Society :1767
5 · 4 · 23 · 17
                              1773,1809

Institutes of Moral Philosophy   : 1769
4 · 3 · 8 · 5

History of the Progress and Termination of the Roman Republic
0 · 9 · 26 · 20   :1783
                              1805,1811

Philip Dormer Stanhope,
          Fourth Earl Of Chesterfield

Letters to His Son :1774
0 13 37 25
                      1778 ,792),81 ·86 ·892, 93,95

Principles of Politeness : 1775
0 5 36 · 13
          1778/2 ,82 · 85.86, 894.
          91,92,93,94 3),95,96,98,99 ,1800

Miscellaneous Works :1777 · 8
0 · 11 ·11 · 7

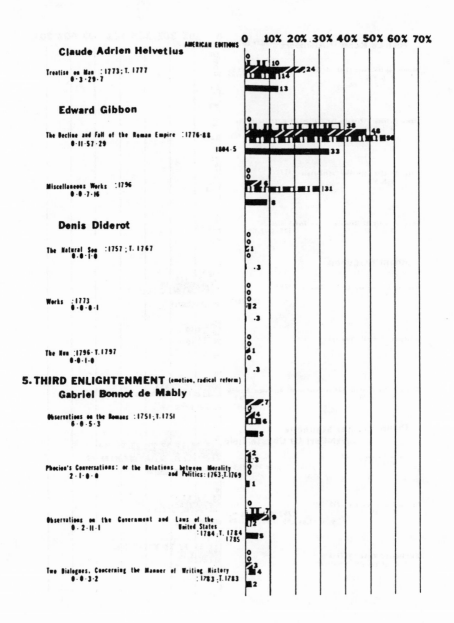

Claude Adrien Helvetius

Treatise on Man : 1773; T. 1777
0 · 3 · 29 · 7

Edward Gibbon

The Decline and Fall of the Roman Empire : 1776-88
0 · 11 · 57 · 29

1884-5

Miscellaneous Works : 1796
0 · 0 · 7 · 16

Denis Diderot

The Natural Son : 1757 ; T. 1767
0 · 0 · 1 · 0

Works : 1773
0 · 0 · 0 · 1

The Nun : 1796 · T. 1797
0 · 0 · 1 · 0

5. THIRD ENLIGHTENMENT (emotion, radical reform)
Gabriel Bonnot de Mably

Observations on the Romans : 1751; T. 1751
6 · 0 · 5 · 3

Phocion's Conversations: or the Relations between Morality
and Politics: 1763; T. 1769
2 · 1 · 0 · 0

Observations on the Government and Laws of the
United States
: 1784; T. 1784
0 · 2 · 11 · 1   1785

Two Dialogues, Concerning the Manner of Writing History
: 1783 ; T. 1783
0 · 0 · 3 · 2

24

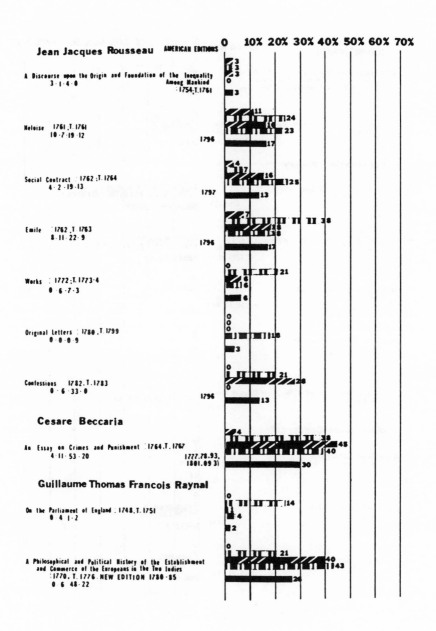

Jean Jacques Rousseau   AMERICAN EDITIONS

A Discourse upon the Origin and Foundation of the Inequality
Among Mankind
3 · 1 · 4 · 0   · 1754 · T · 1761

Neloise   1761 · T · 1761
10 · 7 · 19 · 12

Social Contract   1762 · T · 1764
4 · 2 · 19 · 13

Emile   1762 · T · 1763
8 · 11 · 22 · 9

Works   1772 · T · 1773 · 4
0 · 6 · 7 · 3

Original Letters : 1780 · T · 1799
0 · 0 · 0 · 9

Confessions   1782 · T · 1783
0 · 6 · 33 · 0

Cesare Beccaria

An Essay on Crimes and Punishment : 1764 · T · 1767
4 · 11 · 53 · 20   1777 · 78 · 93 ·
1801 · 09 3)

Guillaume Thomas Francois Raynal

On the Parliament of England : 1748 · T · 1751
0 · 4 · 1 · 2

A Philosophical and Political History of the Establishment
and Commerce of the Europeans in the Two Indies
: 1770 · T · 1776 · NEW EDITION 1780 · 85
0 · 6 · 48 · 22

25

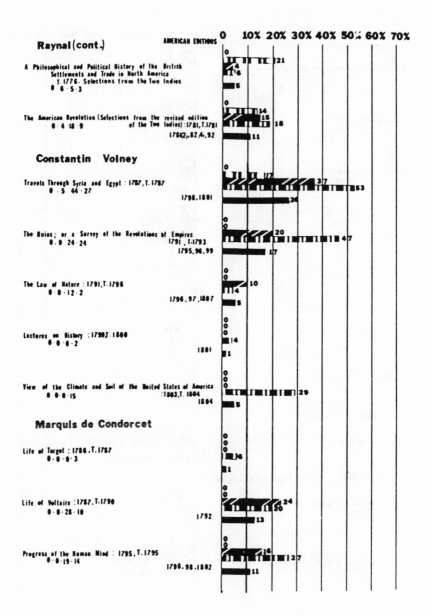

Raynal(cont.)

AMERICAN EDITIONS

0 10% 20% 30% 40% 50% 60% 70%

A Philosophical and Political History of the British
Settlements and Trade in North America
T.1776. Selections from the Two Indies
0 · 6 · 5 · 3

The American Revolution (Selections from the revised edition
0 · 4 ·18 · 9   of the Two Indies) :1781,T.1781
1784(2),82,4,92

Constantin   Volney

Travels Through Syria and Egypt : 1787,T.1787
0 · 5 44 · 27
1798,1801

The Ruins ; or a Survey of the Revolutions of Empires
0 · 0 24 · 24   1791 , T.1793
1795,96,99

The Law of Nature : 1791,T.1796
0 · 0 ·12 · 2
1796,97,1807

Lectures on History : 1799J·1800
0 · 0 · 0 · 2
1801

View of the Climate and Soil of the United States of America
0 · 0 · 0 · 15   :1803,T. 1804
1804

Marquis de Condorcet

Life of Turgot : 1786,T.1787
0 · 0 · 0 · 3

Life of Voltaire :1787,T.1790
0 · 0 · 28 · 10
1792

Progress of the Human Mind : 1795,T.1795
0 · 0 ·19 · 14
1796,98,1802

26

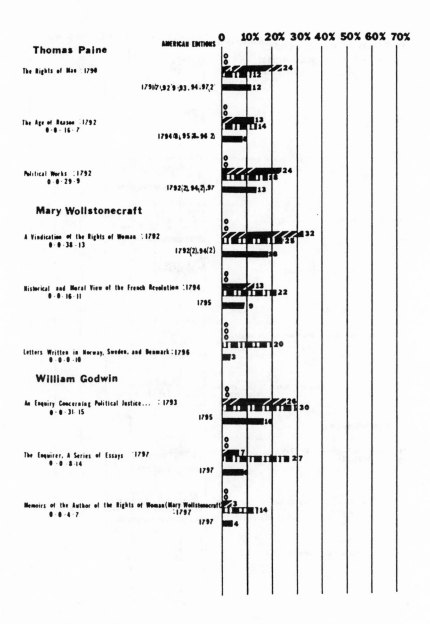

Thomas Paine

AMERICAN EDITIONS   0   10% 20% 30% 40% 50% 60% 70%

The Rights of Man : 1790

1791(7),92'9 :93 ,94 ,97,2'

The Age of Reason : 1792
0 · 0 · 16 · 7

1794(3),95(2),96 2)

Political Works : 1792
0 · 0 · 29 · 9

1792(2),94(2),97

Mary Wollstonecraft

A Vindication of the Rights of Woman : 1792
0 · 0 · 38 · 13

1792(2),94(2)

Historical and Moral View of the French Revolution : 1794
0 · 0 · 16 · 11

1795

Letters Written in Norway, Sweden, and Denmark : 1796
0 · 0 · 0 · 10

William Godwin

An Enquiry Concerning Political Justice... : 1793
0 · 0 · 31 · 15

1795

The Enquirer, A Series of Essays 1797
0 · 0 · 8 · 14

1797

Memoirs of the Author of the Rights of Woman (Mary Wollstonecraft)
:1797
0 · 0 · 4 · 7

1797

27

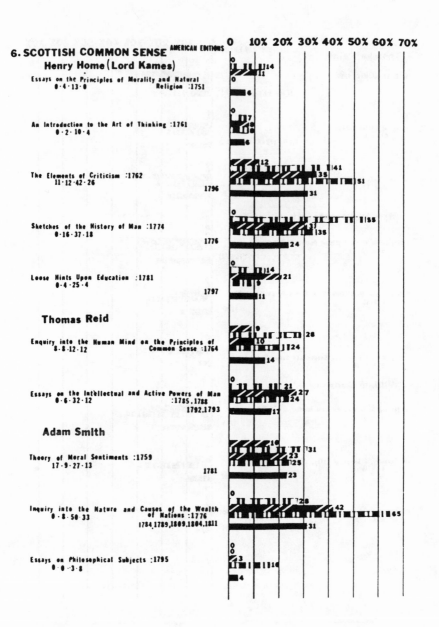

6. SCOTTISH COMMON SENSE AMERICAN EDITIONS

Henry Home (Lord Kames)

Essays on the Principles of Morality and Natural
0·4·13·0   Religion :1751

An Introduction to the Art of Thinking :1761
0·2·10·4

The Elements of Criticism :1762
11·12·42·26

Sketches of the History of Man :1774
0·16·37·18

Loose Hints Upon Education :1781
0·4·25·4

Thomas Reid

Enquiry into the Human Mind on the Principles of
8·8·12·12   Common Sense :1764

Essays on the Intellectual and Active Powers of Man
0·6·32·12   :1785,1788

Adam Smith

Theory of Moral Sentiments :1759
17·9·27·13

Inquiry into the Nature and Causes of the Wealth
0·8·50·33   of Nations :1776

Essays on Philosophical Subjects :1795
0·0·3·8

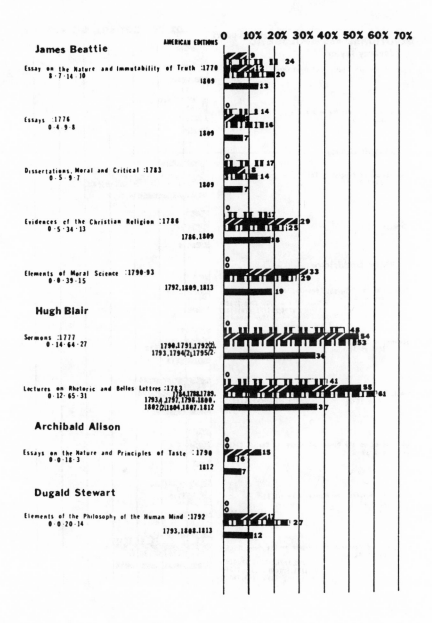

7. DEVOTIONAL and APOLOGETIC
Jeremy Taylor

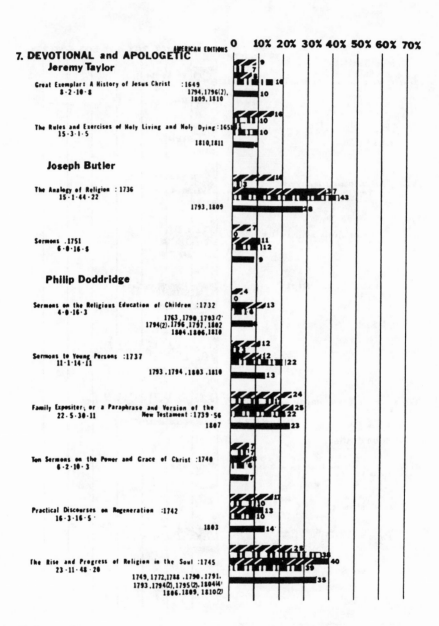

Great Exemplar: A History of Jesus Christ : 1649
8 · 2 · 10 · 8
1794, 1796(2), 1809, 1810

The Rules and Exercises of Holy Living and Holy Dying : 1650
15 · 3 · 1 · 5
1810, 1811

Joseph Butler

The Analogy of Religion : 1736
15 · 1 · 44 · 22
1793, 1809

Sermons .1751
6 · 0 · 16 · 5

Philip Doddridge

Sermons on the Religious Education of Children : 1732
4 · 0 · 16 · 2
1763 , 1790 , 1793 (2)
1794(2), 1796 , 1797 , 1802
1804 , 1806 , 1810

Sermons to Young Persons : 1737
11 · 1 · 14 · 11
1793 , 1794 , 1803 , 1810

Family Expositer, or a Paraphrase and Version of the
22 · 5 · 30 · 11   New Testament : 1739 · 56
1807

Ten Sermons on the Power and Grace of Christ : 1740
6 · 2 · 10 · 3

Practical Discourses on Regeneration : 1742
16 · 3 · 16 · 5
1803

The Rise and Progress of Religion in the Soul : 1745
23 · 11 · 48 · 20
1749, 1772,1788 ,1790 ,1791.
1793 ,1794(2), 1795 (2), 1804(4)
1806, 1809, 1810(2)

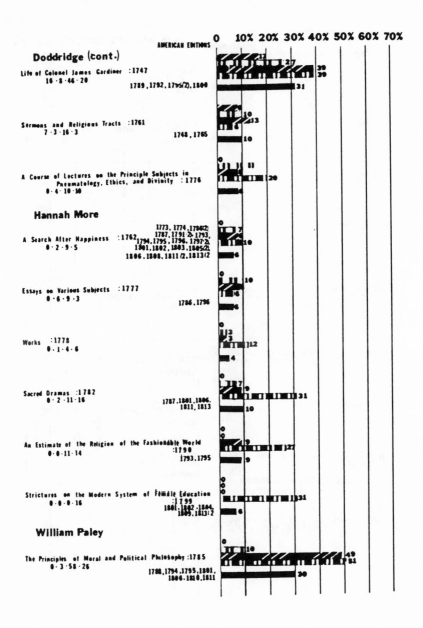

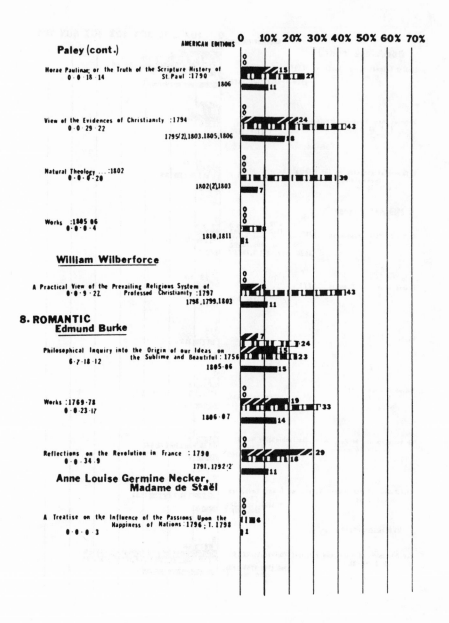

Paley (cont.)

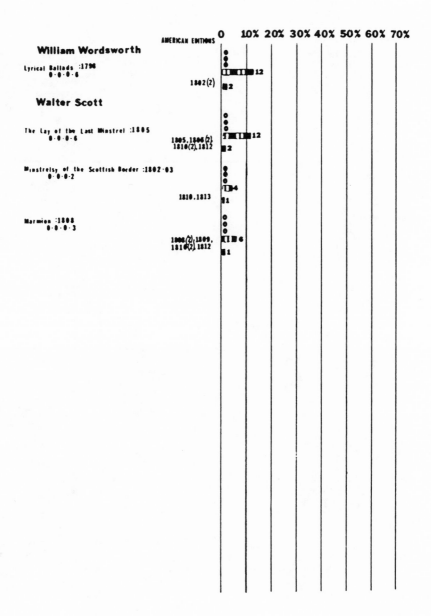

AMERICAN EDITIONS

0   10% 20% 30% 40% 50% 60% 70%

William Wordsworth

Lyrical Ballads : 1798
0 · 0 · 0 · 6   12

1802(2)   2

Walter Scott

The Lay of the Last Minstrel : 1805
0 · 0 · 0 · 6   12

1805, 1806(2)
1810(2), 1812   2

Minstrelsy of the Scottish Border : 1802-03
0 · 0 · 0 · 2   4

1810, 1813   1

Marmion : 1808
0 · 0 · 0 · 3   6

1808(2), 1809,
1810(2), 1812   1

Eden's Constitution: The Paradisiacal Dream and Enlightenment Values in Late Eighteenth-Century Literature of the American Frontier

LESTER H. COHEN

IN A LETTER to Peter Collinson in 1753, Benjamin Franklin recounted his meeting with a "Transylvanian Tartar," actually a Greek Orthodox priest, who had arrived in America in 1748 during a tour around the world. The "Tartar" asked Franklin why he thought the people of so many cultures—Tartars in Asia and Europe, Negroes in Africa, and Indians in the Americas—"continued a wandring [sic] careless Life, and refused to live in Cities, and to cultivate the arts they saw practiced by the civilized part of Mankind." Before Franklin could respond, the "Tartar" offered his own explanation, beginning at the beginning, with Genesis and God's expulsion of Adam and his progeny from Eden. "God make man for Paradise," Franklin quoted the "Tartar," "he make him for to live lazy; man make God angry, God turn him out of Paradise, and bid him work; man no love work; he want to go to Paradise again, he want to live lazy; so all mankind love lazy."[1]

Franklin wrote of this meeting with obvious amusement and a relish for playing with the priest's "broken English" and its implications of the naive and primitive. But Franklin was using his wit to make a point, and he meant to make it circuitously, almost in the form of a parable. The "Tartar" had raised a theme which Franklin had considered at some length, and Franklin meant to use the meeting as a vehicle for presenting his own observations on "the proneness of human Nature to a life of ease, of freedom from care and labour." This was a tendency which Franklin believed characterized America's Indians; indeed, it was a tendency which persistently hindered white Americans' efforts to convert the Indians to the ways of civilization and culture. Refusing to "see the advantages that Arts, Sciences, and compact Society procure us," the Indians perversely (but, of course, understandably) preferred a life in which "almost all their wants are supplied by the spontaneous Productions of Nature, with the addition of very little labour, if hunting and fishing may indeed be considered labour when Game is so plenty. . . ." The Indians "are not deficient in natural understanding," Franklin added with mock exasperation, "and yet they

83

have never shewn any inclination to change their manner of life for ours, or to learn any of our Arts. . . ."

As Franklin saw it, the "Tartar" had tapped one of the deepest wells of human nature: "that the hope of becoming at some time of life free from the necessity of care and Labour, together with the fear of penury, is the mainspring of most peoples [sic] industry." People dreamed of living in spontaneous and bountiful nature, idling away eternity, not only because such a life would be pleasurable, but because the attainment of such a life of paradisiacal ease would in itself betoken the end of Adam's curse and God's requirement that man live by the sweat of his brow.

But while Franklin thought that the paradisiacal dream was an important source of man's motivation, he also saw that it motivated men not to withdraw from work and society but, paradoxically, to pursue them with even greater vigor. He believed that Americans' aspirations seemed to embody a tension between an Edenic dream of idleness amid abundance on the one hand, and a civilized, orderly life based upon hard work and enlightened social values on the other. But Franklin meant in his parable to destroy that tension. He concluded his observations on the quest for paradise by noting that, wonderful as a life of Edenic ease might seem, "as matters [now] stand with us, care and industry seem absolutely necessary to our well-being. . . ." By abruptly ending his playful revery Franklin did not mean to suggest that the hope for the good life had to be abandoned. But he predicated the possibility of attaining that life on the enlightened virtues of "care and industry," dismissing the irrational expectation of paradise for the rational pursuit of civilized society. If "Paradise" were realizable at all, it was only through man's assiduous attention to industry—that is, to the application of his labor to his earthly pursuits.

While Franklin could not endorse the pursuit of the Edenic dream, he could, nevertheless, be excited by another vision, which he translated directly into the context of frontier settlement. To the eminent evangelical minister, George Whitefield, he wrote: "I sometimes wish that you and I were jointly employ'd by the Crown to settle a Colony on the Ohio. What a glorious Thing it would be, to settle in that fine Country a large, Strong Body of Religious and Industrious People."[2] Franklin's sentiment here was consistent with his thoughts on frontier settlement in general. Before emigration to the frontier actually commenced, the settlements would be planned on the drawing board, lands would be surveyed, government would be established in the new areas, and enough supplies would be provided. Colonization, in short, would proceed according to the most judicious reasoning and most educated predictions of which an enlightened people were capable. And the crucial ingredient in this recipe for settlement would be a group of virtuous, industrious settlers, preferably drawn from the established communities of the East.[3]

Franklin's vision of frontier settlement provided an alternative to the Edenic myth. Indeed, his vision embodied a set of values and assumptions which so eloquently spoke to the era's dominant concerns of republican virtue and enlightened rationality that it contained the elements of another myth which rivaled in intensity the ancient myth of paradise. This alternative set of beliefs, convictions, and assumptions constituted what for the present may be called "the myth of the sufficiency of reason."

This essay seeks to accomplish two related aims, one substantive and the other methodological. First, it proposes to demonstrate that the central motif in late eighteenth-century frontier literature was society, not nature. The paradisiacal dream, with its intimations of the irrational and the primitive, played no significant role in the literature of settlement, promotion, or travel. Indeed, whether one interprets that dream as a quest for paradise, as a desire for life in a garden, for idleness amid abundance, for a green world, or for a golden age, one misses the crucial point that the vision of the frontier articulated in this literature presupposed that the frontier would develop, precisely as Franklin had predicted four decades earlier, according to the most enlightened social values of easterners and Europeans, and that the goal of that development was a rational social order.

P. Fourdrinier. A view of Savannah as it stood the 29th of March 1734. Engraving, after Peter Gordon. (*The I.N. Phelps Stokes Collection, Prints Division, New York Public Library*)

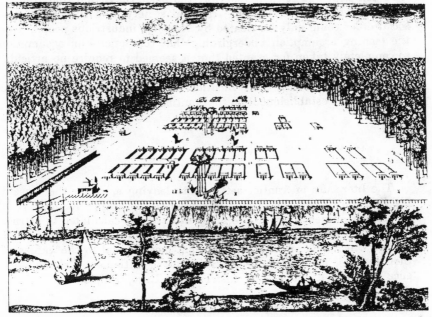

Second, this essay aims to question the interpretations of historians who have relied too heavily upon the literature of the frontier as an index of the "reality" of frontier life. Finding disparities between the accounts of settlers and promoters on the one hand and travelers on the other, and assuming that travelers would more accurately portray frontier conditions because, unlike the promoters, they had no financial stake in western lands, these historians have tended to attribute greater credibility to the more pessimistic, even cynical accounts of the travelers. While common sense recommends this approach, the literary evidence will not sustain its burden. For both the literature of promotion and the literature of travel have the same status for the historian, and neither, in itself, affords a greater insight into "reality." At the same time, by assuming the greater veracity of travel literature the historian fails to see that both bodies of literature rest upon the same assumptions and both articulate the same values.[4]

The criticisms of frontier life that were leveled by travelers (but also by settlers and promoters themselves) reflected less the actual conditions of the frontier than the travelers' chagrin and frustration at the defeat of their own expectations. The literature of the frontier reveals, then, not an irreconcilable conflict between irrational expectations and objective reality,[5] but a fundamental contradiction inherent in the utopian expectation of an enlightened social order—a contradiction inherent in the faith in the possibilities of enlightened rationality itself.

The motives and expectations of promoters, settlers, and travelers were complex, but at their roots lay the basic conviction that frontier society ought to be an orderly, rational society, and that a rational social order could only be created by virtuous, industrious people. And the leading assumption undergirding that conviction—an assumption so completely taken for granted that it seemed to require no articulation—was that the careful application of enlightened rationality to the planning, organization, and execution of settlement was sufficient to guarantee the establishment on the frontier of an ideal community.

I

The literature of frontier settlement—leaving aside for the present the literature of travel—was a promotional literature.[6] Regardless of its actual "influence" on future emigrants, it was calculated to attract prospective settlers by depicting life on the frontier in terms and images which, the promoters felt, would most appeal to the values of their readers. The authors of the literature of settlement and the audience to which it spoke were eastern (and European), and one of the principal appeals that the literature made was the appeal to what seems to be the conservative values of prospective settlers. As Earl Pomeroy has observed of a later period, despite the rhetoric of newness, of the possibility of dramatically altering even the foundations of social life, "the disposition of the settlers was basically to conserve and transport what they had known before." Indeed, promoters lost no opportunity to make precisely that point. As Pomeroy stated it, "The Westerner's perennial plea to the traveler to concede that the West had equalled or surpassed the East in schools, hotels, or civic virtue, revealed the nature of his ambition."[7]

Eighteenth-century promoters, even more than their nineteenth-century counterparts, emphasized the aim of settlers to perpetuate eastern social conventions. In his proposal to establish a colony on the Ohio in 1787, Reverend Manasseh Cutler addressed Congress in terms that would be congenial to an audience imbued with eastern enlightenment ideals. As agent for the Ohio Company, Cutler assured Congress that "a large and immediate settlement of the most robust and industrious people in America . . . would be made systematically" in Ohio.[8] Because the settlement would be carefully planned in advance of actual emigration, the establishment of society would be "systematic and judicious." As a result, the new colony would essentially be a "continuation of the older settlements of the east." If the congressmen were anxious over the possibility of disorder—and clearly they were—Cutler allayed their fears by noting that such care would be taken to ensure social order that the Ohio colony "will serve as a useful model for all settlements which will be founded in the future in the United States."[9] Cutler believed, and took for granted that the congressmen believed, that "systematic and judicious" planning would ensure an orderly society on the frontier, and that the emigration of "robust and industrious" Americans would guarantee social propriety and a commitment to hard work.

The Ohio colony, according to Cutler, would embody the basic features and conventions of eastern society. But that clearly would not be enough. Frontier society would be better than already settled society if only because in Ohio "there is no rubbish to clear away before laying the foundation." But still more important, unlike eastern society, which traced its origins to a preenlightened era, "the first commencement of this settlement will be undertaken by persons inspired with the noblest sentiments, acquainted with the world and with affairs, as well as with every branch of science."[10] The planners and settlers, that is, resembled no group of people as much as the congressmen whom Cutler addressed. Cutler, like Benjamin Franklin, believed in the importance of the physical environment without losing sight of the basic need for industrious, virtuous people who would apply themselves to the cultivation both of the land and of society. Thus Cutler wrote: "[T]his delightful part of the United States" will be "settled upon a wise system and in a well-ordered manner."[11]

Gilbert Imlay, an adventurer and promoter of frontier settlement, is frequently cited for his use of Edenic imagery in his *Topographical Description of the Western Territory* (1792).[12] But Imlay made it clear that, above all, frontier society required lawful and industrious people. At the outset of his work he contrasted "the simple manners, and rational life in these back settlements [of Kentucky], with the distorted and unnatural habits of the Europeans." And it was obvious, he wrote, that the unnatural habits of the Europeans "have flowed no doubt from the universally bad laws which exist" on the old continent.[13] Kentucky, by contrast, was being settled under the rational and benevolent procedures of Virginia law, and "our decisions are governed by acts of the legislature, decreed upon the elementary principles of truth and justice."[14]

Imlay did indeed employ an environmentalist argument, suggesting that people were influenced by—molded by—the significant elements of the environment in which they lived. But his theory was not naturalistic; rather, he was more concerned with the impact of law and government than he was with the impact of nature. Throughout his work, Imlay insisted upon the benign law and form of government under which Kentucky was being settled, suggesting that his strategy for attracting settlers depended more on his arguments for good laws and government than on suggestions of natural fecundity. In Kentucky, he wrote, "the order and quiet, which prevailed in 1784, was sufficient to have induced a stranger to believe that he was living under an old settled government. Such is the science of jurisprudence, when it works upon simple, but substantial springs."[15] Imlay was not promoting nature as much as he was promoting law, order, benign republican government—in short, the principles of the American Revolution and of Enlightenment social values.

Imlay and Cutler were trying to sell land and to populate that land with enough settlers to make property values soar. And Judge William Cooper, founder of the celebrated Cooperstown in the wilderness of upstate New York, unblushingly wrote that his original intent in settling the Otsego Lake area was "for the sole purpose of promoting my interest." He went on to add that self-interest quickly blossomed into a keen attachment to his settlement and its inhabitants.[16]

The promoters' appeal to the profit motive was a crucial strategy in their writings, particularly because financial gain was intimately linked to their views of nature's potentialities. But important as the appeal to profits was, the promoters still found it necessary to base their cases for settlement on arguments for a stable social order. Whatever their personal motives, they felt that they had to promote regular society under republican government. No one, they assumed, would adopt their proposals—neither Congress nor prospective settlers—unless they persuaded people that frontier society would embody the ideals of enlightened rationality. Thus, even if the promoters did not believe their own arguments (and there is no reason to think that they did not), they still found it strategically necessary to present cases that embraced certain assumptions and values—assumptions and values which were aimed at selling not paradise, but society. And in promoting society the promoters emphasized mutuality and reciprocity—in short, the sociability of frontier life.

Employing the language and images of circulation and mutual advantage, Judge Cooper argued that the concentration of industrious people, not nature's bounties, was the key to frontier settlement. "There should be a mutual dependence between the farmer and the villager," he wrote; "the farmer relying upon the villager for the purchase of his produce, and the villager upon the farmer for the sale of the articles of his trade."[17] Cooper's vision embodied the now-classic formulation of the market as a metaphor for community; the community, like the market, was an internally self-regulating system of relations.

The important image in Cooper's work is that of "circulation," of the reciprocal relationships among the inhabitants. He expanded this image as he continued:

> The labour of two or three hundred industrious men concentrated, is like money collected into a bank; when scattered in distant quarters its effects amount to little; when brought together it resembles the heart, from and to which circulation flows, whilst it gives life and health to the remotest extremes.[18]

The power of this circulation metaphor (a metaphor that demonstrates the imaginative interconnectedness of monetary, anatomical, and social theories) lay in its emphatic assertion of the value of ordered society—a society which was intrinsically ordered, like the body's circulatory system, rather than one which might require artificial engineering.

Cooper's circulation metaphor was more than a ploy for economic aggrandizement (though it was that too). It was a crucial symptom of the belief that frontier society could only fail if it were comprised of solitary individuals, lacking the cohesion of social interdependence. Cooper insisted,

> Certainly when the inhabitants are at a distance from each other there is less society, less useful communication upon subjects of common concern, such as the education of children

and the like; there is less polish of manners, more careless-
ness in dress and demeanor, and more languor and indifference in every sort of improvement.

Isolation and dispersal of settlers not only impeded trade, but hindered
the possibility of realizing the ideal of a "compactly built" community
in which

there is a quicker circulation of sentiment; and mutual convenience . . . [where] a kind of city pride arises, and acts
advantageously upon the manners and modes of life; better
houses are built, more comforts introduced, and there is more
civility and civilization.[19]

John Filson's vision, like Cooper's, involved the creation of a community of mutually interdependent citizens. As the man principally
responsible for the Daniel Boone legends (in which Boone, incidentally,
is as much a community-minded republican as he is a rugged
backwoodsman), Filson wanted Kentucky settlers to have "possession of
a country so extensive and fertile" that the land would be transformed
and "inhabited by virtuous and ingenious citizens" who would cultivate
the land as well as commerce, and make Kentucky prosper.[20] One of
the chief advantages of Kentucky, thought Filson, echoing Manasseh
Cutler, was that is was "situated in the central part of the extensive
American empire," a location which would foster trade so "that the
country will be supplied with goods as cheap as if situated but forty
miles from Philadelphia."[21] Filson expected "multitudes" of settlers to
emigrate shortly and exulted that the area "will be exceedingly populous in a short time."[22]

Filson was interested in attracting large numbers of settlers
because, as William Cooper suggested, the worst condition of life on the
frontier was its isolation. The settler on the frontier, Cooper wrote,
hardly desired "a life of savage solitude; he will still desire the society
of his species, and the ordinary comforts of life. . . ."[23] Similarly, Harry
Toulmin, a frontier settler and historian of Kentucky, cautioned prospective settlers not to emigrate singly: they ought to come in
"families," to "form bands of emigration and go strong in society,"
because larger groups would secure "the only circumstance such [wil-
derness] districts can want." Toulmin's point was clear: "Every thing
else is provided with a lavish hand—even with exuberance—but connection, friendship—society must be carried: they are not the growth of
the wilderness."[24] Nature would provide many of man's wants, but
nature could not generate society. And without society, friendship, family, mutual interdependence, settlers would be faced with lives of "sav-

age solitude," and neither trade, nor commerce, nor cultivation of the earth could supply the want of social intercourse.

Gilbert Imlay suggested that, along with the "science of government," "cultivation [is] the most essential to the happiness of men in the wild state which this country is in."[25] Harry Toulmin, following John Dickinson's *Letters From a Pennsylvania Farmer*, saw America as a nation of cultivators, "united by the silken bands of mild government, all respecting the laws, without dreading their powers, because they are equitable."[26] Cultivation, the application of the techniques of civilization to the wilderness, would transform raw nature; and, following another theme of reciprocity, the cultivator would in turn enjoy the beneficent effects of nature transformed, for the labor itself produced the transformation both of nature and of self. "By what invisible power hath this surprising metamorphosis been performed?" asked Harry Toulmin. "By that of the laws and that of [the peoples'] industry."[27]

None of these promoters suggested that nature would spontaneously give rise to fruit that need merely be picked from the vine. None of them hinted that all people need do is go to the frontier and idle away their time without concern for "care and industry." If, as Arthur K. Moore has suggested, there is a hidden appeal to people's irrational expectations of a natural paradise then the appeal is very well hidden indeed. A careful reading of the literature of settlement and promotion makes it difficult to believe that prospective settlers from Europe and the East could have been credulous enough to suppose that life on the frontier would be easy. For, in the first place, the lure presented by these writings was not nature, but civilized society; and, in the second, even promotional literature, filled as it was with joyful and exuberant rhetoric, readily depicted nature's harsher, crueler face.

Emphasizing the need for strenuous labor and know-how in creating a human habitat, promoters underscored the point that building towns and cities, developing trade and manufacturing—extending civilization further westward—were the aims of settlement; and these aims cast doubt on the notion that the frontier was depicted as a natural paradise. Equally important, promoters' descriptions of nature as often echoed William Bradford's "howling wilderness" as they depicted a flowering garden. In fact, the "garden" was not depicted as what already existed; rather, it was what *might* exist, given industry and the arts of civilized society.

William Cooper, for example, saw the first goal of settlement as "*reclaiming* from its rude state the barren wilderness, and scattering the smiling habitation of civilized man in those dreary wastes...."[28] Pictures of "the barren wilderness" and "dreary wastes" could hardly have been calculated to touch peoples' desires for languishing in nature's abundance. To the contrary, while nature scowled it was the

"habitation of civilized man" that "smiled." Thus, "[T]he interest of
every individual from the richest land-holder to the poorest settler con-
spires and contributes to the great primary object," Cooper added, "to
cause the Wilderness to bloom and fructify."[29]

Arguing that the wilderness had no intrinsic value, Harry Toulmin
was interested in the progress that he saw in Kentucky. He saw the
value of the land in its transformation "from dirty stations or forts, and
smoaky [sic] huts . . . into fertile fields, blushing orchards, pleasant
gardens, luxuriant sugar groves, neat and commodious houses, rising
villages, and trading towns."[30] John Filson echoed Toulmin's concerns,
writing that "thus we behold Kentucke, lately an howling wilderness,
the habitation of savages and wild beasts, become a fruitful field. . . ."[31]
Toulmin and Filson described the stages of progress from primitivism
to civilization, from wilderness to culture, historically, even
anthropologically. And the key to progress was, for both, cultivation;
for, as Gilbert Imlay said, cultivation was necessary because of "the
wild state which this country is in."

Nature, of course, was important. Settlers and promoters saw
nature as a field of opportunity—not for its own sake, but for exploitation. Gilbert Imlay succinctly wrote that "it seems this vast extent of
empire is only to be equalled for its sublimity but by the object of its
aggrandizement."[32] Doubtless, a major attraction of frontier nature was
the opportunity it afforded of making money, particularly for those
already wealthy enough to make frontier lands a going concern. This is
why the promoters emphasized the proximity of the frontier to settled
society. It is also why depictions of natural beauty accompanied depictions of natural utility—references to natural resources as economic
resources. It is why William Cooper, in surveying his lands from a
mountain top, saw not the beauty of nature but "where a place of trade
or a village should afterwards be established"; and why on a visit to
Ohio in 1797 the Reverend James Smith saw the future site of Chil-
licothe as "not only a beautiful, but . . . also a most convenient place for
a town. . . ."[33] Smith succinctly articulated the conviction that others
shared, and made clearer what Imlay had meant by the "aggrandizement" of nature. "What Nature denied," Smith wrote, "art then
supplied."[34] Aggrandizement meant the economic exploitation of
nature; but it also meant that nature could be transformed, by art, into
a human habitat.

But if the appeal to profit was designed to attract the wealthy, to
entice the mass of prospective settlers the promoters promoted sociability. The language that dominates the literature of settlement is the
language of community, of "city pride," as Cooper put it, of the "circulation of sentiment," of the kind of sociability that had, it was strongly
implied, gone out of life in the East. The literature of settlement, then,
was at once a depiction of conditions, an appeal for a more sociable

existence, and a critique of eastern society insofar as it had failed to generate sociability.

It was not nature that would regenerate humankind's sentiments and promote a happy social existence; it was, wrote Imlay, "the intercourse of men [that] has added no inconsiderable lustre to the polish of manners...." But even before social life became "polished," even while frontier people still lived in rough log cabins, "in consequence of the friendly disposition which exists among those hospitable people, every neighbour flew to the assistance of each other upon occasions of emergency."[35] Imlay raised the specter of "emergency" precisely in order to deflate it, suggesting that no real emergency could arise when people truly cared about one another.

The influx of population after 1784 created change on the frontier, for then came retired army officers and their families, and "the country soon began to be chequered after that aera with genteel men, which operated both upon the minds and actions of the back woods people, who constituted the first emigrants." The effect of this increase in population was that "the genius of friendship appeared to foster the emanations of virtue...."[36] And concentrations of virtuous, industrious people, as the settlers never tired of repeating, would overcome the dangers of living a life of "savage solitude."

The language of sociability underscored Enlightenment values. Indeed, it signified that settlers and promoters had every intention—or said that they did—of bringing enlightened social values with them and of planting them on the frontier. For man "to resume his pristine dignity" at long last, his condition would have to be "ameliorated." It was not nature, however, but "the perfection of arts [that] will meliorate the condition of man...."[37] Dr. Saugrain, a traveler in Kentucky in 1788, eloquently spoke to the relative importance of nature and society, observing that the lands near Louisville "are splendid, and even amazing in goodness, but no one goes there. I can give no other reason for this unless it be that men wish to be where there are men."[38]

Comfort, civilization, benign republican government, the appearance of stability and permanence, even polish of manners, and, above all, sociability, regularity, hospitality, the mutual concern of all the inhabitants for one another—these were what the promoters promoted. Clearly, then, the hopes and expectations of settlers and promoters were "utopian." But "utopian" ought not to be construed as a synonym for "Edenic" and "paradisiacal," implying the centrality of nature.[39] For if the settlers and promoters sought "Eden," then Eden had a constitution and would be inhabited by virtuous, industrious, and enlightened citizens.

The possibilities of a social utopia seemed endless. Using the skills of enlightened men and bearing the "sentiments" of friendship, hospitality, and virtue, "our amusements flow from the interchange of civilities, and a reciprocal desire of pleasing. . . ." It was, finally, the *"rational* pleasures [which] meliorate the foul; and it is by familiarizing man with uncontaminated felicity, that sordid avarice and vicious habits are to be destroyed."[40]

Spontaneous sociability, ameliorated by the principles of rationality, was the chief appeal of the frontier—at least as the settlers and promoters gauged their audience. They hardly needed to add what every prospective settler should already have known: that "a few years of industry and perseverance will make [one] a man of property."[41] The promoters made it clear that the frontier was emphatically not the place for just anybody, least of all someone who expected nature to provide one's wants. "It is not every emigrant who succeeds," Harry Toulmin wrote:

> no it is only the sober, the honest, and industrious. . . . Others, again, have been led astray by this enchanting scene: their new pride, instead of leading them to the fields, has kept them in idleness: the idea of possessing lands is all that satisfies them: though surrounded by fertility, they have mouldered away their time in inactivity, misinformed husbandry, and ineffectual endeavors.[42]

Toulmin recognized, as Benjamin Franklin had, that some people would be "led astray" by the picture of an Edenic existence. But the last thing he wanted was to attract such people to the frontier. His task, as he saw it, was to disabuse prospective settlers of such irrational expectations, to make them realize that the frontier was a realm of opportunity, of potentiality, but that to fulfill that potentiality people would have to work hard at cultivating the wilderness, society, and the arts and sciences.

II

The literature of settlement and promotion was calculated to attract prospective settlers to emigrate to the frontier. But it would be exceedingly difficult at best to determine whether or not that literature was successful; exceedingly difficult to estimate, for example, how "influential" the literature was on people who might have been wavering in their commitment to emigrate, and even more difficult to judge the influence of the literature on people who might never have considered emigration at all before reading the various "guides," "histories," or "topographical descriptions." But one can uncover the kinds of assumptions that promoters and settlers made about the nature of frontier society and the kinds of strategies they used to promote it. And one can also examine the writings of frontier travelers—again, not in order to arrive at the causal connection between promotional literature and actual emigration, but in order to discover the relationship between the assumptions and perceptions of travelers and those of promoters and settlers.

In comparing the literature of settlement and promotion with the literature of travel, the historian raises certain methodological problems which involve one's own assumptions. Perhaps the most common tendency, in comparing these two modes of literary expression, is to doubt the veracity of promotional writings and at the same time to believe that travelers were, in general, more realistic, more trustworthy, and more accurate in their depictions of frontier life. There are, indeed, good common-sense reasons for tending to value more highly the writings of travelers, not the least of which are those which stem from the nagging suspicion that promoters were trying, above all, to promote land sales, whereas travelers had no financial stake in attracting settlers to the frontier. Indeed, settlers and promoters themselves constantly invoked "the stranger," the mythic "disinterested observer," to witness the truth of their claims. But the historian's tendency to believe travelers more readily than settlers and promoters, taking for granted that travelers were more "objective" or "disinterested," often results in the historian's allowing only pessimistic perceptions to pass for representations of "reality."

Perhaps the most common form generated by this tendency to assume that travelers' perceptions are more believable than those of promoters is the dualistic form "myth" versus "reality." Because they are the expressions of self-interest, the writings of promoters are often interpreted as expressing a "myth" of the frontier, whereas travelers are implicitly accorded a unique insight into "reality." Thus, because travelers frequently expressed the view that life on the frontier bore little or no resemblance to the Edenic garden-world, it is tempting to conclude that the settlers had stretched the truth in their promotional writings. But to separate the literature of settlement and promotion from the literature of travel on the basis of "myth" versus "reality" is to fall prey to a methodological fallacy which has crucial substantive implications. The methodological fallacy lies in separating the two bodies of literature at all, for both have the same status for the historian. Both constitute literary evidence, both articulate perceptions, both reveal assumptions—but neither set of perceptions or assumptions can, in itself, be seen as more closely corresponding to "reality." As recent critics of "myth-symbol" studies have argued, for historians to make statements about historical reality, they need, at the very least, empirical nonliterary data which tend to support or deny a set of perceptions.[43]

This methodological problem has concrete implications for the study of frontier literature, and the problem is exacerbated when one compares promotional literature with travel literature and discovers that neither promoters nor travelers had a uniform view of frontier society. The Reverend James Smith, for example, toured the frontier in 1783 and found himself "in a distant country ... among a people of bad character and entirely destitute of friend or acquaintance. ..."[44] Smith was still more unhappy with the thought, during another tour in 1797, that "if sickness should seize me in a strange land, among a strange people, who will administer me aid and comfort? If the hand of the murderer should take my life, who will carry the fatal tidings to my disconsolate family?"[45] These are not the pictures of a virtuous, hospitable people, cultivating a sociable community on the frontier, people whose greatest aim in life was to rush to the aid of others "on occasions of emergency." They are pictures of a land inhabited by people of "bad character," even murderers.

And yet it was the same Reverend Smith, on the same tour in 1797, only two weeks prior to his expressions of fear of a lonely death, who observed that in Kentucky "the people are kind and hospitable to strangers and plenty is the blessing they enjoy."[46] And it was the same Reverend Smith, traveling in Ohio in 1795, who so exuberantly extolled the virtues of the people of Cincinnati that one might have mistaken him for a property holder and promoter of Ohio lands. "This large and populous town," Smith wrote, "has risen almost instantaneously from nothing, it being (as I was told) only 4 years since it was all in woods. But such is the happy effects of that government in which every trace of vassalage is rooted out and destroyed. ..." At Cincinnati, Smith seemed to find precisely the kind of social order and harmony, based upon a virtuous, hospitable, enlightened citizenry, that promoters like Imlay, Cooper, Toulmin, Filson, and others had advertised.

> [H]ere the honest and industrious farmer cultivates his farm with his own hands, and eats the bread of cheerfulness, and rests contented on his pillow at night. The aged mother instructs her daughters in the useful and pleasing accomplishments of the distaff and the needle. ... The young man ... takes hold of an axe, or follows the plough. The ruddy damsel thinks it no disgrace to wash her clothes, milk her cows, or dress the food for the family.

What picture of social existence, rooted in the natural reciprocity of the family, could better appeal to the enlightened citizen of the new republic? But still greater values issued out of the family settlement: "In a word, it is no disgrace here to engage in any of the honest occupations of life, and the consequence is, trade and manufactures increase, the people live free from want, free from perplexity. . . . Thus they live happy and their end is peace."[47]

Which Reverend Smith is the historian to believe: the one who feared for his life lest he fall ill or be stricken by a murderer, or the one who waxed lyrical over the people of Cincinnati? The answer, perhaps perversely, is both—or neither. But whether one judges his perceptions believable or unbelievable, one goes too far in judging one the expression of "myth" and the other insight into "reality."

It does not help, moreover, to suggest that travelers' views are more credible because their views tended to be less uniform than the views of settlers and promoters. For even the settlers and promoters were very much aware of the uglier aspects of frontier life, and they readily articulated that awareness. Promoters like Harry Toulmin were quick to point out that some settlers could be considered idle, proud, and licentious, and that they "mouldered away their time in inactivity, misinformed husbandry and ineffectual endeavors." Similarly, Judge William Cooper knew of people who "laboured hard all week, but on Sunday they either went hunting or fishing, or else collected in taverns, and loitered away the day, careless of their dress or actions. . . ."[48] There was, as all the settlers and promoters pointed out, the meaner, more miserable sort: "[A] great portion of his time lies vacant, and is usually employed in quarter-races, cock-fights, sauntering in stores and taverns, drinking rum, and spending the residue of his crop."[49]

Settlers, promoters and travelers alike agreed with Harry Toulmin's thought that such "dissipation" "is to be ascribed to some local circumstances."[50] Thus one is left with the banal and not very revealing idea that settlers, promoters, and travelers perceived that some frontier people were mean, avaricious, proud, idle, and licentious, while others were industrious, enlightened, virtuous, and hospitable.

These views suggest that the effort to reduce frontier literature to the categories "myth" and "reality" is a fruitless one unless one relies upon nonliterary evidence. But of equal importance to the methodological fallacy is the substantive problem which arises from it. For if one separates the literature of settlement from the literature of travel one is led to the view that there was a conflict between the irrational paradisiacal dream and a reality which betrayed it. But if one refuses to separate the two bodies of literature, recognizing that both articulated perceptions which reveal underlying assumptions, one realizes that the hopes, expectations, and assumptions of travelers were identical to those of the settlers and promoters. All of them spoke the same language, a language generated by Enlightenment values and founded upon the utopian assumption that the application of human rationality to social problems was sufficient to establish a rational and, therefore, benevolent social order. In criticizing frontier society, travelers did not criticize the settlers for failing to create an earthly Eden rooted in natural wealth and fecundity. They criticized the settlers for failing to create an enlightened social order. In criticizing, as much as in lauding, frontier society, travelers pointed to the same constellation of Enlightenment values to which settlers and promoters pointed. Enlightenment values, in short, constituted a taken-for-granted framework within which travelers articulated their perceptions precisely as did settlers and promoters.

Travelers praised those places on the frontier where they saw the manifest signs of lawfulness, permanent and stable settlement, and virtuous, industrious republicans cultivating society as well as nature. When they criticized frontier society, they criticized the absence of the rational, sociable community that they valued so highly. And, crucially, when they wrote of their disappointments, when they believed that their expectations for an enlightened society were defeated, the travelers implied their growing suspicion that even enlightened rationality was insufficient for creating the kind of society for which rational men had hoped.

Travelers found much to praise on the frontier. Like James Smith, when he remarked on the people and town of Cincinnati, travelers praised frontier society for the same reasons that settlers and promoters did. The layouts of towns seemed to reflect the kind of order and regularity that characterized eastern towns. Travelers' frequent references to checkerboard street plans, for example, evoked images of Philadelphia's grid pattern, and suggested that travelers fully expected rational men to impose physical order on nature's randomness, even when topography resisted such efforts.[51] In emphasizing the value of laying out towns in a regular manner, travelers affirmed Daniel Drake's insightful observation that "curved lines . . . symbolize the country, straight lines the city."[52] Travelers' expectations of order were decidedly "urban," and in praising the planners' good sense in surveying straight lines they lauded what they took to be the fact of prior planning itself.[53]

Similarly, travelers often applauded the planners and settlers for erecting "noble," even "elegant" buildings on the frontier. The buildings to which they were most attracted were public buildings, perceived as the physical signs of permanence and stability, and giving the appearance of what Harry Toulmin called "the apparatus of regulated society."[54] References to brick and stone construction underscored the importance of the permanence that settlers built into the symbolic matrices of legal and constitutional society. Public buildings, moreover, appeared to be the signs of a people who, as advertised, were concerned with matters of common social significance, matters that transcended narrow, individual interests.[55]

The manifest, physical signs of prior planning and social intercourse excited travelers to think that the promise of a new and better society was being realized on the frontier. Here was no desolate wilderness, but towns, or the blueprints and skeletons of towns, with people flocking in only after the "apparatus of regular society" had been established. Travelers' perceptions of overt order, in turn, excited their interest in discovering the virtuous, industrious people whose efforts were, it was presumed, embodied in the external symbols of settled society. But, while travelers had mixed feelings about the frontier people, they were generally disappointed by what they saw. In concentrating on travelers' criticisms two things ought to be remembered: first, that criticism was not universal but varied with "local circumstances"; second—and more important—that in criticizing, travelers revealed less about the reality of frontier society than about the nature of their own perceptions and expectations.

On a visit to his extensive western properties in September, 1784, George Washington reflected that "hitherto, the people of the Western Country having had no excitements to Industry, labour very little."[56] Washington was not alone in his observation. Harry Toulmin had observed people who, "like the Sloth . . . are too lazy to gather food, though they see where it is plenty."[57] Captain John May, surveyor for the Ohio Company, was still harsher. On his journey in 1788, May expressed his utter disappointment at the miserable conditions in which some settlers lived. And what disturbed him most was his sense that the settlers could have bettered their conditions but refused to do so. "[T]his place might be a pretty place of buisness," he wrote, "but the people Do not understand it, in fact the Inhabitants had rather Live like hogs than take a little pains to Live otherwise."[58] In western Kentucky Dr. Saugrain summed up many travelers' comments on the lack of industry among the settlers: "Nearly all the inhabitants pass their time in the chase and in the woods and the rest do just enough to live, what do I say? just enough not to die of hunger." Saugrain concluded with disgust that these frontier people might "pass for the idlest of all America."[59]

These observations are striking not because they portray "reality," but because they express profound chagrin and disappointment; and the chagrin and disappointment are owing to the defeat of the travelers' own expectations. Believing that they would find an enterprising citizenry applying their ingenuity and labor to create farms and towns, trade and manufactures, what they perceived was less than that. Their negative, pessimistic, even cynical judgments, then, are to be seen as functions of their deflated expectations—expectations that had been enormously inflated judging from the crash with which they fell.

It is significant that travelers attributed to the people's indolence and sloth practically every evil that they saw on the frontier; and this attribution to a lack of industry is a good gauge of travelers' expectations and assumptions. John May, for example, did not hesitate to say that the potential for business was being neglected by the people who simply refused to "take a little pains." Similarly, in 1792, after crossing the Oconee River on Georgia's frontier, John Pope came upon a settlement where he perceived the people to be "indolent." The main expressions of the "indolence" which Pope saw, however, were the "Buildings" which "consist of very rough slight Materials, as if intended merely to answer for a Temporary Shelter for a few Sojourners."[60] The inhabitants' miserable dwellings were, as Pope saw it, symptomatic of their lack of industry.

Moses Austin made the same sort of observation in December, 1796, when he noted that "little can be said in favour of the Town of Stanford [in Lincoln County, Kentucky]. it Contins about 20 Hous of Loggs excep a Brick and Stone Hous, has Three small Stores a Tan Yard and Four Taverns." And although Austin had thought that Danville, Kentucky, was well laid out, the town was, nevertheless, "badly Built—Contaning [sic] about 36 Houses the most of which are loggs."[61] On his visit to Greensburgh, Kentucky, in 1789, John May observed that the town "has Thirty odd Logg houses in it and am of opinion there is not thirty beds in the place."[62]

None of these travelers attempted to conceal his disgust at seeing unimproved towns and living conditions that, the travelers thought, reflected indolence and the lack of desire to establish a permanent human habitat. Indeed, precisely as they reported optimistically the use of brick and stone in the construction of public buildings, travelers referred with derision to log cabins, rude huts, and the use of "rough slight Materials." It is interesting, however, that the travelers so readily attributed miserable living conditions to a lack of industry. For this revealed the travelers' assumption that hard work would be sufficient to establish a thriving society, an assumption which they shared with the settlers and promoters.

But the travelers' willingness to attribute to indolence what they saw as the failure of frontier society contains another side. Unwilling to challenge their cherished conviction that industry was sufficient to produce the kind of society for which they hoped, the travelers preferred to see indolence and sloth where there might simply have been poverty. For if hard work was not enough to make people prosperous and society harmonious, then the dream of a thriving society could only become a nightmare of disappointments.

An interesting example of a traveler who allowed his assumptions to guide his perceptions is Dr. Saugrain's thought that a health problem in Louisville, Kentucky, was the result of people's negligence and lack of industry. "Louisville," Saugrain remarked with frustration and contempt, "is a very unhealthy place, and I have no trouble in believing it, considering the negligence of its inhabitants, who let the water stagnate in the lower parts, although it would be little trouble to draw it off."[63] Saugrain's view, while plausible, is single minded. The problem of stagnant water in Louisville, like many health problems on the frontier, was in part the result of difficulties in local government which, on the eighteenth-century frontier, was beset by problems of jurisdiction; and until such jurisdictional problems were resolved the authority and the moneys necessary to remedy specific local difficulties remained problematic.[64]

But this is not the point. The point is that Dr. Saugrain could not think of Louisville's health problem in any category other than that of industry and the people's willingness to apply themselves to a problem, when to correct the problem "would be little trouble." And the same is true of the observations of John May, Moses Austin, and John Pope. These travelers saw a contradiction: they perceived a reality that belied the external signs of ordered, rational, industrious society, a reality that revealed a people lacking in the essential virtue of industry. But the contradiction did not exist between the travelers' perceptions and the reality of frontier life; it existed in the perceptions themselves. It arose from a crisis in the standard of their expectations. Unless one is willing to credit travelers with a privileged insight into reality, the most fruitful interpretation of their criticisms comes from reading them as functions of their utopian expectations.

Several descriptions of the people of Pittsburgh, a frontier city, come very near to the heart of the matter. The reports of David McClure, an exuberant resident of the city, provides a good backdrop for the comments of John Pope and John May. McClure depicted the rapid development of Pittsburgh from a frontier outpost to a thriving city like many settlers described their respective communities. In 1786 McClure observed that "it must appear like enchantment to a stranger... to see, all at once... a town with smoking chimnies, halls lighted up with splendor, ladies and gentlemen assembled, various music, and the magic of the dance."[65] John Pope was, indeed, a stranger to Pittsburgh in 1792; but he was not the stranger whom McClure invoked as a witness to the truth of his observations. Instead, Pope saw a Pittsburgh which was

> inhabited with only some few Exceptions, by Mortals who act as if possessed of a Charter of Exclusive Privilege to filch from, annoy and harrass her Fellow Creatures, particularly the incautious and necessitous.... Goods of every Description are dearer in Pittsburg than in Kentuckey, which I attribute to a Combination of pensioned Scoudrels who infest the Place.[66]

Rather than "ladies and gentlemen" engaged in what Gilbert Imlay thought were "rational pleasures," Pope perceived an avaricious group of scoundrels who took advantage of their fellows, especially "the incautious and necessitous," not to mention touring artists.

John May elaborated Pope's disgust, and May wrote in revealing images. "[T]he inhabitants," he wrote of Pittsburghers in 1788, "are an extravent [i.e., extravagant] lazy set of beings. . . ."[67] A year later May pursued the themes of industry and avarice, writing that Pittsburgh is "intirely destitute of evernly thing butt pride/ they all allow there is no money in the place and I fully believe it for I never saw people so anxious to gitt a Little. and so Loth to part with it. . . ."[68] According to travelers' accounts, avarice was not unique to Pittsburgh, nor was it peculiar to urban areas. Travelers constantly referred with irritation to the presence of men on the make in small settlements and frontier outposts as well as in cities and towns.[69]

These observations on Pittsburgh and its inhabitants reveal an important tension, if not an outright contradiction. John May spoke of the people as being "lazy" and "extravagant," just as John Pope spoke of others as being "indolent, luxurious, fond of gaudy Apparel and pompous Equipage."[70] The pursuit of one's economic self-interest was, by enlightened standards, not only an acceptable enterprise, but a demonstration of one's commitment to cultivating one's occupation. Indeed, travelers criticized settlers for their lack of attention to economic affairs. The enlightened man, of course, ought not to confuse enterprise with avarice, and the enlightened virtue of industry undoubtedly involved moderation. But even if one qualifies these ideas, a tension remains. For if virtuous men properly despised avarice, "extravagance," "luxuriousness," and pomposity, those evils still do not seem to go hand in hand with "laziness," and "indolence," as Pope and May suggested. Even less does the anxiety to get a little money, as May put it, accord with laziness or indolence. Others saw displays of opulence, of the polish of manners and dress, and of the artifacts of eastern society as sure signs of the people's commitment to developing a flourishing and civilized society.[71]

III

Frontier settlers, promoters, and travelers were all caught in the same contradiction of values, although travelers were quicker to express their frustration. At the same time that they criticized frontier people for their lack of industry, travelers also remarked with pleasure on how rapidly trade and manufacturing were developing. At the same time that they condemned the settlers for living like "hogs," refusing to seize the opportunity to make something of the wilderness, travelers also condemned the settlers for creating thriving cities, because land

and commodity prices became inflated and people were on the make. While they mocked the settlers for being too little concerned with matters of behavior, dress, cleanliness, and other conventions of civilized society, they also mocked them for their overrefinement and their absurd efforts to transport the trappings of eastern society to the frontier. They simultaneously criticized the settlers for being idle, indolent, and licentious—rather than dedicating themselves to the task of transforming the wilderness into a productive society—and also for destroying nature.

These criticisms of frontier society, contradictory as they were, reveal an idealized set of expectations which were rooted in Enlightenment assumptions about the nature of society. Settlers, promoters, and travelers alike made these assumptions, so it is no accident that their expectations tended to be similar. These expectations operated on two levels: at one level, settlers and travelers expected frontier society to mirror established society in Europe and the East; at another, less well-articulated level, they expected frontier society to be better than already settled society, more than a continuation of the older settlements. The expectation that frontier society would be better—more rational, orderly, and sociable—than eastern society, reveals the crucial assumption that it *could* be better, for the settlers and travelers believed that social problems would yield to the force of enlightened rationality.

The travelers in particular were frustrated—or, at any rate, they were more willing to express their frustration; and yet frustration was practically guaranteed because the two levels of expectation were mutually incompatible. According to the writings of settlers, promoters, and travelers, the first set of expectations was actually being realized. The new settlements *did* appear to be continuations of the old; and for this appearance the new settlements were praised—but, paradoxically, for this appearance they were also condemned. For it was precisely when the first set of expectations was realized that the second was made impossible. Because the foundation of the new social order consisted of the forms, conventions, and people of the old order, the realization of the new, more sociable society was precluded. But the most important factor in the defeat of expectations was the importation of a way of thinking, and the conviction that that way of thinking could provide for a new society in which, as David McClure put it, "there is all the refinement of the old and more benevolence of heart."[72]

It is important to recognize that the utopian expectation of an enlightened society was not seen as an irrational dream by settlers, promoters, or travelers. There is, in fact, no reason to think of "utopian" expectations or plans as being necessarily irrational. Not even the most disappointed traveler suggested that the planners of settlement (when, indeed, there were planners at all) had acted irrationally.

And this fact in itself made the defeat of expectations all the more severe and difficult to accept. If the disappointed could only have aimed the finger of criticism at irrational dreams and irrational actions in the planning and organizing of settlement, or at the very projection of a new form of civilized society, then they could have reaffirmed their faith in the efficacy of reason to have worked where irrationality had failed. Rather, their criticisms reveal the suspicion that rationality itself was somehow failing, and further, that enlightened modes of rationality might not have the power to bring about their specified intentions.

Moses Austin, one of those travelers who pronounced his pleasure at seeing the signs of cultivation, industry, and commerce on the frontier, nevertheless leveled a telling criticism. Louisville, he wrote, "by nature is beautifull but the handy work of Man has insted of improving destroy.d the works of Nature and made it a detestable place."[73] By "handy work" Austin did not mean irrational actions. He meant the people's arts and artifices, their efforts to transform nature with the instruments of rational civilization. Indeed, he implied a subtle reversal of Reverend Smith's notion that the people's art supplied what nature had denied. For Austin, the people's art reduced what nature had produced.

Austin was not suggesting that "technology" was an evil, nor was he arguing for the preservation of nature's pristine purity. For him, as for settlers and travelers universally, nature was properly to be "improved," transformed pursuant to people's best inclinations to human society. What provoked so much frustration was that in the effort to cultivate or improve nature, human "handy work" inadvertently destroyed it. And this was fearsome: the instruments of rational civilization contained within them the power to transform nature; but whether the result was constructive or destructive seemed beyond human power to anticipate or control.

At Pittsfield, Massachusetts, in 1796, Jeremy Belknap reflected on the change that had come over the countryside since the founding of the settlement. "[T]he land hereabouts were the hunting-ground of the Stockbridge Indians, full of deer and other game," Belknap observed. But "cultivation has gradually destroyed" them.[74] Similarly, John May, writing of Ohio in the summer of 1788, noted that "deer are plentier in this country, than horn cattle are in New England." But May recognized the inevitable consequence of settlement, observing that the presence of the deer "can not be of long duration/ whenever a new country is settled the native inhabitants must flee or die."[75]

Both travelers and settlers were generally dismayed at the wanton destruction and waste of nature, although twentieth-century concerns for the preservation of nature ought not to be read back into the literature of the eighteenth-century frontier. Only a pretwentieth-century

American, like William Cooper, could have invited prospective settlers to perform what today would be considered an act of ecological suicide:

> Leave to Caesar the boast of having killed two million men; let yours be that of having cut down two million trees. . . . To say that you have done all this for your own interest, does not take away the merit; but to render your labors useful to others . . . is the duty to which I now invite you.[76]

In general, however, the destruction of nature meant that the desired balance between nature and society would be upset, and that balance was always viewed as a basic advantage of eighteenth-century society.

What disturbed Austin, Belknap, and May was not the destruction of nature as such; it was that destruction was as intrinsic, inevitable, and unpredictable a dimension of "cultivation" as was construction or improvement. And that same unpredictability seemed to be as true for society as it was for nature. It was as possible to destroy society, to waste human potentialities in the very effort to cultivate a rational community, as it was to destroy nature in the same effort and by the same means.

IV

Settlers and travelers—but especially travelers—had vague intimations of the contradiction that resided in their assumptions and that, therefore, haunted their expectations. Had they proceeded to examine the nature and the depth of their commitment to enlightened values and modes of thought, the effect might have been a crushing blow to those same values and modes of thought. The effect might also have been the development of a new set of social values and new insights into the structure and organization of society. But instead of examining the commitment, settlers and travelers accepted—or resigned themselves to—what they perceived to be the failures of the frontier experiment to live up to their expectations. Because their intimations of the reasons for the failures were merely intimations, they accepted both the failures and the successes with irritation and frustration and even with the suspicion that the aims of enlightened society might be unrealizable in practice. What their acceptance or resignation demonstrates is that, despite the frustration, irritation, and suspicion, they remained committed to the practically limitless possibilities of rationality and hard work. Retaining that faith, Gilbert Imlay could write that "it is physically impossible for man to degenerate into barbarism."[77]

In the most important respect Arthur K. Moore was correct in saying that "the development of society in the West may be regarded as a
grotesque jest at the expense of the Enlightenment...."[78] But it was a
jest that the Enlightenment had played upon itself. It was not Americans' primitivist assumptions or paradisiacal expectations which
undermined Enlightenment values on the frontier. Rather, it was
enlightened thought and practice, and expectations based upon
enlightened rationality, that undermined Enlightenment values—precisely by affirming them. It was this that made the jest grotesque.
Enlightenment values and modes of thought were capable of generat-
ing utopian social visions and expectations. But the same values and
modes of thought were incapable of fulfilling the American project of a
social utopia.

NOTES

1. The following quotations, until otherwise noted, are from Franklin to
Collinson, May 9, 1753, in Leonard W. Labaree, et. al., eds., *The Papers of
Benjamin Franklin* (New Haven, Conn.: Yale Univ. Press, 1964), IV, pp.
479–86.

2. Ibid., VI, pp. 468–69 (July 2, 1756).

3. See, "A Plan for Settling Two Western Colonies" (1754), ibid., V, pp.
456–63. Franklin's ideas on industry and the disinclination of people to work
were associated with his attitudes toward immigrants. See, "Observations Concerning the Increase of Mankind" (1751), ibid., IV, pp. 225–34. See also, ibid.,
IV, pp. 130–33, 484-85: VI, pp. 38ff., 231–32.

4. The theme of naturalism and the categories of "myth" and "reality"
underlie what are generally taken to be the "classics" in the field: Henry Nash
Smith, *Virgin Land: The American West as Symbol and Myth* (Cambridge,
Mass.: Harvard Univ. Press, 1950); Leo Marx, *The Machine in the Garden:
Technology and the Pastoral Ideal in America* (New York: Oxford Univ. Press,
1964): Arthur K. Moore, *The Frontier Mind* (Lexington: Univ. of Kentucky
Press, 1957); Charles L. Sanford, *The Quest for Paradise* (Urbana: Univ. of
Illinois Press, 1961): Richard Slotkin, *Regeneration Through Violence: The
Mythology of the American Frontier, 1600–1860* (Middletown, Conn.: Wesleyan
Univ. Press, 1973).

5. See especially Moore, *Frontier Mind*, especially Chaps. 1, 7, 10, and 11.

6. I am using the terms "settlers" and "promoters" interchangeably except
where such usage might create confusion. Settlers who, like William Cooper
and Harry Toulmin, wrote "guides" or histories used their writings in large
measure to attract future settlers, making them both "settlers" and "promoters."

7. Earl Pomeroy, "Toward a Reorientation of Western History: Continuity
and Environment," *Mississippi Valley Historical Review*, 41, No. 4 (March
1955), 579–600, quoted at pp. 583, 582.

8. [Manasseh Cutler], *A Description of the Soil, Production, Etc., of that
Portion of the United States Situated Between Pennsylvania, and the Rivers
Ohio and Scioto and Lake Erie* (Salem, Mass., 1787: rpt. under the title *Ohio in
1788*, ed., John H. James [Columbus, Ohio, 1888]), p. 16.

9. Ibid., pp. 43–44. Fisher Ames, the sharp-witted Federalist, for example, expressed his fears over the "anarchical notions" of Tennessee's backwoods people, and summarized his disgust with the frontier in general by noting in 1798 that "Kentucky is all alien." In Seth Ames, *The Works of Fisher Ames* (Boston, 1854), I, pp. 233, 248 respectively. With the Louisiana Purchase Ames was outraged by what he saw as President Jefferson's naive optimism over the frontier's possibilities. Ibid., I, pp. 317, 329.

10. Ibid., p. 54.

11. Ibid., p. 45.

12. Gilbert Imlay, *A Topographical Description of the Western Territory of North America* (London, 1792). I have used the Dublin edition of 1793, printed under the title *A Description of the Western Territories of North America.* See Smith, *Virgin Land*, pp. 147–48, and Chap. 11: Moore, *Frontier Mind*, pp. 20–24: Slotkin, *Regeneration Through Violence*, pp. 317–20, 350; Durand Echeverria, *Mirage in the West: A History of the French Image of American Society to 1815* (Princeton, N.J.: Princeton Univ. Press, 1968), pp. 116–18.

13 .Imlay, *Topographical Description*, p. 1.

14. Ibid., p. 15.

15. Ibid., p. 14.

16. William Cooper, *A Guide in the Wilderness, or the History of the First Settlements in the Western Counties of New York, with Useful Instructions to Future Settlers. . . .* (Dublin, 1810), pp. 30–31.

17. Ibid., p. 15.

18. Ibid., p. 16. While political economists like Adam Smith made the circulation metaphor a commonplace by the end of the eighteenth century, its roots lay deeper in English thought. Playing on William Harvey's discovery of the circulation of the blood, Thomas Hobbes, writing in 1651 "Of the Nutrition and Procreation of a Common-wealth," referred to money as "the Bloud of a Commonwealth." Money as a measure of value, Hobbes wrote, "goes round about [the Commonwealth], Nourishing (as it passeth) every part thereof. . . . For naturall Bloud is in like manner made of the fruits of the Earth: and circulating, nourisheth by the way, every Member of the Body of Man." (*Leviathan*, Chap. XXIV)

19. Cooper, *Guide*, p. 16.

20. John Filson, *The Discovery, Settlement and Present State of Kentucke* (1784: facsimile rpt. as *Filson's Kentucke*, ed., Willard R. Jillson [Louisville, Ky., 1930]), p. 107.

21. Ibid., pp. 107, 46–47.

22. Ibid., p. 29.

23. Cooper, *Guide*, p. 5.

24. Willard R. Jillson, ed., *A Transylvania Trilogy . . . Harry Toulmin's 1792 "A History of Kentucky"* (Frankfort, Ky., 1932), p. 182. Hereafter cited as Toulmin, *History*.

25. Imlay, *Topographical Description*, p. 53.

26. Toulmin, *History*, pp. 21–22.

27. Ibid., pp. 22–23.

28. Cooper, *Guide*, p. 2. (Italics added.)

29. Ibid., p. 6.

30. Toulmin, *History*, p. 171.

31. Filson, *Kentucke*, p. 49.

32. Imlay, *Topographical Description*, p. 97.

33. Cooper, *Guide*, pp. 8, 12–24: James Smith, *Tours into Kentucky and the Northwest Territory; Three Journals by the Rev. James Smith of Powhatan County, Virginia, 1783–1795–1797* (n.p., 1907), p. 398. See Labaree, *Papers of Franklin*, V, p. 461.

34. Smith, *Tours*, p. 382.
35. Imlay, *Topographical Description*, pp. 107, 134: see Toulmin, *History*, pp. 22–23.
36. Imlay, *Topographical Descriptions*, pp. 137–38.
37. Ibid., p. 41.
38. Eugene F. Bliss, ed., *Dr. Saugrain's Note-Books, 1788* (n.p., n.d.), p. 8.
39. See, for example, Moore, *Frontier Mind*, p. 31, and Smith, *Virgin Land*, Book Three. By overemphasizing the importance of nature, both authors tend to underestimate the importance of work in the garden, suggesting that one of the principal delights of life in the garden was precisely the absence of the need to work hard. Richard Slotkin, however, is aware of the dialectical relationship between man and nature, a relationship which is founded in labor. See Slotkin, *Regeneration Through Violence*, passim; e.g., p. 273. See also Bernard W. Sheehan, *Seeds of Extinction: Jeffersonian Philanthropy and the American Indian* (New York: Norton, 1974), pp. 26–44.
40. Imlay, *Topographical Description*, p. 139.
41. Ibid., p. 151.
42. Toulmin, *History*, pp. 59–60.
43. See, e.g., Bruce Kuklick, "Myth and Symbol in American Studies," *American Quarterly*, 24, No. 4 (October 1972), 435–50. I do not, obviously, share Kuklick's apparent aversion to "myth-symbol" studies. But his argument, by illuminating some of the faulty assumptions on which they rest, identifies the limits of such studies, and by doing so indicates the directions in which they might profitably proceed.
44. Smith, *Tours*, p. 357.
45. Ibid., p. 389.
46. Ibid., p. 388.
47. Ibid., pp. 376–77.
48. Cooper, *Guide*, p. 30.
49. Toulmin, *History*, p. 55.
50. Ibid., p. 55n.
51. See Dwight Smith, ed., *The Western Journals of John May, 1788, 1789* (Cincinnati, 1961), p. 48. Moses Austin, "A Memorandum of M. Austin's Journey from the Lead Mines in the County of Wythe in the State of Virginia to the Lead Mines in the Province of Louisiana West of the Mississippi," *American Historical Review*, 5, (1899–1900), 523–42: Jeremy Belknap, *Journal of a Tour from Boston to Oneida, June, 1796, by Jeremy Belknap*, ed., George Dexter (Cambridge, Mass., 1882), p. 28: Smith, *Tours*, p. 398: Richard C. Wade, *The Urban Frontier: Pioneer Life in Early Pittsburgh, Cincinnati, Lexington, Louisville, and St. Louis* (Cambridge, Mass.: Harvard Univ. Press, 1959), pp. 27–29.
52. Quoted in Wade, *Urban Frontier*, p. 28.
53. Page Smith has shown that the growth of towns was frequently "not the result of any prior plan": there were many towns "whose growth was cumulative and often fortuitous." In *As a City Upon a Hill: The Town in American History* (New York: Knopf, 1966), p. 17. Drake's observation, although historically inaccurate, nevertheless demonstrates the great value which he placed on prior planning.
54. Toulmin, *History*, p. 183.
55. See, for example, Smith, *Tours*, p. 383: Austin, "Memorandum," p. 527. During the same period travelers in the most settled parts of America spoke of the same phenomena and in the same terms as did frontier travelers. See, for example, Thomas Chapman, *Journal of a Tourist Through the Eastern States* (collected from *Historical Magazine*, n.d. in pamphlet form), p. 17: Timothy Dwight, *Travels; In New England and New York* (New Haven, 1821), passim.

56. Archer B. Hulbert, ed., *Washington and the West, Being George Washington's Diary of September, 1784 Kept During his Journey into the Ohio Basin in the interest of a commercial union between the Great Lakes and the Potomac River* (New York, 1905), p. 99.

57. Toulmin, *History*, p. 54.

58. Smith, *Western Journals*, p. 97.

59. Bliss, *Saugrain's Note-Books*, p. 11.

60. John Pope, *A Tour Through the Southern and Western Territories of the United States of North America* ... (Richmond, 1792), p. 70.

61. Austin, "Memorandum," p. 526.

62. Smith, *Western Journals*, p. 104.

63. Bliss, *Saugrain's Note-Books*, pp. 5–6.

64. Wade, *Urban Frontier*, pp. 72–100. I am indebted to my colleague, Vernard L. Foley, for pointing out that stagnant water, in addition to being a thorny political problem, was also an acute technological problem on the late eighteenth-century frontier.

65. Quoted in ibid., p. 13.

66. Pope, *A Tour*, p. 17.

67. Smith, *Western Journals*, p. 37.

68. Ibid., p. 101.

69. The intersecting themes of unsociability, poverty, idleness, and avarice pervaded the literature of travel. See, for example, Smith, *Tours*, p. 364; Pope, *A Tour*, pp. 12, 43: Nathan Perkins, *A Narrative of a Tour Through the State of Vermont, from April 27 to June 12, 1789* (Woodstock, Vt., 1920), pp. 11–12, 18–19: Bliss, *Saugrain's Note-Books*, p. 18: Smith, *Western Journals*, pp. 31, 39, 53, 97. May summed up the general feeling of disgust in interesting language when he observed that "the Inhabitants of this Country do not live so rationally as the brute Creation." In Smith, *Western Journals*, p. 105.

70. Pope, *A Tour*, p. 70.

71. See, Smith, *Tours*, pp. 372, 395: Imlay, *Topographical Description*, pp. 33–34, 140: Toulmin, *History*, p. 27.

72. Quoted in Wade, *Urban Frontier*, p. 13.

73. Austin, "Memorandum," p. 527.

74. Belknap, *Journal of a Tour*, p. 8.

75. Smith, *Western Journals*, p. 61. (Italics added.) See Filson, *Kentucke*, p. 27: Bliss, *Saugrain's Note-Books*, p. 7.

76. Cooper, *Guide*, p. 2. James Fenimore Cooper, the judge's son, seems to have used his father's *Guide* (for which he wrote an introduction) as the basis for the theme of natural destruction in *The Pioneers* (see, especially, Chaps. xxii and xxiii). In the novel, however, Judge Temple is accorded the good sense to see the immorality of such destruction when Leatherstocking explains it to him.

77. Imlay, *Topographical Description*, p. 54.

78. Moore, *Frontier Mind*, p. 238: see Chap. 10.

MICHAEL T. GILMORE

Eulogy as Symbolic Biography:
The Iconography of Revolutionary Leadership,
1776–1826

Eulogy has been called the oldest form of biography. In eulogy, however, the concrete details that make up the life of a particular person, details essential to even the most uncritical biography, tend to vanish as a result of the didacticism of the genre. The deceased appears less as an individualized figure than as an emblem or symbol contrived for the purpose of instructing an audience. Although the lives described turn out to be much·the same, they nevertheless have value as a revelation of character. By treating the dead as a kind of cultural ideal, the eulogist seeks in effect to compose the collective biography of an entire people. Thus, the true subject of the eulogy is the speaker and his community rather than the character and career of the person nominally portrayed. For just this reason, the eulogies delivered for American revolutionary leaders during the first half-century of the republic's existence yield valuable insights into the ideological and emotional issues that engaged successive generations of their countrymen.

Two systems of allusion were available to American orators who commemorated the illustrious dead: the language of classi-

131

cal antiquity as received through the Commonwealthmen or
radical Whigs; and the evangelical or millennial vocabulary re-
vitalized by the Great Awakening. Each tradition had its models
of what a leader should be, and each helped to shape American
values and standards of conduct. Hopeful that the new nation
would be, in Samuel Adams's words, "the *Christian* Sparta,"
Patriot leaders themselves regularly drew inspiration from both
traditions. Patrick Henry was appealing to this dual inheritance
when he uttered his famous warning to King George at the
height of the Stamp Act crisis: "Tarquin and Caesar each had
his Brutus, Charles the First his Cromwell."[1]

Men do not simply inherit their vocabularies; they also revise

1. Adams quoted in Gordon S. Wood, *The Creation of the American
Republic, 1776–1787* (1969; rpt. New York: Norton, 1972), p. 118;
Henry quoted in H. Trevor Colbourn, *The Lamp of Experience: Whig
History and the Intellectual Origins of the American Revolution* (1965;
rpt. New York: Norton, 1974), p. 150. On the background and evolu-
tion of republican ideology, see, in addition to Wood and Colbourn,
Bernard Bailyn, *The Ideological Origins of the American Revolution*
(Cambridge: Harvard University Press, 1967); J. G. A. Pocock, *The
Machiavellian Moment: Florentine Political Thought and the Atlantic
Republican Tradition* (Princeton: Princeton University Press, 1975);
and Caroline Robbins, *The Eighteenth-Century Commonwealthman:
Studies in the Transmission, Development, and Circumstance of English
Liberal Thought from the Restoration of Charles II until the War with
the Thirteen Colonies* (Cambridge: Harvard University Press, 1959).
On the evangelical tradition, see Alan Heimert, *Religion and the Amer-
ican Mind: From the Great Awakening to the Revolution* (Cambridge:
Harvard University Press, 1966); Heimert and Perry Miller, eds., *The
Great Awakening: Documents Illustrating the Crisis and Its Conse-
quences* (Indianapolis: Bobbs-Merrill, 1967), pp. xiii–lxi; and Richard
L. Bushman, *From Puritan to Yankee: Character and the Social Order
in Connecticut, 1690–1765* (1967; rpt. New York: Norton, 1970). For
the general proposition that Enlightenment ideas were modified in
America and made compatible with Protestant Christianity, see. Henry
F. May, *The Enlightenment in America* (New York: Oxford University
Press, 1976), esp. pp. 153–357. By revolutionary leaders I mean those
individuals who played a prominent part in the War for Independence
in either a civilian or a military capacity. It should be stressed at the
outset that only a few orations for such men were published prior to
1800, and that the eulogists themselves were members of the American
leadership. This study is obviously based on a sampling rather than
a comprehensive survey of elite opinion. I believe, however, that the
emphases isolated here were reflective of broader currents within American culture.

and transform them. The meanings of particular words may be radically altered by the speaker who employs them, or by the context in which they appear. The appeals to Puritan Christianity and classical paganism made by patriotic eulogists in 1776 meant something different by the turn of the century. Originally used to justify revolt against Britain, these appeals were later invoked to legitimize the newly established American state. To speak in terms of the familial imagery then prevalent in political discourse, they were placed at the service of paternal authority, and severed from their previous connection with filial dissent. As American Sons of Liberty became the Founding Fathers, there emerged a rhetorical synthesis of the two traditions that was more appropriate to the celebration of an empire than an authentic republic.

The funeral orations pronounced during the war years naturally took as their theme the justice and glory of the American cause. The orators, in praising their fallen leaders, accordingly dwelt on the revolutionary implications of the two pasts they had inherited. Declaring that war and rebellion were preferable to slavery, they upheld the right of resistance to unjust authority on the basis of republican precedent and their reading of Scripture. They portrayed their subjects as both heroes and saints, martyrs to the rights of Englishmen and the truths of the Christian religion, and they enjoined their hearers to emulate the dead by displaying a similar zeal in defense of virtue and liberty.

The opening salutation commonly set the mood of these early eulogies. William Smith, speaking before the Continental Congress in memory of General Richard Montgomery, began in typical fashion when he addressed the assembled delegates as "Fathers, Brethren, and Countrymen!" Smith's greeting, which recalls the opening lines of Mark Antony's eulogy from *Julius Caesar* (a play well-known to Americans for its portrayal of the decisive moment in Roman history, the transition from the Republic to the Empire), was based on the stylistic convention, the tricolon: an arrangement of words or phrases in a group of three that was perfected in classical antiquity by teachers of rhetoric and popularized in English by writers seeking to reproduce the cadences of Ciceronian Latin.[2] Adopted by orators throughout the revolutionary period, it was a fitting device to introduce a eulogy that treated its subject as a figure worthy of comparison with the greatest heroes of Greece and Rome.

Smith's eulogy was typical in other respects as well. Reminding the Congress that *amor patriae,* "the love of our country," was the most exalted of virtues, he combed two thousand years of history for examples of antique republicans and radical Whigs. Not only did he liken Montgomery to such legendary ancients as Regulus and Cincinnatus — the latter, like his American counterpart, "a *General* from the *plough!*" — he also ranked him with two of the brightest luminaries in the Commonwealth galaxy, John Hampden and Algernon Sidney. Smith's use of the classical past was highly selective, in accordance with the bias of the English libertarians, whose translations and commentaries were the chief source for the American cult of antiquity. The ancient authors he cited most frequently — Cicero, Horace, and Livy — had endeared themselves to the eighteenth century by contrasting the corruption and decay of the Roman Empire with the idealized purity of the early Republic — that golden age of austere morality that had seemingly vanished forever when Caesar crossed the Rubicon to march upon Rome.[3]

2. William Smith, *An Oration in Memory of General Montgomery and of the Officers and Soldiers Who Fell with Him, December 31, 1775, before Quebec; Drawn Up (and Delivered February 19th, 1776) at the Desire of the Honourable Continental Congress* (2nd ed.; Philadelphia, 1776), p. 1. On the tricolon, see Gilbert Highet, *The Classical Tradition: Greek and Roman Influences on Western Literature* (1949; rpt. New York: Oxford University Press, 1970); pp. 112–113, 334–335. For evidence of American familiarity with *Julius Caesar,* see Francois Xavier Martin, *A Funeral Oration on . . . Major-General Richard Caswell* (Newbern, N.C., 1790), pp. 3–4. Martin quotes directly from Antony's eulogy for Caesar as rendered by Shakespeare.

3. Smith, *An Oration,* pp. 3, 20, 12, 11, 4–5, 31, passim; Carl L. Becker, *Everyman His Own Historian: Essays on History and Politics* (New York: F. S. Crofts, 1935), p. 49. See also, in general, Meyer Reinhold, ed., *The Classick Pages: Classical Reading of Eighteenth-Century Americans* (University Park, Pa.: The American Philological Association, 1975). For further evidence of the juxtaposition of ancients and Commonwealthmen, see Perez Morton, *An Oration; Delivered at the King's Chapel in Boston, April 8, 1776, on the Re-Interment of the Remains of the late Most Worshipful Grand-Master, Joseph Warren,*

A comparable world, in the view of Smith and his fellow revolutionists, had been reborn on American shores in the persons of men like Montgomery, himself of Irish origin, who had served with the British forces in Canada and been captivated by "our simplicity of manners, yet uncorrupted by luxury or flagrant vice." How admirable that Montgomery should choose to settle on the banks of the Hudson, and to pursue in rustic retirement "the life of a country gentleman, deriving its most exquisite relish from reflection upon past dangers and past services." To an audience steeped in the classics, such words evoked the Horatian ideal of a rural retreat to which disinterested patriots could retire after a lifetime spent in devotion to country and duty. Clearly America was the place where those agrarian virtues characteristic of the greatest days of the Roman Republic could flourish.[4]

The American setting was also congenial to the cultivation of true religion and piety. Montgomery, according to Smith, was a devout Christian as well as an antique Roman, a man who had taught his heart to "beat *unison* with the harmony of heaven!" Although Smith himself happened to be an Anglican priest with little sympathy for the evangelicalism of the Great Awakening, his celebrations of frugality, industry, and "pure benevolence" could well have been uttered by the Calvinist clergy. He confidently turned to the Bible for proof that the prophets were no less opposed than the ancients to rule by tyrants, and he quoted at length from Isaiah foretelling the downfall of Babylon: "How hath the oppressor ceased! The Lord hath broken the staff of the wicked! He that smote the people in wrath — that ruled the nations in anger — is persecuted, and none hindereth!" Smith even appended a footnote to his published oration in which he quoted an English prelate as saying that "true religion, virtue, and liberty are more intimately connected than men commonly

Esquire . . . (Boston, 1776). "In Fine, to compleat the great Character," Morton said of Warren, "like HARRINGTON he wrote, like CICERO he spoke, like HAMPDEN he lived, and like WOLFE he died," p. 12.

4. Smith, *An Oration*, pp. 18–19. The Horatian ideal is discussed by Howard Mumford Jones, *O Strange New World: American Culture, The Formative Years* (1964; rpt. New York: Viking, 1968), pp. 245–247.

consider." The corresponding theme of his own remarks, he added, was "the reward of *heroes,* in the *Christian's heaven.*"[5]

For both Christians and pagans, Smith declared, the purpose of the eulogy was to encourage the living to imitate the dead — not to worship or deify them. Since men were more prone to imitate than to be instructed, "eminent characters" had "a stronger influence than written precepts." Montgomery's countrymen could show their respect for his memory by consecrating their own lives to the revolutionary cause. "Rome in all her glory would have decreed honors," Smith told his audience; the Congress in justice could do no less.[6]

Smith's oration, apparently the first delivered for an American officer killed in combat, went into a second edition within a matter of months. Although Smith still retained some hope that England would mend her ways,[7] his speech was otherwise representative of the several eulogies for Patriot leaders that have survived from the war years. Chaplains with denominational affiliations less bound to the royal establishment differed little in their choice of models. Israel Evans, an evangelical and militant awakener,[8] saw no conflict between Edwardsean Calvinism and classical republicanism when he commemorated General Enoch Poor of the New Hampshire Brigade in 1780. Dissolving the private man into the public image, Evans also resorted to the ancient authorities as well as the gospel in dignifying his subject. He opened his address with a tricolon — "Friends, Country-men, and Fellow-Soldiers; Favor me, I beseech you, with your attention and candor" — and hailed Greece and Rome as "those sublime patterns of republican wisdom, virtue, and valor." Like others of the revolutionary generation, Evans's understanding of ancient history was thoroughly "Whiggized." Cato the Younger, who had committed suicide at Utica to avoid capture by Caesar, stirred his enthusiasm. Paraphrasing directly from Thomas Gordon's translation of Sallust, the Roman historian who had mercilessly dissected the moral decay of the

5. Smith, *An Oration,* pp. 18, 13, 10, 7–8.
6. Smith, *An Oration,* pp. 10, 36.
7. As it turned out, the Congress considered Smith's position too moderate and voted down a motion to thank him for his address.
8. Evans is mentioned in Heimert, *Religion and the American Mind,* pp. 498, 531. A brief biographical sketch appears on p. 558.

late Republic, Evans told his audience that "Cato fled from fame, but she pursued him with the greater speed. He chose to be virtuous rather than appear so."[9] Evans also drew on Joseph Addison's tragedy *Cato* (1712), the most popular play in eighteenth-century America. In his peroration, he reproduced Addison's words with only slight variation:

> 'Tis not in mortals to command success,
> But we'll do more my friends, we will deserve it.[10]

The example of Poor, who sacrificed private interest to public welfare, suggested comparison to another hero of the classical pantheon, the great Roman patriot Cicero. In his celebrated orations, Cicero had championed resistance to tyrants, and he had saved the Republic by exposing and crushing the Catiline conspiracy. Evans, in praising Poor, declared that the General's selfless conduct "shall procure for him the glorious name of a FATHER to his country" — the title, according to Plutarch, which Rome had given to Cicero for his service in the cause of liberty.[11]

Poor's patriotism, Evans assured his listeners, was nurtured by his religion. "True piety to God" strengthened his resolution in battle, and enabled him to shun intemperance, profanity, and avarice — the besetting vices of armies, equally hateful to virtuous pagans and practicing Christians. His life exemplified

9. Israel Evans, *An Oration, Delivered at Hackinsack, on the Tenth of September, 1780, at the Interment of the Honorable Brigadier Enoch Poor, General of the New Hampshire Brigade* (Newburyport, 1781), pp. 3–6, 9. Sallust is excerpted in Reinhold, *The Classick Pages*, pp. 101–106. The relevant quotation appears on p. 105: Cato "aimed not so much to appear, as to be, a virtuous Man; So that the less he courted Renown, the faster it followed him."

10. Evans, *An Oration*, p. 36. Compare the lines by Portius, Cato's son, from I.ii.44–45: "'Tis not in mortals to command success,/but we'll do more, Sempronius; we'll deserve it." Addison's play was also an important influence on George Washington, Patrick Henry, and Nathan Hale. See Fredric M. Litto, "Addison's *Cato* in the Colonies," *William and Mary Quarterly*, 23 (1966), 431–449.

11. Evans, *An Oration*, p. 27. Cf. Plutarch, *The Lives of the Noble Grecians and Romans*, trans. John Dryden, rev. Arthur Hugh Clough (New York: The Modern Library, n.d.), p. 1054. The so-called Dryden translation (actually by several hands) was first published in 1683.

the lesson "that religion and true courage are no ways inconsistent with each other, but being united, mutually promote
dignity and true glory." By imitating the example of Poor, who
combined moral goodness with love of country, the soldiers of
the American army could be sure of purchasing not only "the
glorious titles of heroes and patriots," but also "a passport . . .
to the regions of eternal happiness."[12]

To the revolutionary eulogists, then, religion and republican
ideology were equally instrumental in preparing the colonists to
depose the British rulers who had infringed upon their liberties.
The two traditions raised up an intrepid leadership and supplied
the vocabularies with which patriotic orators vindicated the
legitimacy of the American cause. Should representatives of
the Crown protest that rebellion was disloyalty to the king,
Americans could answer in the words of Addison's Cato: when
asked, "What is a Roman, that is Caesar's foe?" Cato replies,
"Greater than Caesar; he's a friend to virtue" (II.ii.40–41).
Should Tory clergymen such as Jonathan Boucher assert that
the Scriptures taught passive obedience to rulers, Patriot clergymen could respond in the strains of Isaiah, exulting over the
fall of tyrants. Among the eulogists, it was Israel Evans who
made the most dramatic use of this dual inheritance when he
closed his funeral oration for General Poor with a liturgical
formula and a Latin quotation from Horace:

Now to God the Father, Son, and Holy Spirit, be ascribed, as is
most due, all praise, might, majesty and dominion, from everlasting, and to everlasting. Amen, and Amen.

GLORIA EST PRAEMIUM VIRTUTUS.
DULCE ET DECORUM EST PRO
PATRIA MORI.[13]

The two systems of allusion employed by eulogists for Patriot
leaders were supplemented by a mode of political discourse
habitual to Englishmen on both sides of the Atlantic. At home
and in the colonies, they were accustomed to speak about po-

12. Evans, *An Oration*, pp. 13–14, 26–27, 31–32, 36, passim.
13. Evans, *An Oration*, p. 36.

litical obligation in terms of analogy to the family. The history of the familial metaphor in Western political thought has only recently begun to be studied; its ancestry dates back at least to the ancient Athenians.[14] For seventeenth-century Englishmen, the authority of the metaphor was based on the Word rather than on classical precedent. Their catechisms had taught them that all civil, religious, and natural callings were covered by the biblical injunction to "honor thy father and thy mother." As John Flavel explained in 1692, the Fifth Commandment applied to magistrates and their subjects, ministers and their flocks, household heads and their children, and masters and their servants. Every member of the community at large was expected to act as a godly father toward his subordinates and a dutiful son toward his superiors.[15]

It took Sir Robert Filmer to translate these general sentiments, shared by Puritans and Anglicans alike, into a full-blown defense of the divine right of kings. According to Filmer, all political authority had evolved from the family, and rulers were therefore entitled to the same absolute obedience that children owed to their parents. Adam, in Filmer's view, had been the original father, and his power, descending through the Hebrew patriarchs to the English kings, was sanctioned by God. Filmer's patriarchalism elicited an outspoken response from John Locke in his *Two Treatises on Government* (1689–1690). According to Locke, parenthood was a trust and a duty founded on the weakness of children; parental authority was not absolute because children had rights of their own. Indeed, Locke's contention that consent and contract rather than parenthood were the true foundations of the body politic wholly repudiated the political significance of the Fifth Commandment. Although patriarchalism gradually fell into disfavor as a political doctrine, Locke's warning against reasoning analogically from fami-

14. Gordon J. Schochet, *Patriarchalism in Political Thought: The Authoritarian Family and Political Speculation and Attitudes Especially in Seventeenth-Century England* (New York: Basic Books, 1975), pp. 20–24. Schochet's study is the fullest treatment of the subject, and I am indebted to his book in this and the following paragraph.

15. Flavel is quoted in Schochet, *Patriarchalism in Political Thought*, p. 81.

71

lies was either forgotten or ignored, and Englishmen writing on politics continued to employ the familial metaphor.[16]

It has been shown that this analogical habit of thought was in fact a staple of polemical literature in the period surrounding the revolutionary conflict. Jonathan Mayhew described British kings as "the political FATHERS of their children, and the people their CHILDREN"; John Dickinson urged his countrymen to "behave like dutiful children, who have received unmerited blows from a beloved parent"; Thomas Paine attacked King George as a "wretch . . . with the pretended title FATHER OF HIS PEOPLE"; and John Adams compared England to "a cruel Beldam," capable, like Lady Macbeth, of plucking her nipples from America's toothless gums and dashing out the brains of the infant.[17] These examples suggest the important differences between the filial, paternal, and maternal images used by the colonists.[18] England, the country, was always likened to a mother or parent, never to a father; and womanhood, as a figure of speech, was applied to the nation or land rather than political authority as such. It was George the Third, the pretended father of the empire, who represented the political power of the state. When that power was unjustly exercised, the otherwise dutiful colonists, now transformed into insurgent Sons of Liberty, had the right to oppose and reject it. Sonship, in the context of the Revolution, signified a challenge to, or defiance of, political

16. Schochet, *Patriarchalism in Political Thought*, pp. 115–158. See also Edwin G. Burrows and Michael Wallace, "The American Revolution: The Ideology and Psychology of National Liberation," *Perspectives in American History*, 6 (1972), 167–189.

17. Burrows and Wallace, "The American Revolution," pp. 196–197, 214, 194, 292; generally, pp. 190–306. Quotations are from Mayhew's *The Snare Broken* (1766); Dickinson's *Letters from a Farmer in Pennsylvania* (1768); Paine's *Common Sense* (1776); and the writings of John Adams, who thought so much of the comparison that he used it several times.

18. The differences have been explored from a psychoanalytic point of view by Bruce Mazlish, "Leadership in the American Revolution: The Psychological Dimension," in *Leadership in the American Revolution* (Washington, D.C.: Library of Congress, 1974), pp. 113–133. See esp. pp. 122, 124. Also relevant is Winthrop D. Jordan, "Familial Politics: Thomas Paine and the Killing of the King, 1776," *Journal of American History*, 60 (1973), 294–308.

authority. In the Declaration of Independence, the colonists expressed their "filial" disobedience by addressing their grievances directly to the king. The authors of that document compiled a lengthy list of the crimes committed by the British government, each prefaced by the pronoun "he" — "He has refused," "He has dissolved," "He has ignored," "He has plundered."

Hence the American leaders of 1776, eulogized as heroes and saints, were also described metaphorically as revolutionary sons. And it was precisely the fact of their seditious "sonship" that created problems for patriotic eulogists in the period after independence.[19] Some of these problems can be traced to republican theory, others to events occurring at home and abroad in the 1780s and 1790s.

To Americans whose view of antiquity was colored by the pessimism of the Latin historians, the fates of Greece and Rome underscored the frailty of republican governments. The mixed constitution extolled by Polybius and revered by the Commonwealthmen had not prevented the downfall of Rome, while England offered contemporary proof that no people was safe from degeneracy. The cyclical reading of history, a story of the rise and decline of nations, conditioned Americans to believe that their own republic was dangerously vulnerable to decay and corruption. As they recalled the warnings and lamentations of Sallust and Tacitus, as they brooded on the tragic deaths of Cato and Cicero, Americans could not help but fear for the survival of the republican experiment.[20]

These fears seemed amply confirmed by the turmoil of the eighties and nineties, particularly by the erosion of social and political deference. The Revolution, in the opinion of many,

19. The revolutionists themselves believed they were being "loyal" to their political fathers by upholding the rights of freeborn Englishmen. The fact remains, however, that they were in revolt against established authority. For a discussion of this point from a psychoanalytic perspective, see Mazlish, "Leadership in the American Revolution," p. 124.

20. See John R. Howe, Jr., "Republican Thought and the Political Violence of the 1790's," *American Quarterly*, 19 (1967), 147–165; Wood, *Creation of the American Republic*, pp. 393–429; and Marvin Meyers, "Founding and Revolution: A Commentary on Publius-Madison," in Stanley Elkins and Eric McKitrick, eds., *The Hofstadter Aegis* (New York: Knopf, 1974), pp. 3–35.

had emboldened ignorant and unqualified men to aspire to positions of dominance traditionally reserved for their betters.[21] Growing economic unrest, furthermore, culminated in two armed insurrections within the space of a decade: the uprising of agrarian debtors led by Daniel Shays of Massachusetts in 1786, and the so-called Whiskey Rebellion mounted by farmers in western Pennsylvania in 1794. News from abroad only heightened the anxieties of those who interpreted such occurrences in light of the history of the ancient republics. By the turn of the century, even the warmest friends of the French Revolution saw in its excesses the inevitability of the Polybian cycle of constitutions. The Reign of Terror had created the chaotic conditions essential to the ascendance of Napoleon, a new Caesar who climaxed his rise to power by assuming the title of emperor.[22]

This widespread uneasiness over the future of republican government was reflected in the funeral orations delivered after the war. Eulogists responded to the fears they shared with many of their countrymen by recasting the symbolic lives of the Patriots and altering the public image of American leadership. To be sure, continuities remained between the eulogies delivered in 1776 and those pronounced over the course of the next fifty years. The eulogist for Robert Treat Paine, who had signed the Declaration of Independence, was repeating a commonplace when he observed of his subject in 1814 that "he bore successive bereavements as a man and a christian, he died like a hero and a saint."[23] Officers, signers, and other prominent leaders were as likely as ever to be praised for their piety and compared to republican ancients. A 1792 eulogy asserted that Benjamin

21. Wood, *Creation of the American Republic*, pp. 471–518.
22. On the American response to the French Revolution, see Gary B. Nash, "The American Clergy and the French Revolution," *William and Mary Quarterly*, 22 (1965), 392–412; Richard Buel, Jr., *Securing the Revolution: Ideology in American Politics, 1789–1815* (Ithaca: Cornell University Press, 1972), pp. 1–240; and Eric Foner, *Tom Paine and Revolutionary America* (New York: Oxford University Press, 1976), pp. 253–261.
23. John L. Abbot(?), *Sketch of the Character of the Late Hon. Robert Treat Paine, LL.D.: Extracted from a Sermon, Delivered at the First Church in Boston, the Sabbath after His decease* (Boston, 1814), p. 4. Cf. David Ramsay, *An Eulogium upon Benjamin Rush, M.D.* (Philadelphia, 1813), p. 108.

Franklin outshone Lycurgus as a lawgiver and doer of good and, blandly disregarding Franklin's skeptical deism, attributed to him a belief "in divine Revelation." Samuel Adams's eulogist gilded his character with appropriate quotations from Cicero, Plutarch, and the gospel of St. Matthew. And the orator who commemorated General Charles Cotesworth Pinckney in 1825 spoke for all the eulogists, past and present, when he entreated the living to honor the dead by copying the qualities "which form the incorruptible Patriot, the gallant Soldier, the accomplished Statesman, and the liberal, sincere Christian."[24]

Despite the persistence of these familiar rhetorical strategies, shifts of intention and emphasis began to appear by the middle 1780s. In the eulogies dating from around the time of the Shaysites, traditions previously invoked on behalf of rebellion were used in defense of the public tranquillity — to keep the sons in their place, so to speak, and to buttress paternal authority. Orators appealed to classical antiquity and the Bible in order to reprove ambitious upstarts and to bewail the sins of a restless and seemingly ungovernable people. Even as they continued to praise the Patriots for forcefully resisting "a servile submission to the wills of a few," the eulogists inserted admonitions against less disinterested men who had also toppled authority by resorting to force. The speaker honoring General Nathaniel Greene contrasted his subject with the many who "have waded through seas of blood to the gratification of a lawless ambition, and arrived to the height of power over the ruins of their country . . . Such are the Alexanders, the Caesars, the Tamberlanes, and Koulikhans of history." A decade later, eulogizing the Federalist governor of Connecticut, Azel Backus poured scorn on "those general thieves and butchers, called Heroes and Conquerers," who were taking America on the road of the French Revolution. "The Aristides," he fumed, "the Numa Pompiliuses, the Alfreds, and the Manco Capacs, seem

24. William Smith, *Eulogium on Benjamin Franklin* (Philadelphia, 1792), pp. 7, 37; Thomas Thacher, *A Tribute of Respect to the Memory of Samuel Adams* (Dedham, Mass., 1804), pp. 23–24, 9; Alexander Garden, *Eulogy on General Chs. Cotesworth Pinckney, President-General of the Society of the Cincinnati, Delivered . . . on Tuesday, the First of November, 1825, at St. Philip's Church* (Charleston, S.C., 1825), p. 37.

to be forgotten, in the noise made by the Pericles, the Syllas, the Mariuses, the Catilines, and the Caesars of later ages."[25]

A new note of the jeremiad began to sound in the funeral orations of the eighties and nineties, and still could be heard in the following century. The traditional biblical text reintroduced by conservative divines to preface their eulogies often revealed a partiality for the books composed before and after the Baby- lonian captivity — books full of reproach for the backsliding Israelites. Audiences were reminded that Israel's history between the reigns of David and Solomon and the exile in Babylon was "little more than a narrative of the most distinguished vices." Pessimistic Federalists like Fisher Ames, who clung to the cycli- cal interpretation of history, gloomily turned their hands to composing classical jeremiads. When Ames eulogized George Washington in 1800, he compared the first President to Epami- nondas in "the purity and ardor of his patriotism . . . There, it is to be hoped, the parallel ends: for, Thebes fell with Epami- nondas." Four years later, with the Jeffersonians in power, Ames wrote off the republic completely in his eulogy for Alex- ander Hamilton. "Our Troy has lost her Hector," he lamented, without bothering to qualify the parallel. His audience did not have to be told of Troy's fate after the death of Hector.[26]

Although Ames and Backus were conservative Federalists, the concerns they voiced in their eulogies were exceptional only in degree. And those concerns were dramatically magnified by the realization that the leaders whose lives they commemorated

25. William Hillhouse, *An Oration in Commemoration of General Nathaniel Greene, Delivered before the Connecticut Society of the Cin- cinnati, at New Haven, September 12, 1786* (Brooklyn, N.Y., 1886), pp. 4–5; Azel Backus, *A Sermon, Delivered at the Funeral of His Ex- cellency Oliver Wolcott, Governor of the State of Connecticut* (Litch- field, Conn., 1797), pp. 11, 17. Wolcott was also a signer of the Dec- laration of Independence.

26. Backus, *A Sermon*, p. 3; Fisher Ames, *An Oration on the Sublime Virtues of General George Washington, pronounced . . . on Saturday, the 8th of February 1800*, in Franklin B. Hough, ed., *Washingtoniana: Or, Memorials of the Death of George Washington* (Roxbury, Mass., 1865), II, 52; Ames, *A Sketch of the Character of Alexander Hamilton*, in *A Collection of the Facts and Documents, Relative to the Death of Major-General Alexander Hamilton* (1804; rpt. Boston: Houghton, Mifflin, 1904), p. 249. For a good study of the Federalist literary mind, see Linda K. Kerber, *Federalists in Dissent: Imagery and Ideology in Jeffersonian America* (Ithaca: Cornell University Press, 1970).

had been revolutionaries themselves, disloyal sons to their political father George the Third, the symbolic head of the British
Empire. Hence the eulogists were involved in the paradoxical
situation of upholding public order in the name of men who
had subverted it. Contemporary rebels like Daniel Shays could
not have been far from their minds when they called the roll of
classical demagogues. Yet Shays, too, could claim — as his followers did claim — that he was opposing "a servile submission
to the wills of a few" by championing the rights of countless
yeoman farmers against a handful of oppressive creditors. What
was to prevent disaffected veterans like Shays, or those other
"new men" so despised by the ruling elite, from proclaiming
themselves sons of liberty in their own right? "Happy the country," exclaimed the eulogist for General Greene, referring to the
officers and soldiers of the Continental Army, "that can boast
of such sons."[27] But sonship, in that era of American history,
was associated with resistance to political authority; and the
country was unhappy indeed in having such sons as Daniel
Shays and the insurgents of the Whiskey Rebellion.

Azel Backus, for one, was unhappy with the actual youth of
the nineties. In his eulogy for Oliver Wolcott, he blamed the
waywardness of the rising generation for many of the problems
of the American Israel. Wolcott's character had been formed in
his youth, and his unblemished life confirmed the adage that
the "shape of the sapling" determined the future tree. More
representative of present-day youth, it seemed to Backus, was
the biblical Ishmael, the outcast son of Abraham, "with his
hand against every man, and every man's hand against him."
Native-born Ishmaels (perhaps like the Francophile under-
graduates at nearby Yale) were taking after their Old Testament namesake by abjuring the faith of their ancestors and
"quarrelling not only with the laws of civil society, but the laws
of God." Bewailing the sins of the young had been a favorite
pastime of the Puritan clergy almost since the settlement of
Massachusetts Bay. In the context of the 1790s, however, such
lamentations could be read as a kind of political shorthand in
which filial disobedience stood for political unrest and disaf-

27. Hillhouse, *An Oration*, p. 4.

fection from the newly established American state. The eulogist for John Hancock, speaking in 1793, certainly invited this inference when he informed his listeners that "some must be in authority and others must obey." The people, he added, in words addressed to a new generation of Americans, "may please themselves with the fancy of being superior to restraint, and retaining their own majesty, yet if there are not rulers among them, and these rulers are not honored and obeyed, there can be neither public peace nor private happiness."[28]

These and similar pronouncements implicitly posed the fateful question confronting the American leadership. Was perpetual revolution to become the "lawless law" of a land in which the state rested for its legitimacy on the right to revolution — on "the Right of the People," as enshrined in the Declaration of Independence, "to alter or abolish . . . any Form of Government?"[29] Given the implications of the familial metaphor in American politics, how could the state erected by revolutionary sons command the permanent loyalty of future generations?

Patriotic eulogists devised two related solutions to this troubling dilemma. They created the mystique of the Founding Fathers by holding up the revolutionary leaders to the youth of the country not as insurgent sons but rather as symbols of paternal authority. And while they continued to rely heavily on classical allusions, they turned increasingly to the use of biblical models, particularly to Moses, in order to bind the millennial hopes aroused by the Great Awakening to the new American government. In sum, they transformed the Sons of Liberty into deified Founding Fathers, and they equated the American republic with the kingdom of God on earth in the process of realization.[30]

28. Backus, *A Sermon*, pp. 5, 8; Peter Thacher, *A Sermon Preached to the Society in Brattle Street, Boston, October 20, 1793, and Occasioned by the Death of His Excellency John Hancock Esq.* (Boston, 1793), p. 7.

29. See Meyers, "Founding and Revolution," pp. 24–25. The phrase "lawless law" is used by Meyers.

30. Ernest Lee Tuveson calls this combination of ideas "apocalyptic Whiggism" in *Redeemer Nation: The Idea of America's Millennial Role* (Chicago: The University of Chicago Press, 1968), p. 24. See also Pocock, *The Machiavellian Moment*, pp. 511–512.

The most sustained effort to revise the image of the Patriot leadership, and thus to rewrite, as it were, the collective biography of the early Republic, occurred in the three months following Washington's death on December 14, 1799.[31] In eulogy after eulogy, orators vied with each other in elevating "the first, the greatest of Columbia's sons" to "the distinguished father of his country." The first chief magistrate of the nation was repeatedly hailed as the father of his adoring but often unruly children, a father who composed their quarrels, protected their safety, and accepted with thanks their expressions of filial gratitude. "The father, under God" of our sacred liberties, in the phrase of one eulogist, he was even said by Gouverneur Morris to have had no biological children so that he might claim paternity over the entire American people.[32] Such tributes reaffirmed the political relevance of the Fifth Commandment: their source of inspiration was not an ancient like Cicero, but rather the Hebrew patriarchs of the Old Testament. In the words of one admirer, "Heaven's high decree was that he should be the ruler, the father of that family, which he had rescued from bondage. Having led you in war, he must also conduct you in peace, and roll his vigilant parental eye over you, his beloved children." This passage comes closer in sentiment to the patri-

31. Well over four hundred eulogies have survived from this period. Although Republicans may have been less likely than Federalists to exalt Washington as a symbol of the state, eulogists included members of both parties, and orations were delivered in all sections of the country. Useful studies of the Washington cult have been made by Robert P. Hay, "George Washington: American Moses," *American Quarterly*, 21 (1969), 780–791; Lawrence J. Friedman, *Inventors of the Promised Land* (New York: Knopf, 1975), pp. 44–78; Seymour Martin Lipset, *The First New Nation: The United States in Historical and Comparative Perspective* (1963; rpt. Garden City, N.Y.: Anchor Books, 1967), pp. 18–26; William Alfred Bryan, *George Washington in American Literature, 1775–1865* (New York: Columbia University Press, 1952); and Marcus Cunliffe, *George Washington: Man and Monument* (Boston: Little, Brown, 1958).

32. Peter Van Pelt, *An Oration, in Consequence of the Death of General George Washington* ... (Brooklyn, 1880), pp. 3, 16; John M. Mason, *A Funeral Oration on General Washington* ..., in Hough, ed., *Washingtoniana*, II, 170; Alexander MacWhorter, *A Funeral Sermon, Preached in Newark, December 27, 1799 ... for the Universally Lamented, General Washington* (Newark, 1800), p. 16; Gouverneur Morris, *An Oration upon the Death of General Washington* ..., in Hough, ed., *Washingtoniana*, II, 140.

archalism of Filmer than to the contractual theory of Locke; it suggests that by the turn of the century elements of divine right absolutism had resurfaced in the Washington cult. Washington, the titular head of the Federalist party, was no more. He had become the Founding Father who personified the authority of the American state.[33]

Indeed, the orators of 1800 equated filial piety to Washington's memory with patriotism itself. All civil and political instruction, according to the Reverend Aaron Bancroft, will henceforth "be comprised in one sentence, GO, IMITATE OUR WASHINGTON." Since America was now a "fatherless orphan country," it was imperative to the nation's survival that the young be taught to cherish and emulate Washington's exemplary qualities. "O! like him," implored a representative eulogist, "be thou, brave, prudent, temperate and just. O! Be thou, like him, thy country's shield in war, its ornament in peace." Henry Lee, in the most famous of all the funeral orations, summed up the fondest hopes of his countrymen when he pictured Washington guiding future generations with words of advice delivered from heaven. Shun factionalism, Lee imagined Washington as saying, "reverence religion," and above all, "be American in thought, word, and deed."[34]

Lee's Washington address contained perhaps the most celebrated tricolon in the history of American oratory: "First in war — first in peace — and first in the hearts of his countrymen." Subsequent eulogists eager to present the first president as the equal, if not indeed the superior, of any ancient often repeated Lee's words. He was, the eulogists concurred, a Fabius in prudence, a Cato in integrity, an Aristides in patriotism, and "another Cincinnatus, returning to the plough." It was incum-

33. Van Pelt, *An Oration*, p. 16.
34. Aaron Bancroft, *An Eulogy on the Character of the Late General George Washington* ... (Worcester, Mass., 1800), p. 12; William Clark Frazer, *A Funeral Oration ... in Memory of ... George Washington* (Wilmington, Del., 1800), p. 15; James Madison, *A Discourse on the Death of General Washington* ... (Richmond, Va., 1800), p. 24 (Madison was Bishop of the Protestant Episcopal Church in Virginia and President of William and Mary College); Henry Lee, *Eulogy on Washington, Delivered at the Request of Congress*, in Hough, ed., *Washingtoniana*, I, 73.

bent upon all Americans to publicize the matchless virtues "which have raised our WASHINGTON'S, above every Grecian and Roman name." One speaker confessed himself "strangely mistaken" if Washington's epistolary style did not altogether overshadow that of Pliny or Cicero, and he added that the exploits of Epaminondas "can scarcely form spots in his unclouded SUN." Although Washington prepared for war by studying the tactics of ancient generals like Camillus and Emilius, his mind "soared above imitation," and the orators were certain that "he was himself destined to be a high example to mankind."[35]

Just how high an example became apparent from the construction placed by the eulogists on the precept to "reverence religion" — Washington's parting wisdom, as imagined by Lee (and as actually enunciated in his Farewell Address).[36] Convinced as they were of republicanism's fragility, the eulogists turned to the Puritan past to give a religious sanction and coloring to the American polity, and thus to exempt it from the classical cycle of rise and decay. And finding no divine sanction for patriotism in the annals of the pagan republics, they appropriated the eschatology of the colonial Puritans and proclaimed themselves latter-day Israelites, the people chosen by God to usher in the millennium. Just as the Puritans had likened their own leaders to Old Testament patriarchs, the eulogists of 1800 deified Washington as an American Moses. As a typical speaker explained, using a fittingly familial image, Washington "has been the same to us, as Moses was to the Children of Israel." One zealot even went so far as to hail Moses as "the Washington of Israel." Statements like these, recurring in scores of orations, strengthened the conviction that the American Israel was the eternal republic envisioned but never

35. Lee, *Eulogy*, in Hough, ed., *Washingtoniana*, I, 72: Joseph Story, *Eulogy Delivered at Marblehead, Mass....*, in Hough, ed., *Washingtoniana*, II, 83; Samuel Stanhope Smith, *Oration upon the Death of George Washington ...*, in Hough, ed., *Washingtoniana*, II, 179; Joseph Blyth, *An Oration on the Death of General George Washington ...*, in Hough, ed., *Washingtoniana*, II, 123; MacWhorter, *A Funeral Sermon*, pp. 4, 11; Madison, *A Discourse*, p. 7.

36. Washington stated there that "reason and experience forbid us to expect that national morality can prevail in exclusion of religious principle."

achieved by the ancients. For "if God be for us," the eulogists demanded rhetorically, "who can be against us?"[37]

Still other eulogists interpreted Washington's terrestrial appearance as the second coming of Christ. They enjoined youthful auditors to worship at his tomb and acclaimed the departed leader as "the savior of his country, the messiah of America!" The first president was a kind of mortal god whose character exhibited no flaws, and who had died only after completing his mission of bringing the gospel of freedom to a worshipping nation. "The picture of man in him was perfect," asserted the Reverend Bancroft, "and there is no blot to tarnish its brightness." According to David Tappan, he deserved "to be ranked among Earthly Gods," for he came nearer to "the EXPRESS IMAGE of divine glory" than any other mortal. As late as the 1830s, Gustave de Beaumont could report after visiting this country that "Washington, in America, is not a man but a God."[38]

The patriotic orators who promoted Washington to divine status in order to legitimize the newly instituted government whose authority and power he symbolized did not create a national church. What they did create was a national religion whose cardinal tenet was the divinity of the American republic.[39] They differed, in this respect, from Jonathan Edwards and his fellow awakeners, who had tapped the revolutionary potential in millennialism by turning it against the authority of the colonial churches. Edwards himself, disillusioned by the failure

37. Thaddeus Fiske, *A Sermon, Delivered . . . Immediately Following the Melancholy Intelligence of the Death of General George Washington* . . . (Boston, 1800), p. 10; Eli Forbes, quoted in Hay, "George Washington: American Moses," p. 788; Madison, *A Discourse*, p. 17.

38. Mason, *A Funeral Oration*, in Hough, ed., *Washingtoniana*, II, 117–178; Frazer, *A Funeral Oration*, p. 6; Friedman calls Washington "an immortal mortal" in *Inventors of the Promised Land*, p. 59; Bancroft, *An Eulogy*, pp. 15–16; Tappan is quoted in Bryan, *George Washington in American Literature*, p. 62; Beaumont's *Marie, or Slavery in the United States* is quoted in Lipset, *The First New Nation*, p. 22, n.6.

39. For a thorough and perceptive treatment of American "civil religion" in the revolutionary period, see Catherine L. Albanese, *Sons of the Fathers: The Civil Religion of the American Revolution* (Philadelphia: Temple University Press, 1976).

of the revival, eventually abandoned his faith in the special destiny of the American people. In 1747, for example, he spoke of the worldwide community of believers and identified the "one holy nation" as the universal church of Christ. Yet even in the headiest days of the Great Awakening, Edwards staked his hopes on the country rather than the magistracy, the land rather than the existing state. When he uttered his renowned prophecy of the imminent kingdom, he referred to America as "she," the daughter of Europe:

> The other continent hath slain Christ, and has from age to age shed the blood of the saints and martyrs of Jesus, and has often been as it were deluged with the church's blood: God has therefore probably reserved the honor of building the glorious temple to the daughter, that has not shed so much blood, when those times of the peace and prosperity and glory of the church shall commence, that were typified by the reign of Solomon.[40]

Also at the height of the Great Awakening, Gilbert Tennent denounced the established clergy as "an unconverted ministry." The attacks of Tennent and other evangelicals helped to undermine habits of deference and to weaken "filial" subordination on the part of the people. Sixty years later, in contrast, the Washington eulogists, enjoining the young to be faithful to the "God of our fathers," renewed the covenant in the name of paternal authority. The orators of 1800 who enlisted religion to support the republic neutralized the radical impulse in Edwardsean Calvinism.[41]

One has to go back to the original Puritan theocracy to discover a native equivalent for the union of state and religion proclaimed by the Washington eulogists. When John Winthrop delivered his lay sermon aboard the *Arbella,* he compared himself to Moses as the chief magistrate of a new race of Israelites. Cotton Mather, writing in the waning days of the theocracy,

40. Edwards, *The Visible Union of God's People,* in Heimert and Miller, eds., *The Great Awakening,* pp. 565, 567; Edwards, *Some Thoughts Concerning the Revival,* in Edwards, *The Great Awakening,* ed., C. C. Goen (New Haven: Yale University Press, 1972), p. 355. See also Heimert, *Religion and the American Mind,* pp. 126–127.
41. Mason, *A Funeral Oration,* in Hough, ed., *Washingtoniana,* II, 177.

repeated the analogy by ascribing to Winthrop "a Mosaic Spirit," and he pronounced the first governor of Massachusetts Bay "the Father of New-England." In verses composed in memory of Sir William Phips, Mather even anticipated the famous tribute of Gouverneur Morris: "Write Him not Childless, whose whole People were / Sons, Orphans now, of His Paternal Care." Like the eulogists of 1800, Puritans such as Winthrop and Mather employed familial imagery in speaking of rulers and subjects, and they sanctified paternal authority by variously hailing the New England governors as a Moses, Nehemiah, or King David *redivivus*. The prodigiously learned Mather also ransacked antiquity for apt parallels to the colonial magistracy and declared Winthrop the superior of either Lycurgus or Numa as a lawgiver. The hagiologies of the *Magnalia*, however, were those of an embattled theocrat, not a republican, and hardly suitable for eighteenth-century revolutionists who had cast off the imperial yoke. On the contrary, as applied to the Patriot leadership, they were more appropriate for the rulers of the Roman Empire than the heroes and martyrs of the Roman Republic.[42]

In fact, there was a profound historical irony involved in the excessive veneration of Washington's memory. Although the eulogists failed to realize it, they were effectively duplicating the cult of the Caesars, a cult that had only arisen after the loss of republican freedom. The "divine Julius," upon destroying the Roman Republic, sought to found an absolute monarchy and to legitimize his kingship by having the Senate decree him a god. Under the Empire established by Augustus, Caesar's nephew and appointed heir, it became standard practice to worship the divinized sovereign and formally to acknowledge his godhead after his death. Claiming to be the anointed leader of an elect people, Augustus promulgated the doctrine that Rome had been summoned by providence to civilize the world and inaugurate an earthly millennium. Like their American counterparts, the imperial Romans raised patriotism to a national religion and proclaimed the eternality of their city on a

42. Cotton Mather, *Magnalia Christi Americana* (Hartford, 1853), I, 118–119, 230.

hill.[43] They did so, moreover, while going through the motions of restoring the Republic and presenting themselves as defenders of Roman tradition. The emperors even assumed the title originally bestowed upon Cicero for having risked his life to preserve republican liberty. In Charles Rollin's *Roman History,* the most popular shortcut to the classics of the revolutionary era, Americans could read that "Father of his Country" was "a title afterwards affected by the Emperors, but which Rome, whilst free, gave to no body except Cicero."[44] These were words of ironic relevance for the orators who eulogized Patriot leaders between the death of General Poor in 1780 and that of George Washington two decades later. Although the phrase "father of his country" was itself unchanged, the context had utterly altered its meaning, and the men who spoke it, in imperial Rome as well as America, had betrayed their ideals by making the state an object of worship.

By the turn of the century, then, American eulogists had combined the vocabularies of Christianity and classical paganism with the paternal metaphor to create an iconography of leadership appropriate for a republic on the verge of becoming a continental empire. They employed the identical rhetoric in eulogizing John Adams and Thomas Jefferson when the second and third presidents died — miraculously, it seemed to their countrymen — on July 4, 1826. Following the practice of their predecessors of 1800, the funeral orators who commemorated the two Founders likened them to illustrious ancients and Com-

43. Throughout this paragraph I am indebted to Lily Ross Taylor, *The Divinity of the Roman Emperor* (Middletown, Conn.: American Philological Association, 1931); Charles Norris Cochrane, *Christianity and Classical Culture: A Study of Thought and Action from Augustus to Augustine* (1940: rpt. New York: Oxford University Press, 1972), pp. 1–176; and Moses Hadas, *Hellenistic Culture: Fusion and Diffusion* (1959; rpt. New York: Norton, 1972), pp. 249–263. Cochrane remarks that "the organized society of the empire is the Graeco-Roman counterpart to the New England Kingdom of the Saints; subject, it may be added, to limitations and threatened by dangers which confront all societies in which consecrated egotism (*amor sui*) disguises itself as the love of God" (p. 65).

44. Charles Rollin, *The Roman History from the Foundation of Rome to the Battle of Actium* (London, 1754), XI, 396. This volume was actually written by Mr. Crevier and is described as "the Continuation of Mr. Rollin's Work."

monwealthmen and acclaimed them as the Mosaic deliverers
of a millennial people. As William Wirt put it, after enrolling
"our Great Fathers" in the ranks of Aristides, Cato, Sidney,
and Locke, "they moved all heaven and all earth besides, and
opened a passage . . . through the great deep." The extraordinary coincidence of their joint departure on the fiftieth anniversary of freedom's inception was unanimously construed as a
sign that the republic was under the guidance of "an All-seeing
Providence." The God of Israel was the God of America, Wirt
asserted, and all the orators assigned the responsibility of keeping the covenant to the present generation. America's youth
were exhorted to imitate Adams and Jefferson "as models of
human perfection," and to demonstrate their filial allegiance by
worshipping at the "graves of our political parents." Persuaded
of heaven's approbation as their countrymen pushed westward
toward the Pacific, patriotic eulogists paradoxically affirmed
their republicanism by making father deities out of former
revolutionaries and perpetuating the Augustan cult of the state.[45]

James Madison, one of the last surviving Founding Fathers,
died on June 28, 1836, at the age of eighty-six. On September 9
of that same year Ralph Waldo Emerson published his famous
essay *Nature,* usually regarded as the first major statement of
the American Renaissance. The almost simultaneous occurrence
of the two events points toward a reinterpretation not only of
Emerson's work but of American romanticism in general. For
the celebrated opening sentences of *Nature* could only have been
written in an age saturated with familial rhetoric, an age in
which the most sacred duty imposed on the young was to keep
the faith of the fathers.[46] "Our age is retrospective," Emerson

45. See, in general, *A Selection of Eulogies, Pronounced in the Several
States, in Honor of Those Illustrious Patriots and Statesmen, John
Adams and Thomas Jefferson* (Hartford, 1826). References are to the
eulogies by William Wirt, pp. 394, 385, 401–402; Samuel Smith, p. 88;
William F. Thornton, p. 346; and William Wilkins, p. 350. The most
thorough treatment of this subject is Robert P. Hay, "The Glorious
Departure of the American Patriarchs: Contemporary Reactions to the
Deaths of Jefferson and Adams," *The Journal of Southern History,* 35
(1969), 543–555.

46. For extensive evidence of the persistence of the familial metaphor
in American political discourse, see Rush Welter, *The Mind of America,
1820–1860* (New York: Columbia University Press, 1975), pp. 3–74.

noted. "It builds the sepulchres of the fathers. It writes biographies, histories, and criticism. The foregoing generations beheld God and nature face to face; we, through their eyes. Why should not we also enjoy an original relation to the universe? . . . Let us demand our own works and laws and worship." While Emerson's essay, like the comparable manifestos of the revivalists a century earlier, was religious in tenor, it was also an expression of filial revolt, and filial revolt in America has historically signified political dissidence. The Great Awakening transformed the political landscape of colonial America; and the publication of *Nature,* whatever its author's intentions, had definite political (not to mention artistic) consequences. For the hallmark of the writers who were influenced by Emerson — most notably Thoreau, Hawthorne, and Melville — was their dissent from, and criticism of, the social and political realities of contemporary America.

The attacks on the fathers found in the writings of all these artists, and so often interpreted in recent studies as an index of psychological disorder,[47] can be explained as a conscious protest against existing political authority. Thoreau, Hawthorne, and Melville quarreled with the fathers because the fathers were synonymous with the state, and the state regularly justified its measures in the language that rightfully belonged to its critics — the two systems of allusion that originally inspired the Revolution. In order to articulate their filial dissent, therefore, the American romantics had to recover the revolutionary implications of the dual inheritance appropriated by patriotic orators. They had to perform the radical act of turning Christianity and classical paganism against paternal authority, and to liberate the rhetoric of the Revolution from its current function of reinforcing political loyalty. It was this act of opposition, as carried out in their imaginative literature, that makes the nineteenth-century romantic authors the true successors to the insurgent sons of 1776.

47. For example, Frederick C. Crews, *The Sins of the Fathers: Hawthorne's Psychological Themes* (New York: Oxford University Press, 1966); Quentin Anderson, *The Imperial Self: An Essay in American Literary and Cultural History* (New York: Knopf, 1971); and Edwin Haviland Miller, *Melville: A Biography* (New York: George Braziller, 1975).

One thinks, for instance, of that opening paragraph of *Nature*, with its explicitly millennial language — its reference to beholding God face to face and its hope of regaining paradise through an original, that is to say, an Adamic, relation to the universe. Or "Civil Disobedience" (1849), where Thoreau declaims in the accents of an eighteenth-century Commonwealthman against standing armies and the imperialism of Manifest Destiny, and demands that his compatriots complete the Revolution by abolishing slavery and resisting a tyrannical government, namely their own. Or *The Scarlet Letter* (1850), where the rulers of the Puritan theocracy, with the exception of Arthur Dimmesdale, are all described as elderly men, incapable "of sitting in judgment on an erring woman's heart." In his preface to the romance, Hawthorne points out that the inhabitants of the Salem Custom-House, which displays the heraldry of the federal eagle and symbolizes "Uncle Sam's government," are just as aged as their seventeenth-century counterparts. He thus suggests that in both epochs political authority is paternal if not patriarchal, and that the men who administer the state in America wield the power of figurative fathers over the people.

One thinks, most of all, of Melville, who almost paraphrases Emerson when he writes in *Redburn* (1849) that "the thing that had guided the father, could not guide the son," and whose eponymous hero discovers that the world of the fathers is built on a system of social injustice and oppression. In this early novel, Melville calls for an extension as well as a renewal of the revolutionary heritage, and he postulates a new fraternal order based on the principle that "there is no true sympathy but between equals." Repeatedly alluding to classical ancients and radical Whigs, and employing the language of native millennialism, he makes his case in the very rhetoric used by patriots to sanctify existing institutions. He speaks, for example, of the "unmatchable Tacitus," fondly recalls a childhood history of Rome (presumably Livy's), and praises Cincinnatus, Seneca, Addison, and Socrates, the last of these for having "died the death of a Christian." He mentions, too, the biblical promise of a restoration to Eden, and even accepts the special destiny of the American people; but he rebukes the notion, so dear to his countrymen, that the republic is already the latter-day kingdom. He refers, like Edwards before him, to the New World rather than the current authorities when he utters his own millennial prophecy:

> The other world beyond this, which was longed for by the devout before Columbus' time, was found in the New; and the deep-sea-lead, that first struck these soundings, brought up the soil of Earth's Paradise. Not a Paradise then, or now; but to be made so, at God's good pleasure, and in the fullness and mellowness of time. The seed is sown, and the harvest must come; and our children's children, on the world's jubilee morning, shall all go with their sickles to the reaping.

Melville's *Israel Potter* (1854) establishes beyond question the link between paternal authority and the sovereignty of the state in the work of the American romantics. While recounting the history of Israel's early adventures, Melville emphasizes "the tyranny of his father" in opposing the hero's desire to marry. He spells out the analogy between filial and political rebellion by observing that "ere on just principles, throwing off the yoke of his king, Israel, on equally excusable grounds, emancipated himself from his sire." The legendary fathers of the American republic, Benjamin Franklin and John Paul Jones, are shown to be hypocrites who exploit and abandon Israel Potter; while Ethan Allen, a Roman and a Christian who represents the authentic revolutionary spirit, is seen literally bound in chains. When Israel returns to the "Canaan beyond the sea" after his fifty years of exile, he is almost run over by a "patriotic triumphal car" in a procession honoring the soldiers who fought at Bunker Hill. Melville's dedication "To His Highness the Bunker Hill Monument" clearly indicates that Americans, having made an idolatry of patriotism, have forsaken their republican principles. In light of the iconography of Patriot leadership, it becomes a detail of more than passing interest that Israel Potter comes home on July 4, 1826 — the date of the deaths of Adams and Jefferson.

"Mysterious Obligation": Jefferson's Notes on the State of Virginia

ROBERT A. FERGUSON

The University of Chicago

I

THOMAS JEFFERSON, by any standard, is a major writer of the early Republic, and his one book, *Notes on the State of Virginia,* has been accepted universally as both an American classic and a vital contribution to the political and scientific thought of the eighteenth century. Yet the same book has been virtually ignored as a literary text, and this is true even though *Notes* is a prototype for understanding literary involvement in post-Revolutionary America. Critical neglect began in Jefferson's own seeming disregard. He once threatened to burn the entire first edition of *Notes*—some two hundred copies privately printed at considerable expense. "Do not view me as an author, and attached to what he has written," he warned James Madison. "I am neither."[1] Calling his book a private communication unfit for distribution, he tried hard to prevent its general publication.[2] In subsequent letters, *Notes* became "a poor crayon," "this trifle," "nothing more than the measure of a shadow," and "a bad book . . . the author of which has no other merit than that of thinking as little of it as any man in the world can."[3]

---

[1] TJ to James Madison, 11 May 1785, in Julian P. Boyd, ed., *The Papers of Thomas Jefferson,* 19 vols. (Princeton: Princeton Univ. Press, 1950–74), VIII, 147–48. Cited hereafter as *Papers.* The Princeton edition, projected at sixty volumes, is now complete through 1791. For correspondence and works after this date, I use Andrew A. Lipscomb and Albert E. Bergh, eds., *The Writings of Thomas Jefferson,* 20 vols. (Washington, D.C.: Thomas Jefferson Memorial Association, 1905). Cited hereafter as *Writings.* I have modernized Jefferson's spellings.

[2] Jefferson admonished each of his friends receiving a private copy of *Notes* to avoid all possibility of publication, and he placed inscriptions to this effect in each copy. See *Papers,* VIII, 246. See also TJ to John Page, 4 May 1786, *Papers,* IX, 444.

[3] For these disparaging comments, see in order, TJ to Rev. James Madison, 13 Aug. 1787, *Papers,* XII, 31; TJ to James Madison, 8 Feb. 1786, *Papers,* IX, 264–65; TJ to John Melish, 10 Dec. 1814, *Writings,* XIV, 220; TJ to Alexander Donald, 17 Sept. 1787, *Papers,* XII, 133.

American Literature, Volume 52, Number 3, November 1980. Copyright © 1980 by Duke University Press.

Unfortunately, modern observers have taken these comments at face value instead of placing them in perspective. Even Jefferson's greatest admirers have belittled his creative efforts. Dumas Malone dismisses *Notes* overall as an "unlabored" by-product "tossed off in a few summer weeks." "At no time," Malone tells us of Jefferson, "was he much concerned about its literary form." Gilbert Chinard, in turn, has argued that Jefferson should not be held to standards of authorial planning for a mere random collection, while Merrill Peterson refers to *Notes* as a glorified guidebook, one Jefferson never meant to write.[4]

Nothing could be further from the truth. *Notes* is peculiarly an unfinished work, as its author was the first to point out, but it is neither a haphazard nor an unstructured effort. Jefferson devoted much time and energy to his book from its inception in November 1780 to its official publication in London in 1787. He took enormous pains to insure the accuracy of its contents, and years after publication he continued to revise his own copy with a new edition in mind.[5] In denigrating his own work and shunning publication, he responded as any man of letters would in America in the eighteenth century. The true gentleman addressed his work—usually considered a negligible product of leisure—to a small group of social peers. He never wrote for money, rarely signed what he wrote, and tried to avoid the vulgarity of publication.[6]

[4] Dumas Malone, *Jefferson the Virginian* in *Jefferson and His Times*, 3 vols. (Boston: Little, Brown, 1948–74), I, 376–79; Gilbert Chinard, *Thomas Jefferson: The Apostle of Americanism*, 2nd ed., rev. (Boston: Little, Brown, 1946), pp. 119–20; and Merrill D. Peterson, *Thomas Jefferson and the New Nation, A Biography* (New York: Oxford Univ. Press, 1970), p. 249. Of course, all three writers appreciate the importance of *Notes* as a political, scientific, and historic document and as a crucial sourcebook for examining Jefferson's ideas.

[5] Jefferson began work on *Notes* in November 1780 but was interrupted by official duties as the wartime governor of Virginia. The bulk of the first draft was apparently written in August 1781, though Jefferson made further addenda in the autumn to complete it. In the winter of 1781–82 and again in the winter of 1783–84, he made revisions that trebled the size of the original draft. He used his extensive correspondence to collect additional data from friends. Further changes were completed in Paris before publication—a process Jefferson monitored carefully to insure accuracy. In later years, he kept a personal copy of the London edition of 1787 in which he made numerous marginalia. As late as 1810, he wrote of his plans to revise and enlarge *Notes* in a new edition. These facts can best be drawn from the collection of correspondence regarding *Notes* in E. Millicent Sowerby, *Catalogue of the Library of Thomas Jefferson*, 5 vols. (Washington, D.C.: U.S. Government Printing Office, 1952–59), IV, 301–30. See also William Peden, "Introduction," *Notes on the State of Virginia* (1954; rpt. New York: Norton, 1972), xi–xxv.

[6] William Charvat, *The Profession of Authorship in America, 1800–1870*, ed. Matthew J. Bruccoli (Columbus: Ohio State Univ. Press, 1968), pp. 6–10.

The slow emergence of *Notes* as public book across a six-year period affords an excellent example of the way in which a gentleman's work reached a larger audience in the eighteenth century. Jefferson's friends vied for the right to see copies of the manuscript drafts he started circulating in 1781. Access was tantamount to membership within an inner circle, and ensuing pressures from inside the group led naturally toward private printing and publication.[7] Jefferson abided by all of the conventions, but his correspondence implies that he may have been several jumps ahead of his enthusiastic supporters even as he appeared to lag dutifully a half-step behind.[8] In any event, once the predictable support of Madison, John Adams, and others produced plans for an English edition, Jefferson's behavior resembled that of anxious authors in every age: irritation over delays in publication, anxiety over printing mistakes, and interest in sales.[9]

The writer's private hopes also belie a lack of interest. The decision in 1785 to run off a private edition of two hundred copies included plans for a copy to each student of The College of William and Mary. Jefferson, with his customary faith in the rising generation, acted here with "two great objects" in view: encouragement of slave emancipation in Virginia and the settlement of the state constitution on a new basis (both major topics in *Notes*).[10] It is hard to imagine an author with greater expectations for his text. A man obsessed by notions of design, system, measurement, and style, Jefferson also would have been embarrassed by his biographers' apologies for an apparent absence of form. *Notes,* in fact, possesses a coherent structure that we no longer recognize because of a more general failure to approach the literature of the period on its own terms. We apply our own belletristic standards narrowly and find only weakness in consequence. Placed in the intellectual

---

[7] For the pressures from Jefferson's circle of private readers, see Francis Hopkinson to TJ, 18 Nov. 1784, *Papers*, VII, 535; Charles Thomson to TJ, 6 March 1785, *Papers*, VIII, 16; George Wythe to TJ, 10 Jan. 1786, *Papers*, IX, 165.

[8] Jefferson knew that his own generous distribution of private copies in France was forcing the issue of publication regardless of the advice he sought from friends. See TJ to James Madison, 1 Sept. 1785, *Papers*, VIII, 462.

[9] For the encouragement of Adams and the ever-reliable Madison, see John Adams to TJ, 22 May 1785, *Papers*, VIII, 160, and James Madison to TJ, 15 Nov. 1785, *Papers*, IX, 38. For Jefferson's impatience over delays, his concern over printing accuracy, and his discreet interest in sales, see TJ to Abbé Morellet, 2 July 1787, *Papers*, XI, 529–30, and Jefferson's various letters to his publisher John Stockdale in *Papers*, XI, 107, 183, and XII, 488.

[10] TJ to the Marquis de Chastellux, 7 June 1785, *Papers*, VIII, 184.

context of the day, Jefferson's priorities in *Notes* form part of an unexplored literary aesthetic. His book, like the Declaration of Independence before it, turns upon English common law and the great, humanistic legal compendia of the Enlightenment.

II

The factuality of *Notes* and its circumstantial basis erect major obstacles to modern appreciation. Jefferson's book grew out of a questionnaire circulated during the summer of 1780 to members of the Continental Congress by François Marbois, the secretary of the French legation at Philadelphia. *Notes* was written as a direct response, using the French diplomat's twenty-two explicit queries on the resources of the American states as chapter headings.[11] Detailed answers on manufacturing, demographic patterns, the navigability of rivers, and the nature of animal life fill page after page with charts, measurements, and lists—all suggesting an episodic series of replies to another's questions. In what sense, then, is *Notes* more than a dutiful compilation of information? The very question carries assumptions to guard against. Collection of accurate data— and especially the gathering of information concerning the New World—fascinated eighteenth-century intellectuals. Among Americans in particular, as Daniel Boorstin has pointed out, "the vagueness of the land" and "the scarcity of precise knowledge gave such knowledge as there was a peculiar appeal."[12]

Jefferson's penchant for organized and minute observation coincided with an American quest for certainties; it also met the prevailing intellectual stipulations of European culture. In places *Notes* clearly is meant for an audience of one, George Louis Leclerc, comte de Buffon, the leading French scientist of the day. "Sensible people," Buffon had argued, "will always recognize that the only and true science is the knowledge of facts," and he called for "the exact description of everything" with corresponding, though subordinate, attention given to issues of style. Reportage and literary aspiration went hand in hand. Jefferson accepted Buffon's premises in *Notes*

[11] Marbois' list of twenty-two queries is contained in *Papers*, IV, 166–67.
[12] Daniel J. Boorstin, "The Vagueness of the Land," *The Americans: The National Experience* (New York: Random House, 1965), pp. 221–74, particularly pp. 236–37.

even as he meticulously contested the French philosophe's specific theories about America with massive collections of data.[13] "A patient pursuit of facts," he wrote explaining his procedures, "and cautious combination and comparison of them, is the drudgery to which man is subjected by his Maker, if he wishes to attain sure knowledge."[14]

Nor should we expect a different methodology from a man whose professed heroes were Bacon, Newton, and Locke and whose empiricism, in consequence, assumed that facts properly collected would inevitably lead through inductive reasoning toward unified theory and larger vision. Jefferson spoke disparagingly of his own efforts because he knew *Notes* could only begin the climb toward vision, but, a son of the Enlightenment, he believed strongly in the movement toward larger coherence which factual knowledge would bring. This movement gave his own work shape and meaning. *Notes* was "a poor crayon" in the sense that Jefferson firmly expected the future writers then emerging from The College of William and Mary to use his sketch to "fill up" a complete painting. His book was "the measure of a shadow" in that measurements had to be continued every hour as the sun advanced in order "to furnish another element for calculating the course and motion of this member [Virginia] of our federal system."[15]

Jefferson's explicit analogy here between the Newtonian machinery of Nature and similar laws of causation for human society was, of course, still another standard assumption of the Enlightenment, one that enabled the author of *Notes* to link what he saw in the physical world with what he wanted to see in society. Behind the meteorological charts of rainfall and wind velocity and the

[13] Jean Piveteau, ed., "Buffon et la Méthode," *Oeuvres Philosophiques de Buffon* (Paris: Presses Univ. de France, 1954), pp. 15, 22. See also Peter Gay, *The Enlightenment: An Interpretation,* 2 vols. (1969; rpt. New York: Norton, 1977), II, 152–56. For accounts of Jefferson's controversies with Buffon in *Notes,* see Marie Kimball, *Jefferson: War and Peace, 1776 to 1784* (New York: Coward-McCann, 1947), pp. 279–88, and Ruth Henline, "A Study of *Notes on the State of Virginia* as an Evidence of Jefferson's Reaction against the Theories of the French Naturalists," *Virginia Magazine of History and Biography,* 55 (1947), 233–46.

[14] Thomas Jefferson, *Notes on the State of Virginia,* ed. William Peden (1954; rpt. New York: Norton, 1972), p. 277. All future references in the text are to this edition.

[15] *Papers,* XII, 31, and *Writings,* XIV, 220–21. For even more specific evidence of Jefferson's belief that the minute observations of *Notes* would lead to general theories of solid foundation, see TJ to John W. Campbell, 3 Sept. 1809, *Writings,* XII, 307, and TJ to Lewis Caleb Beck, 16 July 1824, *Writings,* XVI, 71–72.

elaborate comparisons of European and American animal life, *Notes,*
like every other work to come out of the formative period, is
obsessed with the sense of a unique country that Americans were
groping to define. Ideological placement of the Republic is Jefferson's main theme. *Notes* builds slowly through observation of the
natural world and social analysis toward a final peroration on the
subject of country in a closing section improbably labeled public
revenue and expenses. "Young as we are," Jefferson concludes here,
"and with such a country before us to fill with people and with
happiness, we should point in that direction the whole generative
force of nature." What follows is a summation of America's unique
opportunity for creating a new kind of nation based upon peace,
free trade, virtuous citizenship, and careful harmony within the
many advantages Nature has furnished the New World (pp. 174-
76). The controls of a republican government—"one which should
not only be founded on free principles, but in which the powers of
government should be so divided and balanced among several bodies
of magistracy, as that no one could transcend their legal limits,
without being effectually checked and restrained by the others"
(p. 120)—would guarantee appropriate and unparalleled national
growth.

The difficulties in achieving this positive vision involved more
than revolutionary rhetoric. The greatest blunder we make in approaching the works of the formative period is to assume the sense
of country that the Founding Fathers worked so desperately to
create. The year 1781, when *Notes* took shape, was full of confusion and anxiety in America—particularly for a Virginian and most
particularly for Virginia's governor, Thomas Jefferson. Six years
later James Madison would become the Father of the Constitution,
but in 1781 he was a discouraged member of the Continental Congress writing home to Jefferson of his certainty that the Union
would dissolve as the war ended.[16] In Virginia, of course, the war
had just begun in 1781, first with an exploratory raid in January
by British forces under Benedict Arnold and then with a successful
invasion by Cornwallis' army in May that sent Jefferson and his

---

[16] James Madison to TJ, 18 Nov. 1781, in William T. Hutchinson, William M. E.
Rachal, Robert A. Rutland, and Charles F. Hobson, eds., *The Papers of James Madison,*
12 vols. (Chicago: The Univ. of Chicago Press and Charlottesville: Univ. Press of
Virginia, 1962–79), III, 307–08.

state government fleeing from Richmond. Inadequate military preparation, a crop failure throughout the state, runaway inflation, secessionist movements in the Kentucky territory, and insufficient executive power for dealing with any of these emergencies were complications that left Jefferson helpless to act. Nevertheless, he was blamed for the general collapse by an ungrateful legislature that decided in June to investigate his conduct as governor. Six months would pass before the next General Assembly voted "to obviate and to remove all unmerited Censure." In the meantime, one of Jefferson's daughters died, his property was overrun and partially destroyed by the British army, he was personally immobilized for a time by a serious riding accident, and his wife's health continued to decline toward her early death in September 1782, which would leave Jefferson completely traumatized for weeks on end.[17]

Notes on the State of Virginia was written and revised during this bleak period, the darkest in Jefferson's life. In fact, the whole first draft was composed during the second half of 1781 while the prospect of public censure hung over him. Jefferson would later call this threat "a shock on which I had not calculated," and his entire orientation seems to have been shaken by events as he announced his permanent retirement at thirty-eight to farm, family, and books. *Notes* represented an attempt to reorder experience and to control the chaos around him.[18] Never a man of action and always an intellectual, Jefferson clearly welcomed a structured excuse for reappraisal. As he put it himself, "I am at present busily employed for Monsr. Marbois without his knowing it, and have to acknowledge to him the mysterious obligation for making me much better acquainted with my own country than I ever was

[17] The historical facts in this paragraph and Jefferson's place within them are from Dumas Malone, *Jefferson the Virginian*, pp. 327–69. The "Resolution of the House of Delegates, June 12, 1781," seeking an investigation of Jefferson's conduct as governor and the belated "Resolution of Thanks to Jefferson by the Virginia General Assembly, December 12, 1781," are in *Papers*, VI, 88, 135–36.

[18] For an interesting recent essay detailing Jefferson's feelings, see William J. Scheick, "Chaos and Imaginative Order in Thomas Jefferson's *Notes on the State of Virginia*," in *Essays in Early Virginia Literature Honoring Richard Beale Davis*, ed. J. A. Leo Lemay (New York: Burt Franklin, 1977), pp. 221–34. Jefferson's bitter comments concerning his situation at the time are in: TJ to James Monroe, 20 May 1782, *Papers*, VI, 184–85; TJ to George Washington, 28 May 1781, *Papers*, VI, 32–33; TJ to General Lafayette, 4 Aug. 1781, *Papers*, VI, 111–12; TJ to Edmund Randolph, 16 Sept. 1781, *Papers*, VI, 117–18.

before."[19] No one could have been better primed for the task. For years Jefferson had collected information on America, written on what he described as "loose papers, bundled up without order." *Notes* required an organization for these memoranda and soon became, in Jefferson's phrase, "a good occasion to embody their substance."[20]

Everything about Jefferson's personal situation and the ensuing creative process suggests that *Notes* was no casual effort. The book placed him under mysterious obligation, as he tells us, because it led him toward a better sense of country. Moreover, his growth in knowledge happened at least in part because the need to organize earlier and looser writings—"embody their substance"—produced firmer understanding and control. Taken together, Jefferson's statements indicate unexplored levels of clarity and structure in *Notes*, order imposed on chaos. They also suggest the writer's inclination to combine problems of theme and form. The convergence of revolutionary uncertainties with Jefferson's personal difficulties and with the disarray of his "loose papers" pointed toward demands for control on disparate levels. Jefferson's tentative solution was to submerge each problem in a developmental sense of country which supplied republican identity and individual meaning as well as textual coherence to *Notes*. Though the process was fraught with aesthetic complications and confusions, it allowed Jefferson to escape the chaos of the moment and search for incremental meanings within time. Time itself, through Jefferson's optimistic hopes for the future, could suggest an answering promise to anxieties regarding the present and compensate for structural inadequacies within a text that never claimed to attain finality.

The practical difficulty in seeking a view of country in the 1780s was the sheer unruliness of a subject filled with unknowns. When the author of *Notes* describes the Ohio River as the most beautiful on earth (p. 10), it is well to remember that he never traveled far enough west to see it. The notable possibilities of volcanoes along the Mississippi (p. 20) and of carnivorous hairy mammoths extant in the Northwest (pp. 43, 50–54) provide extreme examples of the need to find form in a void. Measuring a half-known world pre-

[19] TJ to the Chevalier D'Anmours, 30 Nov. 1780, *Papers*, IV, 168.
[20] "Autobiography," *Writings*, I, 90–91.

sented related problems. Fearful lest his lists and figures in *Notes* be dismissed as parochial aberrations, Jefferson declares Monticello physically central to Virginia, where "the best average" in data can be expected (p. 76). Ignorant of vital information concerning the Appalachian mountains, he insists upon their orderly appearance: "it is worthy notice that our mountains are not solitary and scattered confusedly over the face of the country; but that they . . . are disposed in ridges one behind another" (p. 18). A similar mechanism projects geometric and artistic unity over the otherwise formless wilderness of western Virginia.[21]

Jefferson knew as well as any modern reader that these devices were superficial, even ludicrous; they were strategies of control, not serious formulations. Time and again in *Notes* he shows sophisticated awareness of an investigator's real problems, confessing that a topic is "unripe" for meaningful response and conceding that his answers are incomplete because phenomena remain inexplicable (pp. 2, 33, 54, 81). "It is impossible," he would later add, "for doubt to have been more tenderly and hesitatingly expressed than it was in the *Notes on Virginia*."[22] His use of Marbois' list of queries as chapter headings underlines this point. The text *as question* warns against false information—"Ignorance is preferable to error" (p. 33). It constantly reminds one that, in the absence of knowledge, inquiry imposes order. Significantly, each admission of an incomplete answer also contains Jefferson's realization that the bulk of the New World remains too remote to allow the use of natural philosophy as the primary structural principle for *Notes*.

Though crucial, the point will escape readers concentrating selectively on Jefferson's eloquent and famous descriptions of the Natural Bridge or the Blue Ridge Gap. Neither interest in the natural world nor general philosophical acceptance of Nature's blueprint for man can compensate the author of *Notes* for his own lack of information. Not surprisingly, Jefferson turned for relief to the mode of intellectual control he knew best, the law. What does surprise one is the rich implementation of this decision within the structure of *Notes*. The civic tones and disjointed forms of early republican literature take on fresh meaning when we realize that

---

21 Here Jefferson's rivers bisect his orderly mountains "at right angles" and move gently eastward toward civilization. *Notes on the State of Virginia*, pp. 18–19.

22 Quoted in Merrill D. Peterson, *Thomas Jefferson and the New Nation*, p. 263.

the legal philosophy of the Enlightenment gave Jefferson more than
an alternative for discursive method; it also provided an ideal solution to his structural problems. Legal formulation assumed a pattern to incremental knowledge that enabled Jefferson to fuse the
organizational needs of *Notes* to a developmental sense of country.

III

Eighteenth-century conceptions of law encouraged both a par-
ticularistic methodology for extracting order from chaos and a
comprehensive view of subject matter. Jefferson, perhaps the best
legal scholar in America in 1781, was thoroughly familiar with the
works behind these assumptions.[23] The Dutch jurist, statesman, and
poet Hugo Grotius had written in 1625 that human reason, not
religious explanation, formed the basis of man's understanding of
natural law. Grotius' confidence in secular inquiry and his insistence that law be presented in "an orderly fashion" and in "a
compendious form" provided the inspiration for Samuel von
Pufendorf's *Of the Law of Nature and Nations* (1673), Jean Jacques
Burlamaqui's *The Principles of Natural and Politic Law* (1747-51),
Baron de Montesquieu's *The Spirit of Laws* (1748), William Blackstone's *Commentaries on the Laws of England* (1765-69), and
related works by Emmerich de Vattel, Lord Kames, Cesare Beccaria,
and others.[24]

Jefferson learned from Pufendorf, among others, that it was
possible through law "to deliver the most comprehensive Definitions
of Things" and to establish in moral science a certainty analogous
to that in mathematics. Clear connections between natural law and
moral science permitted moral entities to be "superadded to natural
Things" through the "imposition" of the reason of "understanding
Beings."[25] Burlamaqui outlined just how man-made or positive law

---

[23] The best analysis of Jefferson's expertise in law is Edward Dumbauld, *Thomas
Jefferson and the Law* (Norman: Univ. of Oklahoma Press, 1978), pp. 10, 28, 33, 75,
88-120, 132-35.

[24] Hugo Grotius, "Prolegomena: 1, 8, 9, 11," *De Jure Belli et Pacis*, trans. William
Whewell, 3 vols. (Cambridge, England: Cambridge Univ. Press, 1853), I, 37, 44-46.
See also Ernst Cassirer, *The Philosophy of the Enlightenment*, trans. Fritz C. A. Koelln
and James P. Pettegrove (1951; rpt. Boston: Beacon Press, 1955), pp. 234-41.

[25] Samuel von Pufendorf, *Of the Law of Nature and Nations*, trans. Basil Kennett,
4th ed. (London: J. Walthoe, 1729), pp. 1-3 (Bk. 1, Ch. 1). See also Leonard Krieger,
The Politics of Discretion: Pufendorf and the Acceptance of Natural Law (Chicago: The
Univ. of Chicago Press, 1965), pp. 52-54.

logically improved upon natural law and guarded the practical
sources of liberty as well as the identity of a culture. Little known
today, Burlamaqui's *The Principles of Natural and Politic Law*
served as a major text among American Revolutionary leaders.[26]
Montesquieu's *The Spirit of Laws,* in turn, showed how the inexplicable diversity of country or countries could be ordered and
then reduced through conceptions of positive law, and Blackstone's
Commentaries represented the great *exemplum* of that accomplishment—a country completely defined though law.[27]

Just about every substantive idea in *Notes on the State of Virginia*
can be traced in one or more of the legal works in question. Of
more immediate concern here, however, is Jefferson's decision to
use the general form of these writings to provide a structure and
organization to *Notes.* The legal treatises of Grotius, Pufendorf,
Burlamaqui, Montesquieu, and Blackstone, though enormous compendia, were consciously written as works of literature addressed
to a general audience. Even a casual modern reader is struck by
the range of subject matter, the reliance upon short headings to
provide narrative structure, and the rapid shifts in rhetorical strategy
from declamatory statement and idle speculation to careful argument, objective proof, and factual narration.

Such combinations were designed to allow sweeping flights in
subject matter within concrete methodical structures which needed
no explanation. Grotius, in his masterpiece *De Jure Belli et Pacis,*
offered the model others followed. "In order to give proofs on
questions respecting this Natural Law," he wrote, "I have made
use of the testimonies of philosophers, historians, poets, and finally
orators . . . as witnesses whose conspiring testimony, proceeding
from innumerable different times and places, must be referred to
some universal cause." At the same time, he promised to "arrange
in due order the matters [he] had to treat of" and to "distinguish

[26] Jean Jacques Burlamaqui, *The Principles of Natural and Politic Law,* trans. Thomas
Nugent, 5th ed., 2 vols. (Cambridge, Mass.: Hilliard, 1807), I, 134-40 (Pt. 2, Ch. 6);
II, 16-24 (Pt. 1, Ch. 3); II, 38-49 (Pt. 1, Ch. 7). For the impact of Burlamaqui's
thought upon Jefferson's writings, see Morton White, *The Philosophy of the American
Revolution* (New York: Oxford Univ. Press, 1978), pp. 39, 161-63, 188. See more
generally, Ray Forrest Harvey, *Jean Jacques Burlamaqui: A Liberal Tradition in American
Constitutionalism* (Chapel Hill: The Univ. of North Carolina Press, 1957).
[27] Baron de Montesquieu, *The Spirit of Laws,* trans. Thomas Nugent, 2 vols. (Cincin-
nati, Clarke and Co., 1873), I, 5-8 (Bk. 1, Ch. 3); William Blackstone, "Introduction,"
Commentaries on the Laws of England, facsimile of the 1st edition of 1765-69 (Chicago:
The Univ. of Chicago Press, 1979), I, 35.

101

clearly things which were really different" through a "concise and didactic mode of treatment" that would enable his reader to grasp the principles involved "at one view."[28] To do so was, in Pufendorf's words, "to rank [the most comprehensive Definitions of Things] agreeably under their proper Classes, subjoining the general Nature and Condition of every Sort of Beings."[29] The prose of the seventeenth- and eighteenth-century legal philosophers constantly aspires toward eloquence of a kind; but to understand its underlying meaning one must concentrate carefully upon the incremental structures supplied by a complex series of chapter and section headings.

Jefferson's use of similar headings in *Notes* solves a number of organizational problems with an ingenuity no one has discussed. As one critic says in summarizing the apparent weaknesses of *Notes*:

[the book] alternates between statistical description and moral exhortation, between sunny affirmation and anxious apprehension. The audience that it addresses is sometimes foreign, one that must be told that Virginia is organized by counties, and sometimes native, one that must be urged to replace its defective constitution and emancipate its slaves. The scope of the book alternately expands to embrace the entire United States and contracts to its ostensible subject, as if Jefferson were still unsure whether the phrase *my country* should have its old Virginian application or its new national one.[30]

All such difficulties were intrinsic to the literature of the early Republic, of course. When a writer of the period tried to define America for Americans, he faced conflicting definitions of loyalty across communal, county, state, and evolving national ties, and he did so knowing that ultimate literary merit would be judged according to the norms of an extrinsic European readership.[31]

---

[28] "Prolegomena: 40, 56, 59," *De Jure Belli et Pacis*, 1, 66, 77–78.

[29] *Of the Law of Nature and Nations*, p. 1.

[30] Thomas Philbrick, "Thomas Jefferson," in *American Literature 1764–1789: The Revolutionary Years*, ed. Everett Emerson (Madison: Univ. of Wisconsin Press, 1977), p. 162.

[31] For the uncertainties involved in the literature of the early Republic, see particularly William L. Hedges, "The Myth of the Republic and the Theory of American Literature," *Prospects: An Annual of American Cultural Studies*, 4 (1979), 101–20, and Lewis P. Simpson, "The Symbolism of Literary Alienation in the Revolutionary Age," in *200 Years of the Republic*, ed. William C. Havard and Joseph L. Bernd (Charlottesville: Univ. Press of Virginia, 1976), pp. 79–100.

Jefferson, a skilled rhetorician well aware of his audiences, uses structure and form to channel the inevitable variations of his discourse. He employs headings to minimize confusion much as the legal writers controlled their expansive subjects, digressions, and juxtapositions in tone and theme.

Marbois' inserted interrogatives were both "Queries proposed to the Author, by a Foreigner of Distinction" (p. 2) and the questions an everyman might ask about the American unknown. Each appears at the beginning of a section of *Notes* as the symbol of a unified audience, and they function as common denominators signifying to each reader—whether Virginia gentleman, French philosophe, or American democrat—the need to adjust and begin again. Nor is it necessarily a sign of poor organization or rigidity, as too many have suggested, that certain headings in *Notes* barely receive answers at all. Many a chapter in Montesquieu's *The Spirit of Laws* was one sentence long.[32] Jefferson understood that the order of headings creates form and narrative structure in such works, and his appreciation of this principle supplies the key to understanding his book. For though he relies upon Marbois' questions, Jefferson freely rearranges their sequence and bases his reorganization on the reasoning of the legal treatises he knew so well.

Grotius had argued that failure to separate instituted or positive law from an initial treatment of natural law had been the major obstacle in previous attempts to reduce jurisprudence to the form of an art or science. *De Jure Belli et Pacis* and the major works of Pufendorf and Burlamaqui accept the distinction as a central organizational premise.[33] To achieve the same effect in *Notes,* Jefferson reorders and divides Marbois' random questions and recasts their meaning in context. The following table presents a quick view of this organization by contrasting Marbois' original order of questions to Jefferson's rearrangement in *Notes:*[34]

[32] Compare, for example, queries three and ten in *Notes on the State of Virginia* with Montesquieu's one-sentence chapters in *The Spirit of Laws,* I, 32 (Bk. 3, Ch. 11); II, 127 (Bk. 24, Ch. 12); and II, 140 (Bk. 25, Ch. 1).

[33] "Prolegomena: 30, 41," *De Jure Belli et Pacis,* I, 60, 66–67.

[34] Marbois' list of questions as Jefferson received them is contained in *Papers,* IV, 166–67.

Marbois' Order   *Jefferson's Order*

(3)	1. An exact description of the limits and boundaries of the state of Virginia?
(6)	2. A notice of its rivers, rivulets, and how far they are navigable?
(13)	3. A notice of the best sea-ports, and how big are the vessels they receive?
(6)	4. A notice of the mountains?
(6)	5. Its cascades and caverns?
(20)(6)	6. A notice of the mines and other subterraneous riches; its trees, plants, fruits, etc.
(21)	7. A notice of all what can increase the progress of human knowledge? [On climate.]
(7)	8. The number of its inhabitants?
(18)	9. The number and condition of the Militia and Regular Troops and their Pay?
(19)	10. The marine?
(22)	11. A description of the Indians established in that state?
(6)	12. A notice of the counties, cities, townships, and villages?
(1)(2)	13. The constitution of the state, and its several charters?
(10)	14. The administration of justice and description of the laws?
(9)	15. The Colleges and Public Establishments, the Roads, Buildings, etc.?
(17)	16. The measures taken with regard of the estates and possessions of the rebels, commonly called Tories?
(8)	17. The different religions received into that state?
(11)	18. The particular customs and manners that may happen to be received in that state? [On slavery.]
(12)	19. The present state of manufactures, commerce, interior and exterior trade?
(14)	20. A notice of the commercial productions particular to the state, and of those objects which the inhabitants are obliged to get from Europe and from other parts of the world?

Marbois' Order	Jefferson's Order
(15)	21. The weights, measures, and the currency of the hard money? Some details relating to the exchange with Europe?
(16)	22. The public income and expences?
(4)	23. The histories of the state, the memorials published in its name in the time of its being a colony, and the pamphlets relating to its interior or exterior affairs present or ancient?

As the table demonstrates, *Notes* opens with accounts of Virginia's boundaries, geography, natural life, and climate (pp. 1–81) based upon queries three, thirteen, twenty, twenty-one, and numerous divisions of query six from Marbois' list. The French diplomat's first two questions on the charters and present constitution of the state, representing civil matters, have been dropped to the second half of the book in Jefferson's thirteenth section (pp. 110–29). These changes and others like them create an elementary structural separation in *Notes* between natural phenomenon and social event. Behind the simplicity of the division, however, appear the same elaborate impulses toward continuity that led Grotius to build a unified view from a series of ordered distinctions. Just as the multiplicity of human law might give rise to a science of jurisprudence, so the bewildering physicality of America could be made to yield a unified republic.

The mysteries in natural phenomena were not to be eliminated, but they could be assigned their places within the intellectual construct of natural law. Every selection of facts depends upon some principle or initiative. For Jefferson the theoretical assumptions of the natural law philosophers—a Nature of uniformity, hierarchy, and larger purpose—provided a necessary sense of order. Indeed, it was easier to infer Nature's general design from a world untouched by human history. To take only the most obvious example from *Notes,* Jefferson's mammoth must still live in theory because explorers have found its bones and extinction would be against Nature's law. As he writes, "such is the economy of nature, that no instance can be produced of her having permitted any one race of her animals to become extinct; of her having formed any link in her great work so weak as to be broken." Indian stories of huge animals in the Northwest operate in this context as "the light of a taper" to "the meridian sun" of natural law (pp. 53-54).

The more difficult connection between natural and political order or between natural law and positive law involved a significant intellectual leap, but it was one which the legal philosophers had made with increasing self-confidence as the eighteenth century progressed. One can see the point of connection most clearly through a particular problem in *Notes*. Jefferson's seventh section involves a discussion of Virginia's climate based upon painstaking tabulations of rainfall, temperature, and wind velocity recorded twice a day across a five-year period (pp. 73-81). And yet the heading for the section comes from Marbois' twenty-first query, which calls far more grandly for "a notice of all what can increase the progress of human knowledge." Narrow meteorological expertise seems an inappropriate response to the question, but it would not have puzzled François Marbois, the French intellectual for whom it was written. In the eighteenth century, climatological factors were extremely relevant to larger discussions of political theory and, hence, to a belief in human progress based upon the forces of political change within the period.

Montesquieu in particular, accepting the general notions that good government should be conformable to Nature and that positive law should build from natural law, emphasized the importance of geophysical elements in describing national identity. "Mankind are influenced by various causes," he wrote in *The Spirit of Laws,* "by the climate, by the religion, by the laws, by the maxims of government, by precedents, morals, and customs; from whence is formed a general spirit of nations." In consequence, a true idea of nationality could only be maintained through a detailed understanding of the many aspects of the physical and social worlds that shaped it. The whole function of Montesquieu's book was to examine the importance of these relationships in creating what inevitably pointed toward a unique sense of country.[35] A descriptive mode based upon particulars promised as much, even as Montesquieu's assumption of an *esprit général* guaranteed final unity within the process. As Peter Gay has suggested in calling Montesquieu the most influential writer of the eighteenth century,

[35] *The Spirit of Laws,* I, 339 (Bk. 19, Ch. 4), and I, 5-8 (Bk. 1, Ch. 3).

coherence emerges in *The Spirit of Laws* through "its author's passion for finding law behind the apparent rule of chance."[36]

Jefferson's personal reliance was profound. While studying law he gave more space in his commonplace book to *The Spirit of Laws* than any other work, and he would later recommend it to his own students as the best general book available on the science of government.[37] In effect, the influence was redoubled because another early intellectual hero in law, Lord Kames, the Scottish jurist and author of *Historical Law Tracts* (1758) and *Principles of Equity* (1760), was a known advocate of Montesquieu's methods. Kames's defense of Scottish nationalism through the uniqueness of Scottish legal traditions prefigures the essential strategy of Jefferson's book.

Notes is a far more coherent text examined in the light of these influences. Mere coverage builds into design if one accepts Montesquieu's belief that effective civil law depends upon issues of climate, geography, and natural wealth.[38] The facts of *Notes* become essential ingredients toward a definition of Americanism that must be reflected in political institutions if the Republic is to survive. Accordingly, each of the early sections on physical circumstances within an assumed natural order contributes to a general American spirit and to "specific principles" of civil government which Jefferson believes "are more peculiar than those of any other in the universe." Political customs and practices represent a unique source of virtue in America because they have evolved away from corrupted European counterparts and because they are composed of "the freest principles of the English constitution" in conjunction with "natural right and natural reason" in a new-world setting (pp. 84–86, 135–37). Excluding section six with its extensive lists of indigenous flora and fauna, Jefferson gives most space in *Notes* to sections thirteen and fourteen—the central rationale of an American polity based upon charters, constitutions, and the laws of the state (pp. 110–49). These sections, like the political chapters of *The*

---

[36] Peter Gay, *The Enlightenment: An Interpretation*, II, 324–25.

[37] Gilbert Chinard, "Introduction," *The Commonplace Book of Thomas Jefferson: A Repertory of His Ideas on Government* (Baltimore: Johns Hopkins Press, 1926), pp. 31–38, 257–96. Jefferson's praise of Montesquieu was qualified by the flaws he found in *The Spirit of Laws*, but his general admiration for the French legal theorist's ideas is clear from TJ to Thomas Mann Randolph, Jr., 30 May 1790, *Papers*, XVI, 449.

[38] *The Spirit of Laws*, I, 7 (Bk. 1, Ch. 3).

Spirit of Laws, form the heart of the book. They supply precision and a higher sense of country against earlier uncertainties. Here Jefferson also delivers his pivotal explanation of the Revolution through precedents extracted from the legal charters of the colonies (pp. 110–18). America's assertion of natural right, he argues, was a response to British disregard of lawful forms and has culminated in thirteen independent states "confederated together into one great republic."

The rest of *Notes* builds structurally out of this fundamental assertion of republicanism. Jefferson proceeds to analyze the theoretical problems of republican government as he has come to understand these problems in legal philosophy. Burlamaqui and Montesquieu both had written that republicanism alone was no assurance of liberty, that only positive law (established legal limits in a mixed constitution) provided that guarantee, and that corruption, luxury, and licentiousness would be particular difficulties in any popular government.[39] In keeping with his mentors' assumptions that rulers would become venal and the people careless, Jefferson warns "it can never be too often repeated, that the time for fixing every essential right on a legal basis is while our rulers are honest and ourselves united" (p. 161). In context the later sections of *Notes* represent a political anatomy, fixing every essential right and isolating each potential problem. Jefferson's description of the Virginia constitution in the second half of section thirteen is peppered with warnings to Virginians and Americans alike to "bind up the several branches of government by certain laws" (pp. 120–29). Section fourteen is dominated by the author's concrete proposals for legal reforms, and each ensuing section offers abbreviated commentary on one or more of these reforms. Again and again, legal formulation offers both a framework of definition and a mechanism of control.

The end of section fourteen and the beginning of fifteen detail the public educational system that Jefferson, Montesquieu, and Burlamaqui all feel is essential to a true republic and that the author

---

[39] *The Principles of Natural and Politic Law,* II, 58–61 (Pt. 2, Ch. 1); II, 68–71 (Pt. 2, Ch. 2); II, 145 (Pt. 3, Ch. 5); and *The Spirit of Laws,* I, 126–44 (Bk. 8); I, 172–86 (Bk. 11, Chs. 4–6); I, 210 (Bk. 12, Ch. 1). Jefferson follows the suggestion in these passages that only a proper disposition of laws in relation to a constitution guarantees liberty.

of *Notes* ties to his legal system of county and ward government (pp. 146–51). This educational system is to insure an essential general knowledge of law. "It is in a republican government that the whole power of education is required," Montesquieu had written, tracing virtue in a citizenry to patriotic feeling and an informed "love of the laws."[40] Sections sixteen, seventeen, and eighteen present a series of measures that will eliminate given threats to republican virtue: recognition of the continuing legal rights of the defeated Tories (pp. 155–56), the guarantee of religious toleration by law within the state (pp. 157–61), and plans for the abolition of slavery (pp. 162–63). Each measure has been raised previously, though briefly, in the plan for legal reform of section fifteen. Here Jefferson explains why his solutions are crucial to the integrity of the Republic and orders his discussion along a continuum of ever-increasing difficulty of implementation, concluding in an image that his Virginia readers could never accept, "the slave rising from the dust . . . with the consent of the masters."

Sections nineteen through twenty-two are more haphazard organizationally because they deal with the vagaries of future danger. Shorter and more episodic, they constitute a loose catalogue of prospective problems and solutions using the terminology of luxury and corruption that any reader of Montesquieu or of the Whig revolutionary writers will recognize (pp. 164–76). Urbanization, industrialization, short-sighted commercial measures, standing armies, and inflation are presented one after the other as potential irritants to the harmony and general spirit of the agrarian republic that Jefferson describes in his peroration at the end of section twenty-two. Section twenty-three, a list of all existing state histories and formal documents (pp. 177–96), gives a last poignant acknowledgment of what *Notes* would never become; it is a rough index of the material an American Blackstone would require to write a commentary instead of a note on the State of Virginia.[41]

[40] *The Spirit of Laws*, I, 38–39 (Bk. 4, Ch. 5); and *The Principles of Natural and Politic Law*, II, 120–22 (Pt. 3, Ch. 2).

[41] Although a commentary could be a book of notes, its formal meaning as used by Blackstone and as presented in Jefferson's own Latin-English dictionary implied more formal and elaborate control. *Notatio* means a marking or observing or a taking notice of. The process leaves a *Nota* or evidence. *Commentatio*, on the other hand, implies more extensive organization and could specifically mean "a description, as of a country, and giving an account of it in writing." Adam Littleton, *Littleton's Latin Dictionary in Four Parts*, 6th ed. (London: J. Walthoe, 1735), and Sowerby, *The Library of Thomas*

IV

The more unified text found within this structural design encourages a new perspective. Theorists, assuming only a sourcebook
for Jeffersonian political thought, have stressed the passages that
affirm the American farmer, Nature's order, and the rising glory
of America; but Jefferson the ideologue is also a careful observer in
his book, and too much of what he sees in Virginia falls short of
the republican ideal that is his central theme. Significantly, the prevailing mood of *Notes* as text is one of profound anxiety.[42] When
Jefferson brags in *Notes* that the Natural Bridge and Blue Ridge
Gap are worth a voyage across the Atlantic to see, he also admits
that his own neighbors lack the wherewithal to travel a few miles
to either location (pp. 19–20). He is generally appalled by the
cultural ignorance and living habits of his fellow countrymen (pp.
152–53), and he designs his scheme of public education to, in his
own words, rake a few geniuses from the rubbish (p. 146). Even
minimal levels of general development, he complains, will be undermined by European immigrants who threaten to reduce the
American citizenry to an "incoherent, distracted mass" (p. 85).
Such views seem out of keeping with our third president's supposed
faith in the people, but they represent only part of a darker side
of *Notes*.

Jefferson the social sophisticate dismisses the towns around him
as of no consequence—they are ephemeral things that rise and fall
in the accidental circumstances of Nature (pp. 108–09)—and he
condemns Virginia's tobacco economy. "It is a culture productive
of infinite wretchedness" (p. 166). Intrinsic political weakness
compounds these social ills. In *Notes* the state's very constitution is
illegitimate, badly conceived, and sadly lacking in "a proper com-
plication of principles" (pp. 120–25). Moreover, Jefferson as former
governor is personally "confounded and dismayed" because current
leaders have readily deserted republican principles in the last stages

---

Jefferson, V, 87. Jefferson, a keen Latin scholar, understood the distinction involved. He
resisted pressures from within his own circle to give *Notes* "a more dignified title."
See, for example, Charles Thomson to TJ, 6 March 1785, *Papers*, VIII, 16.

[42] Thomas Philbrick and William J. Scheick have identified some of the anxious tones
in *Notes* in Philbrick, "Thomas Jefferson," in *American Literature 1764–1789*, p. 166,
and Scheick, "Chaos and Imaginative Order in Jefferson's *Notes*," in *Essays in Early
Virginia Literature*, p. 224.

of the war effort. "Our situation is indeed perilous," he writes, warning against demagoguery, "and I hope my countrymen will be sensible of it" (pp. 126–29). Beyond these immediate problems, Jefferson devotes long pages to theoretical fears of corruption within the state and to the specter of slavery in a republic.[43]

In fact, *Notes* worries the slave issue over three widely separate sections and with growing alarm at each new stage of explanation. Religious tones dominate a hesitant conclusion when it finally comes:

Indeed I tremble for my country when I reflect that God is just: that his justice cannot sleep for ever: that . . . a revolution of the wheel of fortune, an exchange of situation, is among possible events: that it may become probable by supernatural interference! The Almighty has no attribute which can take side with us in such a contest. (p. 163)

Lewis Simpson already has traced this loss of calm and detachment to Jefferson's conviction that slavery would destroy the Republic, but the uncharacteristic switch to apocalyptic terminology also indicates something specific about Jefferson's feelings of helplessness.[44] Of the issues raised in the pessimistic remarks of *Notes*, only slavery resists rational management in Jefferson's hands, and it does so precisely because it defies legal terminology and solution within the intellectual framework of an eighteenth-century lawyer.[45] Slavery exists but outside of law; it becomes, in consequence, a structural incongruity in *Notes* spilling between and among sections.

Jefferson handles his anxieties in every other area by using legal forms to control realities. As he later summarized the vision behind

[43] For Jefferson's frequent comments on corruption and disintegration in the state, see *Notes on the State of Virginia*, pp. 85, 120–21, 148–49, 161. He deals with slavery first in section eight on population (p. 87), then in section fourteen on laws (pp. 138–43), and finally in his discussion of manners and customs in section eighteen (pp. 162–63).

[44] Lewis P. Simpson, *The Dispossessed Garden: Pastoral and History in Southern Literature* (Athens: Univ. of Georgia Press, 1975), pp. 27–30.

[45] John Locke placed slavery completely outside the social compact, and Montesquieu, while analyzing slavery in detail, declared the practice contrary to natural law and to the fundamental principles of *all* societies. Montesquieu found slavery particularly dangerous for a country with moderate laws. It is worth adding that Jefferson wrote *Notes* during the crest of abolitionist movements in both England and France. See John Locke, *Two Treatises of Government* in *The Works of John Locke*, 12th ed., 9 vols. (London: C. and J. Rivington, 1824), IV, 212 (Bk. 1, Ch. 1); and IV, 351–52 (Bk. 2, Ch. 4); Montesquieu, *The Spirit of Laws*, I, 270–83 (Bk. 15, Chs. 1–15). See also Peter Gay, "Abolitionism: A Preliminary Probing," *The Enlightenment: An Interpretation*, II, 407–23.

this procedure, "the elementary republics of the wards, the county republics, the State republics, and the republic of the Union would form a gradation of authorities, standing each on the basis of law."[46] The author of *Notes* can impose his geometrical grid of wards or hundreds upon shifting towns or even upon empty space. His decision to place every essential right on a legal basis represents fixed intelligence in the midst of flux, and his draft of a fundamental constitution for the Commonwealth of Virginia appears in an appendix to show the path of civic virtue in spite of corruption and every danger (pp. 209–22).

That even Jefferson, the most optimistic of Founding Fathers, needed to explain away his fears shows why definitions of country obsessed early Americans. His related ability to sustain optimism through legal formulation also suggests how lawyers came to be the ideological spokesmen of the Republic. It is the assurance behind these imposed solutions that impresses today—an assurance that grew directly out of the contributions of English legal thought to the success of the American Revolution. Jefferson was steeped in the writings of the seventeenth-century English lawyers who had struggled to separate their discipline from other modes of thought and who, succeeding beyond every expectation, had created a whole new political order in the process. In 1625, the year in which Grotius published *De Jure Belli et Pacis,* Jefferson's greatest hero Francis Bacon proclaimed that law-givers and commonwealth builders would be the intellectual champions of the modern world.[47] Meanwhile, Bacon's rival Sir Edward Coke became the embodiment of that proposition by giving form, content, and ascendency to the common law of England. Coke's writings—the four *Institutes,* the thirteen volumes of *Reports,* and his drafts for what became the Parliamentary Petition of Right in 1628—formed the rationale for "the triumph of the Common Law and lawyers over the king" in the Revolution of 1688.[48]

---

[46] TJ to Joseph C. Cabell, 2 Feb. 1816, *Writings*, XIV, 422.

[47] Francis Bacon, "Of Honour and Reputation," *Essays of Counsels Civil and Moral*, in *The Works of Francis Bacon*, ed. James Spedding,. Robert L. Ellis, and Douglas D. Heath, 14 vols. (London: Longman and Co., 1857–74), VI, 505–06.

[48] A summary of the importance of Coke's career both in England and for Colonial American intellectuals is contained in A. E. Dick Howard, *The Road from Runnymede: Magna Carta and Constitutionalism in America* (Charlottesville: The Univ. Press of Virginia, 1968), pp. 117–25. The quotation in the text is from G. M. Trevelyan, *The*

By 1700, within a remarkably short period of time, law had come to represent an independent way of viewing England, a safer alternative to the religious and philosophical examinations that had torn the country apart for most of a century. This new framework was especially attractive to eighteenth-century Americans schooled in the Whig revolutionary tradition. Early Republicans simply *assumed* the efficacy of legal remedies that Englishmen had used more tentatively to make a revolution glorious instead of violent. For Jefferson in particular, with his notorious distrust of theology and metaphysical speculation, law was the perfect ideological tool—at once a justification for rebellion and a model for lasting order.

The intellectual excitement over the possibilities in legal formulation would dominate American thought for decades because the possibilities themselves were so useful. Newton had demonstrated how facts properly observed would lead to a unified vision of scientific law, but the English common law—what Jefferson called "the glory and protection of that country"—was a more practical model to work with.[49] Even conservative English intellectuals like William Blackstone derived the spirit of English legal rights from a golden age of Saxon freedom preceding Norman usurpation. Therefore, the common law could be conveniently separated from the royalist taint and corruption which Revolutionary Americans associated with eighteenth-century British culture in general. As an accumulation of history, custom, and legal procedure, it also provided a flexible, empirical sense of order. "Proceeding warily and undogmatically from case to case, the common law was rich in the prudence of individual cases but poor in theoretical principles; it was adept at solving problems but inept at philosophizing about them."[50] Everything about these intellectual boundaries suited anxious republicans who remained ideologically intense but uncertain of their destinations—so uncertain, in fact, that they would deliberately exclude all mention of the words "federal" and "na-

---

English Revolution, 1688–1689 (1938; rpt. New York: Oxford Univ. Press, 1967), p. 71, but I also refer to Michael Landon's enlargement and explanation of the whole theme in *The Triumph of the Lawyers: Their Role in English Politics, 1678–1689* (University: Univ. of Alabama Press, 1970).

[49] Jefferson, "A Summary View of the Rights of British America, 1774," *Papers*, I, 122.
[50] Boorstin, *The Americans: The National Experience*, p. 41.

tional" as too controversial for the Constitution of the United States.[51] A common-law way of thinking avoided orthodoxies that would split the country, and it gave an effective but loose ideological frame to a growing republic. It was, in short, the basic intellectual analog for the accumulating federalism that would control American expansion for a century.

No early American understood the usefulness of legal examination better than Thomas Jefferson.[52] The very structure of *Notes*— an order through accumulation leaving room for later elaboration— parallels that of the common law, and Jefferson's professional interest in his subject was immense. In an age when practitioners like Patrick Henry and John Marshall joined the Virginia Bar after a few months of reading, Jefferson devoted five full years of rigorous study, even teaching himself Anglo-Saxon in order to trace the common law to its roots.[53] He read Grotius, Pufendorf, Montesquieu, and Beccaria in their original Latin, French, and Italian texts; he mastered everything he could find in the related fields of history, ethics, and oratory; and he collected an enormous law library so complete in ancient statutes and reports that the Virginia courts came to treat it as a depository of public records.[54]

The mystic identification of law and country intrinsic to our national rhetoric is probably the most important legacy of this expertise. Jefferson did more than any other American of his generation to insure that a conception of higher law would dominate political discourse. What is less obvious, however, is the extent to which this rhetoric now masks the compulsive fears that originally gave it meaning. Like most early republicans, Jefferson regarded

[51] James Madison, "June 19–20, 1787," *Notes of Debates in the Federal Convention of 1787*, ed. Adrienne Koch (New York: Norton, 1969), pp. 140–56.

[52] For Jefferson's specific acceptance of both the order *and* the flexibility in what Boorstin calls "the common-law way of thinking," see *Notes on the State of Virginia*, p. 137. Here Jefferson bases his entire revision of Virginia's laws upon English common law, but he carefully resists the "dangerous" inclination to reduce the common law to a single text.

[53] Julian Boyd also raises the discrepancy between Jefferson's preparation and the more superficial legal studies of his contemporaries in "Jefferson's Expression of the American Mind," *The Virginia Quarterly Review*, 50 (1974), 541–42. That Jefferson turned to Anglo-Saxon "for explanation of a multitude of law-terms" is clear from TJ to Herbert Croft, 30 Oct. 1798, *Writings*, XVIII, 363.

[54] See Dumbauld, *Thomas Jefferson and the Law*, pp. 3–17, 121–24. For Jefferson's actual use of Latin, French, and Italian in his legal studies, see Chinard, ed., *The Commonplace Book of Thomas Jefferson*, pp. 47, 257–316, 369.

the uncertainties inherent to his political situation as a perpetual emergency, and he studied law scrupulously because he felt it was the surest mechanism of control in a crisis. Thus, when Jefferson's first inaugural address declares American government to be the strongest on earth because it is "the only one where every man, at the call of the laws, would fly to the standard of the law," it must be understood in light of the potential for emergency within this language and in light of the "anxious and awful presentiments" and "despair" with which Jefferson opens his address.[55]

Because a nation defined through law rested upon a republic obsessed with its own frailty, the same combination of assertion and anxiety necessarily dominated the literature of the period. The prose of early republicans is not so much problem oriented as it is a juxtaposition of problem to solution in cycles of gloom and gladness that never seem to end. *Notes on the State of Virginia* is a type for the manic-depressive tendencies within this process.[56] And Jefferson's creativity is clearest in his use of legal formulation to bridge these extremes through structure and thematic control.

Jefferson's treatment of the American Indian in *Notes* offers a final case in point. Chief Logan's famous speech to Lord Dunmore is evidence that neither intelligence nor sensibility have been lacking in Indian culture. It is also an epitaph for a civilization: "Who is there to mourn for Logan?—Not one" (p. 63). Jefferson's subsequent investigation of Indian burial grounds dramatizes "the melancholy sequel of their history." But there is a larger point to this story of disintegration, and it is one that Jefferson welds to his major concern in *Notes*. Total collapse—"I know of no such thing existing as an Indian monument"—occurs because the Indians "never submitted themselves to any laws, any coercive power, any shadow of government."[57] Jefferson's three sections on the counties, constitutions, and laws of the Republic, with all of their promise

---

[55] "Inauguration Address, March 4, 1801," *Writings*, III, 317–21.

[56] William Hedges comments most forcefully upon the "pronounced manic-depressive tendencies" in early American literature in "Charles Brockden Brown and the Culture of Contradictions," *Early American Literature*, 9 (1974), 137.

[57] *Notes on the State of Virginia*, pp. 92–97. Critics looking for the revolutionary Jefferson have tended to stress his suggestion in these pages that no law among the American Indians is preferable to too much law among civilized Europeans. What they overlook is that the full context of Jefferson's remarks shows his support for what he presents as a separate generalization: "great societies cannot exist without government."

of order and all of their fear of current weakness, follow directly upon the warning explicit in this secular jeremiad.

Jefferson's fascination with law is crucial to the craft of such passages in a marriage of solution and problem that helps to explain why lawyers would remain so central to literary endeavor in the first forty years of our national history. Although it is an untold story, attorneys controlled a number of the first major literary journals and wrote some of the country's first important novels, plays, and poems. Their inevitable subject was our national identity, and no other vocational group came close to matching their contribution either in quality or quantity. *Notes on the State of Virginia* is, in this sense, more than an American classic; it is also a gauge for examining a literature in which legal thought controls mental adventure. Here as elsewhere, Thomas Paine's *Common Sense* in 1775 anticipated how so many would later think. "In America," wrote the prophet of revolution, "the law is king."[58]

[58] Thomas Paine, *Common Sense* in *The Complete Writings of Thomas Paine*, ed. Philip S. Foner, 2 vols. (New York: The Citadel Press, 1945), I, 29.

ROADS TO HAPPINESS: RHETORICAL AND PHILOSOPHICAL DESIGN IN JEFFERSON'S *NOTES ON THE STATE OF VIRGINIA*

HAROLD HELLENBRAND
California State University, San Bernardino

I

It is commonplace now to observe that Thomas Jefferson's *Notes on the State of Virginia* has been one of the stepchildren of American literature.[1] Regarded by some as a simple, if factually tedious polemic against European perceptions of America as a degenerate environment, it also has been dismissed by others as either a guidebook or a "reference-type work" (Commager 36–45, Sandford 51). Fortunately, recent scholarship especially has helped to right perceptions of the form of the book. Clayton Lewis has analyzed the discursive "process of observation and evolving hypothesis" that organizes Jefferson's Queries and that, in effect, links his rhetorical style to late Enlightenment conceptions of nature as energetic and functional (672). And Robert Ferguson has argued that the volume recalls both the note-like chapters and the somewhat determinist philosophy of Montesquieu's *Spirit of the Laws*, in which the physical and social environment conditions—and controls—man's behavior (390–93, 396–99).[2] In other words, *Notes* has emerged as a literary text that is rooted in the discursive forms as well as the philosophical assumptions of eighteenth-century literature that is concerned with the operations of nature and the origins of natural and civil law.

Still, Jefferson's indebtedness to theorists of natural and positive (civil) law—and specifically to Montesquieu—can be overstated.

3

For instance, as Joyce Appleby reminds us, Jefferson did not agree with Montesquieu's argument that only if a republic were small could it endure (309). Our understanding of *Notes* must be tempered, then, by an awareness of how Jefferson reconciled his inheritance of rhetorical and philosophical conventions in *Notes* with his own peculiar stylistic habits and intellectual beliefs. Specifically, we must look more closely at his conception of nature; we must see how nature was, for him, not only energetic and evolving but also profoundly stable in its core and its fundamental laws, as it was in his "Declaration of Independence." For, this paradoxical attitude affected the premises of geological, social, and biological arguments in individual Queries as well as the logical arrangement of *Notes* as a whole. Let us begin with nature in Queries IV and V since these sections, detailing "the flow of the Potomac through the Blue Ridge and the Natural Bridge," are in many ways the *ground* of Jefferson's ideas in *Notes* (Ogburn 142).

For Jefferson, "the first glance" of the passage of the Potomac through the Blue Ridge

> hurries our senses into the opinion that this earth has been created in time, that the mountains were formed first, that the rivers began to flow afterwards . . . The piles of rocks on each hand, the evident marks of their disrupture and avulsion from their beds by the most powerful agents of nature, corroborate this impression.

Evidently what must be guarded against is the seeming fact "that hurries our senses into . . . opinion" (*Notes* 19); for, Jefferson continues, ". . . the distant finishing which nature has given to the picture is of a very different character. It is a true contrast to the fore-ground. It is as placid and delightful, as that is wild and tremendous." Through the cloven Ridge one could see a "small catch of blue horizon" that provided the viewer with a feeling of respite and a measure of control over "the riot and tumult roaring around." "Here," Jefferson concluded, "the eye composes itself; and that way, too, the road happens to lead" (*Notes* 19). Clayton Lewis has suggested that this sequence leaves us with the "implication" that natural "processes tend to restore order, harmony, and composure" in the observant human mind (674–75). Actually, this impression of order and peace is a direct result of Jefferson's own assumptions about the inmost stability and quiescence of nature, beneath its superficial processes and changes. For, despite the geological impression afforded by the violent passage of the river, Jefferson resisted inducing that the whole "earth has been created in time," in a series of massive cataclysms. Why? Because the placid prospect, gained by traveling imaginatively down the "road," served as a reminder of the largely static uniformity and order of nature that, in effect, framed and made convulsions of minor magnitude both emotionally bearable and aesthetically pleasing. Elsewhere in *Notes* Jefferson dismissed theories of a "universal deluge" or continental upheaval as interpretations of how the crust of the earth possibly had been formed. In "all the aeras of history," he could discover no proof of "natural agents" equal to such tumult (*Notes* 31–33).[3] And so, when he characterized the strata of the gap as "monuments of a war between rivers and mountains, which must have shaken the earth to its center," he celebrated energy and convulsion, yes, but convulsion embraced aesthetically by a peaceful distance and geologically by a harmonious nature (*Notes* 19–20).[4]

The description of the Natural Bridge repeated this strategy of first giving the tumult and terror of experience and then stepping back, as it were, to appreciate the picture that "nature's god" designed. Atop the Bridge, one fell "involuntarily" to hands and knees when approaching the edge to peer over. "Looking down from this height about a minute, gave me a violent headache," Jefferson reported. But "this painful sensation" was relieved quickly by a "pleasing view" of the distant Blue Ridge and Short Hills. And once a person descended from the Bridge and left behind the "emotions, arising from the sublime" and painful experience of glancing downward, he could admire the arch, "so beautiful[,] . . . so elevated, so light, and springing, as it were, up to heaven." The fissure beneath the Bridge, which led the eye to the far ranges, could be followed to an impressive limestone cavern (*Notes* 24–25).

From sublime sensations of confusion and pain to a calmer appreciation of far prospects and of the arch itself "springing up to heaven": geologically as well as aesthetically, the stages of this experience suggested that nature was never appreciated completely until its harmony was recollected and invoked, even when one stood transfixed before the most turbulent or frightening scenes. And this model of experience—especially as the eye moved away, following the Potomac or the fissure beneath the Bridge—applied to more than just sensing and understanding nature; it explained as well the process of feeling and comprehending human nature. For, the stability of nature's inmost order was, for

Jefferson, more than just analogous with the basic laws of human nature; it was almost coincident, as the rhetorical design of his "Declaration of Independence" suggested just several years earlier.

We recall that the preamble of the "Declaration" took care to show "a decent respect to the opinions of mankind." Apparently, it would avoid rash arguments that might inflame the "senses" and excite "opinion." Yet, in the penultimate paragraph of his "Original Rough Draught," Jefferson accused the British people— those "unfeeling brethren"—of planning to "deluge us in blood" and of delivering "the last stab to agonizing affection." He indicted them, in effect, for attempting fratricide. This act resulted necessarily in the avulsion of American from British brother, in revolution. Still, even this tumult was framed by harmony. After all, Jefferson ended the paragraph by imagining travel along another path, here the "road to glory & happiness" that "we will climb . . . in a separate state" ("Original" 423, 427). And this buoyant prospect was sponsored not by violent convulsion but rather by "the laws of nature & of nature's god" that underlay the Americans' decision—and feeling—to revolt. More importantly, such laws represented a fundamental moral and ethical order that existed outside the aberrations of history. In geology as well as politics, then, concord might be temporarily out of sight but never—for Jefferson—out of mind, even in the midst of discord.

The road leading out of chaos and into happiness was central to Jefferson's rhetorical and philosophical design; indeed, it recurred in his first "Inaugural" as well as in his discussion of agriculture in *Notes,* as we shall see. The "Declaration" implied, of course, that the achievement of "glory & happiness"—imagined spatially as the goal of the "road"—depended on how thoroughly "the laws of nature & of nature's god" were, in fact, made the "ends" of particular government. And the effective establishment of natural laws in the republic depended, in part, on how clearly they were articulated at the start: thus we read of "sacred and undeniable truths" in the second paragraph—equal creation of all men and "the preservation of life, & liberty, & the pursuit of happiness," among them ("Original" 423–24). Twenty-five years later, in his first "Inaugural Address," Jefferson pronounced once more upon the "sum of good government." Here though, he wrote from within the confines of the history of a republic, not from before its commencement. He based what he said, therefore, not on intuitions about and aspirations for natural law but rather on those major principles of civil law that experience suggested were needed to guarantee natural rights and the durability of the republic itself. The principles cited included "equal and exact justice," avoidance of "entangling alliances" abroad, respect for the constitutional competency of state governments, establishment of a militia, and "economy in public expense." "These principles," Jefferson concluded,

> form ye bright constellation which has gone before, & guided our steps, thro' an age of Revolution and Reform. The wisdom of our Sages, & blood of our Heroes, have been devoted to their attainment . . . in moments of error or alarm, let us hasten to retrace our steps and to regain the road which alone leads to Peace, Liberty, & Safety.

Despite the different historical context, the structure of the rhetoric again detailed a path out of tumult and into harmony; and this brightening prospect recalled those that we have examined already. It, too, consisted of principles of balance and stability that antedated the present era of "Revolution and Reform" and, in essence, transcended the process of history even though—paradoxically perhaps—they were discovered by historical figures, "Sages" and "Heroes" (Jefferson, "Address" 197–99).

2

This insistence that stable principles existed untainted by the agents of history—and that they were, nonetheless, discernible from within history itself—motivated more than just the rhetorical designs of *Notes* and Jefferson's major political pronouncements; and it was more than just analogous to his projection of an ideal core, of a uniform and universal creation, behind observable nature. It also charged his dissent from Virginia's Constitution in *Notes* and affected profoundly the substance of other arguments there as well—particularly about the virtue of farming and even of those races destined, he believed, to farm America.[5] Jefferson's thought about nature and human nature—we can begin to see—was profoundly dualistic, perceiving (and fearing) phenomenal turbulence, intuiting (and longing for) inner composure and harmony.

To begin, he was perturbed by the too–large share of representatives that the eastern section of the state wangled for itself; he was upset, too, by the disproportionate powers that devolved upon the legislature, including the implicit power to declare itself a "quorum"—or tyranny—of one, after the precedent of the Roman republics. But evidently what troubled him most—given the length of the complaint—was simply the means by which this Constitution had been constituted: by the legislature of 1776, not by an extraordinary convention. Such a Constitution, he felt, only awaited abrogation by some tyrant or tyrannical faction, some agents within history, within the structure of financial and political intrigue that evolved, alas, in the processes of all governments. Then, the people of Virginia would have no "fundamental rights" at all. A constitutional convention, invoked by a two-thirds vote within two of the three branches of government and then elected by the people, could approximate—more closely than the legislature—the kind of ideal agency that was required to recognize natural rights—and order—and could then translate such founding principles into the state's civil law (*Notes* 118–29).

Further, in the late 1780s and periodically through the rest of his life, Jefferson suggested that national constitutional conventions be called every nineteen years—that is, according to his calculus, every political generation.[6] At first, we might be tempted to observe that this plan promised nothing but turmoil and ceaseless change. But actually, Jefferson thought that such a procedure could postpone indefinitely the necessity for bloody revolution; it could reverse the degeneration of temporal government from its founding principles by enabling the people in the republic to recognize and re-assert the convergence of natural law with civil law in an orderly manner and at predictable periods.[7] Also, as the nation grew in size and its people changed in character, such conventions could inflect the wording of the Constitution to check the aberrant tendencies of the people's temperament by accenting those natural rights and laws that, previously, had been only tacitly recognized. (See, for instance, Jefferson's hedging phrase "among these" before the list of rights in the "Declaration.") Clearly, Jefferson exhibited remarkable faith in the integrity of both the people and their constitutional representatives; for, these constitutional epiphanies, these cyclical interruptions of history, would disclose the people's essential power as well as character.

Constitutional principles, even those as convergent as possible with natural rights and laws, could not by themselves calm Jefferson's anxieties for a Virginian and an American republic. After all,

did not equilibrium depend cyclically—and perhaps ultimately—
on the people, not just on government, not just on constitutions?
Thus, he hoped to encourage the people to adopt occupations that
corresponded with the character of the land and thereby with the
fundamental principles of nature in America. These basic principles—stable and orderly in themselves—would further buttress
the republic against the turbulence and convulsions of history.
Once more, he believed that such principles could be confirmed
either by moral intuition or by an elementary knowledge of history and philosophy;[8] and he expressed himself in a rhetoric that,
again, treated time as a spatial path. "Young as we are, and with
such a country before us to fill with people and with happiness,
we should point in that direction the whole generative force of
nature," Jefferson wrote (*Notes* 174–75). In other words, to arrive
at "happiness"—here, an even and productive distribution of people over nature—the nation should follow the road (westward?) to
"the cultivation of the earth." Why? Simply because "cultivators
. . . are the most virtuous and independant citizens" (*Notes* 175).

Jefferson's dedication to farming, especially in Query XIX,
should need no further comment. For years, it has been recognized
as the nutriment of his "middle landscape." And along with an
educated populace, it was a guarantor of his designs for a republican democracy that would honor the governmental competency of
its "grassroots." Yet, we must turn to this section again to understand thoroughly the logic and fervor of Jefferson's effort to subordinate creatures of history—the American people and their use
of the land—to the essential, unchanging "laws of nature & of
nature's god."

"Those who labor in the earth," he intoned, "are the chosen
people of God, if ever he had a chosen people, whose breasts he
made his peculiar deposit for substantial and genuine virtue"
(*Notes* 164–65). This famous homily about farming epitomized to
Leo Marx the poetic strain in Jefferson's thought (19, 124–29).
The farmer's pastoral world, a place of peace and self-sufficiency,
seemed but a Virginian version of Virgil's arcadia in the *Eclogues.*
Indeed, Marx has written that the Query had "more in common
with Virgil's poetry than with [Adam Smith's] *The Wealth of Nations.*" The larger world of tumult—of politics, war, and ceaseless
change—was forgotten as the tiller lived in diurnal contact with
the cycles of nature and, beyond nature, with God. In fact, Jefferson advanced as an undoubted principle the proposition that
"corruption of morals in the mass of cultivators is a phaenomenon

of which no age nor nation has furnished an example" (*Notes* 165).

Obviously, much is assumed in this assertion beyond the pastoral myth of ancient poetry. Again, nature (or more precisely, man's relation with it, as a tiller) is a bedrock of harmony and stability, never decaying in the "mass" despite, perhaps, small cracks and crevices. This attitude is not surprising. After all, for Jefferson, fundamental nature could never decay in the "mass." Recall his geology: even the riven passage of the Potomac through the Blue Ridge, when viewed against the horizon, confirmed the essential calm of nature.

Let us look at this homily with a social—not a pastoral—context in mind now. Occasionally, we forget that a whole family was to work the Virginian farm of Jefferson's imagination.[9] And from time to time, yeomen would meet either to raise one another's buildings or to elect delegates to distant assemblies. The tiller's world was thus a communal one arranged in townships and villages; it was not a landscape occupied by solitary and wandering shepherds. We recall that Jefferson wrote about the "genuine virtue" and the "germ of virtue" in the farmers' "breasts" and "hearts"; implicitly, he praised their social morals. He described farmers in the very terms of moral sense philosophy and moral rationalism that he turned to throughout his writings after the 1770s, as Garry Wills and Morton White have demonstrated at considerable length.[10] Jefferson's farmer would be a responsible political and social creature because the soil, somehow, nurtured the social sense that was, yes, in all men but that unfortunately was, as Francis Hutcheson himself admitted, thwarted at times by ignorance and selfishness (132, 176, 182).

The soil nurtured this best nature—the social nature—in man. And the metaphor of courtship suggested the socioeconomic and theological implications of this nurture. "We have an immensity of land courting the industry of the husbandman," Jefferson observed (*Notes* 164). In the terms of this metaphor, as Annette Kolodny has shown, the honorable choice for the "husbandman" was to betroth the "courting" suitor, to join his "industry" to the land (27).[11] Then, a nation of farmers would consummate nature's courtship.[12] Never would such a union be debilitating since the "sacred fire" of virtue that God implanted in the farmers' breasts was actually replenished by constant contact with the soil. Thus, husbandry of nature linked man not only to the "laws of nature" but also to "nature's god." And miraculously, it also reaped more than it spent. Only if farmers turned their "industry" to manufacture and abandoned the land "might [virtue] escape the face of the earth" (*Notes* 165).

The personification of nature ("face," "courting") and the description of the farmer as a "husbandman" implied that moral, financial, even sexual economies would capitalize or devalue as one. In fact, reinforcing Jefferson's worry that the American might deplete his "industry" and "sacred fire" in commercial processes that were not tied to nature's virtuous order was a sexual anxiety, which revealed his sexual politics. In the 1780s, Jefferson thought fidelity to the marriage bed, like faithfulness to the soil, essential to the happiness and stability of a republic. After all, fidelity enabled a person, as well as a nation, to control passion. And presumably, since faithfulness seemed to beget frugality, man would be freed to spend reasonable amounts of energy in other useful pursuits, as he wrote to his friend Maury (409–10). To Charles Bellini in 1785, Jefferson described "conjugal love," sustained by the moral sense and characterized by restraint, as a principal source of American happiness (*Papers*, vol. 8: 368–69). Without such love, the republic could not remain secure. Witness France: its people plunged themselves into all sorts of "pursuits which nourish and invigorate all our bad passions." Once so enlivened, these feelings slowly diminished the capacity of a people to maintain interest in political and financial matters. The balance of social goals disturbed, the harmony of the sexes undone, craving inevitably begat dependence. There was no checking the thirst for passion, Jefferson lamented, once it was indulged. Its passions unchecked, a society would lapse into either anarchy or tyranny since a nation could not be more controlled and rational than its individual members—and families.[13]

Thus, the yeoman family was not only the basic demographic unit but a central symbol of the Virginia that Jefferson projected in *Notes*. One can—and should—argue that this family actually reflected the sociological character of the Virginia that already was.[14] Yet, Jefferson himself was a plantation and slave owner (and an often absentee one at that), and a widower as well. And so, the yeoman family also assumed the place and power of a wish-fulfillment in his thinking, connecting him—and the society that he envisioned—to the rectitude, order, and sustenance—the "sacred fire"—of nature. The role of woman, personified as nature and socialized as wife, was to nourish the husbandman's moral nature; woman-as-wife literally and figuratively grounded male endeavor in virtue and order. The farmer and his fellows constituted the polity and were the visible principals of the work force; they were a fraternity of independence.

Ironically, there was no place for women in this fraternal polity. Why? Because the bonds that tied men and women were not always rational and moderate, not always frugal and faithful, not—in a word—conjugal. Helplessly, Jefferson watched the French queen lead her aristocracy to its doom in the 1780s all because, he believed, they were thoroughly entranced by her wealth and charms.[15] Needless to say, the Virginian considered enthrallment an innately feminine power and did not appear to wonder whether its source could also be in men (*Autobiography, Works* vol. 1: 150–52). One recalls his early and late idealization of male mentors and affectionate friends—Small, Wythe, Randolph, Fauquier —and, much later, the role of teachers in his projected University; and alternately, one thinks, perhaps, of the pain caused him by his jilted love for Rebecca Burwell and, of course, by the premature death of his own wife. Brother with brother, male friend with male friend, and father with mature son were the temperate and affectionate models for a people engaged in republican politics. As I have said, women nourished husbands and sons; women prepared men for the world beyond the home while domesticated nature warmed and sustained the "sacred fire" of virtue. But then were not women dependent on men? And did not Jefferson himself say, in his description of manufacture, that dependence begat venality? This matter of sexual dependence in the home did not seem to bother Jefferson; it was, for him, a lesser evil. Somehow, the home, outside of the polity yet the very spring of it, would escape the tyranny of bifurcated roles implicit in manufacture and even in slavery.[16]

3

Jefferson's penchant for adjusting government, constitutions, and the social and economic character of the people to the "first principles" of nature that he rather regularly intuited shows how literally he conceived of America as nature's nation. This tendency, though, caused him many philosophical and political problems since nature and human nature, in their temporal forms and historical processes, constantly seemed to diverge from what he believed to be their stable essences and harmonious laws. Indian culture, whose dependence on nature he idealized at times, was not the least of his stumbling blocks in *Notes*. And collectively, the Indians only constituted one example of Jefferson's tentative effort to correlate racial nature with the physical nature of America.

Against foreign theorists who argued the deficiency of the red race in America—nature's *children* indeed—Jefferson contended, as we well know, that whites and reds shared the same "moral sense." "Crimes," he reported, "are very rare among them," although they resisted "the merest shadow of government" even more than white republicans did (*Notes* 93). To indict Indian behavior, he possibly suspected, might have exposed all America, which was the Indians' habitat, to criticism as a poor environment for whites, too. Buffon, for one, observed the low number of Indians in America and their relatively undeveloped culture—no architecture to speak of, certainly no substantial literature. And he concluded that they "lack ardor for their females"; further, since "consequently [they] have no love for their fellow men . . . [,] the most intimate of all ties, the family connection, binds them therefore but loosely together; between family and family," he continued, "there is no tie at all, hence they have no communion, no commonwealth, no state of society" (*Notes* 58–60).[17]

To all this, Jefferson retorted bluntly on two fronts. First, he intended to show that Buffon did not understand the law of nature as it applied to family life; and then he suggested that all culture was a function of one of nature's mathematical—and hence, incontrovertible—laws. Society—yes, even Indian society—was a function of natural law properly conceived. Buffon, alas, saw sex ("ardor for their females") as the pinion of family life; and he saw the family ("the most intimate of all ties") as the basic unit of society. Jefferson agreed about the importance of the family, but he did not see passion or some insatiable hungering after sex as particularly caring, intimate, or moral. Instead, he emphasized the Indians' parental solicitude. This feeling was the proper measure of the togetherness of a family and the key to a society that did not require governmental compulsion to cohere. No one, he felt, could possibly dispute the Indian's "affectionate" care for his children and his loyalty to his tribesmen. True, moving outward from family and kin, an Indian's solicitude weakened visibly until it became barely effectual in the most distant circles of acquaintanceship, for intensity of care was often a function of emotional proximity, much as the pull of gravity followed a similar law.

Humans, red and white, instituted laws and treaties to compensate for this natural falling off of feeling (*Notes* 60).

To account for the low density of the Indians and their relatively undeveloped (by European standards) culture, Jefferson first hypothesized that the women (not the men, interestingly) were infecund. Soon however, he had doubts about the wisdom of this thesis and expunged it from the manuscript of *Notes*. Emphasizing infecundity might lead people to deduce that the land which nurtured the Indians was itself infertile or malnourishing; and they might assume, therefore, that Indian men were carnal spendthrifts, wasting "industry" in sex without a productive goal. Both deductions would burden transplanted whites with the hypothesis of degeneration in the New World. Instead, in a passage which was somewhat hasty and vague, given the significance of the subject, Jefferson speculated that "obstacles of want and habit" limited the numbers of the Indians (*Notes* 63–65, 93, 96; and note 3 on p. 280). The land, for instance, was difficult to farm without good tools; and it was virtually infinite, there being few natural boundaries to pen tribes in, press them side by side, and force competition and an exchange of ideas. Consequently, men and women were plagued with arduous labor, which dampened ardor. And without numbers, which "produce emulation" and "multiply the chances of improvement," the Indians had never actually had the chance to improve culturally; Europeans, of course, had had such opportunities north of the Alps and in the compact Grecian and Roman peninsulas. Despite these physical and social impediments, Indians still were content with the subsistence economy afforded by such low numbers. For, more people would force them to abandon traditionally nomadic ways and adopt a specialized and productive agriculture unless, of course, they were willing to face starvation. As for the hardships that economic change would cause, as well as the cultural disruption, the Indians sensed them and opted instead for quiet continuity.

Jefferson sympathized with this attachment to equilibrium on the land; nevertheless, he also thought that it served the interests of whites and reds for the Indians to change their ways gradually. Once they abandoned foraging for farming, more of American nature could be brought under the benign influence of republican domestication. And whites, leaving their settlements as numbers grew, could work tracts that once were needed for the uneconomical habits of Indian subsistence. The success of Virginia and

America—of the whole republican experiment in the New World —depended on the ability of the nation to avoid simultaneously the corruption of a people too concentrated in manufactures and cities and the meanness of one too scattered in foraging and nomadic camps. Only yeoman farming could insure a "happy" congruence of political and social behavior with the "sacred fire" of nature and—in an almost Malthusian sense—with the full productive yield of the land (*Notes* 64–65, 83–85, 92–93, 146, 162–63).[18]

This anxiousness about the distribution of people over the land—and even the fear about the effect of sexuality on political life—betrayed the depth of Jefferson's concern for the durability of the republic; and it betrayed too the social conservatism behind his assumptions—and constant invocations—of "the laws of nature." To survive, the republic had to be as uniform, as homogeneous as possible in its social and economic agents. (Of course, Montesquieu had valued homogeneity, too.) Evidently, a nation worked together best when it was a uniform people. That such thinking was tautological did not bother Jefferson. He calculated that, at the present rate of growth, Virginia's level of density would attain Britain's of the 1780s in ninety-five years. This figure he reached by excluding new immigrants (*Notes* 83–84). For doubtlessly, he observed, among the newcomers would be "heterogeneous, incoherent, distracted mass" who were fleeing the "absolute monarchies" of Europe (*Notes* 84–85). Even if they had good intentions, they would be a political pestilence, carriers of tyrannical and servile habits. How could they not make a motley mass of Virginia and corrupt the republican experiment? Through the rear door of immigration would return the evil specters—the imbalances—that the Revolution had tried to exorcise once and for all.

This argument against immigration developed out of Jefferson's understanding of the effect of nature on individual character and on species. No amount of manna, he said, could ever make a mouse into a mammoth; and merely introducing a stranger to the farther shores of America could not undo years of ingrained habits. Change came slowly and according to the limits that nature itself imposed on the mind and on species. If only foreign children came, perhaps republican America could wean them from their biological parents and the tyranny of habits. But adults could not forget "the principles of government they leave, imbibed in their youth; or if able to throw them off," Jefferson feared, "it will be in exchange for an unbounded licentiousness, passing, as is usual, from one extreme to another. It would be a miracle were they to stop at the precise point of liberty." Worse, Jefferson concluded, "These principles, with their language, they will transmit to their children." Faction would be sewn into the promised land because education—school—could not instill liberty in those who had not also grown up to liberty in the public and domestic realms of the Revolutionary era (*Notes* 82–85).

But Jefferson fretted not just about the effect of nature on character but also about the fundamental nature of character itself—and more specifically, the nature of race. Although he rarely broke silence on this topic, he seemed to believe that few peoples, even in their adult capacities, had the natural heritage to manage the natural laws and rights so central to American republicanism. The Anglo-Saxons and their British descendants, especially those who separated themselves in America, did. After all, parliaments were the ancestors of Congress. But few peoples had such republican principles in their blood. Unlike Crèvecoeur and Samuel Stanhope Smith, Jefferson had little hope that the American land and republican institutions could transmute humankind into a homogeneous folk who were all capable of recognizing—and incorporating in charters—"the laws of nature & of nature's god" that Jefferson valued so dearly. No, he did not look favorably on "that strange mixture of blood" that emerged from the various conjugations of European types and, occasionally, Europeans with blacks (Crèvecoeur 43–44). Nor did he believe that America was shaping a "national countenance" in its inhabitants (Smith 47, 97).[19]

To the contrary, the success of Jefferson's family-nation in *Notes* depended largely on the careful screening of all applicants for utopia, not on their sudden metamorphosis. Apparently, as he said, he wished to strain the fine particles of Anglo-Saxon heritage out of the yet unwinnowed world so that one people, indivisible and uncorrupted, could rediscover in themselves "the freest principles of the English constitution"; then they could perceive the source and dependence of these principles in nature. Indeed, he said that "every species of government has its specific principles. Ours perhaps are more peculiar than those of any other in the universe" (*Notes* 84). Did "species" and "universe" suggest that he was classifying governments according to some largely unstated biological or racial standard?[20] The moral sense, which above all else made a republic possible, was preeminently, although not peculiarly, an Anglo-Saxon and Germanic feature. (Recall, as a contrast, Jefferson's hope that the Indians would meld with the whites of the republic.) The Norman invasion had repressed it, subjected it to several centuries of unfortunate hybridizing. Only careful weeding now could give it the room that it needed to grow; and then nurture could help it to flower in Virginia and, hopefully, in the far fields of America.

In a far more Teutonic-centric way than he could have supposed at this juncture in the eighteenth century, Jefferson believed that the nature of America was intended, ideally, for the human nature of the Anglo-Saxon people—and reasonable facsimiles. Pointedly, the only blacks whom he considered as indigenous to his adopted continent were the "Albinos," and they were an "anomaly of nature," "uncommonly shrewd, quick in their apprehensions and reply" (*Notes* 70–71). Just why Jefferson fixed on blacks as particularly unassimilable in America is a complex question. Winthrop Jordan has suggested that the traits which Jefferson ascribed to blacks, lassitude and promiscuity primarily, were projections of his own psychic anxieties (458–61). He was, in other words, guilty of social and psychological scapegoating. And as promiscuity and laziness were generally the antitheses of the Protestant work ethic, many other Anglo-Saxons similarly projected their own temptations and indulgences onto blacks.

Still, historians of Jefferson's racial consciousness—and conscience—remind us that he did call slavery a "blot on our country" (*Notes* 87). This "blot" was an irreducible otherness, an irremediable and fixed mark of difference. In passion and anger whites could be suffused with red, even with a whiter white, a lividness (*Notes* 138–39). These unending variations were, to him, intriguing and beautiful, as Winthrop Jordan has remarked (478–81). And white, as it expressed the tints of emotions and thoughts that streamed through the mind, was thus an honest or transparent tone. However, black revealed only an "eternal monotony," an impenetrable fixity. Black was the opposite of white, obviously, in this allegorical spectrum of pigments. And severe opposition tested a republic crucially, for it inevitably undermined uniformity and consensus. Manufacturer and laborer, master and slave, white and black, these were pairs of opposites that drained men—at both ends of the pole—of their energy for sustaining independence.[21] Whether black inferiority made the race a completely different variety of the human species, or whether the differences were too minute and transient to be catalogued precisely beyond color, Jefferson did not doubt that blacks and whites should develop separate republics which complemented their respective talents (*Notes* 138–39, 162–63).

Jefferson's attitudes towards blacks as well as women suggested a fear that the republic might not endure heterogeneity and conflict or, in a word, humanity itself. For, he conceived of them, really, as opposites of the white man whom he hoped would be Virginia's agricultural republican living by the consensus, constitutions, and generational revolutions that grounded, that stabilized, political change in nature's nation. Blacks and women appeared in his philosophy largely as monotonous creatures chained each to a physical sign and an accompanying physiological function. In a sense, women became their sexual organs which, if not domesticated, could enthrall and debilitate the yeoman. And blacks, who were undeniably moral creatures and who suffered terribly in their Middle Passage and often cruel enslavement, still were summed up by their color, which suggested intellectual dullness and otherness. These signs—sex organs and pigment—were natural vehicles of the moral and cultural anxieties that Jefferson seemingly wished as much to dismiss as to remedy in his projected republic.

For Jefferson, the success of the republic depended then on how closely constitutional and civil law converged with the first principles that he intuited in nature; and attaining this convergence depended on how thoroughly the new nation contoured the moral nature of its people to make the most of the productive capacity of its land. Many years after he completed *Notes,* Jefferson still struggled with the two demons of American republicanism: manufacture and slavery. And significantly, he proposed the same solution for both: take manufacture out of cities and subordinate it within the rural rhythms and requirements of the yeoman household; take slaves out of plantations and place them individually in the yeoman houses of the West until the nation could afford to expatriate them.[22] In both instances, the yeoman home—or precisely, the yeoman family married to the moral economy of nature—would prove magically capable of absorbing the disturbances of history.[23]

Such a vision is almost poignant in its effort to disarm change and to dilute heterogeneity. Still, we must see that as early as *Notes* Jefferson was not dedicated either exclusively or blindly to a pastoral and homogeneous world. *Notes* did acknowledge, albeit reluctantly, the mixed origins of the people, the small chance for a restrictive policy towards newcomers, and even the popularity of trade and manufacture (85, 174–75). Hence, Jefferson was forced by circumstance to achieve a version of the "complex pastoral" even in *Notes*: his ideal republic was compromised from the start by its immersion in history, in time and politics. To cure this disease of history, the republic would have to immunize itself, so to speak, by absorbing small doses of industry, of slavery too, into its yeoman households. Otherwise, if not diffused, manufacture and servitude would grow into festering "sores" that would sap the "strength" of the body politic and soon eat "to the heart of its laws and constitution" (*Notes* 165).

4

The design of the whole book embodies the mixed intentions of this complex pastoral, as well as the doubleness of Jefferson's attitude toward phenomenal nature and its stable core. Contained within several of the Queries are passages of scientific theory (alluding to the stability of nature in the mass, the limited character of species) and of social belief (suggesting the divinity of farming, the harmony of racial homogeneity). Yet *Notes* has no philosophical preamble, no introduction really to its method or subject. Hence, these passages are largely submerged beneath an articulation of seemingly factual evidence—beginning with geological nature and ending with society and history—that can appear haphazard in what it touches upon and tentative or reticent in its conclusions. As Ferguson has suggested, both the rhetorical strategy and political methodology appear to be "incremental" (388); history, pragmatism, and observation—phenomena and process—are foregrounded in a book premised, in epiphanies, on visions of geological and social changelessness.[24]

Nonetheless, André Morellet's French translation of *Notes* forced Jefferson to admit, obliquely, that his book did have a rhetorical and philosophical design. Dorothy Medlin has observed that Morellet arranged the Queries within four divisions: geography, animals, peoples, and customs (87–89). He gathered the Virginian's scattered comments about blacks and Indians into consecutive sentences and paragraphs. Thus, the Frenchman was formally direct and, as a result, almost doctrinal in subjects about which Jefferson himself was especially intent on having diffuseness imply his tentativeness and reticence. Although he often said that his book was inelegant, that it was mere patchwork, he still told friends that he did not like the liberties that Morellet had taken with it; Morellet, he believed, had butchered his creation.[25] But what did the Frenchman damage really? His four divisions did away with the ad hoc appearance of the Queries; his revisions threatened to subordinate the American's factual method to an a priori organization. And Jefferson's vanity, curiously, was invested in the appearance of *Notes* as an assemblage of—yes—notes, a series of rambling inquiries suffused but not explicitly ordered by methodical reasoning and intuition.

We should recall that the author adopted a similar pose toward his "Declaration of Independence." That paper, he announced, was impersonal, a record of the "American mind"; yet, was he not offended at the changes that Congress made? Jefferson adopted the question and answer format of *Notes* as a deliberate artifice. After all, he need not have preserved, as much as he did, the program of Francois Marbois' original questions. But this for-mat—besides recalling the structure of legal treatises by Grotius, Montesquieu, and others—also reminded readers intermittently that the entire book was an American's no-nonsense response to European curiosity. As Jefferson said in *Notes*, European pro-ponents of American degeneration had made an unfortunate al-though rather typical rhetorical—and philosophical—error in the design of their treatises: "I am induced to suspect, there has been more eloquence than sound reasoning displayed in support of this theory; that it has been one of those cases where the judgment has been seduced by a glowing pen." Had not Buffon himself been swept away, Jefferson concluded, by his own "vivid imagination and bewitching language"? And so, Jefferson—ever the sensible American—confided that he based his prose on "what I have seen" and "on the information of those [even] better acquainted" with the facts of the New World. Yes, as in his "Declaration," he would submit "facts" to a "candid world" while foreswearing the pomp, flattery, and theoretical conceit of a "glowing pen" (*Notes* 59, 63, 64).[26]

Jefferson's apparent dedication to facts and incremental knowl-edge was itself, of course, a rhetorical design with political and philosophical implications. He took his stance on a bedrock of belief: nature, in its geological essence and fundamental moral laws, was changeless. What changed was mankind's ability to see this changelessness and to form society accordingly. Consequently, roads to happiness might branch and even detour for a time, but they all afforded partial vistas of the same brightening prospect.

NOTES

1. Lewis 668–69, Ferguson 381–406, Ogburn, Jr. 141–50.
2. See, too, Marx's account of how nature determined the order of the Queries and his foray into Query XIX, 19, 118–120, 124–29.
3. Also see Jefferson to Charles Thomson, Dec. 17, 1786, *Papers*, vol. 10: 608–609.
4. On Jefferson's geology see Boorstin, *The Lost World*, 30–33.
5. For the political evolution of Americans' reliance on constitutional conventions, see Wood, ch. 8.
6. Jefferson to Madison, Sept. 6, 1789, *Papers*, vol. 15: 393–95; to Kerchival, July 12, 1816, *Works*, vol. 12: 11–15.
7. See Peterson 438–41.
8. White discusses these two modes of proving basic principles—and their tension—in Jefferson's and Burlamaqui's thought, ch. 1, 76–78, 161–70.
9. Jefferson, "Bill," 1777, *Papers*, vol. 2: 139–40.
10. See White on "moral rationalists," 99–107, 161–70.
11. See as well Tichi, ch. 3, particularly 93–94.
12. In *Liberty's Daughters*, Norton reports eighteenth-century pregnancy figures that, along with the experience of Jefferson's wife, ground this sexual metaphor (71–73).
13. Jefferson to Maury, Aug. 19, 1785, *Papers*, vol. 8: 409–10.
14. Sydnor 35–42, 60–61, 67–73, 83–85; Boorstin, *The Americans*, 116–23.
15. Kerber remarks the politics of "effeminacy" charges (21–32).
16. On the pervasiveness of this cult of domesticity in eighteenth-century political prose, see Norton, 63–64, 243, 248–50; Kerber, 283.
17. Sheehan, 66–70.
18. Jefferson to Monroe, July 9, 1786, *Papers*, vol. 10: 112–13. Malthus, 105–106, 117–19.
19. My argument here follows Jordan, 486–90.
20. Chinard has pointed to the relation of biology to nationalism in Jefferson's thought (124–26).
21. Morgan, 5–29. Davis, 558–62.
22. Miller, ch. 25.
23. Jefferson to Austin, Jan. 9, 1816, Ford, vol. 11: 500–505; to Holmes, Apr. 22, 1820; to Gallatin, Dec. 26, 1820; to Sparks, Feb. 4, 1824, Ford, vol. 12: 158–60, 187–89, 334–38.
24. Lewis 672–73, 675–76. Also, see Boorstin, *Lost World* for related remarks on Jefferson's positivist bias and the problems thereby created for his noumenal tendencies (130 and 139).
25. To Charles Thomson, June 21, 1785, *Papers*, vol. 8: 245–46; to Wythe, Aug. 13, 1786, vol. 10: 243. See Peden's useful account, "Introduction," *Notes*, xvi–xx.

26. Echeverria remarks the "... a priori hypotheses" that characterized Buffon's style (10–11).

WORKS CITED

Appleby, Joyce. "What Is Still American in the Political Philosophy of Thomas Jefferson?" *William and Mary Quarterly* 39 (1982): 287–309.
Boorstin, Daniel. *The Americans: The Colonial Experience.* New York: Random House, 1958.
_____. *The Lost World of Thomas Jefferson.* New York: Henry Holt, 1948.
Chinard, Gilbert. *Thomas Jefferson: The Apostle of Americanism.* Ann Arbor: Univ. of Michigan Press, 1914.
Commager, Henry S. *Jefferson, Nationalism, and the Enlightenment.* New York: George Braziller, 1975.
Crèvecoeur, J. Hector St. Jean de. *Letters From an American Farmer.* 1782; rpt. New York: Dutton, 1971.
Davis, David Brion. *The Problem of Slavery in the Age of Revolution.* Ithaca: Cornell Univ. Press, 1975.
Echeverria, Durand. *Mirage in the West: A History of the French Image of America to 1815.* Princeton: Princeton Univ. Press, 1968.
Ferguson, Robert. " 'Mysterious Obligation': Jefferson's *Notes on the State of Virginia*," *American Literature* 52 (1980): 381–406.
Hutcheson, Francis. *Illustrations on the Moral Sense.* Cambridge: Belknap, 1971.
Jefferson, Thomas. *Notes on the State of Virginia*, ed. William Peden. New York: Norton, 1972.
_____. *The Papers of Thomas Jefferson*, ed. Julian Boyd. Princeton: Princeton Univ. Press, 1950, vols. 1, 2, 8, 10, and 15.
_____. *The Works of Thomas Jefferson*, ed. Paul Leicester Ford. New York: Putnam, 1905, vols. 1, 9, 11, and 12.
Jordan, Winthrop. *White Over Black: American Attitudes Toward the Negro.* New York: Norton, 1977.
Kerber, Linda. *Women of the Republic.* Chapel Hill: Univ. of North Carolina Press, 1980.
Kolodny, Annette. *The Lay of the Land.* Chapel Hill: Univ. of North Carolina Press, 1975.
Lewis, Clayton W. "Style in Jefferson's *Notes on the State of Virginia*," *Southern Review* 14 (1978): 668–76.
Malthus, Thomas. *An Essay on the Principle of Population.* 1798; rpt. Baltimore: Pelican, 1970.

Marx, Leo. *The Machine in the Garden*. New York: Oxford Univ. Press, 1973.

Medlin, Dorothy. "Thomas Jefferson, André Morellet, and the French Version of *Notes on the State of Virginia*," *William and Mary Quarterly* 35 (1978): 85–99.

Miller, John C. *The Wolf By the Ears: Thomas Jefferson and Slavery*. New York: Free Press, 1977.

Morgan, Edmund. "Slavery and Freedom: The American Paradox," *Journal of American History* 59 (1972): 5–29.

Norton, Mary B. *Liberty's Daughters*. Boston: Little, Brown, 1980.

Ogburn, Floyd O., Jr. "Structure and Meaning in Thomas Jefferson's *Notes on the State of Virginia*," *Early American Literature* 15 (1980): 141–50.

Peterson, Merrill, "The Sovereignty of the Living Generation," *Virginia Quarterly Review* 52 (1976): 437–47.

Sandford, Charles B. *Thomas Jefferson and His Library*. Hamden, Connecticut: Archon, 1977.

Sheehan, Bernard. *Seeds of Extinction*. New York: Norton, 1974.

Smith, Samuel Stanhope. *An Essay on the Causes and Variety of Complexion and Figure in the Human Species*. Cambridge: Harvard Univ. Press, 1965.

Sydnor, Charles. *American Revolutionaries in the Making*. New York: Free Press, 1967.

Tichi, Cecilia. *New World, New Earth*. New Haven: Yale Univ. Press, 1979.

White, Morton. *The Philosophy of the American Revolution*. New York: Oxford Univ. Press, 1978.

Wills, Garry. *Inventing America: Jefferson's "Declaration of Independence."* Garden City: Doubleday, 1978.

Wood, Gordon. *The Creation of the American Republic: 1776–1787*. New York: Norton, 1972.

FEMALE AUTHORSHIP AND
AUTHORITY: THE CASE OF
SUKEY VICKERY

CATHY N. DAVIDSON

Michigan State University

Nathaniel Hawthorne, who railed against the "damned mob of scrib-bling women," even less chivalrously urged that these women be forbidden to write upon penalty of having their faces "deeply scarified with an oyster shell" (Bell 175).[1] Implicit in his hostility is the assumption that nineteenth-century America somehow provided special opportunities to its women authors that it denied to its men, and that the demands and rewards of authorship were different for one sex than for the other. Hawthorne's crude counsel bespeaks, in short, his sense of a double standard that—at least in fiction—worked against men. Similar suspicions have been voiced by such twentieth-century critics as Ann Douglas, Leslie A. Fiedler, and Henry Nash Smith, who not only denounce the nineteenth-century women authors as scribblers but also accuse them of cultivating a mass audience by perpetrating an insipid sentimentality and by reducing the moral dimension of their work to a simple advocacy of passivity, conformity, and even hypocrisy.

Other scholars, however, have recently examined sentimental fiction in a different and, I think, more revealing light. Nina Baym, for example, in *Woman's Fiction: A Guide to Novels By and About Women in America, 1820–1870*, assesses these novels as tales about the "triumph" of the "feminine will," while both Dee Garrison and Jane P. Tompkins read selected nineteenth-century women's novels as subversive texts which question traditional values and traditional systems of authority. Or Mary Kelley, in *Private Woman, Public Stage: Literary Domesticity in Nineteenth-Century America*, looks beyond the bestseller successes of numerous nineteenth-century women authors to see the ambivalence about self and society that characterizes their work. As Kelley notes, although a substantial body of women writers achieved an unprecedented fame in the mid-nineteenth century, "as private women they were uncomfortable in the world beyond the home. At best they felt ambivalent, at worst

4

that they simply did not belong there" (29). By juxtaposing the private and public statements of such writers and by contrasting the sales they achieved for their publishers with the relatively modest royalties they often earned for themselves, Kelley documents conditions of authorship that few (even of Hawthorne's disposition) could envy.

But it is not my purpose to weigh further either the artistic success of these mid-century women or the impediments to that success. Rather, I wish to examine the tradition out of which they came. More specifically, I consider one test case as representative of the quandaries and contradictions that faced the would-be woman author (and particularly the novelist) in the early republic. On the largest level, to write a work of fiction was to author both a book and a vision of the world in a society that largely denied women the authority that such authoring implies. Moreover, the novel as an emerging art form was both socially and morally suspect and was considered to be less appropriate for women (as either readers or writers) than for men. But even if the novel had been seen as the most innocent of forms, there would have still been something dubious in women writing them. In the division of labor of the time, the pen, almost as much as the sword, was deemed an implement of a man's trade.

I would also here stress that I am not positing for the early national period a different double standard than the one Hawthorne suspected. There was not so much an obvious bias favoring the male novelist over the female novelist as, rather, a distinct suspicion of both. Not even Charles Brockden Brown, who is often erroneously termed America's first professional novelist, could support himself solely by his fiction. Neither did America's first bestselling novelists, Susanna Haswell Rowson or Hannah Webster Foster, particularly profit from their craft. Both Rowson's *Charlotte* (1794) and Foster's *The Coquette* (1797) had gone through numerous editions and had sold upwards of 30,000 copies by the first decade of the nineteenth century, yet each author was still required to supplement whatever profit her fiction brought her with other employment such as writing, directing, and performing for an itinerant theatre troupe; writing and performing songs; producing advice tracts and nonfiction studies of geography or grammar; or running a ladies' academy. Rowson, moreover, was one of the most prolific fiction writers in early America, at least partly to compensate for the financial failures of her husband. But because eighteenth-century married women had virtually no legal or contractual powers, it was the alcoholic, irresponsible William Rowson who handled his wife's business dealings with her publisher, Mathew Carey, and who received the wages of her labors.[2]

Rowson and Foster were America's only two bestselling novelists prior to 1820. More typical of the early woman writer was Sukey Vickery (1779–1821), who wrote but one novel, a book that the world little noted and did not long remember.[3] Vickery, who had early achieved some success as a minor poet, published *Emily Hamilton* while still in her early twenties but then, as a wife and mother, wrote no more. Nevertheless, her extant papers provide a fascinating glimpse of the sociology of female authorship in the first years of the republic. In her letter to her publisher, Isaiah Thomas, Junior; in the poems published in Thomas' *Massachusetts Spy*; in her few surviving letters; in the poignant diary entries written after she had ceased her literary career in favor of marriage and the mothering of nine children; in her one novel, *Emily Hamilton* (1803); and in the one published critical review of that novel, we can make out some of the forces that shaped the life and career of one of America's first novelists.

I

Sukey Vickery lived most of her life in Leicester, Massachusetts, a town of almost one thousand in Worcester County. Little is known of her early life except that she was born late in the marriage of Benjamin and Susannah Barter Vickery, had only one sibling, and, as a young woman, attended the Leicester Academy (Bennett 8–18, Bemis 29).[4] This academy was co-educational and, in principle at least, strove for equality in education by teaching from basically the same textbooks to both male and female pupils. Young women students, however, generally did not read the classics in their original language but in translation, and, a further distinction, only young men entered the Upper School, essentially a college-preparatory curriculum which stressed Latin and Greek, advanced mathematics, chemistry, and philosophy (Washburn 19–34). It is difficult to determine just how good Sukey Vickery's education might have been, but we do know that she attended at least the summer session at Leicester Academy, and it is also clear that, in her later life, she attempted to pass on to her daughters an education that far surpassed the severely restricted form of "female education" commonly provided by ladies' academies and by summer schools for girls. The typical fare at these institutions was comprised of such subjects as needlework, elocution, music, manners, painting, and refined composition—or, in Lydia Maria Child's memorable phrase, "a series of 'man traps'" (94).

Sukey Vickery's poetry, published between 1801 and 1803 in Thomas'

Massachusetts Spy and under the pseudonym of "Fidelia," demonstrates a certain familiarity with both the ancient classics and contemporary British literature. Written primarily in the popular Della Cruscan mode, the poems range from public political and didactic pieces, such as "Lines, Addressed to John Adams, Esq. late President of the United States" or "Address to Piety," to more personal verses such as "To the Memory of Miss H. who departed this life on the 6th of July, after a short illness." Vickery's verse is clearly derivative in form and tone and to a modern reader seems both overinflated and underdeveloped. But it was not unappreciated in its own time. One anonymous Vermont reviewer, in a "Tribute to Merit," found Fidelia's poetry to be far superior to that of the English Della Cruscans as well as to the "*low* poetry which now abounds in European publications, under the name of *ballads*, in which simplicity is much too simple" (3). Other pseudonymous responses (by "Theodorus," "Eugene," and "Frederic," published in the *Massachusetts Spy*) similarly praised Fidelia's poems and solicited, in somewhat the same vein as the admired verse, more lines from her pen. On June 10, 1801, "Theodorus" urged: "O never cease thy charming strain—/But strike thy well strung harp again" (4).

Celebrated locally as a poet, Sukey Vickery still retained the anonymity allowed her by her pen name. Yet she was less willing to be known as the author of her one novel, *Emily Hamilton*, a work that she also very much wanted to publish. The chief roots of such authorial ambivalence are easily discerned. On the one hand, the novel might earn its author some cash (a desired possibility alluded to in the sketchiest terms in her letter to Isaiah Thomas, Jr.). On the other hand, the novel was not at all respectable as an art form. For example, in the same year that *Emily Hamilton* appeared, the Reverend Samuel Miller could denounce the reading of fiction in terms that effectively sum up the established judgment of the time: "It may, with confidence, be pronounced, that no one was ever an extensive and especially an habitual reader of novels, even supposing them to be all well selected, without suffering both intellectual and moral injury, and of course incurring a diminution of happiness" (2:179). A veritable host of other critics also condemned the new genre as being morally, socially, politically, and/or religiously suspect.[5] As James McHenry, writing retrospectively in 1824, observed: "To us it appears as if it were but yesterday, that the grave, the serious, the religious, and the prudent considered novel reading as an employment utterly beneath the dignity of the human mind.... In those days, it was almost as disreputable to be detected reading a novel, as to be found betting at a cock-fight, or a gaming table. Those who had sons,"

McHenry continued, "would have supposed them forever incapacitated for any useful pursuit in life, if they exhibited an inclination for novel reading; and those who had daughters who exhibited such an inclination, would have considered them as totally unfitted for ever becoming good wives or mothers" (1–2). In such a social climate, a young woman (and especially an unmarried woman) had little to gain by being identified as the author of a novel.

Sukey Vickery, in her letter of February 13, 1802 to Isaiah Thomas, Jr., categorically refuses to be so identified. Thomas had already published Vickery's poetry and was interested in her novel, which had been presented to him by an intermediary, one Mr. Greenwood. Vickery, too, wanted to see the book in print but only if it was in no way attributable to her. Indeed, her letter so implicitly and explicitly addresses the inherent contradictions of early American novel-writing in general and of female authorship in particular that it deserves to be quoted in full:

> Sir,
> Your very obliging letter entitles you to my sincere thanks. The flattering compliments you have bestowed on my trifling production[s?] are greater, I am conscious, than they deserve. Had I known Mr. Greenwood would have mentioned my name as the authoress of the Novel, I believe I never should have ventured to have had it thus exposed. It is, and ever has been, my wish to remain unknown. To his friendship, I consider myself in many respects greatly indebted, and in his judgment I place some confidence. On supposition the little work above alluded to ever should appear in print, I shall never consent to have my name or that of Fidelia appear to it. The novel is written in letters and founded principally on facts, some of which I have heard from persons with whom I am connected. I have been careful not to write any thing that could have a tendency to injure the mind of the young and inexperienced. I have written the whole of it at hours of leisure, and the greater part after the family had retired to rest. I am quite ignorant of the manner of disposing of copy rights, and a faint hope that I might possibly gain something by it induced me to mention it in confidence to Mr. Greenwood.

> I will transcribe it as soon as possible for your perusal, should it be thought unfit for publication, I shall rest satisfied with the decision of your superior judgment, and repose sufficient confidence in your honor to believe my name will never be exposed as the occasion.
>
> Yours with respect,
> S. V.[6]

Vickery, in this ambivalent apology for her art, also employs several arguments that were, by the beginning of the nineteenth century, standard in the prefaces of American fiction. The first of these, the claim that the book was "founded principally on facts," served to counter a residual Puritanical notion that fiction, being by definition false, was necessarily and inescapably morally reprehensible. That particular charge was so established that even the first American novel, William Hill Brown's *The Power of Sympathy* (1789), was, on the title page, "FOUNDED in TRUTH." But truth had its dangers, too. Brown was apparently threatened with a legal action, and Vickery may well have feared the repercussions of too obviously voicing truths that others would prefer to leave hidden, which could be another reason why she insisted upon anonymity.[7] A surviving letter, written by Vickery on July 29, 1799 to Adeline Hartwell, details at length the sad life of one Mrs. Anderson, a virtuous woman brought to the verge of death by marriage to a violent, profligate, and emotionally abusive drunkard. There is in *Emily Hamilton* a "Mrs. Henderson" portrayed in almost the same terms as those that Vickery used in her letter to describe Mrs. Anderson (114–19).

A second conventional defense in Vickery's letter to Thomas is the assertion that her book would not "injure the mind of the young and inexperienced." The author here denies the single most common charge against fiction, that it threatened the virtue of the "unwary." The claim advanced in the letter was also, it might be noted, considerably expanded in Vickery's Introduction to *Emily Hamilton*:

> Novel reading is frequently mentioned as being in the highest degree prejudicial to young minds, by giving them wrong ideas of the world, and setting their tastes so high, as to occasion a disrelish for those scenes in which they are necessitated to take a part. The observation will, in many respects, hold good, and there have been instances of the ruin of many young persons, produced by the erroneous ideas of romantic felicity, imbibed from an early attachment to this kind of reading. Novels, however, ought not to be indiscriminately condemned, since many of them afford an innocent and instructive amusement, and being written in the best style furnish the young reader with elegant language and ideas. Those which carry us too far from real life, and fill the imagination with a thousand enchanting images which it is impossible ever to realize, conveying at the same time an idea of perfect earthly happiness, ought never to be read till the judgment is sufficiently mature to separate the truth from the fiction of the story. But those which are founded on interesting scenes in

real life, may be calculated to afford moral instruction to the youthful mind, in the most pleasing manner. (iii–iv)

That there was some need for such a defense is further demonstrated by Thomas' incorporating this whole passage into his subscription advertisements for the novel.

The contention that fiction was a tissue of lies and a corrupter of innocence had to be faced by any novelist, male or female, in the new republic. We might also note the stance from which those charges were typically answered—a pre-Romantic posture of humility and a deferring to the reader or critic. Essentially the same statements and stances can be found in the prefaces or on the title pages of dozens of other novels of the time, those written by men as well as by women. What does seem distinctly "feminine" in Vickery's letter, however, is her insistence that the book was composed in her leisure time, after the "family had retired." The same claim, which was also advanced by Vickery's contemporary, the socially conservative novelist Mrs. S. S. B. K. Wood, would be voiced much more frequently by the women novelists of mid-nineteenth-century America. We see in Vickery, then, an early version of what later becomes almost an official pose for the woman novelist, a careful pretense of amateurism despite (for the later writers) even the professional success of being a prolific, bestselling author. Authorship, obviously, should not distract a woman from her real duties, her more "useful" domestic pursuits. And what is true for the writer is, by implication, true for the reader as well. Fiction, for women especially, was marginal. The book—being read or being written—should be taken up only after the real work was done.[8]

I I

As the poet Fidelia publishing in the weekly section of the *Massachusetts Spy*, "Blossoms of Parnassus," Sukey Vickery did not challenge the ethos of her time. Poetry as a form was well established. There was nothing revolutionary in Fidelia's heroic couplets. But *Emily Hamilton* was a different matter. To start with, the novel as a genre was new in America and was not vested in classical learning and elitist values.[9] Quite the contrary. As Mikhail Bakhtin and, more recently, Walter L. Reed have argued at length, the emerging novel tended to be viewed as subversive and even anti-literary in every western country in which the form appeared (Bakhtin 3–40, Reed 1–41). Certainly it was in America. For some forty years before the first American novel was published, official spokesmen—clergymen, political leaders, college professors—were denouncing the form, partly inspired, as Emory Elliott and Terence Martin have argued, by Scottish Common Sense philosophy. Nor did the chorus of condemnation cease with the appearance of *The Power of Sympathy.* The early American novelist worked, consequently, not within an approved tradition such as neoclassical poetry but against all such traditions. To turn to fiction was to entertain, overtly or covertly, questions about the status quo, and for the writers particularly those questions were inescapable: they came with the territory.

In this context, the contrast between the verse and the fiction of Sukey Vickery is striking. Her Fidelia poetry (both that published as the "Blossoms of Parnassus" and that still unpublished at the time of her death) was, as noted, marked only by its rigorous conventionality, whereas her novel, *Emily Hamilton,* is one of the most sustained critiques of sexual mores written in America during the early national period. The novel anticipates *The Scarlet Letter* in its sympathetic portrayal of a woman who transgresses against her marriage vows but whose transgression is shown to have, as much as Hester Prynne's, a justification of its own. *Emily Hamilton* is also especially noteworthy in that it calculatingly compromises the conventional sexual double standard on which the sentimental novel and particularly the tale of seduction typically turned.

"It has ever been my opinion," Emily Hamilton writes to her friend Mary Carter, "that the world has been too rigid, much too rigid, as respects the female sex" (97–98). The world's problem (and woman's) derives for Emily squarely from the obvious injustice of holding a woman accountable for even the "suspicion" of any impropriety while allowing a flagrantly offending man to go free. He, not she, should be condemned and treated "with as much detestation and abhorrence as the robber and assassin" (98). Mary Carter responds to her friend's letter in much the same vein, insisting that she "could never see the propriety" of the "assertion" (inspired by Samuel Richardson's *Pamela*) that a "reformed rake makes the best husband." By the same logic, Mary argues, "might it not be said with equal justice, that if a certain description of females were reformed, they would make the best wives?" (108).

It is not just occasional statements but the whole novel that calls into question the established relationships between the sexes. More specifically, *Emily Hamilton,* an epistolary novel made up of some seventy letters among three young women, centers on marriage and particularly on what Lawrence Stone has described as the "affectional marriage" that came increasingly into prominence in the latter half of the eighteenth century. Each of the young women begins the novel single; each ends wed. Each must strike in marriage some balance between the socially acceptable and the personally suitable, a tension that perfectly reflects the ongoing changes in marriage as an institution that Stone has so amply documented in England and that historians such as Nancy F. Cott and Carl N. Degler have similarly assessed in America. Each character provides a possible pattern for the reader contemplating—prospectively, retrospectively, or in wish-fulfillment—her own marriage. Indeed, by portraying a range of possibilities (from unions entered into fully by one's own free choice to those forced upon unwilling participants by tyrannical and financially motivated parents), Vickery provides different paradigms for marriage even as she also portrays the complex social nexus in which any paradigm must be realized. But perhaps most radical in her taxonomy of matrimony is her determined focus on the role of women in choosing a partner and taking responsibility for the consequences of that choice as opposed to simply sitting back and awaiting the happy event. The most disastrous relationship in the novel is also the one in which a young woman is deprived (through emotional and financial blackmail, along with a forced incarceration) of volition.

The pattern for women most obviously valorized in *Emily Hamilton* is the one first presented through the character Eliza, whose capable management of her own life—not to mention her wry appraisal of her circumstances and her suitors—makes her one of the most appealing characters in the novel. Exhibiting what Henri Petter has praised as a certain pluck and "sprightliness," Eliza simply refuses to be victimized by a love affair gone awry and so becomes an effective model for others in the book (particularly the title character) and for its female readers too (180–82). When Cutler, the man Eliza loves, deserts her, she re-judges him according to his most recent action and realizes that his abdication represents no great loss. Vickery thereby counters the sentimental notion that a woman's emotional wellbeing must be in the hands of the man who first engages her affections.

Writing to Emily, Eliza uses a language that deliberately ironizes the usual sentimental reactions to romantic betrayal: "Mr. Cutler has made a very important discovery, and I confess I wonder that he had not made it long ago. He was at Boston about six weeks since, and discovered by the sparkling eyes and dimpled cheeks of Miss Maria Willson that it was not in the power of Eliza Anderson to make him happy, as he had long foolishly imagined. . . . He was all love, tenderness and submission; she agreed to accept him, and made him sole master of her fortune, which, by the way, was more than three times as much as mine" (127). Far from being devastated, Eliza simply refuses to let her former lover's faithlessness circumscribe her own life. As she also emphasizes, it is his too obvious commitment to the premise that marriage should be socially advantageous that proves him worthless as a prospective mate, just as it also undercuts all such calculated marriages—the one she does not enter as well as the one he does. Instead of mourning his defection, she can anticipate "twenty" other suitors distinctly more suitable. She settles, however, for just one, and soon turns to Selwyn who has, quite sentimentally and equally ineffectually, long worshipped the lovely Eliza. More to the point, Selwyn is shown to be a worthy character who respects the woman he adores. Although her correspondence falls off sharply after her wedding, we are given to believe that it is a good marriage and that Eliza wisely refused to sorrow and pine in the usual sentimental fashion.

Vickery differently reverses gender-expectations in the story of Mary Carter and Mr. Gray. In this marriage plot, it is the man who is cast as the heartbroken lover grieving over the demise of his ideal woman, the beautiful Sophia, who has recently succumbed to consumption. Emily Hamilton sympathizes with Mr. Gray's bereavement but also notices the striking resemblance between the deceased Sophia and Emily's friend, Mary, a virtuous orphan, and slyly arranges a meeting between Mary and the mourning lover. The strategem works; a match ensues. Once more a marriage promises to be congenial. Once more that marriage is portrayed realistically instead of in "happy ever after" fairy tale terms. With such unions figuring prominently in its admittedly discursive plot, *Emily Hamilton* is surprisingly hard-headed in matters of the heart and encourages its women readers to follow the example of those characters who learn early on that good will, common sense, mutual esteem, and a realistic appraisal of possible marriage partners can promote personal happiness, whereas impossible dreams, proper passivity, necessary disappointment, and sentimental sorrow do not.

It is Emily Hamilton who gives her name to the book; who is by far the most prolific correspondent in the novel; and who learns, in the course of the novel, from the various happy and unhappy marriages she witnesses and reports. This same character is also most at the center of various romantic episodes in the novel, either as confidant or participant. And as with Eliza, Emily, too, finds her first try at romance unsatisfactory and is required to adjust her expectations. She is briefly wooed by Lambert, who—amiable, handsome, from a good family and possessed of a fortune—readily wins the approval of her parents and who, for a brief time, also appeals to Emily. But Lambert soon proves to be the stock seducer of much sentimental fiction. The timely arrival of a letter reveals to Emily that her suitor has come to her straight from a dubious involvement with "an artless, inexperienced girl, whose only error proceeded from loving [him] too well" (97). Appalled at his behavior, Emily rebuffs him: "I never will listen to any man who meanly triumphs in the ruin of my sex" (97). She counsels him to wed the unfortunate girl, to which he first responds that he "cannot submit to marry one so much below my rank in life" (103), and then, even more dubiously, that his "pride will not suffer [him] to stoop so low" as to marry a woman no longer a virgin. "If your pride was not too great to prevent you from committing a crime," Emily cogently responds, "I should not think it ought to be too great to prevent you from making atonement for it" (104). It is a convincing argument, but Lambert is not swayed. His refusal to do right by poor Betsey is one more sign of an increasingly obvious degeneracy that eventually brings him to imprisonment and a sentence of death.

Considering the percentage of children conceived out of wedlock in Vickery's day (higher, some demographers estimate, than at any time in American history except for our own era), there is a definite point to Vickery's premise that *both* partners are culpable in a seduction and that both are responsible for the consequences.[10] But the Lambert subplot serves another function in the novel. Emily's parents are horrified when they discover just what sort of marriage they had proposed for their daughter, and the father apologizes that he "never wished [her] to sacrifice inclination to duty" (105). Other fathers could feel differently. The theme of meddling parents is common in early American fiction and is examined in *Emily Hamilton* through clearly positive and negative cases.[11] In other words, the story of Emily and Lambert (resolved happily for Emily at least) anticipates the very different story of Edward Belmont and Clara Belknap. These two, both described as attractive, sensitive, decent young people, are thrown into the unhappiest of unions by calculating fathers who view the conjunction of one's daughter to the other's son as a kind of joint stock venture.

The resultant sorrows of the two main partners in that venture are revealed in bits and pieces throughout the novel, but the whole sad story is finally put together in the final missive of the book. Writing to her friend Mary and telling of her recent marriage to Belmont, Emily repeats his account of his previous union with Clara. Neither partner, Belmont acknowledged, loved nor even desired the other. The motive for the match was provided by two materialistic fathers, each determined to see his child joined to a suitably prosperous mate. Dutiful children, the young couple soon acceded to the parental pressure relentlessly applied. After the ceremony, Belmont attempted to make the best of a bad situation, and for a time Clara could feign happiness in his presence despite the fact that "her heart was devoted to another" (239). As Belmont notes: "When I was with her, she was all gaiety and cheerfulness, but if I came in to her apartment suddenly, I found her melancholy and dejected" (240). More telling still, in her sleep she murmured another's name. Belmont, sensitive to his wife's real feelings and the consequent nature of their relationship, realized that "if she has married me only in obedience to her parents' will, and against her own inclination, I must be wretched" (240). She has. He is. Some time after the marriage he discovers that she was earlier secretly engaged to a soldier, LeFabre, a man even Belmont acknowledges as "an amiable young Frenchman," but one too poor to gain the approval of Clara's father. Despite her best efforts, Clara continues to love this other man whom she had earlier admitted into her "intimacy." That "intimacy" (a word used repeatedly in the novel) is gradually resumed after the marriage, as the two former lovers first attempt to be proper friends but soon find their continuing passion too strong to resist. When Clara again has "private interviews with LeFabre, frequently in the absence" of her husband (156), she is obviously violating the established proprieties of wifely conduct, even if technically (and in the fiction of the time it is often impossible to tell) no adultery occurs.

The soldier in eighteenth- and early nineteenth-century American literature is regularly portrayed (no doubt with some justice) as the main opponent of female virtue, and in the iconography of much early American fiction, foreign soldiers—British in novels set during the Revolution, French during the Terror—especially signify a threat to American innocence. But Sukey Vickery's Frenchman is no standard seducer, no more than Clara is the standard victim of the seducer's wiles. LeFabre is rendered utterly abject by his beloved's forced marriage to another man. He contemplates suicide, which surely testifies to dashed hopes instead of disappointed schemes. Nor can Belmont condemn either his wife or her erstwhile and continuing lover. The husband admits that he married mostly from parental respect and because he previously believed that passionate love was "only to be found in the imaginations of poets and novelists" (239). After marriage, however, he can recognize that even though he "had reason to believe [Clara] had a sincere friendship for me. . . , friendship alone, in a wife, is too cold" (243). And just how cold, he, she, and the marriage all are he still better discovers when he rescues the lovely Emily Hamilton from drowning and begins to fall in love with her. Tasting for himself thwarted desire, he also can much better understand the devastation his wife must be experiencing: "I had now some conception of what Clara had suffered, and all my compassion was awakened. I wished we could part, or that we had never seen each other. Honor, religion and duty compelled me to give up every idea of [Emily], but I could not erase [her] from my mind" (246). Neither Belmont's compassion nor Clara's struggle to accept her condition nor the birth of two children can save this sorry union, and the impasse of impossible loves is resolved only through Clara's untimely death.

Belmont's sister, viewing the situation as an outsider, blames the whole messy marriage on Clara: "She could, by marrying [my brother], not only possess all the elegancies of life, but have it in her power to continue her intimacy with LeFabre at his return" (154). The husband, however (and even though he was himself disgraced by public displays of affection between his wife and LeFabre), apportions responsibility differently. Overhearing, after the marriage, a conversation between the two conniving fathers, Belmont learns that Clara had written to LeFabre begging him to return and carry her off before she was forced to wed another. Her father had intercepted the letter and shut up his daughter without pen or paper. Yet she had still somehow managed another letter, this one to Edward Belmont, telling him of her love for LeFabre and begging Edward to call off the match. Again the letter had been intercepted by the father who promised his daughter that she would be disowned by the family and abandoned in shame and penury if she did anything further to prevent the match. "I was too old and too wise," this parent confided to the other, "to mind the tears of a foolish girl, and I'll warrant she thanks me for it now." "It's no matter," both fathers agree, "whether married people love each other or not, if they only mind the main chance. I'll warrant they won't quarrel as long as they have money enough" (241–42). Reported in the final letter of the volume, this callous prediction is proven wrong by the whole preceding novel, just as the purely materialistic considerations on which it is based are shown to be totally bankrupt. Belmont knows where the blame for his past suffering—and Clara's—mostly lies. Looking forward to a different kind of marriage with Emily, he can also hope that Clara might achieve in death the happiness she did not have with him.

Despite her unusually sympathetic portrayal of a woman who continues a (possibly) illicit liaison after matrimony, Vickery does not totally exonerate Clara Belmont but, paradoxically, blames her for the very blamelessness that precipitated her plight. In other words, Clara's tragedy is that she is too much the conventional female, not too little, and, good sentimental heroine that she is, she concedes her fate to the men around her: she turns to the soldier she loves, hoping he will rescue her from marriage; to the fiancé to whom she is unwillingly betrothed, hoping he will call off the match; to the father she honors, hoping he will have an unlikely change of heart. Never does she make any overt declarations of independence whereby she might save herself. In metaphoric terms, she is seduced, seduced into the materially motivated marriage that she cannot subsequently endure. The iconography of seduction is further suggested by her final fate. Like other victims of other seductions in other sentimental fictions, Clara dies young, unhappy, despised by a censorious community—and a community appalled not by her feminine passivity but by her perceived sexual transgressions. Sukey Vickery, however, puts the primal fault before the marriage, not after it. The irony here is striking. Unlike Eliza and unlike Emily Hamilton (in the Lambert plot), Clara Belmont has done what she thought she was supposed to do. She consented to a socially acceptable match and yielded to filial duty. The result, for all involved, is disaster.

Emily Hamilton, at least in this respect, is a remarkable novel. Despite considerable awkwardness of plotting (coincidence figures mightily), the book is a psychologically astute anatomy of marriage—both those that work and those that do not. In its analysis of the latter, it is particularly sympathetic towards a woman who has clearly transgressed against accepted sexual strictures. That state of affairs is highly unusual in the fiction of the time. *Emily Hamilton* is one of the very few early American novels in which a woman's sexuality is not inextricably conjoined with the seduction plot and a consequent demonstration of the wages of sin. In both William Hill Brown's *Ira and Isabella* (1807) and Leonora Sansay's *Laura* (1809), it will be remembered, a woman cohabitates with a man without benefit of matrimony and without suffering immediate disgrace and death, while Samuel Woodworth's *The Champions of Freedom, or The Mysterious Chief* (1816) portrays the male, not the female, as a seduced young innocent. But Sukey Vickery's portrayal of Clara Belmont stands out even in this atypical company. More sinned against than sinning, Clara evokes her husband's sympathy as well as the reader's. She is not a socially defiant Hester Prynne, certainly, but then Belmont is not a cruel, vengeful Chillingworth, either. We must notice that he does not enter into his second marriage without explaining to Miss Hamilton the circumstances of his first, which is a way of exonerating Clara's memory and expiating his role in the woe that was her marriage even as it portends a happier union with Emily.

III

As earlier noted, the author argued in her introduction that novel reading could be "prejudicial to young minds, by giving them wrong ideas of the world" (iii). In the novel itself, Vickery diligently avoids the danger that she here describes. *Emily Hamilton*, as a romance, is remarkably realistic. Passion must be weighed, and so—witness the arranged marriage of Clara and Edward—must reason. On one level the plot can be reduced to a didactic demonstration of the claims of sensibility over self-indulgent sentiment or crude calculation. But Vickery in the same Introduction also insists that novels "afford an innocent and instructive amusement" (iv). Here is one of the first overt statements by an American novelist that an important function of fiction is, simply, to amuse. In England at this same time fiction's importance as a source of entertainment was widely acknowledged, but in America intellectual and moral edification were the primary justifications for novel reading until well into the nineteenth century.[12] This defense of the *dulce* is, however, tempered even in its very formulation by an appeal to the *utile* as well. The "amusement" is "instructive" and should promote a higher level of literacy ("elegant language and ideas") among the book's readers.

The last claim need not be dismissed as pure advertising. Reading was one important mode of feminine education in the early nineteenth century. Hannah More, for example, observed: "Ladies . . . though they have never been taught a rule of syntax, yet, by a quick facility in profiting from the best books and the best company, hardly ever violate one." As More argued, in *Strictures on the Modern System of Female Education*, women could achieve an "elegant and perspicuous arrangement of style, without having studied any of the laws of composition" (I:26). A good novel might be, then, a particularly effective way of improving a young woman's literary skills, especially since, as Charles Brockden Brown noted, many readers of novels read no other material besides novels ("Novel-Reading," 405). As Brown implies, a substantial portion of the audience of the novel was effectively excluded from other literary forms. This fact is hardly surprising; after all, in what other literary form could a marginally middle-class reader peruse the lives, the loves, the daily comings and goings of characters much like herself or see, in the case of *Emily Hamilton*, such characters learn (often the hard way) that money alone cannot insure one's wellbeing? As Emily observes: "Neither wealth nor honor can confer real happiness; it is to be found only in the mind" (218)—a reassuring maxim for a reader whose wealth must be largely mental.

Unhappily, the social and literary lessons that might have been garnered from *Emily Hamilton* were limited mostly by the limited sale of the book itself. Isaiah Thomas, Jr., originally sought to sell the novel by subscription:

> The work will be neatly printed on good paper and a fair type, in a 12mo. Volume, and will make about 300 pages. The price to sub-

scribers will be 75 cents, neatly bound and lettered. Those who subscribe for Six copies shall be entitled to a Seventh gratis. Should there
be 300 subscribers, and the Subscription Papers be returned in season, the names shall appear in the work. Those who do not get their
Books within six months after they are published, must pay the same
price as Nonsubscribers.[13]

The list of subscribers was not included in the published volume. In fact,
Thomas's objective of three hundred subscribers was highly optimistic.
No early American novel came close to that number. Of the four early
novels bound with subscription lists, only Herman Mann's *The Female
Review* reached even 200 names. The novel as a genre simply was not
established enough to be able to lay an advance claim upon American
readers.

The price of the volume, it might also be noted, well may have limited
its sales. Although seventy-five cents for a leather-bound duodecimo volume of approximately three hundred pages may seem a small sum, it was
not. In Massachusetts at that time a common day laborer earned between fifty cents and a dollar a day. Or put in more immediate and local
terms, Vickery's classmate, diarist Ethan Allen Greenwood, earned $3.00
a month in 1799 at his first teaching job in Massachusetts. A young man
like Greenwood well might be the kind of person expected to subscribe
to *Emily Hamilton,* especially since he was an avid reader. But even
assuming that room and board were free with his teaching appointment,
Greenwood's $3.00 per month would not purchase many luxuries. A
night at the theatre was $.75; a dinner at a local tavern $.37; and a
stage coach journey of only ten miles cost approximately a dollar. There
would be little left, at the end of a typical month, for a copy of *Emily
Hamilton.*[14]

Despite a number of advertisements in the *Massachusetts Spy, Emily
Hamilton* did not sell well. Fifty copies of the book, for example, were
sent to Thomas' Walpole shop in 1803, and three years later more than
half still remained on the shelves. A few copies of the first printing were
available at Thomas' shop in Boston, as well as at the Worcester store, in
1813, a full ten years after the publication date. The novel was never
reprinted, and Sukey Vickery's faint hope of possible gain (with emphasis
on the "faint") proved all too prophetic. Neither did the novel receive
much attention in the press, and one anonymous review in the *Monthly
Anthology and Boston Review* in May 1805 did little to encourage sales.
The circumstances of that review, however, do cast an interesting light on
the sociology of female authorship in the early national period.

Thomas had apparently sent the book to the Boston magazine accompanied by a note, at least partly specious, in which he described the author as a mere girl of eighteen who took up writing to support her family: "This volume was sent to us," the review begins, "as the production of a 'country girl, about eighteen years of age, residing in an obscure town, and by her needle maintaining her aged parents'" (267). The printer, it seems, perpetrated a sentimental story with which to place Vickery, as much as possible, within an acceptable ideology of female labor. She thereby becomes an innocent, self-sacrificing daughter whose pen is barely distinguishable from her needle. The only problem is that the "facts" in the account are mostly fictions. Vickery was twenty-four, not eighteen; Vickery's father, who appears to have been the area's only tailor and who was prosperous enough to buy himself a small farm in Worcester County, was hardly indigent. The publisher had simply composed his own author, one without social authority and in no position to challenge—through, say, her portrait of a woman who has a husband and a lover, too—the accepted customs of her country. That he did so not to counter the book but to sell it only ironically highlights the portrait provided.

The age demanded such portraits. The ruse worked, for the anonymous reviewer (possibly the Reverend John Pierce of Brookline) attests that he is being much kinder to the book than he might otherwise have been:[15]

> Either of these circumstances [i.e., Vickery's age or her family's penury] would have interested us in [the novel's] favour, but we could not view them thus combined without an earnest wish for the success of the author. We do not recollect any American female, except Mrs. Rowson, who has written a novel which can be read with any pleasure; and we are not disposed to encourage the exertions of females to become known as authors, unless convinced that the amusement and instruction which they can furnish will extend beyond the circle of their own partial friends. Considering however the age at which it was written, and the peculiar embarrassments of the author, the novel before us is deserving of commendation. The style evidently displays the youth of the author, though more simple and correct, than that in which young ladies generally write. The sentiments are common, but just; and though the incidents are neither very numerous nor interesting, they evince considerable ingenuity. (267–68)

Considering the reviewer's disposition to discourage female authorship and his gratuitous dismissal of the exertions of all women other than Mrs. Rowson, his comments are surprisingly gentle—unless one also considers the possibility that all he read of the book was Thomas' fiction as to its author (after all, the sentiments expressed in the novel would not likely be found either common or just by this reviewer).

The early reviewer can grudgingly commend Vickery's artistic intentions even as he condemns her actual accomplishment with the faintest of praise. And no one has subsequently questioned that first critical judgment. Thus Henri Petter commends a few characters and scenes in the novel but still relegates it to the category of the second rank, while Lillie D. Loshe includes the book only in her bibliography, and Herbert Ross Brown mentions it only in passing. Even John B. Bennett, the one person to write an extended biography of the author, dismisses *Emily Hamilton*. The novel, he argues, "never rises above a dead level of sentimental conventionality."[16] Yet, as we have seen, *Emily Hamilton* challenges the sentimental conventions of the early novel as consistently as any other novel of the time.

This is not to argue that Sukey Vickery is an earlier Hawthorne or that, under different social circumstances, she might have become one. The question is moot. We know that this author wrote only one novel and after that nothing, not even another ode by Fidelia. A year after the publication of *Emily Hamilton*, Sukey Vickery married Samuel Watson, who ran a clothier's shop in Leicester and who went on to become the first manufacturer of woolen cloth in the area. Later, after his first wife's death, Watson would also become a Representative to the General Court (Bemis 29). But during his marriage to Sukey, he led a more precarious existence, continually leasing out buildings and equipment, regularly trying to launch himself into a larger business career, and regularly landing in near-bankruptcy, while new children were just as regularly added to his family. His wife's only literary endeavor during the years between 1804 and her death in 1821 was to bestow upon her seven daughters and two sons names with an obviously literary cast: Harriot, Eliza, Sarah, Caroline, Clarissa, Marianne, Henry, Edward, Maria—a number of which come from *Emily Hamilton* itself.

Yet something more still remains. Among Sukey Vickery's papers are two pages torn from what seems to have been a complete diary. The handwriting is elegant and assured, the prose carefully edited, the phrasing striking in its simple eloquence. The contents of this brief excerpt, the first entry dated Monday, December 18, 1815, are directed specifically to the six children she had already borne (the oldest, Harriot, was then aged ten). The busy mother works hard to make time in her day for her daughters' education. She "instruct[ed] Harriot in Arithmetic—attended to Eliza's improvement in writing—Taught Amanda for the first time to make strait marks with a pen." On the following day, the erstwhile novelist and poet celebrated her oldest daughter's first spinning, "eleven skains," watched over by the mother, a project that reached completion after "five days, excepting the time she has been hindered by doing some necessary work about the house." Sukey also "attended to their writing half an hour this evening—Earnestly wish I could devote more time to them." Subsequent days report lessons in arithmetic, and Sukey Vickery's attempt to make learning a pleasure in the hope that her daughters will continue their education in the future.

Why does just this portion of the diary survive? Did Vickery save one excerpt as a kind of explanation as to why her literary production ceased entirely after her marriage? Did some descendant select out this portion to make that same apology or, equally plausible, to counter the literary excesses of the author as a young woman with a portrait of the matron as ever diligent mother? We do not know. But there is certainly a "literariness," perfectly befitting the author of *Emily Hamilton*, in the entry for December 18, 1815:

> Could the dear creatures know the interest I feel in all that concerns them, and any anxious wishes for their improvement and future usefulness, it would be a sufficient stimulus to their ambition. Taught them the probable reason of the twinkling of the stars—All such information is communicated and received with delight—It makes me happy to find one hour I can spare for the improvement of my children.

From the improvement of the minds of the "young and inexperienced" who she assumed, in her initial letter to Thomas, would be her readers to the improvement of the minds of her own growing brood of children, Sukey Vickery had shifted her immediate audience but not her authorial intention.

Writing in 1809, Charles Brockden Brown generalized about the divided lives of would-be literary women: "Of that numerous class of females, who have cultivated their minds with science and literature, without publishing their labours, and who consequently are unknown to general inquirers; how many have preserved the balance immoveable between the opposite demands of the kitchen, the drawing room, the nursery, and the library? We may safely answer from our own experience, not one" (245). Sukey Vickery was no exception to this rule. Effaced on her own title page by her reservations about being a "woman novelist," Vickery was even more effaced from the world of literature by marriage and a family. Perhaps it was no great loss. Certainly her novel did not sell well, not enough to bring its author either fame or fortune. Certainly the novel has its flaws in characterization and construction. Nevertheless, *Emily Hamilton*, now as then, challenges the named or anonymous authorities (such as the reviewer in the *Monthly Anthology*) who would write women into their place. The proper response to that writing, Vickery haltingly realized, was to portray feminine transgressions as forced declarations of independence. Thus, as with Hawthorne, a woman's sin defines her community as much as the community defines the sin. It is not, however, just the novel but the whole life of Sukey Vickery—dutiful daughter, determined student, pseudonymous poet, anonymous novelist, diligent housewife, and concerned mother—that suggests the larger sociology of female authorship in the early national period. Forty-two years old when she died, she left behind nine children, a handful of personal papers, poetry, and one intriguing novel too long unread.

ACKNOWLEDGMENTS

I am grateful to the American Antiquarian Society for a Kate B. and Hall James Peterson Fellowship that facilitated the writing of this essay, and I also thank the staff of the Society, and especially Georgia B. Bumgardner, Marie E. Lamoureux, and Kathleen A. Major, for their expert assistance. I am grateful, too, to the staff of the Leicester (Massachusetts) Public Library for helping me to locate the copy of *Emily Hamilton* formerly owned by Vickery's eldest daughter.

NOTES

1. The full quotation reads: "*All* women, as author's [sic], are feeble and tiresome. I wish they were forbidden to write, on pain of having their faces deeply scarified with an oyster shell" (quoted in Bell 175).

2. Seven transactions between Carey and William Rowson are recorded in the former's account books (Manuscript Department, American Antiquarian Society), none between Carey and the author herself. See Cott (21, 77–78), Kerber (123–34), and Norton (45–50) for excellent discussions of the *feme* [sic] *covert*.

3. Vickery is representative in that she published only one novel in the course of her lifetime, just as the typical early printer published no more than one American novel, for financial but also often for moral reasons. For example, in his personal copy of *Emily Hamilton* (American Antiquarian Society), Isaiah Thomas, Senior, rationalized that "the perusal of Novels generally tend[s] to *enlighten* than to *distract* the mind," but he also warned that it "behoves .... heads of families ... to expel [immoral] Books from their Homes." Vickery was also typical in that she published her novel with a local printer, as did over sixty percent of American novelists prior to 1820. According to Charvat, by 1840, because of the centralization of capital-intensive publishing, only six percent of American fiction was still published locally (*Literary Publishing* 26).

4. Bennett's detailed account of Vickery's life and works was invaluable to my research, but I have corrected throughout this essay numerous errors in that early study.

5. For a survey of the negative evaluation of American fiction, see the discussions by Charvat (especially *Origins* 7–26 and 134–63), Orians, and Palmer.

6. The "Mr. Greenwood" of Vickery's letter remains a mystery. Several men with that family name resided in Leicester at the time, including another alumnus of Leicester Academy, painter Ethan Allen Greenwood (who mentions neither "Fidelia" nor Sukey Vickery in his diary).

7. The first American novel may not have been "banned in Boston" as was long supposed, but, as Walser has shown, Perez Morton (whose name was changed to "Martin" in the plot) attempted to suppress the novel that accused him of an illicit (and, by the standards of the time, incestuous) relationship with his wife's younger sister (65–74).

8. For example, in her diary Elizabeth Drinker juxtaposed accounts of her fiction reading with long lists of household chores "to shew that I have not spent the day reading," while diarist Julia Cowles apologized: "Been so much engaged in read[ing] 'Grandison' that other things have been neglected, especially my journal" (40–41).

9. Ong has argued that women's forms of discourse, such as the sentimental novel, derive from organic, folk narrative traditions and differ structurally from men's literary traditions, which are derived from classically-based forms of public sermonics and formal oratory, a notion much earlier advanced by Abigail Adams, who felt women had "more delicate Sensations" and could better portray a "true Similitud" than men, who were "warpt by Education" and who "judge amiss from previous prejudice and refering all things to the model of the ancients" (3: 52).

10. The controversial issue of premarital pregnancy has been explored by Smith and Hindus and is summarized by Degler (20). An equally important demographic phenomenon, however, was the extraordinarily high birthrate in America in 1800, approximately 7.04 live births per adult woman, a figure that declined by fifty percent over the next century. The novel may not have *caused* such patterns but it did reflect them and, additionally, encouraged the woman reader to take some measure of control over reproductive decisions. For other relevant demographic statistics, see the studies by Coale and Zelnick, Sanderson, and Wells.

11. For a discussion of the cruel parent motif in early American fiction, see Petter (188–209) and, for an overview of the larger, changing social attitudes towards parenting, Fliegelman.

12. Both Thomas Moore and Laetitia Aikin justified fiction on the grounds that it amused the reader but, as Gallaway and Cairns (90–94) have shown, theirs was not the prevailing sentiment.

13. This advertisement appeared in the *Massachusetts Spy* on October 20, 1802 and was reprinted on December 1, 1802; December 29, 1802; and January 5, 1803. On March 2, 1803 Thomas requested that "gentlemen holding subscription papers for *Emily Hamilton*, a New Novel, are requested to return them immediately to this office." (Note that Thomas assumes subscribers will be "gentlemen.") Thomas advertised the novel weekly in the *Massachusetts Spy* from June 8, 1803 to July 27, 1803 (with the exception of the July 13 issue), along with popular titles from his press such as Plutarch's *Lives* and Perry's *Spelling Book*, and then followed up with an individual ad for Vickery's novel that ran six times between late August and October, 1803.

14. The accounts in the back of Greenwood's diary (twenty-one octavo volumes for the years 1801–1810) corroborate the U.S. Department of Labor figures for wages and expenses (53, 57, and 137). Teachers' wages fluctuated from between $ .67 per week for a "qualified woman teacher" in Connecticut in 1798 and $20.00 per month for a "man of

culture and experience" (133–34). Although Greenwood earned $14.00 per month at his second teaching job, he still could not afford to buy books and so, like thousands of Americans, he borrowed them. He belonged to the Social Friends Library, the Adelphi (fraternity) Library, and an unnamed circulating library and read nearly a volume a day.

15. The authority for identifying the reviewer as the Reverend John Pierce (Vickery's former teacher at Leicester Academy) rests on a remark inscribed within the copy of *Emily Hamilton* donated to the Leicester Public Library by Vickery's eldest daughter, Harriot.

16. See Petter (180–82), Loshe (111), Brown (11–12, 38–39, 40–41, and 160), and Bennett (65).

WORKS CITED

Adams, Abigail. *Adams Family Correspondence, Vol. III*, ed. L. H. Butterfield and Marc Friedlander. Cambridge: Harvard Univ. Press, 1973.

Aikin, Laetitia [Mrs. Barbauld]. "Preface" to *British Novelists*. London, 1810.

Bakhtin, M. H. *The Dialogic Imagination*, ed. and trans. Michael Holquist. Austin: Univ. of Texas Press, 1981.

Baym, Nina. *Woman's Fiction*. Ithaca: Cornell Univ. Press, 1978.

Bell, Michael Davitt. *Hawthorne and the Historical Romance of New England*. Princeton: Princeton Univ. Press, 1971.

Bemis, Julia Draper, and Alonzo Amasa Bemis, comp. *History and Genealogy of the Watson Family*. Spencer, Mass., 1894.

Bennett, John B. "A Young Lady of Worcester County." Unpublished M.A. thesis, Wesleyan Univ., 1942.

Brown, Charles Brockden. "Female Learning." *Literary Magazine* 1 (1804): 245.

———. "Novel-Reading." *Literary Magazine* 1 (1804): 405.

Brown, Herbert Ross. *The Sentimental Novel in America*. Durham: Duke Univ. Press, 1940.

Brown, William Hill. *The Power of Sympathy: Or, The Triumph of Nature. Founded in Truth*. Worcester, Mass., 1789.

Cairns, William B. *British Criticism of American Writings, 1783–1815*. Madison: Univ. of Wisconsin Press, 1918.

Carey, Mathew. "Account Books." Manuscript Department, American Antiquarian Society.

Charvat, William. *Literary Publishing in America, 1790–1850*. Philadelphia: Univ. of Pennsylvania Press, 1959.

———. *The Origins of American Critical Thought, 1810–1835*. Philadelphia: Univ. of Pennsylvania Press, 1936.

Child, Lydia Maria. *The American Frugal Housewife*. Boston, 1833.

Coale, Ansley J., and Melvin Zelnick. *New Estimates of Fertility and Population in the United States*. Princeton: Princeton Univ. Press, 1963.

Cott, Nancy F. *The Bonds of Womanhood: "Woman's Sphere" in New England, 1780–1835*. New Haven: Yale Univ. Press, 1977.

Cowles, Julia. *The Diaries of Julia Cowles: A Connecticut Record, 1797–1803*, ed. Anna Roosevelt Cowles and Laura Hadley Moseley. New Haven: Yale Univ. Press, 1931.
Degler, Carl N. *At Odds: Women and the Family in America from the Revolution to the Present*. New York: Oxford Univ. Press, 1980.
Douglas, Ann. *The Feminization of American Culture*. New York: Knopf, 1977.
Drinker, Elizabeth. Diary entry, 29 February 1796. Historical Society of Pennsylvania.
Elliott, Emory. *Revolutionary Writers: Literature and Authority in the New Republic, 1725–1810*. New York: Oxford Univ. Press, 1982.
"Eugene." "To Fidelia." *Massachusetts Spy, or Worcester Gazette* 30 (October 27, 1801).
Fiedler, Leslie A. *Love and Death in the American Novel*. Rev. ed. New York: Dell, 1967.
Fliegelman, Jay. *Prodigals and Pilgrims: The American Revolution Against Patriarchal Authority*. New York: Cambridge Univ. Press, 1982.
"Frederic." "Sonnet to Fidelia." *Massachusetts Spy, or Worcester Gazette* 31 (September 7, 1802).
Gallaway, W. F., Jr. "The Conservative Attitude Toward Fiction, 1770–1830." *PMLA* 55 (1940): 1041–59.
Garrison, Dee. "Immoral Fiction in the Late Victorian Library." *American Quarterly* 28 (1976): 71–89.
Greenwood, Ethan Allen. Diary, 1801–1810. Manuscript Department, American Antiquarian Society.
History of Wages in the United States from Colonial Times to 1928. Washington, D.C.: U. S. Department of Labor, 1929.
Kelley, Mary. *Private Woman, Public Stage*. New York: Oxford Univ. Press, 1984.
Kerber, Linda K. *Women of the Republic: Intellect and Ideology in Revolutionary America*. Chapel Hill: Univ. of North Carolina Press, 1980.
Loshe, Lillie D. *The Early American Novel*. 1907; rpt. New York: Frederick Ungar, 1966.
McHenry, James. "On the Causes of the Present Popularity of Novel Writing." *American Monthly Magazine* 2 (1824): 1–8.
Mann, Herman. *The Female Review: or, Memoirs of an American Young Lady*. Dedham, Mass., 1797.
Martin, Terence. *The Instructed Vision: Scottish Common Sense Philosophy and the Origins of American Fiction*. Bloomington: Indiana Univ. Press, 1961.
Miller, Samuel E. *A Brief Retrospect of the Eighteenth Century*. New York, 1803.
Moore, Thomas. *A View of the Commencement and Progress of the Romance*. London, 1798.
More, Hannah. *Strictures on the Modern System of Female Education*. New York, 1813.
Norton, Mary Beth. *Liberty's Daughters: The Revolutionary Experience of American Women, 1750–1800*. Boston: Little, Brown, 1980.

Ong, Walter J. *Orality and Literacy: The Technologizing of the Word.* New York: Methuen, 1982.

Orians, G. Harrison. "Censure of Fiction in American Romances and Magazines, 1789–1810." *PMLA* 52 (1937): 195–214.

Palmer, Ormond E. "Some Attitudes Toward Fiction in America to 1870, and a Bit Beyond." Diss. Univ. of Chicago, 1952.

Petter, Henri. *The Early American Novel.* Columbus: Ohio State Univ. Press, 1971.

Reed, Walter L. *An Exemplary History of the Novel.* Chicago: Univ. of Chicago Press, 1981.

Rev. of *Emily Hamilton. Monthly Anthology and Boston Review* 3 (1805): 267–68.

Sanderson, Warren C. "Quantitative Aspects of Marriage Fertility and Family Limitation in Nineteenth-Century America: Another Application of the Coale Specifications." *Demography* 16 (1979): 339–58.

Smith, Daniel Scott and Michael S. Hindus. "Premarital Pregnancy in America, 1640–1971: An Overview and Interpretation." *Journal of Interdisciplinary History* 5 (1975): 537–70.

Smith, Henry Nash. *Democracy and the Novel: Popular Resistance to Classic American Writers.* New York: Oxford Univ. Press, 1978.

Spurlin, Paul M. "Readership in the American Enlightenment." In Charles G. S. Williams, ed., *Literature and History in the Age of Ideas.* Columbus: Ohio State Univ. Press, 1975.

Stone, Lawrence. *The Family, Sex, and Marriage in England: 1500–1800.* New York: Harper, 1977.

"Theodorus." "To Fidelia." *Massachusetts Spy, or Worcester Gazette* 30 (June 10, 1801).

Thomas, Isaiah, Jr. Advertisement for *Emily Hamilton. Massachusetts Spy, or Worcester Gazette* 32 (June 8, 1803–July 27, 1803).

———. Advertisement for Subscriptions for *Emily Hamilton. Massachusetts Spy, or Worcester Gazette* 31–32 (October 20, 1802; December 1, 1802; December 29, 1802; and January 5, 1803).

Thomas, Isaiah, Sr. "Accounts of Stock, Thomas and Andrews, Boston, 1811"; "Accounts, Worcester, 1813"; "Exchange Book, Walpole, NH, 1803"; and "Thomas and Thomas's Stock, Debts & c., Walpole, NH, May 1, 1806." Thomas Papers. Manuscript Department, American Antiquarian Society.

Tompkins, Jane P. *Sensational Designs: The Cultural Work of American Fiction, 1789–1860.* New York: Oxford Univ. Press, 1985.

"Tribute to Merit." [Brattleborough, Vermont] *Federal Galaxy* 5 (August 21, 1801).

Vickery, Sukey to Adeline Hartwell, July 29, 1799. Vickery Papers. Manuscript Department, American Antiquarian Society.

———. to Isaiah Thomas, Jr., February 13, 1802. Vickery Papers, American Antiquarian Society.

———. "Address to Piety." *Massachusetts Spy, or Worcester Gazette* 30 (May 13, 1801).

———. "Diary." Vickery Papers, American Antiquarian Society.

———. *Emily Hamilton, A Novel. Founded on Incidents in Real Life. By a Young Lady of Worcester County.* Worcester, 1803.

———. "Lines, Addressed to John Adams, Esq. late President of the United States." *Massachusetts Spy, or Worcester Gazette* 30 (April 15, 1801).

———. "To the Memory of Miss H. who departed this life on the 6th of July, after a short illness." *Massachusetts Spy, or Worcester Gazette* 30 (August 19, 1801).

Walser, Richard E. "Boston's Reception of the First American Novel." *Early American Literature* 17 (1982): 65–74.

Washburn, Emory. *Brief Sketch of the History of Leicester Academy.* Boston, 1855.

Wells, Robert V. "Family Size and Fertility Control in Eighteenth-Century America: A Study of Quaker Families." *Population Studies* 25 (1971): 73–82.

The Republican Wife: Virtue and Seduction in the Early Republic

Jan Lewis

WHEN the American colonists commenced rebellion against the British government and assumed the separate and equal station to which they believed the laws of God and nature both entitled them, they found in marriage—"that SOCIAL UNION, which the beneficent Creator instituted for the happiness of Man,"—a metaphor for their ideal of social and political relationships. In the republic envisioned by American writers, citizens were to be bound together not by patriarchy's duty or liberalism's self-interest, but by affection, and it was, they believed, marriage, more than any other institution, that trained citizens in this virtue. Thus "L," writing in the *Royal American Magazine* in 1774, explained why this "social union is so essential to human happiness." The married man, he wrote, "by giving pleasure . . . receives it back again with increase. By this endearing intercourse of friendship and communication of pleasure, the tender feelings and soft passions of the soul are awakened with all the ardour of love and benevolence. . . . In this happy state, man feels a growing attachment to human nature, and love to his country."[1] Marriage was the very pattern from which the cloth of republican society was to be cut.

Revolutionary-era writers held up the loving partnership of man and wife in opposition to patriarchal dominion as the republican model for social and political relationships. The essays, stories, poems, and novels

Ms. Lewis is a member of the Department of History at Rutgers University, Newark. She wishes to thank the National Endowment for the Humanities for a Fellowship for Independent Study and Research, and Ruth H. Bloch, Jay Fliegelman, Drew R. McCoy, and, especially, Norma Basch for their advice.

[1] "Thoughts on Matrimony," *Royal American Magazine* (Boston), Jan. 1774, 9. Historians have explored the anti-patriarchal dimensions of the Revolution. See Jay Fliegelman, *Prodigals and Pilgrims: The American Revolution against Patriarchal Authority, 1750-1800* (New York, 1982); Edwin G. Burrows and Michael Wallace, "The American Revolution: The Ideology and Psychology of National Liberation," *Perspectives in American History*, VI (1972), 167-306; Winthrop D. Jordan, "Familial Politics: Thomas Paine and the Killing of the King, 1776," *Journal of American History*, LX (1973), 294-308; and Melvin Yazawa, *From Colonies to Commonwealth: Familial Ideology and the Beginnings of the American Republic* (Baltimore, 1985). Fliegelman has noted that the Revolutionary generation found in the "affectionate union" of marriage an alternative to the patriarchal model of political relationships (*Prodigals*, chap. 4).

163

that established this model created in republican marriage an ideal that drew upon recent social trends and infused them with political meaning; in so doing, their authors created for women an important new political role, not so much as a mother, as Linda K. Kerber has suggested,[2] but, rather, as a wife. As an indispensable half of the conjugal union that served as the ideal for political as well as familial relationships, the Republican Wife exemplified the strengths and weaknesses of the Revolutionary era's notion of woman's role and, indeed, of republicanism itself; neither can be understood fully except in the context of the other.

Because historians have begun to question whether American political discourse in the period 1775-1815 can be understood in terms of republicanism alone, it is important to note that the adjective "republican" will be used here much as Americans of the period used it—to signify not only classical republicanism but also that fusion of civic humanism and evangelical ardor achieved by Americans at the eve of the Revolution. The key to republicanism is virtue, the self-sacrificial and disinterested quality that was prized in both sacred and secular traditions.[3] The premium that

[2] Linda K. Kerber coined the term "Republican Motherhood" to describe the peculiar political mission assigned to American women in the Revolutionary era. In an influential article and book she used the term to characterize the indirect political role that women were to play by "raising sons and disciplining husbands to be virtuous citizens of the republic" ("The Republican Mother: Women and the Enlightenment—An American Perspective," *American Quarterly*, XXVIII [1976], 187-205, quotation on p. 203, and *Women of the Republic: Intellect and Ideology in Revolutionary America* [Chapel Hill, N.C., 1980]). Although Kerber focused upon the domestic rather than the maternal character of woman's political participation, her term has taken on a life of its own and is often assumed to say more about motherhood than Kerber herself ever claimed. (See, for example, Mary Beth Norton, "The Evolution of White Women's Experience in Early America," *American Historical Review*, LXXXIX [1984], 616-619; Jane Rendall, *The Origins of Modern Feminism: Women in Britain, France, and the United States, 1780-1860* [New York, 1984], chap. 2, and *passim;* and Mary P. Ryan, *Womanhood in America: From Colonial Times to the Present*, 3d ed. [New York, 1983], 101-104.) Indeed, as Ruth H. Bloch first suggested, comparatively little attention was paid in the period 1785-1815 to the republican dimensions of motherhood, in relation to woman's other roles ("American Feminine Ideals in Transition: The Rise of the Moral Mother, 1785-1815," *Feminist Studies*, IV [1978], 125-126, n. 67). More recently Kerber has argued that "republican motherhood was a conceptualization which grafted the language of liberal individualism onto the inherited discourse of civic humanism," which could not, in and of itself, "effectively describe an active role for women in the republic" ("The Republican Ideology of the Revolutionary Generation," *Am. Qtly.*, XXXVII [1985], 486, 484). The argument here is that American republicanism offered women a role as wives. It was left to liberalism, as Kerber suggests, to extol the political dimensions of motherhood.

[3] See especially Gordon S. Wood, *The Creation of the American Republic. 1776-1787* (Chapel Hill, N.C., 1969); his analysis of the meaning of republicanism informs this essay. For a discussion of the meaning of virtue to contemporary Americans see Ruth H. Bloch, "The Gendered Meanings of Virtue in Revolutionary America," *Signs: Journal of Women in Culture and Society*, XIII (forthcom-

republican thought placed upon disinterestedness has obscured the revolutionary nature of its views about women. To be sure, republican theorists were unwilling to think of women, or any other group, as having different and perhaps antagonistic interests;[4] hence, they did not address women as a separate group. Republicanism assumed, however, that America's dawning glory would cast its beneficent rays upon the whole of society, a new and different society in which women would be required to play a new and unprecedented role.

If we would understand the role designed for women in the early national era, we must look to that body of Anglo-American literature that addressed political issues indirectly and found a wide and appreciative audience among the rapidly expanding reading public. Jay Fliegelman has shown that when we read those popular literary, pedagogical, and didactic works for their political meaning, we gain a new perspective on both the development of political thought in the eighteenth century and the intimate connections between family and polity in eighteenth-century thought. Much of the commentary about woman's nature and her proper role can be found in novels and in the fiction and essays of the growing number of popular magazines.[5]

---

ing). A useful review of the literature of republicanism is provided by Robert E. Shalhope, "Republicanism and Early American Historiography," *William and Mary Quarterly*, 3d Ser., XXXIX (1982), 334-356. Although republicanism can be described as a wholly secular ideology, and the exact contributions of religious thought and feeling to it are certainly debated, its religious dimension must be recognized; as a popular ideology—that is, as one that was expressed in fiction and magazines by writers who reflected more than they shaped its key beliefs— republicanism was an amalgam of secular and sacred elements. Perhaps its ability to tap so many in-some-ways-contradictory roots explains republicanism's broad and enduring appeal.

[4] See Wood, *Creation*, esp. 53-65, for the republican hostility to "interest." For the history of women in the era of the Revolution see Gerda Lerner, "The Lady and the Mill Girl: Changes in the Status of Women in the Age of Jackson," in *The Majority Finds Its Past: Placing Women in History* (New York, 1979), 15-30; Joan Hoff Wilson, "The Illusion of Change: Women and the American Revolution," in Alfred F. Young, ed., *The American Revolution: Explorations in the History of American Radicalism* (DeKalb, Ill., 1976), 383-445; Mary Beth Norton, *Liberty's Daughters: The Revolutionary Experience of American Women* (New York, 1980); and Kerber, *Women of the Republic*. For a review of this literature see Norton, "Women's Experience," *AHR*, LXXXIX (1984), 593-619.

[5] Fliegelman, *Prodigals*. For the growth of literacy see Kenneth A. Lockridge, *Literacy in Colonial New England: An Enquiry into the Social Context of Literacy in the Early Modern West* (New York, 1974). For the tastes of the American reading public see David Lundberg and Henry F. May, "The Enlightened Reader in America," *Am. Qtly.*, XXVII (1976), 262-293; Garry Wills, *Inventing America: Jefferson's Declaration of Independence* (Garden City, N.Y., 1978), esp. pt. 4; and Herbert Ross Brown, *The Sentimental Novel in America, 1789-1860* (Durham, N.C., 1940), esp. chap. 1. The relevance of literature to an understanding of women's history has been explored by Mary Sumner Benson, *Women in Eigh-*

Americans drew no clear distinctions between that which was "fiction" and that which was not, between works addressed to men and works addressed to women, or even between British literature and original American creations; nor should we. Moreover, what concerns us here is the meaning that American men and women might derive from popular literature. The moral message in what might seem a diverse body of works was remarkably consistent. Magazine editors, for example, aimed both to instruct and to entertain, devoting their periodicals to "knowledge and entertainment," "entertaining knowledge and instructions," and "amusement and instruction." They and their readers could find knowledge entertaining and a properly written piece of fiction instructive.[6] Indeed, fiction served to illustrate the workings of character. In the moral world of the eighteenth century, character was all, and the study of character was an important aspect of moral philosophy, itself a branch of post-Newtonian natural science.[7] Here art and science might fuse.

Similarly, although some periodicals seem to have been addressed primarily to men and others to women, most welcomed both sexes as readers and authors and printed articles that presumably were of interest to both sexes.[8] In fact, no magazines intended exclusively for women were published in America until early in the nineteenth century.[9] The themes of courtship, marriage, and seduction figured to a greater or lesser extent in a wide range of early national publications, not only the *Boston Women's Magazine* but also, for example, Paine's *Pennsylvania Magazine* and Webster's *American Magazine*. The topic of marriage was not reserved to women or their magazines, for it was an issue of public, indeed political, import.

Finally, we must note that much of what was read in America had been written in Britain. Popular British novels were brought out in American editions, and American editors, unable to fill their periodicals with original works, borrowed freely from each other and from their British counterparts.[10] Yet what matters is not only the origin and intent of such works

---

teenth-Century America (Port Washington, N.Y., 1966 [orig. publ. New York, 1935]), and Janet Wilson James, *Changing Ideas about Women in the United States. 1776-1825* (New York, 1981).

[6] *General Magazine and Impartial Review of Knowledge and Entertainment* (Baltimore), 1798; *Ladies Magazine, and Repository of Entertaining Knowledge* (Philadelphia), 1792; and *New York Weekly Museum, or Polite Repository of Amusement and Instruction,* 1814.

[7] See Gordon S. Wood, "Conspiracy and the Paranoid Style: Causality and Deceit in the Eighteenth Century," *WMQ,* 3d Ser., XXXIX (1982), 414, and *passim.*

[8] See, for example, *American Magazine* (New York), Dec. 1787, 3, welcoming "fair readers" as both subscribers and correspondents.

[9] Frank Luther Mott, *A History of American Magazines, 1741-1850* (Cambridge, Mass., 1957), 139.

[10] For the popularity of British works in America see Fliegelman, *Prodigals,* chap.

but also the lessons Americans might have derived from them. Bernard Bailyn has shown the special meaning British political writings may have had for Americans immersed in an imperial crisis.[11] So also with the popular literature of marriage.

Indeed, a British work might be edited for the American audience in ways that would make it more applicable to the American situation. In *Clarissa*, the novel of the patriarchal family par excellence, the heroine is, as Fliegelman has put it, "purely a victim caught between two tyrannies," that of the father and that of the seducer. Although Richardson held the disobedient daughter partly responsible for her sad fate, eighteenth-century American editions of the book removed that assessment of the heroine from both the subtitle and the introduction, making Clarissa instead the innocent victim of male arrogance, imperiousness, and design. Yet *Clarissa* was more than a seduction story; it was a political parable with particular lessons for Americans, as a fearful John Adams recognized when he observed that "Democracy is Lovelace and the people are Clarissa."[12]

Americans who aimed for the separate station of a viable republic would have to learn better than Clarissa how to resist the tyrannies and seductions that republican theorists were certain they faced. Because eighteenth-century thought placed the family and the state on one continuum, that of "society," and did not yet—as the nineteenth century would—erect a barrier between the private sphere of the family and the public one of the world, it could dramatize issues of authority in terms of relationships between members of a family.[13] Accordingly, the young woman's quest for a suitable husband and her attempt to navigate between the eighteenth-century's Scylla of overweening power and its Charybdis of seductive liberty was the nation's plot as well.

Americans, successfully completing a revolution against one sort of tyranny, were bound to conclude that their young men and women also could achieve independence. The anti-patriarchalism of Revolutionary ideology dictated that tyranny presented the most immediate and obvious threat to American happiness, and patriarchal domination the chief obstacle to happy and virtuous marriage. According to the republican view, patriarchs such as "The Inexorable Father" who was "unfeeling as adamant, hard of heart as the nether mill stone," threatened always to block the happiness of their children; in this case, the father refused to let

---

2. For the reprinting of British articles in American magazines see Mott, *History*, 14-15.

[11] In particular, Bailyn, *The Ideological Origins of the American Revolution* (Cambridge, Mass., 1967), and *The Origins of American Politics* (New York, 1967).

[12] Fliegelman, *Prodigals*, 83-88; the quotation is from p. 87 and refers to abridgments only; Adams is quoted on p. 237.

[13] See n. 1, above, and Richard Sennett, *The Fall of Public Man* (New York, 1977).

his daughter marry a promising young physician who was too honest to enrich himself by overcharging his patients.[14]

So resonant was this anti-patriarchal theme that well after the Revolution American magazines published articles excoriating "parents . . . who are daily offering up the honour and happiness of their children at the shrine of interest and ambition,"[15] much as the British government had sacrificed its American colonies. Instead, "marriages should be contracted from motives of affection, rather than of interest." Fortunately, such unions were possible in "happy America," where partible inheritance—"provided our conduct does not render us unworthy"—formed "the basis of equality and the incitement to industry and caution." If America's sons and daughters were educated to "virtue and good morality," they would choose to marry for love rather than interest.[16] Being capable of exercising sound judgment, children were not obligated to obey the injunctions of narrow-minded or rapacious parents.

The rhetoric of marriage bears the same relationship to the prevailing customs as does republican ideology to the events it sought to shape and define: in each case, the terms of analysis explained long-range trends by turning them into dramas enacted by villains and heroes—or, more commonly, heroines. Historians of the family have shown that parental control of marriage declined over the course of the eighteenth century, while children's autonomy increased.[17] That trend had its roots in the

[14] *Massachusetts Magazine* (Boston), Oct. 1791, 619-620. See similarly "The Unfeeling Father," *ibid.*, May 1792, 286, and "The Precipitate Lover," *Gentleman and Lady's Town and Country Magazine* (Boston), Oct. 1794, 227-232.

[15] "Essay on Parental Care and Filial Duty," *New York Magazine*, Jan. 1794, 49. This article may well have originated in Britain, for it speaks of "rich and noble parents." See also "On the Treatment of the Fair Sex," *Lady's Magazine and Musical Repository* (New York), Apr. 1801, 214: "It has been remarked, that the public affairs of most nations have been conducted with more or less elegance, dexterity, and success, as they respectively restrain or give freedom to their women." Such articles had as their object proving (or bringing about) American superiority, of which the status of women was deemed a fit measure. See also Wood, *Creation*, 46-48, 97-107.

[16] "Improvements Suggested in Female Education," *N.Y. Mag.*, N.S., Aug. 1797, 407; "Lindor to Caroline," *Mass. Mag.*, May 1792, 312, 313. See also "On Marriage," *Gent. and Lady's Mag.*, Mar. 1789, 85-86; "On Parental Authority," *Ladies Mag.* (Philadelphia), Oct. 1792, 239; and "The Censor," *Christian's, Scholar's, and Farmer's Magazine* (Elizabethtown, N.J.), Apr.-May 1790, 49.

[17] See Daniel Scott Smith, "Parental Power and Marriage Patterns: An Analysis of Historical Trends in Hingham, Massachusetts," *Journal of Marriage and the Family*, XXXV (1973), 419-428; Robert A. Gross, *The Minutemen and Their World* (New York, 1976), 98-102; Daniel Blake Smith, *Inside the Great House: Planter Family Life in Eighteenth-Century Chesapeake Society* (Ithaca, N.Y., 1980), chap. 4; and Jan Lewis, *The Pursuit of Happiness: Family and Values in Jefferson's Virginia* (New York, 1983), 187-203. See also Randolph Trumbach, *The Rise of the Egalitarian Family: Aristocratic Kinship and Domestic Relations in Eighteenth-

Reformation; Protestantism, with its insistence that "mutual comfort" was one of marriage's primary purposes, had licensed the consensual, affectionate union.[18] Although American Puritan ministers still retained for parents, by virtue of their supposedly superior wisdom, a key role in selecting their children's mates, they nonetheless recognized that "marriage is one of the weightiest actions of a person's life, and as the Yoke fellow is suitable or unsuitable, so that condition is like to be very comfortable or uncomfortable." Nor did wealth establish a potential spouse's suitability. As Cotton Mather rhymed it, "The Wretch that is alone to *Mammon* Wed, / May chance to find a *Satan* in the Bed."[19] Interest alone, whether personal or dynastic, had never been an acceptable basis for marriage in the colonies; what changed were, on the one hand, determinations of who was best qualified, the parents or the children, to recognize merit in a potential spouse and, on the other, perceptions of how likely the affections of marriage were, in and of themselves, to assure lasting happiness. During the eighteenth century, parents grew less willing or able to exert the full range of pressures at their command to shape their children's destinies; the balance tipped in favor of the younger generation's discretion.

Thus rhetoric that implicitly likened late eighteenth-century parents to designing court ministers, bent upon subjecting their dependents, grossly exaggerated the control that parents retained over their children's marriages and, in fact, overstated the power parents had held a century earlier. Nonetheless, the rhetoric of marriage, much like that of politics, served both to expose underlying fears and to legitimate and encourage patterns that had already come to prevail.

Republican theorists endeavored to show how, in a post-patriarchal world, citizens could govern themselves, how they could form a society bound by love rather than fear. Because they deemed marriage the school of affection, authors who wrote about the institution were addressing one of their age's most pressing questions: how to make citizens fit for a republic. For example, if the choice of a mate were, or should be, the individual's, he or she must know how to select wisely. And if the parents no longer did, or should, have control, substitute parents could still give

---

Century England (New York, 1978), chap. 2, and Lawrence Stone, *The Family, Sex, and Marriage in England, 1500-1800* (New York, 1977), chaps. 7, 8.

[18] See Stone, *Family,* 135-142; Steven Ozment, *When Fathers Ruled: Family Life in Reformation Europe* (Cambridge, Mass., 1983), chap. 1; Laurel Thatcher Ulrich, *Good Wives: Image and Reality in the Lives of Women in Northern New England, 1650-1750* (New York, 1982), chap. 6; John Demos, *A Little Commonwealth: Family Life in Plymouth Colony* (New York, 1970), 82-99, 150-170; and Edmund S. Morgan, *The Puritan Family: Religion and Domestic Relations in Seventeenth-Century New England* (New York, 1966 [orig. publ. Boston, 1944]), chap. 2. See also Jean-Louis Flandrin, *Families in Former Times: Kinship, Household and Sexuality,* trans. Richard Southern (Cambridge, 1979), 145-173.

[19] Benjamin Wadsworth, *The Well-Ordered Family* (Boston, 1712), 42; Cotton Mather, *Eureka; or A Vertuous Woman Found* . . . (Boston, 1703), 3.

advice, which they did at great length in numerous tracts and essays. Parents did not abdicate; rather, they refashioned themselves into friendly paternalists who exerted influence in their families by more subtle, psychological means and in the wider world by words of friendly counsel.[20] Thus the author of "A Father's Advice to his Daughters" recommended that his own daughters and those of other men "place confidence in those who have shown affection for you in your early days, when you were incapable of making them any return."[21] Yet even those dethroned patriarchs who posed as kind advisors believed they best served young men and women by enabling them to choose wisely their own partners.

What sort of man made the ideal husband? He was republican virtue incarnate, moderation personified. He was "devout without superstition, and pious without melancholy, . . . careful without avarice, [manifesting] a kind of unconcernedness without negligence." He should be well educated but not "a pedant." A woman should look for "virtuous conduct, good temper, discretion, regularity and industry," and a "mild and even" disposition.[22] Unlike her European sisters, who supposedly married to raise their status, the American maid aimed at—and hoped to maintain— a happy medium, a domestic version of that steadily improving yet never-changing society that Gordon S. Wood has identified as the ideal society of republican dreams. Thus the happily married woman would find that her husband "would always be the same, and always pleasing."[23]

The good husband was like the good citizen; he wed "not by interest but by choice," and "he treats his wife with delicacy as a woman, with tenderness as a friend." He "ever studied the happiness of the woman he loved more than his own."[24] In fact, the ideal husband resembled more than a little the popular portrait of the Revolutionary War officer, which is precisely the occupation Royall Tyler chose for the hero of his play *The Contrast*. To ensure that the officer/suitor's character could not be mistaken, Tyler dubbed him "Colonel Manly" and gave him such quintes-

[20] See Lewis, *Pursuit of Happiness*, 175-187; Jane Turner Censer, *North Carolina Planters and Their Children, 1800-1860* (Baton Rouge, La., 1984), esp. 60-64, 68-70; and Fliegelman, *Prodigals*, 259-266.

[21] *Christian's Mag.*, Feb.-Mar. 1790, 697. This article is an extract from *A Father's Legacy to His Daughters* by Dr. John Gregory of Edinburgh. Originally appearing in England in 1774, it proved one of the most popular books published in this era in America, where it went through at least 15 editions and sold more than 20,000 copies. See Benson, *Women in Eighteenth-Century America*, 59-60, and Fliegelman, *Prodigals*, 39.

[22] "The Maid's Husband," *Baltimore Weekly Magazine*, May 20, 1801, 297; "On the Choice of a Husband," *Columbian Magazine or Monthly Miscellany* (Philadelphia), Feb. 1788, 67; "On the Choice of a Wife," *Gent. and Lady's Mag.*, Apr. 1789, 147; "Choice of a Husband," *Columbian Mag.*, Feb. 1788, 65.

[23] "Maid's Husband," *Baltimore Wkly. Mag.*, May 20, 1801, 297. Wood, *Creation*, 70-75.

[24] "Character of a Good Husband," *Mass. Mag.*, Mar. 1789, 177; "The Suspicious Lover," *ibid.*, Sept. 9, 1796, 495.

REPUBLICAN WIFE 697

sentially republican opinions as that ancient Greece declined because "the common good was lost in the pursuit of private interest" and that "the man who can plant thorns in the bosom of an unsuspecting girl is more detestable than a common robber, in the same proportion as private violence is more despicable than open force, and money of less value than happiness."[25] The qualities that made a man honorable in public life, then, distinguished him as a potential husband as well.

Men, likewise, were supposed to select republicans as their life partners. As the author of "On the Choice of a Wife" put it, "virtue, wisdom, presence of mind, patience, vigour, capacity, and application, are not *sexual* qualities; they belong to all who have duties to perform and evils to endure." Echoing standard Protestant assumptions, Americans and the British writers they chose to republish argued that the most important considerations in the selection of a wife were her "qualifications as a *companion* and a *helper*."[26] The choice was difficult, for women were not equally qualified. Suitors should be wary of frivolity and mere physical beauty or what the author of "The Intrinsic Merits of Women" called "the fashionable follies of the age." It was not that all women were suspect but that only certain types—great beauties, heiresses, and coquettes—were likely to be dangerous. Thus "the husbands of beauties are the most miserable of husbands. . . . Vexed by the vanity, exhausted by the extravagance, tortured by the inconstancy . . . life, instead of a blessing, becomes to them a purgatory." The republican gloss is equally evident in the simple reminder that "riches . . . will never alone afford happiness to their possessors."[27]

Men and women both were thus advised to seek for their mates what we can recognize as embodiments of republican ideology. They were warned at even greater length to avoid certain notorious types, those associated with the despicable aspects of European court life: flatterers, deceivers, flirts, fops, coxcombs, coquettes, and all persons lacking in honor and virtue. Indeed, writers devoted so much effort to delineating the characteristics of the coxcomb and coquette that one cannot help suspecting that the type, rather than presenting a bona fide threat to naive American beaux and belles, served as a distillation, much like the tyrannical ruler or the designing minister, of what the age most feared. Flirts and fops, coxcombs and coquettes romp through the pages of republican literature with abandon. Their names are code words that signify luxury, vice, and deceit; their presence in a story points almost without exception to an

[25] Royall Tyler, *The Contrast: A Comedy in Five Acts* (Boston, 1920 [orig. publ. Philadelphia, 1790]), 80, 82.

[26] *Boston Weekly Magazine*, Dec. 29, 1804, 37; printed also in *Lady's Mag.* (New York), Mar. 1802, 168, 165. The articles are selections from *Letters from a Father to His Son* (1794) by John Aiken, an English physician, quoted in James, *Changing Ideas*, 143-144.

[27] *Christian's Mag.*, Dec. 1789–Jan. 1790, 628, 627. "Thoughts on the Choice of a Wife," *Columbian Mag.*, Mar. 1792, 176. See also "On the Choice of a Wife," *Christian's Mag.*, Aug.-Sept. 1790, 351-353.

171

unhappy ending. They promise ruin not only for themselves and their victims but also for the infant nation, for they practice habits that were commonly believed to spell the death of republics. So reasoned the author of "The Philosophy of Coquetry": "so long as the sensualities and pride of one sex shall delight in luxurious habits and ostentatious living; so long as the vanities of the other shall be gratified by splendid personal decorations, costly refinements, and glittering equipages—or, more philosophically speaking, so long as we shall be enslaved in a refined state of society, by numerous and factitious wants, we shall look in vain for disinterested alliances, and an union of the sexes resulting from mental attachment."[28]

Reform began with the individual; a republican society required virtuous men and women. That belief permeates the purportedly "True Story" of "Eugenia—or the Coquette." The girl of the title had parents who were "dissipated and luxurious. . . . [T]hey looked forward to immense wealth. . . . Pride, pomp, and luxury dazzled their eyes." Indeed, "without a particle of principle, [Eugenia's] father countenanced depredation, at a time when the hirelings of tyranny were not sparing in the arts of devastation." In this republican vision a nation could be no better than the individuals who constitute it. In this story a sad fate for the nation is averted when Eugenia, who has inherited her parents' vices, jilts the decent young man who had courted her, freeing him to marry "a woman, who boasts only those real charms. . . . which constitute the perfect wife. . . . [A]s she never experienced the deceit of a fop, so he congratulates himself that he has escaped from the smiles of a coquette." Significantly, Eugenia herself is almost incidental to the story. It is her parents, stand-ins for a corrupt British government, and their ability to thwart a truly affectionate union that are most feared. In such a view, to fall for a coquette is to surrender republican virtue, and to flirt is to commit an act of treason.[29]

When courtship and marriage are infused with political meaning, women inevitably and inescapably become political beings. Make no mistake: these first formulations of a feminine political role were not fundamentally feminist. They were not devised by women in particular, nor was their aim primarily to enhance the position of women. The dynamic, rather, was republican and anti-patriarchal: it juxtaposed the virtuous, independent child and the oppressive, corrupting parent, and it found in the union of two virtuous individuals the true end of society and the fit paradigm for political life. Such a conceptualization of the relationship between family and polity represents more a subtle shift than a clean break from earlier models. When Puritans designated the family "a little

[28] *N.Y. Mag.*, N.S., Nov. 1796, 583. The classic example, of course, is Hannah Foster's *The Coquette; or, The History of Eliza Wharton* . . . (Boston, 1797).

[29] *Columbian Mag.*, Nov. 1792, 334-335. See also "The Flirt. A Moral Tale," *ibid.*, June 1791, 389-391; "A Vindication of the Fair Sex, Against the Charge of Preferring Coxcombs to Men of Worth and Genius," *ibid.*, July 1792, 28-30; and "The Ladies New Catechism," *Baltimore Wkly. Mag.*, May 20, 1801, 303.

commonwealth," they meant it to be "a schoole wherein the first principles and grounds of government and subjection are learned: whereby men are fitted to greater matters in Church or commonwealth."[30] In such a family the relationship between parent and child was most important.

When anti-patriarchalists in the eighteenth century substituted marriage for parenthood as the fundamental familial relationship, they did not, however, question the assumption that the family was but the society in miniature. Society still appeared as the family writ large, with the same sorts of relationships deemed appropriate for both the as-yet-undifferentiated spheres of home and world. Yet in shifting interest from the parent-child nexus to the husband-wife bond, eighteenth-century authors necessarily raised women to a new moral and political stature. When the key relationship in a society is that between father and son or ruler and subject, women may conveniently be ignored; when the most important relationship is between conjugal equals, and when the family is still seen as the correlative of the larger society, then women can no longer be overlooked. If the affectionate union between a man and his wife, freely entered into, without tyrannical interference, is the model for all the relationships in the society and the polity, then the wife, as an indispensable half of the marital union, is a political creature.

To the extent that the success of the republican endeavor rested upon the character of citizens, republicanism demanded virtue of women, not because it numbered them as citizens but because it recognized how intimately women, in consensual unions, were connected to men. A virtuous man required a virtuous mate. Moreover, republicanism called upon every means at its disposal to assure male virtue. That obsession with virtue, deriving its force from the fusion of Protestant and republican notions of character, persisted long after the Revolution had been won and the Constitution ratified. Well into the nineteenth century, Americans linked the fate of their nation to the virtues of its people.[31] Even if, as several historians have suggested, certain thinkers, before the end of the eighteenth century, had embraced liberalism and its premise of the self-interested individual,[32] popular writers and, presumably, their audience had not. One writer put it emphatically: "Private vices are *not* public

[30] William Gouge, *Of Domesticall Duties* (London, 1622), quoted in Demos, *Little Commonwealth*, xix.

[31] See Perry Miller, "From the Covenant to the Revival," in James Ward Smith and A. Leland Jamison, eds., *The Shaping of American Religion* (Princeton, N.J., 1961), 322-368. For the legacy of republicanism see Drew R. McCoy, *The Elusive Republic: Political Economy in Jeffersonian America* (Chapel Hill, N.C., 1980).

[32] See, for example, Joyce Appleby, "Commercial Farming and the 'Agrarian Myth' in the Early Republic," *JAH*, LXVIII (1982), 833-849, and "What Is Still American in the Political Philosophy of Thomas Jefferson?" *WMQ*, 3d Ser., XXXIX (1982), 287-309; John Patrick Diggins, *The Lost Soul of American Politics: Virtue, Self-Interest, and the Foundations of Liberalism* (New York, 1984); and Isaac Kramnick, "Republican Revisionism Revisited," *AHR*, LXXXVII (1982), 629-664.

benefits." That rejection of Bernard Mandeville infused much of the early
national literature, and that conceptualization of society—which continued to see the family as the microcosm of the wider world and to insist that
"public good must grow out of private virtue"[33]—held out a significant
role for women.

"A woman of virtue and prudence is a public good—a public benefac-
tor." She has the power to make "public decency . . . a fashion—and public
virtue the only example." And how is woman to accomplish that great
end? By her influence over the manners of men. Indeed, "nothing short of
a general reformation of manners would take place, were the ladies to use
their power in discouraging our licentious manners." Such a role might
seem trivial did Americans not consider "the general reformation of
manners" one of the young nation's most important goals, and did they not
think women fully capable of contributing to it. Women might begin by
reforming themselves, for "there is not a more certain test of national
depravity, than that which presents itself in the degeneracy of female
manners."[34]

Male manners, however, were of more concern, and in changing them
women were to play their most important role. So argued men, such as the
essayist who held that women who were the beneficiaries of a "virtuous
and refined education" might contribute "no less to public good than to
private happiness. A gentleman, who at present must degrade himself into
a fop or a coxcomb in order to please the ladies, would soon find that their
favor could not be gained but by exerting every manly talent in public and
private life." That same view could be expressed by a woman—for
example, Miss C. Hutchings, who assured her fellow boarding-school
graduates of the influence of "female manners on society in general":
"were all women rational, unaffected and virtuous, coxcombs, flatterers
and libertines would no longer exist." Such arguments rested on several
important new assumptions. First, although the concern with "manners"
betokened an upper-class emphasis upon gentility, the insistence that
women are—or can be—a moral force transforms manners into mores,
into the moral foundation of the society. Thus "it is . . . to the virtues of
the fair . . . that society must be indebted for its moral, as well as its natural
preservation."[35] Second, women play their moral role not by denying

[33] *Gent. and Lady's Mag.*, July 1789, 311; "Review of the Boarding School,"
Columbian Phenix and Boston Review, May 1800, 278. See also "The Reflector No.
V," *Ladies' Monitor* (New York), Dec. 5, 1801, 124-125.
[34] "Scheme for Increasing the Power of the Fair Sex," *Ladies Mag.* (Philadelphia),
June 1792, 22, 24, reprinted in *Baltimore Wkly. Mag.*, Apr. 1, 1801, 241; "The
Reflector No. IX," *Ladies' Monitor*, Jan 2, 1802, 156.
[35] "The Influence of the Female Sex on the Enjoyments of Social Life,"
Christian's Mag., Oct.-Nov. 1789, 497, reprinted in *Columbian Mag.*, Mar. 1790,
153-154; "Influence of the Female Character on Society in General," *Boston Wkly.
Mag.*, Oct. 30, 1802, 3; "Reflector No. IX," *Ladies' Monitor*, Jan. 2, 1802, 156.

their sexuality, by becoming "passionless,"[36] but by using it to tempt men to be good.

This conceptualization of female influence seems to have intrigued men and women in the decades just after the Revolution. Magazines printed and reprinted numbers of articles with similar titles and sentiments: "Female Influence," "Scheme for Increasing the Power of the Fair Sex," "The Influence of the Female Sex on the Enjoyments of Social Life," "The Power of Beauty, and the Influence the Fair Sex might have in Reforming the Manners of the World."[37] These, with a host of similar articles, argued that the potential for beneficial female influence was almost unlimited.

The height of a woman's influence was reached during the period of "love and courtship," which, "it is universally allowed, invest a lady with more authority than in any other situation that falls to the lot of human beings." A young man who addressed his classmates at Columbia College's commencement elaborated: "She can mold the taste, the manners, and the conduct of her admirers, according to her pleasure." Moreover, "she can, even to a great degree, change their tempers and dispositions, and superinduce habits entirely new." Thus it was not in childhood that a man was most malleable; rather, it was when, grown to maturity, he sought the favors of a young lady that he was most susceptible to influence. "By the judicious management of this noble passion [love], a passion with which the truly accomplished of the fair sex never fail of inspiring men, what almost miraculous reformations may be brought about?"[38]

Once she had seduced him into virtue, the married woman's task was to preserve her husband in the exalted state to which her influence had raised him. "It rests with her, not only to confirm those virtuous habits which he has already acquired, but also to excite his perseverance in the paths of rectitude."[39] The boldness of this formulation is stunning. What earlier

[36] On the changing conceptualization of woman's nature see Ruth H. Bloch, "Untangling the Roots of Modern Sex Roles: A Survey of Four Centuries of Change," *Signs*, IV (1978), 237-252, and "Feminine Ideals," *Feminist Studies*, IV (1978), 101-126; Catherine M. Scholten, *Childbearing in American Society, 1650-1850* (New York, 1985); and Nancy F. Cott, "Passionlessness: An Interpretation of Victorian Sexual Ideology, 1790-1850," *Signs*, IV (1978), 219-236.

[37] "An Oration delivered at the Annual Commencement of Columbia College," *N.Y. Mag.*, May 1795, 297-305; *Ladies Mag.* (Philadelphia), June 1792, 22-24, and *Baltimore Wkly. Mag.*, Apr. 1, 1801, 241; *Christian's Mag.*, Oct.-Nov. 1789, 496-497; *Columbian Mag.*, Mar. 1790, 153-154; *Boston Wkly. Mag.*, Mar. 3, 1804, 73-74.

[38] "Female Influence," *N.Y. Mag.*, May 1795, 299, 300. See similarly Benjamin Rush, "Thoughts upon Female Education, Accommodated to the Present State of Society, Manners, and Government in the United States of America," in Frederick Rudolph, ed., *Essays on Education in the Early Republic* (Cambridge, Mass., 1965), 25-40. See also Rush's "A Plan for the Establishment of Public Schools and the Diffusion of Knowledge in Pennsylvania," *ibid.*, 21-22.

[39] "Female Influence," *N.Y. Mag.*, May 1795, 300.

Americans perceived as Eve's most dangerous characteristic, her seduc-
tiveness, is here transformed into her capacity for virtue. Woman was to
lead man into rectitude, to lure him to the exercise of manly virtue. What
miraculous reformations became possible when the attraction between the
sexes, which for millennia had been considered the cause of the fall of
mankind, could be transformed into the bedrock of the nation! Women
indeed had great power—nothing less than the ability, as one magazine
implored, "to make our young men, not in empty words, but in deed and
in truth, republicans."[40]

That was why so much importance was attached to the education of
women. Passion could and must be tempered by reason. If Eve's daughters
could deserve, as one young woman put it, to be "extolled for the beauties
of their minds instead of their persons . . . , then would mankind enjoy
that happiness which was first intended for the happy pair in Paradise."
Were women properly educated, "then will the halcyon days dawn, and
human nature appear in its highest beauty and perfection." Few topics
excited more interest in the early national period than education, for it
seemed to hold the key to making "our women virtuous and respectable;
our men brave, honest, and honorable—and the *American* People in
general *an* EXAMPLE *of* HONOUR *and* VIRTUE to the rest of the
world."[41] Writers were not always clear or certain about whether the
American people were naturally virtuous or whether, instead, they merely
had unusual potential to be so; hence the extremes of millennial hope and
overwhelming fear, as men and women envisioned both the prospect of
paradise on earth and the potential for disastrous failure.[42]

Unless we recognize how grandiose American expectations could be
and how terrifying was the possibility that they might not be realized, we
cannot fully appreciate how central female education was to the republican
agenda. While it is true that some reformers advocated educating women
so that they, in turn, could teach their children,[43] the more important

[40] "Female Economy," *Ladies' Literary Cabinet* (New York), July 8, 1820, 67. See
also "Woman," *N.Y. Wkly. Museum*, Aug. 27, 1814, 132.

[41] "Clio," "On Female Education," *N.Y. Mag.*, Sept. 1794, 570; "The Gossip
No. XXVII," *Boston Wkly. Mag.*, May 28, 1803, 125. See also "On Female
Education," *Royal Am. Mag.*, Jan. 1774, 10, and *Ladies' Lit. Cab.*, Aug. 12, 1820,
112. For the importance that republicans attached to education see Lawrence A.
Cremin, *American Education: The National Experience, 1783-1876* (New York,
1980), 103-148. See also the essays in Rudolph, ed., *Essays on Education*.

[42] Wood, *Creation*, chap. 3; Miller, "Covenant to Revival," in Smith and Jamison,
eds., *Shaping of American Religion*, 322-368; Charles Royster, *A Revolutionary
People at War: The Continental Army and American Character, 1775-1783* (Chapel
Hill, N.C., 1979). See also "Education," *Am. Mag.*, Dec. 1787, 22-26.

[43] For example, "Review of the Cultivation of Female Intellect in the United
States," *Virginia Evangelical and Literary Magazine* (Richmond), May 1827, 244,
June 1827, 292, as well as the works cited in n. 39, above. See also Kerber,
"Daughters of Columbia: Educating Women for the Republic, 1787-1805," in
Stanley Elkins and Eric McKitrick, eds., *The Hofstadter Aegis: A Memorial* (New
York, 1974), 36-59.

consideration, always, was to make women into fit companions for republican men and, especially, reliable guarantors of masculine virtue. Hence, as one man put it, "would the females keep in view the influence they possess over our education, they would not fail to perceive an attention to their own as nearly connected with the welfare of mankind. . . . Do they admire and respect the man of sense, and treat with contempt the coxcomb and the fop, [a young man] will, to recommend himself to their esteem, form himself to usefulness and virtue."[44] No one argued that women were naturally more virtuous or pure than men; rather, they had the capacity to overcome weakness and become good.

Nor, certainly, were all women natural republicans; the books and magazines of the age are populated with as many coquettes and flirts as coxcombs and fops. Human nature was malleable, and if it could be bent toward the good, to make a republican, it might also be warped toward evil,[45] creating a coxcomb or coquette. Obviously, those who believed in the malleability of character rejected Calvinistic assumptions about innate depravity, and nowhere is their departure from the older orthodoxy more clear than in their expectations of feminine virtue. Thus one essayist advised women of the enormous power they had at their disposal: "as *Milton* says, *The world lies all before them,* and it is theirs to mould into what shape they please."[46]

That paraphrase and application of the penultimate lines of *Paradise Lost* are a good deal more sanguine than the original. So optimistic a reading of Milton, with its suggestion that the world was Eve's to make, even into a new paradise, drew upon millennial hopes that had become an integral part of American culture.[47] To be sure, such expectations did not always express a literal belief in the imminence of Christ's thousand-year reign, and they were often dampened by a lurking fear that they might not be realized. Still, the Revolution unloosed a flood of optimism—so much, in fact, that some Americans could begin to think of themselves as "new" men, veritable American Adams, given the opportunity to make the world and themselves anew. As Paine put it, America "has it in her choice to do, and to live as she pleases. The world is in her hands." This persistent strain in American thought is well known to students of American culture.[48] Yet there could be no Adam without an Eve; in the garden, as described in Genesis and by Milton, Adam had a companion who sinned first. Without Eve, Adam presumably would have remained in Paradise; that reminder of

[44] "On Love," *General Mag. and Review,* June 1798, 22.

[45] Fliegelman, *Prodigals,* 15.

[46] "The Power of Beauty, and the Influence the Fair Sex might have in Reforming the Manners of the World," *Boston Wkly. Mag.,* Mar. 3, 1804, 74.

[47] See Ruth H. Bloch, *Visionary Republic: Millennial Themes in American Thought, 1756-1800* (New York, 1985).

[48] "The Crisis, No. 15," in Howard Fast, ed., *The Selected Work of Tom Paine* and *Citizen Tom Paine* (New York, 1946), 84. See, in particular, R.W.B. Lewis, *The American Adam: Innocence, Tragedy, and Tradition in the Nineteenth Century* (Chicago, 1955), and D. H. Lawrence, *Studies in Classic American Literature* (New York, 1923).

woman's unhappy role in effecting human destiny had never been far from the minds of Puritan ministers such as Cotton Mather.[49] To the extent that the Fall was the most compelling of all biblical episodes for Puritans, woman played a central, and unenviable, role in the central drama of mankind. Milton's version of the Fall achieved wide popularity in America at the end of the eighteenth century, and not just among the heirs of the Puritans;[50] his Eve, although more sympathetic than the stock Puritan version, still bore primary responsibility for the great calamity.

Thus, to move to a more helpful view of human potential, it was necessary first to come to terms with the Fall. Several avenues were available. One was to shift the focus of religion from Fall to Redemption; that path was taken, particularly in the nineteenth century, as American Protestantism became more Christocentric.[51] Another option was for Adam, in effect, to go his own way, without Eve, remaking the world as an all-male paradise; classic American literature, written by men, followed that route in the nineteenth century.[52] But Americans of the late eighteenth century, steeped as they were in orthodox readings of the Bible, and reminded of them by Milton, could not remake Adam and give the story of the Fall a happier ending without first remaking the woman who had been first in sin. And that is precisely what they did.

Some revamped Eve clearly and consciously, offering new exegeses of Genesis, as did the author of "The Nobility of Woman Kind," who reasoned that "the man gave us death; not the woman. The woman did amiss ignorantly and from deception: But the man knew, that he did amiss." Judith Sargent Murray, writing in the *Massachusetts Magazine* under the pen name "Constantia," offered an even more positive assessment of Eve's brief residence in Eden. Eve's motive in eating the forbidden fruit, Murray suggested, was admirable; she hungered for knowledge. Even though Adam could see that his mate had grown no wiser, he nonetheless tasted the fruit himself. His motive? "A base pusillanimous attachment to a woman! . . . Thus it should seem, that all the arts of the grand deceiver . . , were requisite to mislead our general mother, while the

[49] See, for example, Cotton Mather, *Ornaments for the Daughters of Zion; or, The Character and Happiness of a Vertuous Woman* . . . (Cambridge, Mass., 1692), 1. See also Scholten, *Childbearing,* 12.

[50] George F. Sensabaugh details the spread of Milton's works in America. Although his picture of connubial bliss was occasionally referred to in American publications before the Revolution, it was the final quarter of the century and especially its last decades that brought "American acceptance of Milton's authority on a national scale" (*Milton in Early America* [Princeton, N.J., 1964], 98, and *passim*).

[51] See H. Richard Niebuhr, *The Kingdom of God in America* (New York, 1937), chaps. 3 and 4, and Ann Douglas, *The Feminization of American Culture* (New York, 1977), chap. 4. See also Fliegelman's brilliant analysis of "The Familial Politics of the Fortunate Fall," in *Prodigals,* chap. 3.

[52] See Leslie A. Fiedler, *Love and Death in the American Novel* (New York, 1960), and Lawrence, *Studies.*

father of mankind forfeited his own, and relinquished the happiness of posterity, merely in compliance with the blandishments of a female."[53] Thus could common assumptions about feminine moral weakness and masculine intellectual strength be turned cleverly on their heads.

Still, most writers who wished to revise popular evaluations of Eve did not take so assertively feminist a tack as to reinterpret the story of the Fall. For one reason, they might be refuted by traditional readings that kept a culpable sensuality, both feminine and masculine, at the center of the story.[54] Instead, those who were inclined to paint the first mother in more flattering hues tended to focus not so much upon her unhappy departure from Eden as upon her more pleasing qualities when she was still there. Here Americans took their cue from Milton, and in the years just after the Revolution his Eve "began to emerge as a pattern of womanly perfection."[55] Sometimes an author quoted Milton directly, as did Dr. John Gregory, an Edinburgh physician whose *Legacy* to his daughters was popular in America: "Milton had my idea, when he says of Eve 'Grace was in all her steps. / Heaven in her eye. In every gesture dignity and love'." Samuel Low, author of the play *The Politician Out-witted*, must have assumed that his audience would recognize his source when he quoted the same lines, without attribution, to describe his heroine.[56]

Often Milton's influence was indirect but unmistakable; his "fair angelic Eve," created "for softness . . . and sweet attractive grace,"[57] served as model for the ideal woman who would display "softness and delicacy of manners, unaffecting beauty, unassuming worth, modesty happily blended with good humour." The Miltonic influence is also clear in a poem entitled "Female Character," published in 1792:

Queen of every gentle passion,
Tender sympathy and love;
Perfect work of Heav'nly fashion,
Miniature of charms above.

Love and grace in rich profusion,
Soft'ning man's ferocious soul;

[53] *Royal Am. Mag.*, Mar. 1775, 104; "On the Equality of the Sexes," *Mass. Mag.*, Apr. 1790, 224-225. See also "On Woman," *Boston Wkly. Mag.*, July 21, 1804, 153: "if our first parents were at all to be blamed, Adam was by far the most culpable."

[54] For example, "The Passenger No. XXXI," *Boston Wkly. Mag.*, Sept. 15, 1804, 185, and "On the Forbidden Fruit," *Mass. Mag.*, Oct. 1791, 617-618.

[55] Sensabaugh, *Milton*, 115.

[56] Reprinted, without attribution, under the title "A Father's Advice to his Daughters," *Christian's Mag.*, June-July 1789, 191; *The Politician Out-witted*, in Montrose J. Moses, ed., *Representative Plays by American Dramatists* (New York, 1918, 1946), I, 372.

[57] *Paradise Lost*, bk. 5, line 74, bk. 4, line 298.

All creation's fair conclusion,
Form'd to beautify the whole.[58]

Woman is the last of God's works, created not, as the pre-Miltonic tradition had it, to bring about man's fall, but rather to remind him, after that event, of the paradise they had once shared and hoped still to regain.[59]

Jay Fliegelman has noted that Milton's description of Eve played an important role in "the secularization and feminization of 'grace'" in the eighteenth century as the word took on an aesthetic meaning.[60] By the same token, woman, "Heav'n's last best gift," promised salvation; she, like Christ, pointed the way toward redemption. Yet it is redemption with a difference, for when sacred history is rewritten in such a way—as American popular writers would have it—that woman is gracious and man has not yet sinned, then we can imagine the time before the Fall when the world was Paradise and our first parents

In naked majesty seemed lords of all,
And worthy seemed, for in their looks divine
The image of their glorious Maker shone . . . [61]

It was to this image of prelapsarian godliness that Americans, in the era just after the American Revolution, responded.

The Republican Wife, then, was Eve, and republican marriage represented Paradise, a veritable "heaven on earth." Taking their model from Milton's hymn to wedded love in Book IV of *Paradise Lost*, American publications described marriage in unabashedly Edenic terms. "The house of the married man is his paradise. . . . In the existence of a married man, there is no termination[;] when death overtakes him, he is only translated from one heaven to another."[62] Marriage is "the highest state of human felicity, and resembles that of the beneficent beings above." For this reason the choice of a marriage partner was so important. A correspondent to the *Christian's, Scholar's, and Farmer's Magazine* put it simply: "The Choice of a Wife" was one "on which not only [mankind's] present welfare, but even their everlasting felicity may depend."[63]

[58] "On Masculine Manners in the Fair Sex," *Boston Wkly. Mag.*, May 5, 1804, 109; *N.Y. Mag.*, May 1792.

[59] See Diane Kelsey McColley, *Milton's Eve* (Urbana, Ill., 1983).

[60] Fliegelman, *Prodigals*, 130. See also "On the Difference between Grace and Beauty," *Royal Am. Mag.*, Feb. 1775, 43-45.

[61] *Paradise Lost*, bk. 5, line 19, bk. 4, lines 290-293.

[62] "On Matrimonial Felicity," *Gent. and Lady's Mag.*, Sept. 1784, 194; "The Felicity of Matrimony," *ibid.*, Aug. 1789, 375-376, reprinted in *N.Y. Mag.*, N.S., Sept. 1797, 474. For direct references to Milton see "On Love," *Ladies Mag.* (Philadelphia), June 1792, 34-35, and Sensabaugh, *Milton*, notes on 42, 111-113, 195-200.

[63] "Letter from Eliza," *Pennsylvania Magazine* (Philadelphia), Apr. 1776, 168;

The Edenic vision of marriage, then, served to bridge the anti-patriarchalism of the eighteenth century and the domesticity of the nineteenth. If the patriarchal model of familial relationships was suited to a hierarchically organized society, and if, as Nancy F. Cott has suggested,[64] domesticity went hand in hand with mid-nineteenth-century democratic liberalism, the Edenic vision fit just as nicely with the canons of republicanism. Like republicanism itself, Edenic republican marriage presented itself as egalitarian. Republican characterizations of marriage echoed with the words *equal, mutual,* and *reciprocal,* and marriage was described as a friendship between equals. An essay "Addressed to the Ladies," for example, urged "every young married woman to seek the friend of her heart in the husband of her affection. There, and there only, is that true equality, both of rank and fortune, and cemented by mutual interests, and mutual . . . pledges to be found. . . . There and there only will she be sure to meet with reciprocal confidence, unfeigned attachment and tender solicitude to soothe every care." Indeed, no word better summarizes republican notions of marriage than *friendship.* "Marriage is, or should be, the most perfect state of friendship. Mutual interest produces mutual assistance." Another writer defined the good marriage in almost the same words as "the highest instance of human friendship." In fact, "love" was nothing more than "friendship raised to its highest pitch."[65]

Marriage, quite simply, was friendship exalted. Its pleasures derived from "mutual return of *conjugal love*. . . . When two minds are . . . engaged by the ties of reciprocal sincerity, each alternately receives and communicates a transport that is inconceivable to all, but those that are in this situation." Marriage was intended, another writer concluded, "to be the basis and the cement of those numberless tender sympathies, mutual endearments and interchanges of love between the mutual parties themselves, which make up not the morality only, but even the chief happiness of conjugal life." Marriage was moral because it fused "virtuous love and friendship; the one supplying it with a constant rapture, the other regulating it by the rules of reason." True marriage was quite unlike "those unnatural and disproportionate matches that are daily made upon worldly views, where interest or lust are the only motives."[66] True marriage was

---

Christian's Mag., Aug.-Sept. 1790, 351-353. See similarly "On Matrimonial Felicity," *Gent. and Lady's Mag.,* Sept. 1784, 193-194.

[64] Cott, *The Bonds of Womanhood: "Woman's Sphere" in New England, 1780-1835* (New Haven, Conn. 1977), 65.

[65] "On Friendship," *Christian's Mag.,* June-July 1790, 226; "Praise of Marriage," *Boston Wkly. Mag.,* Apr. 7, 1804, 93; "On Marriage," *General Mag. and Review,* July 1798, 42; "Reflections on Marriage Unions," *N.Y. Mag.,* Oct. 1790, 561. See also "Gossip No. XXXII," *Boston Wkly. Mag.,* July 9, 1803, 149; "Conjugal Love," *Mass. Mag.,* Feb. 1792, 102; and "Philo. No. XIV," *ibid.,* Nov. 1790, 664: "Friendship is the reciprocal attachment of two persons of the same sex. *Love* of two persons of different sexes."

[66] "Conjugal Love," *Mass. Mag.,* Feb. 1792, 102; "On the Pleasures Arising from a Union Between the Sexes," *Columbian Mag.,* Jan. 1787, 244.

proportionate; put another way, it was symmetrical. Indeed, the mutuality and reciprocity that republicans so prized were inconceivable in an asymmetrical union—the "slavery" of so-called barbaric cultures, in which women were thoroughly subordinated to men.[67] That republican marriage was symmetrical does not mean that it was fully egalitarian; rather, men and women were opposite sides of the same coin or, as a popular fable had it, two halves of a being that had once been sundered. Neither could be whole until it found its other half.[68] Nor could the halves be fully moral when separate, for Eve's love and Adam's reason were equally necessary to the prelapsarian vision. As heirs to the Enlightenment, American republicans sought the happy medium between—or, more precisely, a fusion of—passion and intellect, head and heart. Eighteenth-century moral philosophy, as it was popularized in American magazines, taught both that passion must be regulated by reason[69] and that "no real felicity can exist independent of susceptibility and affection, and the heart of him who is cold to the soothing voice of friendship, dead to the melting strains of love, and senseless to the plaintive pleadings of distress, is a mansion only calculated for demoniac spirits, or a cheerless dwelling for disgust and spleen."[70] Adam and Eve, reason and love, are each indispensable, and the symmetrical marriage brings them together.

[67] For the assertion that the subordination or "slavery" of women was characteristic of barbaric cultures see, for example, "On the Treatment of the Fair Sex," *Lady's Mag.* (New York), Apr. 1801, 214-215; "An Occasional Letter on the Female Sex," *Penn. Mag.*, Aug. 1775, 362-364; "Domestic Life of the Arabs," *General Mag. and Review*, July 1798, 34-36; and "The Influence of the Female Sex on the Enjoyments of Social Life," *Columbian Mag.*, Mar. 1790, 153-154: "Matrimony, among savages, having no object but propagation and slavery, is a very humbling state for the female sex." On the other hand, the position of women in societies characterized by commerce, large cities, and an advanced, complex civilization was not necessarily more enviable. See, for example, "Marriage Ceremonies of different Countries Compared," *ibid.*, June 1787, 491: "The trade of fortune-hunting . . . seem[s] to be confined to the old crowded cities, while the tedious peculiarities of European settlements of fortunes, &c are scarcely understood by the inhabitants of America." Americans saw their society—and its women—poised somewhere between barbarity and excessive economic and cultural development with its attendant corruptions. See McCoy, *Elusive Republic*, chap. 1. See also "Education," *Am. Mag.*, Dec. 1787, 22-26. To be sure, the cyclical view of the rise and fall of civilizations, which McCoy illuminates, and the linear Christian eschatology are inconsistent; nonetheless, both sorts of cultural analysis appeared side by side in the era's magazines. Perhaps the pessimistic cyclical paradigm only made the more hopeful Christian one more appealing.

[68] "On Marriage," *General Mag. and Review*, July 1798, 43.

[69] For example, *Boston Wkly. Mag.*, Sept. 24, 1803, 193, and "On the Government of the Passions," *Mass. Mag.*, July 1796, 402-404. See also Wills, *Inventing America*.

[70] "On the Duties which we Owe to Society," *Lady's Mag.* (New York), Jan. 1801, 16.

For this reason—that in checking passion and socializing reason the conjugal union made mankind truly virtuous—marriage was the model for society. The single life, according to John Witherspoon, writing as "Epaminondas" in the *Pennsylvania Magazine* on the eve of the Revolution, "narrows the mind and closes the heart." He asserted unequivocally the "absolute necessity of marriage for the service of the state."[71] The pure love of marriage formed the basis for "social virtue," for "while other passions concentrate man on himself, love makes him live in another, subdues selfishness, and reveals to him the pleasure of ministering to the object of his love. . . . The lover becomes a husband, a parent, a citizen." The "marriage institution," then, "is the first to produce moral order." For that reason, "marriage has ever been considered by every wise state the sinew of its strength and the foundation of its true greatness." Marriage formed the basis of all other relationships, both in the family, because it led to parenthood, and in the society, because it schooled men in the disinterested benevolence that was supposed by republican ideologues to constitute virtue.[72] In sum, as an essayist in the *Key* put it, "nothing is so honourable as MARRIAGE, nothing so comfortable both to body and mind. . . . It is marriage alone that knits and binds all the sinews of society together and makes the life of man honourable to himself, useful to others, and grateful to the God of nature. . . . Is there anything on earth nearer heaven?" Lest that promise of heaven-on-earth be insufficient to persuade his readers, the writer continued: "That MAN who resolves to live without WOMAN, or that WOMAN who resolves to live without MAN, are [*sic*] ENEMIES TO THE COMMUNITY in which they dwell, INJURIOUS TO THEMSELVES, DESTRUCTIVE TO THE WORLD, APOSTATES TO NATURE, and REBELS AGAINST HEAVEN AND EARTH."[73] The man or woman who proposed to live alone, then, was heretic and traitor both.[74]

Like republicanism, the doctrine of symmetrical marriage subordinated individual interest to the greater good of the whole. Accordingly, marriages based upon interest were to be loathed; true marriage was the model for disinterested benevolence. Unlike the canon of domesticity, in which "women's self-renunciation was called upon to remedy men's

[71] "Reflections on Marriage," *Penn. Mag.*, Sept. 1775, 411, 408, later published as "Letters on Marriage" in *The Works of the Rev. John Witherspoon . . .* , 2d ed. (Philadelphia, 1802), IV, 161-183.

[72] "On Love," *N.Y. Mag.*, June 1791, 311; "A Second Vindication of the Rights of Woman," *Ladies' Monitor*, Aug. 15, 1801, 12; "The Reflector No. 1," *ibid.*, Nov. 7, 1801, 92. See also "On Matrimonial Felicity," *Gent. and Lady's Mag.*, Sept. 1784, 193-194; "On Love," *Ladies Mag.* (Philadelphia), June 1792, 34-37; "Fashionable Miscellany," *Baltimore Wkly. Mag.*, July 12, 1800, 91-92; and "On Marriage," *General Mag. and Review*, July 1798, 41-45.

[73] "From the Genius of Liberty," *Key* (Fredericktown, Md.), Apr. 14, 1798, 105-106.

[74] Numerous articles attacked bachelors while pitying spinsters. See, for example, *Columbian Mag.*, Apr. 1790, 213-214, and *Mass. Mag.*, July 1791, 410-411.

self-alienation,"[75] idealized republican marriage required men and women both to display virtue. Male and female were two halves of one whole whose name was concord; the ideal marriage was a scene of prelapsarian harmony. As the author of "On the Necessity of Domestic Concord" noted, "peace" was more important even than "plenty."[76] In order for "harmony" and "concord" to prevail, husband and wife were to be of one mind; they could not disagree.[77] To prevent a conflict-filled marriage, one must choose one's mate wisely; probably no consideration was more important than "a similarity of sentiments and dispositions," for where there is "an union of souls, and a consistent harmony of mental ideas . . . discord will keep at an awful distance, and an universal sympathy, productive of an ineffable bliss, will ever attend them. . . . O happiness divine! source of concordant minds!" An essayist in *New York Magazine* expressed the same idea more matter-of-factly: "There cannot be too near an equality, too exact a harmony, betwixt a married couple." Indeed, "the idea of power on either side should be totally banished."[78]

Conjugal affection, then, was not coercive. Nor did it admit of any "selfish or sensual alloy." Marriage was the republic in miniature; it was chaste, disinterested, and free from the exercise of arbitrary power. And, like republican citizens, husband and wife were most likely to find happiness when, as Witherspoon suggested, they shared the same rank, the same education, and the same habits of life.[79]

It is tempting to suppose that the ideology of the republican marriage was but the rhetorical manifestation of the newly affectionate conjugal union, and that both rhetoric and reality represented positive and progressive change.[80] Yet we must remember that republicanism, like Janus,

[75] Cott, *Bonds*, 90. The model of self-denying femininity was the mother; the idealization of motherhood, hence, was more characteristic of 19th-century domesticity than of late 18th-century republicanism.

[76] *Key*, Apr. 7, 1798, 93.

[77] "Fashionable Miscellany," *Baltimore Wkly. Mag.*, July 12, 1800, 92; "Remarks on Family Government," *Mass. Mag.*, June 1791, 352-353; "A Panegyric on the Delights of Matrimony," *ibid.*, Oct. 1793, 610-612. See also "From a Mother to her Daughter, Just on the Point of Marriage," *Boston Wkly. Mag.*, May 5, 1804, 109-110, and "Conduct of St. Augustin's Mother Monica," *Christian's Mag.*, Oct.-Nov. 1790, 429-430.

[78] "A Short Sermon on Marriage," *Baltimore Wkly. Mag.*, Apr. 8, 1801, 249, printed earlier in *Ladies Mag.* (Philadelphia), Aug. 1792, 108-110; "On Marriage," *N.Y. Mag.*, N.S., Dec. 1796, 656.

[79] "On Conjugal Affection," *Ladies Mag.* (Philadelphia), Sept. 1792, 176. "I consider a parity of understanding and temper to be as necessary towards forming a happy marriage, as an equality of years, rank, and fortune" ("Letters," in *Works of Witherspoon*, IV, 169).

[80] See, for example, D. B. Smith, *Great House*, chap. 4; Trumbach, *Egalitarian Family*, chap. 2; Stone, *Family*, chap. 8; D. S. Smith, "Parental Power," *Jour. Marriage and Family*, XXXV (1973), 419-428; and Ellen K. Rothman, *Hands and Hearts: A History of Courtship in America* (New York, 1984), chap. 1. Of course,

looked to the past as well as to the future; it focused more upon the welfare of the society than the well-being of the individual. Thus it had an implicitly anti-individualistic dimension,[81] one that was exposed whenever conflict arose. We can see that tendency in the ideal of marital concord, which could be—and was—used to legitimate both coverture and the exclusion of women from direct participation in politics. Indeed, the rhetoric of harmony seems almost a gloss upon the doctrine of marital unity—the English common law fiction that in marriage the husband and wife are one, and the husband is the one.[82] It has puzzled some historians that American Revolutionaries did not jettison coverture along with other pieces of undemocratic British baggage such as primogeniture and entail.[83] Yet republican theorists prized harmony above all else; they created the ideal of the affectionate marriage not so much to liberate the individual as to assure concord in the family, the building-block of society.

Republicanism aimed to avoid conflict. Hence, using the same principle that predicted that small republics would be the most harmonious,[84] those who applied the theory to the family suggested that husband and wife should share similar dispositions, beliefs, and interests, that they should be as one. Even so, conflict might arise, and the recommendations republicans made to restore harmony in such unfortunate cases expose the limitations of the republican model for family and polity alike.

The ideal, of course, was equality; no good republican would have disagreed with the egalitarian sentiments expressed by the woman who styled herself "A Matrimonial Republican." "The obedience between man and wife," she wrote, "is, or ought to be mutual."[85] The catch was in the "ought to be," for here the weaknesses in the republican ideal show through. What, for example, was a wife with an errant husband to do? Although it was certainly true that "man has no more right to sin with impunity than woman," husbands seemed to fall more often, and it became a wife's duty to lure her errant mate back to rectitude with "the charm of good humour and uncomplaining sweetness." In other words, only

---

heightened expectations of marriage may have worked against the end they sought to secure; see Lewis, *Pursuit of Happiness*, 187-204, and Cott, *Bonds*, 76-83.

[81] Wood, *Creation*, esp. 70-75. Consider also J.G.A. Pocock's famous description of the American Revolution as "the last great act of the Renaissance" ("Virtue and Commerce in the Eighteenth Century," *Journal of Interdisciplinary History*, III [1972], 120).

[82] For coverture see Norma Basch, *In the Eyes of the Law: Women, Marriage, and Property in Nineteenth-Century New York* (Ithaca, N.Y., 1982), chaps. 1 and 2, and "Equity vs. Equality: Emerging Concepts of Women's Political Status in the Age of Jackson," *Journal of the Early Republic*, III (1983), 297-318. For the justification for excluding women from politics see, for example, "Remarks on Female Politicians," *Ladies' Monitor*, May 29, 1802, 324-325.

[83] For example, Kerber, *Women of the Republic*, 119-121, 135-136.

[84] Wood, *Creation*, 58, 356. See also "Reflections on Marriage Unions," *N.Y. Mag.*, Oct. 1790, 561-562.

[85] "On Matrimonial Obedience," *Ladies Mag.* (Philadelphia), July 1792, 66.

redoubled feminine virtue could reclaim a husband from masculine vice. "Dispute not with him, be the occasion what it will," advised one writer.[86] Better to let errors go unremarked, warned another, than to "strike too often the unharmonious string." Indeed, "the best way of a married woman to carry her points is to yield sometimes."[87] Harmony, then, took precedence over equality; in the interest of concord a woman would sometimes have to forbear.

But why not the husband? In a truly reciprocal marriage would not the two parties compromise? Almost all essayists who addressed the issue of conflict in marriage argued that it was the wife who had to bend. The responsibility for anchoring marriage fell disproportionately to women because they were, supposedly, more compliant than men,[88] or, at least, they would find it "necessary, for political purposes, to consider man as the superior authority."[89] The symmetrical marriage thus gave way, under

[86] "The Gossip No. XV," *Boston Wkly. Mag.*, Feb. 5, 1803, 61; "Rules and Maxims for promoting Matrimonial Happiness," *Gent. and Lady's Mag.*, May 1784, 28. Although occasional articles and stories describe the failings of bad wives, most focus upon deficient husbands. For a description of a bad wife see "The Extravagant Wife: An American Tale," *Mass. Mag.*, July 7, 1791, 425-426. For bad husbands see "The Matron," *Gent. and Lady's Mag.*, Dec. 1789, 581-583; "Genuine Letter from an Injured Wife to Her Husband," *Christian's Mag.*, June-July 1789, 242-243; "The History of Adrastus and Camilla," *Ladies' Monitor*, Mar. 20, 1802, 241; "A Female Character," *Ladies Mag.* (Philadelphia), Sept. 1792, 182; "Conjugal Prudence," *N.Y. Mag.*, Mar. 1791, 127-128; and "Harriot," *Mass. Mag.*, Jan. 1789, 3-7.

[87] "Advice to Married Ladies," *Mass. Mag.*, June 1793, 331-332; "A Letter to a very good natured Lady married to a very ill natured Man," *Christian's Mag.*, Aug.-Sept. 1789, 319-320.

[88] "Woman: An Apologue," *Columbian Phenix*, July 1800, 438-439. See also "Letter to good natured Lady," *Christian's Mag.*, Aug.-Sept. 1789, 319-320; Wm. Alexander, M.D., "On the Happy Influence Arising from Female Society," *Mass. Mag.*, July 1795, 220-223; and "Female Biography," *Baltimore Wkly. Mag.*, Aug. 9, 1800, 125.

[89] "An Address to the Ladies," *Am. Mag.*, Mar. 1788, 245. There was no consensus on whether those differences between men and women that led to the expectation that women would defer to male authority were innate or merely convenient. Some writers were themselves uncertain, as was "The Gentleman at Large," who concluded that women were morally equal to men; that their minds had a "nice and delicate texture," which proved that "the situation for which Heaven designed them in this world is of a nature the most benevolent and engaging," while "the more rugged and invidious offices of life were appropriated to man, as being better suited to his firm and sturdy disposition"; and that women should "voluntarily" adopt certain responsibilities in the home (*Columbian Phenix*, May 1800, 266-269). Most writers, however, seem to have adopted a symmetrical, different-but-equal model of gender, which could manifest itself—as early as 1788—as a fully articulated version of "separate spheres." (See "An Address to the Ladies," *Am. Mag.*, Mar. 1788, 241-246; Miss M. Warner, "Rights of Woman," *Boston Wkly. Mag.*, Oct. 30, 1802, 2; Miss P. W. Jackson, "Concluding Address, at exhibition at Mrs. Rowson's Academy," *ibid.*, Oct. 29, 1803, 2-3; and "Gentleman

very little pressure, to a disproportionate one in which the wife, in order to maintain domestic tranquillity, was expected to defer.

Deference, of course, was the solution republicans offered for the problem of conflict in the polity; persons deficient in judgment or inferior in status, they believed, should simply yield to those of superior wisdom. Yet although, as Wood has shown, Federalists offered the Constitution as a "republican remedy" for the republican vice of disharmony, no similar rearrangement was forthcoming for the family. Indeed, as Americans showed increasing acceptance of conflict in the market and the polity, they became less willing to tolerate it at home.[90]

The insistence upon feminine deference revealed fears about conflict in the society and nation, and not merely concern about unhappy marriages. Indeed, very few of the essays that enjoined women to complaisance mentioned those character flaws we might expect women to have confronted most frequently in their mates: irritability, distasteful habits, slovenliness, insensitivity, an inability to earn an adequate income, or even the arbitrary exercise of power. Rather, the single failing that drew the most censure—and also the most extravagant claims for the power of female influence—was infidelity. Stories with titles like "The Way to Reclaim Him. A Moral Tale" purported to show how supreme feminine virtue could recall an errant husband to the path of rectitude. In that story, as in such another as "Conjugal Prudence," the wronged wife won back her wayward husband by embracing, literally, his mistress and illegitimate offspring, and by insisting upon an education for the children and an annuity (and, implicitly, banishment) for the mistress. Such acts of generosity never failed. The husband in the former story clasped his wife to his breast, "murmured out . . . 'Excellent woman! matchless wife!'"and promised "to remain immutably attached to her alone to the last moment of his existence." Similarly, the husband in the latter exclaimed, "'Thou heavenly woman! . . . is it *thus* thou upbraidest me for my infidelity to the most amiable woman that ever existed! O, my love, forgive!—but that's impossible! I am, I will be only yours'."[91]

The authors of such stories seem to be exploring the farthest reaches of

---

at Large," *Columbian Phenix,* May 1800, 266-269.) But because these distinctions were grounded in a religio-cultural metaphor of the first parents, rather than in science, they were quite flexible, could be put to any number of uses, and were quite inconsistent. For an analysis of the "paradoxes and contradictions" in late eighteenth-century depictions of femininity, see Mary Poovey, *The Proper Lady and the Woman Writer: Ideology as Style in the Works of Mary Wollstonecraft, Mary Shelley, and Jane Austen* (Chicago, 1984), chap. 1, quotation on p. 15.

[90] Wood, *Creation,* chap. 11. Consider the premise of Carl N. Degler, *At Odds: Women and the Family in America from the Revolution to the Present* (New York, 1980); Cott, *Bonds,* 98-99; and Tocqueville's classic analysis of the origins of individualism in *Democracy in America,* ed. Phillips Bradley (New York, 1980), II, 98-99.

[91] *Gent. and Lady's Mag.,* Nov. 1784, 299-302, quotation on p. 302; *N.Y. Mag.,* Mar. 1791, 127-128, quotation on p. 128.

self-abasing virtue; they imagine the most extreme instances of domestic cruelty a wife might endure in order to see whether the depths of depravity may be exceeded by the heights of virtue. When the answer is yes, the resolution takes the form of a conversion, with the husband confessing his sins and the wife playing the part, in the words of another contrite fictional husband, of "my guardian angel sent by heaven to prevent my ruin."[92] Stripped of her original culpability, Eve is easily transformed into Christ's surrogate, able to work a sinner's "reformation." "Trust me," the wronged wife says. "I assure you, that search the habitable globe, you will meet with no woman more inclined to serve, love, obey, and oblige you, than your Emilia."[93] Like Christ, the wife has to suffer, and like him, she redeems.

It was, however, equally possible for women to suffer yet not redeem. That was the sad fate of the heroine of Susanna Rowson's *Sarah; or, The Exemplary Wife*, a novel in which "virtue is represented, in all her native simplicity and beauty; and vice . . . is exhibited in her own proper ugliness and deformity." Although "the story is far from being improbable,"[94] it is really a parable, with virtue pitted against vice. Virtue is represented by Sarah, a lovely young woman who is forced by mercenary relatives to wed a reprobate, somewhat as if Clarissa had been made, against her will, to marry Lovelace. Although her husband kept a mistress, even bringing her into the home he shared with his wife, and although he despised Sarah for her goodness, she never wavered in her patience, charity, or virtue. When her husband bankrupted himself and even her clothing was claimed by his creditors, she entered into service to support him and herself. And when she discovered his illegitimate child, "said she calmly . . . 'if the child owes its being to you, give orders that it be brought home, and I will see it is properly taken care of; but let me entreat you not to add to the offence already committed against religion and morality, the unpardonable one of leaving your offspring to perish'." Whereupon the errant husband exploded, " 'D—n-t—n. . . . Of all the plagues a man can have, a moralizing, sentimental, canting, hypocritical wife is the worst'." After years of such trials, Sarah died, secure in her conviction that "even in thought she had never dishonoured her husband." Thereupon he married his mistress.[95] Here there is no conversion; virtue will not prevail. Nevertheless, "who of

[92] "Conjugal Affection," *Gent. and Lady's Mag.*, Feb. 1789, 4. The repentant husband wished "every man blessed with a wife like thee to break his fall whenever he deviated from virtue's paths."

[93] "Genuine Letter from an Injured Wife to her Husband," *Christian's Mag.*, June-July 1789, 242-243. See also "Harriot," *Mass. Mag.*, Jan. 1789, 3-7; "A Female Character," *Ladies Mag.* (Philadelphia), Sept. 1792, 182; "Emilia," *N.Y. Mag.*, Oct. 1793, 592-595; and "History of Adrastus and Camilla," *Ladies' Monitor*, Mar. 20, 1802, 241.

[94] As announced in *Boston Wkly. Mag.*, June 16, 1804, 136. The novel was serialized in the magazine in 1804 as "Sincerity, a Novel, by a 'Lady of Massachusetts'," but published as *Sarah* (Boston, 1813).

[95] *Boston Wkly. Mag.*, May 19, 1804, 120, June 30, 1804, 144.

common reflection but would prefer the death of Sarah, resigned as she was, and upheld by faith and hope, to all the splendors, wealth and honors ever heaped upon the heroine in the last pages of a novel" in which a heroine met only an earthly reward?[96] To put it another way, Susanna Rowson expressed doubt about whether feminine virtue *could* prevail in a corrupt world.

The doctrine of the Republican Wife suggested that a good wife could influence a susceptible man; *Sarah* raised the question whether she could reclaim, as well, a man who was confirmed in viciousness. The answer was that she could not. Here was a fundamental dilemma for the new nation: how could virtue be exacted from the vicious? Republican ideology offered a number of plausible ways to encourage the good to be more so; chief among them were education, benevolent reform, and female influence.[97] But it faced an insurmountable obstacle when it confronted men who were beyond all hope of reformation. The problem was infidelity, not merely the faithlessness of a spouse but apostasy itself—the unpardonable sin; for it, republicanism had no cure.

Republican advocacy of virtue was powerless before persons who had no conscience. How bedeviling this problem was can be seen when we examine the conventional seduction story. Tales such as *Charlotte Temple* and *The Coquette* may be considered as not very subtle warnings to young women without dowries that their value lay in their virginity; if they would be sought after on the marriage market, they must keep that commodity intact. The sentimental tale of seduction thus has been seen as an instrument of bourgeois respectability and middle-class conformity.[98] Such a view is not untrue, for surely no early nineteenth-century girl enhanced her marriage prospects by squandering her virginity. Chastity *was* esteemed, but for republican as much as bourgeois reasons. Consider "Reflections on Chastity, or Female Honour," a brief definition printed in at least three magazines before 1800: "What Bravery is in man, Chastity is in woman. This virtue, by making them triumph over every wicked attempt to dishonour them, bestows on them, as the first reward of

---

[96] Rowson, *Sarah,* iii.

[97] On education see Kerber, *Women of the Republic,* chap. 7; Norton, *Liberty's Daughters,* chap. 9; and Ann D. Gordon, "The Young Ladies Academy of Philadelphia," in Carol Ruth Berkin and Mary Beth Norton [eds.], *Women of America: A History* (Boston, 1979), 68-91. For benevolent activities see Suzanne Lebsock, *The Free Women of Petersburg: Status and Culture in a Southern Town, 1784-1860* (New York, 1984), chap. 7. For examples of women's benevolent organizations see Fred J. Hood, *Reformed America: The Middle and Southern States, 1783-1837* (University, Ala., 1980), 151, 153, 167, and "Religious," *Boston Wkly. Mag.,* Dec. 15, 1804, 29.

[98] See Christopher Hill, "Clarissa Harlowe and Her Times," *Essays in Criticism,* V (1955), 330-331; Wendy Martin, "Profile: Susanna Rowson, Early American Novelist," *Women's Studies,* II (1974), 6-7; and Ian Pierre Watt, *The Rise of the Novel: Studies in Defoe, Richardson, and Fielding* (Berkeley, Calif., 1957). See also Cott, "Passionlessness," *Signs,* IV (1978), 219-236.

victory, an universal esteem."[99] Once again we see the symmetrical expectations of men and women; in this case, chastity is the feminine version of the absolute standard of courage expected of Revolutionary War soldiers. For patriots like the Reverend Robert Cooper, cowardice was sin; thus he warned in 1775 that "if . . . you would escape deep guilt before God, and lasting contempt among men, forward you must go. . . . You have, in a word, no alternative, but either to venture your lives bravely, or attempt to save them ignominiously; to run the hazard of dying like heroes, or be certain of living like cowards."[100] Bravery, like chastity, was an absolute; it allowed not the slightest deviation nor tolerated any taint.

Brave men and chaste women were expected to "triumph over every wicked attempt to dishonour them." What Charles Royster has said of this Revolutionary attachment to exacting standards of bravery applies to chastity as well: it reflected an evangelical tendency to establish dichotomies between good and evil, salvation and grace, God and Satan. To waver in one's courage was to fall from grace; similarly, to surrender one's chastity was to sin. Americans of the Revolutionary era held out an impossible standard of purity for women and men both. Yet the Continental army, as Royster has shown, would come to a more workable notion of human capability, as would the political theorists who framed the Constitution. Standards of female virtue, however, fully as unrealistic as the expectation that no soldier would ever feel fear or no citizen advance his own interest, only became more rigid.[101]

In many ways chastity was a fit emblem for republicanism, which, when infused with evangelical ardor, could demand absolute and undeviating virtue from its citizens. Hence we must read the era's popular literature of seduction not merely as cautionary tales addressed to young women but also as political tracts in which men and women explored the possibilities for virtue in a corrupt world. Surely it is significant that the most popular novel of the early national period—indeed, the most popular American novel of all until the publication of *Uncle Tom's Cabin*—was *Charlotte*

[99] *Royal Am. Mag.*, Feb. 1775, 61; *Mass. Mag.*, Oct. 1791, 629-630; *Key*, Feb. 17, 1798, 44.

[100] Quoted in Royster, *Revolutionary People*, 225.

[101] *Ibid.*, 27-31, 47-49, 224-230, and *passim*. For other discussions of chastity see "On the loss of Chastity," *N.Y. Mag.*, N.S., Apr. 1797, 213; "The Gossip No. 25," *Boston Wkly. Mag.*, May 7, 1803, 113; "On Female Chastity," *ibid.*, Nov. 24, 1804, 18; and "An Address to the Ladies," *Am. Mag.*, Mar. 1788, 241-246: "chastity really exists in the mind; and when this fountain is pure, the words and actions that flow from it will be chaste and delicate" (p. 242). The best discussion of the origins of the ideal of chastity is Cott, "Passionlessness," *Signs*, IV (1978), 219-236. There is some debate about how fully American women abided by this ideal. (See, for example, Carl N. Degler, "What Ought to Be and What Was: Women's Sexuality in the Nineteenth Century," *AHR*, LXXIX [1974], 1467-1490, and Peter Gay, *The Bourgeois Experience: Victoria to Freud*. Vol. I: *Education of the Senses* [New York, 1984].) But there is no question about the pervasiveness of the ideology.

Temple, Susanna Rowson's classic tale of seduction and abandonment.[102] In this novel it takes not one but two designing men to seduce Charlotte from the path of virtue. The work is begun by Montraville, a Lovelace type who is drawn to the innocent young woman he ensnares but is unwilling to make a disadvantageous match; it is completed by his "friend" Belcour, whose only apparent motivation is to destroy both Charlotte and her faithless lover. Under such an assault, Charlotte's innocence stands not a chance.[103]

Like Charlotte and her forerunner Clarissa Harlowe, the heroines of the sentimental tales of seduction are all sympathetic. Eliza Wharton, *The Coquette,* seemed "to possess both the virtues and the graces"; her weaknesses were "an air of gaiety in her appearance and deportment" and a fatal naïveté.[104] Indeed, the flaws ascribed to the unfortunate heroines were traits that republicans usually valued: "a heart . . . formed of sensibility"; "unsuspecting innocence"; "innocent herself, she expected to find others so"; a mind "pure and unsullied"; "innocence and simplicity"; "amiable, ingenuous and sensible."[105] Pure, innocent, without guile, such young women are nothing less than contemporary versions of Eve; they are endowed with her attributes and given her signs. The unfortunate Amelia, for example, is "one of the fairest blossoms in the garden of society," while Almira is "as beautiful as the daughters of Paradise, as gentle as the breezes of spring; her mind was spotless, and her manners artless."[106] Such innocence fell once from Paradise, and it was destined to fall again and again in countless tales of seduction in the early republic.[107]

[102] Susanna Haswell Rowson, *Charlotte Temple: A Tale of Truth* (Philadelphia, 1794). For the popularity of *Charlotte Temple* see Francis W. Halsey's introduction to the 1905 New York edition, and Fliegelman, *Prodigals,* 261-262.

[103] As Fliegelman notes, Charlotte's parents—who are cast in the affectionate, post-patriarchal mold—might, in theory, have protected her, and in falling, she broke their hearts; but paternalism, no more than patriarchalism, represented an acceptable option for post-Revolutionary Americans (*Prodigals,* 261-262).

[104] Foster, *Coquette,* 62.

[105] "Copy of a Letter from Miss —— to M——," *Penn. Mag.,* Mar. 1775, 114; "Innocence Betrayed," *Lady's Miscellany* (New York), Aug. 24, 1811, 282; "Story of Philenia," *Mass. Mag.,* Dec. 1791, 729; "Maltilda," *Key,* Apr. 14, 1798, 107; "The Fatal Effects of Seduction," *Gent. and Lady's Mag.,* June 1789, 250, "Melancholy Tale of Seduction," *Mass. Mag.,* Apr. 1795, 41.

[106] "The Sorrows of Amelia," *Baltimore Wkly. Mag.,* July 5, 1800, 87; "Treachery and Infidelity Punished," *Gent. and Lady's Mag.,* Aug. 1789, 340.

[107] Other seduction tales include "Gossip No. LIV," *Boston Wkly. Mag.,* Feb. 18, 1804, 65; "Advice to the Unguarded Fair of this Metropolis," *Gent. and Lady's Mag.,* Nov. 1789, 547-548; "Passenger No. XI," *Boston Wkly. Mag.,* Dec. 10, 1803, 25; and "The Gossip No. XXV," *ibid.,* May 7, 1803, 113. See also the stories in n. 105. For different readings of the literature of seduction, in particular *The Coquette,* see Cathy N. Davidson, *Revolution and the Word: The Rise of the Novel in America* (New York, 1986), esp. chap. 6, and Carroll Smith-Rosenberg, "Reinterpreting Antebellum Culture" (paper presented at the annual meeting of the Organization of American Historians, 1987).

We have seen that feminine influence had its limits; no wife could expect to triumph over a thoroughly corrupted man on this side of the grave. Likewise, feminine innocence was at the mercy of masculine vice. No matter how many times the story of the Fall was reenacted, it came out the same way, as a correspondent to the *Gentleman and Lady's Town and Country Magazine* was well aware: "Most angelic and ever-admir'd blossoms of earthly eminence—how few are the instances of thy pure innocence ever reaching the summit of that bliss, uninjured, for which thy Maker intended it." Why? Because of "the wicked designs of artful men, more ravenous than the hungry lions, which go about seeking whom they may devour." Thus he cautioned "the fair daughters of Eve," but could his warning against the "seducers of female excellence" have any more success than God's to Adam and Eve?[108]

How closely the seduction story was modeled upon that of the Fall is even more apparent in a tale entitled "Treachery and Infidelity Punished." Almira, the picture of innocence and "as beautiful as the daughters of Paradise," is seduced by one Lothario: "Oh! the base dissembler—had ingratiated himself too far in her affections: with fondness she listened to his deceitful tales, and with too great avidity devoured his insinuating discourse."[109] Like her mother Eve, Almira fell, for like Eve, she faced the most artful of deceivers, Satan himself, barely disguised.

Without question, most of the fictional seducers are satanic; they are described in terms that leave no doubt about their true nature. Seducers are "those reptiles, those anamacules [*sic*], who really come under the class of non-descripts in creation." Even when the deceiver is not a snake, he is animal-like, "a lordly brute [who] fixed his cruel fangs" on one who was "gay . . . lovely . . . innocent . . . happy."[110] The seducer "stalks through the polite world like a satiated lion, who wants only the impulse of hunger to sacrifice another victim." The "vile seducer" is indeed subhuman, for he lacks the ability to love. Instead, he perverts affection, preying upon the credulity of the innocent; "falsehood guides [his] tongue, whilst an infamous baseness, under a plausible appearance of love or friendship conceals a heart destitute of every feeling."[111] Indeed, the seducer is the enemy of love, and much like the Devil who envied Adam and Eve their innocent bliss, he plots its destruction.

Hannah Foster modeled Eliza Wharton's seducer at least as much on Satan as on Lovelace. Jealous of the minister Eliza seems to prefer and angered by her virtuous friends, Sanford sets out to trap the lovely girl who has caught his eye. The responsibility is hers, he claims: "If she will

[108] "Advice to the Unguarded Fair of this Metropolis," *Gent. and Lady's Mag.*, Nov. 1789, 547-548.
[109] "Treachery and Infidelity Punished," *ibid.*, Aug. 1789, 340-341.
[110] "Gossip No. XXV," *Boston Wkly. Mag.*, July 30, 1803, 161; "The Seducer," *ibid.*, May 18, 1805, 117.
[111] "On Seduction," *Mass. Mag.*, May 1792, 308; "General Characteristics of Modern Novels," *Boston Wkly. Mag.*, Aug. 24, 1805, 174; "A Virtuous and Prudent Conduct Recommended," *Ladies Mag.* (Philadelphia), Nov. 1792, 265.

play with a lion, let her beware of his paw, I say."[112] *Charlotte Temple's* Belcour is cut from the same cloth, as are Sidney in "Charles and Amelia, or the Unfortunate Lovers," and Orlando, who contrives Narcissa's fall. In each case, most of the plot is devoted to the stratagems used to "ensnare" the heroine's virtue.[113] Such men, surely, are beyond the compass of normal experience. Each is attracted only to the most singularly virtuous of girls and is not satisfied until he has succeeded in ruining her. Judith Sargent Murray wrote that it was hard to "conceive of turpitude so *enormous, as that which must excite a being, deliberately to perpetrate the murder of the peace of a fellow creature, without a single apparent motive to stimulate a deed of such atrocity.*"[114] But it should not have been difficult at all; loathsome as the creature was, his prototype could be found in Genesis.

For this reason—that seduction tales essentially reenact the Fall, with the victim cast as Eve and the seducer as Satan himself—we should not read such tales too literally. While they certainly reinforced emerging Victorian standards of sexuality, it is doubtful that this was the primary objective. Rather, they represent another chapter in the early nineteenth century's secularization of religion. In them, the seducer is a secularized—but nonetheless recognizable—version of Satan.[115] The real subject of the seduction stories is not whether young girls should resist sexual temptation, but what hope innocence has in a corrupt world. The answer was grim, and mankind's—not merely Eve's—repeated fall had grave implications not only for women but for all of American society. That was the lesson of "The Seducer: Addressed to the Fair Daughters of America." Its author, typically, was incredulous that a being so depraved as the "base seducer" could exist: "Such a one is a monster in creation. . . . To obtain his desires, he practices every art of dissimulation, and he does not hesitiate to violate the most solemn engagements. Falsehood and perjury become familiar to him. . . . Virtue is sacrificed to his lust." Yet it is not only his innocent victim who suffers, for "the peace of individuals, families, and societies is destroyed. . . . Such are more dangerous to meet than bears bereaved of their whelps. They ought like ravenous wolves to be hunted from civilized society."[116] The satanic seducer was an enemy to society, the snake in the grass of the infant republic.

[112] Foster, *Coquette*, 82.

[113] Rowson, *Charlotte Temple; General Mag. and Review*, July 1798, 33-36; "The History of Narcissa," *Mass. Mag.*, Mar. 1792, 179-181.

[114] Murray, *The Gleaner* (Boston, 1798), II, 55. See also "Melancholy Tale of Seduction," *Mass. Mag.*, Apr. 1795, 40-42; "An Admonition to those who glory in seducing the affection of the fair, and then deserting them," *Columbian Mag.*, Nov. 1792, 303; and "On the Power of Love," *Ladies Mag.* (Philadelphia), Nov. 1792, 255-256.

[115] See also Wood, "Conspiracy and Paranoid Style," *WMQ*, 3d Ser., XXXIX (1982), 420-421.

[116] *Baltimore Wkly. Mag.*, Mar. 25, 1801, 231.

To the list of republicanism's stock villains, to the tyrannical ruler and the designing courtier, we thus must add several other names: those of the coxcomb, the coquette, and—most of all—the vile seducer. All threatened the consensual union that served as the metaphor of what republicans wanted their society to be. Yet if republicanism found ways to vanquish the tyrant and banish the sycophant, it was powerless when confronted by this most insinuating and devilish seducer. He put republicanism, as a system of belief, on trial—and he won. He revealed republicanism's fatal flaw; although it could imagine ways by which reasonably virtuous men and women could make each other more so and might live with each other in harmony, it was utterly baffled by confirmed depravity. In some ways, republicanism represented a quarrel with Genesis. So long as republican-minded men and women could rewrite sacred history in such a way that the Fall never took place and Eve was never tempted, they could imagine themselves inhabiting an earthly paradise, living with their mates in a prelapsarian bliss. But the men and women who were the heirs of the Reformation could never fully forget the Fall; they knew that, when tempted by a deceiver of satanic proportions, humankind would fall and fall again.

The best solution they could devise for the inevitability of sin was the metaphor of republican marriage, in which like-minded and virtuous men and women would guide each other's steps along the paths of rectitude. Yet in their fiction they were drawn irresistibly to the seduction story, and there virtue—and the republic—fell. Most of this discourse, naturally, was expressed in codes; because it was so metaphorical, we cannot read it literally. Clearly, it was not merely sexual lust that republicans found so threatening, but immoderate desires of all kinds, ambition and self-interest chief among them. The vile seducer represented republicanism's inability to come to terms with power, which it tended to equate with evil.

Still, because women figured so prominently in it, we must ask what bearing the literature of republican marriage had for actual republican women. We see embedded in these works many of the themes that historians have already exposed: a growing acceptance of affection as the only proper basis of marriage, increasing respect for feminine virtue, the feminization of religion, the idealization of chastity, and, finally, a growing interest in the possibilities for feminine influence. These themes are all compressed into the person of the Republican Wife: affectionate, virtuous, chaste, and capable of enormous moral authority over her husband. The Republican Wife represented, in the ideology at least, a real and important role. Yet even as an image, she was limited. Indeed, she led to a dead end, for her capability always depended upon masculine suscepti-bility. She had no more power than man allowed, and even if republican doctrine suggested that men ought to welcome feminine influence, that doctrine held no sway over those who did not subscribe to its credo. That generalization, of course, describes the fundamental weakness in repub-licanism; it had no power over those who were not or did not want to be virtuous.

In that sense republicanism served women no more poorly than it did men: all were baffled by unalloyed vice. Even though republicanism enhanced woman's status and legitimated improvements in her education as well as her entry into benevolent reform movements,[117] it also placed implicit checks upon her power. And it confronted her with the image of the seduced maid, condemned to fall repeatedly in tale after tale, seemingly incapable of learning from her experience. Women who wanted more status, influence, or power would have to look for another model. Thus the ideal of the wife would give way, by perhaps 1830, to that of the mother. Men might not be malleable, but children were, and they seemed to offer a more promising opportunity for the exercise of influence. Yet before that transition could be effected, the many elements that brought it about would have to fall into place: not merely a sentimental conception of motherhood—already widely shared by the end of the eighteenth century, as Ruth Bloch has shown—but also the removal of the father's place of work from the home, new views on the nature of childhood and child rearing, and, perhaps most important of all, an acceptance of childhood conversion.[118] This shifting of emphasis from woman-as-wife to that of woman-as-mother had important implications for reform, for it rested upon the assumption that women had a special role to play as mothers and that, consequently, they represented a separate interest.

This transition in the conceptualization of woman's nature and her role would have parallels in other aspects of early national life. The 1820s and 1830s may represent a watershed, for not only would the Republican Wife be replaced by the Victorian mother, but in other ways as well the republican synthesis would dissolve, yielding to a more fragmented social vision. In politics, the semblance of an era of good feelings would give way to the second party system. Reform, also, would pass on to a new and more militant phase, beyond benevolence; vague plans for colonization or the eventual abolition of slavery would yield to immediatism, and hopeful schemes to "civilize" the Indian tribes would be replaced by the reality of the reservation. The republic of harmony proved ephemeral; it simply could not work, for it faltered in the face of intransigent slaveholders, Indians who did not want to be white, drunkards who would not give up the bottle, and, most simply, men who would not reform. When confronted by such enormous obstacles, the Republican Wife, like the theory that begot her and like the original woman in whose image she was cast, tasted of the fruit of knowledge and, inevitably, fell.

[117] See n. 97, above.
[118] See Bloch, "Feminine Ideals," *Feminist Studies,* IV (1978); Anne Louise Kuhn, *The Mother's Role in Childhood Education: New England Concepts, 1830-1860* (New Haven, Conn., 1947); Mary P. Ryan, *The Empire of the Mother: American Writing about Domesticity, 1830-1860* (New York, 1982); Bernard Wishy, *The Child and the Republic: The Dawn of Modern American Child Nurture* (Philadelphia, 1968); Cott, *Bonds;* and Douglas, *Feminization of Culture.*

AMERICAN FEMININE
IDEALS IN TRANSITION:
THE RISE OF THE MORAL MOTHER, 1785-1815

RUTH H. BLOCH

Motherhood has long held a special place of honor in the symbolism of American life. Still a dominant value today, the ideal of motherhood probably achieved its quintessential expression in the writings of the mid-nineteenth century. Women, according to the prevailing Victorian image, were supremely virtuous, pious, tender, and understanding. Although women were also idealized as virgins, wives, and Christians, it was above all as mothers that women were attributed social influence as the chief transmitters of religious and moral values. Indeed, other respectable female roles—wife, charity worker, teacher, sentimental writer—were in large part culturally defined as extensions of motherhood, all similarly regarded as nurturant, empathic, and morally directive.[1]

The Victorian maternal ideal was first manifest as part of the culture of the most articulate, Anglo-American, Protestant, middle and upper classes. Some of its features, particularly its asexuality, probably never permeated as deeply into the culture of other American groups. However, the high evaluation of maternal influence was destined in time to command a far wider allegiance. By the mid-twentieth century, it would be difficult to identify a more pervasive "all-American" ideal.

Even among the social groups who gained cultural dominance in the Victorian era, however, motherhood had not always been a dominant feminine ideal. Indeed, in seventeenth- and early eighteenth-century literature written and read in America, motherhood was singularly unidealized, usually disregarded as a subject, and even at times actually denigrated. Partially because pre-Victorian writers understated the importance of motherhood, historians of the colonial period have also given the subject far less attention than more overtly economic forms of female labor, women's legal status, and the more common literary depiction of women as wives and Christians. Moreover, the widely acknowledged "transitional" phase between mid-eighteenth and mid-nineteenth century

197

attitudes toward motherhood has received surprisingly little examination. Recently, the valuable work of Linda Kerber and Nancy Cott has begun to fill this scholarly gap, but primarily because they focus on other, broader issues—Kerber on views of women in late eighteenth-century republican ideology and Cott on a wide constellation of changes in New England women's lives between 1780 and 1835—neither author has given extended attention to changing conceptions of motherhood per se. In particular, no one has yet analyzed the wide range of printed literature circulating in America between the late seventeenth and the early nineteenth centuries, much of it British in origin, that bore on the question of mothering. The relationship between this literature and the consciousness (much less behavior) of even its limited readership is, of course, highly problematic; and many unanswered questions about mothering in this period remain. Yet even when viewed narrowly as the "official" culture of dominant groups, this body of literature reveals a change in attitudes of great and continuing significance to the history of American women.[2]

* * * * * *

Prior to the late eighteenth century, two, essentially mutually exclusive, ideal images of women appeared in the literature written and read in America. The first, that of woman as "help-meet," has been the most extensively described by modern historians.[3] It was the earliest and most indigenously American literary ideal, associated above all with New England Puritanism and, later; with significant modifications, with a part of the American Enlightenment. In its Puritan version, the help-meet ideal laid great stress on the value of female subordination to men, a position justified both by Old Testament patriarchal models and by general cultural assumptions that women were weaker in reason; more prone to uncontrolled emotional extremes; and in need, therefore, of practical, moral, and intellectual guidance from men. Yet while thus proclaiming female mental inferiority and insisting on the wife's duty to obey her husband (except when he violated divine law), Puritan literature tended to downplay qualitative differences between the sexes and to uphold similar ideal standards for both men and women. Faith, virtue, wisdom, sobriety, industry, mutual love and fidelity in marriage, and joint obligations to children were typically enjoined on both sexes. Good wives, who were above all defined as pious, frugal, and hardworking, were especially valued for the help they could be to men in furthering both spiritual and worldly concerns.

Some eighteenth-century Enlightenment writings on women published in America also minimized differences between the sexes and emphasized the usefulness of sensible, industrious wives. These writings, however, often revised the earlier help-meet ideal by simultaneously stressing female rational capabilities, advocating more serious education for women, and urging greater equality in marriage. In their defense of women, these authors, even more than the Puritans, tended to place special emphasis on the practical value of diligent housewives.[4]

The second feminine ideal that appeared in the eighteenth-century literature emphasized ornamental refinement.[5] Whereas the help-meet ideal tended to downplay sexual distinctions and to stress the utility of good housewives, this more upper-class ideal instead concentrated on feminine graces and dwelt on the charms of female social companionship in polite company. It came to America primarily by means of imported English literature, especially sentimental romances, and didactic pieces on female education and etiquette, many of which were popular enough to be reprinted in America. Eighteenth-century periodicals, largely extracted from contemporary English magazines, were also full of articles conveying an ornamental image of women. According to this vision, often described in highly ornate eighteenth-century prose and verse, women were exquisite beings—beautiful, delicate, pure, and refined. Although modesty and piety constituted key features of this ideal, as they did of the help-meet image, charm and fashionable female "accomplishments" such as musical performance, drawing, and speaking French tended to be incorporated as well. Originally associated with the chivalric tradition of romantic love, this image of ornamental refinement still retained aristocratic overtones and probably strongly appealed to those elements of the eighteenth-century English and American prosperous middle-classes aspiring to gentility.

* * * * * *

Both of these eighteenth-century feminine ideals, the help-meet and the ornament, dwelt primarily on woman's relationships to God and man as Christian, wife, and social companion. Neither placed much emphasis on motherhood. In practically all of the literature on women circulating in America prior to the late eighteenth century, the theme of motherhood tended either to be ignored altogether in favor of such topics as courtship or marriage, or it was subsumed among a variety of other religious and domestic obligations shared with men. This is not to say that women, in reality, had no special maternal relationships to their children; women not only gave birth, they usually nursed and tended small children far more than men. Yet despite this actual behavior, motherhood received less normative emphasis and symbolic appreciation in early American literature than did many other aspects of women's lives.

Throughout most of the colonial period, relationships between mothers and infants rarely drew literary attention. Although we know that mothers generally took care of their babies, their behavior for the most part evidently remained ascriptively controlled, dictated by custom passed down from one generation to the next without any felt need for written scrutiny. Inasmuch as mothering became a matter for literary treatment at all, it was far from idealized. Puritan writers whose works circulated in New England did occasionally turn to the subject, but the main maternal functions that aroused their commentary were regarded as biological givens: childbearing and breastfeeding.

Childbirth, God's special curse on the daughters of Eve, received notice from Puritan writers because, above all, it raised the specter of death. In an age when women often died in delivery, and infants frequently thereafter, ministers viewed pregnancy primarily as an occasion to exhort women to guard their health and, more importantly, to seek their spiritual salvation.[6] Partly in response to this high risk of mortality, fertile women who successfully bore many children also drew some special recognition.[7]

The only other aspect of mothers' relationships with infants to receive much attention in early American literature was breastfeeding. Ministers addressed this issue specifically in order to urge mothers to nurse their own children. During this period, it was still customary for many urban and landed families throughout western Europe to send babies to suckle wet nurses, and, although the evidence on colonial America is sketchy, in the eighteenth century, wet-nursing seems to have made a few inroads on this side of the Atlantic as well.[8] The Puritan clergy strenuously objected to this practice, insisting that mothers who chose not to nurse their babies opposed the clear will of God as revealed in both Scripture and nature. Ministers commonly cited Biblical examples of mothers suckling babies and also pointed out that God obviously designed the breasts on the female body for this use. To defy this divine intention constituted a basic violation of a mother's calling, a clear-cut sign of sinful sloth, vanity, and selfishness. On occasion this religious case against wet-nursing joined with a medical one, that maternal breastfeeding less often endangered the physical health of the child. Only rarely, and evidently only in imported English treatises, was the impact of wet-nursing upon a child's character raised as a noteworthy consideration. American writers who condemned the practice stressed the importance of the child's health and, especially, the mother's duty to God, not the value of an affective relationship between mother and child.[9]

This absence of literary emphasis on emotional bonds between mothers and children is no indication, of course, that such attachments did not actually exist. Even the act of sending a child out to a wet nurse is not evidence that a mother was indifferent to her baby's health and happiness.[10] Indeed, although maternal love was seldom a theme in early American literature, it seems to have been largely taken for granted. Several Puritan ministers issued warnings against "a Mother's excessive fondness," the tendency for mothers to spoil or "cocker," their children, "to as it were smoother their Children in their Embraces."[11] The observation that mothers were particularly tender toward their children, however, more often gave rise to criticism than commendation. Cotton Mather's printed funeral sermon for his own mother, which gave almost sentimental homage to maternal comfort, was a rare departure from this tendency to devalue what seemed distinctive about a mother's love. Yet even there, in characteristically Puritan fashion, the overriding theme of Mather's sermon was that God is still a "better comforter." " What," he asked, "is the best of *Mothers* weigh'd in the Ballance with such a *Father*?"[12]

In keeping with this highly patriarchal Puritan God, early American literature on childrearing gave as much or more notice and appreciation to fathers as to mothers. Compared with the paucity of written material on infancy, there was a great deal to be read about childhood education after the nursing stage. During the seventeenth and eighteenth centuries, children were attracting increased attention as objects of artistic, literary, religious, and pedagogical concern throughout the western world.[13] In New England, where Puritans took an especially vital interest in socialization that would maximize chances of religious conversion, sermons and treatises on family life meticulously enumerated parental responsibilities. Practically all these works assumed that parental obligation was either vested primarily in fathers or shared by both parents without sexual distinction.

Puritan writings on the family generally divided into separate sections that defined ideal relationships between husband and wife, parent and child, and master and servant, specifying the mutual obligations of each figure within the complementary pairs. The main tasks encumbant upon the parent, in addition to insuring the child's physical well-being, were to provide baptism, prayer, religious instruction, and assistance in the choice of a calling and a spouse. Because "parent" was itself a genderless term, these works often conveyed the impression that mothers and fathers

ideally performed much the same role.[14] Indeed, those few works
that dealt separately with specifically maternal responsibilities—
usually as one small part of sermons on virtuous women—reiterated
many of the same duties that other works on childrearing commonly assigned to fathers as well. Good mothers were described
as caring, pious, and wise; they prayed for their children, instructed
and catechised them, reproved their sins; and they served as examples of virtue and faith.[15] None of these were distinctively maternal obligations. At the most, writers would point out that because
mothers had closer contact with small children, they had special
opportunities to make lasting impressions on young minds.[16] At
times, however, commentators actually denigrated the value of
this early maternal influence, insisting that fathers subsequently
undertook the more serious and ultimately most beneficial education of their children. As Cotton Mather once expounded upon
the proverb "A wise son maketh a glad father, but a foolish son
is the heaviness of his mother," applying it to children of both
sexes:

> ... it may be worth while to Enquire, Why 'tis rather the Gladness of the
> *Father* than of the *Mother*, that is here mentioned upon the *Wise Child*?
> Unto this I answer; 'Tis because the *Father* ordinarily has most *Share* in
> procuring, and most *Sense* in perceiving, the *Wisdom* of his Children. When
> Children are come to such *Maturity*, that their Wisdom does become Observ-
> able, ordinarily the *Mother* has more dismissed them from her Conversation
> than the *Father* has from *his*. . . . But if you go on to Enquire, Why 'tis
> rather the Sadness of the *Mother*, than of the *Father*, that is mentioned
> upon the Foolish Child? Unto this I answer; 'Tis because when Children
> miscarry the *Mother* is ordinarily most *Blamed* for *It*: People will be most
> ready to say, and very *Often* say it very *Justly* too, 'Twas her making Fools
> of them, that betray'd them into the Sinful Folly. . . .[17]

Those works that outlined the more neutral "parent's" obligations were, moreover, often heavily patriarchal in tone, not only
employing the pronoun "he," but also drawing from such Biblical
models as Abraham, Joshua, and David.[18] At times, specifically
paternal duties such as presiding over family worship received
special emphasis. Other works on the upbringing of children were
explicitly addressed to fathers alone, while only one book published
in America prior to the late eighteenth century, an edition of *The
Mother's Catechism* attributed to the English cleric John Willison,
was designed specifically for mothers.[19] Indeed, ministers often
felt it necessary to make a special point that mothers were not
"exempted" from the duty to participate in the religious education
of their children.[20] Others noted a tendency among children to

respect their mothers less than their fathers and reminded them of the Fifth Commandment injunction to honor both parents equally. William Gouge, the English Puritan whose treatise on family life was well known in New England, even sympathetically acknowledged that, at least for boys, the duty to honor mothers despite their manifold female deficiencies was "the truest triall of a childes subjection."[21]

This devaluation of motherhood was, on the one hand, an integral part of broader cultural assumptions about the inferiority of women. The traditional view that women were less rational, less capable of controlling emotions than men, helped to explain not only their unfitness for civil and ecclesiastical leadership and their need to be deferential in marriage, but also their subordinate parental status. Certain qualities regarded as essential to good childrearing, such as self-discipline and theological understanding, were deemed more characteristic of men; and the Protestant Reformation even further accentuated the value of these supposedly masculine traits. Moreover, by abandoning certain Catholic and aristocratic traditions that had enhanced the position of women—such as the worship of Mary and the female saints and the extensive education of at least some privileged women—Puritanism in some ways actually lowered the status of women. At a time when the domestic socialization of children was becoming a matter of greater cultural scrutiny than before throughout the western European world, the paternal role, in particular, drew pronounced emphasis and respect.

On the other hand, despite this elevation of fathers over mothers, the standard against which they were measured was essentially the same. Although mothers had more weaknesses to overcome, as "parents" they were supposed to strive toward an identical ideal. No differentiated maternal role received extended definition. Only childbearing, breastfeeding, and the preliminary education of very small children drew notice as uniquely maternal obligations. Partially because Puritans believed that infants were depraved and that the truly decisive process of conversion only began later on, these early years of predominantly maternal care aroused minimal interest relative to the later period of serious religious instruction that involved fathers as well.

The lack of emphasis on motherhood in seventeenth- and eighteenth-century Puritan literature reflected, in addition, certain social realities of family life. Fathers not only wielded superior intellectual and moral authority as men, but they also worked in sufficient proximity to their children to take an active part in childrearing. Craftsmen and tradesmen typically conducted their

203

businesses at home; even farmers worked close by and often spent long winter months indoors. Furthermore, although the term "parent" referred to mothers and fathers, other adult figures frequently lived with children and undoubtedly shared childrearing obligations, thereby further diffusing the parental role. Colonial households, for example, often included servants, many of them adolescents sent by their parents to learn practical skills from other adults.[22] Writings on familial obligations typically advised masters to treat servants as they would their own children; servants, in turn, were enjoined to aid in the religious education of the young.[23] Their involvement in the life of a growing child may well have further undermined the uniqueness of the maternal relationship.

Mothers, moreover, much like fathers and servants, typically engaged in other activities in addition to childrearing. Not only were rudimentary household tasks demanding occupations; but women also had to produce many of their own commodities for domestic use in this preindustrial, and still relatively uncommercial, economy. They often helped their husbands with the craft or trade, and on occasion even owned and managed enterprises inherited from deceased husbands or fathers.[24] If parenthood was not regarded as a predominantly maternal responsibility, neither was motherhood the primary occupation of women.

The prevailing image of women as wives, or "help-meets," rather than mothers, then, while partly a result of deprecatory opinions about both women and children, also accurately described major aspects of women's lives. The more fanciful ornamental ideal of female refinement sought, to the contrary, to elevate women above all the banalities of work. Yet even while taking the otherwise nearly opposite perspective on women, this ideal, too, tended to disregard motherhood in preference for other defining characteristics. The rearing of children was evidently considered a far too mundane and undistinguished feature of a woman's married life to warrant idealization from either point of view.

* * * * * *

The second volume of Samuel Richardson's novel *Pamela* more than any other work first heralded the new, idealized conception of motherhood. Here the new ex-servant girl Pamela settles into her married life with the country squire Mr. B. and takes on the at once serious and pleasurable task of rearing their children. Although the plot actually revolves around other, more suspenseful themes, the novel dwells periodically on Mrs. B.'s maternal virtue: she unsuccessfully pleads with her husband to allow her to breastfeed her baby; she jeopardizes her own health to nurse her son when he contracts smallpox (probably a consequence of using the wet nurse); she studiously engaged in a detailed examination of Locke's *Thoughts on Education*; and, in the closing scene of the novel, she recounts moral tales to enraptured children clustered about her in the nursery.

One suspects that the popularity of *Pamela* was due far less to this domestic sequel than to the passionate romance of the first volume. Yet this work, which appeared in its first American edition as early as 1744, offered a preliminary sketch of a feminine ideal that by the turn of the century had become widespread— particularly in more explicitly didactic religious, educational, and medical literature. By transforming the virginal chambermaid Pamela into the wise matron Mrs. B., Richardson merged parts of the older ideals of domestic competence and ornamental purity with the new image of the moral mother.

Although anticipated by Richardson, this new maternal ideal gained ascendancy in America only toward the end of the eighteenth century. It emerged in the context of an expanding literature on various aspects of women's lives, including female education, courtship, and marriage. Children, too, always objects of great concern in Puritan literature, received ever more specialized and detailed attention over the course of the eighteenth century.[25] The difference between these post-Revolutionary commentaries and earlier publications on women and children was not, however, merely a difference in number but a difference in kind. To be sure, in the literature on women the older help-meet and ornamental ideals were still much in evidence; and in literature on childrearing the genderless "parent" was still an object of address. However, an altered conception of motherhood developed alongside these traditional views. Between 1785 and 1815, large numbers of reprinted British and indigenously American works began to appear that stressed the unique value of the maternal role. Not only did the still popular *Pamela* articulate this new theme, but so did many contemporary books and magazines published in America on such subjects as family religion, children's health and morality, and female manners and education. It was taken up, moreover, by late eighteenth-century Enlightenment rationalists and evangelical Protestants both, groups representing broad Anglo-American intellectual orientations that became increasingly polarized near the end of the century. Although they tended to define it somewhat differently, the value of moral motherhood was one of the few things about which many on both sides agreed.

During the late eighteenth century, writers began to dwell on the critical importance of proper maternal care during infancy.

What had earlier been left to custom for the first time became a matter of widespread written analysis and prescriptive advice. Opposition to wet-nursing, for example, although always pronounced in Puritan America, now enlisted the support of many physicians and other secular commentators who advanced the cause of maternal breastfeeding on far more comprehensive grounds. Mothers who chose not to nurse their own children were still regarded as essentially profane and were now often charged with violating Enlightenment natural law as well as the Protestant will of God. The child's health became an even more salient factor in these discussions than it had been earlier. And, in addition to extending these older arguments, late eighteenth-century authors introduced a new set of objections to wet-nursing. They began, for example, to stress the detrimental effects upon the child's character. The strict Calvinist doctrine of infant depravity began giving way to the more environmentalist psychology of the Enlightenment, and many writers came to portray the newborn baby's mind as infinitely impressionable, as "a blank sheet of paper," "spotless as new-fallen snow," capable of being "easily moulded into any Form."[26]   Earlier European medical theorists had warned that a nurse could convey bad character, or "humour," through the physical medium of milk, an argument that had never caught on in Puritan America.[27]   Now several writers contended that those who nursed babies wielded determining psychological influence, not so much through the milk itself (although the metaphor was on occasion employed) but, more significantly, through their personal interaction. Wet nurses, they argued, could not be trusted to implant desirable characters because they felt less affection for babies than natural mothers and because they might be mentally or morally deficient. "What prudent mother," asked the Rhode Island minister Enos Hitchcock, "will trust the commencement of the education of her child in the hands of a mercenary nurse . . . who knows little more than how to yield nourishment to an infant [?]"[28]   Borrowing an expression from Rousseau, a New York midwife named Mary Watkins protested that, in addition, wet-nursing violated "the rights of the mother to see her infant love another woman as well or better than herself."[29] Mindful that "even upon the breast infants are susceptible of impressions," authorities encouraged nursing mothers to be "double careful" of their tempers, "to indulge no ideas but what are chearful, and no sentiments but what are kindly."[30]   Indeed, several advised that even if a mother proved incapable of breastfeeding, she should never send her baby away from home to nurse. Rather she herself nevertheless should assume primary control over the physical and emotional care of her child, either by feeding it manually or by keeping a wet nurse on hand under her close supervision.[31]

In another major revision of the case against wet-nursing, writers began to recommend maternal breastfeeding not only as a necessary religious duty, but also as a source of physical and psychological fulfillment for the mother as well as the child. Nursing, as well as infant care generally, came to be viewed as an exquisite pleasure, as an invaluable opportunity to delight in the charms of innocent infancy. Far from requiring physical sacrifice, many authors suggested, breastfeeding actually enhanced the mother's health; nursing mothers became more radiant, contented, graceful, and "harmonious."[32]   And, contrary to fashionable opinion, men would find these mothers more attractive as well. As the widely read English physician Hugh Smith phrased this often highly sentimental appeal, "a chaste and tender wife, with a little one at her breast is certainly to her husband the most exquisitely enchanting object upon earth."[33]

Not only were mothers strongly advised to feed their own children, but for the first time they were also furnished with extensive written information about how to do it. They were instructed how to overcome physical problems such as sore nipples, how to use manual devices like the "pot" and the "boat," how often to feed, when to wean, and so on. Medical experts also addressed mothers on various other aspects of infant care. Handbooks on child nurture and disease began to become widely available during this period. Most of these were American reprints of slightly earlier works by well-known English and Scotch obstetricians, but in the early nineteenth century, indigenous American publications also began to appear. These works urged mothers to tend closely to their small children—not just to nurse them competently when sick, but to clothe them loosely rather than swaddle them, to keep them meticulously clean, to exercise them regularly outdoors, to keep them on a special diet for years, and (some texts said) to feed them on demand rather than on schedule.[34]

Although we know next to nothing about actual childrearing practices, most of these admonitions seem aimed toward increasing the amount of attention paid by mothers to small children. Infant care came to be viewed as an exacting occupation, one requiring not only heightened concentration, but also special expertise. Tasks that had earlier been regulated by unwritten custom now began to be matters for extended analysis and deliberate, rational manipulation. A few of the British physicians openly deplored the superstitious ignorance of most mothers

207

and believed themselves to be on a mission of scientific enlightenment.[35] This medical condescension could, however, also backfire
as mothers themselves came to take pride in their craft. *The
Maternal Physician*, for example, a book of advice written by an
American mother of eight, spoke more directly from the voice of
experience. Acknowledging her debt to the books by the doctors,
she adds: ". . . these gentlemen must pardon me if I think, after
all, that a mother is her child's best physician, in all ordinary cases;
and that none but a mother can tell how to *nurse* an infant as it
ought to be nursed."[36]

Several of these popular medical handbooks on childcare contained sections offering advice on the psychological as well as the
physical management of small children. The dominant message
was that mothers should establish gentle but firm moral discipline
as early as possible. Just as the impressionability of infant minds
became grounds for objecting to wet nurses, so prevailing assumptions about the continuing malleability of small children's characters served to heighten the responsibility assigned to mothers
throughout these first formative years. Many writers warned
against entrusting children to servants, who were commonly
characterized as careless, ignorant, and even potentially corrupt.
William Buchan, the author of the manual *Advice to Mothers*,
described the far-reaching ramifications of this early maternal
moral custody:

Everything great or good in future life, must be the effect of early impressions; and by whom are those impressions to be made but by mothers, who
are most interested in the consequences? Their instructions and example will
have a lasting influence and of course, will go farther to form the morals,
than all the eloquence of the pulpit, the efforts of schoolmasters, or the
corrective power of the civil magistrate, who may, indeed, punish crimes,
but cannot implant the seeds of virtue.[37]

Not surprisingly, ministers and secular moralists as well as medical
experts often took up this theme, exhorting mothers to use their
power to "ingraft," "sow," and "root" steadfast principles of virtue in impressionable young minds.[38] "Weighty beyond expression is the charge devolved on the female parent," solemnly observed the New Hampshire minister Jesse Appleton, "It is not
within the province of human wisdom to calculate all the happy
consequences resulting from the perservering assiduity of mother-
ers."[39]

As writers thus accorded more significance to maternal care
during the first years of life, they in effect upgraded the status
of what had always been a female role. For mothers traditionally

had been entrusted with very small children, particularly in America where wet-nursing was relatively rare from the outset. The change in conceptions of motherhood involved, however, not simply a higher evaluation of an age-old occupation but also a substantive redefinition of the maternal role. Many responsibilities that had earlier been assigned to fathers or to parents jointly became transferred to mothers alone. Whereas Puritan writers had portrayed fathers as taking an active, even primary role in childhood education once the children became capable of rational thought and moral discrimination, now fathers began to recede into the background in writings about the domestic education of children.

By the turn of the century, Protestant clergymen frequently stressed the religious influence of mothers without reference to any subsequent paternal intervention at all. Whereas past literature on childhood education had been primarily addressed to fathers, now books and magazines catering to women offered advice on the moral upbringing, discipline, and education of growing children.[40] Catechisms, instructive dialogues, and moral stories for children began to feature mothers in the instructive role. One anonymous publication entitled *The Mother's Gift*, for example, a work that went into several American editions in the late eighteenth and early nineteenth centuries, contained both a catechism and several heavily didactic stories about children's lives in which fathers scarcely appear.[41] Mrs. Elizabeth Helme, the English author of another such educational manual for mothers called *Maternal Instruction* reprinted in New York in 1804, introduced her work by explaining, "As I regard an informed mother the most proper and attractive of all teachers, I have chosen that character as the principal, in the following sheets."[42] A new Quaker catechism similarly cast "mother" as the questioner, as did other, less formal educational dialogues.[43] Even the earlier *Mother's Catechism* by John Willison now enjoyed an impressive revival.[44] Nor were all of these works aimed solely at the religious and moral education of children. Practical information on the use of tools and money; basic skills such as reading and arithmetic; and even more advanced subjects such as history, biography, geography, science, and art all fell within the range of what at least some authors regarded as the mother's appropriate educational role.[45] Although this early maternal instruction scarcely substituted for the more formal education that children, especially boys, would receive later on, professional teachers were evidently to take up where mothers left off. "Business, and many cares, call the father abroad," explained a New Hampshire clergyman, "but home is the mother's province—here she reigns sole mistress the greatest part of her life."[46] Fathers, concurred an English author widely read in America, "can afford but little leisure to superintend the education of their children."[47] Indeed, just as a few Puritan commentators had seen fit to remind mothers that they, too, bore some responsibilities for childhood education, now an occasional work made the reverse point that fathers should not simply leave the rearing of children entirely to mothers alone.[48]

The literature that entrusted mothers with such wide-ranging physical, psychological, religious, and intellectual custody over the young in part accurately reflected concrete social changes that greatly expanded and specialized the maternal role. These structural changes occurred first and far more rapidly in England, still the source of much that was read in America even after the Revolution, but the indigenous as well as the imported literature also spoke to a long-range social process beginning in America. A real, although very gradual, realignment in the familial division of labor loosely coincided with this cultural redefinition of motherhood; and it occurred first among the same literate, commercial middle-class groups that provided the largest literary market. Whereas earlier mothers had often shared parental responsibilities with servants and fathers, by the late eighteenth century, these other figures had begun to withdraw from the domestic scene. Fewer middle-class households contained servants than they had earlier. Those who did become servants in the late eighteenth century, moreover, now usually came from much lower social and cultural backgrounds than their employers, a difference which undoubtedly contributed to the frequency of later warnings against their influence on children.[49] The structural change that altered parental roles the most, however, was the gradual physical removal of the father's place of work from the home, a process already under way in eighteenth-century America among tradesmen, craftsmen, manufacturers, and professionals (if not the majority of farmers), and one that in England was rapidly accelerating with the beginnings of industrialization. Fathers and their assistants who worked outside the domestic premises no longer had continuous contact with children. In the absence of these other parental figures, childrearing responsibilities slowly became less diffused, more exclusively focused on mothers.[50]

Not only did mothers rear children more by themselves, but simultaneously—and for similar reasons—women became more exclusively preoccupied with their maternal roles. Although literature at the turn of the century still stressed the value of wives who were frugal "economisers," women were becoming less vitally engaged in economic production. Those whose husbands worked away from home could less directly assist their labor. And although the textile industry continued to provide work for some, usually unmarried, women in their homes, the decline of the domestic system of production was already under way in both England and America by the early nineteenth century.[51] Home manufacturing for domestic use, while still a major activity of most women, was becoming a less demanding job in settled regions as more goods became available at affordable prices on the expanding commercial market. As women were relieved of much of their former economic role and at the same time left in primary care of children, motherhood understandably came to be a more salient feature of adult female life. Still another interrelated development, also associated with increased material comfort as well as some expansion of literacy, was the growth of a female, middle-class reading public in England and America.[52] These more leisured women provided a ready market for authors, many of whom themselves were women, who spoke to their special concerns as mothers.

As women came to be seen as the primary childrearers, motherhood often came to be viewed as a powerful vehicle through which women wielded broad social influence. Physicians and other writers delivering advice on childcare often pointed to the socially beneficial effects of good mothering, some even holding out the possibility of a wholesale "revolution" in human manners and morals.[53] As both Nancy Cott and Ann Douglas have recently observed, New England ministers who spoke to an increasingly female constituency in this period were especially taken with this vision of maternal moral influence permeating throughout society.[54] "Mothers do, in a sense, hold the reins of government and sway the ensigns of national prosperity and glory," the Reverend William Lyman typically glorified the role, "yea, they give direction to the moral sentiments of our rising hopes, and contribute to form their moral state."[55] This was, of course, a particularly compelling argument to those seeking to justify the restriction of women to the ever-narrowing domestic sphere. Characterizing the important responsibilities of motherhood, the minister Thomas Barnard, for example, took a direct swipe at Mary Wollstonecraft's feminist polemic, A Vindication of the Rights of Woman. "These are not the fancied, but the real 'Rights of Women.' They give them an extensive power over the fortunes of man in every generation."[56] Yet such argumentation, far from being confined to antifeminists, carried weight even with Wollstonecraft herself who, while insisting that women were capable of other achievements as well, also stressed that "the rearing of children—that is, the laying a [sic] foundation of sound health both of body and mind in the rising generation . . . [is] the peculiar destination of women."[57]

As motherhood was deemed a more demanding responsibility than it had been earlier, the complementary view arose that women, in particular, were eminently suited to rear children. Not only were they endowed with the physiology to bear and nurse babies, but, an increasing number of writers suggested, they also possessed the requisite mental qualities to take charge of the minds and morals of growing children. Challenging the traditionally vaunted moral, and often even intellectual, superiority of men, authors increasingly celebrated examples of female piety, learning, courage, and benevolence.[58] Women often came to be depicted not only as virtuous in themselves, but as more virtuous than men, indeed, as the main "conservators of morals" in society by means of their beneficial influence on both men and children.[59] Even New England clergymen regarded "the superior sensibility of females," their "better qualities" of tenderness, compassion, patience, and fortitude as inclining them more naturally toward Christianity than men.[60] In part, this exaltation of female piety came as an appreciative response to the ministers' increasingly female congregations, but it also reflected broad intellectual changes extending far beyond the New England churches. For during this period the qualities traditionally associated with women, particularly emotionalism, came to be more highly valued throughout Anglo-American culture. Not only religion, which became more revivalistic and softer in doctrine, but sentimental and romantic literature as well as other, less popular artistic and intellectual movements all registered this shift. No longer grounds for disparagement, the supposedly natural susceptibility of women to "the heart" now became viewed as the foundation of their superior virtue.

In accord with this newly elevated characterization of female emotions, maternal fondness and tenderness toward children—behavior that had often provoked criticism from Puritan writers—now received highly sentimental acclaim. In *Pamela*, for example, when Richardson describes Mrs. B. disagreeing with a few points in Locke's *Thoughts on Education*, her objections arise from her own more gentle and indulgent approach to children. Around the turn of the century many authors presented tenderness as the primary component of good mothering, indeed, as the very quality most essential to the cultivation of morality in children.[61] In sentimental poetry carried by magazines—flowery verses bearing such titles as "A Mother's Address to a Dying Infant," "Sweet

Infant," "Mother to Child"—this adulation of maternal love achieved its most maudlin expression.[62]

Although writers still warned against the tendency of mothers
to spoil their children, they no longer relied so much on the father's corrective influence as on the mother's own ability to
achieve self-control. At times authors even envisioned the tender
mother softening the "too rough and severe Passions of the Father."[63] Although paternal tenderness, too, could give rise to
sentimental praise, fathers often appeared as excessively harsh
and authoritarian—in fiction, for example, frequently cast in the
roles of arranging unhappy marriages for their children.[64] An
anonymous volume on women published in Philadelphia in 1797
drew the following extravagant contrast between the feelings of
fathers and mothers:

> Where are the tender feelings, the cries, the powerful emotions of na-
> ture? Where is the sentiment, at once sublime and pathetic, that carries
> every feeling to excess? Is it to be found in the frosty indifference and the
> rigid severity, of so many fathers? No; it is in the warm impassioned bosom
> of the mother. . . .
>
> These great expressions of nature, these heartrending emotions, which
> fill us at once with wonder, compassion and terror, always have belonged,
> and always will belong only to women. They possess . . . an inexpressible
> something, which carried them beyond themselves. They seem to discover
> to us new souls, above the standard of humanity.[65]

Significantly, many writers of the period incorporated a sentimental conception of maternal feelings into more overtly feminist
arguments for female intellectual equality.[66] Indeed, the conviction that women innately possessed the best physical, emotional,
and moral qualifications for rearing children did not preclude a
simultaneous commitment to more extensive female education
among feminists and nonfeminists alike. With increasing frequency, in fact, motherhood itself was presented as a compelling
reason for improved female education. Raised in opposition to
"vain" and "frivolous" instruction in the genteel social ornaments
such as music and French, the argument that girls needed to be
prepared for future maternal responsibilities carried a distinctively
middle-class, anti-aristocratic, and utilitarian ring. As historian
Linda Kerber has emphasized, this appeal had a special resonance
in the newly republican United States where motherhood offered
an acceptable outlet for female talent and patriotism despite wom-
en's exclusion from politics.[67] Far from an essentially indigenous
response to the Revolution, however, it was an argument that became popular among middle-class ideologues on both sides of the

Atlantic. Moreover, while in the long run it generally supported conservative desires to keep women in the home, in this transitional period the maternal ideal often lent support to contradictory points of view on female education and social roles.

On the one hand, the ideal served to strengthen the Enlightenment feminist case for a more intellectually rigorous education for women. According to this line of thought, women, too, possessed human reason and with an advanced education would not only better fulfill their human potential and perhaps even make valuable contributions outside the home; but they would, in addition, handle themselves more rationally as mothers and pass valuable knowledge on to their children.[68] On the other hand, however, the responsibilities of motherhood could support the case for a more serious, but also more specialized, domestic education for women. This was an implicit message of much of the accumulating body of medical and educational childrearing literature addressed to mothers which deplored women's ignorance about the practical details of rearing children. Most writers proposing systematic programs of female education did not recommend the actual study of childcare, but many did cite the influence of mothers as a primary reason to tailor curricula to domestic utility. Benjamin Rush, for example, in his *Thoughts upon Female Education*, held that knowledge of foreign languages and musical instruments had no real use even for affluent American women who, unlike their British counterparts, were, as wives and mothers, vitally engaged in managing households and shaping the "manners and character" of the new republic. Their education should instead concentrate on handwriting, bookkeeping, "the more useful branches of literature," and, especially, Christianity.[69] This emphasis on religious instruction as essential preparation for female domestic responsibilities characterized the writings of various Christian apologists, including several English authors widely read in America around the turn of the century. Whereas Enlightenment feminists like Wollstonecraft argued that the development of female intellect best enabled women to become good mothers as well as the equals of men in other respects, these religious figures stressed the cultivation of female piety, as well as instruction in other "basics," to render women most capable as wives and mothers operating within an exclusively domestic context. Compared with more genteel writers who also viewed female piety as a central component of true feminine refinement, these generally middle-class Protestants laid far greater stress on the practical domestic utility of female Christian virtue. Hannah More, for example, the famous English Evangelical author of cheap religious tracts, described the care of families as "the profession of ladies" comparable to the demanding professions of men. Decrying the idle vanity of female ornamentation and intellectual prowess, she advocated "a predominance of those more sober studies, which, not having display for the object will not bring celebrity, but improve usefulness."[70] She warned adolescent girls that only religious women make desirable wives: ". . . how can a man of any understanding, (whatever his own religious professions may be) trust that woman with the care of his family, and the education of his children, who wants herself the best incentive to a virtuous life. . . ?[71]

It was this evangelical perspective on motherhood, with its stress on women's religiosity rather than reason and its emphasis on the importance of their exclusively domestic role, that reigned supreme in the Victorian period. Emerging out of this earlier time of flux, this view began to achieve predominance after the turn of the century, bolstered by an upsurge of religious revivalism and a conservative reaction, especially in the churches, against the radicalism of the French Revolution. Indeed, insofar as eighteenth-century feminism involved a non-Christian rationalism, it probably always appealed to a limited base.[72] The evangelical maternal ideal drew from a much more popular and indigenous Protestant tradition, one that began a resurgence in the early nineteenth century with the revivals and the organization of many voluntary "benevolent" associations. Even nonrevialist "liberal" Protestants were infected with much of this evangelical spirit and similarly promoted this new maternal ideal.[73] The evangelical image of the moral mother triumphed in part because it presented a compelling synthesis of the old and the new. In certain respects it constituted an updated version of the older feminine ideal of help-meet, with its downplaying of female intellect and its emphasis on domestic usefulness and Christian virtue. It also incorporated key features of the ideal of ornamental refinement, particularly its sentimental conception of feminine purity. In other respects, however, the evangelical ideal of the moral mother sharply diverged from these earlier predecessors and conformed more closely to Enlightenment feminist conceptions of women. This is, of course, particularly true of their common elevation of the maternal role. Indeed it is ironic that influential evangelical polemicists sought to discredit feminism by characterizing it not only as anti-Christian, promiscuous, and vain, but as antimotherhood as well.[74] For although Enlightenment feminists and evangelical Protestants might disagree about how mothering stood in relation to other female intellectual, economic, domestic, and religious pursuits, they generally agreed about the imperative natural calling, the serious educational requirements, and the extensive social utility of motherhood.

In the long run, the rise of the moral mother, even in its more conservative evangelical version, had ambiguous effects on the status of women. On the one hand, it provided both ideological justification and incentive for the contraction of female activity into the preoccupations of motherhood. The newfound emphasis on the maternal role became an integral part of the rigid sexual differentiation that became so characteristic of nineteenth-century, middle-class Protestant culture. Women came to be perceived as, essentially, "moral mothers," not only in relation to their children, but also in their other major supportive and didactic roles as teachers, charity workers, and sentimental writers. Moreover, the personality traits stereotypically associated with these nineteeenth-century women—the emotionalism, selflessness, and empathy that characteristically contrasted to male rationalism, competitiveness, and individualism—may well have been reinforced by the psychological repercussions of such intensively maternal nurture. For, as psychoanalytic sociologists have suggested, when mothers rear children virtually alone, the psychological responses of the sexes widely diverge: girls become more interdependent and expressive, and boys tend to become more independent and emotionally self-contained.[75] Through this cycle of mutual reinforcement, then, the social, cultural, and psychological impact of the elevation of the maternal role limited the range of acceptable female pursuits and helped to generate highly distinctive and restrictive feminine and masculine styles.

On the other hand, however, the rise of the moral mother also played its part in the long-range upgrading of the social status of women. The abortive rationalist feminism of the late eighteenth century may be more to the taste of contemporary women, but the evangelical ideal of motherhood also broke with tradition by attributing to women strong moral authority and granting them an important field of special expertise. It entitled them to considerable autonomy within what came to be defined as the "woman's sphere," and it even helped to create both the legitimacy and the solidarity necessary for later, more successful, feminist agitation.[76]

NOTES

[1] See especially Anne L. Kuhn, *The Mother's Role in Childhood Education* (New Haven: Yale University Press, 1947); Barbara Welter, "The Cult of True Womanhood: 1820-1860," *American Quarterly* 18 (Summer 1966): 151-74; Kathryn Kish Sklar, *Catherine Beecher* (New Haven: Yale University Press, 1973); Ann Douglas, *The Feminization of American Culture* (New York: Knopf, 1977).

[2] Elizabeth Anthony Dexter, *Colonial Women of Affairs* (New York: Houghton Mifflin Co., 1924); Julia Cherry Spruil, *Women's Life and Work in the Southern Colonies* (Chapel Hill: University of North Carolina Press, 1938); Mary Sumner Benson, *Women in Eighteenth-Century America* (New York: Columbia University Press, 1935); Edmund S. Morgan, *The Puritan Family*, rev. ed. (New York: Harper and Row, 1966); John Demos, *A Little Commonwealth* (New York: Oxford University Press, 1970); Mary P. Ryan, *Womanhood in America* (New York: New Viewpoints, 1975), pp. 21-135; Laurel Thatcher Ulrich, "Vertuous Women Found: New England Ministerial Literature, 1668-1735," *American Quarterly* 28 (Spring 1976): 20-40; Margaret W. Masson, "The Typology of the Female as a Model for the Regenerate: Puritan Preaching, 1690-1730," *Signs* 2 (Winter 1976): 304-15.

For examples of the more recent trend see Linda K. Kerber, "Daughters of Columbia: Educating Women for the Republic, 1787-1805," in *The Hofstadter Aegis: A Memorial*, eds. Stanley Elkins and Eric McKitrick (New York: Knopf, 1974), pp. 36-59; Linda K. Kerber, "The Republican Mother: Women and the Enlightenment—An American Perspective," *American Quarterly* 28 (Summer 1976): 187-205; Nancy F. Cott, *The Bonds of Womanhood* (New Haven: Yale University Press, 1977), pp. 46-47, 58-62, 85-92, and passim.

[3] This portrait of the Puritan "help-meet" ideal is drawn from Morgan, Ryan, Ulrich, and from my own reading of numerous Puritan published sermons and treatises on women and family life. More extensive documentation on many points in this paper is available from the author upon request.

[4] A few examples are Benjamin Franklin, *Reflections on Courtship and Marriage* (Philadelphia: B. Franklin, 1746); John Witherspoon, "Letters on Marriage," in *A Series of Letters on Courtship and Marriage* (Springfield, Mass.: F. Stebbins, 1798); "On the Choice of a Wife," *The Columbian Magazine and the Universal Asylum* 8 (March 1792): 176-79.

[5] This genteel ideal has received far less scholarly treatment than the help-meet, although it has been observed by Ryan and Benson. Also see Robert Middlekauff, *Ancients and Axioms* (New Haven: Yale University Press, 1963), pp. 106-108, 167-68. This sketch draws primarily from my own reading of the eighteenth-century sources.

[6] John Oliver, *A Present for Teeming Women* (Boston: Benjamin Harris, 1694); Cotton Mather, *Elizabeth on her Holy Retirement* (Boston: B. Green, 1710). Also see Catherine M. Scholten, " 'On the Importance of the Obstetrick Art': Changing Customs of Childbirth in America, 1760 to 1825," *William and Mary Quarterly* 34 (July 1977): 426-45.

[7] Benjamin Colman, *Some of the Honours that Religion Does unto the Fruitful Mothers in Israel* (Boston: B. Green, 1715).

[8] The evidence on wet-nursing in western Europe is summarized in Edward Shorter, *The Making of the Modern Family* (New York: Basic Books, 1975), pp. 175-77. For some scattered evidence on American wetnursing, see Joseph E. Illick, "Child-Rearing in Seventeenth-Century England and America," in *The History of Childhood*, ed. Lloyd deMause (New York: Harper and Row, 1974), p. 325; Carl Bridenbaugh, *Cities in Revolt* (New York: Oxford University Press, 1955), p. 149; Spruill, *Women's Life and Work*, pp. 55-57.

[9] A few examples of numerous admonitions against wetnursing are Robert Cleaver,

A Godlie Forme of Householde Government (London: Felix Kingston, 1598), pp. 235-39; William Gouge, *Of Domesticall Duties* (London: John Haviland, 1622), pp. 507-17; Cotton Mather, *Ornaments for the Daughters of Zion* (Cambridge, Mass.: Samuel Phillips, 1692), p. 93; Benajmin Wadsworth, *The Well-Ordered Family* (Boston: B. Green, 1712), p. 46; Sophia Hume, *An Exhortation to the Inhaibtants of South-Carolina* (Philadelphia: William Bradford, 1748?), pp. 119-24. Cleaver and Gouge very briefly mention psychological effects.

[10]Many contemporary historians, primarily of Europe, have come to this dubious conclusion. Their case is based on at least two faulty assumptions: The first is that caring mothers should have known that wetnursing was medically dangerous, and the second is that a lack of written attention to maternal affection means that it did not exist. See especially David Hunt, *Parents and Children in History* (New York: Harper and Row, 1970); Lloyd de Mause "The Evolution of Childhood," *History of Childhood Quarterly* 1 (1974): 503-75; and Shorter, *The Making of the Modern Family.*

[11]Cleaver, *A Godlie Forme,* pp. 60, 297; John Taylor, *The Value of a Child* (Philadelphia: B. Franklin and D. Hall, 1753), p. 7; Mather, *Ornaments,* p. 95; Cotton Mather, *Help for Distressed Parents* (Boston: John Allen, 1795), pp. 8-9; Philip Doddridge, *Sermons on the Religious Education of Children,* 4th ed. (Boston: Kneeland, 1763).

[12]Cotton Mather, *Maternal Consolations* (Boston: T. Fleet, 1714), pp. 18, 21. Another unusual funeral sermon by a mourning son that praises maternal tenderness is Thomas Foxcroft, *A Sermon Preach'd at Cambridge, After the Funeral of Mrs. Elizabeth Foxcroft* (Boston: B. Green, 1721).

[13]See especially Phillipe Ariès, *Centuries of Childhood,* trans. Robert Baldick (New York: Vintage Books, 1962).

[14]This genre included numerous works. The best summary is Morgan, *Puritan Family,* pp. 65-108. Other historians have noted the relatively undifferentiated parental roles prescribed in Puritan literature. See Ryan, *Womanhood in America,* p. 60; Ulrich, "Vertuous Women Found," p. 39; Masson, "Typology of Female," pp. 306-307.

[15]For a few of many examples, see Mather, *Ornaments,* pp. 88-89; Mather, *Maternal,* pp. 11-15; Foxcroft, *A Sermon*; and Benjamin Colman, *The Honour and Happiness of the Vertuous Woman* (Boston: B. Green, 1716).

[16]See, for example, Gouge, *Of Domesticall Duties,* pp. 546-47; Increase Mather, *Call from Heaven to the Present and Succeeding Generations* (Boston: John Foster, 1679), p. 23; Taylor, *The Value of a Child,* p. 3.

[17]Cotton Mather, *Help,* pp. 8-9. Also see Cleaver, *A Godlie Forme,* pp. 60-61; Gouge, *Of Domesticall Duties,* pp. 259-60; John Robinson, "Of Children and their education," in *New Essayes or Observations Divine and Morall* (n.p., 1628), p. 306.

[18]See, for example, Richard Mather, *A Farewell Exhortation to the Church and People of Dorchester in New-England* (Cambridge, Mass.: S. Green, 1657), p. 11; Cotton Mather, *Cares about the Nurseries* (Boston: n.p., 1702), pp. 4-8; Benjamin Bass, *Parents and Children Advised and Exhorted to their Duty* (Newport: James Franklin, 1730).

[19]One now obscure edition of *The Mother's Catechism*—possibly not by Willison but by Richard Baxter—was printed in Boston in 1729. Puritan works written explicitly for fathers are numerous. A few examples are Deodat Lawson, *The Duty & Property of a Religious Householder* (Boston: B. Green, 1693); Cotton Mather, *A Family-Sacrifice* (Boston: B. Green and J. Allen, 1703); Joseph Buckminister, *Heads of Families, to resolve for their Households, no less than for themselves, that they will serve the Lord* (Boston: S. Kneeland, 1759).

[20]Richard Baxter, *A Christian Directory* (London: Robert White, 1673), p. 548; Richard Mather, *A Farewel Exhortation,* p. 13; Cotton Mather, *Cares,* pp. 44-45.

[21]Gouge, *Of Domesticall Duties,* pp. 486-87. Also see Foxcroft, *A Sermon,* pp. 8, 18.

[22]Morgan, *Puritan Family,* pp. 75-79, and Demos, *Little Commonwealth,* pp. 70-75.

[23]Morgan, *Puritan Family,* pp. 117-18. For servants' responsibilities to children, see

Cotton Mather, *Corderius Americanus* (Boston: J. Allen, 1708), pp. 12-13.

[24]On women in the colonial economy, see especially Dexter, *Colonial Women*. She, however, exaggerates the extent and autonomy of women engaged in nondomestic work. See Mary Beth Norton, "Eighteenth-Century American Women in Peace and War: The Case of the Loyalists," *William and Mary Quarterly*, 3d ser. 33 (July 1976): 386-409.

[25]Gusti Wiesenfeld Frankel, "Between Parent and Child in Colonial New England: Analysis of the Religious Child-Oriented Literature and Selected Children's Works" (unpublished doctoral thesis, University of Minnesota, 1977). I am indebted to Gusti Wisenfeld Frankel of the Hebrew University for conversation and tips on other aspects of this paper as well.

[26]Hugh Smith, *Letters to Married Women, on Nursing and the Management of Children* (Philadelphia: Mathew Carey, 1792), p. 121; Elizabeth Griffiths, "Letters to Ladies—Married and Single. With Useful Advice," *New York Weekly Magazine* I (September 1795), p. 92; Clark Brown, *The Importance of the early and proper education of children* (Newbedford: John Spooner, 1795), p. 17; Enos Hitchcock, *A Discourse on Education* (Providence: Bennett Wheeler, 1785), p. 6. This evolving perspective on child psychology owed much to the long-term influence of such philosophers as Locke and Rousseau, although much of their work did not circulate widely in eighteenth-century America. See David Lundberg and Henry F. May, "The Enlightened Reader in America: 1700 to 1813," *American Quarterly* 28 (Summer 1976): 262-71 and appendix.

[27]Cleaver, *A Godlie Forme*, p. 237, is the only example I know of a work read in America using the "humour" theory. Others explicitly dismissed it. See Nicholas Culpeper, *A Directory for Midwives* (London: George Sawbridge, 1675), pp. 152-60, and Hume, *An Exhortation*, p. 120.

[28]Enos Hitchcock, *Memoirs of the Bloomsgrove Family* (Boston: Thomas and Andrews, 1790) I: 79.

[29]Mary Watkins, *Maternal Solicitude, or, Lady's Manual, &c.* (New York: H. C. Southwick, 1809), pp. 9-10.

[31]Henry Home (Lord Kames), *Sketches of the History of Man* (Edinburgh: W. Strahan and T. Cadell, 1778), p. 92; Smith, *Letters to Married Women*, p. 51.

[31]Smith, *Letters to Married Women*, p. 51; William Buchan, *Domestic Medicine* (Boston: Joseph Bumstead, 1793), pp. 3, 23-35; *The Maternal Physician* (New York: Isaac Riley, 1811; reprint ed., New York: Arno Press, 1972), p. 14.

[32]"The Advantage of Maternal Nurture," *The Weekly Visitor, or, Ladies' Miscellany* II (May 1804): 260-61. Also see Richard Polwhele, "On the Domestic Character of Women," *The New York Magazine, or, Literary Repository* 7 (November 1796): 600-602; Henry Home, *Loose Hints upon Education* (Edinburgh: John Bell, 1782), p. 44; Watkins, *Maternal Solicitude*, pp. 8-9.

[33]Smith, *Letters to Married Women*, p. 60.

[34]This paragraph is drawn from numerous pieces of medical literature printed (or reprinted) in America. Salient examples include: Dr. Willich, "Method of Treating that Excruciating Complaint incident to Married Ladies,—Sore Nipples," *The Weekly Visitor, or, Ladies Miscellany* II (March 1804): 196; George Wallis, *The Art of Preventing Disease, and Restoring Health* (New York: Samuel Campbell, 1794), pp. 114-28; Michael Underwood, *A Treatise on the Diseases of Children with General Directions for the Management of Infants from the Birth* (Philadelphia: T. Dobson, 1793), pp. 327-404; William Cadogan, *An Essay upon Nursing and the Management of Children* (Boston: Cox and Berry, 1772), pp. 10-49; Alexander Hamilton, *Management of Female Complaints, and of Children in Early Infancy* (Philadelphia: A Bartram, 1806), pp. 225-42; William Buchan, *Advice to Mothers* (Philadelphia: J. Bioren, 1804); Buchan, *Domestic*; Smith, *Letters to Married Women*; Samuel Kennedy Jennings, *Married Lady's Companion, or Poor Man's Friend* (Richmond, Va.: T. Nichol-

son, 1804); Watkins, *Maternal Solicitude*, pp. 7-18; anon. *Maternal Physician*, pp. 5-28, 93-135. The last three are American. Many of these prescriptions were also in Locke's *Some Thoughts concerning Education* and were taken up in other, nonmedical, books such as Richardson's *Pamela* and Enos Hitchcock's *Memoirs.*

[35]Cadogan, *An Essay upon Nursing*, pp. 3-5; Underwood, *A Treatise on Diseases*, pp. 1-2, 335-37; Buchan, *Domestic*, pp. 4-5.

[36]Anon., *Maternal Physician*, p. 7.

[37]Buchan, *Advice*, p. 294.

[38]George Strebeck, *A Sermon on the Character of the Virtuous Woman* (New York: n.p. 1800), p. 23; John Burton, *Lectures on Female Education and Manners* (Elizabethtown, N.J.: S. Kollock, 1799), p. 54; Griffiths, "Letters to Ladies," pp. 91-92, 99-100; Thomas Barnard, *A Sermon preached before the Salem Female Charitable Society* (Salem: William Carlton, 1803), p. 13; Hitchcock, *Memoirs*, I: 47-48.

[39]Jesse Appleton, *A Discourse delivered before the members of the Portsmouth Female Asylum* (Portsmouth: S. Whidden, 1806), p. 15.

[40]Aside from the medical literature noted above, see, for example, anon., *Advice to the Fair Sex* (Philadelphia: Robert Cochran, 1803), pp. 121-33; Jane West, *Letters to a Young Lady* (Troy, N.Y.: O. Penniman & Co., 1806), pp. 406-41; [Judith Sargeant Murray], "On the Domestic Education of Children," *The Massachusetts Magazine* 2 (June 1790): 275-77.

[41]Anon., *The Mother's Gift* (Worcester: Isaiah Thomas, 1787).

[42]Elizabeth Helme, *Maternal Instruction, or Family Conversations* (New York: James Oram, 1804).

[43]Anon., *Early Christian Instructions in the form of a Diagloue between a Mother and Child* (Philadelphia: James P. Parke, 1807); Priscilla Wakefield, *Domestic Recreation* (Philadelphia: Jacob Johnson, 1803); [Mary Jane Kilner], *Familiar Dialogues for the Instruction and Amusement of Children of four and five* (Boston: Hall and Hiller, 1804). On mothers in Quaker literature, see J. William Frost, *The Quaker Family in Colonial America* (New York: St. Martin's Press, 1973), p. 85.

[44]After one American edition in 1729, it went into 14 new editions between 1783 and 1811.

[45]See, for example, Helme, *Maternal Instruction*; Wakefield, *Domestic Recreation*; Kilner, *Familiar Dialogues*; Griffiths, "Letters to Ladies"; anon, *The Mother's Remarks on A Set of Cuts for Children* (Philadelphia: Jacob Johnson, 1803).

[46]John Cosens Ogden, *The Female Guide* (Concord: George Hough, 1793), p. 8.

[47]Burton, *Lectures on Female Education*, p. 55.

[48]Jennings, *Married Ladies*, pp. 123-25; anon., *The Parent's Friend* (Philadelphia: Jane Aitken, 1803), pp. xi-xiii.

[49]Cott, *Bonds of Womanhood*, pp. 48-50. On changes in class composition see Lawrence W. Towner, " 'A Fondness for Freedom': Servant Protest in Puritan Society," *William and Mary Quarterly* 3rd ser. 19 (April 1962): 213-15.

[50]On parental role differentiation due to fathers leaving home to work, see Cott, *Bonds of Womanhood*, especially p. 46. This phenomenon has received more extended analysis in its relation to the Industrial Revolution, which in America occurred only later. See especially Neil J. Smelser, *Social Change in the Industrial Revolution* (Chicago: University of Chicago Press, 1959), pp. 180-312.

[51]On home manufacturing in America, see Cott, *Bonds of Womanhood*, pp. 19-62. For England, see Alice Clark, *Working Life of Women in the Seventeenth Century* (London: Frank Cass and Co., 1919); Ivy Pinchbeck, *Women Workers and the Industrial Revolution*, rev. ed. (London: Frank Cass and Co., 1969).

[52]Ian Watt makes this argument in *The Rise of the Novel* (Berkeley: University of California Press, 1957), pp. 43-45. Ann Douglas, in *Feminization*, also makes this case for a later period in America. On literacy, see Kenneth A. Lockridge, *Literacy in Colo-*

nial *New England* (New York: Norton, 1974), pp. 38-42. Note especially the Boston figures.

[53]See, for example, Smith, *Letters to Married Women*, p. 129; Buchan, *Advice*, p. 4; Jennings, *Married Lady's Companion*, p. 5; *Maternal Physician*, p. 278.

[54]Cott, *Bonds of Womanhood*, pp. 85-86, 147-48; Douglas, *Feminization*, passim.

[55]William Lyman, *A Virtuous Woman the Bond of Domestic Union* (New London: S. Green, 1802), p. 22.

[56]Barnard, *A Sermon*, p. 14.

[57]Mary Wollstonecraft, *A Vindication of the Rights of Woman* (London, 1792; reprint ed., New York: Norton, 1967), p. 280.

[58]New England clergymen now frequently stressed such female virtues. For a more complete discussion and listing of such clerical writings, see Cott, *Bonds of Womanhood*, pp. 126-59, and her bibliography. In addition, numerous secular comparative histories and biographies of women began to appear that emphasized these qualities.

[59]Examples are numerous. A few are: "Scheme for encreasing the power of the Fair Sex," *The Baltimore Weekly Magazine* I (April 1801): 241-42; *The Female Advocate* (New Haven: Thomas Green and Son, 1801), p. 14; "On the Influence of Women," *The Literary Magazine and American Register* V (June 1806): 403-408; Thomas Branagan, *The Excellency of the Female Character Vindicated* (New York: Samuel Wood, 1807), pp. 61-62, 111-12.

[60]See, for example, Samuel Worcester, *Female Love to Christ* (Salem: Pool and Palfray, 1809), p. 14; Daniel Dana, *A Discourse delivered May 22, 1804, before the Members of the Female Charitable Society of Newburyport* (Newburyport: Edmund M. Blunt, 1804), pp. 15-19; Timothy Woodbridge, *A Sermon, preached April 20th, 1813, in compliance with a request of the Gloucester Female Society* (Boston: Samuel T. Armstrong, 1813), pp. 18-19; Daniel Chaplin, *A Discourse delivered before the Charitable Female Society in Groton* (Andover: Flagg and Gould, 1814), pp. 8-10.

[61]See, for example, anon., *The Mother's Gift*; Griffiths, "Letters to Ladies," [Murray], "On Domestic Education," pp. 275-77; Worcester, *Female Love*, p. 7.

[62]"A Mothers Address," *The Weekly Visitor, or, Ladies Miscellany* 2 (August 1804): 344; "Sweet Infant," *The Lady's Weekly Miscellany* 8 (November 1808): 63; "The Mother to her Child," *The Lady's Weekly Miscellany* 7 (May 1808): 64.

[63]Anon., *Family-Religion Revived* (New Haven: James Parker, 1775), p. 96. Also Smith, *Letters to Married Women*, p. 123.

[64]Examples of sentimentalized paternal foundness are: Mason Locke Weems, *Hymen's recruiting sergeant* (Philadelphia: R. Cochran, 1802); "On the Happiness of Domestic Life," *The American Museum* 1 (February 1787): 156-58; for examples of tyrannical fathers, see "Honour Eclipsed by Love," *The Boston Magazine* 2 (August 1785): 293-95; M. Imbert, "The Power of Love and Filial Duty," *The New-York Magazine; or, Literary Repository* 2 (August 1791): 468-75; "On Parental Authority," *The Ladies Magazine* 1 (October 1792): 237-41.

[65]Anon., *Sketches of the History, Disposition, Accomplishments, Employments, Customs and Importance of the Fair Sex* (Philadelphia: Samuel Samson, 1797), pp. 103-104.

[66]Judith Sargeant Murray, *The Gleaner* (Boston: I. Thomas and E. T. Andrews, 1798) 3: 223-24; [Murray], "On Domestic Education"; anon., "Maternal Affection: Extract from the Beauties of Wollstoncraft [sic]," *The Lady's Weekly Miscellany* 7 (April 1808): 14-15; William Boyd, *Woman: A poem* (Boston: John W. Folsom, 1796), p. 9; *The Female Character Vindicated* (Leominster: Charles Prentiss, 1796), p. 10; anon., *Female Advocate*, pp. 33-34.

[67]See Kerber, "Daughters of Columbia," and "Republican Mother," Contrary to Kerber's impression, however, still only a small minority of those advocating improved female education stressed the responsibilities of mothers. Prospects of improvement in

the quality of women's companionship, personal fulfillment, and even intellectual contributions to society were still more often invoked.

68A few outstanding examples are: Wollstonecraft, *Vindication*, pp. 32-33, 280; Murray, *Gleaner*, 2: 6-7, 3: 188-224; *Female Advocate*, pp. 33-34; "Oration upon Female Education," in *The American Preceptor*, ed. Caleb Bingham (Boston: Manning and Loring, 1813), pp. 47-51; "Plan for the Emancipation of the Fair Sex," *Lady's Magazine and Musical Repository* 3 (January 1802): 43-44; "Present Mode of Female Education Considered," *The Lady's Weekly Miscellany* 7 (June 1808): 43-44; "On the Supposed Superiority of the Masculine Understanding," *The Columbian Magazine and the Universal Asylum* 7 (July 1791): 11.

69Benjamin Rush, "Thoughts upon Female Education," in *Essays on Education in the Early Republic*, ed. Frederick Rudolph (Cambridge, Mass.: Harvard University Press, 1965), pp. 25-40. Also see Noah Webster, "On the Education of Youth," *A Collection of Essays and Fugitiv Writings* (Boston: I. Thomas and E. T. Andrews, 1790), pp. 27-30; Hitchcock, *Memoirs*, 2: 23-94, 289-300. Hitchcock drew from Rousseau in his stress on female domesticity, but, like other Americans in this period, thought more highly of female intellect.

70Hannah More, *Strictures on the Modern Ssytem of Female Education* (London: R. Cadell and W. Davies, 1799) 1: 97-98, 2: 2.

71Hannah More, "Essays for Young Ladies," in *The Lady's Pocket Library* (Philadelphia: Mathew Carey, 1792), p. 67.

72Henry F. May, *The Enlightenment in America* (New York: Oxford University Press, 1976), pp. 153-304, passim.

73Douglas, *Feminization*, passim. She, however, wrongly associates such views with northeastern liberal (later Unitarian) Protestants alone. Most of the religious figures cited in this paper were decidedly evangelical (either English Low Church Anglicans or American "moderate" revivalist Calvinists in the Congregational or Presbyterian Churches). Significantly, some of the next-generation Victorian "liberals" featured in Douglas' book, such as the Beecher siblings, came from strong evangelical backgrounds.

74See especially Timothy Dwight, as "Morpheus," *New-England Palladium*, March 15, 1802. As cited in Kerber, "Daughters of Columbia," p. 52.

75See especially Nancy Chodorow, *The Reproduction of Mothering* (Berkeley: University of California Press, 1978). Many essays by Talcott Parsons have also drawn this connection. Fred Weinstein and Gerald M. Platt's *The Wish to be Free* (Berkeley: University of California Press, 1969) is a historical work largely organized in these terms, but it focuses on male personality.

76Cott, *Bonds of Womanhood*, pp. 160-96.

WORDS AS SOCIAL CONTROL: NOAH WEBSTER AND THE CREATION OF THE *AMERICAN DICTIONARY*

RICHARD M. ROLLINS
Ohio State University

"I FINISHED WRITING MY DICTIONARY IN JANUARY, 1825," Noah Webster once recalled. It was a solemn moment:

> When I had come to the last word, I was seized with a trembling which made it somewhat difficult to hold my pen steady for writing. The cause seems to have been the thought that I might not then live to finish the work, or the thought that I was so near the end of my labors. But I summoned the strength to finish the last word, and then walking about the room a few minutes I recovered.[1]

So ended twenty-five years of constant, daily labor. The finished product was, by all standards, a monumental achievement. With 70,000 entries, all written out by his own hand, it was a massive work, the last major dictionary ever compiled by a single individual.[2] It has become, in the form of its successors, an integral part of American culture. As early as the mid-nineteenth century the name Webster had become synonymous with a dictionary.[3]

Virtually everyone believes that the *American Dictionary of the English Language* was a nationalistic tract. So pervasive is this belief that many historians, like Oscar Handlin and John D. Hicks, discuss the work in the context of rising nationalism without really stating that the work was thus

---

[1]Undated quote in Emily E. F. Ford, *Notes on the Life of Noah Webster* (New York: Private Printing, 1912), Vol. I, 293.

[2]Robert Keith Leavitt, *Noah's Ark: New England Yankees and the Endless Quest* (Springfield. Mass.: G. and C. Merriam Company, 1947).

[3]Horace E. Scudder, *Noah Webster* (Boston: Houghton Mifflin, 1888).

motivated.[4] They write as if Webster's nationalism was common knowledge and that there could be no other explanation for his work. Others have made clearer statements concerning the subject. Charles Beard called the dictionary a high note of nationalism;[5] Merle Curti and his associates portrayed it as a patriotic effort,[6] while John Krout and Dixon Ryan Fox fit it nicely into their narrative of the completion of American Independence.[7] Even Lawrence J. Friedman, who correctly notes Webster's alienation, portrays the dictionary as a patriotic work.[8] Those who have concentrated on Webster or the dictionary itself have been even more adamant in their conclusions. Homer D. Babbidge represents the attitude and methodology most commentators employ. He consistently confuses Webster's nationalistic statements of the 1780s with his later work, as if nothing occurred between 1783 and 1841.[9]

Nationalism is too simple an explanation. When the work is considered within the context of Noah Webster's life, it becomes apparent that it was stimulated by much more than patriotism. That was undoubtedly an important factor in his early conceptions, but the *American Dictionary* was the product of a lifetime. It reflected the events and inheritances of that human life and contained all the biases, concerns, and ideals of a specific individual. Indeed, it was an extension of his whole personality, and one must read it carefully to understand the tale it tells. Webster's main motivation for writing and publishing it was not to celebrate American life or to expand independence. Instead, he sought to counteract social disruption and reestablish the deferential world order that he believed was disintegrating.

*   *   *

Over the course of his eighty-four years, Noah Webster changed from an optimistic revolutionary in the 1780s, convinced that man could perfect himself and that America was the site of a future utopia,[10] to a pessimistic

---

[4]Oscar Handlin, *The History of the United States* (New York: Holt, Rinehart and Winston, 1967), Vol. I, 393, and John D. Hicks, George E. Mowry and Robert L. Burke, *A History of American Democracy*, 3rd ed. (Boston: Houghton Mifflin, 1966), 185.

[5]Charles A. Beard, *The Rise of American Civilization* (New York: Macmillan, 1940), 766.

[6]Merle Curti, Richard H. Shryock, Thomas C. Cochran, and Fred Harvey Harrington, *A History of American Civilization* (New York: Harper, 1953), 165.

[7]John A. Krout and Dixon Ryan Fox, *The Completion of American Independence, 1790-1830* (New York: Quadrangle, 1944), 33.

[8]Lawrence J. Friedman, *Inventors of the Promised Land* (New York: Knopf, 1975), 30-41.

[9]Homer D. Babbidge, Jr., ed., *Noah Webster: On Being American. Selected Writings, 1783-1828* (New York: Praeger, 1967). See also Harry R. Warfel, *Noah Webster: Schoolmaster to America* (New York: Octagon, 1936), 353.

[10]Webster also advocated universal white male suffrage, complete religious toleration, equal distribution of property (including confiscation of landed estates), and the abolition of slavery. For an analysis of Webster's writings in relation to revolutionary ideology as outlined by

critic of man and society. His buoyant nationalism dissolved under the pressures of the events of the 1780s and 1790s. The question that commanded his attention during the last fifty years of his life was the conflict between freedom and order. As with many others who perceived themselves as America's moral stewards after 1800, his answer to that problem was that all Americans should submit their hearts and minds to an authoritarian God and mold themselves in the image of Quiet Christians. Good citizens were not disruptive; they were obedient to the wishes of a social leadership consisting of pious, elderly property owners. Webster's definitions of words, both in his private correspondence and in the dictionary itself, as well as his method of etymology, reflect this view. If Americans would only see the world through the eyes and mind of Noah Webster as set forth in his dictionary, Christian peace and tranquillity would reign. Webster's main motivation was social control, and his dictionary was a means of achieving it.

The change in Webster began in the 1780s. Dissent in Connecticut, Shays' Rebellion in Massachusetts, chaotic election procedures in the South, and economic instability convinced him that an authority capable of enforcing order was necessary, that the Articles of Confederation must be replaced. In 1787, the Pennsylvania delegation to the Constitutional Convention asked him to write a defense of the new government. Webster happily complied, expressing his view of the new system as a balance between revolutionary ideals and social stability.[11]

The development of Webster's interest in language coincided with an emerging emphasis on order. Throughout his life he exhibited a dualistic attitude toward language. It was a subject worthy of study by all Americans for its own sake, but also a means to a greater end. In 1789 he published the first significant American essay on linguistics, *Dissertations on the English Language....*[12] His concept of language as a tool of social change had emerged. Webster believed that cultural as well as political independence was necessary for the new nation to survive. Like Schlegel, Grimm, Horne Tooke, and other Europeans, Webster believed that a connection between

---

Bernard Bailyn and Gordon S. Wood, see Richard M. Rollins, "Noah Webster: Propagandist for the Revolution," *Connecticut History*, forthcoming, or Richard M. Rollins, "The Long Journey of Noah Webster" (Diss., Michigan State University, 1976). The best source of information on Webster's early life is an unpublished autobiographical fragment: [Noah Webster], "Memoir of Noah Webster," Webster Family Papers, Box 1, Yale Univ. Archives. For a complete listing of all his work, see Edwin A. Carpenter, ed., *A Bibliography of the Writings of Noah Webster* (New York: New York Public Library, 1958).

[11] [Noah Webster], *An Examination into the Leading Principles of the Federal Constitution* ... (Philadelphia: Pritchard and Hill, 1787). See also Webster's *Diary*, The Papers of Noah Webster, Manuscripts and Archives, New York Public Library (archive hereafter cited as NYPL).

[12] Noah Webster, *Dissertations on the English Language* ... (Boston: Isaiah Thomas and Company, 1789).

language and the nation existed. "A *national language* is a bond of *national union*," he said, and it should "be employed to render the people of this country national. . . ."[13]

Yet Webster's anxiety increased in response to the events of the 1790s. The growth of the democratic societies, mob violence, the activities of Genêt and his supporters, and especially the political battles and public vituperation dismayed him. The terror in France was a turning point. Shocked by the widespread use of the guillotine, Webster became convinced that man was innately depraved and that the expansion of human freedom and self-reliance brought only anarchy, chaos, murder, and brutality. Events in France seemed a portent of America's future, and thus he opposed efforts at progressive social change. The great experiment had produced only a people characterized by corruption, vice, deceit, and debauchery.[14]

On July Fourth of 1798 Webster gave an oration in New Haven in which he summarized the events of the previous twenty years and predicted the nation's future. It amounted to little more than a call for imposition of authority and a means of enforcing its wishes. Utopia had become a frightening den of iniquity; agitation and dissent must cease, a source of cohesion must be found. "Let us never forget that the cornerstone of all republican government is," he said, "that the will of every citizen is controlled by the laws of supreme will of the state."[15]

His criticism of the developing nation after 1798 was profound. The concept of equality seemed fallacious,[16] and democracy threatened civilization itself.[17] Only fatherly figures of authority could be trusted to govern. People would be freer and happier "if all were deprived of the right of suffrage until they were forty-five years of age, and if no man was eligible to an important office until he was fifty. . . ." All power should be vested in "our old men, who have lost their ambitions chiefly and have learnt wisdom by experience."[18]

Conversion to evangelical Protestantism in 1808 provided Webster with more detailed explanations of all his fears. With men like John Jay, Stephen Van Rensselaer, Timothy Dwight, John Cotton Smith, and Elias Boudinot, Webster believed that religion provided the only viable basis for civilization. They saw themselves as "their brother's keepers," and were determined to

[13]Ibid., 397. Webster's use of italics is inconsistent throughout his dictionary.

[14]See especially Letter To Timothy Pickering, July 7, 1797, Ford, *Notes*, I, 422 and *Minerva*, July 12, Aug. 14, 1797.

[15]Noah Webster, "An Oration, Pronounced before the Citizens of New Haven . . . ," *Commercial Advertiser*, July 24, 1798.

[16]Noah Webster, *An Oration, Pronounced before the Citizens of New Haven, on the Anniversary of the Declaration of Independence; July, 1802* (New Haven: William W. Morse, 1802), 16.

[17]Letter to Oliver Wolcott, Sept. 16, 1800, *Ford*, I, 504–06.

[18]Letter to Benjamin Rush, Dec. 15, 1800, ibid., 479.

oversee America's return to tranquillity through their own moral stewardship. They formed large organizations, including the American Bible Society, the American Tract Society, and the American Sunday School Union
in order to spread their doctrines of Quiet Christian deference and to
enhance public acquiescence.[19] In everything he wrote after 1808, from ordinary school books to evangelical tracts and including his own version of the
Holy Bible, Webster proclaimed that fearful worship of God was the first
step to civil order, that government should be run by the elderly, pious, and
wealthy. He summed up his conception of the influence of religion on behavior and society:

> Real religion implies a habitual sense of divine presence, and a fear of offending the
> Supreme Being, subdues and controls all the turbulent passions; and nothing is
> seen in the Christian, but meekness, forbearance, and kindness, accompanied by a
> serenity of mind and a desire to please, as uniform as they are cheering to families
> and friends.[20]

Americans should not agitate for social change but must instead be
obedient followers of the law as laid down by the moral stewards. All would
be chaos without total obedience to God:

> . . . we are cast on the ocean of life, without chart, or compass, or rudder—nay, we
> are ignorant of our own port—we know not where we are bound—we have not a
> ray of light to guide us in the tempestuous sea—not a hope to cheer us amidst the
> distresses of this world, or tranquillize the soul in its passage into the next—and all
> beyond the present state, is annihilation or despair![21]

In this frame of mind, far from one of exuberant nationalism, Webster wrote
his dictionary.

[19]Several studies of the religious benevolence movement in the early nineteenth century have
been written. Most stress the social control aspect; these include Charles S. Griffin, *Their
Brother's Keepers: Moral Stewardship in the United States, 1815–1865* (New Brunswick: Rut-
gers Univ. Press, 1964), and "Religious Benevolence as Social Control, 1815–1860," *Mississippi
Valley Historical Review,* 64 (Dec. 1957), 423–44; Stephen E. Berk, *Calvinism versus
Democracy: Timothy Dwight and the Origins of American Evangelical Orthodoxy* (Hamden,
Conn.: Archon Books, 1974); M. J. Heale, "Humanitarianism in the Early Republic: The Moral
Reformers of New York, 1776–1825," *Journal of American Studies,* 2 (Oct. 1968), 161–75; W.
David Lewis, "The Reformers as Conservatives: Protestant Counter-Subversion in the Early
Republic," in Stanley Coben and Lorman Ratner, eds., *The Development of an American Cul-
ture* (Englewood Cliffs, N.J.: Prentice-Hall, 1970); and Raymond A. Mohl, *Poverty in New
York, 1783–1825* (New York: Oxford Univ. Press, 1970). For a skeptical analysis, see Lois W.
Banner, "Religious Benevolence as Social Control: A Critique of an Interpretation," *Journal of
American History,* 60 (June 1973), 23–41.
[20]Noah Webster, *Letter from Noah Webster, Esq., of New Haven, Connecticut, to a friend in
Explanation and Defense of the Distinguishing Doctrines of the Gospel* (New York: J. Seymour,
1809), 22.
[21]Noah Webster, "Letter to a Young Gentleman Commencing his Education," *A Collection
of Papers on Political, Literary and Moral Subjects* (New York: Webster and Clark, 1843), 86.
This essay was first published in 1823.

It is natural to draw direct links between Webster's early nationalism and his *American Dictionary*. And of course Webster encouraged this in the title and in his preface to his most famous work. He noted that the chief glory of a nation arose from its authors and stated that American writers were equal to Englishmen. He even named those on this side of the Atlantic whom he considered comparable to the best of Europe. Franklin, Washington, Adams, Jay, Madison, Marshall, Dwight, Trumbull, and Irving were his more well-known favorites. Nonetheless, the nationalist context is insufficient to explain the book. Perhaps as an indication of what was to come, Webster did not mention the internationally famous American who symbolized all that he loathed, Thomas Jefferson. Thomas Paine and other earlier American celebrators of democracy and freedom were also neglected. As George Krapp, the most respected twentieth-century student of the development of the English language has noted, merely naming Franklin, Washington, and others as authorities "is quite a different matter from the narrow patriotic zeal which was rampant in the years immediately following the Revolution."[22]

In addition, Webster himself indicated that his views had changed. "It is not only important, but, in a degree necessary," he said in the opening pages, "that the people of this country, should have an *American Dictionary* of the English language. . . ." He did not advocate the development of a new language, or even a new dialect. Instead, he perceived himself to be writing merely an "American" dictionary of the English language, which is different from creating a whole new language. And he further explained his position, noting that the body of the language was basically the same as that of England. He added a revealing statement: "It is desirable to perpetuate that sameness."[23]

Thus the end product of Webster's toils was anything but a new "American tongue." He included only about fifty Americanisms, a fact which prompted H. L. Mencken to label Webster an incompetent observer of his own country.[24] The lexicographer's nationalism had in fact reached a low point in 1814, when he helped draft the first circular calling for the Hartford Convention.[25] In that year he also denounced the Constitution as naive and wildly democratic, ridiculed the concept of universal white male suffrage, and called for division of the union into three separate countries.[26]

[22]George Phillip Krapp, *The English Language in America* (New York: Ungar, 1925), 338.
[23]Noah Webster, *An American Dictionary of the English Language* . . . (New York: S. Converse, 1828), [iii]. Hereafter cited as *A. D.*
[24]H. L. Mencken, *The American Language: An Inquiry into the Development of English in the United States* (New York: Knopf, 1923), 42.
[25]From Joseph Lyman, Jan. 5, 1814, Ford, *Notes,* II, 124. Carpenter, *Bibliography,* 363, indicates that Webster was the author of this letter.
[26]Noah Webster, *An Oration, Pronounced Before the Knox and Warren Branches of the Washington Benevolence Society, at Amherst* . . . (Northampton, Mass.: William Butler, 1814).

The *American Dictionary* was perfectly acceptable in England. The first edition of 2,500 copies was quickly followed by an English edition of 3,000, and one major student of lexicography had noted that Webster's crowning achievement was quite suitable for use in America and England.[27] Indeed, his dictionary was received more warmly across the Atlantic than in the United States. Warfel stated that "soon Webster became the standard in England. . . ." When his publisher went bankrupt, copies of the English edition were sold without change in America.[28]

Yet another incident suggests that his dictionary was not a nationalistic tract. When the second American edition was published in 1841, he sent a copy to Queen Victoria. Significantly, he told the person carrying it to her that "our common language is one of the ties that binds the two nations together; I hope the works I have executed will manifest to the British nation that the Americans are not willing to suffer it to degenerate on this side of the Atlantic."[29] Half a century earlier he had despised England and all that it stood for. Now he told the Queen that he hoped his dictionary might furnish evidence that the "genuine descendants of English ancestors born on the west of the Atlantic, have not forgotten either the land or the language of their fathers."[30]

* * *

Webster made his intentions in the dictionary explicit. The values expressed within the work were his. "In many cases, I have given brief sentences of my own," he declared, "and often presenting some important maxim or sentiment in religion, morality, law or civil policy. . . ."[31]

While Webster's work in etymology exhibited the influence of his social and political values, he sincerely believed that it was new, scholarly, and in fact the most important part of his work. As Laird correctly notes, of all the causes he supported over his long life, and they were legion, "none was dearer to him than was the pursuit of etymologies, and in nothing so much as in his vast synopsis of 'language affinities' . . . did he repose his hopes for the gratitude and admiration of society."[32] As early as 1806 Webster had vowed to "make one effort to dissolve the chains of illusions" surrounding the development of language.[33] A year later he had begun to compile the dic-

---

[27]George H. McKnight, *The Evolution of the English Language: From Chaucer to the Twentieth Century* (New York: Dover, 1968).

[28]Warfel, *Webster*, 361, 365.

[29]Letter to Andrew Stevenson, June 22, 1841, The Papers of Noah Webster, Box 1, NYPL.

[30]Letter to Her Majesty, Victoria, Queen of Great Britain, June 22, 1841, The Papers of Noah Webster, Box 1, NYPL.

[31]*A. D.* n. p.

[32]Charlton Laird, "Etymology, Anglo-Saxon, and Noah Webster," *American Speech* (Feb. 1946), 3.

[33]Noah Webster, *A Compendious Dictionary of the English Language* . . . (New Haven: Hudson and Goodwin, 1806), xxiii.

tionary by concentrating merely on definitions and correcting errors in orthography. This had led him "gradually and almost insensibly" to investigate the origin of the English language. He had been surprised to learn that the path of development of all European languages was an unexplored subject. All other etymologists had "wandered into the field of conjecture, venturing to substitute opinions for evidence. . . ."[34] By 1809 he had concluded that language had begun in Asia and migrated outward.[35] At about this time, Webster stopped working on definitions and orthography and spent ten years compiling his synopsis of the affinities of languages,[36] on which his etymology in his dictionary was based. Four years before his death he still believed that his work was superior to any others and that any other etymology, including those by "the German scholars, the most accurate philologists in Europe, appears to be wholly deficient."[37]

Yet, according to modern etymologists, it was Webster who was in error, not the Europeans. In fact, his etymology has been judged a failure.[38] George Krapp has come close to explaining Webster's errors. "In short," he said, "it was really spiritual, not phonological truth in which Webster was primarily interested." He seems to have thought "that the truth of a word, that is the primitive and original radical value of the word, was equivalent to the truth of the idea."[39]

Webster's etymology was a literal extrapolation of Scriptural truth, the only concrete truth, as far as he was concerned, into another field. Since 1808 he had believed that the Bible was factually correct, and that it must be accepted as such. Without it, there was no basis for civilization itself. Thus his rejection of European etymologists is no mystery. Their scientific attempts to unravel the development of language led away from the story of the Tower of Babel. They were challenging the validity of the Bible, the only rock upon which peace and tranquillity could be secured.

In 1806, as he began his etymological studies, Webster commented specifically on this subject. He believed that etymology illuminated not just the origins of words but the development of human history as well. The etymology of the languages of Europe "will throw no inconsiderable light on the origin and history of the several nations who people it, and confirm in no small degree, the scriptures account of the dispersion of men."[40]

[34]"To the Friends of Literature in the United States," Harry R. Warfel, *The Letters of Noah Webster* (New York: Library Publishers, 1953), 272.
[35]Letter to Thomas Dawes, July 25, 1809, ibid., 343.
[36]Letter to John Jay, Nov., 1821, *Ford*, II, 160–61.
[37]Noah Webster, *Observations on Language* . . . (New York: S. Babcock, 1839), 5.
[38]Webster's etymology has been heavily criticized by nearly all experts in the field. The most recent and thorough student of lexicography, Joseph Friend, *The Development of American Lexicography*, 1798–1864 (Paris: Mouton, 1967), summarizes their analyses.
[39]Krapp, *Language*, 365.
[40]Webster, *Compendious Dictionary*, xix.

In the final analysis, Webster had no choice but to write Christian etymology, regardless of the methodology and insights of other authors. The only ultimate truth was contained in the Scriptures, and it dictated the mere truth of words. Beside Christ, Schlegel and Grimm were insignificant. They challenged the validity of Christianity, and if the authority of the Scriptures was demolished, there was simply no hope for mankind. Without literal belief in Biblical truth, he said in 1823, "we are cast on the ocean of life, without chart, or compass, or rudder." Only "annihilation and despair" could result if the Scriptures were found invalid in any area.[41] Given this vision, Webster was incapable of seeing the development of language in any framework of explanation other than that set forth in the Bible.

Webster introduced his etymology with a literal belief in the origin of language according to Genesis. Vocal sounds, he noted, were used to communicate between Adam and Eve. "Hence we may infer that language was bestowed on Adam, in the same manner as all his other faculties and knowledge, by supernatural power; or in other words was of divine origin. . . ." "It is therefore probable that *language* as well as the faculty of speech, was the immediate gift of God."[42] Webster then traced the Biblical story of the development of man, which was the basis for all the deviations of the words in the two volumes.[43] As Joseph Friend notes, no amount of hard work, not even the labor of a quarter of a century, could overcome the limitations imposed by this Scriptural literalism.[44] He accepted without question the story of the Tower of Babel and the confusion of tongues. Before that time all mankind had spoken a common language, which Webster called "Chaldee," and which modern etymologists agree was a fantasy. When those in Babel were dispersed, they divided into three groups, each led by a son of Noah: Shem, Ham, and Japheth. The last had eventually migrated to Northern Europe, and thus all the languages of that area were labeled "Japhetic." This development, believed Webster, could be traced through the existence of certain words that reappeared in several languages, as well as through the existence of words with similar construction and meaning in various languages.

One example of Webster's etymology will illustrate both his change in viewpoint over time and his authoritarian cast of mind. In 1789 he had remarked that the word "God" had come from the concept "good," and that His nature was the explanation of that derivation.[45] In 1826 he specifically rejected that idea. Instead, he noted that "Supreme Being" was taken from

[41] Webster, "Young Gentleman," 86.
[42] Letter to David McClure, Oct. 25, 1836, Warfel, *Letters*, 454.
[43] *A. D.*, (vii).
[44] Friend, *Development*, 76.
[45] Webster, *Dissertations*, 399.

"supremacy or power." Thus "God" was "equivalent to lord or ruler, from some root signifying to press or exert force."[46]

* * *

In attempting to understand the *American Dictionary* and the man who wrote it, we must recall that Webster's view of language was dualistic. It was, of course, to be studied for its own sake, but it was also something much more. Language, he believed, influenced opinion and behavior. If people had a clear understanding of "equality," they would act in certain ways. Language could be used as a means to a greater end. It could be altered and manipulated, and in so doing, one could affect millions of people. Although he never explicitly said so, Webster assumed this from the very beginning of his work. It is implicit in his early attempts—later repudiated—to forge an "American tongue" as a way of encouraging independence from a vile and corrupt England, and to further his utopian dreams. Even in 1788 he could conceptualize the use of language in purifying society. In that year he called for studies which would "show how far truth and accuracy of thinking are concerned in a clear understanding of *words*." Language should be studied "if it can be proved that *mere use of words* has led nations into error, and still continues the delusion...."[47] As early at 1790 he was engaged in manipulation of language as a means of influencing opinion and behavior. He had just completed another book, he told a friend. "I have introduced into it some definitions, relative to the slave trade," he said, "calculated to impress upon young minds the detestableness of the trade."[48]

Webster's disillusionment with man and society was accompanied by the conclusion that the definition of words played a role in American development. "There is one remarkable circumstance in our own history which seems to have escaped observation," he noted in 1838, "which is, the mischievous effect of the indefinite application of terms." A year later he wrote an essay in which he summed up his entire life's work in linguistics, philology, etymology, and lexicography. "It is obvious to my mind, that popular errors proceeding from a misunderstanding of words," he said, "are among the efficient causes of our political disorders...."[49]

The thought process which led to etymological error also led to certain definitions. His correspondence and publications offer the opportunity to ob-

[46] *A. D.*
[47] Noah Webster, "A Dissertation concerning the influence of Language on opinions and of opinions on Language," *American Magazine* (May 1788), 399.
[48] Letter to J. Pemberton, March 15, 1790, Historical Society of Pennsylvania Archives.
[49] Noah Webster, *Observations*, 31-32.

serve the way in which definitions were formed. Indeed, examples of the influence of social events and opinions abound, including the formulation of definitions which appeared almost intact decades later in his dictionaries. They reveal that his strong social and political values and his longing for public submission to authority dictated what he believed should be the correct understanding of important words.

He wrote that an incorrect understanding of the word "pension" had been partially responsible for social discord in the 1780s. Congress had granted a pension to officers who had served in the Continental Army. Many had protested, and a convention held in Middletown, Connecticut, had called for its repeal. This unrest had distressed Webster. It had been "a remarkable, but unfortunate instance of the use of the word, in a sense so indefinite that the people at large made no distinction between *pensions* granted as a provision for old officers, and *pensions* granted for the purpose of bribery for favor and support." Obviously Webster thought that the half-pay for officers was the first type of pension, while to the convention it was the second kind. In his dictionary he was careful to say that it meant "to grant an annual allowance from the public treasury to a person for past services. . . ." No example of the misunderstanding of words, he noted, was as important as that surrounding the phrase "union of church and state." He understood the aversion of many Americans to the unification of ecclesiastical and civil authority because of the European experience. Along with many others, Webster had spoken in favor of their separation in the 1780s. But times had changed, and by 1838 his conception of that relationship had also changed. Now the union of the two meant that "all laws must have *religion for their basis.*" In this sense, there was a strong need for a "union of civil and ecclesiastical powers; in support of the laws and institutions."[50] This union was the seedbed of Quiet Christians and the heart of his concept of social relations.

"Jacobinism," "democrat," and "republican" were prominent words that Webster's biases led him to define in significant ways. The first, he said in 1799, was not merely the philosophy of a French political faction. It was instead "an opposition to established government and institutions, and an attempt to overthrow them, by private accusations or by violent or illegal means."[51] "Democrat" was "synonymous with the word *Jacobian* in France. . . ." Democratic organizations arose from the attempt to "control our government by private associations." By 1800 the word signified "a person who attempts undue opposition to our influence over government by means of private clubs, secret intrigues, or by public popular meetings which

---

[50] *Middletown* (Conn.) *Constitution,* Dec. 5, 1838.
[51] *Commercial Advertiser,* Oct. 21, 1799.

are extraneous to the Constitution."[52] "Republicans," on the other hand, were "friends of our Representative Governments, who believe that no influence whatever should be exercised in a state which is directly authorized by and developed by legislation."[53] Similar definitions appeared in his dictionary.

A key word, the definition of which he felt could influence action, was "free." Most Americans were convinced that all men were free to act according to their own wills. The idea that this abstract condition was natural and was a basic part of American life was widely upheld, or so thought Noah Webster. To him it was absurd, and in fact "contributed to the popular licentiousness, which often disturbs the public peace, and even threatens extensive evils in this country." A misunderstanding of "free" threatened the permanency of government, because it led people to feel that somehow individuals were "*above* the constitutional authorities."[54] It was also simply incorrect. Instead, all individuals, from the time of their birth, were subject to the demands of their parents, of God, and of the government of the country in which they lived.[55] There would be fewer problems in society, said Noah Webster, if Americans understood that "*No person is born free,* in the general acception of the word *free.*"[56]

"Equality" and "equal" were also crucial terms. "Nothing can be more obvious than that by the appointment of the creator, in the constitution of man and of human society," he wrote a few months before his death, "the conditions of men must be different and *unequal.*"[57] The common American assumption that all men must be equal in conditions in which they lived was false. The Declaration of Independence was wrong when it began by affirming as a self-evident truth that "all men are born *equal.*" That was the work of the infamous idealist, Thomas Jefferson, and as a universal proposition had to be rejected. In their intellectual and physical powers men were born "*unequal,*" and hence inequality was a basic part of human life. Webster said that most of the men of the earlier generation had maintained that each person was born with an "equal natural right to liberty and protection. . . ," something far different than total equality, an idea that led to agitation over the right of suffrage.[58] The founders had believed in equality of opportunity, with which Webster had no argument. "But *equality of condition* is a very different thing and dependent on circumstances over which government and laws have no control."[59]

[52]Letter to Joseph Priestley, 1800, Warfel, *Letters,* 208.
[53]Ibid., 207–08.
[54]*Middletown Constitution,* Dec. 5, 1838.
[55]Noah Webster, "Discourse delivered before the Connecticut Historical Society on April 21, 1840," 29, Connecticut Historical Society.
[56]Letter to Daniel Webster, n.d., Warfel, *Letters,* 482.
[57]Letter to James Kent, Feb. 7, 1843, The Papers of Noah Webster, Box 8, NYPL.
[58]*Commercial Advertiser,* Jan. 20, 1835.
[59]Webster, "Discourse," 30.

Most importantly, when people expected equality of condition, it led inevitably to opposition to authority, chaos, and ultimately anarchy. Misunderstanding of the words *"free* and *equal"* influenced "the more ignorant and turbulent part of the community" to become "emboldened" and to "take the law into their own hands, or to trample both constitution and law under their feet."[60] The very concept of equality of condition could culminate in disaster:

> . . . It is not for the interest and safety of society that all men should be equal. Perfect equality, if such a state could be supposed practicable, would render due subordination impossible, and dissolve society. All men in a community are equally entitled to protection, and the secure enjoyment of their rights. . . . Superiority in natural and acquired endowments, and in authority derived from the laws, is essential to the existence of social order, and of personal safety.[61]

In his dictionary Webster listed nineteen definitions of the words "equal" and "equality." His faith in equality among men is conspicuous only by its absence.

* * *

Webster's emphasis on Quiet Christian behavior appears throughout the definitions in the *American Dictionary* itself. The reader is reminded of his divinely-directed role in life and the values by which he should live. The fear of God, absolute and rigid controller of all things, the depravity of man, and the character traits of meekness, humility, passivity, and wholehearted submission to proper authority are celebrated in the definitions of hundreds and perhaps thousands of words. This was done in two ways: either through definitions outlining deferential conduct, or through quotes illustrating the meaning of the word. He defined "author," for instance, as "One who produces, creates, or brings into being. . . ." Webster could have stopped there, with an objective statement, as other lexicographers did. Instead he added "as, God is the *author* of the Universe," thus reminding the reader of His fearful power.[62]

Webster interjected his obsession with authority into the most intimate of human relationships. The verb form of "love" was "a sense to be pleased with," to which he added a significant set of examples of its usage, again designed to instruct the Quiet Christian:

> The Christian *loves* his Bible. In short, we *love* whatever gives us pleasure and de-

[60] *Middletown Constitution,* Dec. 5, 1838.

[61] Ibid.

[62] The *American Dictionary* was unpaginated, but definitions may be found in their correct alphabetical order. The original edition has recently been reissued: Rosalie Slater, ed., *Noah Webster's First Edition of an American Dictionary of the English Language* (Anaheim, California: Foundation for American Christian Education, 1967).

light, whether animal or intellectual; and if our hearts are right, we *love* God above all things, as the sum of all excellence and all the attributes which can communicate happiness to intelligent beings. In other words, the Christian *loves* God with the love of complacency in his attributes, the love of benevolence towards the interests of his kingdom, and the love of gratitude for favors received.

The noun form of "love" was also used in a similar way. Webster gives another example of the use of religion in forming deferential, Quiet Christian personalities and demeanor:

The *love* of God is the first duty of man, and this springs from just views of his attributes or excellencies of character, which afford the highest delight to the sanctified heart. Esteem and reverence constitute ingredients in this affection, and a fear of offending him is the inseparable effect.

The dictionary also evidenced Webster's disgust with politicians and politics. He defined them as men "of artifice or deep contrivance" rather than people engaged in government or management of affairs. The adjective form of "politician" meant "cunning; using artifice." His own longing for a return to some former time before the rise of democratic politics was indicated in his definition of "polity." He quoted Ezra Stiles, who said, "were the whole Christian world to revert back to the original model, how far more simple, uniform and beautiful would the church appear, and how far more agreeable to the ecclesiastical *polity* instituted by the holy apostles."

The Quiet Christian image appears throughout the dictionary. "Laws" were "the *laws* which enjoin the duties of piety and morality, and prescribed by God and found in the Scriptures." Under "submission" Webster again insists that the Quiet Christian should be full of "resignation," meaning "entire and cheerful *submission* to the will of God [which] is a Christian duty of prime excellence." The only individual who could be "esteemed really and permanently happy" is the one "who enjoys a peace of mind in the favor of God," not unlike the mental tranquillity he had found in 1808. Defining "improve," he commands that "it is the duty . . . of a good man to *improve* in grace and piety." He tells us that "the distribution of the Scriptures may be the *instrument* of a vastly extensive reformation in morals and religion." Webster's view of the family appears in his definition of "marriage" as "instituted by God himself, for the sexes, for promoting domestic felicity and for securing the maintenance and education of children." The helplessness of a man is accented when he tells us under "meritorious" that "we rely for salvation on the *meritorious* obedience and suffering of Christ."

The dictionary is saturated with commands to be quiescent. Only a few examples will suffice as a general indication of the flavor of the work. "Good breeding forbids us to use *offensive* words." "A man is *profane* when he takes the name of God in vain, or treats sacred things with abuse and irreverence." "*Perfect rectitude* belongs only to the Supreme Being. The more nearly the *rectitude* of men approaches to the standard of divine law, the more exalted and dignified is their character. Want of *rectitude* is not only sinful, but debasing." "Freedom" is defined in one sense as "violation of the rules of decorum," while Webster warns us to "beware of what are called innocent *freedoms.*" Webster's denial of freedom and advocacy of submission to authority is consistent. "Freedom" in another sense is defined as "license."

"Duty" is a key concept, and in defining it Webster commands us to obey virtually any authority:

> That which a person owes to another; that which a person is bound, by any natural, moral or legal obligation, to pay, do or perform. Obedience to princes, magistrates and the laws is the *duty* of every citizen and subject; obedience, respect and kindness to parents are the *duties* of children; fidelity to friends is a *duty;* reverence, obedience and prayer to God are indisputable *duties;* the government and religious instruction of children are *duties* of parents which they cannot neglect without guilt.

"Submission" was synonymous with "obedience," and *"submission* of children to their parents is an indispensible duty." "Government" meant "control; restraint." In this definition he added that "Children are often ruined by a neglect of *government* in parents." Under "inferior" Webster commands us to "Pay due respect to those who are superior in station, and due civility to those who are *inferior."*

"Liberty" is one of the most revealing terms in the *American Dictionary.* His first definition was simply "freedom from restraint...." To this, however, he added some interesting distinctions. Most important were the two types of liberty that John Winthrop had spoken of in 1645. *"Natural liberty"* meant the "power of acting as one thinks fit, without any restraint or control, except from the laws of nature." Like Winthrop, he emphasized that this condition was impractical and was always "abridged by the establishment of government." He was not speaking of the Lockean notion of a government as a compact between men, but of the need for restraint on human liberty. *"Civil liberty,"* on the other hand, was the liberty "of men in a state of society" in which natural liberty was "abridged and restrained" not to enhance cooperation or distribution of goods, but for "the safety and interest of the society, state or nation." Civil liberty he stated was "secured by established laws, which restrain every man from injuring or controlling others." He was undoubtedly thinking of the turmoil since the 1780s when he noted that "the restraints of law are essential to *civil liberty."*

Perhaps the most revealing definition in the entire two-volume work was that of "education." This one small paragraph in many ways summed up much of Webster's life. Education had always been of interest to him, not only for its own value, but as a means of social change of one sort or another. In the early 1780s it had been an instrument of increasing both cultural independence from England and reform as well, and these two motivations were behind his first attempt to Americanize the schools systematically. After

1808 Webster had seen schools as institutions for producing Quiet Christians, as a means of insuring tranquillity by teaching a specific form of conduct.[42] Through them discipline could be instilled and the unruly passions of men checked and limited. His definition of education did not stress the increase of learning, of understanding or comprehending the world. Value-laden words emphasizing this side of education appear only twice: "enlighten the understanding," and "arts and science." The second occurrence is almost thrown in as if an afterthought. But terms espousing authoritarian control appear nine times in the space of three sentences: "formation of manners," "discipline," "correct the temper," "form the manners and habits of youth," "fit them for usefulness in their future stations," "manners," "religious *education*," "immense responsibility," "duties." And this is not counting the use of "instruction," a term he chose instead of "learning" or other, less authority-laden terms. Finally, notice that an education in manners, arts and science is merely "important." A religious education, with all its overtones of the Quiet Christian, is "indispensible."

One last definition demonstrates the interrelationship between religion, politics, behavior, and language that existed in Webster's mind. Under "reason," he quotes an author who said "God brings good out of evil, and therefore it were but *reason* we should trust God to govern his own world." Implicit is the notion that man should follow God's laws, not his own reason. Thus reason was used to advocate its opposite.

* * *

Every phase of the *American Dictionary* affirms the author's concern with authority and social control; exuberant nationalism is absent. The same obsession appears in the dedication of the work. One might expect a man who labored for twenty-five years on a single book to acknowledge the role played by those who influenced him. Modern scholars usually mention the work of those who came before them or others in the field. But, of course, Webster could not do that. If Webster had been a strong nationalist, as most historians have said, one might expect long paeans to American freedom, or celebrations of the heroes of the Revolution. But the *American Dictionary* was a product of Webster's evolving ideas about America. The work exhibited the values and beliefs of the evangelical movement of the early nineteenth century whose major emphasis was limiting human actions, not of the nationalistic fervor of the late eighteenth century. In his dedication Webster said:

> To the great and benevolent Being, who during the preparation of this work, has sustained a feeble constitution, amidst obstacles and toils, disappointments, infirmities and depression; who has twice borne me and my manuscripts in safety across the Atlantic, and given me strength and resolution to bring the work to a close, I would present the tribute of my most grateful acknowledgments.[44]

[43]Noah Webster, *A Plea for a Miserable World . . .* (Boston: Ezra Lincoln, 1820).
[44]*A. D.*, (v).

Statistics and the State: Changing Social Thought and the Emergence of a Quantitative Mentality in America, 1790 to 1820

Patricia Cline Cohen

A growing predilection and respect for "statisticks" and "authentic facts" marked the public thought of the young American republic. Formerly a matter of interest to a mere handful of colonists—compulsive counters and measurers like Ezra Stiles and Thomas Jefferson—the compiling of figures and facts became, in the early nineteenth century, a common mode of reportage that both reflected and promoted a novel way of thinking about society and state. This development is evidenced by some two dozen statistical gazetteers and manuals published between the 1790s and the 1820s, as well as in repeated efforts to expand the federal census. These undertakings testify to the rising appeal of certain kinds of "authentic facts" to men who sought to comprehend and in a measure to direct the social changes of their time. The sponsors and authors of these efforts to account by counting favored pure empirical description, though their practice in that regard was often less than perfect. They championed an inductive approach intended to eliminate theorizing and speculation. They popularized a new word, "statisticks"—defined as salient facts about state and society—to express their sense of the relationship between factual knowledge and the business of government. To open up an unexplored dimension of the historical problem of modernization, this essay describes this phenomenon and suggests its significance for changing ideas about the character of politics and society in the new republic.[1]

Today the word statistics can refer broadly to any collection of numerical data or to the branch of mathematics that deals with the analysis of

Ms. Cohen is a member of the Department of History at the University of California, Santa Barbara. She wishes to thank Winthrop D. Jordan, Martha T. Blauvelt, and Morton Borden for helpful criticism of earlier versions of this article. Research was supported by a grant from the Fred Harris Daniels fund at the American Antiquarian Society.

[1] Certain kinds of quantitative data were collected sporadically before the American Revolution. James H. Cassedy has described the use of numbers in demographic thought in the 17th and 18th centuries, and George Rosen has done the same for medicine through 1850. See Cassedy, *Demography in Early America: Beginnings of the Statistical Mind, 1600-1800* (Cambridge, Mass., 1969), and Rosen,

aggregate data. But the original sense of the word, the one that prevailed until the 1820s, was quite different: it meant simply "a statement or view of the civil condition of a people."[2] Statistics did not necessarily entail numbers, and at first only descriptive facts about the civil relations of men could be termed "statistical." Other types of facts and data—for example, records of meteorological observations—were not considered statistical, and that sort of miscellaneous material will not be treated here. Men of the new republic—the specification of gender is intentional—limited statistics to facts about population, wealth, trade, industry, occupations, and civil and religious institutions, and argued that these were the data most appropriate for assessing the American experiment in republican government.[3] They collected such data in three distinct sorts of endeavors: statistical gazetteers compiled by private individuals; government projects, chiefly the census; and commercial reference works such as statistical manuals and almanacs, devoted to disseminating a potpourri of facts.

Although the word "statisticks" was not formally inducted into American English until 1803, when it first appeared in a Philadelphia dictionary,

---

"Problems in the Application of Statistical Analysis to Questions of Health, 1700-1880," *Bulletin of the History of Medicine*, XXIX (1955), 27-45. Robert C. Davis has traced the enthusiasm for quantitative statistics through the antebellum decades ("The Beginnings of American Social Research," in George H. Daniels, ed., *Nineteenth-Century American Science: A Reappraisal* [Evanston, Ill., 1972], 152-178).

Modernization theory continues to draw fire as an inadequate conceptual tool for analyzing historical change. I use the word here only to suggest in summary form the transformation of social and economic experience in America during the late 18th and early 19th centuries. Although no consensus exists on the exact nature of that transformation, many historians agree that swift commercial development and concomitant changes in values and *mentalité* marked the years between 1790 and 1820. The history of statistics illuminates one aspect of the interplay between economic change and *mentalité*.

[2] Noah Webster, *A Compendious Dictionary of the English Language . . .* (New Haven, Conn., 1806). Americans universally gave credit to Sir John Sinclair of Scotland for coining the word "statisticks," after a German word for the study of the state. But there were a few before Sinclair who used the word in the 1770s and 1780s in England. Sinclair himself claimed he invented the word; see his *Statistical Account of Scotland . . .* (Edinburgh, 1791-1799), XX, lxv-lxvi. For the German and English development of statistics see M. J. Cullen, *The Statistical Movement in Early Victorian Britain: The Foundations of Empirical Social Research* (New York, 1975), 9-11; Paul F. Lazarsfeld, "Notes on the History of Quantification in Sociology—Trends, Sources and Problems," *Isis*, LII (1951), 277-333; and Anthony Oberschall, ed., *The Establishment of Empirical Sociology: Studies in Continuity, Discontinuity, and Institutionalization* (New York, 1972).

[3] In 19th-century America, females reputedly had no head for figures, and statistics had a masculine aura. When common schools spread in the 1820s and 1830s, educators debated about the level of training in arithmetic appropriate for girls;

"authentic facts" about civil society had been accumulated throughout the 1790s by authors of state and local gazetteers.[4] The infancy of the United States stimulated an outpouring of descriptive books the purpose of which was to inform the public and especially men in public life—statists—about the nature of American society. Neither the state governments nor the federal government yet felt obliged to engage in broad fact-finding missions, and so the task was first taken up by private individuals.

The forerunners of the gazetteers were works of geography, travel, and natural and civil history by such authors as William Douglass, Peter Kalm, and Thomas Jefferson.[5] But the post-1790 gazetteers departed from their precursors in significant ways. The earlier works often included quantified facts about civil society but were casual and imprecise. The gazetteers of the 1790s, in contrast, were likely to give sets of facts about population and trade and to express interest in trends. Implicit in the new style was an assumption of historical progress: the facts of today were important to know because they presaged the improvements of tomorrow. The emphasis on sets of facts turned large sections of civil histories into dry reference works, and the driest of them assumed the title "gazetteer" or, after 1803, a "statistical view" or "statistical account."[6]

---

very few advocated that they should follow the boys past the basic operations. The author is at work on a study of women and arithmetic in the 19th century.

[4] John Walker, A Critical Pronouncing Dictionary and Expositor of the English Language . . . (Philadelphia, 1803), s.v. "Statisticks." The earlier English edition of Walker's work (London, 1791) did not contain the word.

[5] William Douglass, A Summary, Historical and Political, of the First Planting, Progressive Improvements, and Present State of the British Settlements in North-America . . . (London, 1771); Thomas Jefferson, Notes on the State of Virginia, ed. William Peden (Chapel Hill, N.C., 1955). For a discussion of the traditional literary form of geographical description and travel in America see Kathryn and Philip Whitford, "Timothy Dwight's Place in Eighteenth-Century American Science," American Philosophical Society, Proceedings, CXIV (1970), 60-71.

[6] Works representative of the genre include Jeremy Belknap, The History of New-Hampshire, 3 vols. (Philadelphia, 1784-1792); Samuel Williams, The Natural and Civil History of Vermont (Walpole, N.H., 1794); W[illiam] Winterbotham, A Geographical, Commercial, and Philosophical View of the Present Situation of the United States . . . (New York, 1795); Benjamin Davies, Some Account of the City of Philadelphia . . . (Philadelphia, 1794); James Sullivan, The History of the District of Maine (Boston, 1795); David Ramsay, A Sketch of the Soil, Climate, Weather, and Diseases of South Carolina . . . (Charleston, S.C., 1796); [Charles Williamson], A Description of the Genesee Country, Its Rapidly Progressive Population and Improvements . . . (Albany, N.Y., 1798); [John Peck], Facts and Calculations Respecting the Population and Territory of the United States [Boston, 1799]; A Topographical and Statistical Account of the Province of Louisiana (Baltimore, 1803); [Samuel L. Mitchell], The Picture of New York (New York, 1807); Joseph Scott, A Geographical Description of the States of Maryland and Delaware (Philadelphia, 1807); James

Authors of gazetteers often called attention to features that set their volumes apart from earlier works of description and travel. Some apologized for the dull prose that the new factual approach obliged them to adopt. Others explained their innovative methods of collecting data. And in what became a repeating refrain, almost all of them proudly proclaimed that only "authentic facts," unsullied by personal opinion, were admitted to their texts. For example, Samuel Williams, a Vermont clergyman and almanac writer, warned readers of his *Natural and Civil History of Vermont* that they would find

a minuteness of dates, facts, and circumstances, not common in European productions; and not very entertaining in itself. This method was adopted with choice, and by design. Persuaded that the American commonwealth is yet in the early years of its infancy, and unable to comprehend to what extent, magnitude, and dignity it may arise; the author of these sheets views the history of a particular state, rather as a collection of facts, circumstances, and records, than as a compleat and finished historical production. The more important the *United States* shall become in the future periods of time, of the more importance it will be to be able to find a minute and authentic account of the facts, proceedings, and transactions, from whence the grand fabric

---

Dean, *An Alphabetical Atlas, or Gazetteer of Vermont* ... (Montpelier, Vt., 1808); David Ramsay, *The History of South Carolina* ... (Charleston, S.C. 1809); Timothy Dwight, *A Statistical Account of the City of New-Haven* (Connecticut Academy of Arts and Sciences, *Memoirs*, I[New Haven, Conn., 1811]); James Morris, *A Statistical Account of Several Towns in the County of Litchfield* (ibid. [1815]); Sterling Goodenow, *A Brief Topographical and Statistical Manual of the State of New-York* ... (New York, 1811); James Mease, *The Picture of Philadelphia* ... (Philadelphia, 1811); Jervis Cutler, *A Topographical Description of the State of Ohio, Indiana Territory, and Louisiana* (Boston, 1812); Horatio Gates Spafford, *A Gazetteer of the State of New-York* ... (Albany, N.Y., 1813); Rodolphus Dickinson, *A Geographical and Statistical View of Massachusetts Proper* (Greenfield, Mass., 1813); Daniel Drake, *Natural and Statistical View, or Picture of Cincinnati and the Miami Country* ... (Cincinnati, Ohio, 1815); Moses Greenleaf, *A Statistical View of the District of Maine* ... (Boston, 1816); Samuel R. Brown, *The Western Gazetteer* ... (Auburn, N.Y., 1817); D[avid] B[ailie] Warden, *A Statistical, Political, and Historical Account of the United States of North America* ... (Edinburgh and Philadelphia, 1819); David D. Field, *A Statistical Account of the County of Middlesex in Connecticut* (Middletown, Conn., 1819); John Preston, *A Statistical Report of the County of Albany, for the Year 1820* (Albany, N.Y., 1823); Timothy Dwight, *Travels; in New-England and New-York* (New Haven, Conn., 1821); Frederick Hall, *A Statistical Account of the Town of Middlebury, in the State of Vermont* (Boston, 1821); John Melish, *A Statistical View of the United States* ... (New York, 1825); *A General Outline of the United States of North America, Her Resources and Prospects, with a Statistical Comparison* (Philadelphia, 1825); and Robert Mills, *Statistics of South Carolina* ... (Charleston, S.C., 1826).

arose. To collect and record such facts and proceedings . . . is what I have attempted.[7]

Williams did not discuss his method for collecting facts, but other authors did. Jeremy Belknap devoted the final book of his three-volume *History of New-Hampshire* to a compendium of facts which he had gathered by an intensive one-man investigation. He scoured the countryside, talked to prominent local people, searched public record offices, sometimes surveyed land himself, and circulated a letter of inquiry to local clergymen and "other gentlemen of public character," so "that no source of information might be left unexplored." The response to the letter was not gratifying, Belknap admitted, but the idea of sending out questionnaires to solicit factual information was so new in 1792 that it was unreasonable to expect many replies.[8]

In South Carolina later in the decade David Ramsay encountered similar difficulties with the same method. In 1798 he began circulating inquiries to elderly people in his state to secure information he feared was "fast hastening to oblivion." It was not unique personal histories he sought but detailed accounts of the population growth and economic development of the informant's area. One reply to his survey was so thorough that Ramsay printed it as a thirty-page appendix to his *History of South Carolina*, intending it to serve as an inspirational model. Co-authored by a clergyman and a physician, the "Statistical Account of Edistoe Island" covered the gamut of statistics with a description of the situation, soil, and settlement of their island; the major crops and rate of cultivation per field hand; the current prices of land and labor; a census of inhabitants conducted for the occasion; a register of white births, deaths, and marriages over sixteen years; and a similar register for slave births on one plantation. Ramsay promised to devote a book to the statistics of the state if volunteers would furnish similar data: "If this proposal should be carried into effect a collection of facts useful to philosophers, legislators, physicians, and divines, would be brought to light."[9] His project did not materialize for nearly two decades, when Robert Mills circularized leading South Carolina gentlemen and assembled the results in a book designed to inform politicians as well as to attract emigrants to the state. By then, the method pioneered by Belknap and Ramsay, that of asking local men of substance

---

[7] Samuel Williams, *The Natural and Civil History of Vermont . . . in Two Volumes*, 2d ed. (Burlington, Vt., 1809), I, 12-13. Williams was more mathematical than most of his contemporaries; in addition to the series of Vermont almanacs in the 1790s, he prepared an edition of Nicholas Pike's *New and Complete System of Arithmetick* (Newburyport, Mass., 1788).

[8] Belknap, *History of New-Hampshire*, III, 3.

[9] Ramsay, *History of South Carolina*, I, vii-xii, II, 539-568.

[10] Mills, *Statistics of South Carolina*. The fact that no one worried whether lead-

for first-hand information, had become much more familiar and success-ful.[10]

Claims to complete accuracy recur in prefaces of many local histories. Authors of gazetteers took pains to assure readers that only "authentic facts," facts that had been verified, were fit for inclusion in their books. Facts were carefully distinguished from opinions and estimates, and sever-al authors presented wildly eclectic data as if to prove that no pre-conceived theory dictated their selection. Some compilers went so far as to boast that they had eliminated commentary altogether: facts should be permitted to speak for themselves, without interpretation or amplifica-tion. "In composing a work like the present," wrote James Mease in *The Picture of Philadelphia* (1811), "the author is of opinion that the chief ob-ject ought to be the multiplication of facts, and that the reflections arising out of them, should be left to the reader." Mease offered such information as the number of gallons of oil used in city lamps per year (14,355) and the number of printed sheets put out by the eight daily newspapers (8,328) in contrast to the number put out by the nine weekly papers (7,058). His readers were left perfectly free to draw their own conclusions from these facts. Rodolphus Dickinson boasted of the "merit of impartiality" con-ferred by the facts and numbers in his *Geographical and Statistical View of Massachusetts Proper* (1813), and David Warden asserted that he had "sel-dom indulged in discussion or speculation" in his ambitious three-volume work, *A Statistical, Political and Historical Account of the United States of North America* (1819), as if such indulgence were a vice. Rather, he wanted "to put his readers in possession of a full and authentic collection of the most interesting facts regarding the population, industry, wealth, power and resources of the United States."[11] Facts had come to be seen as ante-rior, indeed antithetical, to opinions and theories. Facts were objective and indisputable; opinions were idiosyncratic and debatable.

An extension of this respect for facts was the idea that if only enough facts were known, disagreement on public issues would end. "Whence arises the diversity of opinion?" asked the editor of the *Literary Magazine and American Register* in an article of 1804. The answer lay in indolence, dogmatism, and "a want of certain data": "Did all men know alike, though imperfectly, their opinions must be the same"—apparently a mark and desideratum of a healthy society.[12] Social facts and figures took on critical political importance in the 1790s, when dogmatic differences of opinion split Congress into a worrisome division that verged on being a party sys-

---

ing gentlemen were reliable sources of accurate statistical information indicates the extent to which local elites were still assumed to dominate the civil relations of their communities.

[11] Mease, *Picture of Philadelphia*, xi, 25, 357; Dickinson, *Geographical and Statis-tical View*, 2; Warden, *Statistical, Political, and Historical Account*, i.

[12] *Literary Magazine and American Register*, I (Feb. 1804), 388-392.

tem. Political parties were unwelcome in the 1790s because they were thought to violate the ideal of virtuous, impartial solons legislating for the common good. Granted that the country was large and diverse, still commitment lingered to the norm of a single public interest, a general public happiness. To square the recognized reality of social heterogeneity to that older norm or concept, proponents of statistics argued that a comprehensive knowledge of general social facts could be the new foundation of the common good. Knowing the exact dimensions of heterogeneity would compensate for the lack of homogeneity in the diverse United States. If only law-makers knew enough facts, differences of opinion would evaporate and the correct course of action would be clear. Facts would dispel the factious spirit.[13]

"Authentic facts" were thus held to be the essential foundation of good government. Authors of gazetteers and statistical accounts constantly advertised the value of their works for the makers of public law and policy. Wise governmental actions would flow from certain knowledge, whereas uncertain, speculative, or theoretical assertions led inevitably to conflicts of opinion. Noah Webster spelled out this antipathy between facts and factions in 1794: "Another cause of violent parties is frequently a difference of opinion of *speculative* questions, or those whose real tendency to secure public happiness is *equivocal.*—When measures are obviously good, and clearly tend to advance public weal, there will seldom be much division of opinion of the propriety of adopting them. All parties unite in pursuing the public interest, when it is clearly visible. But when it is doubtful what will be the ultimate effect of a measure, men will differ in opinion . . . "[14] Like Webster, Timothy Dwight of Yale assumed that the common good could be agreed upon and advanced by statistics. In a sermon of 1795 on *The True Means of Establishing Public Happiness,* he maintained that in order to "promote the general good," men must have knowledge derived from close observation of facts. Webster, Dwight, and other statistical writers appealed to facts to bury the doctrinal political disputes of the 1780s and 1790s and to create consensus on the principles of public happiness and the means of pursuing it.[15]

---

[13] A major Antifederalist worry in 1788 was the absence of a homogeneous common good in a large republic. Gordon S. Wood discusses the Federalist solution to this problem as one where men of uncommon talent would rise to the top in government and by their gifts correctly intuit the common good. He does not discuss the importance of statistics to this new natural aristocracy (*The Creation of the American Republic, 1776-1787* [Chapel Hill, N.C., 1969], 499-518, 605-615).

[14] Noah Webster, *The Revolution in France, Considered in Respect to Its Progress and Effects by an American* (New York, 1794), 43.

[15] (New Haven, Conn., 1795), 23. Benjamin Silliman's funeral eulogy of Dwight in 1817 called special attention to his delight in "statisticks" and his abhorrence of "mere speculation" (*A Sketch of the Life and Character of President Dwight, Delivered as an Eulogium* [New Haven, Conn., 1817], 33-34).

Dwight's statistical work illustrated one way by which numbers could promote unity. In 1796 he began collecting materials for a descriptive guidebook of the northeast which was published in four volumes after his death. His goal was to assemble data that would mark the improvements of the age; growth of population, career opportunities for Yale graduates, the price of food in New Haven—all answered his purpose. The minuteness of detail "in all probability may be disagreeable to a considerable class of readers," Dwight politely conceded, perhaps in reference to the ladies, but another group, so described that most patriotic male readers would recognize themselves in it, was bound to be enthusiastic: "Men, who unite curiosity with expansive views, usually find not a little pleasure in comparing the different degrees of improvement, which a country attains at different stages of its history."[16] Thus it was not only the *certainty* of facts about society that allowed men to reach agreement, as Dwight had argued in his sermon. Consensus would also be aided by the particular kinds of facts that men like Dwight were likely to discover when they went out with notebook in hand. Dwight's facts indicated improvement and expansion, and very often took a quantitative form. Men of expansive views took pleasure in statistics, according to Dwight; they found personal happiness in contemplating the rising state of public happiness.

Dwight and Webster joined forces in the most ambitious of the privately undertaken statistical surveys in the young republic. Both were members of the newly formed Connecticut Academy of Arts and Sciences; under their prompting, the academy sent a circular letter to every town in the state requesting quantitative answers to thirty-two "heads of inquiry."[17] The questions included not only predictable ones about population, number of houses and other buildings, and manufactures, but also inquiries about "instances of suicide in the last twenty years," the number of clergymen and amount of their salaries, and the number of carriages and coaches. The academy's grand yet vague purpose was to contribute "to the collection and propagation of useful knowledge" by publishing a multivolume statistical history of Connecticut. After ten years, however, only thirty towns had returned answers, of varying quality and utility, and the only two to be published sold so few copies that the series was discontinued. Dwight himself was the author of one of the two completed books, *A Statistical Account of the City of New-Haven*.[18] But surprisingly, this longtime champion of empirical fact-gathering confessed to encountering difficulty in carrying out his assignment: "The public will naturally ask why the answer has been so long delayed. The true reason is, that every man, here, is closely engaged in his own business; and that no man of business is,

---

[16] Dwight, *Travels*, I, 12.
[17] The circular was reprinted in the Conn. Academy of Arts and Sciences, *Memoirs*, I (1811), pt. ii, vi-xi.
[18] The other was Morris, *Statistical Account of . . . Towns in . . . Litchfield*.

ordinarily, willing to write on subjects, unconnected with his personal concerns. My own situation, to those who know it, would fairly excuse me from the undertaking. I have made the attempt, because I was convinced, that it would be made by no other person. As this account is drawn up in circumstances of extreme inconvenience, the Academy will, I doubt not, readily excuse its imperfections."[19]

Dwight had discovered that systematic collection of data was an onerous and time-consuming task. In view of the difficulties that beset even the most dedicated voluntary efforts, political men began to suggest that government take on the job. If facts were essential to good government, if certain knowledge promised to restore political harmony, then governments should conduct inquiries of their own.

American statists were of course familiar with official censuses and trade statistics. Throughout the second century of colonial rule, Britain's Board of Trade had repeatedly requested reports on population and foreign trade, and colonial governors and customs officials had tried valiantly to supply the numbers in the face of frequent opposition from colonial subjects who worried that the figures would be used to measure military strength or to raise taxes.[20] Trade statistics, a by-product of the collecting of customs duties, were seriously deficient owing to tax evasion and smuggling. Yet however inaccurate the numbers might be, at the least Americans knew that modern states considered it important to gauge the size of their population and the extent of their foreign trade.

Accordingly, the new federal government paid attention only to those two sorts of statistical information. A law of 1789 required customs officials to record the volume and dollar value of trade passing the national boundaries, again chiefly as the by-product of the system of import and export duties. And the new constitution mandated a periodic count of free and enslaved persons, the express purpose of which was to determine the numerical basis for representation in the lower house of Congress.[21]

The founders of the republic took little interest in expanding the scope of economic statistics. From 1791 on, the Treasury Department aggregated customs records for the use of Congress but made no attempt to monitor the internal trade and manufacturing of the United States. Even among the leading proponents of commercial development in the 1790s— that circle of nationally minded men where one would most expect to find

[19] Dwight, *Statistical Account*, 1.

[20] Robert V. Wells, *The Population of the British Colonies in America before 1776: A Survey of Census Data* (Princeton, N.J., 1975), is an invaluable guide to official provincial censuses of the colonial era.

[21] John Cummings, "Statistical Work of the Federal Government of the United States," in John Koren, ed., *The History of Statistics: Their Development and Progress in Many Countries . . .* (New York, 1918), 571-689.

a well-developed taste for and grasp of facts and figures—there was no one who yet saw a need for systematic collection of data. Tench Coxe was probably the most sophisticated political economist in the federal government and, as Alexander Hamilton's right-hand man, was in a position to appreciate the utility of quantitative economic facts. Periodically he issued reports and papers on the state of the economy for the use of Congress, sprinkling them so liberally with numbers and quantities (culled mostly from import and export records) that his work has been characterized as betraying "more than a trace of fact-benumbed pedantry."[22] But the close reader of these reports will detect a substantial amount of hypothesis, unsupported generalization, and guesswork beneath the superficial glitter of definite numbers. Coxe studded his writings with numerical tidbits to support sweeping statements about the progress of manufactures and the balance of trade, but the numbers were often slender and random—a survey of the home manufactures of twenty Virginia families taken "indiscriminately," or a count of manufacturing establishments in one Pennsylvania town[23]—leading political opponents to doubt that he had escaped the realm of mere opinion.[24] Political economy would not acquire a strong empirical bent until 1810, when the first census of manufactures was taken.[25]

In contrast, a few congressmen immediately appreciated the decennial census as a tool for gathering facts about the civil relations of Americans. Information about people, rather than products, seemed to them the means to achieve consensus on national political goals and measures. But others in Congress disagreed, and thwarted their efforts. The debates on

[22] Jacob E. Cooke, *Tench Coxe and the Early Republic* (Chapel Hill, N.C., 1978), 213. Many of Coxe's essays were drawn together in *A View of the United States of America* (Philadelphia, 1794), which Cooke likens to a statistical abstract in its ability to lose a reader's interest.

[23] *Ibid.*, 260, 312-313.

[24] Sometimes Coxe simply declared his statements to be the truth, offering no supporting evidence. At one such point, in a copy of his essay *Reflexions on the State of the Union* (Philadelphia, 1792), bearing South Carolina Sen. Pierce Butler's autograph, a hostile 18th-century hand noted in the margin that "the position is not supported by Argum[en]t nor founded in facts," and on the next page, "Declamation—not argument," blasting Coxe's prediction that the South would languish without domestic iron manufacture. See pp. 5 and 6 in the American Antiquarian Society's copy. It does not appear that the marginal notes and Butler's name are in the same handwriting, and since Butler and Coxe were long-time friends, it seems especially unlikely that the marginal notes were Butler's.

[25] By 1810 Coxe was considerably more sensitive to the necessity for accurate statistics on the economy. He assembled the results of the 1810 manufacturing census and discussed their imperfections with sophistication (*A Statement of the Arts and Manufactures of the United States of America for the Year 1810* [Philadelphia, 1814], xxv).

the censuses of 1790 and 1800 show how controversial the statistical approach to government was.[26]

The foremost advocate of expanding the census in 1790 beyond the basic constitutional stipulation was James Madison, at that time a strongly nationalist representative from Virginia. Madison served on the committee responsible for drawing up the "enumeration bill" and got his elaborated census schedule onto the House floor for debate. His proposal called for classifying the population into five categories—free white males over and under the age of sixteen, free white females, free blacks, and slaves—and for identifying each working person by occupation. These categories were hardly an unusual or sophisticated way of classifying the population, for many colonial censuses ordered by the Board of Trade had sought as much and more. Separating free persons from slaves was essential, since a slave was only three-fifths of a person for the purposes of representation in Congress. But the rest was more than the Constitution required. Distinguishing free blacks from whites, females from males, and boys from men, as Madison proposed, had the effect of identifying the group that most mattered: free adult white males—the workers, voters, and soldiers of the nation. Congress agreed with Madison on these priorities and wrote the five categories into the first census.

Madison's proposal to report occupations, however, encountered stiff resistance. In its defense, Madison offered what probably seemed to him to be a simple truism: "In order to accommodate our laws to the real situation of our constituents, we ought to be acquainted with that situation." He reminded his colleagues that in earlier debates on bills that concerned the agricultural, commercial, and manufacturing interests, "did they not wish then to know the relative proportion of each, and the exact number of every division, in order that they might rest their arguments on facts, instead of assertions and conjectures? Will any gentleman pretend to doubt, but our regulations would have been better accommodated to the real state of the society than they are?"[27]

House members did in fact profess that doubt. Samuel Livermore of New Hampshire offered serious objections to the feasibility of a census of occupations, protesting that it would be very difficult to decide exactly what occupation many people had. His constituents, for example, often had two or three, depending on the season. Livermore "was confident the

---

[26] The best recent account of the development of the United States census is Davis, "Beginnings of American Social Research," in Daniels, ed., *Nineteenth-Century American Science*, 154-156. Edward Clark Lunt, "Key to the Publications of the United States Census, 1790-1887," includes a good history (American Statistical Association, *Publications*, N.S., I[1888], 63-125).

[27] The debates were printed in the *Congressional Register* (New York, 1790), III, no. 4, a publication of brief duration based on the shorthand notes of Thomas Lloyd. The dates of the key discussions were Jan. 25 and Feb. 2, 1790 (*ibid.*, 167-168, 205-208).

distinction which the gentleman wished to make, could not be performed," and he opposed the extra expense and labor. Worse, he "apprehended it would excite the jealousy of the people; they would suspect that
government was so particular, in order to learn their ability to bear the
burthen of direct or other taxes," and so they would refuse to cooperate.
Another critic, John Page of Virginia, also thought the proposed census
would "occasion an alarm" among the people, for "they would suppose the
government intended something, by putting the union to this additional
expence, beside gratifying an idle curiosity." Page contended that even if
congressmen were "acquainted with the minutiae, they would not be benefited by it."[28]

Over such resistance the House passed Madison's plan intact, but the
Senate approved only the five basic categories of sex and race as legitimate
objects of inquiry.[29] Lacking a report of Senate debates comparable to the
Congressional Register transcript for the House, we have no record of
specific objections to a tally of occupations. Virtually the only source for
Senate debates in the First Congress, the journal of Senator William Maclay of Pennsylvania, treats the enumeration bill more as a vehicle for
expressing personal enmity than as an issue of substance in its own right.
Maclay moved to reject the entire proposed "lengthy schedule," for reasons undisclosed. The debate focused on a trivial detail, and in the end the
bill was consigned to committee. "The debate was scarce worth mentioning," Maclay said, except insofar as the debaters scored points for parliamentary prowess. When the bill emerged from committee, the tally of
occupations was gone.[30]

[28] *Ibid.*, 206. No congressman raised the traditional religious objection to any
census: the sin of David, who brought a plague upon Israel by "numbering" the
people (1 Sam. 24, 1 Chron. 21). On three occasions colonial governors blamed
the biblical prohibition for their inability to administer a census, but it is not clear
to what extent they were accurately reflecting a popular concern. For two instances, see letters to the Lords of Trade from the New York governor of 1712
and the New Jersey governor of 1726 in an 1870 congressional report on the
history of the census, U.S. Congress, *House Reports*, 41st Cong., 2d sess., no. 3, Jan.
18, 1870, 29. In 1763 the Lords of Trade singled out Massachusetts for a special
census and encountered great reluctance on the part of both houses of the assembly. Thomas Hutchinson thought that "religious scruples," specifically the sin of
David, lay behind the objections, but the assembly's record of debates fails to
mention sin at all. Hutchinson, *History of the Colony and Province of Massachusetts-
Bay*, ed. Lawrence Shaw Mayo (Cambridge, Mass., 1936), III, 75; *Journals of the
Honourable House of Representatives . . . of Massachusetts-Bay in New-England, 1763-
1764*, XL (Boston, 1970), 44, 48, 99, 103, 260, 266; Josiah H. Benton, Jr., *Early
Census Making in Massachusetts, 1643-1765 . . .* (Boston, 1905), 31-65.

[29] *Journal of the Second Session of the Senate of the United States of America . . .* (New
York, 1790), 25-28, and *passim*.

[30] Edgar S. Maclay, ed., *The Journal of William Maclay: United States Senator from
Pennsylvania, 1789-1791* (New York, 1890), 194-195, 197-198, quotation on p.

In a bitter letter to Jefferson, Madison stated that his plan "was thrown out by the Senate as a waste of trouble and supplying materials for idle people to make a book." Along with these objections to the count of occupations as trivial and useless, he identified an anti-quantitative strain in the negative vote, for he warned Jefferson to "judge by this little experiment of the reception likely to be given to so great an idea as that explained in your letter of September," a reference to Jefferson's developing ideas on the illegitimacy of one generation binding future generations to political contracts, ideas rooted in tenuous mathematical extrapolations from bills of mortality.[31] The Senate was barely able to grasp the advantage of knowing the number of men over the age of sixteen and could find no value in a census of occupations. The idea that political theory could be mathematically constructed from demographic observation was sure to be greeted with scorn, as Madison suspected.[32]

When Congress designed the census of 1800, efforts were made to transform it into an unprecedentedly ambitious social survey. Madison had once suggested merely adding occupations and had been called visionary for his trouble; proponents now evinced a heady enthusiasm for inquiring into other characteristics of the population—age, nativity, and marital status, as well as occupation. Belief in the necessity and appropriateness of "authentic facts" for comprehending America had grown during the previous decade. Statistically-minded men felt encouraged to appeal to the government to conduct a fact-gathering foray into every home in the republic. Two learned societies each petitioned Congress to serve science by enlarging the census. Dwight, speaking for the Connecticut Academy of Arts and Sciences, and Jefferson, as president of the American Philosophical Society, each submitted memorials elaborating on the value of diverse quantitative facts about the population. "To present and future generations," Dwight contended, "it will be highly gratifying to observe the progress of population in this country, and to be able to trace the proportion of its increase from native Americans, and from foreigners emigrating at successive periods; to observe the progress or decline of various occupations; the effects of population, luxury, mechanic arts, the

---

195. The small detail debated on Feb. 9 was whether a commissioner or a federal marshal should be in charge of the census in each district.

[31] Madison to Jefferson, Feb. 14, 1790, in *Letters and Other Writings of James Madison . . .* , I (Philadelphia, 1865), 507. For Jefferson's letter of Sept. 6, 1789, to Madison see Julian P. Boyd *et al.*, eds., *The Papers of Thomas Jefferson*, XV (Princeton, N.J., 1958), 392-398.

[32] Scholars of a later, more quantitative era have been generally receptive to Jefferson's ideas uniting political theory with demographic calculations, but Garry Wills exposes the logical fallacies in Jefferson's calculations in *Inventing America: Jefferson's Declaration of Independence* (Garden City, N.Y., 1978), 123-128. Wills pictures Jefferson as an inveterate calculator, swept away by the possibilities of making politics a quantitative science.

cultivation of lands, and the draining of marshes, on the health and longevity of the citizens of the United States."[33] Congress, however, was not convinced that future generations would be gratified to have such information. The 1800 census differed from its predecessor only in refining the age classification of the free white population into five categories for both sexes. This format was repeated for the 1810 census as well. That no one was interested in learning either the sexes or ages of black Americans, whether slave or free, testifies to the relative unimportance of blacks in the hierarchy of social ranking as well as in the eyes of science.

Why did all but a few congressmen of 1790 and the early 1800s fail to see an opportunity in the census? In the midst of a developing cluster of ideas associating good government and knowledge of the common good with facts and statistics, why did they refuse to take advantage of an information-gathering mechanism that could have yielded a wealth of facts? The reasons for resistance can be culled from the statements of the legislators themselves. Many of them believed that Congress had no authority to collect more than the most basic facts—certainly a legitimate sentiment at a time when the limits of governmental power were still under exploration. Alexander White of Virginia felt compelled to reject a plunge into social research, however attractive the possibilities, simply because the Constitution did not expressly authorize such activity. Another Virginian, John Page, held that this sort of knowledge was more appropriately the province of historians and philosophers, and not politicians, who were concerned with immediate policy. Page thought a census of occupations worse than useless because it would spark alarm among the people, who would naturally imagine a sinister purpose in the plan. Livermore agreed: "so particular a detail might excite some disagreeable ideas in the minds of the people." Americans' experience with colonial censuses had shown that a distant government could use information in ways adverse to the public interest. Members of Congress understandably wanted to exercise caution, and too few shared Madison's enthusiasm for "marking the progress of the society."[34]

Even if most congressmen could accept Madison's observation that to legislate wisely for the people Congress must know their true situation, still it did not follow that a division of the people into agricultural, commercial, and manufacturing interests would constitute an appropriate way to classify American society. One representative, Theodore Sedgwick of Massachusetts, wanted to expand the list to include the learned profes-

[33] U.S. Senate, 6th Cong., 1st sess., 1799-1800, *Memorial of the Connecticut Academy of Arts and Sciences; also, The Memorial of the American Philosophical Society . . . printed for the use of the Senate* (Philadelphia, 1800), 3.

[34] *Cong. Reg.*, III, 167-168, 207. The *Boston Gazette*, Feb. 8, 1790, and the *Herald of Freedom, and the Federal Advertiser* (Boston), Feb. 5, 9, 1790, printed the speeches of Madison, Alexander White, Roger Sherman, Fisher Ames, and Theodore Sedgwick.

sions, particularly lawyers, as a distinct class. Madison professed agreement but pointed out that the learned professions could never properly be "objects of legislative attention" in the way his three basic categories presumably were. Others, like Livermore, wanted to abandon the list of occupations, because they were persuaded that no such distinctions could be drawn. In truth, the boundaries dividing agriculture, commerce, and manufacturing were often vague and overlapping in the eighteenth century. The activity of a Chesapeake tobacco grower was at once agricultural and commercial; a New England farmer who made shoes in winter was both a farmer and a manufacturer. While Madison spoke of measuring "the growth of every interest," Livermore denied that separate interests could be distinguished.[35]

Clashing here were two notions of the common good. The opponents of a census of occupations did not see a need to determine the relative weights of economic interests: the very idea conflicted with the traditional principle of a common good that embraced the entire community. The object of wise governmental policy was to foster the happiness of society as a harmonious whole; this notion arose from eighteenth-century ideas of an organic society. Madison, on the other hand, thought a census revealing the "several classes" of America would allow Congress to adapt legislation to reality. In his view, the common good could no longer be known solely through the agency of talented leaders somehow divining the genius of the people. Statistical writers of the 1790s echoed Madison's idea that empirical knowledge was now essential for determining the common good. For example, Timothy Dwight, in his sermon of 1795, expressed no doubt about the existence of one transcendent public happiness, which he thought could be served by collecting statistics. By insisting on the value of survey data, men like Madison and Dwight were subtly shifting the grounds underlying the traditional idea of a common good. It was a short step from Dwight's position to the idea that public happiness was best thought of as the sum of many individual happinesses, that the common good was really the greatest good for the greatest number.[36]

That step was not taken in the 1790s. In arguing for a census of occupations Madison approached the position that the interests and strengths of competing groups should be weighed before legislation was enacted. But the imprecise boundaries of the groups he named prevented him from following through with the logic of an empirically determined common good. There were other ways to classify the population by economic interest—divisions of relative wealth, debtors and creditors, employers and

[35] *Herald of Freedom*, Feb. 9, 1790; *Cong. Reg.*, III, 206.
[36] For a discussion of the effect of post-Revolutionary economic changes on the conception of the common good see J. E. Crowley, *This Sheba, Self: The Conceptualization of Economic Life in Eighteenth-Century America* (Baltimore, 1794), 151-157.

employees—and these would find favor with political economists in later times when the empirical common good had been transformed to the majoritarian version, the greatest good for the greatest number. This view, which became an aphorism in mid-nineteenth-century political thought, implied a quantitative assessment of a measured good that benefited some known proportion of the population. A census of occupations would reveal the proportions of competing groups only if it were decided that agriculture, commerce, and manufacturing were in fact separable groups constituting the most meaningful distinctions in the social order. In 1820 that step was finally taken; the federal census of that year required that each household be labelled as belonging to one and only one sector of the economy. The common good was being broken into constituent parts, and the social order could now be comprehended through arithmetic.

How had this change come about? One answer that satisfies common sense is that the census categories of occupation directly reflected the increasing specialization of economic activity, but the change also reflected burgeoning interest in perfecting a "science of statistics."[37] Thus an anonymous writer in the *North American Review* in 1816, commenting on Moses Greenleaf's *Statistical View of the District of Maine*, remarked that in times past "little information was sufficient, to provide for the wants and exigencies of the community, as men were not divided into so many classes, having distinct interests, as they are at the present."[38] The emergence of such interests, together with the government's increasing acceptance of responsibility for fostering economic growth, demanded that accurate and comprehensive statistics be made available in readily accessible form. For similar reasons, journals like *Niles' Weekly Register* made statistical tables a regular feature from 1811, declaring them to be "among the most useful and interesting articles we can possibly insert."[39] The output of state gazetteers rose sharply, and almanacs, the staple of every man's reading, began to be garnished with facts and figures.[40] By 1820, when Secretary of

[37] Quotation from *Niles' Weekly Register*, XIV (1818), 142.
[38] *North American Review and Miscellaneous Journal*, III (1816), 364, 367-368.
[39] *Niles' Wkly. Reg.*, I (1811), 16.
[40] One quick way to monitor changing trends in almanacs is to read through a chronological checklist that outlines the contents of a series of these annual books. In the bibliography of James A. Bear, Jr., and Mary Caperton Bear, *A Checklist of Virginia Almanacs, 1732-1850* (Charlottesville, Va., 1962), one learns that Virginia almanacs from 1812, 1814, 1815, 1817, and 1818 included population tables, whereas none earlier had done so. Almanac-makers occasionally suggested that the purchaser keep his almanacs and stitch them together to form a set for reference. The 1817 almanac of Elijah Middlebrook suggested that the owner add his own notes on the local price of labor, the value of his produce, and the expense of living, with the reminder that "fact, accuracy & conciseness are requisite." The series of almanacs, sewn together, would form a personal quantitative record of

State John Quincy Adams sat down to plan the federal census, statistics had become familiar ingredients in writings about American society, no longer requiring apologies or justifications.

The statistical manual, a new sort of book intended to satisfy the public's appetite for facts and figures, made its appearance in 1806 and was perfected by 1818, perfection being defined as strict adherence to the objectivity of bare numbers. Three such works were published during that period. The first was Samuel Blodget, Jr.'s *Economica: A Statistical Manual for the United States,* published in the nation's capital. Blodget, an erstwhile insurance man with interests in Washington real estate, announced that his book would "embrace every statistical point yet in our power," but his points turned out to be only those few statistics collected by the federal government, for he compiled them solely from census reports and Treasury documents on exports and imports.[41] What he offered was no more than a convenient collection of existing data.

That in itself was sufficient justification for the book, for in 1806 there was no other even remotely comparable compilation. But Blodget's work was flawed, in the eyes of contemporaries, by the dogmatic and opinionated text that accompanied, but made little reference to, the numerical data. Blodget had emphatic views on such subjects as the public debt, narcotic drinks, southern indolence, the fair sex, and slavery, and he argued those with slight regard to quantitative facts. For example, he presented figures comparing the price of a slave to the worth of a free person, but observed that "this estimate, as far as it is opposed to slavery, corresponds with that of every other rational calculating economist. But is this a subject for cold calculation? No, it is the cause of feeling! of humanity! of virtue!"[42] While Blodget's was by no means an unusual view of slavery in 1806, it was thought to be out of place in a book that claimed to be a "statistical manual." Though credited as a pioneer by other statistical writers of the 1810s, Blodget was sharply criticized by them for being inexact and inaccurate. One writer observed that he had an "ardent" and "speculative" mind: consequently, his statistics were imprecise and his conception of the subject was indistinct and undiscriminating. Another complained that Blodget was "deficient in the details" and gave too many of his own estimates.[43]

The next quantitative manual, Timothy Pitkin's *Statistical View of the Commerce of the United States of America,* published in 1816, proposed to

---

one's life, most appropriately shelved next to the family Bible with its personal record of vital events (*An Agricultural and Economical Almanack for 1817* [New Haven, Conn., 1816], preface).

[41] Samuel Blodget, Jr., *Economica: A Statistical Manual for the United States of America* (Washington, D.C., 1806), 8.

[42] *Ibid.,* 80.

[43] *No. Am. Rev.,* III (1816), 349; Adam Seybert, *Statistical Annals ...* (Philadelphia, 1818), v.

remedy the deficiencies of its ill-fated predecessor. Pitkin, a congressman from Connecticut, intended his compilation primarily for the use of merchants and statists but maintained that anyone could peruse it with profit, for "every individual must feel an interest, in obtaining a knowledge of the wealth and resources of his own country."[44] This confidence that commercial statistics commanded universal appeal marks a new development in social thought, and the theme was picked up and elaborated on by the anonymous reviewer of Pitkin's manual in the North American Review. The reviewer argued that the growing complexity and interdependence of society demanded accurate statistical information. Where once a few great men determined the course of history, while the rest of the population—huntsmen, fishermen, shepherds—was inconsequential, under the post-Revolutionary "arrangements of society" the mass of men with their combined "intellectual, moral, and physical powers" set the direction and pace of progress. The inequality of those powers, resulting from the growth of commerce and the concomitant concentration of wealth, meant to the reviewer that the "general will" had to be studied in its component parts. Manuals like Pitkin's, the reviewer declared, admirably revealed "the internal proportions of power and of influence" in the body politic. They should therefore "be studied by all who aspire to regulate, or improve the state of the nation; and even by all who would judge rightly of their duties as citizens." The benefits of such books of "Political Arithmetick" lay in the harmony of thought they would promote, according to the reviewer: "As men approximate towards certainty in their judgments concerning the facts which indicate the condition of the nation, parties will be likely to draw nearer to each other in their plans of policy." In view of their social and political utility, such compilations amounted to "something more than the gratification of mere curiosity"—the charge levelled by Madison's opponents nearly thirty years earlier; they should be required reading for citizens, legislators, and commercial men alike, because statistics were essential for calculating "the force of the nation."[45]

Two years later, Adam Seybert, a Pennsylvania physician and, like Pitkin, a member of Congress, published his Statistical Annals. Noting that Pitkin's book was excellent yet limited, Seybert pushed beyond the realm of commerce to include detailed data on population, the public lands, the post office, and the military. In a further improvement, he often transformed sets of large numbers into ratios such as the proportion of free persons to slaves, or males to females, an innovation that the North American Review hailed as a great boon to memory and understanding.[46]

Seybert addressed his "authentic book of reference" to two sets of readers. First were the legislators, to whom he dedicated the book, who would

[44] Timothy Pitkin, A Statistical View of the Commerce of the United States of America in Connection with Agriculture and Manufactures . . . (Hartford, Conn., 1816), iii.
[45] No. Am. Rev., III (1816), 345-354.
[46] Ibid., IX (1819), 223; Dictionary of American Biography, s.v. "Seybert, Adam."

learn not only the facts they needed in order to govern well but would also read in the statistics the measure of their success: "The state of civilized society and the resources of nations, are the tests by which we can ascertain the tendency of the government. It is to the condition of the people, in relation to their increase, their moral and physical circumstances, their happiness and comfort, their genius and industry, that we must look for the proofs of a mild and free, or of a cruel and despotic government."[47] The other audience consisted of those people, both in the United States and abroad, who entertained "errors and misrepresentations" about the condition and progress of the country and who needed to be set straight. Perhaps with this readership in mind, Seybert managed to get the book circulated in Britain and translated into French in 1820.

The prestigious *Edinburgh Review* rendered a mixed verdict on Seybert's volume in a lengthy article of 1820. The critic credited it with giving "a pretty complete picture of America" but complained that the book had a disagreeably chauvinistic air that was, in his view, unwarranted. Since Seybert's book contained very little textual commentary, the charge related to the contents of the tables, which featured standard statistics of growth and progress. The critic challenged whether records of population, imports and exports, taxes, and the like could justify national pride, when culture, genius, science, and art were missing both from the statistical tables and from American society. The typical American, according to the *Review*, was "vulgar and arithmetical," and in danger of becoming vain if he took such quantitative boasts seriously, when in fact they were "unspeakably ludicrous."[48]

The American press, by contrast, viewed Seybert's work as a monumental tribute to the virtues and accomplishments of America.[49] Seybert did not need to wave the flag; his facts spoke for themselves, communicating national pride to native and foreign reader alike. While the Scottish critic thought that Seybert's measurement constituted a false claim to greatness, American proponents of statistics agreed that grandeur could be captured by numbers. Statistics signalled America's rising power and glory; numbers commanded respect because they measured and weighed the very aspects of American life of which the people of the republic were most proud. Statists in the 1810s valued data that revealed material growth, progress, improvement, and abundance. Their choice of statistical facts was informed by a quantitative notion of achievement: more people, more trade, more daily newspapers, more gallons of lamp oil. No opinionated comment was necessary because the choice of facts already carried the assumption that *more* meant *better*.

At the end of the second decade of the nineteenth century, statistics

[47] Seybert, *Statistical Annals*, 1.
[48] *Edinburgh Review*, XXXIII (Jan. 1820), 69-80.
[49] *No. Am. Rev.*, IX (1819), 217-239.

were usually employed to evidence social and economic progress, but on occasion there appeared sprouts of a new crop of quantitative facts, the results of applying numerical measurement to social problems. By the antebellum reform decades, this application would become commonplace. In the late 1810s a few governmental bodies began to commission surveys and enlist statistics to serve a variety of reform purposes. In 1817, for example, the Boston School Committee conducted an unprecedented ward-by-ward survey of children in and out of school, though with results that were deflating to all who prided themselves on the city's educational system.[50] In 1821 the Massachusetts legislature appointed a committee to survey the condition of the state's paupers, and the committee complied with an exactness on the number of poor and the sums spent for relief that set a model for future investigations.[51] A few private societies also adopted the same tactic for measuring the problems they were dedicated to solving and for evaluating the effects of their endeavors. In 1816 the Massachusetts Society for the Suppression of Intemperance built their anti-drink argument on a quantitative scaffolding, summoning "well-authenticated" facts to show the numbers of dollars and lives wasted by alcohol. Their publications up to that time had relied on morality and sermonizing to carry their temperance message.[52] The Philadelphia Society for Alleviating the Miseries of Public Prisons appointed a committee in 1816 to prepare a statistical overview of the miseries of prisons; a year later, their short pamphlet was presented to the public. Confident that numbers spoke for themselves, alongside one table detailing large numbers of prisoners still awaiting trial the committee observed that "having presented these reflections and truths to public notice, and beseeching a particular regard to their importance, we leave the subject to a virtuous community."[53] In 1817 the Boston Society for the Moral and Religious Instruction of the Poor surveyed the dimensions of irreligion in Boston by sending gentlemen to impoverished abodes to inquire how many attended

[50] The committee found that only a very small fraction of the children of the town were attending school (Stanley K. Schultz, *The Culture Factory: Boston Public Schools, 1798-1860* [New York, 1973], 32). Details of the survey are in Joseph M. Wightman, *Annals of the Boston Primary School Committee* (Boston, 1860), 20-28.

[51] David J. Rothman terms this report (called the Quincy report) and its close imitator, the 1824 Yates report of New York, "path-forging" and "exceptionally thorough" (*Discovery of the Asylum: Social Order and Disorder in the New Republic* [Boston, 1971], 157-161, 307).

[52] Jesse Appleton, *An Address delivered before the Massachusetts Society for the Suppression of Intemperance* (Boston, 1816), 1-7. For the nonstatistical moral-suasion temperance argument see John T. Kirkland, *A Sermon Delivered before the Massachusetts Society for the Suppression of Intemperance* (Boston, 1814).

[53] Philadelphia Society for Alleviating the Miseries of Public Prisons, *A Statistical View of the Operation of the Penal Code of Pennsylvania* . . . (Philadelphia, 1817), 6.

public worship and how many owned Bibles. The findings convinced many citizens to subscribe to the society's program for distributing Bibles and setting up Sunday schools. In 1818 the society proudly reported on the number of new pupils, the average attendance at the schools, and the scriptural verses, hymns, and catechisms the pauper children had committed to memory since the preceding February: 54,029 verses, 1,899 hymns, and 17,779 answers to catechism.[54] A way had been found to quantify piety.

This account of the rising popularity of statistics in the new republic allows a fresh angle of vision on the question of how Americans confronted the economic expansion that quickened after political independence. In the 1790s, statistical thought offered a way to mediate between political ideas based on a homogeneous social order and economic realities that were fast undermining homogeneity. Inventories of descriptive facts about society were touted as providing an authentic, objective basis for ascertaining the common good. Complete possession of the facts, it was hoped, would eliminate factionalism and allow government to rule in the best interest of the public. Further, collections of social data were thought to constitute the proper scientific proof that the new experiment in republicanism did indeed benefit all citizens. By 1820, the subject matter of statistics had shifted somewhat, indicating alterations in the conception of the common good and in the proof of the republican pudding. Statistical information took on a specifically quantitative connotation and narrowed its focus to measurable facts about society. This meant that the benefits of republicanism were now most readily demonstrated by appeals to quantifiable facts, notably of demographic or economic character. The celebration of growth so evident in compilations of the 1810s thus became closely tied to the celebration of republican institutions, but at the same time statistical writers abandoned the idea that they were elucidating a single common good and moved toward an acceptance of competing economic interests. Avid collectors of statistics had come to recognize that distinctions and divisions in American society legitimately existed and had to be reckoned with. The particular distinctions they made—for example, between agriculture, commerce, and manufacturing—they regarded as inherent in their social order; empiricism, they insisted, was objective and value-free. But of course their empiricism was freighted with unacknowledged values. The kinds of things they did *not* count and calculate in 1820—for instance, the number of slaveowners, black mortality, the incidence of crime, female illiteracy—tells as much about them and their society as the things they chose to notice.

[54] *Annual Report* . . . (Boston, 1817), and *Second Annual Report* (Boston, 1818), 10.

"I have the itch of Botany, of Chemistry, of Mathematics . . . strong upon me": the Science of Benjamin Henry Latrobe

DARWIN H. STAPLETON

Mellon Bibliographer, American Philosophical Society Library

and

EDWARD C. CARTER II*

Librarian, American Philosophical Society

From the years of his English and German schooling through the years of his great professional achievements in the United States, Benjamin Henry Latrobe's life was filled with scientific endeavor. Latrobe is generally remembered as an architect who directed the construction of the Capitol and the White House during parts of the first two decades of the nineteenth century, and as the designer and engineer of many other public and private projects. But Latrobe was also a dedicated natural historian whose publications appeared in the *Transactions* of the American Philosophical Society, and whose professional activities were infused with scientific ideas. As a product of what was possibly the best educational system in Europe, Latrobe possessed an informed and inquisitive mind, and he conversed on equal terms with leading American and European men of science

such as Thomas Jefferson, William Maclure, and Constantin F. C. Volney.

1. SCIENCE IN THE LIFE OF BENJAMIN HENRY LATROBE

Benjamin Henry Latrobe was born in 1764 in a Moravian community at Fulneck in Northern England.[1] The Moravian faith had its origins in the Hussite rebellions of the fifteenth century in central Europe, but it did not flourish until the 1720s when a flock of its adherents were taken under the protection of Count Zinzendorf in Saxony. Thereafter the Moravians developed a strong evangelical movement which spread their faith to the rest of Europe, the Americas, and Africa. The Moravians also had an educational system which was among the best in the Western world in the latter eighteenth century.

Adhering to the principles of Amos Commenius (1592–1672), the Moravians developed a rigorous and stimulating curriculum. All Moravian children were expected to enroll in school at an early age and to follow their education as far as their personal talent could take them. The church provided support for those children whose families could not afford to keep them in school. The link between faith and education was particularly

* This paper is an expansion of an earlier version read by Edward Carter at the April 1977 Spring General Meeting of the American Philosophical Society. The authors thank Charlotte Porter and Charles E. Brownell for analyses supplied for the preparation of that earlier paper.

PROCEEDINGS OF THE AMERICAN PHILOSOPHICAL SOCIETY, VOL. 128, NO. 3, 1984

173

261

strong because of the Moravian habit of founding entire new communities which were centered on their academic institutions.[2]

Fulneck, Latrobe's birthplace, was such a community, and Latrobe's parents were directors of the school. Accordingly, at three years of age their son began his formal education, probably with two hours of spelling and reading five days of every week.[3] At twelve years of age, like his older brother Christian Ignatius and some other Fulneck boys, Benjamin Henry was sent to Germany for higher education. From 1776 to 1782 he was at the paedagogium in Niesky, and in 1782 to 1783 at the seminary in Barby.[4]

All of the classes which Latrobe attended are not known, but the subjects taught at the two German schools are well documented. At Niesky there was a heavy emphasis on learning languages, particularly Latin and Greek, but with attention given to Hebrew and French. Greek and Hebrew lessons focused on biblical texts, and Cicero and other classics were read in Latin. Substantial attention was also given to mathematics, geometry, trigonometry, history and geography, and there were a few classes in writing, drawing, and music.[5] At Barby there was greater concentration on theological studies, since most of the students at the seminary intended to go into the ministry, but there were also medical and legal studies for prospective doctors and lawyers.[6]

Latrobe was introduced to the sciences (in addition to the mathematical disciplines) while at Niesky and Barby. Natural history was taught at Niesky while he was there, and at Barby he had instruction in natural philosophy, which included physics and botany. The seminary had a cabinet of natural history, an astronomical observatory, and a pneumatic apparatus for experiments.[7]

The major intellectual force behind the scientific activity at Barby appears to have been Friedrich Adam Scholler, a teacher there from 1754 to 1769, and director of the

seminary from 1772 to 1782. Scholler's major interest was botany, and in 1775 he published a Flora Barbiensis. Scholler was succeeded as director by Johan Gottfried Cunow (formerly at Niesky), who taught mathematics and physics.[8]

Outside of the classroom, study of the sciences was a major avocation of the Niesky and Barby students. Notably, C. G. von Brinkmann, who was in Latrobe's class, compiled a manuscript Flora Niskyensis in 1782. Christian Ignatius La Trobe, who preceded his brother at both schools, also exhibited a strong interest in natural history.[9]

According to the Moravian plan of education, each student was to select his vocation, presumably well-prepared for the choice by the wide variety of the curriculum. Students not choosing the ministerial, medical, or legal professions were encouraged to arrange an apprenticeship, and by 17 years of age they were to begin work if their studies were completed. Apparently Latrobe announced his interest in architecture and engineering, and for a time (probably in 1781 or 1782) studied under a Silesian engineer of river improvements.[10]

It is now known that at about the same time he had reached some conclusions regarding his own religious convictions which were incompatible with Moravian theology, and after deliberations of some months (during which he was provisionally admitted to Barby) church officials decided not to allow him to continue his studies. He was sent back to England.[11]

For the next eleven years Latrobe lived in London, probably with his parents at first, then with his brother, and finally (after their marriage in 1790) with his new wife. He was employed as a clerk in the Stamp Office of the Treasury from 1784 to 1792 or 1793, but apparently had no difficulty combining that position with the pursuit of his architectural and engineering career.[12]

According to Latrobe's later statements he spent some time in the 1780s studying under

John Smeaton, perhaps the most respected engineer of the time.[13] The circumstance is not unlikely, since Smeaton spent a portion of each year in London. His office was at Gray's Inn, close to the Stamp Office's quarters at Lincoln's Inn and to Latrobe's residence.[14] Latrobe later mentioned writing a report for Smeaton on the drainage of the Lincolnshire and Cambridgeshire fens, one of Smeaton's commissions in 1782–84. If Latrobe did have an association with Smeaton, he was exposed to an active member of the Royal Society of London, the foremost scientific society of Britain. Smeaton had strong interests in astronomy, scientific instrumentation, and mathematics, and published several articles in the Society's *Transactions.*[15]

Latrobe's professional development continued throughout the remainder of his English years. He later recalled work on Rye Harbour and on the Basingstoke Canal, projects supervised by Smeaton's former assistant, William Jessop.[16] He then spent two years in the office of Samuel Pepys Cockerell, the architect of many public buildings in London, and finally went to work on his own about 1791. He had a public appointment (Surveyor of the Police Offices), some private commissions, and a canal consultation in the next four years.

In addition to his continued acquisition of professional knowledge, some of which may be classed as "engineering and architectural science," Latrobe continued to have a strong interest in natural history. The evidence for his interest comes, paradoxically enough, only from the time of his actual departure from England in 1795. From that point Latrobe's journals and letters survive in sufficient quantity to ascertain that he had never lost the passion for flora and fauna which he acquired in Germany.

Latrobe left England because neither his personal life nor his professional career fared well. His wife died in childbirth in 1793; at about the same time he seems to have lost his position as Surveyor of the Police Offices, and little further work was forthcoming. Emigration to the United States had some appeal to him since his mother had been raised in the Moravian community of Bethlehem, Pennsylvania and she willed him some nearby lands at her death in 1794. Latrobe also had definite republican sympathies which undoubtedly focused his attention on the "land of liberty" during the heightened political tensions of the 1790s in England.

Consigning his two children to the care of his wife's family and leaving his other personal affairs in shambles, Latrobe left England for America in November 1795. He was a passenger on the American vessel *Eliza* which, due to the inept direction of its captain, required nearly four months to make the Atlantic passage. Latrobe spent a considerable portion of the voyage observing and recording things of scientific interest. His journals and sketchbooks contain a description of the volcanic cone Pico in the Azores, and an attempt to measure its altitude; comments on the appearance and behavior of dolphins; a discussion of gulfweed and the Gulf Stream; and descriptions of a whale, an albacore, barnacles, and other animals.[17]

Perhaps the most remarkable aspects of Latrobe's observations are the watercolor paintings which he often made. Carefully delineated and labeled, they exhibit his skill in technical rendering and his knowledge of the style of illustrations in technical publications and encyclopedias. They reflect as well his years of drawing experience, first as a student at Niesky and Barby where drawing was part of the curriculum, and thereafter as a follower of the British Picturesque movement.[18]

After his arrival at Norfolk, Virginia in March 1796 Latrobe continued to include scientific observations in his journals and sketchbooks. His keen eye recorded (among others) insects, fish, flowers, and general landscape features (figs. 1, 2). Perhaps most striking was his interest in the life of wasps, bees, and ants. He devoted hours to watching their behavior, and took what might be termed an engineer's interest in their dwellings and their compartments for eggs and larvae. Eventually he wrote a paper on the mud-dauber wasp which was published in both the United States and Britain.[19]

Late in 1797 and early in 1798 Latrobe made acquaintances with three men of geological bent: Giambattista Scandella, Constantin-Francois de Chasseboeuf (comte de) Volney, and William Maclure. He met Scandella and Maclure when they visited Richmond, and Volney on his brief trip to Philadelphia in 1798. All of them came to be members of the American Philosophical Society, and Volney and Maclure helped lay the foundations for the study of American geology.[20] While Latrobe had previously made only sparse geological observations, he now devoted considerable time to them.[21] His last activity in Virginia, before removing his residence to Philadelphia, on 1 December 1798, was a geological excursion with William Maclure. The two men examined the coal fields west of Richmond "to ascertain the succession of strata between Richmond, and the extent of the coal country."[22]

Latrobe had found Virginia society not to be intellectually stimulating, particularly in scientific topics. He wrote to Scandella that "I have the itch of Botany, of Chemistry, of Mathematics, of general Literature strong upon me yet, and yawn at perpetual political or legal discussion."[23] With limited professional prospects in Virginia as well, his attention turned to Philadelphia as the most likely place for employment and mental inspiration. When he was appointed architect of the Bank of Pennsylvania in the latter part of 1798, he had few regrets about leaving his first American home.

Latrobe traveled to Philadelphia with Maclure, stopping on the way "to investigate the nature of the soil and stratification of the Stone at Fredericsburg on the Rappahannoc, and from George town to the little falls, on the Potowmac." For the next four months Latrobe lived with Maclure's family, which must have facilitated his entrance into the scientific community of Philadelphia.[24]

On 21 December 1798 the first of Latrobe's papers was read at a meeting of the American Philosophical Society. He discussed a pattern of wind-blown sand deposition at Cape Henry in Virginia and noted that it was creating a geological formation similar to those which geologists had assumed were water-formed. The paper was referred to one of the Society's members for consideration, and a few days later it was approved for publication in the Society's *Transactions*.[25]

Latrobe plunged into Philadelphia not only in architecture and science, but also in engineering. Soon after his arrival he was asked to give his professional opinion about a group of springs as a source of fresh drinking water for the city's inhabitants, and he proceeded to write a pamphlet which outlined the city's water problem and a likely solution for it. In January he became the consulting engineer to the committee of the city councils which was looking into a water system, and his plan was eventually adopted. For the next two years he was largely employed in constructing the Philadelphia Waterworks, the first comprehensive urban waterworks in North America.[26]

Well-established in Philadelphia, Latrobe became an active member of the city's scientific community. He was elected a member of the American Philosophical Society on 19 July 1799 along with William Maclure, John Redman Coxe, Thomas Peters Smith, and three others. For the next four years Latrobe frequently attended meetings, and from 1800 to 1805 he served on the Society's governing council.[27]

It seems apparent that the active membership of the society had considerable regard for Latrobe's scientific ability. Of the

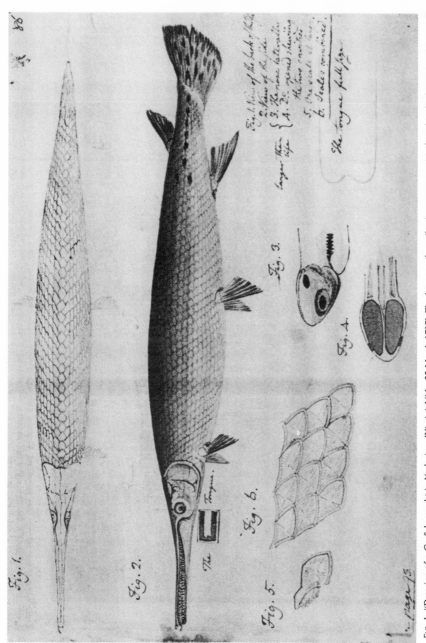

FIG. 1. "Drawing of a Garfish caught in York river [Virginia]" [c. 25 March 1797]. The longnosed gar (Lepisosteus osseus) is found in freshwater in the eastern United States, and brackish or salt water in the southern part of its range. He was intrigued by their vicious appearance, commenting that "nothing seems capable of escaping so formidable a machine." Latrobe dissected two specimens for detailed study. Edward C. Carter II, John C. Van Horne, and Charles E. Brownell, eds., *Latrobe's View of America, 1795–1820* (New Haven, Conn., Yale University Press, 1985).

FIG. 2. "Extraordinary appearances in the Heavens, and on Earth," 2 August 1797. Latrobe's primary concern here was to illustrate a remarkable, fan-like double rainbow that he saw near Richmond, Virginia. Although he was of the opinion that the phenomenon was caused by something other than sunlight ("perhaps electrical fluid"), the accuracy of his rendering indicates that it was a rare combination of primary and secondary rainbows with "rays" caused by shadows of clouds (or cloud debris) between Latrobe and the sun. Carter et al., eds., *Latrobe's View of America.*

seven papers which he presented to the Society after his election five were chosen for publication in the *Transactions*.[28] He also received nineteen committee assignments; most frequently the committees were established to judge the publishability of a paper. For example, he was twice a committee of one to report on papers of the eminent botanist Benjamin Smith Barton. But he was also chosen to serve on committees considering Society operations, including the preparation of volumes IV and V of the *Transactions*.[29]

Latrobe was also a member of the Chemical Society of Philadelphia, which had been founded in 1792 by James Woodhouse, a professor at the University of Pennsylvania. The extent of Latrobe's participation in the meetings of the Chemical Society is unknown due to the scarcity of documents relating to it. However, he apparently took advantage of the Society's offer of free mineral analysis in 1800, and in 1805 he attended the public eulogy of Joseph Priestley which the Chemical Society co-sponsored.[31]

Through his membership in these scientific societies Latrobe became acquainted with several prominent men of American science, and his letterbooks and journals indicate that he had continuing scientific discussions with them. He was a friend of Thomas Jefferson, John Vaughan, Charles Willson Peale, Robert Hare, and Thomas Peters Smith; he also conversed with Robert Patterson, Adam Seybert, and Robert Leslie.[32]

Changes in Latrobe's professional life during and after 1803 reduced his contact with this circle of savants (except for Jefferson, to whom he drew closer). His architectural and engineering commissions grew far more demanding when he assumed the positions of Surveyor of the Public Buildings (1803), Engineer to the Navy Department (1804), and Engineer of the Chesapeake and Delaware Canal (1804). Reflecting on these appointments, he wrote to Charles Willson Peale in the summer of 1805: "My time is at present fully occupied by professional engagements, that I have no time to attend to the more pleasant and morally improving study of nature."[33] The press of business also required Latrobe to move his family, first to Delaware in 1803–05, then to Washington in 1807, with interludes in Philadelphia with his wife's family.[34] These changes of residence reduced Latrobe's level of activity in the American Philosophical Society. From 1804 to 1808 he attended only four meetings and thereafter none. His letterbooks record his attempt to keep up with Society business, largely by correspondence with Peale and Vaughan, but even that contact ceased after 1808.

Thus Latrobe found through experience what historians have since deduced from the records: that Philadelphia was the center of American science during this period.[35] By moving Latrobe was separated from that mainstream of American science which he had found so stimulating in comparison with Virginia.

In spite of his isolation Latrobe retained his scientific interests. In 1807 and 1808 he submitted papers to the American Philosophical Society. In 1809 he recorded in his sketchbook his fascination with galls of the sumac shrub formed by the gall fly. From 1809 to 1813 he corresponded on scientific topics with Erick Bollmann, a European-trained physician and chemist. In 1814 he exchanged several letters with Thomas Cooper, the former assistant to Joseph Priestley who was then professor at Dickinson College. Latrobe also contributed an article on road construction to Cooper's journal, *The Emporium of Arts and Sciences*.[36]

To some extent, as well, Latrobe found that Washington had a scientific community, however fragmented and ephemeral compared to Philadelphia's. The scientific axis of the city in 1807–09, for example, must have been Thomas Jefferson and Joel Barlow, both of whom had decided intellectual and scientific tastes. Latrobe was frequently in their company. It was undoubtedly through Barlow that Latrobe met Robert Fulton late in 1807, and several years later, the Portuguese botanist Jose Francisco Correa de Serra.[37]

Latrobe was also in contact with nascent scientific agencies of the federal government.[38] He often dealt with William Thornton, first head of the Patent Office (1802), although the two men frequently quarreled. Thornton had a Scottish medical degree and his interests ranged from natural history to steam engineering in a manner similar to Latrobe's.[39] Latrobe was a friend of William Tatham, a self-described surveyor and engineer, who had intermittent connections with the Coast Survey. Tatham had a large collection of maps, instruments, and books which he attempted to sell to Congress.[40] Latrobe also came to know Colonel Jonathan Williams, the first superintendent of the military academy at West Point. Williams was a founder of the first military science society in the United States, the Military Philosophical Society, and Latrobe joined it at William's request.[41]

From late in 1813 to the spring of 1815 Latrobe lived in Pittsburgh directing the construction of steamboats. Thereafter he returned to Washington for two years, then spent the remainder of his life (before his death in 1820) living in Baltimore and New Orleans. His projects consumed his energies, and his ties with the larger scientific community were few. It appears that he had no connection with the Chemical and Physiological Society in Pittsburgh, although he did participate in the founding of the new Columbian Institute in Washington in 1816.[42]

The most impressive evidence of his continued scientific interests in these years is in his sketchbooks and journals, particularly those covering his voyages to and from New Orleans and his stay in New Orleans, from late 1818 to the spring of 1820. On his first voyage from Baltimore to New Orleans, for example, he described a species of shearwaters, further examined the gulfweed (his journals recorded his first encounter with it in 1796), recorded an unusual geological formation in the Bahamas, described the flora and fauna of an island in Louisiana, and considered the discharge of the Mississippi River through its alluvial fan.[43] (fig. 3)

But the record of Latrobe's enormous appetite for science was soon to end. In the course of directing the final stage of constructing the New Orleans Waterworks (the reason for moving to the city) he contracted yellow fever and died on 3 September 1820.[44]

2. LATROBE'S SCIENTIFIC CONCEPTS

Latrobe's science was fundamentally Baconian; that is, experimental, empirical, descriptive, and lacking hypotheses.[45] Baconianism was the framework which dominated British science in the latter eighteenth century, and it was unquestioned orthodoxy in American science during the early nineteenth century.[46] It also fit well with Latrobe's vocation, since both architecture and engineering were still guided by precedent rather than theory.

Latrobe's scientific publications consisted largely of his careful observations of things and processes. Even in geology where he acknowledged the validity of a general theory (Neptunism) he emphasized that careful observation of current processes led one to a different conclusion about the origin of certain rock formations than the theory would have suggested.[47]

Latrobe's Baconianism was connected to the broader stream of ideas known as the Enlightenment, which flourished in America as well as Europe. Like Thomas Jefferson and Joel Barlow, his friends, Latrobe believed that man was essentially a rational being whom God expected to extend knowledge and refine human society.[48] Latrobe exhib-

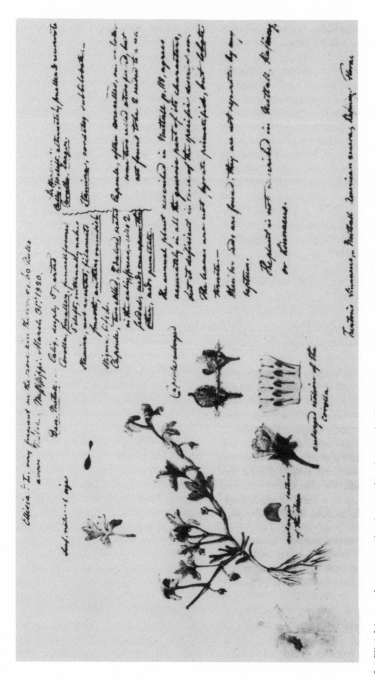

FIG. 3. "Ellisia? L. very frequent on the shore and in the woods, 60 miles above Natchez, Mississippi, March 31st, 1820." Latrobe carefully observed and drew *Ellisia* (L.), a member of the waterleaf family, on his trip to New Orleans in the winter and spring of 1820. Although Latrobe's notes indicate that he believed he had found a new species, there is only one species in the genus. Carter et al., eds. *Latrobe's View of America*.

ited Enlightenment values in his comments on religion, capital punishment, education, and city planning.[49]

He did modify one concept of Enlightenment science, the "great chain of being," which suggested that careful study of the world's flora and fauna would yield a continuous range of God's creation from the insensitive and unthinking (rocks and minerals) to the most rational and sensitive (man). Some philosophers took this concept to the extreme of stating that only man was capable of reasoning and of expressing the higher emotions of love and affection.[50] Latrobe agreed with the existence of the chain, and took some interest in the problem of what creatures linked the animal and vegetable kingdoms. He studied two candidates for the position: the freshwater polyp or *Hydra*, and the barnacle.

In assuming the existence of the chain, however, Latrobe did not agree that man's position at the head was proof of a monopoly on reason, love, or affection. He saw such qualities in other creatures. In his paper on the blue wasps, or daubers, of Virginia he described how they placed comparable amounts of captured, but living spiders in each of the cells which the adult wasps made for their eggs. Latrobe weighed and counted the accumulated spiders in several cells, and concluded that the parent wasps placed the same weight in each cell, even if the number of spiders varied. (He also commented on the wasps' cruelty in sealing the living spiders in the cells so that the larval wasps could eat them.)

Latrobe went on to relate how he damaged a group of cells which a wasp had under construction, and how the wasp first rebuilt the damaged cells before continuing with the project.[52] He concluded: "If it should be necessary to break through the barrier antiently traced between reason and instinct, the oeconomy of the whole class of *hymenoptera*, and particularly of the wasps, may contribute to it."[53]

Latrobe also discussed affection in birds and various emotions in ants and plants.[54] Having attributed reason and higher emotions to creatures lower on the chain than man, Latrobe might have gone further and noted that some animal qualities, such as the cruelty which he had observed in the wasps, also appeared in man, which was highest on the chain. Latrobe was, in fact, appalled by many aspects of Negro slavery in America.[55] But if he was troubled by such ideas he did not discuss them in terms of the chain of being, and they did not alter his image of man as capable of rational improvement.

If Latrobe was essentially a child of the Enlightenment, it must also be recognized that he was influenced by the rise of Romanticism. For example, Latrobe is credited with designing and erecting some of the earliest Gothic buildings in America. (The Gothic revival is usually associated with Romanticism in architecture.[56]) If one can speak of Romantic science, as well, Latrobe exhibited two aspects of it.[57]

The first aspect was a fascination with unusual symbiotic and prey-predator relationships. In his publications he described the relationships of wasp and spider species, and of alewives and crustaceans.[58] In his journals and sketchbooks he considered the sumac shrub and its gall fly, hogs and rattlesnakes, mosquitoes and humans, gulfweed and crabs, and remoras and sharks.[59] In this approach to natural history Latrobe did not have an ecological or "balance-of-nature" point of view, but instead he focused on the one-sided, cruel, and even violent qualities of relationships between species.

Similarly, though he was an avowed uniformitarian in geology, it was the dramatic catastrophic events which often caught his fancy. Note the manner in which he described the formation of the breccia quarried for the Capitol in Washington:

Suppose against the Cotocktin mountain an immense pebble beach to be heaped up by the ocean, formed of marbles of all descriptions and of all sizes, from grains of sand to masses of two or three hundred weight. . . . Imagine these pebbles rounded and mingled by attrition for ages, and then to have been left, and cemented by some matter filling all interstices, sometimes of the most lively green, generally of a beautiful red, so as to become a solid mass. Suppose then that the valley become the bed of a mighty torrent running from S.W. to N.E. over this cemented mass, wearing it down in the direction of its current unequally, according to the velocity of its veins; and employing, (as in all our rivers) the agency of loose stones, to whirl deep basins into the solid mass, and thus giving to the rocks, now separated into distinct masses, that specific character, which the rocks of all our rapids acquire by the action of the water, *and which character cannot possibly be mistaken, or derived from any other known agency.*[60]

Latrobe's Romanticism also took another turn. As a watercolor painter in the Picturesque style, he was already a proto-Romantic.[61] His paintings sometimes expressed his peculiar desire to visualize vast extents of landscape, far beyond that possible at any actual site. In his "Essay on Landscape," which was written as a guide to watercolor painting, he described his desire.

When you stand upon the summit of a hill, and see an extensive country of woods and fields without interruption spread before you, you look at it with pleasure. . . . But this pleasure is perhaps very much derived from a sort of consciousness of superiority of position to all the monotony below you. But turn yourself so as to include in your view a wide expanse of Water, contrasting by its cool blue surface, the waving, and many colored carpet of the Earth, your pleasure is immediately doubled, or rather a new and much greater pleasure arises. An historical effect is produced. The trade and cultivation of the country croud into the mind, the imagination runs up the invisible creeks, and visits the half seen habitations. A thousand circumstances are fancied which are not beheld, and the indications of what probably exists, give the pleasure which its view would afford.[62]

In a similar fashion, much of Latrobe's interest in geology might be described as

topographical, since he sketched and described phenomena which covered large portions of the Atlantic seaboard. He was particularly concerned with the Fall Line, which he believed to be the location of the shoreline of the ocean in a previous age, and the Coastal Plain, which he conceived of as a flatland whose valleys and other variations were entirely caused by erosion.[63] In another leap of imagination he even contended that the topography of North America east of the Mississippi River was a gigantic example of mineral structure, such that the stratification and deposition of rocks were in the pattern of an enormous crystal.[64]

In sum, Latrobe's science was consonant with the intellectual patterns of his age. Within those patterns he developed his own versions of current theories and demonstrated unique approaches of his own.

3. THE SCIENCE OF ENGINEERING

Botany, entomology, and geology were areas in which Latrobe was a competent amateur, and he merited the respect of the American Philosophical Society for his knowledge of those fields. But when he was elected to the Society it was as "Benjamin Henry Latrobe, Engineer," and the members demonstrated, by his committee assignments, considerable regard for his knowledge of his profession.[65] Certainly Latrobe understood and practiced the engineering "science" of his day.

By the meaning of his era, an engineer's science included sound knowledge of precedents, a thorough knowledge of available texts, and careful measurement and observation. In discussing the qualifications for the position of engineer to the State of Virginia, for example, Latrobe commented:

It is desired that the Person to be employed shall be a compleat civil Engineer, and not only understand the principles on which roads ought to be laid out and constructed but that he shall also be perfectly acquainted with the much more difficult and rare Science necessary to lay out and construct a Canal.[66]

Although he was not offering himself for the Virginia position, Latrobe was the engineer of two canals and he obviously thought of himself as a model candidate for the job.[67] Modern historians concur that Latrobe was one of the finest American engineers of the era.[68]

Of what elements did the science of the "compleat civil Engineer" consist, if Latrobe is taken as an example? The accurate and knowledgeable use of surveying instruments was one criterion. In the later eighteenth century, theodolites (transits), spirit levels, sextants, circumferentors, and measuring rods and chains were made with increasing precision. To use them required competence in geometry and trigonometry.[69] Latrobe had a theodolite made for him by Jesse Ramsden, the greatest English scientific instrument-maker of the age.[70] He also owned spirit levels, a sextant, a circumferentor, and a surveyor's compass, and he took care to have them repaired and in good order.[71]

Latrobe used his instruments numerous times, but most significantly for the Susquehanna River survey of 1801 (from which he produced a remarkably accurate map of the lower 40 miles of the river) and for the Chesapeake and Delaware Canal survey of 1803–04.[72] During the latter project Latrobe demonstrated his standards for surveying by describing the abilities of the other members of the survey team. He praised one for his "great accuracy," and called another "a good Mathematician," but a third he found inadequate because he was "without any method in his mode of keeping his field book . . . and without the proper instruments."[73] (fig. 4)

Once surveys were made, or after preliminary sketches of structures were prepared, Latrobe transformed his data into scaled drawings with the aid of drawing instruments, which he called "mathematical in-struments."[74] This was a significant step in itself, because most engineers of his era worked from full-scale drawings, if any at all. Celebrated steam engineer Oliver Evans, a contemporary engineer (and an unfriendly critic), is reported to have credited Latrobe with the introduction to America of a higher standard of "mechanical drawing."[75]

In conjunction with surveying, Latrobe sometimes sampled a site in other ways. In rivers and harbors he practiced the ancient method of determining depths by dropping a weighted line or probing with a pole.[76] He also practiced boring into the soil to determine subsurface conditions, and urged others to follow his example.[77] In any riverine work he determined the lines of high and low water, relying on personal observation or local informants.[78] (fig. 5) Such casual determinations of flood levels were probably not very accurate, being based on an insufficient period of time.[79]

In at least two instances Latrobe attempted to measure a stream's discharge, a significant problem in eighteenth and nineteenth century hydrology. He took a section (area) of each stream, clocked the velocity of the water, and found a result in terms of the flow (quantity) of cubic feet of water per hour ($AV = Q$). Latrobe knew the approximate nature of the results obtained by this formula and did not rely heavily on its results.[80] Considering the supply of water available for the Chesapeake and Delaware Canal feeder, he stated:

> To estimate the quantity of water which any of these three creeks discharge is not practicable. The differences of opinion which in all cases of large streams have existed between the most eminent men of science are well known . . . and exhibited themselves particularly in the case of the Forth and Clyde navigation.[81]

As this indicates, Latrobe was informed of developments in European hydrology, and he probably had the most advanced knowledge of this science in the United States. His

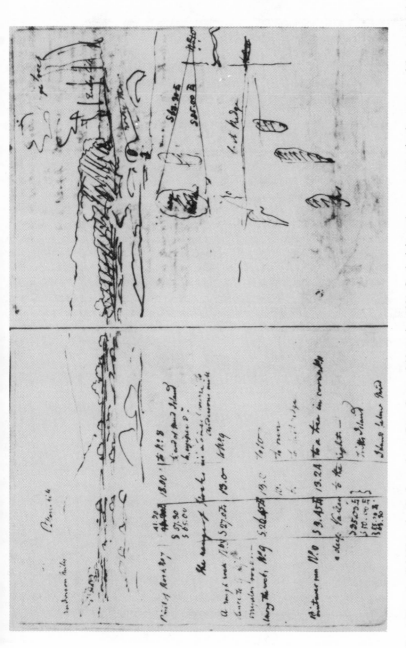

FIG. 4. From the Field Notes for the Susquehanna River Survey, 2 November 1801. On the left are the survey notes for the segment of the river just below Columbia and Wrights Ferry. In the first column is a description of each survey station, in the second column is a series of angles taken from those stations, in the third column is the measurement (in two-pole chains) to the next stations and some other points, and in the fourth column are the points sighted from the survey stations. Across the top of both pages is a panoramic view of the east side of the section of the river containing the stations. On the right is an imaginary bird's-eye-view of the west shoreline and islands, with the sightlines from station no. 10 drawn in. These two pages are representative of Latrobe's survey technique, and are remarkable evidence of how he combined careful survey evidence with nonverbal landscape rendering to create survey maps. Field Book 2, 14/B5, *The Microfiche Edition.*

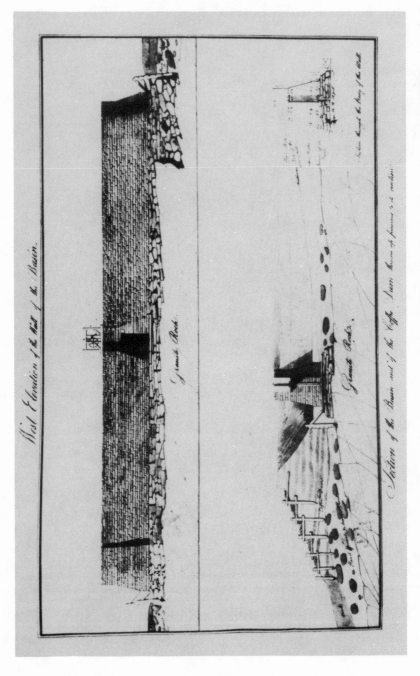

FIG. 5. "West Elevation of the Wall of the Basin; Section of the Basin and of the Coffre Dam thrown up previous to its erection," [1800]. In order to firmly anchor the west wall of the Philadelphia Waterworks' settling basin, Latrobe had the foundation excavated to bedrock. In this pair of sections he was careful to note the surface geology of the bed of the Schuylkill River: blue mud, hard gravel, and loose rock, and granite. (Historical Society of Pennsylvania.)

training under Smeaton and Jessop put him in touch with the best English hydrologic engineering, and he read further in Continental works by Belidor, Fabré, Proni, Eytelwein, Kaestner, and Bernoulli.[82]

Latrobe himself developed a general theory of the changes occurring in Atlantic coastal rivers. Observing the rapid accumulation of sediment in tidal estuaries, he attributed it to the agricultural development of the hinterland and, as proof, noted that the greatest deposits lay where the river currents were slowed by the action of the tide. Commenting on the Delaware, Potomac, and other rivers, Latrobe asserted that the process was irreversible, and although careful engineering might alter the depth of deposit at some locations within the tidal areas, the rate could not be changed. Latrobe took this position in the face of Eastern merchants' growing anxiety. In his opinion, only ignorant or unscrupulous engineers promoted "permanent" solutions to the problem.[83]

Latrobe also occasionally called geological knowledge to his aid in engineering problems. By examination of rock strata he ascertained the practicality of tunnels, predicted the ease of excavations, and located useful types of rock for quarrying. He even based his opinion of the strength of wrought iron on the type of iron ore used in its manufacture.[84]

The most explicit statement of Latrobe's engineering science was in acoustics. He wrote two papers on the transmission and reflection of sound waves in auditoriums: the first (believed to date from 1803) was a response to a query about the plans for the new Arch Street Meeting House of Philadelphia, and the second was an addendum to the acoustics article in the American edition of *The Edinburgh Encyclopedia* in 1812. In both cases Latrobe tried to establish the best form of a room for public speaking, and showed some knowledge of the literature on acoustics. But the latter paper also demonstrated that his experience with the halls of the Capitol in Washington gave him more confidence in handling such issues as the speed of sound and the role of echoes in reinforcing a speaker's voice.[85]

If Latrobe possessed and practiced engineering science in surveying, drawing, hydrology, geology, and acoustics, he had less interest in the science of other areas of his profession. His papers reveal only occasional interest in strengths of materials, or concern with determining distribution of stresses. Perhaps, as in his comment on the method of determining stream discharge, he recognized that scientific consideration of such matters was in a formative period.[86] Instead, Latrobe relied on the English tradition of a hierarchy of building materials (from best to least acceptable being stone, brick, iron, and wood), and dealt with stress patterns by overbuilding. On occasion he criticized tradition, but he normally did not depart from it.[87]

Similarly, Latrobe did not exhibit significantly deeper understanding of science in his work with steam engines. Although he was intimately familiar with them (twice he reported to the American Philosophical Society on steam engines), and he was considered by many to be one of the American experts on the subject, it was the engines' practical, operational aspects which concerned him.[88] In his long dispute with Oliver Evans over the value of "high" versus "low" pressure, Latrobe contended neither on grounds of theory nor of experiment, but rather upon past experience.[89]

4. CONCLUSION

The study of Benjamin Henry Latrobe's papers reveals a wide range of ways in which he drew on science for intellectual challenge, professional activities and leisure. There were few Americans of his time who could match his scientific education and breadth of reading and, indeed, it was only at the meetings of the American Philosophical Society that he regularly met his peers. Yet Latrobe was an amateur in science and his interests seldom ran deep except in periods of enthusiasm (e.g., his geological studies after meeting Scandella, Volney, and Maclure) or enforced leisure (e.g., his ocean voyages).

What we have in the Latrobe papers is the record of an informed amateur whose life and career drew on his experience on two continents, and spanned the formative years of the American scientific community. Like his contemporary Thomas Jefferson, Benjamin Henry Latrobe represents the heights of an era when intellectual gentlemen formed the elite of American science. With the publication of a substantial body of Latrobe's papers, historians should be able to use his activities and ideas as a convenient benchmark for that era.[90]

NOTES

1. "Baptisms at the Chapel of the United Brethren, at Fulneck," Fulneck Congregational Archives, Pudsey, Yorkshire, England.
2. For example, Herrnhut in Germany, and Bethlehem and Salem in North America.
3. Joseph Jackson, 9 August 1767, to Okerhousen, "Sundry Papers and Accounts," Moravian Church House Archives, London; "List of Teachers & Boys in the Oeconomy, with Timetable of School," Fulneck Archives.
4. Fulneck Congregational Diary, 17 September 1776, Fulneck Archives; D. Paul Kölbing, ed., Die Feier des 150 jährigen Bestehens des theologischen Seminariums der Brüdergemeine in Gnadenfeld am 24. Mai 1904 (Leipzig, Verlag von Friedrich Jansa, 1904), 75; Fetter Lane Congregational Diary, 28 August 1783, Moravian Church House Archives, London.
5. Heinrich Casmir Gottlief Graf zu Lynar, Nachricht von dem Ursprung und Fortgange, und hauptsächlich von der gegenwärtigen Berfassung der Brüder-Unitat (Halle, Johan Jacob Curt, 1781), 145–147; Geschichte des Padagogiums der evangelischen Brüder-Unität (Nisky, privately printed, 1859), 8–9, 16–17; Niesky syllabus for 1779, rubric 4. B. KV. a. 7, Archiv der Bruder-Unitat, Herrnhut, East Germany. We gratefully acknowledge the generosity of I. Baldauf, chief archivist at Herrnhut, who has provided us with copies of manuscripts relating to Latrobe's years at Niesky and Barby.
6. Lynar, Nachricht von dem Ursprung, 148, 150–51.
7. Ibid., 151; Hermann Plitt, Das Theologische Seminarium de Evandelischen Brüder-Unität in seinem Angang und Fortgang (Leipzig, C. Kummer, 1854), 54, 56.
8. Köbling, ed., Die Feier, 65, 75; Plitt, Das Theologische, 54; E. R. Meyer, Schleiermachers und C. G. von Brinkmanns Gang durch die Brüdergemeine (Leipzig, Friedrich Tanza, 1905), 94–95; Latrobe, 11 December 1810, to Law and Jones, 80/D7, Edward C. Carter and Thomas E. Jeffrey, eds., The Microfiche Edition of The Papers of Benjamin Henry Latrobe (Clifton, N.J., James T. White & Co., 1976) (hereafter The Microfiche Edition).
9. Meyer, Schleiermachers, 94; journal of C. I. La Trobe, 22 December 1788, 15 August 1789, John Rylands

Library, Manchester, England. Although his family generally wrote their surname "La Trobe," Benjamin Henry Latrobe seems always to have written it "Latrobe."
10. Gillian Lindt Gollin, Moravians in Two Worlds: A Study of Changing Communities (New York, Columbia University Press, 1967), 83; Latrobe 10 June 1816, to the Mayor and Corporation of the City of New Orleans, 225/Cl, The Microfiche Edition.
In the letter cited above, Latrobe notes that when he was "scarce 17 years old" he had "the good fortune to become acquainted with the eminent hydraulic engineer, Riedel" of Silesia. We know that Latrobe was at the Moravian community of Gnadenfrey in Silesia in 1782, and it seems likely that Latrobe is referring to Heinrich August Riedel (1749–1812), a Prussian engineer and architect who had a distinguished career in both private and public capacities. At an earlier time Latrobe had also mentioned his discussions with "skillful engineers in the Prussian service." Minutes of the Elder Brethren's Meeting, 6 August 1782, Archiv der Brüder-Unität; Johan Christoph Adelung, Fortsetzung und Ergänzungen zu Christian Gottlieb Jöchers allgemeinem Gelehrten-Lexico. Reprint. 6 vols. (Hildesheim, Georg Olms Verlagsbuchhandlung, 1960), 6: 2112; B. H. Latrobe, ed. and trans., Characteristic Anecdotes and Miscellaneous Authentic Papers, Tending to Illustrate the Character of Frederick II, Late King of Prussia (London, John Stockdale, 1788), 11n.
11. Minutes of the Elder Brethren's Meeting, 11 August 1782, 19 March 1783, 27 March 1783, 26 June 1783, Archiv der Brüder-Unität.
12. For BHL's position in the Stamp Office, see the editions, 1785–1792, of The Court and City Register and The Royal Kalendar.
13. Latrobe, 20 January 1811, to Moore, in John C. Van Horne et al., eds., The Correspondence and Miscellaneous Papers of Benjamin Henry Latrobe, 3 vols. (New Haven, Conn., Yale University Press, in press), vol. 3 (hereafter Correspondence); Latrobe, 3 September 1817, to Seaton, ibid.; Benjamin Henry Latrobe, Opinion on a Project for Removing the Obstructions to a Ship Navigation to Georgetown, Col. (Washington, W. Cooper, 1812), 17. Although we

have found that Latrobe is usually reliable in statements about his early life, Darwin Stapleton's search of Smeaton's surviving papers and drawings in 1978 revealed no mention of Latrobe.

14. Denis Smith, "The Professional Correspondence of John Smeaton: An eighteenth-century consulting engineering practice," *Newcomen Society Transactions* 47 (1974–75, 1975–76): 179–80. The Stamp Office was at Lincoln's Inn until 1787, when it was moved to Somerset House. Latrobe lived on Fetter Lane 1783–1786, Rolls Buildings 1786–1788/89, and Staples Inn Buildings from 1788/89 until his marriage.

15. Latrobe, 20 January 1811, to Moore, *Correspondence,* 3; Joseph Banks et al., eds., *Reports of the late John Smeaton, F. R. S.,* 3 vols. (London, Longman, Hurst, Rees, Orme, and Brown, 1812), 1: 72–87; Smeaton, 9 March 1784, vol. 4, "Machine Letters" of John Smeaton, Institution of Civil Engineers, London; drawings of improvements of Lincolnshire fens, c. 1782–1784, collection of Smeaton drawings, ff. 99, 103–05, vol. 6, Library of the Royal Society, London; s.v. "Smeaton, John," in Sir Leslie Stephen and Sir Sidney Lee, eds., *Dictionary of National Biography,* 21 vols., reprint (Oxford, Oxford University Press, 1967–68).

16. Latrobe, *Opinion on a Project,* 17; Latrobe, 19 August 1805, to Gilpin, 42/G14, *The Microfiche Edition;* D. Swann, "The Engineers of English Port Improvements, 1660–1830: Part II," *Transport History* 1 (1968): 260; P. A. L. Vine, *London's Lost Route to Basingstoke: The Story of the Basingstoke Canal* (Newton Abbot, David & Charles, 1968), 42, 44.

17. Edward C. Carter II, ed., *The Virginia Journals of Benjamin Henry Latrobe, 1795-1798,* 2 vols. (New Haven, Conn., Yale University Press, 1977) 1: 28, 29, 37, 38, 43–47, 49–52, 63–65, and plate 5 with annotation.

18. Ibid., 1: 457–66; Lynar, *Nachricht von dem Ursprung,* 147; Plitt, *Das Theologische,* 56.

19. Carter, ed., *Virginia Journals,* 1: 157n, 157–60, 176–78, 186–89, 239–42; 2: 502–03.

20. Ibid., 2: 328, 341, 357. It seems likely that Latrobe met Volney in Philadelphia during his first visit there in March and April of 1798. See the sketches of Maclure and Volney in Charles Gillispie, ed., *Dictionary of Scientific Biography.* 14 vols. (New York, Charles Scribner's Sons, 1970–1976).

21. Carter ed., *Virginia Journals,* 1: 123, 145, 174–75; 2: 346–50, 373, 379, 390–414, 516–17. Modern comments on Latrobe's geology appear ibid., 2: 384–90; and Stephen F. Lintner and Darwin H. Stapleton, "Geological Theory and Practice in the Career of Benjamin Henry Latrobe," in Cecil J. Schneer, ed., *Two Hundred Years of Geology in America.* Proceedings of the New Hampshire Bicentennial Conference on the History of Geology in America. (Hanover, N.H., The University Press of New England, 1979), 107–19.

22. Carter, ed., *Virginia Journals,* 2: 453–54, 516–17.

23. Ibid., 2: 341. For a general discussion of Latrobe's views of Virginia society, see: Lee W. Formwalt,

"An English Immigrant Views American Society: Benjamin Henry Latrobe's Virginia Years, 1796–1798," *The Virginia Magazine of History and Biography* 85 (October, 1977): 387–410.

24. Edward C. Carter II, John C. Van Horne and Lee W. Formwalt, eds., *The Journals of Benjamin Henry Latrobe, 1799-1820: From Philadelphia to New Orleans* (New Haven, Conn., Yale University Press, 1980), 7.

25. B. Henry Latrobe, "Memoir on the Sand-hills of Cape Henry in Virginia," *Trans. Amer. Phil. Soc.* 4 (1799): 439–443, plate, in *Correspondence,* 1; minutes of the American Philosophical Society, 21 December 1798, 27 December 1798, American Philosophical Society, Philadelphia, Pa.

26. Darwin H. Stapleton, ed., *The Engineering Drawings of Benjamin Henry Latrobe* (New Haven, Conn., Yale University Press, 1980), 28–36.

27. Minutes of the American Philosophical Society, 19 July 1799, 3 January 1800, 1 January 1802. On 1 May 1800 Latrobe married Mary Elizabeth Hazlehurst (1771–1841) the daughter of a Philadelphia merchant. Within a few months the children of his first wife were brought to America to join his household. Thereafter Mary bore six children, only three of whom survived to adulthood.

28. Papers by Benjamin Henry Latrobe in the *Transactions* of the American Philosophical Society other than cited in note 25: "A Drawing and Description of the Clupea Tyrannus and Oniscus Praegustator," 5 (1802): 77–81, plate; "On two species of Sphex, inhabiting Virginia and Pennsylvania, and probably extending throughout the United States," 6 (1809): 73–78, with plate; "First Report of Benjamin Henry Latrobe, to the American Philosophical Society, held at Philadelphia; in answer to the enquiry of the Society of Rotterdam, 'Whether any, and what improvements have been made in the construction of Steam-Engines in America?'" 6 (1809): 89–98, plates, all in *Correspondence,* 1; "An account of the Freestone quarries on the Potomac and Rappahannoc rivers," 6 (1809): 283–93, in *Correspondence,* 2; "Observations on the foregoing communications [on buildings in India]," 6 (1809): 384–91.

29. Minutes of the American Philosophical Society, 1 November 1799, 15 November 1799, 6 December 1799, 7 February 1800, 6 February 1801, 21 September 1801, 18 December 1801, 15 January 1802, 7 May 1802, 16 July 1802, 21 January 1803, 18 February 1803, 4 March 1803, 15 April 1803, 20 May 1803, 20 July 1804.

30. 6 February 1807, 10 February 1807, 17 June 1808, ibid.

31. Latrobe, 27 June 1807, to Robert Hare, 69/F10, 69/F13; Latrobe, 5 January 1805, to Thomas Jefferson, *Correspondence,* 2; Latrobe, 18 January 1817, to Gales & Seaton, *Correspondence,* 3; Edgar F. Smith, *Chemistry in America* (New York and London, D. Appleton and Company, 1914), 12, 45–47, 76. Latrobe is not on the list of members of the Chemical Society of Philadelphia compiled by Wyndham

Miles in "Early Chemical Societies," *Chymia* 3 (1950): 107–08, but Miles acknowledges that the list is "undoubtedly far from complete."

32. See Latrobe's letters to Jefferson, Vaughan, Peale, Hare, Patterson, and Seybert in *The Microfiche Edition.* Latrobe refers to Smith in his Journals, 15 March 1800, and in Latrobe, 18 January 1817, to Gales & Seaton, *Correspondence,* 3. Leslie and Latrobe had been at several American Philosophical Society meetings together and had served on the same committees, yet Leslie was severely critical of Latrobe: Robert Leslie, 10 January 1803, to Thomas Jefferson, Jefferson Papers, Library of Congress, Washington, D.C.
All of the persons mentioned are noticed in the *Dictionary of American Biography* or the *Dictionary of Scientific Biography,* or both, except Smith and Leslie. For them, see Tom Taylor, ed., *Autobiographical Recollections. By the Late Charles Robert Leslie* (Boston, Ticknor and Fields, 1860), 1; Greville Bathe and Dorothy Bathe, *Oliver Evans* (Philadelphia, Historical Society of Pennsylvania, 1935), 26; Wyndham Miles, "Thomas Peters Smith," *Journal of Chemical Education* 30 (1953): 184–88; Smith, *Chemistry in America,* 12–46.

33. Latrobe, 29 July 1805, to Peale, 42/B5, *The Microfiche Edition.*

34. Talbot Hamlin, *Benjamin Henry Latrobe* (New York, Oxford University Press, 1955), 203, 208, 305.

35. E.g., John C. Greene, "Science, Learning, and Utility: Patterns of Organization in the Early American Republic," in Alexandra Oleson and Sanborn C. Brown, *The Pursuit of Knowledge in the Early American Republic: American Scientific and Learned Societies from Colonial Times to the Civil War* (Baltimore and London, The Johns Hopkins University Press, 1976), 2–5.

36. *The Emporium of the Arts and Sciences,* new series 3 (1814): 284–97, plate, in *Correspondence,* 3.

37. Edward T. Martin, *Thomas Jefferson: Scientist* (New York, Henry Schuman, 1952); Henry F. May, *The Enlightenment in America* (New York, Oxford University Press, 1976), 238–43; Richard Beale Davis, "The Abbé Correa in America, 1812–1820," *Transactions* of the American Philosophical Society, new series 40 (1955): 95–96; H. W. Dickinson, *Robert Fulton: Engineer and Artist, His Life and Works* (London, John Lane, 1913), 206; Latrobe, 28 December 1807 to Fulton, *Correspondence,* 2.

38. A. Hunter Dupree, *Science in the Federal Government: A History of Policies and Activities to 1940* (Cambridge, Mass., The Belknap Press, 1957), 29–31.

39. Elinor Stearns and David N. Yerkes, *William Thornton: A Renaissance Man in the Federal City* (Washington, American Institute of Architects Federation, 1976).

40. G. Melvin Herndon, *William Tatham, 1752-1819: American Versatile* (Johnson City, Tenn., East Tennessee State University, 1973); Latrobe, 30 July 1805, to Smith, *Correspondence,* 2.

41. Hamlin, *Benjamin Henry Latrobe,* 359; Latrobe, 24

November 1807, to Roosevelt, 60/E3, *The Microfiche Edition.*

42. Dupree, *Science in the Federal Government,* 34; John O'Connor, Jr., "Pittsburgh's First Chemical Society," *Science* 44 (July 7, 1916): 11–14; Edward H. Hahn, "Science in Pittsburgh, 1813–1848," *Western Pennsylvania Historical Magazine* 55 (1962): 69, Minutes of the Columbian Institute, 8 August 1816, 4 November 1816, 226/D4–G6, *The Microfiche Edition.*

43. Carter et al., eds., *Journals,* 149, 151–53, 162–64; Latrobe, Sketchbook XIV, 28 December 1818, 259/B1, *The Microfiche Edition.*

44. Hamlin, *Benjamin Henry Latrobe,* 528.

45. Latrobe stated that "Lord Bacon had pointed out the true road to Science—or which is synonymous, to truth, by way of experiment . . . ," Carter, ed., *Virginia Journals,* 2: 417.

46. George H. Daniels, *American Science in the Age of Jackson* (New York and London, Columbia University Press, 1968), ch. III; Robert E. Schofield, *Mechanism and Materialism: British Natural Philosophy in An Age of Reason* (Princeton, N.J.: Princeton University Press, 1970), 3, 265.

47. Latrobe, "Memoir on the Sand-hills of Cape Henry in Virginia," and "An account of the Freestone quarries."

48. May, *The Enlightenment in America,* 239–43, 287–302, 310–12.

49. Carter, ed., *Virginia Journals,* 1: 75, 78, 191–93, 2: 379–81, 414–28; Hamlin, *Benjamin Henry Latrobe,* 583–85; Latrobe, "Remarks on the Plan of the town of Nescopeck, Pennsylv.," 30 March 1805, *Correspondence,* 2.

50. Arthur O. Lovejoy, *The Great Chain of Being: A Study of the History of an Idea* (New York, 1960).

51. Ibid., pp. 231–36; Carter, ed., *Virginia Journals,* 1: plate 5 and notes; 2: 504–05, 507.

52. Latrobe, "On Two Species of Sphex." A slightly edited version of this paper appeared in the *Philosophical Magazine,* 25 (June–September, 1806): 236–41, a British journal of science.

53. Latrobe, "On Two Species of Sphex," 77.

54. Carter, ed., *Virginia Journals,* 1: 186–87, 244–45; 2: 500, 507.

55. Formwalt, "An English Immigrant Views American Society," 404, 406.

56. Hamlin, *Benjamin Henry Latrobe,* 151–52, 245–47, 345–48. It is perhaps relevant in this context to note that Friedrich Schleiermacher, author of "two of the chief manifestos of early German Romanticism," passed through the Moravian schools of Niesky and Barby only a few years after Latrobe. Lovejoy, *The Great Chain,* 307–11; Meyer, *Schleiermachers.*

57. Robert E. Schofield and Wesley C. Williams, eds., *Man and the Frame of Nature: Confluent Styles in the Arts and Sciences* (Ann Arbor, Mich., 1974), 156–70.

58. Latrobe, "A Drawing and Description of the Clupea Tyrannus and Oniscus Praegustator", and "On Two Species of Sphex."

59. Carter, ed., *Virginia Journals*, 1: 110, 182; Latrobe, Sketchbook XI, 15 September 1809, 256/C3, *The Microfiche Edition*; Sketchbook XIV, 29 September 1819, 259/D2, *The Microfiche Edition*; Carter, et al., eds., *Journals*, 3: 151, 305–08.

60. Latrobe, 18 January 1817, to Gales and Seaton, *Correspondence*, 3.

61. Carter, ed., *Virginia Journals*, 2: 459–61; Hamlin, *Benjamin Henry Latrobe*, 245–46.

62. Carter, ed., *Virginia Journals*, 2: 473.

63. In discussing the upper Delmarva Peninsula, which he surveyed for the Chesapeake and Delaware Canal Company, he commented:

> It will be easy to comprehend the present state of the Land between the two Bays, if we suppose the whole peninsula to have been once a plain composed of soft alluvial soil extending from the foot of the Granite hills to the ocean, and gently declining from the North west, to the South east. In the course of many centuries the water falling upon the surface and discharging itself into either Bay as accident or some unknown cause directed would wash this plain into vallies.

Latrobe, Reports of the Engineer, 21 October 1803, 170/C10, *The Microfiche Edition*.

64. Latrobe, 5 October 1810, to Thomas, *Correspondence*, 2.

65. Minutes of the American Philosophical Society, 19 July 1779.

66. Latrobe, 8 April 1816, to Madison, *Correspondence*, 3, also printed in Edward C. Carter II, with Darwin H. Stapleton, and Lee W. Formwalt, "Benjamin Henry Latrobe and Public Works," *Essays in Public Works History* 3 (1976): 22–29. In the letter Latrobe used the word "science" eight times to refer to a higher level of engineering.

67. The Chesapeake and Delaware (1803–06), and Washington (1810–17) canals.

68. Hamlin, *Benjamin Henry Latrobe*, 544–65; Daniel H. Calhoun, *The American Civil Engineer: Origins and Conflict* (Cambridge, Mass., MIT, 1964), 16–23; Carroll W. Pursell, Jr., *Early Stationary Steam Engines in America: A Study of the Migration of a Technology* (Washington, Smithsonian, 1969), 31–37.

69. A. W. Richeson, *English Land Measuring to 1800: Instruments and Practices* (Cambridge, Mass., The MIT Press, 1966), 160, 187–88. See Latrobe's calculations relative to Hadley's quadrant in Carter, ed., *Virginia Journals*, 1: 213–220.

70. Richeson, *English Land Measuring*, 169–72; Latrobe, 26 October 1803, to Gale, *Correspondence*, 1.

71. Latrobe, 10 March 1804, to Voight, *Correspondence*, 1; Latrobe, 20 May 1810, to Briggs, 75/B9, *The Microfiche Edition*; Latrobe, bankruptcy petition, 19 December 1817, 235/B3, *The Microfiche Edition*.

72. The surviving survey books are those from the Susquehanna River survey, 1801, 14/A1, *The Microfiche Edition*, and the New Castle town survey, 1804–05, 175/E1, *The Microfiche Edition*.

73. Latrobe, 19 October 1803, to Gilpin, *Correspondence*, 1.

74. Latrobe appreciated good drawing instruments but found that none were made in the United States. Latrobe, 6 March 1811, to De Cabre, *Correspondence*, 3.

75. Eugene S. Ferguson, ed., *Early Engineering Reminiscences (1815–1840) of George Escol Sellers*. United States National Museum Bulletin 238. (Washington, 1965), 38; and additional notes supplied to the authors by Mr. Ferguson.

76. [Albert Gallatin], *Report of the Secretary of the Treasury on the subject of Roads and Canals* (Reprint, New York, 1968), 94; Latrobe, 23 April 1804, to Tatnall, 31/D5, *The Microfiche Edition*; Latrobe, 9 February 1818, to Harper, 235/E5, *The Microfiche Edition*; Latrobe, 24 October 1801, to Poulson, in *Poulson's American Daily Advertiser*, 164/A2, *The Microfiche Edition*.

77. Latrobe, 2 August 1806, to De Mun, *Correspondence*, 2; Latrobe, 30 March 1810, to Cochran, 74/A12, *The Microfiche Edition*; Wash. Canal Co., account, 25 September 1810, with Latrobe, 78/E5, *The Microfiche Edition*; Latrobe, 16 August 1812, to Henry Latrobe, 102/B12, *The Microfiche Edition*; Latrobe, 19 August 1815, to Randle, *Correspondence*, 3.

78. See, for example, the notations on Latrobe's drawings of the basin of the Philadelphia Waterworks. Stapleton, ed., *The Engineering Drawings of Benjamin Henry Latrobe*, 151, plate 7.

On one occasion Latrobe walked several miles in a rainstorm to observe the quantity of water which had to be contained by culverts on the Chesapeake and Delaware Canal feeder. Latrobe, 26 August 1804, to Gilpin, 34/G7, *The Microfiche Edition*.

79. See the comment in W. B. Langbein, *Hydrology and Environmental Aspects of the Erie Canal (1817–99)*. Geological Survey Water-Supply Paper 2038. (Washington, 1976), 36. This publication was brought to our attention by Stephen Lintner.

80. Latrobe, Reports of the Engineer, 26 January 1804, 171/B9, *The Microfiche Edition*; Latrobe, "Report on the Improvement of Jones' Falls, Baltimore," 31 May 1818, 236/D1, *The Microfiche Edition*; Asit K. Biswas, *History of Hydrology* (New York, 1970), 262–69, 280, 285–88; Arthur H. Frazier, *Water Current Meters*. Smithsonian Studies in History and Technology, 28. (Washington, Smithsonian Institution, 1974), 6–8.

81. Latrobe, Reports of the Engineer, 26 January 1804, 171/B9, *The Microfiche Edition*.

82. B. Henry Latrobe, *Remarks on the Address of the Committee of the Delaware and Schuylkill Canal Company* (Philadelphia, 1799), 10–11; Latrobe, *Opinion on a Project*, iv, 21, 24–25; Latrobe, 8 February 1814, to Cooper, *Correspondence*, 3; Latrobe, "Essay on the means of preventing, meeting and repairing the calamities occasioned by inundations," 10 June 1816, 224/G14, *The Microfiche Edition*.

83. Latrobe, *Opinion on a Project*; Latrobe, 25 May 1807,

to Fitzsimmons, and 6 June 1807, to Fitzsimmons, *Correspondence,* 2, 57/D2, *The Microfiche Edition;* Latrobe, 3 February 1810, to Bates, 73/F1, *The Microfiche Edition;* Latrobe, "Report on the Improvement of Jones' Falls, Baltimore," 31 May 1818, 236/ D1, *The Microfiche Edition.*

84. Lintner and Stapleton, "Geological Theory and Practice"; Latrobe, 4 January 1813, to Greenleaf, *Correspondence,* 3.

85. Latrobe, "Remarks on the best form of a room for hearing and speaking," c. 1803, American Philosophical Society Archives, *Correspondence,* 1; Latrobe, "Note," s.v., "Acoustics," in *The Edinburgh Encyclopedia.* 1st American ed. 18 vols. (Philadelphia, 1812–31), *Correspondence,* 3. We have relied upon William B. Forbush III's study of Latrobe's acoustical writings for these remarks. Readers wanting an extended consideration of those writings should consult *Correspondence,* 3.

86. Hans Straub, *A History of Civil Engineering.* Erwin Rockwell, trans. (Cambridge, Mass., MIT; 1964), ch. VI; Schuyler Warmflash, "Benjamin H. Latrobe: The Interplay of Architecture and Engineering in His Building Designs," M.A. thesis, Hunter College of The City University of New York, 1982.

87. Latrobe, "Observations on the foregoing communications," 388–90.

88. Latrobe, 19 April 1799, to Patterson, 162/A1, *The Microfiche Edition;* Latrobe, "First Report of Benjamin Henry Latrobe," 89–98; Pursell, *Early Stationary Steam Engines in America,* 34. Latrobe submitted a paper to the American Philosophical Society on his experiments on the varying temperature of the water in the boiler of the Schuylkill engine of the Philadelphia Waterworks, but the paper was not printed and the manuscript has not been preserved. Minutes of the American Philosophical Society, 4 March 1803.

89. E.g., Latrobe, 17 January 1814, to Ingersoll, *Correspondence,* 3; Latrobe, 8 April 1814, to the Editor, Pittsburgh *Gazette,* 15 April 1814.

90. Especially *The Microfiche Edition* (note 8); *The Correspondence* (note 13); *The Virginia Journals* (note 17); *The Journals of Benjamin Henry Latrobe, 1799–1820: From Philadelphia to New Orleans* (note 24), and Edward C. Carter II, John C. Van Horne, and Charles E. Brownell, eds., *Latrobe's View of America, 1795–1820: Selections from the Watercolors and Sketches* (New Haven, Conn., Yale University Press, 1985).

The Changing Social Climate, 1790-1810 and the Pennsylvania Academy of the Fine Arts

Lee I. Schreiber

On the 26th day of December, 1805, 71 prominent Pennsylvanians agreed to incorporate an association to be known as the Pennsylvania Academy of the Fine Arts stating their purpose in a single paragraph:

> The object of this association is to promote the cultivation of the Fine Arts, in the United States of America, by introducing correct and elegant Copies, from works of the first Masters, in Sculpture and painting, and, by thus facilitating the access of such Standards and also by occasionally conferring moderate but honorable premiums, and otherwise assisting the Studies and exciting the efforts of the artists, gradually to unfold, enlighten and invigorate the talents of our Countrymen.[1]

Although every 18th century attempt to establish a long-lasting academy of fine arts ended in failure, this group of 68 laymen and three artists agreed that there was not a more favorable climate for such an undertaking because public opinion had changed regarding the value of art in America. Consequently, they concluded, public patronage would support such an institution.[2] Within five years from the date of their agreement they were proved right and their chief spokesman Joseph Hopkinson was able to publicly point with pride to the Pennsylvania Academy's accomplishments and to its public support reflecting the public's change in opinion.[3]

To understand Hopkinson's references to change in public opinion one must go back a decade and more. It was true that American artists had achieved some respectability after the War of Independence, especially those neo-classical artists who specialized in painting American history, but it was not until the 1790s that the status of artists was elevated beyond that of mere artisans. It was only after the ratification of the Constitution that they were called upon to help glorify the new nation. Statesmen, editors, poets, and civic leaders all appealed to the artist to use his "divine gift" to aid in the campaign to honor and exalt the new republic. Intellectuals, political figures, and civic leaders began to recognize artists as more than craftsmen. Some people now referred to them as "intellectuals and creators" and said that they could "help promote the happiness of man." Artists were now seen by many to be members of a profession "not only honorable but useful to our country;" they could also aid the republic by helping the people in the "acquiring of good taste."[4]

Not everyone, however, believed that art was beneficial. Many wealthy and articulate citizens of varied political leanings, disapproved of art and

361

condemned art patronage as symptoms of social decay.

There was a strong, and often prevalent, sentiment among Americans that art was dangerous because of its past association with the aristocracy and their ecclesiastical allies. Furthermore, these critics often equated art with luxury; and luxury, they claimed, led to degradation and decadence. The prevailing thought among intellectuals, in Europe and America, was that decadence had caused the collapse of the great republics of antiquity; and many Americans, consequently, were much concerned with the effects of luxury upon their infant society.

Certainly, the long and continuing verbal battle over the value or usefulness of art was not conducive to the establishment of artistic institutions at that time. In addition, Philadelphia society was split politically toward the end of the century and this split was reflected within the artistic community.[5]

Although some prominent persons and great numbers of the lower classes were outspoken pro-French Jeffersonians, most of Philadelphia's leading citizens were to be found in the camp of the pro-English forces. Some individuals, in spite of their strong feelings favoring a particular faction, tried to dissipate the air of suspicion and fear that had permeated the city. The well-known Jeffersonian artist Charles Willson Peale and the noted Federalist lawyer Joseph Hopkinson appealed to both Parties for unity. Hopkinson wrote the song, *Hail Columbia,* as a plea against disharmony, and nowhere was disharmony more acute than among the artists and their patrons. For in the artistic community, the situation was further complicated by the presence of both English and French nationals.[6]

As American involvement in the war between England and France drew closer, the foreign artists gravitated into partisan national groups and engaged in constant bitter debate. Soon this verbal warfare became a fight over the values of monarchy as contrasted with republicanism. Hindsight makes it appear obvious that an association of such violently opposed factions could not possibly remain intact, yet Charles Willson Peale, the constant nationalist who continually sought to elevate the status of art and artists, still tried to maintain enough unity to keep the first attempts at an academy alive.[7]

If it were possible for anyone to have brought the opposing artists together, it would have been Peale. For no single person had more influence at that time among artists, and no artist enjoyed more respect among the artists' patrons. Not only was he the outstanding Philadelphia artist of the period, he was also known to all as a hero of the Revolution where he served both as a soldier in battle and as council delegate in Philadelphia. He had been acclaimed for his role in Washington's Inauguration, and was noted as an inventor and as the originator of the nationally famous Peale's Museum. Above all was his reputation as the portraitist and associate of George Washington.

It was Peale, more than anyone else, who tried to establish and maintain an academy of art in the midst of the acrimonious debates over the value of art. Perhaps he wished to defend the artist's newly-won status by establishing academic and professional artistic institutions. Perhaps, as he later wrote in a letter to Thomas Jefferson, his motives were to "promote a public benefit," and "to promote fine arts in our country." Or possibly Peale, like other public spirited Philadelphians, was desirous of obtaining for his city the first American academy of art.[8]

Whatever his motivation, Peale, although openly known as a republican friend to Jefferson and the Corsican artist and revolutionist Ceracchi was able to interest artists of opposing political views to unite in order to form an association. However, the disputes between Federalists and Republicans in the capital city were to prove too bitter to permit the new organization to survive.

On December 29, 1794, Peale and 28 other professional and amateur artists met at Peale's Museum inside the Philosophical Hall, to form "an association of Artists in America for the protection and encouragement of the Fine Arts." The meeting unanimously elected the Reverend Burgess Allison of Bordentown, New Jersey as chairman and Richard C. Claibourne of Virginia as secretary. The society adopted the name Columbianum and stated at the meeting that:

We the undersigned, from an ernest [sic] desire to promote, to the utmost of our abilities, the Fine Arts—now in their infancy in America—mutually promise and agree, to use our utmost effort to establish a School or Academy of Architecture, sculpture, Painting &c., within the United States.[9]

The new organization was not the first attempt to establish an art school in Philadelphia. Private art schools had been in existence there since colonial days, and a community of artists had developed in the city before the Revolution. In 1780, Alexandre Quesnay opened an "academy of drawing," and later Robert Edge Pine had instituted a school where serious students could copy from his recently acquired collection of antiques. This collection included a much-discussed plaster cast of the *Medici Venus* which was "kept *shut in a case*...as the manners of our country...would not tolerate a public exhibition of such a figure."[10]

The presence of an artistic community and a history of established drawing schools, though of importance in precedent, was not, in itself, enough to insure success for the new Academy. Peale had misjudged both the intensity of the political debate, and the force and sonority of those who feared art and art patronage. Those Americans who feared so much for the survival of the republic included among their ranks many who looked upon art as a most dangerous threat.

For the most part this group of nay-sayers were wealthy well-educated Federalists who, as they explained, "sought to promote only institutions based upon honor and utility." Clearly these anxious patriotic gentlemen had to be reassured that the promotion of fine arts was not hazardous to the nation's health, but there was little reason for such reassurance in Philadelphia where "political fanaticism...at its acme" reigned among all ranks of society.[11]

The vicious published polemics and heated arguments which took place outide the Columbianum were sometimes directed against members of the society, especially when the artist was a Frenchman or bore a French-sounding name. William Cobbett, the Francophobe editor of the Philadelphia newspaper *Porcupine's Gazette,* was especially caustic in his column which he wrote under the by-line of "Peter Porcupine."[12]

Although he had already lost one libel suit in 1793 to Benjamin Rush (pleaded by Joseph Hopkinson), Cobbett continued to write in the same manner as he kept up his war against the French. The French, he claimed, "have spies in every nook and corner of this extensive country."[13] And the "French" artists, especially Benjamin Latrobe, he insisted, were part of the group most dangerous to the security of America. Beneath the caption "A Farce and a Fire," he described, with heavy humour, a play performed in the city of Richmond where fire happened to sweep the playhouse the night after the performance:

The author is La Trobe, the son of an old seditious dissenter; and I am informed that he is now employed in the erecting of a *Penitentiary House*, of which he is likey to be the *first* inmate.[14]

It was obvious that in Philadelphia, no matter how distinguished a French artist might be, the English artist ranked higher. In the eyes of Federalist dominated "Society," French artists were primarily republican revolutionaries and their suporters were considered dupes or worse. As Benjamin Latrobe complained in his journal, on april 26, 1798, "to be civilly received by the fahionable people, and to be invited to the President's, it is necessary to [first] visit the British ambassador."[15]

Peale and his closest associates labored unceasingly to keep the association functioning. But despite Peale's activity, despite his membership on every society committee, Peale's republican sentiments proved too much for the English-born artists. Recently arrived in America, these British artists desired the Columbianum Society to be modeled after the royal Academy, with Washington as the honorary leader in the same manner that King George was the honorary patron of the royal Academy in London.

Under the leadership of Peale and the Corsican artists Geracchi, the Society rejected the English model. This action, coupled with Peale's proposal for a study class where students would draw from a living model, proved to be too much for the British artists.[16] They withdrew from the Society in a group to found a counter organization, after submitting the following resolution on February 2, 1795:

We whose names are hereunto subscribed, highly disapproving of the inconsistant and indecent motion brought forward at the last meeting of the Association of Artists of Philadelphia, take the liberty of informing them that we consider ourselves no longer of that Association, and do accordingly personally and openly give in our resignation.[17]

In this resolution the dissident artists referred to their former associates as members of an "Association of Artists of Philadelphia." The reason for this peculiar avoidance of the organization's name became apparent when the eight English artists formed a rival association and retained the name "Columbianum" for themselves. The new organization called upon the artistic community to support their cause and to join the rebel group. But nearly all of the Philadelphia artists rallied behind the parent group, especially after they intimated the support of Gilbert Stuart from England.[18] The tiny rebel division gradually withered away, while the victors began their plans for a public exhibition of paintings.[19]

The Columbianum soon amended their original agreement to restrict membership to artists only. They now voted to admit members who would contribute financially to the organization. This added financial support enabled the society to undertake the long-desired program of a life study class. In addition to copying from plaster casts, the students could now study and copy from the living figure.[20]

Scarcely a decade had passed since the copy of the *Medici Venus* was kept locked in a case and it was no easy matter to find a male model. The idea of a female model was too exotic a concept to ever enter a Philadelphia drawing master's mind in the 1790s. Female nude models were used in some European drawing schools with shocking effect upon visiting American artists. The New England artist James Guild described his reaction to this unexpected event as follows: "...the first subject we had was—a young lady stripped to the beef and placed on a pedestal, and we twenty Artists sitting around drawing her beautiful figure, perfectly naked: *Se Sie____!*"[21]

One of the founders of the Pennsylvania Academy of the Fine Arts, Horace Binney, in a speech honoring the Academy later in the next century, recalled that "Peale, finding nobody who would exhibit his person for hire to students...bared his own handsome torso for the class."[22]

Although the association did succeed for a time in banding artists and students together organizationally, it slowly faded away. One explanation has been advanced that the Columbianum's failure was due to "financial difficulties and depletion of teachers with the loss of the English artists." Why a "depletion of teachers" is given as a reason is difficult to understand since there appears to be no evidence for such an assertion.[23] On the other hand, the "financial difficulties" which arose with the departure of the British artists are quite easy to understand. It was to be expected that wealthy Federalist support would cease once Republican Francophils assumed undisputed control of the society.

In 1803, Peale wrote a letter to his friend Thomas Jefferson concerning plans for a new academy. He admitted that the loss of the English artists was unfortunate but did not feel that their departure was the only reason for the end of the Columbianum. Instead he emphasized the fact that the social climate at the time was not conducive to success. Somewhat wistfully, he wrote:

In Philadelphia public spirit is wanting for such encouragement...when we attempted a like institution. I endeavored for some time to keep it up as a tender beautiful plant—that if cherished would in future produce good fruit.... I was abused by writers to whom I never deigned to make reply.[24]

The description of the atmosphere in Philadelphia at the time was true. Public spirit *was* wanting and many writers *did* abuse artists and the arts. Most of the abuse arose from concern over the safety of the infant republic and doubts concerning the usefulness of art in a republican society. Added to this fire was the fuel provided by the dispute within artistic circles between the Republican and Federalist partisans.

The pervasive thought among Americans, radical or conservative, was preservation of the republic with its popular government and its moral and social ideals. The opponents of art and art patronage welcomed the "disposition to study nature which is always safe," but questioned, even into the 19th century, whether the country had yet reached "the point that calls for or justifies" an establishment dealing with the study of fine arts.[25] Later in the century, John Adams was still wondering, "are we not in too great a hurry, in our zeal for the fine arts?"[26]

Athens, Rome, Florence and Venice were historic reminders of republics fallen to decay and despotism. The question constantly arose: was it possible that the arts could be employed to further national virtue or were they alien to republican ideals? "Is it possible to enlist the 'fine arts' on the side of truth, of virtue, of piety, or even of honor?" wondered John Adams, and added, "From the dawn of history they have been prostituted to the service of superstition and despotism."[27]

Independence gave native artists a new social role. Eager to assist in portraying the history of the Revolution and its heroes, the artists were, however, denied the traditional forms of patronage which had developed in Western society. Lacking an established church and aristocracy, native artists were forced to look elsewhere for patronage. But elite patronage would be forthcoming only after there had developed an audience that was convinced of the value of art. Until this had been accomplished the patronage necessary for the establishment and survival of artistic institutions would not long continue.

During the turbulent formative years of the nation, art was often equated with wealth and luxury and it was common knowledge that the combination of wealth and luxury led, inevitably, to decadence. Therefore, value judgments on a particular work of art were often made only in relation to the value of art itself. Consequently, articulate Americans, pro or con on the value of art, voiced their opinions in terms of morality, virtue, utility and need.

The negative views of the utility or need for art were often accompanied by expressions of fear that art was the constant companion of luxury. Since luxury led to loss of virtue (the backbone of republicanism), it was obvious that luxury must be avoided at all cost, because loss of virtue, in turn, led to final destruction.

Tench Coxe, prominent member of the wealthy Coxe family of Philadelphia, and (at this time) an ardent Federalist, urged immigrants to come to the United States where they must succeed if engaged in "useful occupations." At the same time he warned that Americans were not concerned with the "fine, superfluous, or luxurious."[28] In an essay dated 1790, about one year after Coxe's warning, the noted Philadelphia physician Benjamin Rush pointed out that "painting and sculpture flourish chiefly in wealthy and luxurious countries."[29] Previously, Abigail Adams, among others, had cautioned against the "bad effects" of refinement and the "extravagance pervading all classes."[30]

Americans in the post-revolutionary period were not entirely convinced that the new republic could last. Republican Rome and Greece had succumbed, and in each instance, after an age marked by luxury and decadence. So there was much to be said for pursuing a conservative program. Why not play safe and avoid any possible source of societal decay? Even Peale the Republican yea-sayer, sometimes questioned the advisability of exploring ideas that had not been tested by American experience. On the other side, the Federalist *Monthly Anthology*, like Peale, was sometimes ambivalent concerning the safety of sensual delights.[31] Richard Price, a financial expert who was also well known for his philosophic writings, summed up the fears of many when he wrote that if the people deviate from "Simplicity of Manners into luxury...the governments must become corrupt and tyrannical."[32]

But not all Americans agreed. Many well-known public figures rejected these views and members of both political parties advanced contrary opinions. Benjamin Latrobe was but one among the Republicans who claimed that "the history of Grecian art refutes the vulgar opinion that the arts are incompatible with liberty" and he pointed out that "...Greece was free when the arts flourished."[33]

Among the Federalists, some of Philadelphia's most distinguished citizens agreed with Joseph Hopkinson that the idea of luxury weakening a nation "was absolutely false."[34] Among those who agreed there was, however, a large group who, while concurring with this conclusion, admitted that wealth and affluence led to a desire for luxury and this could lead to corruption of republican virtue. This particular group sought to prove that the way to overcome this evil was to channel luxury into "correct taste" which, then, would strengthen the ideals that were necessary for continued virtue, usefulness and good government. Thereby, corruption and decadence would be so weakened that despotism could not flourish:

It is obvious to all, who attend to human nature, or the history of human society; and it is verified by observing the state of manners in our own country, that affluence and prosperity are ever attended by a correspondent passion for amusement and pleasure in their diversified forms. It is equally obvious, that whatever serves to correct and regulate this passion is an additional security to the publick and private morals.[35]

The editors of the *Monthly Anthology* were well aware, as they informed their readers, that "we are becoming familiar with Wealth" and that "Out of Wealth grows luxury." Nevertheless they urged the support of every effort "to promote the love of Letters and the Arts," since "if the enjoyments of literature and good taste are not emulated," we shall be exposed to that "enervating and debasing luxury, the object of which is sensual indulgence...its immediate effect, vice...and its ultimate issue, public degradation and ruin."[36]

During the first decade of the 19th century more and more editors, essayists and other writers joined the growing number of those demanding that steps be taken to insure the "creation of good taste," and that necessary procedures be established for the "encouragement of learning and patronage." A swelling chorus of voices was heard, too, calling for whatever programs might be necessary to obtain a "higher degree of excellence," and for the funds necessary to finance such programs to be raised through the "munificence of merchants" since the government "has been so niggardly."[37]

Since the American Revolution patriots, had called upon artists to assist in exposing the "horrid deeds of our enemies" and to extol the virtues of Americans.[38] With the birth of the nation the war between yea-sayers and nay-sayers began over the value or need for art in a republic. At first, the opposing forces seemed to be of equal strength, but by the opening years of the 19th century it became evident that the pessimists were losing the war. Sniping and occasional broadsides continued, but as early as 1797 toasts were offered in restaurants to the honor of the Arts.[39] By 1805, when the Pennsylvania Academy of the Fine Arts held its first meeting, the pro-art forces were dominant even within the Federalist ranks.[40]

One reason for the victory of those who favored the development of art was that so many of America's leading spokesmen were motivated by cultural nationalism. There was a long-present feeling in America of cultural inferiority which began with the nation's founding. Immediately after the the Peace of Paris, the drive to provide the republic's superior virtue over the decadent monarchies of Europe began. Acutely aware of their shortcomings in the Arts, Americans boasted to the world of American "genius," citing in the area of the fine arts such noted American painters as West, Copley, and Stuart. All the while, at home, the same spokesmen stressed the values of art and urged "the development of a native culture that would prove to the world the advantages of the American system."[41]

Whether optimistic or pessimistic about the result of artistic development and art patronage, all citizens were quick to defend American "genius." Some Americans admitted to their countrymen that they did not yet compare favorably with Europeans in the arts of achitecture, sculpture and painting. But, although we lagged behind, as Jefferson pointed out, Americans excused the lag as a result of the efforts of building a new nation in the wilderness.[42]

The rapid progress in economic development and the accompanying accumulation of wealth appeared to make most Americans even more self-conscious concerning their admitted deficiency of culture. Defensively, Americans spoke of their need as a nation to develop a strong economy and were often incensed at European writers who derided American culture. Federalist or Republican, Americans continually defended their "pursuits of more immediate utility and profit," and replied vigorously to the European charges that culture could not ever advance to any great height in America because it was known that "particular climates have a particular fitness for the production of genius,"[43] and that "the liberal arts cannot thrive out of Europe."[44]

In reply to the European theory which held that the Americans were savage in their manners because they were inhabitants of a new world in the West, and that the ocean voyage westward resulted in degeneration, Americans were quick to counter that they were equal in genius "in proportion to their population."[45] George Clymer, Revolutionary War hero and a leader in Philadelphia banking and Federalist Party circles, raised his voice in protest that "no nation has the proud monopoly of genius; wherever there are men, there genius is to be found."[46] And some defended American genius by claiming a New World *special genius* which stressed usefulness and virtue.[47]

By the early years of the 19th century, enough advances had been made in the arts that self-conscious Americans could sometimes take the offensive against the European critics. European books that dealt with "travels through the United States" still enraged American readers; but now, Americans could point to achievements where Europeans were lacking. It was especially gratifying to all Americans when Englishmen could be shown to be lagging in any area of culture or knowledge.

American citizens now occasionally called Englishmen "provincial" and contemptuously derided their lack of knowledge of art, of geography and of nationalities.[48] The *New York Chronicle Express* on May 23, 1803, printed an article praising the establishment of the Art Academy in New York and followed with an article the next day maliciously asking, "how it must exate astonishment to reflect that there is no public gallery of pictures in London."[49]

Evidence of cultural inferiority and its accompanying tendency toward overcompensation continued in American life through the 19th century. There appears to be little doubt that this complex was a significant force in the establishment of American cultural institutions. Although some citizens still saw no good in the cultivation of art or its institutions, most Americans soon came to favor the view that art was useful in a republic.

Whatever their reasons as former opponents, the "worriers" tended toward resignation to the inevitable. John Adams fretted over the question of art and morality and concluded: "It is in vain to think of restraining the fine arts. Luxury will follow riches and the fine arts will come with luxury in spite of all that wisdom can do."[50] Lonely voices of opposition would continue to be raised, but by the middle of the first decade of the new century the victory of art was secure.

At last the political, social, and intellectual climate of Philadelphia seemed ready for an academy of the fine arts. The idea for another attempt to establish an academy began, as could be expected, with Charles Willson Peale. The midwives at the actual birth of the new infant Academy, however, were the enthusiastic former Columbianum members Joseph Hopkinson and Peale's artist son Rembrandt. Rembrandt had enlisted Hopkinson's aid in an effort to obtain a building suitable to display a shipment of paintings recently imported by a Dutch merchant. Instead, Hopkinson persuaded the artist to use such a room to display the works of native artists.[51]

Enthusiastic responses from his friends, particularly among members of the bar, led Hopkinson to convince the elder Peale to issue a call for a meeting for the purpose of organizing an academy to be devoted to the fine arts. Meanwhile, Hopkinson explained, "he would get the lawyers to make a subscription."[52]

Peale subsequently called several meetings at his home and many subscriptions were obtained, but, of all the fund raisers, Hopkinson was the most industrious and most successful. While the subscribers were being solicit, plans were already being formulated for the new organization. The Peales visualized the new society to be structured as a school for artists, but unlike the European prototype the American model would include the

289

public among its members. They also suggested that the Academy should exhibit and sell to the public, thus laying the foundation for public patronage.[53] Before the group had formally convened, Peale outlined the plan of the organizing committee to his son Raphael:

The proposal is to import casts, and begin a gallery of figures and paintings, beginning with an exhibition; to receive paintings that may be offered for sale, and if sold to take a commission in such sales.... This is the first part of the plan, and out of this will arise the Academy, drawing from Models, and afterwards from life.[54]

In other words, Peale visualized an art gallery which would sell contemporary paintings for the immediate benefit of the artist and raise funds for the establishment of a school for artists. However, the laymen shareholders had a different concept and were soon to treat the Academy and its gallery as their own private and exclusive "gentleman's" club.

On June 21, 1805, the first meeting of the Academy membership took place. The work of the indefatigable Hopkinson in securing support among his fellow lawyers was apparent. Of the 71 subscribers assembled, more than 40 represented the bench and bar.[55] Many prominent Philadelphians remarked upon Hopkinson's enthusiastic labors in behalf of the Academy. Peale was among the first to applaud Hopkinson's efforts to make the long-sought dream come true.[56]

Hopkinson was not alone in his zeal. To establish an art academy would be a triumph for any city, and pride in one's city and rivalry between cities was common in the early days of nationhood. It is possible that much of the impetus and response of prominent Philadelphians toward an academy was due to the establishment of an academy in New York in December 1802. Peale, among others, when discussing a new Academy, had remarked that he wished Philadelphia to be the seat of art in America. These sentiments of local pride had been echoed by such outstanding civic leaders as Nicholas Biddle, William Meredith and, of course, Joseph Hopkinson.[57] Richard Rush was but one of many local voices that were raised in support "with the pride of a Philadelphian."[58] Similar sentiments of local pride and civic rivalry had been voiced in New York during the campaign to institute an academy in that city. The mayor of New York and first president of the New York Academy, Edward Livingstone, had appealed to New York pride in 1803, and one year prior Edward Savage had entreated fellow New Yorkers to found an institution to exhibit such prints and paintings "that would rival Peale's museum in Philadelphia."[59]

Wealthy Philadelphians did more than voice their expressions of support in terms of public spirit. They responded zealously with financial aid. On June 13, Peale was able to write Jefferson that "we hope soon to build a building to display casts and paintings," and by June 21 he was able to report, "We have upwards of $2400 subscribed." Three days later he was able to add, "our subscriptions amount to $2500."[60]

Immediately after the June 21 meeting, negotiations began in order to secure building lots suitable for the construction of an appropriate building. Peale's Museum had demonstrated that "an elegant building, with a changing exhibition of objects of unusual interest, could be self-supporting as well as an important cultural attraction."[61] The laymen organizers of the PAFA were money-minded gentlemen and the element of self-support was possibly a key reason for the haste to erect a building. The newly-formed association was made up overwhelmingly of businessmen and lawyers; and the lawyers, themselves, were often engaged in other business endeavors. Most all of them came from wealthy families whose income was derived from various business enterprises. The President and 10 of his 12 directors could be included in the above description. Only two artists were elected as members of the Board. This ratio of artists to businessmen on the board of the Academy, except for a very few years, was to continue as such thereafter.[62]

Fired by their successful start and full of optimism, a committee was formed consisting of Peale, Hopkinson, and William Meredith to secure "meritorious" casts for exhibiton and for study. With just enough funds for the purchase of the castings and with no place to house them, the committee, undaunted, wrote General John Armstrong, the United States Minister to France, for help in obtaining suitable casts in Paris. This request was directed to him because they relied, so they said, "on your good wile [sic] to our City and to your desire to encourage any understanding that has for its object the improvement of our country."[63]

A second letter was sent the same day to the legation secretary, the 18 year old fellow Philadelphian, scion of one of Philadelphia's most distinguished and wealthy families, Nicholas Biddle. The committee stressed the fact that they were "anxious to have the best that...money can procure," and included in the letter a list of statues desired, the price to be paid for each, and "a Bill of Exchange to repay the expence [sic]." This letter too, like the letter to Armstrong, also emphasized the recipient's good will toward improvement of the city. They were aware, they explained, that Biddle was "interested, as we know you are, in everything which gives improvement and honor to your native City."[64]

The precocious youngster took immediate action by enlisting the support of his countrymen in France. Next, he obtained the advice and help of noted French and Italian artists and as legation secretary he used his official contacts to employ the services of French government functionaries whenever necessary. He reported his avid interest back to the committee as due to "the willingness with which I will contribute all my excertions toward an establishment so honorable to our city."[65]

In the preamble of the charter, the incorporators had stressed their concern with usefulness and the educational enlightenment so necessary to the pursuit of "good taste."[66] The Pennsylvania Legislature echoed the founder's views and added, "It is in the manifest of free government to cherish and encourage institutions of such nature."[67] If legislators do, as they often profess, reflect the opinions of their constituents, then by 1806 public had accepted the usefulness of art toward the pursuit of republican virtue.

On April 15, 1807, the Academy was opened "with good attendance," and tribute was paid to the directors for the number and selection of casts chosen from the "choicest pieces of statuary in Europe." The Boston magazine *Monthly Anthology* reported that the collection "gave universal satisfaction."[68]

At the gala opening the main address was given by George Clymer, who had been elected as the Academy's first president the previous year by a special election committee. Clymer, after gently chiding the directors for overspending available funds, praised anew the native-born artistic geniuses. He replied once again to foreign detractors and those who might still object to "a departure from accustomed simplicity." Pleading for understanding, Clymer asked: "But if luxury be a consequential evil of the progress of our country, a better question would be, how is it to be understood?...Philosophy and the laws would here teach in vain."[69]

Editors and writers, artists and patrons, men of affairs both here and abroad, concurred with Clymer's remarks and sent messages of support to the new Academy. "Remarker" in the *Monthly Anthology* noted: "The encouragement of learning, the patronage of genius are subjects, of which, though we hear much in our country, we have not yet a perfect understanding." The author then called for the judicious use of patronage, pointing out that "many of our distinguished citizens without patronage would have been forever confined to the humble pursuits of their fathers!"[70] These thoughts were echoed by letter writers who noted the number of fellow Americans in Paris and the dearth of patronage in the United States.[71]

It was humiliating to many Americans that their fellow citizens were forced to travel to Europe in order to improve themselves or to gain knowledge necessary for certain chosen professions. Correspondents throughout the nation hailed the creation of any institution that would assist in the development of native genius. In America, "proof already existed of a pure taste," and of "the peculiar genius of our people" but, critics complained, "they have been obliged to seek abroad for those means of improvement."[72]

Hence, the opening of the Academy brought expressions of approval and delight not only from Philadelphians but from far-off areas and occasioned passionate pleas for patronage to secure and maintain the institution. Three years after the formal opening, Hopkinson was to refer to Philadelphia merchants as "the restorers of learning and fine arts...the benefactors to whom every civilized man is grateful." And Charles Jared Ingersoll, eminent Philadelphia author and politican, in an address before the American Philosophical Society in 1823, summed up the uniqueness of arts and sciences in America with the conclusion that "Public funds for the education of the whole community are endowments exclusively American."[73]

The enthusiastic response to the initial exhibition convinced the Academy Directors to keep the gallery open for daily viewing. The price of admission was 25 cents and doors were open to all, "daily except Sunday 9-3 P.M.," and on Mondays when "ladies only will be admitted."[74] Since the exhibits included many nude statues, Mondays were reserved "with tender gallantry, for ladies exclusively."[75]

Daily exhibitions proved successful from their inception and public interest continued to be maintained by means of continual additions to the permanent collection. The continuing popularity of Peale's Museum was a constant diagram of success to the Academy Directors. He had proved that frequent changing of exhibits and the acquisition of new displays would continue to bring the public to his doors. The lesson was well learned by the PAFA directors.[76]

By July, 1809, Peale was able to write to Benjamin West that "the number of visitors to the Academy has given us upwards of $100 per month since we hung up your pictures. Subscribers to the Institution have become so numerous as to enable us to pay off our debts." He ended the letter with the prophecy that the Academy "promises to become a nursery to the genius of America."[77]

Peale's prophecy proved to be correct. The Pennsylvania Academy of the Fine Arts became the first institution of its kind to achieve lasting success. It became the model for other like-minded institutions and earned recognition as a leading force in the development of art and artists within this nation.

Notes

[1]Photostatic copy of the original Agreement of Incorporation, Archives of the Pennsylvania Academy of the Fine Arts, hereinafter cited as PAFA.

[2]Lee L. Schreiber, "The Philadelphia Elite in the Development of the Pennsylvania Academy of the Fine Arts," unpublished doctoral dissertation, Temple University, Philadelphia, Pa., March, 1977, 1-31.

[3]Joseph Hopkinson, "Annual Discourse delivered before the Pennsylvania Academy of the Fine Arts on the 13th of November, 1810 in Philadelphia," First Annual Exhibition of the Society of Artists of the United States (Philadelphia, 1811), 6-11. Hereinafter cited as "Annual Discourse."

[4]Charles Willson Peale (Scientific and Descriptive) Catalogue (Philadelphia, 1796). Microfilm, Paley Library, Temple University I.V.; Letter from J. Allen Smith (of South Carolina) to William Tilghman, James Gibson and P.F. Glentworth, December 21, 1807. Archives, PAFA.

[5]Neil Harris, The Artist in American Society (New York, 1966), 28.

[6]Hopkinson Papers, Historical Society of Pennsylvania, hereinafter cited as HSP.

[7]Peale Papers, HSP; Biographical material relating to Charles Willson Peale, unless otherwise noted, has been taken from Charles Coleman Sellers, Charles Willson Peale (New York, 1969).

[8]Charles Willson Peale to Thomas Jefferson, January 25, 1803. Peale Papers, HSP.

[9]"Original Agreement," Peale Papers, HSP.

[10]Charles Coleman Sellers, Charles Willson Peale (New York, 1969), 268; Joseph Hopkinson, May 6, 1833, quoted in Helen W. Henderson, The Pennsylvania Academy of Fine Arts and other Collections of Philadelphia (Boston, 1911), 31.

[11]J. Allen Smith to William Tilghman, James Gibson, and P.F. Glentworth, December 21, 1807, Archives, PAFA; Harris, Artist in Society, 28; Benjamin Henry Latrobe, April 26, 1798 entry in The Journal of Latrobe (New York, 1905), 86.

[12]Porcupine's Gazette, 1798-1799.

[13]Porcupine's Gazette, April 3, 1798.

[14]Porcupine's Gazette, April 3, 1798.

[15]Latrobe, 86; "Two notable victims of social exclusion were John Nicholson and Charles Willson Peale," cited in Roland M. Baumann, "John Swanwick: Spokesman for 'Merchant Republicanism' in Philadelphia, 1790-1798," The Pennsylvania Magazine of History and Biography, 97, (Philadelphia, 1973), No.2, 143.

[16]Sellers, C.W. Peale, 269.

[17]"Journal," Peale Papers, HSP, 8.

[18]Sellers, C.W. Peale, 270.

[19]"Notes Files of Records Pertaining to the Pennsylvania Academy of Fine Arts," HSP.

[20]Manuscript of original agreement and amendments, "Minutes of Society," Peale Papers, HSP.

21"The Travel Diary of James Guild," *Vermont Historical Society Proceedings* (New Series V., 1937), 250-313.

22Quoted in "The First American Art Academy," *Lippencott's Magazine*, 9 (February 1872), 145.

23*Catalogue of the Heritage Collection,* Archives, PAFA.

24Peale to Jefferson, January 25, 1803, Peale Papers, HSP.

25*Monthly Anthology,* May 1807, 230.

26John Adams to Benjamin Waterhouse, February 26, 1817; Adrienne Koch and William Peder (eds.), *Selected Writings of John and John Qunicy Adams* (New York, 1946), 199, 200.

27Koch and Peder, *Selected Writings,* 199, 200.

28*American Museum,* July 1790, 40.

29Benjamin Rush, *Essays, Literary, Moral and Philosophical* (Philadelphia, 1770-1790, 2nd edit., Philadelphia, 1806).

30Abigail Adams to Thomas Jefferson, January 29, 1787; Eliza House to Jefferson, July 24, 1786; Julian P. Boyd (ed.) *Papers of Thomas Jefferson* (Princeton, 1953), II, 86; X, 167.

31Peale, *(Scientific and Descriptive) Catalogue,* IV; "Editor's Address," *Monthly Anthology,* May 1807, 231.

32Richard Price to Thomas Jefferson, March 21, 1785; Boyd, *Jefferson Papers,* VIII, 53.

33B. Henry Latrobe, "Anniversary Oration pronounced before the Society of Artists of the United States," *First Annual Exhibition of the Society of Artists of the United States* (Philadelphia, 1811).

34Joseph Hopkinson, Essay: "A Defense of Luxury," May 3, 1788, Hopkinson Papers, HSP.

35*Monthly Anthology,* May 1807, 231.

36*Monthly Anthology,* May 1807, 4.

37*American Museum,* March 1787, 297; *Monthly Anthology,* May 1807, 243.

38Quoted in Harris, *Artist in Society,* 28.

39*Aurora General Advertiser,* January 18, 1797.

40Talbot Hamlin, *Benjamin Henry Latrobe* (New York, 1955), 128.

41Lillian B. Miller, *Patrons and Patriotism* (Chicago, 1966), vii, viii, 5; Jefferson to Charles Bellini, September 30, 1785;, Boyd, *Jefferson Papers,* VIII, 569.

42A number of historians have, smewhat apologetically, explained the dearth of art in America during its early years by resting their case on the fact that the colonists were too busy conquering the wilderness to have time to create works of art. See Arthur M. Schlesinger, *The Birth of the Nation* (New York, 1968), 206; or Clinton Rossiter, *The First American Revolution* (New York, 1953), 189.

43Samuel Miller, *A Brief Retrospect of the Eighteenth Century* (New York, 1803; rpt. New York, 1970), 428.

44Hopkinson, "Annual Discourse," 8.

45"Thoughts on American Genius," *American Museum,* March 1787, 206.

46*Paulson's Daily Advertiser,* April 21, 1807.

47*American Museum,* July 1790, 40; Philip Freneau, under the pen-name Robert Slender, O.S.M. [Initials stand for "one of the swinish multitude,"] *Letters on Various Subjects* (Philadelphia, 1799), Letter No. 2, 18; *Port-Folio,* April 20, 1805, 18.

48Hopkinson, "Annual Discourse," 18; Latrobe, *Journal,* 156.

49Quoted in George Gates Raddin, Jr., *The New York of Hocquet Caritat and his Associates 1797-1817* (Dover Advance Press, 1954), 53.

50Adams to Waterhouse, February 26, 1817, Koch and Peder, *Selected Writings* 199-200.

51Sellers, *C.W. Peale,* 321.

52Peale to Raphael Peale, June 6, 1805, Correspondence of Charles Willson Peale, HSP.

53Peale Papers, HSP.

54Peale to Raphael Peale, June 6, 1805, Peale Correspondence, HSP.

55"The First American Art Academy," Archives PAFA.

56Hopkinson Papers, V., HSP.

57The American Academy of Fine Arts opened in 1803 in New York City was already moribund by the date of Hopkinson's speech in 1810, and deceased by 1826. Peale to John Hawkins, quoted in J. Thomas Scharf and Thomas Westcott, *History of Philadelphia* (Philadelphia, 1884), II, 1070; C.W. Peale, Jos. Hopkinson, Wm. Meredithy to Nicholas Biddle, Esq., July 8, 1805, Archives, PAFA; Biddle to Peale, Hopkinson and Meredith, October 24, 1805, Archives, PAF.

58Richard Rush to Hopkinson, February 16, 1805, Hopkinson Papers, HSP.

[59]Edward Livingstone in *The Spectator*, January 26, 1803, quoted in Raddin, 51; Raddin, 39; letter to Peter Irving in *The Morning Chronicle05, Archives, PAF.*

[58]Richard Rush to Hopkinson, February 16, 1805, Hopkinson Papers, HSP.

[59]Edward Livingstone in *The Spectator*, January 26, 1803, quoted in Raddin, 51; Raddin, 39; letter to Peter Irving in *The Morning Chronicle* stated that "New Yorkers had no intentions of being out rivaled by Philadelphians...," quoted in Raddin, 41.

[61]Sellers, *C.W. Peale*, 321, 322.

[62]"Notes and Letters of Charles Willson Peale," Peale Papers, HSP.

[63]Peale, Hopkinson and Meredith to Gen. John Armstrong, July 8, 1805, Archives, PAFA.

[64]Peale, Hopkinson and Meredith to Nicholas Biddle, July 8, 1805, together with original "List of Statues," Archives, PAFA.

[65]Biddle to Peale, Hopkinson and Meredith, October 24, Archives, PAFA.

[66]"Transcribed from the Original Academy Charter," December 26, 1805, Archives, PAFA.

[67]"Exemplification, Articles of Incorporation," May 28, 1806, certified copy by Timothy Matlack, Master of Rolls, "as an act of the Commonwealth of Pennsylvania, May 24, 1806." Archives, PAFA.

[68]*Monthly Anthology*, April 1807, 216.

[69]"Original rough minutes of meeting for purpose of electing officers," June 2, 1806, Archives, PAFA; George Clymer, Address upon the opening of the Pennsylvania Academy of Fine Arts, rpt. under heading "Literary and Philosophical Intelligence," *Monthly Anthology*, April 1807, 216.

[70]"Remarker, No. 21," *Monthly Anthology*, May 1807, 243.

[71]"Letter from Paris," *Monthly Anthology*, May 1807, 237.

[72]J. Allen Smith to Tilghman, Gibson and Glentworth, December 21, 1807. Archives, PAFA. Hopkinson, "Annual Discourse," 8.

[73]Prince Hoar to Biddle, October 15, 1807, Archives, PAFA. Hopkinson, "Annual Discourse," 13. C.J. Ingersol, *A Discourse Concerning the Influence of America on the Mind* (Philadelphia, 1823), 5-6.

[74]Advertisement in *Paulson's Daily Advertiser*, April 21, 1807.

[75]Quoted in William Henry Noble, Jr., *Philadelphia's Treasure Houses* (Philadelphia, 1950), 67.

[76]Within an advertisement printed in the *Aurora General Advertiser*, January 2, 1797, Peale emphasized that "the constant visitor will always find some additions...."

[77]Peale to West, July 4, 1808, Peale Papers, HSP.

Professor Schreiber is on the history faculty at Temple University. He is president of the Delaware Valley American Culture Association.

THE WANING OF AN ENLIGHTENMENT IDEAL: CHARLES WILLSON PEALE'S PHILADELPHIA MUSEUM, 1790-1820

Sidney Hart and David C. Ward

On April 24, 1794, Charles Willson Peale (1741-1827) (Figure 1) "respectfully" informed the public that "he should bid adieu to Portrait Painting" and he recommended his artist sons Raphaelle and Rembrandt to those desiring portraits. Peale did continue to paint to the end of his life but his hitherto prodigious output of commissioned portraits dwindled to a yearly handful of portraits of his family, special friends, and the occasional notable American or European.[1]

Mr. Hart is associate editor and Mr. Ward is assistant editor at the Peale Family Papers, National Portrait Gallery, Smithsonian Institution. They would like to thank Dr. Lillian B. Miller, Editor, Peale Family Papers, National Portrait Gallery, Smithsonian Institution, for encouraging this paper. The authors would also like to thank Milton M. Klein and Toby A. Appel for their comments. An earlier version of this paper was presented at the joint national meeting of the National Council on Public History and the Society for History in the Federal Government in Washington, D.C., on April 24, 1987.

[1] *Dunlap and Claypoole's American Daily Advertiser*, Apr. 24, 1794. The definitive biography of Peale is Charles Coleman Sellers, *Charles Willson Peale* (New York 1969). Sellers has focused more tightly on the museum in *Mr. Peale's Museum: Charles Willson Peale and the First Popular Museum of Natural Science and Art* (New York 1980). To avoid needless repetition of notes it can be assumed that general details about Peale's life can be found in either or both of these works.

The Peale Family Papers project at the National Portrait Gallery, Smithsonian Institution, is in the process of publishing a seven-volume letterpress edition of *The Selected Papers of Charles Willson Peale and His Family*. Volume 2, *Charles Willson Peale: The Artist as Museum Keeper, 1791-1810*, ed. Lillian B. Miller, Sidney Hart, and David C. Ward (New Haven, Conn. 1988), covers the period discussed in this paper. The

Peale did not, however, abandon his active role in the cultural life of Philadelphia and the new nation; if anything, his withdrawal from painting was followed by a period of increased activity and creativity in which Peale worked to establish and improve the organizations which would support and advance the artistic, scientific, and intellectual needs of Americans. Among scientists, he was a bulwark of the American Philosophical Society, faithfully attending meetings, contributing prize essays and papers, and serving as one of the society's officers. In the arts, Peale was instrumental in efforts, first with the abortive Columbianum and later successfully with the Pennsylvania Academy of the Fine Arts, to establish a permanent institution to improve, promote, and exhibit the work of American artists. Overshadowing all these—and a multiplicity of other activities—was Peale's most important contribution to Philadelphia's, and indeed America's, culture: the establishment and operation of the Philadelphia museum or, as it was familiarly known, Peale's museum. As Peale put it in his retirement announcement, he was leaving his artistic career because "It is his fixed determination to encrease the subjects of the Museum with all his powers, whilst life and health will admit of it"[2] (Figure 2).

The museum began as an offshoot of Peale's efforts to run a portrait gallery to display his paintings. A chance remark from a friend that the public might also pay to see some natural history specimens that Peale had on hand ultimately led to the creation of a museum housing collections of art, science, natural history, and technology. Peale's receptivity to the idea of expanding a portrait gallery into a museum was not simply because such a museum might produce revenue. Beyond the necessity to make money and support his large family was Peale's drive to make the museum one of America's preeminent cultural institutions. This drive followed logically from his world view, a view that grew out of his career as an artisan and artist

---

Peale Family Papers has also published a complete edition of Peale papers in microfiche: Lillian B. Miller, ed., *The Collected Papers of Charles Willson Peale and His Family: A Guide and Index to the Microfiche Edition* (Millwood, N.Y.: Kraus Microform 1980). Subsequent references to the microfiche edition will be given as F: followed by the alphanumeric code used to identify and locate documents in the edition and on the microfiche.

[2] *Dunlap and Claypoole's American Daily Advertiser*, Apr. 24, 1794. For Peale's role in Philadelphia's cultural life, see Sellers, *Charles Willson Peale*; for the cultural environment in Philadelphia, see Daniel J. Boorstin, *The Lost World of Thomas Jefferson* (1948; rep. Boston 1960), 8-26, and Edgar P. Richardson, "The Athens of America, 1800-1825," in Russell F. Weigley, ed., *Philadelphia: A 300-Year History* (New York 1982), 208-257.

Figure 1

Self-Portrait (With Spectacles). Charles Willson Peale, 1804 [?]. Oil on canvas. The Pennsylvania Academy of the Fine Arts, Philadelphia. Henry D. Gilpin Fund.

and reflected eighteenth-century Enlightenment and republican ideas about order, harmony, and civic virtue.[3]

This article will examine Charles Willson Peale's attempts to obtain government support for his museum during the years 1790 to 1820. For Peale, governmental support for educational and cultural institutions was essential for an enlightened, republican society. The changing nature of American culture in the first years of the nineteenth century, however, made Peale's efforts problematic and ultimately fruitless. We will argue that Peale's museum was an institution arising out of the ideals of the eighteenth-century Enlightenment; that its continued existence into the nineteenth century as an educational institution was hampered by changing cultural and intellectual values that focused on the specific and specialized rather than the general and universal; that these changing values precluded continued local and state government support; and that its opportunity to obtain national support was blocked by a political ideology—Jeffersonianism—that rigidly circumscribed the area of society into which the national government would intervene. Existing studies of Peale's museum have been both presentist and ahistorical in their explanations of why Peale was unable to obtain governmental support and ensure the long-term survival of his museum. By placing the museum in the ideological and political context of the early nineteenth century, we will suggest another hypothesis—namely, that Charles Willson Peale, a man of the eighteenth-century Enlightenment who believed in unity and harmony, found himself in conflict with the ideals of the new century, one in which the universal and general categories of the Enlightenment would be broken down into distinct and separate spheres of thought and action. In terms of Peale's greatest creation—his Philadelphia museum—this meant, as he feared, the absence of governmental support; his museum would not be a permanent institution for posterity but would last little more than twenty years after his death.

---

[3] Peale's own account of the founding of the museum is in his Autobiography, 107-108, F:IIC. On Enlightenment thought in the late eighteenth century, see Henry F. May, *The Enlightenment in America* (New York 1976), 153-277; for Philadelphia specifically, see 197-222. The world of the artisan in eighteenth-century Philadelphia has been detailed in Eric Foner, *Tom Paine and Revolutionary America* (New York 1976), 19-69. For the interconnection of Peale's artisanal background and faith in the progress of enlightenment, see Sidney Hart, "'To encrease the comforts of Life': Charles Willson Peale and the Mechanical Arts," *Pennsylvania Magazine of History and Biography*, 110 (July 1986), 323-357.

Figure 2

The Artist in His Museum. Charles Willson Peale, 1822. Oil on canvas.
The Pennsylvania Academy of the Fine Arts, Philadelphia. Presented by Mrs.
Joseph Harrison.

In its philosophy, organization, and arrangement, Peale's Philadelphia museum embodied much of the spirit of the eighteenth-century Enlightenment. The basic tenets of the Enlightenment's cosmology were all demonstrated in graphic display. The Linnaean classification of species indicated the order, harmony, and regularity of nature and also testified to man's ability to perceive its complexities and present them in a systematic way. The species were also displayed as links in a "great chain of being," which depicted a static universe of ascending life forms from the simplest organism to man. Peale conceived of his museum and its displays as a "world in miniature" in which life in its variegated but ultimately harmonious forms would be on view. Peale had "no doubt" that his "assemblage of nature . . . when critically examined" would be "found to be a part of a great whole, combined together by unchangeable laws of infinite wisdom . . . ."[4]

It is worth noting that Peale seriously considered displaying the embalmed corpses of eminent men to show the highest level of the natural world. When this proved unworkable a substitute was found in Peale's portraits, which lined the walls, significantly displayed *above* the natural history specimens. The harmonies of the mechanical world were also represented in displays of the latest technology. In addition to the fascination of watching intricate and complicated mechanisms working harmoniously, the inventions made the point that progress had been made, and would continue to be made, in the material conditions of mankind through the application of man's rational powers to solve or ameliorate the problems of living, a key tenet of Enlightenment thought (Figure 3).[5]

In its organization and operation Peale's museum was democratic and popular, reflecting the proprietor's ideological and political views. During the American Revolution Peale had been a radical republican who in his art and actions supported the colonial cause and

---

[4] "World in miniature": Peale, Autobiography, 272, F:IIC; Peale's course of lectures on natural history, which he delivered at the museum, had as its central thesis the depiction of a harmonious animal kingdom, F:IID/3-26; Peale to Isaac Weaver, Feb. 11, 1802, in Miller, Hart, and Ward, eds., *Peale: The Artist as Museum Keeper*, 396-398.

[5] The organization of the museum and Peale's interest in displaying embalmed corpses is detailed in an untitled broadside by Peale, dated 1792, F:IID/lB8-11. A graphic representation of the main exhibition area of the museum, with the portraits displayed above the cabinets, is Titian Ramsay Peale's painting "The Long Room" (1822, Detroit Institute of Arts).

Figure 3

The Long Room. Charles Wilson Peale and Titian Ramsay Peale II, 1822. Ink and watercolor on paper. The Detroit Institute of Arts, The Founders Society; Director's Fund.

This study for C.W. Peale's *The Artist in His Museum* provides an accurate depiction of the arrangement of the museum's main exhibition space. Note the portraits hanging above the glass cases which held the specimens.

the democratization of American culture and society. He was a soldier in the militia and a member of Philadelphia's political committees and societies, which actively promoted and supported the most radical ideas and policies of the American Revolution, including the Pennsylvania constitution of 1776. His commitment to republican ideology and democratic polity was well known. As heir to both the Enlightenment and the American Revolution, Peale believed that improvement in knowledge led necessarily to improvement in character and that republics could survive only with an educated and virtuous citizenry. Peale's major justification in seeking state support for his museum was predicated on the republican concept of civic virtue. In his memorial to the Pennsylvania legislature in 1795 he defined his museum as an educational institution and then pointed out what for the legislators surely would be a well-known republican formulation: "In a country where institutions all depend upon the virtue of the people, which in its turn is secured only as they are well informed, the promotion of knowledge is the First of duties." For men such as Peale the American Revolution provided the opportunity to create an intellectual and cultural renaissance, perhaps even a secular millennium, in which ignorance and superstition would give way to reason and truth. Only Peale's fear of the still strong influence of organized religion kept him from calling his museum a "Temple of Wisdom." But the museum's function nonetheless would be to educate and teach virtue to the public by demonstrating the benevolence of the Creator and the order, harmony, and beauty of His creation. It was a matter of faith to the proprietor that "nothing which human invention has yet found out, can so forcibly impress sentiments of piety, and a reverence for the supreme Creator" as a well-organized museum.[6]

In dramatic contrast to traditional European practice, the museum was open to the public without restriction except for the payment of an admission fee of twenty-five cents; additional fees were sometimes imposed for special exhibits—such as the mastodon display—and events such as lectures and concerts. In Peale's museum, again unlike the state-run museums and collections in Europe, the specimens and artifacts were not hidden in drawers or storerooms,

---

[6] May, *American Enlightenment*, 338-340; Peale, "Memorial to the Pennsylvania Legislature," Dec. 26, 1795, in Miller, Hart, and Ward, eds., *Peale: The Artist as Museum Keeper*, 136-138; for "Temple of Wisdom" and Peale's concern about religious opposition to the museum, see Peale to Andrew Ellicott, Feb. 28, 1802, F:IIA/25C3-6; Peale to Isaac Weaver, Feb. 11, 1802, in Miller, Hart, and Ward, eds., *Peale: The Artist as Museum Keeper*, 396-398.

accessible only to the learned and privileged. Rather, Peale's overriding goal was to disseminate knowledge to as wide an audience as possible. Peale (and his workers) were expert taxidermists, adept at preserving and displaying animal specimens (Figure 4). Peale was a pioneer in the use of the habitat group in which animals were displayed in a life-like manner in realistic settings made to duplicate nature as closely as possible (Figures 5 and 6). The clear intention was to attract the eye of interested laymen, so that they would learn more about the natural world. Peale did not assume knowledge and expertise about what was displayed so he added labels and descriptions to the exhibits in order to facilitate the public's education; to further inform and orient the visitor Peale published *A Guide to the Philadelphia Museum* which he distributed free of charge. The scholar, too, was not neglected since Peale's expert taxidermy and display of natural history specimens, all arranged in the best scientific and taxonomic order, were calculated to facilitate scientific observation and analysis; the museum was frequently used by science classes at the University of Pennsylvania as well as by prominent individual scientists. Peale's intention, besides universal education, was also to make his museum a public institution in a democratic state. In his mind this meant that he had to compel "the unwise as [well] as the learned to feel the importance of a well organized Museum, before . . . [he could have] any pretention or expectation of getting any aid from our Public bodies."[7]

---

[7] Peale discussed his admission policy and contrasted it with European practice in a letter to William Findley, Feb. 18, 1800, F:IIA/23A6-10; Peale, Autobiography, 318, F:IIC. See also Richard D. Altick, *The Shows of London* (Cambridge, Mass. 1978), 26-27; Edward Miller, *That Noble Cabinet: A History of the British Museum* (Athens, Ohio 1974), 62-63, 92; Toby Anita Appel, "The Cuvier-Geoffroy Debate and the Structure of Nineteenth Century French Zoology" (Ph.D. diss., Princeton University 1975), 38-41; and Peale's Museum, *A Guide to the Philadelphia Museum* (Philadelphia 1804 and subsequent editions). For Peale's intention to compel the "unwise" as well as the "learned," see Peale to Phillipe Rose Roume, Dec. 25, 1803, F:IIA/29C6-8.

Peale's primary purpose in charging an admission fee was to obtain revenue for his family and the museum's support. An additional reason cited by Peale for the fee was to control the crowds that would result if he allowed free admission to the museum. There may also have been a class component to Peale's admission fee since the amount required was sufficiently high to exclude those at the bottom of Philadelphia's social structure. This may be evidence, then, of the attempt by the "respectable" classes in Philadelphia (including artisans and mechanics) to demarcate themselves from the culture and physical lives of the poorer classes. Peale to William Findley, Feb. 18, 1800, F:IIA/23A6-10; Susan G. Davis, *Parades and Power: Street Theatre in Nineteenth-Century Philadelphia* (Philadelphia 1986).

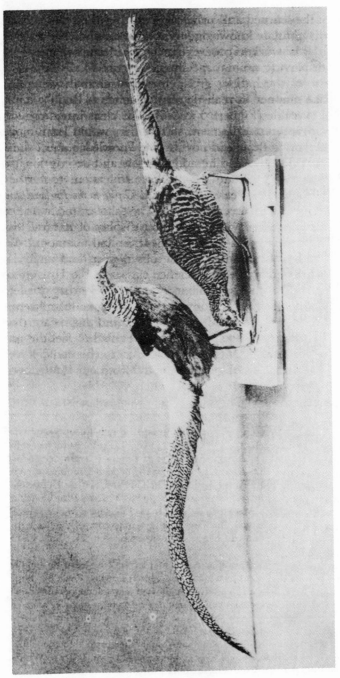

Figure 4

Golden Pheasants. Museum of Comparative Zoology, Harvard University, Cambridge, Massachusetts.

The pheasants were given to George Washington by the Marquis de Lafayette in 1786, and a year later, when they died, donated by Washington to Peale's museum.

Figure 5

White-Headed Eagle. Alexander Lawson, 1811. Hand-colored engraving and etching on paper. Library, The Academy of Natural Sciences of Philadelphia (Collection 79, II: 28).

Lawson's engraving was taken from Alexander Wilson's drawing for his *American Ornithology* (9 volumes, 1808-1813). Wilson, whose drawing of the eagle was undoubtedly based on the specimen in Peale's museum, utilized the museum's well-organized and extensive bird collection for his study of American birds, citing museum catalogue numbers so that readers could refer to actual specimens. Wilson's drawings not only provide a documentary record of the museum's bird collection, but give a good indication of the habitat exhibit form in Peale's museum.

Figure 6

Dusky Wolf Devouring a Mule Deer Head. Titian Ramsay Peale II, 1820. Watercolor on paper. American Philosophical Society, Philadelphia.

Charles Wilson Peale's son made this drawing while on the Long Expedition, and arranged for the specimens to be brought back to the museum to create a mount similar to the drawing. It is one of the only illustrations of a museum habitat group.

The museum soon became highly popular among not only Philadelphians but all Americans and foreign visitors, achieving its founder's goal of involving large numbers of people in a democratic cultural and intellectual experience. One indication of the museum's national (and indeed international) popularity and renown was the range and extent of the individuals who donated specimens and artifacts to it. Peale received items from such disparate people as local Pennsylvania artisans and farmers and the most eminent scientists in the United States and Europe. Geographically, items came to the museum from the settled areas of the east coast but also from the frontier regions of North (Figure 7) and South America, the Pacific Islands, and the Orient. It was this far-flung network of donors, acting independently and voluntarily, that provided both the mundane and exotic items that made up the museum's collections. The two-volume list of accessions, totaling some 192 closely written manuscript pages, is testimony to the general desire of the age to collect, classify, and observe the elements of the physical and man-made worlds. During the second decade of the nineteenth century, the museum contained (among other things) 269 paintings, 1,824 birds, 250 quadrupeds, 650 fishes, over 1,000 shells, and 313 books in the library; according to one authority the total number of all objects was over 100,000.[8]

Further evidence about the museum's popularity can be found in figures for the institution's income and attendance. After some shaky years in the 1790s when the museum brought in revenues fluctuating from $1,172 to $3,301 a year, income traced a continuously upward path during the first two decades of the nineteenth century: $2,910 was received in 1800; $4,213 in 1805; $8,380 in 1810; $9,905 in 1815; and $11,924 in 1816, the peak year. Lacking other evidence, rough figures for annual attendance can be derived from the museum's receipts since Peale depended solely on visitors for income; he received no subsidies and apparently did not accept (or was not offered) cash donations (Figure 8). A precise figure for attendance cannot be derived from the receipts because Peale had special admission packages such as yearly tickets and charged additional fees for special exhibits or events. Given an admission fee of 25 cents, however, a rough count of the number of visitors can be extrapolated from the

---

[8] Peale's Museum, 1803-1842, Records & Accessions, F:XIA/3-5. David C. Ward is working on an analysis of the accessions list to create a collective biography of museum donors. The totals of the museum's collection are in Sellers, *Charles Willson Peale*, 346.

Figure 7

Plains Hunting Shirt, 1806-1807. Peabody Museum of Archaeology and Ethnology, Harvard University, Cambridge, Massachusetts (HU 53041).

The hunting shirt was probably part of the collection of artifacts and objects from the Lewis and Clark expedition that Thomas Jefferson donated to the museum in 1809.

Figure 8

Ticket to the Museum. Engraved by Charles Willson Peale, 1788. Peale family descent to Elise Peale Patterson de Gelpi-Toro.

figures for yearly revenue. This gives an attendance of 11,620 people in 1800, 16,862 in 1805, 33,520 in 1810, and 39,620 in 1815. The peak year of 1816 may have seen 47,696 people enter the museum, this in a city whose population was 69,403 in 1800 and 91,874 in 1810.[9]

Despite the museum's popular success, almost from the beginning Peale realized that his vision for it was beyond the capacity of any one person to realize and, moreover, that if he continued expanding his collections the museum would soon become an institution of general value to the city, the state, and the republic as a whole. In 1792 he published an address "To the Citizens of the United States of America" in *Dunlap's American Daily Advertiser* expressing his gratitude to those who donated specimens, indicating his desire to expand his collections, and admitting that his "design" was "so vast" as to be "far beyond the slender abilities of an individual . . . ." His hope was that the importance and magnitude "of the object" would attract more public support and "enable him to raise this tender plant, until it shall grow into full maturity, and become a *National Museum*." Peale's conception of the utility of the museum meant that state aid was not only desirable but imperative because the museum contributed to the general welfare. Additionally, public support for the museum would be valuable in ensuring its growth and prosperity and in providing for its continuity once he and his family were gone. State aid, in Peale's view, was the only means to provide funds for the day-to-day operation of the museum as well as the solid institutional foundation which would ensure its future.[10]

In looking to receive government support Peale was influenced by European precedent and practice. Peale well knew of the European policy of state aid for institutions devoted to learning and science. Peale also had received the encouragement of European scientists and statesmen that he should and would receive state support. For example, after a private audience with Jefferson in 1805, the naturalist Alexander von Humboldt reported to Peale that he found it inconceivable that the American government would not make the museum a national institution. Similarly, the French envoy Phillipe Rose Roume wrote to Peale, using the image of the enlightening sun

---

[9] Museum attendance is calculated from the tables of museum income in 1808-1819. Peale's Museum, Current Expenditures, F:XIA/5; Susan Edith Klepp, "Philadelphia in Transition: A Demographic History of the City and Its Occupational Groups, 1720-1830" (Ph.D. diss., University of Pennsylvania 1980), 342.

[10] Peale, "To the Citizens of the United States of America," *Dunlap's American Daily Advertiser*, Jan. 13, 1792.

to describe the effect of the museum on the American people and concluding that Peale's efforts had entitled him to the "droit incontestable" of public support.[11]

At the time Peale founded his museum he did not feel it necessary to delineate with precision its public and private nature because political and economic theory allowed a blurring of these categories with regard to activities and institutions viewed as promoting the general welfare. It was understood in post-revolutionary America that activities which could be shown as eventually useful to the community, and which would not otherwise be undertaken, should be given encouragement by the state. Americans looked to the state governments as the guardians and promoters of the public interest; nor was the term public interest construed in a narrow sense. Projects in agriculture, manufacturing, commerce, the arts and science, and education were to be given careful consideration when seeking state aid. In his 1803 address to the Massachusetts legislature, Governor Caleb Strong noted that in the ideal commonwealth a wise government, its power resting in the people, would direct and aid diverse pursuits so that private advantage and the public good would "concur." In his address to the same legislature a few years later, Elbridge Gerry declared that state aid and patronage to varied pursuits "cannot be too much encouraged and supported." A political economist of the early nineteenth century argued that even special interests and monopolies were not to be denied aid if it could be shown that the "general interest of the community is still the object in view . . . [or that there would be as much reason] for the interest of the community to make the grant, as for . . . [the special interest or individual] to receive it." Local and state governments frequently intervened in such privately sponsored economic enterprises as turnpikes, canals, banks, and bridges which were regarded as essential public services requiring support or guarantees beyond the capacity of individuals; state legislatures also aided private universities and colleges in the post-revolutionary era. The American Philosophical Society, America's first learned society, was perhaps Peale's model with regard to the question of state patronage of science and education. Before the revolution the society's greatest source of income was the Pennsylvania assembly, and the legislature continued to aid the society, although to a

---

[11] Von Humboldt's conviction that the Jefferson administration would aid Peale is in Peale's Diary, 20, F:IID/19-20; see also Phillipe Rose Roume to Peale, Jan. 4, 1802, in Miller, Hart, and Ward, eds., *Peale: The Artist as Museum Keeper*, 381-386.

lesser extent, after independence. In a similar example, which Peale probably knew about, the government of Massachusetts had founded and then aided the American Academy of Arts and Sciences.[12]

Given this practice and climate of opinion it was reasonable that Peale should attempt to demonstrate that his museum was one of the institutions that contributed to the general welfare of society and seek aid from the state and national governments. Peale conducted a campaign in the press to create a nationwide awareness of his museum and its beneficial consequences for American society. He published a series of appeals to the American public like the one already mentioned and he wrote or commissioned other articles for the press arguing in favor of such positions as the public benefits of natural history museums. In order to disseminate information about the museum and natural history to the public more efficiently, Peale acquired a printing press in 1804. As he wrote to a fellow naturalist, having a press "will enable me to do many useful things to defuse Knowledge of Natural History and show the importance of such an Institution. This must be done, before I can exert to obtain government patronage." This educational campaign was intended to buttress Peale's more direct appeals for state aid such as in 1792 when he submitted his first memorial to the Pennsylvania state legislature. This appeal requested that a committee be appointed to visit his museum and determine the "proper pecuniary aid" to be contributed by the state. The legislature tabled the memorial, perhaps, as Peale optimistically believed, because it was simply submitted too late in the session. Not discouraged, Peale made several more attempts during the 1790s to obtain aid from Pennsylvania, but while he did receive favorable responses from legislative committees, he was not successful in getting the legislature to act in his favor.[13]

Having failed to obtain direct financial aid from the legislature, Peale's next campaign for state aid, beginning in the winter of 1800, was to obtain a larger building for his museum and its increasing number of specimens. There were two suitable buildings available:

---

[12] Oscar Handlin and Mary Flug Handlin, *Commonwealth: A Study of the Role of Government in the American Economy: Massachusetts, 1774-1861* (New York 1947), 53-56, 104; Governor Elbridge Gerry to the Massachusetts House and Senate, *Salem Gazette*, June 12, 1810; George Rogers Taylor, *The Transportation Revolution, 1815-1860* (New York 1951), 378-383; Brooke Hindle, *The Pursuit of Science in Revolutionary America, 1735-1789* (Chapel Hill, N.C. 1956), 140.

[13] Peale to Dr. Edward Stevens, June 28, 1805, F:IIA/35A11-13; Miller, Hart, and Ward, eds., *Peale: The Artist as Museum Keeper*, 19, 24, 83, 85, 138.

Independence Hall, which was vacant following the shift of Pennsylvania's capital to Lancaster; and Congress Hall, which would become vacant when the federal government left the city the following spring. Peale published an address in the newspapers to the "People of America and Citizens of Philadelphia." Philadelphians, he wrote, should be proud of the museum, but he warned them that if they would not "make exertions to foster an important school for their own and their children's use . . . some other city in the Union will rejoice in receiving my labours." And he reminded all Americans that "England, France, Italy, not only boast of their Museums, but cherish them from the public funds." Peale submitted a memorial to the state legislature "praying the loan of one of the unoccupied buildings in the city of Philadelphia . . . ." On February 24, 1800, the petition was read in the lower house of the legislature, tabled, and no further action was taken.[14]

Peale did not allow these setbacks to divert him from overseeing the expansion and improvement of the museum. Most importantly, in 1801 he learned of a significant find of fossil bones in New York state. With an interest-free loan from the American Philosophical Society, Peale organized an expedition that succeeded in exhuming and eventually reconstructing two almost complete skeletons of the American mastodon (Figure 9). The exhumation of the mastodon can be considered the first organized scientific expedition in the United States and Peale's accurate recreation of the skeletons was of immense importance in the history of paleontology (Figure 10). It is worth noting that in constructing the skeletons Peale pioneered modern museum practice and techniques by using carved models to substitute for missing bones and carefully noting which sections of the skeleton were man-made. The mastodon enormously increased the reputation, prestige, and popularity of the museum; as a result, overcrowding became an even more severe problem. To solve the problem of the museum's lack of space, once again Peale sought government patronage.[15]

---

[14] Peale, "Address to the Public," Philadelphia *Aurora General Advertiser*, Jan. 27, 1800. See also Peale's letters soliciting state support for the museum to William Findley, Feb. 18, 1800, F:IIA/23A6-10; Thomas McKean, Mar. 3, 1800, F:IIA/23B3-4; and Timothy Matlack, Mar. 9, 1800, F:IIA/23B5-6.

[15] The scientific background to the exhumation of the mastodon and an assessment of Peale's achievement is found in a headnote introduction, written by David C. Ward, to the relevant documents, in Miller, Hart, and Ward, eds., *Peale: The Artist as Museum Keeper*, 308-313; see also John C. Greene, *The Death of Adam: Evolution and Its Impact on Western Thought* (Ames, Iowa 1959), 112-115; and George Gaylord Simpson, "The Beginnings of Vertebrate Paleontology in North America," *American Philosophical Society Proceedings*, 86 (Sept. 1942), 130-188.

On January 12, 1802, Peale wrote to President Jefferson (Figure 11) about his desire to make his museum a permanent public institution. Although he emphasized the utility of such an institution, Peale's description became lyrical as he "imagined" a great collection which "in one view" would "enlighten the minds of . . . [his] countrymen" by exhibiting the "wonderful and various beauties of Nature." Such an institution would prove to be "more powerful to humanize the mind, promote harmony, and aid virtue, than any other School yet imagened." And as a result, his arduous labor in collecting and preserving specimens would not end in their dispersal after his death, but "would be crown'd in a National Establishment . . . ." He wanted to know Jefferson's "sentiments" about "whether the United States would give an encouragement, and make provision for the establishment of this Museum in the City of Washington."[16]

Jefferson, in his reply four days later, acknowledged the great value of Peale's collection, and praised the museum keeper's "unwearied perseverance & skill" in collecting and preserving specimens. He wished that the museum "could be made public property," but feared that Peale would allow his (Jefferson's) "partiality" to the museum "to excite false expectations . . . which might eventually be disappointed." Jefferson explained that the issue rested on "one of the great questions which has divided political opinion in this country . . . Whether Congress are authorised by the constitution to apply the public money to any but the purposes specially enumerated in the Constitution?" Members of his own party, Jeffersonian Republicans, who limited Congress to those powers enumerated—strict constructionists in modern parlance—"have always denied that Congress have any power to establish a National academy." But some of these Republicans, Jefferson added, "still wish Congress had power to favor science, and that an amendment should be proposed to the constitution, giving them such power specifically." Jefferson further noted that if a majority of the Congress believed that the national government had the power to establish a national university, Peale's museum would be purchased as the first step toward creating such an institution. But as an astute politician Jefferson knew that a majority in Congress were strict constructionists. Indeed, when Joel Barlow proposed a plan for a national university in 1807, which Jefferson

---

[16] Peale to Thomas Jefferson, Jan. 12, 1802, F:IIA/25A14-B3.

Figure 9

The Exhumation of the Mastodon. Charles Willson Peale, 1806-1808. Oil on canvas. The Peale Museum, Baltimore.

Peale's history painting shows the extent of the equipment, manpower, and organization that was necessary to exhume the skeletons. Peale, holding a drawing of one of the bones, directs operations in the right foreground.

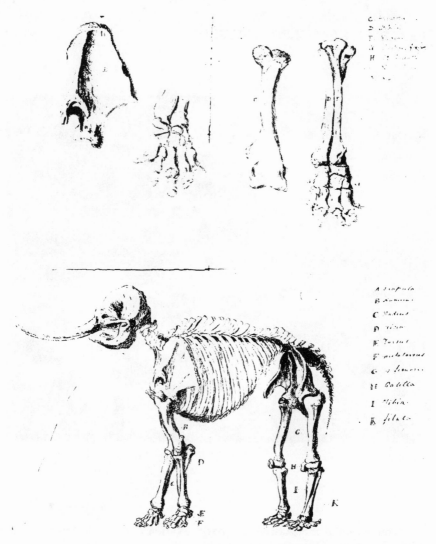

Figure 10

Working Sketch of the Mastodon. Rembrandt Peale, 1801. Ink and water-color on paper. American Philosophical Society, Philadelphia.

In 1806 the French naturalist and paleontologist Georges Cuvier wrote that it was the work of the Peales in recovering, assembling, and describing the skeletons that made his classification of the extinct American mastodon possible.

Figure 11

Thomas Jefferson. Rembrandt Peale, c. 1800. Oil on canvas. White House Collection.

favored and viewed as a "means" of satisfying his friend Peale and nationalizing the museum, it went down to defeat in Congress.[17]

Bowing to political realities, Peale accepted Jefferson's judgment with respect "to an Application to congress," and in February 1802 he reopened his campaign for state support by presenting memorials to the house and senate of Pennsylvania seeking aid in obtaining a larger building for his museum. The legislature this time responded positively and granted Peale the use of the vacant Independence Hall (or State House as it was also known). Peale welcomed the legislature's action, little suspecting that it would be virtually the only support he would receive from the state. Indeed, just in order to keep Independence Hall, Peale would have to regularly lobby the legislature for their continued support, and perform a variety of other tasks such as maintaining order in the State House yard, a popular gathering place for drunks and prostitutes. In addition, starting in 1815 he had to pay a rental fee (previously he had only to maintain the building), a fee which would increase regularly and be the subject of much wrangling between the Peales and the state, and later the city of Philadelphia.[18]

Peale's dream that his museum would become a public institution was never attained. Its collections were sold and dispersed, and after the museum was purchased by P.T. Barnum in 1848, fires in 1851 and 1865 destroyed most of the collection. Existing explanations of the reasons for the museum's ultimate failure rely on the notion that the museum was ahead of its time and—there are two versions to this argument—that it was the forerunner of either P.T. Barnum or the twentieth-century Smithsonian Institution. Historians who see Peale as the forerunner of Barnum argue that, contrary to Peale's stated intentions, the museum was never a serious educational institution and that Peale was merely a "showman" who earned a good income by exploiting the public's fascination with unusual and exotic displays. One historian of science, who at least acknowledges Peale's goal of making the museum an institution of public education, nonetheless concludes that the "reality fell short of the ideal" and that the

---

[17] Thomas Jefferson to Peale, Jan. 16, 1802, F:IIA/25B7-8; Peale to Thomas Jefferson, Dec. 13, 1806, F:IIA/39F4-5; Dumas Malone, *Jefferson the President: Second Term, 1805-1809* (Boston 1974), 554-555.

[18] Peale to Thomas Jefferson, Jan. 21, 1802, F:IIA/25C1-2; Miller, Hart, and Ward, eds., *Peale: The Artist as Museum Keeper*, 390-392, 393-396; Edward M. Riley, "The Independence Hall Group," in *Historic Philadelphia: From the Founding Until the Early Nineteenth Century*, American Philosophical Society *Transactions*, 43 (Mar. 1953), 30-33.

legislators, like most of the visitors, "regarded the museum as a kind of show . . . [and] were impressed by Peale's financial success but took it as proof that his museum did not need public support." The view comparing Peale's museum to the Smithsonian is far more complimentary: the reality did achieve the ideal, but society was not ready to support that ideal. The two components of that ideal, which have been realized in the twentieth century, are Peale's democratic concept of a museum of all classes, the research scientist as well as the general public, and his method of displaying specimens in habitat groups, which satisfied the specialist and provided, in Peale's terms, "rational amusement" for the populace. In this interpretation, Peale's museum failed because it was ahead of its time—a twentieth-century institution that could not obtain public support in the nineteenth century.[19]

Both these interpretations are ahistorical and fail to treat Peale in context. An incident in 1806 illustrates the point that Peale was very much a man of his time, but one who did not perceive that times were changing. The American Philosophical Society had permitted Peale to borrow its elephant skeleton to display alongside the mastodon but only on the understanding that he not advertise the elephant. The society knew full well that Peale depended on publicity and advertisements for attendance and income; their attitude indicates that they resented the commercial aspect of the museum. Superficially, the incident would seem to confirm that Peale was a precursor of Barnum: Peale as nineteenth-century showman. For Peale, however, the categories were not so easily defined. The ideal in Peale's time—the eighteenth-century Enlightenment—was to unify separate realms of behavior and knowledge. Peale sought to close the gap between popular entertainment and scientific knowledge, and considered it proper and desirable to advertise an attraction if that would bring people into the museum for enlightenment.[20]

In Peale's mind the commercial dimension was far less distinct from the public realm than it would be in the nineteenth and twenti-

---

[19] George H. Daniels, *Science in American Society: A Social History* (New York 1971), 130, 160; John C. Greene, *American Science in the Age of Jefferson* (Ames, Iowa 1984), 26-27. Greene cites no evidence to support the summation that the museum was regarded as merely a show. Neil Harris, *Humbug: The Art of P.T. Barnum* (Boston 1973), covers the rise of the sensational displays and exhibits of the late nineteenth century.

[20] American Philosophical Society, *Early Proceedings of the American Philosophical Society* (Philadelphia 1884), 381.

eth centuries. In 1800 he wrote William Findley, a Pennsylvania state legislator, arguing that his museum be made a state institution. Peale believed it was his duty to come to the legislature at a time when he was still able to aid in the further development of the museum and make it an important educational institution "by blending the amusing & the useful." As for his own individual gain or profit, he believed that he did "not ask for any advantage" for himself "which will not produce greater benefits for the State." He saw no inconsistency in the legislature making the museum a public institution and also "allowing profits" to him and his heirs. That the state legislators viewed the museum as a "show" which earned a profit did not mean that Peale conceived of himself as acting as a showman. Rather Peale's conceptions of public/private and education/amusement had not evolved (as they were beginning to for the legislators) into their separate and distinct nineteenth-century realms; in the fluid situation of the early years of the century the two parties were speaking across each other in different languages.[21]

Peale's very sense of an educational institution derived from the Enlightenment's sense of the unity and utility of knowledge. In many ways, the history of his museum mirrors the experiences of eighteenth-century learned societies in America. The most prominent of these societies—the American Philosophical Society—was established as a general body of learning in the expectation that the knowledge it generated would have application in such important areas of society as agriculture, manufacturing, and commerce. Benjamin Franklin's (Figure 12) circular letter of 1743 proposing the Philosophical Society set forth a long list of activities that would be the legitimate concerns of the new society. The list included investigations of plants, cures for diseases, labor saving mechanical inventions, "Arts, Trades, Manufactures . . . Surveys, Maps and Charts," husbandry, and "New Improvements in Planting." For Franklin, all of these miscellaneous investigations into "the Nature of Things" were a unity because they would "increase the Power of Man over Matter, and multiply the Conveniences or Pleasures of Life." Similarly, Peale's vision for his museum was that it become a repository in which "every art and every science should be taught . . . . To this central magazine of knowledge, all the learned and ingenious would flock, as well to gain,

---

[21] Peale to William Findley, Feb. 18, 1800, F:IIA/23A6-10. The development of distinct public and private spheres is surveyed in Richard Sennett, *The Fall of Public Man* (New York 1976).

Figure 12

Benjamin Franklin. Charles Willson Peale, 1785. Oil on canvas. The Pennsylvania Academy of the Fine Arts, Philadelphia.

as to communicate, information." Man would thus be able to achieve the same mastery and power as Franklin had envisioned: to know "from the combination of certain things the results" by comparing "the present with the past," to "calculate the revolution of the Planets," to "produce by the labor of the hands various and wonderful works of art, and with knowledge of the . . . lever, the screw, & the wedge . . . make machines to lessen labour, and multiply the conveniences & comforts of Life." All this man is able to accomplish when he has at hand, as in a museum, the "subjects" of "nature" with which to "analize & know the component parts . . . by actual experiments." The inclusiveness of Peale's museum thus reflected the all but pervasive belief in the Enlightenment that all knowledge had unity and utility. This belief was an Enlightenment axiom that reached its highest expression in Diderot's *Encyclopedia*, which had as its goal to collect, classify, and disseminate the universal body of knowledge. The eighteenth century's learned societies shared this objective and Peale's museum—the world in miniature—was an even more explicit statement of this philosophy and one which came close to translating the ideal into reality.[22]

Toward the end of the eighteenth century this vision of unity began to unravel; the pattern is clearly shown in the histories of the American Academy of Arts and Sciences and the American Philosophical Society. The founders of these institutions had expected that their organizations would be making significant contributions to society. But by the late eighteenth century these organizations were being criticized as too general, too "universal," in their programs and research. In the last decade of the century organizations limited in scope to specific aspects of manufacturing or agriculture, such as the advancement of an industry or the improvement of a breed, were formed in nearly all the states in order to address specific economic or scientific needs of American society. The multiplication of these societies by 1800 is seen as an indication that the broad, universal approach to knowledge formulated in the Enlightenment had broken down. To a great degree, Peale's argument for the public support of

---

[22] For the Enlightenment's ideal or "faith" in the "great unity of human knowledge" and the view of science as "a kind of cosmic education," see Charles C. Gillispie, "The Natural History of Industry," in A. E. Musson, ed., *Science, Technology, and Economic Growth in the Eighteenth Century* (London 1972), 131-132; and Franklin's circular letter, quoted in Boorstin, *The Lost World of Thomas Jefferson*, 9-11; see also Charles Willson Peale, *Discourse Introductory to a Course of Lectures on the Science of Nature* (Philadelphia 1800), 35; and Miller, Hart, and Ward, eds., *Peale: The Artist as Museum Keeper*, 706-707.

his museum was predicated on the public utility of the museum, which in turn looked back to the old Enlightenment faith that all knowledge was unified and useful, and that all classes of people— "the unwise as [well] as the learned"—would appreciate and value the "importance of a well organized Museum . . . ." With a large segment of the public suspicious that scientists were more interested in abstract research than in knowledge that would have practical application, it was not possible to build a great deal of public support for science in general. On the other hand, it was indicative also of the elitist attitudes of American scientists and their distrust of popular science when more and more of them in the early nineteenth century dismissed as unworthy Peale's belief that the public's interest in the curious and unusual, used with care, could contribute to the popularity of science. Peale failed in his attempt to turn popular opinion in America to the support of science, and also in his attempt to get scientists to seek popular support. The museum's failure was in part a consequence of its being in an age of great scientific discovery but one in which science was not widely appreciated by the general public. The unpopularity of science, and the scientists' distrust of popularity, was in part a consequence of the breakdown of the unified view of knowledge and science that prevailed during the Enlightenment. Government support on the state or local level would also not be possible once the Enlightenment's unified view no longer prevailed. The breakdown of this unity undermined the support the museum would need in the nineteenth century if it were to be made into a public institution.[23]

The importance of Peale's museum was long minimized by scholars who saw Peale's activity as a museum "showman" as a declension from his career as an artist. Subsequent work, most notably by Charles Coleman Sellers, has refuted this negative interpretation and established the importance of the museum in the history of American culture. Sellers also correctly saw that Peale's operation of the museum was the logical consequence of an integrated and coherent world view; the exhibition of the unities and harmonies of nature was a natural outgrowth of much that went into his painting. But in arguing the case for the importance of the museum, Sellers and others have

---

[23] Peale to Philippe Rose Roume, Dec. 25, 1803, F:IIA/29C6-8; John C. Greene, "Science and the Public in the Age of Jefferson," *Isis*, 49 (Mar. 1958), 13-26; Daniels, *Science in American Society*, 152-156; Hindle, *The Pursuit of Science in Revolutionary America*, 357-359; Greene, *American Science in the Age of Jefferson*, 4-26.

perhaps gone too far in stressing the prototypical aspects of the institution. In a kind of Whig interpretation of museums, the Peale museum is almost seen as a twentieth-century museum in eighteenth- and nineteenth-century Philadelphia because of its anticipation of modern museum techniques. What we have demonstrated is the extent to which Peale's conception of the museum straddled two worlds, an ultimately untenable situation. While the layout of the museum did anticipate modern practice, the philosophy underlying its operation was rooted in an eighteenth-century Enlightenment conception of the unity and utility of all knowledge. In the nineteenth century the "universalism" of Peale's "world in miniature" would be increasingly questioned by those who, skeptical of such all-inclusive visions, would only support institutions and interests that were able to demonstrate an immediate practical utility to the state and society. Through unceasing effort Peale was able to keep the museum operating but a culture increasingly unresponsive to his claim to serve the general good meant that he would be unable to complete his life's task and ensure that his museum would be handed down to posterity.

College Founding in the
New Republic, 1776–1800

DAVID W. ROBSON

DURING THE TWENTY-FIVE YEARS, 1776–1800, sixteen colleges opened in the United States that still operate today.[1] They almost tripled the total number of the nation's colleges. The increase demonstrated the augmenting American interest in higher education and also the restless, expansive urge of the American people, for with the exceptions of the College of Charleston and St. John's College in the Chesapeake port of Annapolis,[2] these institutions arose on the edge of settlement: in upstate New York, the district of Maine, northeastern Georgia, western Massachusetts, and even in the Territory South of the Ohio, two years before it became the state of Tennessee. Indeed, their location on the frontier was one of the primary determinants of these colleges' character, for it led these colleges to develop functions, commitments, and curricular and atmospheric traits that differed somewhat from those of the established, seaboard colleges.

Just as these new institutions were frontier colleges, they were also republican colleges. During the Revolutionary movement the colonial colleges had become politicized; the majority had embraced what Bernard Bailyn and others have called the Commonwealth Whig ideology of politics. Consequently, by the mid-1760s, college educators emphasized the link between higher education and virtuous leadership of the state. For example, the supporters of Rhode Island College, clearly intending to train Baptist ministers, found it necessary in petitioning the legislature for a charter to note:

> Whereas, Institutions for liberal education are highly beneficial to society by forming the rising generation to virtue, knowledge, and useful literature, and thus, preserving in a community a succession of men qualified for discharging the offices of life with usefulness and reputation. . . a public school or seminary. . . would be for the general advantage and honor of the government.

This sentiment did not fade in the post-war period. Yale's Ezra Stiles made the same connection in even stronger terms in 1783, having had his convictions sharpened by Revolution:

> The cultivation of literature will greatly promote the public welfare. In every community, while provision is made that all should be taught to read the Scriptures,

---

Mr. Robson is an historian of early America living in Laramie, Wyoming.

Fall 1983 323

and the very useful parts of common education, a good proportion should be carried through the higher branches of literature . . . [for they] will form the civilian, the judge, the senator, the patrician, the man of useful eminence in society. . . . It would be for the public emolument should there always be found a sufficient number of men in the community at large of vast and profound erudition, and perfect acquaintance with the whole system of public affairs, to illuminate the public councils. . . .[4]

Founded then, at the height of the republican experiment, these new colleges joined with their established peers in the effort to produce good citizens in and leaders of the new nation. The Revolutionary legacy acted as a force for continuity between the new, frontier colleges and the older, seaboard institutions.

The focus here is on the interplay between the disrupting influence of the frontier and the continuity produced by the political legacy of the Revolution in three areas of collegiate life: founding motives, the nature of the curriculum, and the aspirations and concerns of the students.

When men of the post-Revolutionary generation convened to consider founding a college, they faced the question of what the college should do for the students. The Revolution had influenced the colleges in the settled areas to aspire to produce virtuous citizens, fit members in and leaders of the new republic. The goals of the new colleges had to be similar. This was both a case of seeking common ground and equal respectability with the existing colleges and one of sincere conviction on the part of college founders. James Bowdoin, the patron of Bowdoin College in the District of Maine, was certain that education was responsible for "Constitution, laws, religion, and morals, which pursued in all their ramifications determine the fate of a country; whether it shall be virtuous, prosperous, and happy, or vicious, unfortunate, and wretched." A supporter of Franklin, the ethnically-oriented new college in Lancaster, Pennsylvania, asserted that

The Germans, on account of their peculiar virtues, have hitherto been very necessary members of the Republic; but they have not considered that a true Republican must also possess education, so as to take part in directing the rudder of government, and to give his children the opportunity of rising to the higher levels of republican utility.

University of North Carolina advocates held that "nothing can be more conducive to the existence of liberty, than such a system of education as gives every citizen the opportunity of gaining knowledge and fitting him for places of trust." The idea of a virtuous republican education also appeared in support of Union College, the University of Vermont, and Washington College in Maryland.[5]

The charters of Virginia's Washington College and Hampden-Sydney, Pennsylvania's Dickinson, and Blount College in Tennessee proclaimed the necessity of a proper education of youth to preserve happiness, tranquility, prosperity, and a "succession of able and honest men, for discharging the various offices and duties of the community. . . ." The argument was best phrased in the charter of the University of Georgia:

As it is the distinguishing happiness of Free governments that civil order should be the result of choice and not necessity, and the common wishes of the people become the law of the land, their public prosperity and even existence much depends on suitably forming the minds and morals of the citizens. . . . This is an influence beyond the stretch of laws and can be claimed only by religion and education. It should therefore be among the first objects of those who wish well to the national prosperity to encourage and support the principles of religion and morality, and to early place the youth under the forming hand of society that by instruction they may be molded to the love of virtue and good order.[6]

A recognition that collegiate education played a part in shaping the political attitudes of students and that it therefore must aspire to insure the viability of the republican form of government thus linked the founding motives of the new colleges to the educational purposes of the old.

This concern for promoting republicanism was not the only motive for college founding. Another important goal of the new colleges was "civilizing" the frontiersmen. These new institutions were remote from established centers of learning and culture. Their founders were anxious that the colleges bring the people they served up to the level prevailing in the established centers. This desire received support from two separate sources. First, college founders were often clergy or devout laymen educated at established colleges who looked at the frontier as both an opportunity and a challenge. It was an opportunity in that they could take the orthodox gospel into the unsettled areas to minister to hundreds of thousands of the unchurched. It was a challenge in that they had to use both that gospel and education to prevent the frontier from descending into barbarism through lack of culture and religion.[7] Secondly, frontiersmen themselves recognized their lack of culture and polish, a defect they earnestly desired to correct. To be sure, they did not wish to emulate completely the characteristics of Easterners. Many of them would not have left the settled areas had they felt comfortable there. Rather, they wanted a minimum of polish, enough to be considered as Americans, not savages.

The civilizing theme, then, loomed large in the founders' minds. Benjamin Rush hoped that Dickinson and Franklin would "humanize even the half-civilized inhabitants of the western counties of Pennsylvania." The Dutch Reformed missionary Michael Schlatter, also interested in Franklin College, had long felt that the Germans needed education; "if there are no schools, provided with qualified schoolmasters, of which there are almost none, or very few, will not the children who are not instructed in reading and writing, in two or at least in three generations, become like the pagan aborigines?" The founders of Greeneville College in Tennessee, Kentucky's Transylvania College, and the University of Georgia wanted to avoid "degenerating into ignorance and barbarism." The desire of the supporters of Maine's Bowdoin College, and Union College in upstate New York to provide higher education for residents of their areas at lower cost than would be possible if they attended the established schools was implicit recognition of the need for civilization.[8]

329

And the desire to establish a uniform identity with the rest of the nation was apparent in the attitude of the legislatures of Vermont and North Carolina, each holding that the ratification of the Constitution required the establishment of a college in the state.[9]

Even what appeared to be state political disputes were at least partially offshoots of the desire to civilize the frontier. In Pennsylvania Benjamin Rush had backed off from his enthusiastic republicanism after 1776, disheartened by popular excesses in the name of democracy. Resolving to help change the state constitution, Rush urged the founding of both Dickinson and Franklin as moderating influences in democratic territory, as intellectual counterweights to Philadelphia. Rush admitted he was counting on "my German brethren [who are] . . . the future reservoirs and vehicles to posterity, of a great part of the knowledge, virtue, and religion of Pennsylvania. . . . [On you] I rely chiefly to outvote, to outwork, and to out pray the anti-Federalists in our state." For Rush, part of the frontier's barbarity was its inclination toward democracy. He hoped the college would reform the area.[10]

After the revolution South Carolina wanted colleges; the question was where. The natural location was Charleston, but the backcountrymen had acquired power and, just as they had succeeded in moving the capital from Charleston to Columbia and in disestablishing the Anglican church, so they forced a compromise on the education issue. In 1785 the legislature decided to establish three colleges, at Winnesborough and Camden in the backcountry, and at Charleston. Perhaps the frontiersmen were precipitous, for only the Charleston school survived the eighteenth century.[11]

The foundation motives of these new colleges are significant. They demonstrate that the political character of higher education, attributable at the older institutions to changes embraced in the Revolutionary movement, was built in at the start of the frontier colleges. Laymen, and even governments, joined with politicized sectarian ministers to use all the colleges to produce fit leaders of the state as well as the church. Yet the motives also reveal that if the political goals were the same, what was needed to achieve them was not. On the frontier civilizing the students was a prerequisite to politicizing them. College founders recognized this and campaigned against barbarism as well as for republicanism.

The political legacy of the Revolution and the cultural demands of the frontier carried over into the college curriculum. In the main, the new colleges sought to emulate the old. Ten of the fourteen whose pre-1800 curricula are known[12] borrowed from established American colleges. This imitation meant that their basic curricula were much the same—a foundation in the classics, studies in English and possibly modern languages, an expanding role for mathematics and natural sciences, and the Revolution everywhere produced a heightened recognition of the worth of history and government in producing good citizens. But the frontier intervened to thwart the effort to reproduce the established colleges' curricula. The reasons were many. The limited initial assets of many colleges did not allow the total implementation of the desired curriculum. The one-man domination of most new colleges, invariably by a clerical president who might or might not be sympathetic to all branches of learning, produced the same result. Then, too, the curricular models these men chose were sometimes out of date, reflecting the more limited educational focus of their own college days. Finally there were the conditions imposed by the frontiersmen themselves. Often they needed grammar school education to prepare them for college. Moreover, despite their cultural yearnings, they were often more interested in the practical, useful skills than in "civilized" trappings. Mathematics, construction arts, bookkeeping, and the rudiments of law and medicine often had more allure than the learned languages, metaphysics, or moral philosophy. How the various frontier colleges overcame these obstacles differentiated them from the seaboard colleges and, to a degree, from each other.

Two of the frontier colleges used curricular models other than those of the established colleges and enjoyed little success before the turn of the century. Franklin College started in 1787 with several professors to offer bilingual instruction to Pennsylvania's Germans, thus following no American model. The college soon experienced many problems. German instruction was intended to produce ministers for the local churches, demonstrating the local clerical founders' affinity for German pietism, but the religious atmosphere drove off both students, most of whom enrolled only in the English school, and many financial backers, who did not believe German-speaking ministers would promote Americanism. Financial distress brought faculty resignations and separation of the German and English schools in 1788. Both continued only as academies.[13]

Dickinson College was American in form but had no clear antecedent. Benjamin Rush, acquainted with the colleges in Philadelphia and Princeton, was active in Dickinson's founding, but indifferent thereafter. Charles Nisbet, the Scots-Presbyterian minister who presided over the college, came out of the same environment that had produced John Witherspoon and shared the Common Sense Philosophy with him, but had little influence with the trustees. They shaped the curriculum on their own, at first following the older colleges. Dickinson's program was three years, including the republican classics and full courses in both natural philosophy, mathematics, and astronomy, and in moral philosophy, history, and chronology. Rhetoric, belles-lettres, and criticism also received attention. Nisbet's moral philosophy and public law lectures emphasized politics, covering such topics as the law of nature and nations, political parties, the forms of government, and the citizen's role in it. The trustees institutionalized republicanism in 1798 when they authorized a special set of lectures on the virtues of republican government, the federal system, state and local government, America's superiority to ancient republics, and of its extension to any size territory. These courses indicate that Dickinson embraced Enlightenment science and study in English, while trying to maintain a republican flavor in its moral, historical, and political offering. It aimed both to civilize its students and to

331

make them good citizens. But in 1798 the college faltered. The frontier students, who had always wanted their "book-learning" fast, demanded a full collegiate course in one year. Despite Nisbet's protests, the trustees capitulated, thereby dramatically reducing the value of the education. This was an extreme reaction to frontier conditions and one that left the college in a troubled limbo between respectability and infamy for some years.[14]

Dickinson and Franklin were exceptions. The rest of the colleges followed established American models. But how the colleges implemented their curricula depended on their environments and leadership. Despite many variations a pattern emerges. The new college founded in an area that had previously sent its sons to an established institution usually stuck closely to the plan of studies followed at that institution. Where settlement was too recent to have allowed college attendance, the new colleges were more inclined to experiment with their curricula.

In the North Harvard, Yale, the College of Philadelphia, and Princeton were "successful" institutions. Bowdoin, Williams, Washington College in Chestertown, Maryland, and Union were all close enough to these "established" colleges to be competitors for students. They thus followed quite closely their educational examples. A brief analysis of the Williams and Union curricular atmosphere reveals how this process worked.

The Connecticut River Valley in the eighteenth century was a Yale Congregationalist preserve; not surprisingly, many Williams College trustees were Yale-educated. In choosing a president they sought the advice of Yale's Ezra Stiles, who recommended his long-time tutor Ebenezer Fitch. Fitch brought Stiles' curriculum to Williams; the 1795 laws of Williams followed closely the 1787 laws of Yale. In both colleges the freshmen worked principally in classical languages and English; sophomores continued those studies and added logic, rhetoric, geography, and some branches of arithmetic and geometry; juniors continued mathematics with such subjects as trigonometry and surveying, while also beginning natural philosophy and astronomy; and seniors studied metaphysics, ethics, history and civil policy. Like Stiles, Fitch encouraged English composition and frequent forensic disputation. The only significant variations from New Haven practice were the hiring of a French instructor to supplement the Yale-educated tutors, the addition of chemistry to the field of natural philosophy, and Fitch's theological slant, for he had New Divinity leanings and sometimes had his students read Samuel Hopkins' *System of Divinity*. Early Williams was an upriver outpost of Yale.[15]

The Hudson River Valley was fertile field for the Dutch Reformed and the Presbyterians. Union, led by Princetonians John Blair Smith and Jonathan Edwards, Jr., stuck closely to Nassau's example, which meant emphasis on humanities, not science. In fact, the reading of Enfield's *Natural Philosophy* and some few demonstrations with the aid of scientific apparatus constituted Union's commitment to the sciences, and mathematics did not go as far as fluxions.[16] But the languages were important throughout the curriculum.

Students read a wide variety of Latin authors, French could be substituted for Greek, and English introduced Blair's *Lectures,* Rollin, the *Tatler,* the *Guardian,* and the works of Milton and Addison. In history and moral philosophy Union shone. Reading was diverse and extensive, including Hume, Dugald Stewart's *Philosophy of the Mind,* Priestley, Paley, David Ramsay's *History of the American Revolution,* Robertson's history of Scotland, Gibbon, Ferguson, Jefferson's *Notes on the State of Virginia,* Burke, Vattel, Burlamaqui, Blackstone, Doddridge, Hutcheson, and the *Transactions* of the American Philosophical Society. All shades of opinion on things divine, moral, and political appeared. Union's curriculum, closely related to Princeton's, was dominated by old disciplines, yet full of the latest scholarship.[17]

In the South this replication also prevailed, but here some colleges arose in areas so newly settled and so remote from established institutions that their use of the "older" college's curriculum did not conform to a single pattern. An institution such as Hampden-Sydney drew leadership from Princeton graduates of the 1750s and 1760s who perpetuated what they had learned to produce a curriculum rather out of date by Princeton standards, especially those of the 1790s. The University of North Carolina used the Princeton model as a base on which to build an innovative curriculum unlike anything in existence at the established colleges by 1800. And the University of Georgia made use of many years of Yale tradition to develop a curriculum largely New Haven based but with some new twists demanded by its frontier student body. The theme of basic continuity between seaboard and frontier colleges, yet with some differences attributable to the frontier influence, emerges once more.

Hampden-Sydney was the first new Southern college, founded in an area that had sent its Presbyterian sons desiring an education to Princeton. The college began as an academy in 1776 under the direction of Samuel Stanhope Smith, and five other Princetonians were among the trustees. When it received degree granting power in 1783, Samuel's brother John Blair led the college. He was a member of the first Princeton class to matriculate under John Witherspoon, but he chose to keep in place the curriculum his brother had installed, that of Princeton in the early 1760s reduced to three years, for Hampden-Sydney had no freshman class. Actually this produced little curricular alteration, for Princeton students used the senior year for review, undertaking no new studies. The classics dominated both systems: Horace, Cicero's *Orations,* Xenophon, Lucian, and the Greek Testament were staples for all classes. The differences between the curricula were slight: Princeton gave some consideration to natural philosophy while Hampden-Sydney did not, but the Virginia college spent more time with history and chronology than did Princeton. The Hampden-Sydney students did read John Witherspoon's moral philosophy lectures, which fostered both religion and virtue, and were the element of Witherspoon's Princeton most necessary to a college competing with it in Virginia's dissenting community. This program changed little when Archibald Alexander became the college's second president, for, although he had been educated at Virginia's Liberty Hall Academy, his mentor, William Graham, was Princeton, class of 1773. Hampden-Sydney, then, chose to match Princeton as closely as possible in an effort to compete for students, but even by the mid-1780s its curriculum no longer matched that of Nassau, which had incorporated much mathematics and science, and more modern authors in many other subjects.[18]

The University of North Carolina did not slavishly follow Princeton's example, even though it was in Carolina's backcountry, where Presbyterian influence had previously pushed those interested in higher education toward the New Jersey College. William Davie and Samuel McCorkle, both Nassau graduates, determined the original curriculum, which was recognizably Princetonian, with extra features, especially in the sciences. It provided for study of the classics, mathematics, history, and moral philosophy—standard Princeton fare. In addition, the president was to give weekly lectures on agriculture, mineralogy, botany, zoology, architecture, and commerce. This program was a blend of traditional arts and new sciences, differing but slightly from Princeton's, but it was quickly modified. Shortly after the college opened Professor Charles Harris wrote that the trend was toward the practical, that the dead languages were to be dropped. By the end of 1795 a new curriculum placed much more emphasis on English, history, and natural science, while the traditional studies received ambitious upgrading. Rhetoric and belles-lettres incorporated the latest texts. Moral and political philosophy and history would use Paley, Montesquieu, Vattel, Burlamaqui, Priestley, Millot, Hume, the United States Constitution and those of modern Europe; all were recommended reading at Princeton but were not part of the curriculum. These works indicate an earnest effort to teach both piety and rationality, Commonwealth Whig and traditional history, and they demonstrated a great concern for the law. But the most significant new departures included a professorship of chemistry and the philosophies of medicine, the agricultural and the mechanic arts. Natural science ventured into optics, hydrostatics, hydraulics, and magnetism, thus going beyond Princeton. Language instruction emphasized English, with Latin confined to Virgil, Cicero, and Horace, Greek to Lucian and Xenophon. Even the translation of classics to English placed greatest importance on "the spirit and elegance of the translation. . . ." A separate degree program for those desiring to concentrate on English and the sciences enhanced the practical emphasis. The designer of the curriculum, trustee William R. Davie, explained the purpose of separate degrees: "The ruling or leading principle in our plan of education is that the student may apply himself to those branches of learning and science alone which are absolutely necessary to fit him for his destined profession or occupation in life." Too little money and too few professors prevented the full enactment of the program in the eighteenth century, but plainly the University of North Carolina recognized the desirability of a practical education and was not afraid to experiment to attract students.[19]

Franklin College, eventually the University of Georgia, was patterned after

Yale, probably because of the influence of Yale alumni Governor Lyman Hall and Abraham Baldwin, who together convinced the state legislature in 1785 to authorize a university and to appropriate land to endow it. Both men corresponded with Ezra Stiles about the proposed college. When the college finally opened in 1801, Baldwin hired as president Josiah Meigs, recently deposed professor of natural philosophy at Yale. Meigs might have been expected to bring contemporary Yale practice to bear on the new college, replicating the curriculum of Timothy Dwight. However, Meigs had trained and taught under Stiles, and he never got along with Dwight, so it was a slightly older curriculum that he brought south.[20]

There were basic similarities between Stiles' Yale and Meigs' Franklin. At both colleges freshmen and sophomores concentrated on Latin, Greek, mathematics, and a smattering of English. Juniors and seniors turned to belles-lettres, the laws of nations, logic, moral philosophy, and natural philosophy. Many of the readings were the same, such as Nicholas Pike's *New and Complete System of Arithmetic*, William Enfield's *Institutes of Natural Philosophy*, and Joseph Priestley's *Lectures on History*. At both schools forensic disputations were important for sharpening young minds.

But the intellectual fare at Franklin went somewhat beyond that at Yale. Meigs' talents lay in the sciences, and he was both politically and religiously more liberal than Stiles. These characteristics found expression in the curriculum. There was more mathematics at Franklin than at Yale, and more of it was applied, as in bookkeeping. Franklin science included experimental natural philosophy, chemistry, and Linnaen botany; none of these appeared at Yale for some years. Classical language readings included not only traditional fare, but also Gibbon's *Decline and Fall of the Roman Empire* and Gordon's Tacitus; English brought reading in Pope, Swift, Addison, and the normal Blair's *Rhetoric*; and political readings included the Locke, Montesquieu, and Vattel in use at Yale, as well as Hume's *History of England*, Adam Smith, and Blackstone. Religious works ran the gamut from pietists to skeptics. Franklin College, with no competition for students, set out to bring all the trappings of civilized society to the frontier. To do it, Meigs based the curriculum on established practice and then innovated. He probably tried to do too much, as the subsequent history of the college shows. He may not have taught as thoroughly as Yale's Stiles or Dwight, but the frontier bred ambition as well as emulation. Meigs personified its spirit.[21]

The political legacy of the Revolution, with its emphasis on education for citizenship, and the frontier, with its concern for civilization, including religion, virtue, culture, and practical skills, were major influences on the motives of foundation and the curricula of the new colleges. They had their effect on the colleges' informal, extracurricular activities as well. For the most part, and in common with the established seaboard colleges, those activities embraced politics. The stances taken on political issues at both groups of colleges tended to draw them closer together, to create a common bond. But once more the frontier atmosphere intervened to prevent complete identity, for students at the new colleges were as preoccupied with the question of who they were as with the public issues that confronted them as members of the new republic.

The frontier college communities were interested in politics, but most had not been caught up in the ideological concerns of the Revolution,[22] so they focused instead on state and nation building, on backcountry issues, and on the special meaning for the frontier of the French Revolution's alleged disorder and deism. Another issue of paramount concern for the new colleges' students, at least, was that of civilization; the problem of developing a distinctive identity that was recognizably American, yet revealed them as frontiersmen. Both separately, and in their interrelation, the questions of politics and civilization were the major ones concerning the new colleges before 1800.

Yet, the political atmosphere prevailing at the new colleges was similar to that of the seaboard institutions. In general, concerns were local before the ratification of the Constitution. The response to the actions of the new government was one of interest but not of partisanship. Then, in the mid-1790s, the altering character of the French Revolution, and the attitudes of the Republicans and Federalists toward it, affected the campuses.[23] The new frontier college communities mirrored the old, and their reaction to the French Revolution brought them even closer to the established college communities' beliefs.

The political climate of the frontier colleges had as its base the inculcation of public virtue, a legacy from the Revolution shared by all the colleges. It appeared in the founders' motives and in the texts chosen for moral philosophy and history. Moreover, frontier college presidents all believed they were educating for citizenship. Dickinson's Charles Nisbet and Washington's William Smith, for instance, expressed sentiments best elaborated by John Blair Smith, of Hampden-Sydney and Union:

In our republic, where all men have the same advantages and the same difficulties, and where the path to the gaining of offices and honors has been open to all men, a wide dissemination of knowledge has been absolutely necessary. It nourishes freedom, erases servitude, stands up against autocratic domination. It explores and sanctifies the rights of man. It considers liberty of supreme value. . . . Education utilizes the history of other nations for the benefit of our country. It conjures up from what is most worthy in the past, such examples as to show the way to those who have the power of making our laws. Thus officeholders of the republic are trained for their very important duty, and legislators merit greatly in their achievements.[24]

In this atmosphere the new college communities of the 1780s, Washington's in Maryland, Hampden-Sydney's and Liberty Hall's in Virginia, Dickinson's and Franklin's in Pennsylvania, viewed the adoption of the Constitution and the beginning of the new government. Their presidents generally approved of the Constitution. Only Liberty Hall's William Graham disliked the document (so strongly that his interest in politics ceased), claiming it violated Virginia's rights over internal taxes and trade. Graham may have reflected popular sentiment in the backcountry, for John Blair Smith's vigorous support of the Constitution provoked an outburst from Patrick Henry and the suspicion of the Hampden-Sydney trustees, and Charles Nisbet's pro-Constitution sentiments prompted an adverse reaction in Carlisle, only the first of many times the townspeople would oppose his politics.[25]

The frontier colleges' pro-Constitution spirit resembled that of the established colleges. Columbia's William Samuel Johnson was a member of the Federal Convention who figured prominently in the drafting of the Constitution. President James Madison of William and Mary shared many of the pro-Constitution sentiments of his more famous cousin. Yale's Ezra Stiles, Princeton's John Witherspoon, and the College of Rhode Island's James Manning also proclaimed their support for the new instrument of government.[26]

Only Dickinson College's students have left us records of their concerns at this time and we may use them to illustrate activities at all the colleges. Their debate topics reveal a slight, but wide-ranging interest in politics. They considered local issues such as "whether the wheelbarrow law in this state is a good law and calculated to produce the desired effects?" and "whether the ends of government can be better obtained by a single convention or assembly or by two or more branches [of government]?" but also considered the more abstract question "Is the people's retaining too much power in government likely to produce as much evil as the giving up too much power?" On the commencement platform the speakers' major interest was the role of virtue in the new republic. The 1789 orations included those on "The Necessity of Virtue in Representatives and Governors," "The Usefulness of a Sense of Honor and Reputation," and "The Necessity of Morals as a Bond of Society."[27]

Dickinson's political interest after the ratification of the Constitution remained spread between local and national issues. The question "Are the individual slaveholders of America justified in continuing to hold their negroes in slavery in the present situation of American affairs or not?" signalled the start of a continuing interest in the topic.[28] Other national questions included "Is the Susquehenna preferable to the Potomac for the permanent seat of the government of the U.S.?" and "Is the cultivation of the ground more advantageous to the Atlantic states than the nurture of manufactures?" State issues debated included the merits of voice vote versus secret ballot in elections, whether property qualifications were necessary to state franchise, whether a representative should be bound by the will of his constituents, and whether a lawyer ought to be a member of a legislature.[29] Neither debates nor orations indicated partisanship.

Toward the French Revolution, the chief foreign interest of Americans at this time, initial reaction varied. Neither Dickinson nor Hampden-Sydney students debated the Revolution in its early stages, but Transylvania, the University of North Carolina, and Williams all were sites of Revolutionary sympathy. The appearance in the settled areas of precisely this kind of activity led the Federalists and the eastern Calvinist clergy to make common cause against the alleged evil influences of the French Revolution. The dangers of deism and disorder seemed even worse on the frontier where institutions were few and there was little organized religion. For this reason, the college educators on the frontier, Calvinist clergy transplanted from the east, strove manfully to counteract pro-Revolutionary sentiment.

College presidents and professors took the lead in the anti-French campaign. North Carolina's David Caldwell exhibited a staunch Presbyterian-based Federalism that countered the irreligion of his faculty. Bowdoin's Joseph McKeen backed John Adams firmly, reviewing American foreign policy to demonstrate the duplicity of the French. By the late 1790s Theodore Sedgewick and President Ebenezer Fitch had restored the proper order to Williams; students eagerly followed state and national campaigns to see if Federalists had won. Union's John Blair Smith, according to student George Bancker, son of one of New York's regents, was using his 1796 moral philosophy lectures to turn his students into Federalists: "He lectures daily upon Federalism and tries to prove that the Alien and Sedition Bills are constitutional. . . . The poor Democrats cannot escape. They get it from every quarter; newspapers, presidents of college, and every hot-headed, or rather English, Federal abuses them."[30]

The best example of the anti-French campaign occurred at Dickinson where Charles Nisbet's antipathy to the Revolution apparently preceded its excesses in 1792 and 1793. The college's 1792 commencement featured orations on "The Necessity of Knowledge and Virtue in Free Government," "The Pernicious Consequences of Skepticism," "The Danger of Relying on the Principle of Self-interest in Political Establishments," and "The Influence of Education on National Happiness." These topics betrayed a general disquietude, a sense of impending crisis. The natural refuge for the Calvinist was an exaltation of virtue, both public and private, and this too was reflected.[31]

Student debates, orations, and Nisbet's own remarks over the rest of the decade charted the progress of the anti-French struggle. In mid-1793, by asking "Were the French justified in beheading Louis XVI?" the students defined the battle. Then followed a flurry of questions bearing on the Revolution and its meaning for America: "Whether men who have been governed by laws are not more wicked when freed from their restraint than those who have never been restrained by them?"; "Whether it would be prudent for America under her present circumstances to declare war on Britain under hers?"; "Ought republican governments to encourage the manufacture of luxuries?"; "Is it consistent with the interest and dignity of a republic to admit foreigners to legislative and executive office?"; "Civil and military appointments ought not to be united in the same person in a well-regulated republic." Implicit in these questions were the spectres of the French mob and the Whiskey rebels, of the loss of American virtue, of the folly of war with Great Britain, and of the rise of Napoleon. Twenty years earlier, many of these questions were asked regarding the establishment, not the preservation, of republican government.[32]

In 1795 Nisbet informed his philosophy class that "the French have done all in their power to make all things appear equal . . . to release the vicious from all fear of punishment." Commencement that year again emphasized virtue and the fear of deism; orations considered "The Importance of a Good Education," "Civil Liberty," "The Necessity of Moral Virtue," and "The Necessity of Religion for the Support of the Civil Government." The following year students wondered if "It is just in some cases for one nation to declare war against another," a subject considered at the 1797 commencement and debated again in 1798. All this indicated a Federalist sympathy, one documented by a laudatory address sent to President Adams in 1798, commending him for averting open warfare and congratulating him on "the measures that have been pursued to maintain a policy of neutrality and peace." With this anti-French, pro-Federalist sentiment peaked. The students in the 1798 commencement simply reviewed "The Politics of the Times and the French Revolution," while the Belles-Lettres Society left the issue by debating "whether or no it is right for Americans to rejoice at the downfall of France?"[33]

The political preoccupations of the 1780s and 1790s served in many ways to link the extracurricular atmosphere of the frontier colleges to that of the seaboard schools. Speculation on the meaning and implications of the Constitution, and later of the French Revolution, was inevitable given the political legacy of the American revolt. But another theme appears in the records left by the backcountry collegians, the search for an identity in which could be blended the desirable traits of frontier life with what these students perceived as mainstream Americanism. Typical of this concern, and illustrating its longevity, was a letter from Greeneville student James Campbell to his sister in 1811:

. . . I have not, however, acquired any politeness. On the contrary my manners have become more rough and unpolished than they were . . . I would wish you to write me before the end of the session and give me a lecture on politeness for, depend upon it, I have forgotten everything you learnt me.[34]

Some political issues of special significance to the backcountry disclosed the search. Questions arose concerning an act for the recovery of debts, the excise tax, internal improvements, whether total ownership of land should be limited to 1,000 acres, and ultimately "Whether would it be most consistent with the interest of the United States for it to continue with its present government or for each state to be governed by its own legislature?" Moreover, the repeated debates on the justice and propriety of Negro slavery suggest that the issue was of special concern to the frontier. That the heightened sense of equality characteristic of the frontier was offended by slavery was confirmed by a North Carolina debate on "whether have not the Africans as good a right to enslave the Americans as the Americans have to enslave the Africans?"

Another racial question haunting the frontier was that of the Indians. Frontiersmen resembled other Americans when they asked if "the Europeans were justified in driving out the native Americans and taking possession of the land for themselves?" Then came the local question, "Whether it is justifiable · to drive off the Indians or not?" Deciding that it was, the debates then shifted to immediate policy and practice: "Whether is the war now carried on against the Indians just?"; "Is the treaty made with the Indians by General Wayne profitable to the United States?"; "Would it be politic in the government to give a premium for all Indian scalps?"; "the lands in the western territories ought to be taken from the Indians without giving them any restitution."[35]

Troubled by their relations with the Negro, the Indian, and the rest of the nation, the frontier college students may have sensed some irony in their constantly reiterated question, "Whether mankind in the savage or civilized state enjoys the most happiness?" The question was symptomatic of the identity problems reflected in other debates. On the one hand, students hastened to participate in the political concerns of the nation, and they indulged in common philosophical speculations with their peers: "Whether all children who die in infancy before they know their right hand from their left, or distinguishing good and evil, will be saved or not?"; "Is matter eternal?"; "Whether is honor or interest the most likely motive to action?"; "Whether is liberal education or riches the greatest recommendation?"; "Whether a man in public or private life enjoys the most happiness?"; and "Is the study of ancient or modern history the most advantageous?"[36] These questions and others like them were asked at institutions old and new, east and west. They gave the students the chance to think about what they had learned from ethics, moral philosophy, and divinity. That they were asked in both old and new colleges demonstrates the common bond of learning uniting the two, and shows that both country and city people shared convictions on the desirability of such knowledge.

On the other hand, there were questions, some even asked at both frontier and lowcountry colleges, that showed a different concern and were less symptomatic of unity. When a frontier student asked "Which is more preferable, country or city life?" it probably did not reflect pastoral supremacy. So, too, the question "Whether solitude or society is best adapted to form a useful character?" It took on greater meaning on the sparsely settled frontier. The Hampden-Sydney student's query "Whether is the contemplation of the works of nature or art most calculated to improve and please the mind?" combined with that of "Whether is the lowcountry or the backcountry the most eligible seat?" to show deep reserve about his surroundings, where works of art outside nature were few. A debate on whether "Is duelling consistent with the laws of honor and justice?" was significant in a society where the legal institutions were weak, where personal honor was important, and where most men were armed. Students in such a society might well ask also "Whether the trial by jury is best calculated to produce justice and equity in society?" or "Whether do men's moral characters become better in proportion as the society in which they live becomes more civilized?" because these were questions that they wanted answered. The very act of attending college was a commitment to civilization as well as to learning, a statement that they wanted some of the trappings of society they or their parents had left behind. There was perhaps a little hope, a little fear, and a double meaning in their asking of the question that lay at the heart of the new republic, "Whether is there a natural aristocracy or are all men naturally created equal?"[37]

If all men were so created, then there would probably not be much difficulty in establishing themselves as Americans. Distinctions of culture or place would matter little. Much could be comprehended under the title American.

This analysis of college founding in the new republic demonstrates that both continuity and diversity characterized higher education in the last quarter of the eighteenth century. The older seaboard colleges were politicized in the course of the American Revolutionary movement and the ideas those college communities developed about the role of the college in bringing about a republican nation, about the proper curriculum to inculcate republicanism, about the political activism of the members of the community, all carried over to the new institutions, providing a bond to unite American higher education in the service of republican government. Yet the frontier's influence acted to disrupt the continuity in higher education. The consciousness of the wide cultural gap existing between seaboard and frontier prompted college founders to be as concerned with civilizing students as with republicanizing them. It kept the new colleges from accurately replicating the standard seaboard curriculum and fostered a keen local appreciation for the modern, the scientific, the practical, which seaboard residents could assimilate at institutions other than colleges. But most of all, the frontier was responsible for a different mood among backcountry students than that possessed by their seaboard peers. For on the frontier, students had to decide what kind of Americans they were as well as what a good American should know.

Even though somewhat different in their functions, services, and mood, frontier and seaboard colleges joined in enjoying unprecedented prestige in the post-Revolutionary period. Americans at that time united their political, moral, and religious values under the banner of republicanism, and the college became the institution charged with the dissemination of its truths to the young. It was the highpoint of early American higher education.

But it could not last. The union of values began to break down almost as soon as it formed, and by the first years of the nineteenth century parochialism, denominationalism, and educational conservatism were the characteristics of college founding and the frontier colleges led the retreat.[38] Never again would the relationship between the college and the national ethos be quite as close as it was in the years of the new republic.

NOTES

1. Debate over what constitutes college founding is perpetual among those concerned with the history of higher education. In this discussion, the inclusion of a college rests on the date it received a charter granting it the power to award college degrees. The sixteen colleges included are: Washington College in Maryland (1782); Liberty Hall Academy in Virginia (1782—now Washington and Lee University); Hampden-Sydney

College in Virginia (1783); Transylvania Seminary in Virginia (1783—the area became Kentucky in 1792); Dickinson College in Pennsylvania (1784); St. John's College in Maryland (1784); the University of Georgia (1785); the College of Charleston in South Carolina (1785); Franklin College in Pennsylvania (1787—now Franklin and Marshall College); the University of North Carolina (1789); the University of Vermont (1791); Williams College in Massachusetts (1793); Bowdoin College in Massachusetts (1794—the area became Maine in 1820); Greenville College in Tennessee (1794—now Tusculum College); Blount College in Tennessee (1794—now the University of Tennessee, Knoxville); Union College in New York (1795). Two of these colleges, St. John's in Annapolis and the College of Charleston, are not included in the discussion that follows, for several reasons. They were urban institutions; they did not partake of the frontier influence; they were run by Anglicans or American Episcopalians and did not conform to the usual curricular practices of post-Revolutionary American higher education. For a convenient listing of the colleges established in America before 1820, see Jurgen Herbst, *From Crisis to Crisis: American College Government, 1636–1819* (Cambridge, Mass., 1982), pp. 244–53.

2. These two colleges are not included in the discussion that follows, for several reasons. They were urban institutions; they did not partake of the frontier influence; they were run by Anglicans or American Episcopalians; they also did not conform to the usual curricular practices of post-Revolutionary American higher education; there is some doubt that the College of Charleston offered a college-level curriculum at any time before 1800.

3. See Bernard Bailyn, *The Ideological Origins of the American Revolution* (Cambridge, Mass., 1967), Ch. 1–4, and Gordon Wood, *The Creation of the American Republic, 1776–1787* (Chapel Hill, 1969), Part I, for thorough expositions of the Commonwealth Whig ideology and its adoption by the Revolutionaries. For a discussion of the ways in which the colonial colleges adopted this ideology, see David W. Robson, "Higher Education in the Emerging American Republic, 1750–1800" (Ph. D. diss., Yale University, 1974), pp. 436–37.

4. Reuben A. Guild, *A History of Brown University, with Illustrative Documents* (Providence, 1867), p. 122; Ezra Stiles, *The United States Elevated to Glory and Honor* (New Haven, 1783), reprinted in John W. Thornton (ed.), *Pulpit of the American Revolution* (Boston, 1860), pp. 436–37.

5. Robert L. Volz, *Governor Bowdoin and His Family: A Guide to an Exhibition* (Brunswick, Me., 1969), pp. 31–32; Franklin College Trustees' Circular of January 19, 1787, quoted in Frederick S. Klein, *The Spiritual and Educational Background of Franklin and Marshall College* (Lancaster, Pa., 1939), p. 34; *North Carolina Journal* (July 10, 1793), quoted in R.D.W. Connor (comp.), *A Documentary History of the University of North Carolina, 1776–1799* ([2 vols.] Chapel Hill, 1953), I, p. 226; "Minutes of the Albany-Schenectady Town Meeting, 1794" (Union College Archives, Schaeffer Library); Ira Allen, "Memorial to the Assembly of New York, January 27, 1792" (University of Vermont Archives, Bailey Library); William Smith, *An Account of Washington College* (Philadelphia, 1784), p. 4.

6. William Kilty, ed., *The Laws of Maryland*, ([2 vols.] Annapolis, 1799–1800), Ch. 8, 1782; Alexander Dallas, ed., *The Laws of the Commonwealth of Pennsylvania* ([4 vols.] Philadelphia, 1797–1803), I, p. 815; George Roulstone, ed., *The Laws of the State of Tennessee* (Knoxville, 1803), pp. 43–44; William W. Hening, ed., *The Statutes at Large, Being a Collection of All the Laws of Virginia* v. 11 (13 vols., Richmond, 1809–1823), pp. 271–74; "Charter of the University of Georgia" (University of Georgia Archives, University Library).

7. Perry Miller, "From the Covenant to the Revival," in James W. Smith and A. Leland Jamieson (eds.), *Religion in American Life: The Shaping of American Religion* (Princeton, 1961), 352–53; Howard G. Miller, *The Revolutionary College: American Presbyterian Higher Education, 1707–1837* (New York, 1976), pp. 103–89.

8. Benjamin Rush to John Dickinson, May 5, 1787, in Lyman Butterfield, (ed.), *The Letters of Benjamin Rush* ([2 vols.], Princeton, 1951), I, 416; Michael Schlatter's "Appeal," quoted in Klein, *Franklin and Marshall*, 13; Kentucky Academy Papers, Shane Collection (Presbyterian Historical Society, Philadelphia), #8; Roulstone, *Laws of Tennessee*, I, pp. 44–45; E. Merton Coulter, *College Life in the Old South* (2nd ed., Athens, 1951), pp. 4–5; "Extracts from the Journal of the House of Representatives," in Acts of the General Court of Massachusetts Concerning Bowdoin College (Bowdoin College Archives, College Library), February 7, 1788, June 3, 1791; Calvin Durfee, *A History of Williams College* (Boston, 1860), p. 62; "Albany-Schenectady Town Meeting, 1794."

9. Connor, *Doc. Hist. U.N.C.*, I, pp. 22–23, 109; F. H. Dewart et al. (eds.), *State Papers of Vermont* v. 4 (8 vols., Montpelier, 1908–1939), p. 127.

10. J. Bell Whitfield "Bulwark of Liberty," in *Bulwark of Liberty*, Volume I of the *Boyd Lee Spahr Lectures in Americana* ([4 vols. thus far] Carlisle, 1950–   ); David F. Hawke, *Benjamin Rush: Revolutionary Gadfly* (Indianapolis, 1971), pp. 338–57; Rush to John Armstrong, March 9, 1783, in Butterfield, *Letters of Rush*, I, pp. 294–96; Rush to Henry Muhlenburg, ?, 1788, quoted in Klein, *Franklin and Marshall*, pp. 48–49.

11. J. H. Easterby, *A History of the College of Charleston* (Charleston, 1935), p. 17.

12. I can find no evidence of Greeneville College's pre-1800 curriculum. The University of Vermont, although planning, had developed no course of study by 1800.

13. Joseph H. Dubbs, *A History of Franklin and Marshall College* (Lancaster, Pa., 1903), p. 46, 71-75; Klein, *Franklin and Marshall*, p. 61, 53-54.

14. James H. Morgan, *Dickinson College* (Carlisle, 1933), pp. 131-32; Charles Coleman Sellers, *Dickinson College: A History* (Middletown, Conn., 1973), pp. 82-85, 91-95, 123-24; The *Carlisle Gazette*, Dec. 20, 1786; "Dickinson College, Trustees' Minutes" (Dickinson College Archives, Boyd Lee Spahr Library), Apr. 26, 1796, June 20, 1798; Samuel Mahon, "Notes of Dr. Nisbet's Lectures, December 1788-May 1789, Volume I, Moral Philosophy" (Dickinson College Archives); John Young, "Nisbet's Metaphysics and Public Law Lectures" (Dickinson College Archives); Charles Nisbet to Board of Trustees, July 29, Sept. 25, 1799 (Dickinson College Archives); Joseph B. Smith, "A Frontier Experiment in Higher Education," in *Bulwark of Liberty*, pp. 90-91.

15. Leverett Spring, *A History of Williams College* (Boston and New York, 1917), pp. 32-33, 39-40; "Williams College, Free School and College Records" (Williams College Archives, College Library), Aug. 6, 1793, Aug. 20, 1794, Sept. 2, 1795; "Laws of Yale College, 1787" (Yale University Archives, Yale University Library); "The Laws of Williams College, 1795" (Williams College Archives), pp. 19-20; Durfee, *History of Williams*, pp. 69-72, 65, 84; Increase N. Tarbox, ed., *The Diary of Thomas Robbins, 1796-1854* v. 1 ([12 vols.] Boston, 1886), p. 1, 6, 15, 16. The full title of Hopkins work is *The System of Doctrines Contained in Divine Revelation, Explained and Defended Showing their Consistence and Connection with Each Other* (Boston, 1793).

16. William Enfield, *Institutes of Natural Philosophy, Theoretical, and Experimental* (London, 1775); fluxions described what modern mathematicians refer to as differentials in calculus, hence fluxions was also used to mean the Newtonian calculus.

17. "Laws and Regulations for the Government of Union College, 1795" (Union College Archives, Schaeffer Library); "Union College Trustees' Minutes" (Union College Archives), Jan. 20, Apr. 30, Sept. 3, 1799; Samuel B. Fortenbaugh, Jr., *In Order to Form a More Perfect Union: An Inquiry into the Origins of a College* (Schenectady, 1978), pp. 104-05; the trustees had to ask Jonathan Edwards, Jr., to upgrade the English offering, apparently to no avail: cf. "The Laws of Union College, 1802" (Union College Archives). Texts referred to are: Hugh Blair, *Lectures on Rhetoric and Belles-Lettres* ([2 vols.] London, 1783; Philadelphia, 1784); Charles Rollin, *The Method of Teaching and Studying the Belles-Lettres* (3rd ed., London, 1742); *The Poetical Works of John Milton* (London, 1695; Philadelphia, 1791); *The Works of Joseph Addison* ([4 vols.] London, 1721); David Hume, *The History of England from the invasion of Julius Caesar to the Revolution in MDCLXXXVIII* ([6 vols.] London, 1754-1762; [2 vols.] Philadelphia, 1795); Dugald Stewart, *Elements of the Philosophy of the Mind* ([3 vols.] Edinburgh, 1792-1827; [Vol. I] Philadelphia, 1793); Joseph Priestley, *Lectures on History and General Policy* (Birmingham, 1788); William Paley, *The Principles of Moral and Political Philosophy* (London, 1785; 7th ed., corrected, Philadelphia, 1788); David Ramsay, *The History of the American Revolution* (2 vols., Philadelphia, 1788); William Robertson, *The History of Scotland during the Reigns of Queen Mary and King James VI till His Accession to the Crown of England* ([2 vols.] London, 1759); Edward Gibbon, *The History of the Decline and Fall of the Roman Empire* ([1st Eng. trans., 6 vols.] London, 1776-1788); Adam Ferguson, *An Essay on the History of Civil Society* (Edinburgh, 1767; Philadelphia, 1773); Thomas Jefferson, *Notes on the State of Virginia* (Philadelphia, 1788); *The Works of Edmund Burke* ([8 vols.] London, 1792-1827); Emerich de Vattel, *The Law of Nations* ([2 vols.] London, 1759-1760; New York, 1796); Jean Jacques Burlamaqui, *The Principles of Natural and Political Law* ([2 vols.] London, 1748-1752; 4th ed., Boston, 1792); Sir William Blackstone, *Commentaries on the Laws of England* ([4 vols.] Oxford, 1765-1769; Philadelphia, 1771); Philip Doddridge, *A Course of Lectures on . . . Pneumatology, Ethics, and Divinity* (London, 1762); Francis Hutcheson, *A Short Introduction to Moral Philosophy* (Glasgow, 1747; 5th ed., Philadelphia, 1788); American Philosophical Society, *Transactions* (Philadelphia, 1771-   ).

18. Herbert C. Bradshaw, *A History of Prince Edward County, Virginia, 1754-1954* (Richmond, 1955), p. 141; Donald R. Come, "The Influence of Princeton on Higher Education in the South before 1825," *William and Mary Quarterly*, 3rd series, v. 2 (1945): 371-74 [hereafter cited as *WMQ*; 3rd series unless otherwise indicated]; William H. Foote, *Sketches of Virginia, Historical and Biographical*, v. 1 ([2 vols.] Philadelphia, 1850-1856), p. 397, 404; James W. Alexander, *The Life of Archibald Alexander* (New York, 1854), p. 200; The *Virginia Gazette* (Dixon & Hunter), Oct. 7, 1775; "Hampden-Sydney Records" (Hampden-Sydney College Archives, Eggleston Library), June 23, 1784, Sept. 2, 1785; Samuel Blair, *An Account of the College of New Jersey* (Woodbridge, N.J., 1764), pp. 24-25; Francis L. Broderick, "Pulpit, Physics, and Politics: The Curriculum of the College of New Jersey, 1746-1794," *WMQ*, v. 6 (1949): 61-63; "College Laws, 1794" (Princeton University Archives, Firestone Library), p. 57.

19. Come, "The Influence of Princeton:" 383; "Trustees' Minutes, Feb. 6, 1795," "Charles W. Harris to Dr.

Charles Harris, Apr. 18, 1795," in Connor, *Doc. Hist. U.N.C.*, I, pp. 360-61, 387-89; Kemp Battle, *A History of the University of North Carolina* v. 1 ([2 vols.] Raleigh, 1907-1912), pp. 94-97, quotation from p. 97; "College Laws, 1794" (Princeton Univ. Archives), 37n. Works not previously identified are: Charles Secondat, Baron de Montesquieu, *The Spirit of Laws* (1st Eng. trans., London, 1752) and Claude F. X. Millot, *Elements of General History* ([5 vols.] London, 1778-1779; 5 vols., Worcester, 1789).

20. Thomas W. Reed, "History of the University of Georgia" ([19 vols.] unpublished Ms., Univ. of Georgia Archives), I, p. 6; E. Merton Coulter, *Georgia: A Short History* (Chapel Hill, 1947), pp. 188-89, 96, 107; Henry C. White, *Abraham Baldwin* (Athens, 1926), pp. 154-71; Ezra Stiles, "Literary Diary" (Yale Univ. Archives), XII, p. 5, 137; XIII, p. 102-03; William M. Meigs, *The Life of Josiah Meigs* (Philadelphia, 1887), pp. 40-43.

21. O. Burton Adams, "Yale Influence on the Formation of the University of Georgia," *Georgia Historical Quarterly*, 51 (1967): 180-81; Coulter, *College Life in the Old South*, pp. 15-16; "University of Georgia Trustees' Minutes" (Univ. of Georgia Archives), June 1801; "Minutes of the Senatus Academicus" (Univ. of Georgia Archives), Nov. 27, 1800; Ezra Stiles, "Yale College Memoranda, 1793-1794" (Yale Univ. Archives). Works not previously identified are: Nicholas Pike, *A New and Complete System of Arithmetic* (Newburyport, Mass., 1788); Thomas Gordon, trans., *The Works of Tacitus* ([2 vols.] London, 1728); *The Works of Alexander Pope* ([2 vols.] London, 1717-1735); *The Works of Jonathan Swift* (4 vols., Dublin, 1735); John Locke, *An Essay Concerning Human Understanding* (London, 1690); Adam Smith, *An Inquiry into the Nature and Causes of Wealth Among Nations* ([2 vols.] London, 1776; 3 vols., Philadelphia, 1789).

22. Robson, "Higher Education:" 117-50; Miller, *The Revolutionary College*, pp. 112-22.

23. Robson, "Higher Education:" 170-205.

24. Charles Nisbet, *An Address to the Students of Dickinson College* (Carlisle, 1786), p. 6; Nisbet, *The Usefulness and Importance of Human Learning* (Carlisle, 1786), pp. 17-18; Smith, *Account of Washington College*, p. 18; John Blair Smith, "On the Education of Youth, May 1, 1796," trans. Norman B. Johnson (Union College Archives).

25. Alexander, *Life of Alexander*, pp. 17-18; Hugh B. Grigsby, "The Founders of Washington College," *Washington and Lee Historical Papers*, 2 (1890), pp. 23-29; Foote, *Sketches of Virginia*, I, pp. 431-32; Smith, "A Frontier Experiment:" 93-94.

26. Max Farrand (ed.), *The Records of the Federal Convention* (revised ed. [4 vols.] New Haven, 1937), I, pp. 461-62; II, pp. 346-47, 376, 428; Charles R. Crowe, "James Madison and the Republic of Virtue." *Journal of Southern History*, 30 (1964): 60-62; Ezra Stiles, "Literary Diary," v. 13 (Ms. Yale Univ. Library) pp. 102-03, 165, 312, 366; XIV, p. 52; ALS, James Manning to Hezekiah Smith, June 10, 1788 (Ms. Brown Univ. Library).

27. "Belles-Lettres Society Minutes, 1786-1806" (Dickinson College Archives), July 20, Dec. 8, 1787, Sept. 20, 1789; *The Carlisle Gazette*, June 10, 1789.

28. "Belles Lettres Society Minutes," June 20, 1789: cf. Aug. ?, 1790, Aug. 4, 1792, July 26, 1794, Dec. 16, 1795, Dec. 9, 1797, Nov. 10, 1798.

29. Ibid., Dec. 12, 1789, Jan. 2, Mar. 19, July 10, ?, 1790.

30. Battle, *History of U.N.C.*, I, pp. 136-49; Joseph McKeen, *Two Discourses Delivered at Beverley, May 9, 1798* (Salem, Mass., 1798); Durfee, *History of Williams*, pp. 111-12; George Bancker to Abraham Bancker, Dec. 10, 1798 (Union College Archives).

31. The *Carlisle Gazette*, May 9, 1792.

32. "Belles-Lettres Society Minutes," Aug. 31, Dec. 14, 24, 1793, Feb. 27, Mar. 22, July 12, 1794.

33. Quoted in Smith, "Frontier Experiment:" 94; *Kline's Carlisle Weekly Gazette*, Oct. 7, 1795, Oct. 4, 1797, Oct. 3, 1798; "Belles-Lettres Society Minutes," Mar. 19, 1796, Apr. 28, Dec. 8, 1798; "The Address of the Students of Dickinson College to the President of the United States," *The Universal Gazette* (Philadelphia), July 12, 1798.

34. Quoted in Allen E. Reagan, *A History of Tusculum College, 1744-1944* (Bristol, Tenn., 1944), pp. 20-21.

35. Connor, *Doc. Hist. U.N.C.*, I, p. 504, 491; II, p. 140, 270, 127, 250; "Belles-Lettres Society Minutes," Mar. 2, 1793, June 20, Aug. 1, 1795, Jan. 13, 1796; "Union Society Minutes" (Hampden-Sydney College Archives), July 19, 1793, Nov. 27, 1795, Jan. 22, 1796; for an analysis of the problems of the west and their implication for western self-definition, see Edmund S. Morgan, "Conflict and Consensus in the American Revolution," in Stephen G. Kurtz and James H. Hutson (eds.), *Essays on the American Revolution* (Chapel Hill, 1973), pp. 297-306.

36. The question of civilization arose repeatedly: cf. "Belles-Lettres Society Minutes," Mar. 30, 1798, Jan. 19, Nov. 23, 1799; Connor, *Doc. Hist. U.N.C.*, I, p. 488, 489, 495; II, p. 150, for example; "Belles-Lettres Society Minutes," Jan. 6, Mar. 9, 1797; "Union Society Minutes," Mar. 3, 1792, Jan. 26, 1793; Connor, *Doc. Hist. U.N.C.*, I, p. 498; II, p. 125.

37. "Records of the Calliopian Society" (Union College Archives), Aug. 20, 1795, Apr. 3, 1797; "Union Society Minutes," Feb. 24, 1792, Dec. 4, 1795; Connor, *Doc. Hist. U.N.C.*, I, p. 487; II, p. 274; "Belles-Lettres Society Minutes," Aug. 1, Oct. ?, 1788.
38. Richard Hofstadter and Walter P. Metzger, *The Development of Academic Freedom in the United States* (New York, 1955), pp. 209-22; Miller, *The Revolutionary College*, pp. 191-285; Steven J. Novak, *The Rights of Youth: American Colleges and Student Revolt, 1798-1815* (Cambridge, Mass., 1977), *passim*.

THOMAS JEFFERSON AND A "NATIONAL" UNIVERSITY

The Hidden Agenda for Virginia

by NEIL MCDOWELL SHAWEN*

THOMAS JEFFERSON's belief in public education was an important corollary to his basic political philosophy. He regarded an informed citizenry not only as a prerequisite to the sound exercise of political rights but as a guarantor of individual liberties cherished in a democracy against the ambition and potential tyranny of those entrusted with power. To Jefferson's republican mind the central government was to maintain a delicate balance of power, "too weak to aid the wolves, and yet strong enough to protect the sheep." [1] Accordingly, he advocated local support and control of schools and saw the federal establishment less as an active promoter of programs than as an "unexacting landlord" or "disinterested policeman" [2] sworn to ward off "local egoisms," [3] sectional jealousies, and other forces of disunity which threatened the body politic as a whole.

One might assume, therefore, that the last institution Jefferson would have wished to see introduced into the American experiment in democracy was a national university on the order of the one endorsed by George Washington, controlled by the very central government of which he was so suspicious. But for a time Jefferson did indeed, both in public pronouncement and private correspondence, support the concept of a national university.[4]

Despite his recurring fears of unbridled federalism, Jefferson's evolving nationalism broadened his republicanism enough to accommodate for a time the notion of a national university. Even as he agonized over constitutional sanctions, his actions in founding the United States Military Academy, in

---

*Mr. Shawen is an assistant professor of adult and continuing education at the University of Virginia.

[1] Daniel J. Boorstin, *The Lost World of Thomas Jefferson* (New York, 1948), p. 190.

[2] Dumas Malone, *Jefferson and His Time* (6 vols.; Boston, 1948-81), IV, 22.

[3] Boorstin, *Lost World*, p. 192.

[4] Several early historians view Jefferson's endorsement of a national university as inconsistent with his emphasis on local government, states' rights, and a restricted role of federal government. The reaction of Charles W. Nason is illustrative: "It must become a matter of wonder that Jefferson, the staunch defender of the rights of the individual states and ever looking with a jealous eye at any tendency toward centralization, should, nevertheless, be an advocate of a great national system of instruction embracing the secondary and higher education of the whole country, culminating in a National University located at the capital city" (Nason, "Jefferson and Washington on National Education," *Education*, XIX [Nov. 1898], 158). Later historians deny any such inconsistency, citing the nationalistic theme of his republicanism.

purchasing Louisiana, in establishing the 1807 Embargo, and in calling for roads, canals, and other internal improvements indicate his recognition that the general government alone could take certain steps to promote interstate communication and to ensure America's place within the community of nations. Merrill D. Peterson describes a subtle shift in Jefferson's thought on the subject:

> The American Revolution was a national as well as a democratic movement. ...It was accompanied by a still shadowy but developing consciousness of common experience and common culture, of unifying habits, beliefs, and aspirations, all parts of the process by which a people comes to identify itself as a nation. If, as was true, Jefferson's *amor patriae* was more Virginian than American or continental in 1776, the transmutation of provincial loyalties into unifying national loyalties ... had already begun in him. He began to see that America was the place where Enlightenment dreams, which were only dreams in the Old World, might be realized.[5]

Jefferson's endorsement of a national university was, then, an act of cultural nationalism, as he sought to light an academic signal fire in the Western Hemisphere which could be seen in Britain and on the Continent. It was, moreover, an internal improvement designed to open channels of national interchange. He invited the youth of the several states to "come and drink of the cup of knowledge and fraternize with us."[6]

Dumas Malone and other recent historians have noted that Jefferson, although often appearing a visionary theorist, was capable of demonstrating a remarkable pragmatism or political opportunism.[7] While perhaps at odds with his distaste for federal consolidation, his support of a national university was in keeping with a nationalistic strain in his republicanism, and was manifested when other of his goals for public education encountered a specific set of circumstances.

Examined here is Jefferson's temporary endorsement of a national university in the larger context of a lifelong interest in public education for his native Virginia, with specific reference to his efforts toward founding a university in his state. Detailed attention is paid not only to a variety of contemporary schemes for the establishment of a national university in America but to changing historical situations and a location criterion which the man applied in rebuffing or embracing each plan. Finally, this study

---

[5] Peterson, *Thomas Jefferson and the American Revolution* (Williamsburg, 1976), p. 11.

[6] Jefferson to Joseph Priestley, 18 Jan. 1800 (Andrew A. Lipscomb and Albert Ellery Bergh, eds., *The Writings of Thomas Jefferson* [20 vols.; Washington, D.C., 1903-4], X, 138-43).

[7] Malone, *Jefferson and His Time*, IV, 102.

considers Jefferson's stance in terms of a hidden agenda, which the opportunistic educational reformer held for the promotion of first-rate higher education in his own state.

Although still a relatively young man in 1789, Thomas Jefferson had already had a distinguished career in public service to the fledgling republic, including the drafting of the Declaration of Independence and a ministry to France. He had suffered setbacks, however, as an agent of educational change in Virginia. His 1779 revisal of the state's archaic law code had met with mixed success: A bill for the introduction of a broad system of free, locally controlled, elementary schools for white boys and girls; district grammar schools; and a modern university boasting truly advanced scholarship suffered a lingering death before the legislature. A separate measure, which would have secularized the governance and curriculum of William and Mary College, increased the number of its professorships, brought instruction in modern languages and applied sciences, and otherwise enabled the school to become the highest level in his three-tiered public system, met with a similar fate.[8] The college was deemed private in nature, portending issues raised in the *Dartmouth v. Woodward* case (1819). Its charter and governing board were considered beyond the jurisdiction of the Virginia General Assembly. Jefferson rejected this position, pointing to the college's royal charter and continuous, if unsystematic, financial support from the colonial legislature as proof of the institution's public character and the appropriateness of its continued control by state lawmakers.

As wartime governor of Virginia, Jefferson, serving as a member of his alma mater's board of visitors, managed to effect certain of the changes he had attempted through legislation. He was restricted, however, to those institutional areas that were within the purview of the board and not covered by its charter. By the time Jefferson left for France in 1784 to serve as minister under the Articles of Confederation, he had become increasingly impatient with "a College . . . just well enough endowed to draw out the miserable existence to which a miserable constitution [charter] has doomed it."[9]

---

[8] The texts of these bills, numbered Bill 79 and Bill 80, along with a Bill 81 calling for the creation of a state library in Richmond, appear in Roy J. Honeywell, *The Educational Work of Thomas Jefferson* (Cambridge, Mass., 1931), pp. 199-210.

For helpful discussion of the confusing revisal period in Virginia legislative history, see Charles T. Cullen, "Completing the Revisal of the Laws in Post-Revolutionary Virginia," *Virginia Magazine of History and Biography*, LXXXII (1974), 84-99.

[9] Jefferson to Priestley, 18 Jan. 1800 (Lipscomb and Bergh, *Writings*, X, 138-43).

Years later, the prime mover of the William and Mary board summarized his efforts: "I was appointed Governor of the Commonwealth and retired from the legislature. Being elected also one of the visitors of William and Mary College, a self-electing body, I effected, during my resi-

During his ministry to France (1784-89), Jefferson associated with leading philosophes of the Enlightenment, visited universities in Great Britain and on the Continent, and became familiar with a variety of European systems for national higher education. While his own correspondence during the period suggests no interest in a national system for his own country, it does indicate growing concern for the status of higher education in Virginia. His boyhood friend and the president of William and Mary College, Bishop James Madison, kept him abreast of the continuing constraints posed by the school's charter, financial problems wrought by the war, and decline in the school's prestige brought by disestablishment of the Church of England and the shifting of Virginia's capital from Williamsburg to Richmond.[10] Jefferson's *Notes on the State of Virginia*, compiled during this period, suggests that his disenchantment with the Tidewater college may have extended beyond academic and financial matters to its physical location. He found Williamsburg "the hottest part of Virginia"; noted its meager population, "never . . . above 1800 inhabitants"; and could find little good to say about its architecture: "The only public buildings worthy mention are the Capitol, the Palace, the College, and the Hospital for Lunatics. . . . The College and Hospital are rude, mis-shapen piles, which, but that they have roofs, would be taken for brick-kilns." [11]

Jefferson had by this time become sufficiently disillusioned by William and Mary College to feel that Virginia's intellectual elite deserved a better fate. He returned from France in 1789 with new plans stimulated by European models and, Roy J. Honeywell concludes, a determination to place his idealized university at a healthier, more central location where he could give its creation and development his personal attention.[12]

Jefferson's tour of duty in Paris exposed him to several specific, albeit fantastic, plans for the establishment of an educational system for the United

---

dence in Williamsburg that year, a change in the organization of that institution, by abolishing the grammar school and the two professorships of divinity and oriental languages, and substituting a professorship of law and police, one of anatomy, medicine, and chemistry, and one of modern languages; and the charter confining us to six professorships, we added the law of nature and nations and the fine arts, to the duties of the moral professor, and natural history to those of the professor of mathematics and natural philosophy" (Thomas Jefferson, *Autobiography of Thomas Jefferson*, ed. Dumas Malone [New York, 1959], p. 63).

[10] Bishop James Madison to Jefferson, 17 Jan., 30 Mar. 1800; Jefferson to Bishop Madison, 6 Jan. 1800 (Thomas Jefferson Papers, Library of Congress [hereafter cited as Jefferson Papers]).

Madison, a cousin of the president of the same name, was a classmate of Jefferson's at Rev. James Maury's school in Louisa County. See John Peter Carey, "Influences on Thomas Jefferson's Theory and Practice of Higher Education" (Ph.D. diss., University of Michigan, 1969), p. 202.

[11] Thomas Jefferson, *Notes on the State of Virginia*, ed. William Peden (Chapel Hill, 1955), pp. 108, 150-53, 279 n.

[12] Honeywell, *Educational Work*, p. 56.

States. As a result of these schemes, three of which were French in origin and two homegrown, Jefferson came to be associated with the cause of a national university. The details and historical setting for these plans, his reaction to each, and the relationship of that reaction to his own desires for higher education in Virginia reveal underlying reasons for his endorsement of a national university.

The first of these projects, masterminded by one Quesnay de Beaurepaire, was initiated while Jefferson was still in Paris. Quesnay, the grandson of a distinguished economist and court physician to Louis XV, had access to the highest social circles of prerevolutionary France. Equipped with his grandfather's interest in science and an ample share of wanderlust, Quesnay set off on something of a lark to serve under Lafayette in the American Revolution. While he achieved the rank of captain and assisted Virginia colonists with military and naval operations in the Chesapeake Bay, he also manifested a susceptibility to illness and imprudent business ventures. Forced to abandon his military pretensions, he resurfaced in Richmond. Impressed by the state capital Jefferson had just succeeded in locating there, Quesnay was approached by John Page about the possibility of headquartering in Richmond an academy for the arts and sciences patterned after the famous French Academy. Page gave assurances of popular financial support and promised Quesnay the presidency of the new institution.

The Richmond Academy was not only to be linked with similar academies in London and Paris but was to have branch campuses in Baltimore, Philadelphia, and New York. The plan called for French scholars to investigate and catalogue America's natural resources as well as to supervise study in a myriad of subjects—painting and sculpture, foreign languages, experimental sciences, medicine, architecture, natural history. Scholarly publications featuring research in these fields were to be shared with European academies in a steady stream of information across the Atlantic. There was a profit motive as well, since corporations were expected to appear to develop resources uncovered by the project. American students were to learn by field-based activities, which would fill the coffers of the academy and its stockholders. The Richmond Academy, at least as Quesnay glorified it in his memoirs, was to be at once a storehouse of information on American flora and fauna, a network of schools for the dissemination of knowledge, a wildcat business scheme, and an international clearinghouse for higher learning.

John Page's promise of financial support was realized. Largely through his own entrepreneurial zeal, Quesnay amassed private donations amounting to some 60,000 francs, nearly one hundred of the donors being prominent

Virginians. With the venture capitalized, the cornerstone of the academy's main building in Richmond was laid with all appropriate ceremony in June 1786.

Among the individuals associated with the enterprise were patriot Thomas Paine, French playwright Beaumarchais, scientist Lavoisier, philosopher-cynic La Rochefoucauld, and Richmond mayor John Harvie, who Quesnay was careful to note was "allié à la Famille de son Excellence M. Jefferson." Lest he be accused of competing with the college in Williamsburg, Quesnay also claimed the backing of William and Mary president Bishop Madison. The resourceful Frenchman clearly left no semiprecious stone unturned; he was even able to interest Benjamin Franklin's daughter (but apparently not Franklin himself) in the Philadelphia phase of the venture. With building underway and the nomination of a Dr. Jean Rouvelle, professor of science, promising the beginning of a faculty, Quesnay returned to France to win the patronage of other leading figures in Paris, including Monsieur Jefferson.[13]

The Richmond Academy progressed no further after its auspicious beginning. The French Revolution, breaking in 1789, spelled an end to French funding and doomed Quesnay and his academy to oblivion.

Jefferson's reaction to Quesnay's undertaking is most revealing. Herbert B. Adams and David M. R. Culbreth conclude that Jefferson was initially sympathetic to the academy scheme, noting that Quesnay listed among his supporters or "councillors" Thomas Jefferson, minister to France, residing in Paris.[14] There is some basis for this supposition. The liberal list of subjects to be taught, the emphasis on research in the sciences, and the broad dissemination of knowledge touted by the Richmond Academy were all reflected in Jefferson's concept of a university. It is more likely, however, that Quesnay took the liberty of publicizing the minister's support without his prior consent and that any similarity between the Richmond Academy and Jefferson's later efforts was the result of his familiarity with French institutions in general and not of an attraction to Quesnay's plan in particular. At any rate, the tone of Jefferson's 1788 reply to Quesnay is one of

---

[13] Quesnay de Beaurepaire, "Memoir concerning the Academy of the Arts and Sciences of the United States of America at Richmond, Virginia," trans. Rosewell Page, in *Eighteenth Annual Report of the Library Board of the Virginia State Library, 1920-21* (Richmond, 1922), pp. 5-50. For further discussion of Quesnay's adventures in America, see John G. Roberts, "Poet, Patriot and Pedagogue," *Arts in Virginia*, VI, no. 2 (1966), 23-31.

[14] Adams, *Thomas Jefferson and the University of Virginia* (Washington, D.C., 1888), p. 27; Culbreth, *The University of Virginia, Memories of Her Student-Life and Professors* (New York and Washington, D.C., 1908), p. 80; Philip Alexander Bruce, *History of the University of Virginia, 1819-1919: The Lengthened Shadow of One Man*, I (New York, 1920), 55-59.

cautious indifference: "I beg you . . . not to alter your plan in any part of it on my account, but permit me to pursue mine of being absolutely neutral." What made Jefferson so lukewarm to the idea? Certainly, his objection was based in part on Virginia's depressed postwar economy; he claimed that the plan was too grandiose, "too extensive for the poverty of the country."[15] As wartime governor, Jefferson had presided over his state's military and financial collapse and had seen his own educational reforms die in the aftermath. While he decried the pathetic trickle of Virginia news to Paris,[16] he knew only too well from correspondence with Edmund Randolph, James Madison, Bishop Madison, George Wythe, his nephew Peter Carr, and others that Virginia's ability to launch an undertaking like Quesnay's was still far off. Jefferson probably had doubts about Quesnay as well. Less a scholar than a promoter and devotee of the polite arts, Quesnay had been associated with lesser schools of dance and drama. Quesnay must have struck Jefferson as something of a charlatan and his Richmond Academy as just the latest in a rash of "petty *academies* . . . which," he later wrote John Adams, "are starting up in every neighborhood, and where one or two men, possessing Latin and sometimes Greek, a knowledge of the globes, and the first six books of Euclid, imagine and communicate this as the sum of science." [17]

His formal objection to Quesnay, however, was that foreign professors would be lured to America with exaggerated hopes, which might be dashed by the country's simple lifestyle:

> Knowing how much people going to America overrate the resources of living there, I have made a point never to encourage any person to go there, that I may not partake of the censure which may follow their disappointment.[18]

There is something very peculiar in this position. Jefferson was forever inviting individuals to come to America and to relocate in Virginia. Indeed, the number of individuals who accepted his invitations not only to Virginia but to Monticello contributed to his chronic financial problems. Consideration of a second French-laid educational plan for Virginia suggests that he had other, more substantive, objections to the Quesnay scheme, which he was not yet prepared to commit to paper.

In December 1793 Jefferson resigned from Washington's cabinet to return to Monticello. But as his opposition to Hamiltonian Federalism continued to draw him into the limelight as the leader of a growing opposition

[15] Jefferson to Quesnay de Beaurepaire, 6 Jan. 1788 (Lipscomb and Bergh, *Writings*, VI, 412).
[16] Malone, *Jefferson and His Time*, II, 17.
[17] Jefferson to Adams, 5 July 1814 (Lipscomb and Bergh, *Writings*, XIV, 150-51).
[18] Jefferson to Quesnay de Beaurepaire, 6 Jan. 1788 (ibid., VI, 412).

party, his interest in higher education for his state and nation led to involvement in that sphere. In 1794 Jefferson received a remarkable communication from Sir Francis D'Ivernois, a Geneva-born scholar whom Jefferson had known since his Paris days. D'Ivernois proposed nothing less than the mass immigration of the faculty of the University of Geneva to America. A revolution in Geneva had placed power in the hands of an aristocracy averse to the more leveling doctrines of that faculty, and its members scurried to find other, politically safer employment. In simultaneous letters to Jefferson and John Adams, D'Ivernois indicated that three of the faculty seemed definitely interested: Pierre Prevost, a physicist known for his work with heat radiation, and the brothers Pictet, one of whom must have been the "monsieur Pictet, Citoyen de Genève" whom Quesnay de Beaurepaire listed as a confederate in the earlier Richmond Academy scheme. D'Ivernois believed, however, that the entire faculty could be lured to the United States by the promise of gainful academic employment.[19]

At one time, Jefferson might have rejected a plan "to translate the Academy of Geneva in a body to this country." He had always respected the faculty itself but felt that the tense political situation in Geneva had been a major drawback to the institution:

> I do not count on any advantage to be derived, in Geneva, from a familiar acquaintance with the principles of that government. The late revolution has rendered it a tyrannical aristocracy, more likely to give ill than good ideas to an American.[20]

By 1791, however, he was more optimistic:

> The sciences are there [Geneva] more modernized than anywhere else. There, too, the spirit of republicanism is strong with the body of the inhabitants: but that of aristocracy is strong also with a particular class.[21]

Three years later, Jefferson was intrigued by the notion of uprooting a brilliant group of scholars parched by Geneva's political climate and transplanting it in America.

While D'Ivernois's letter did not suggest where in America the Geneva band might be relocated, there was no doubt in Jefferson's mind that the site should be somewhere in Virginia. Here was an opportunity to accom-

---

[19] Jefferson to Wilson C. Nicholas, 22 Nov. 1794 (ibid., IX, 291-93); Jefferson to George Washington, 23 Feb. 1795 (ibid., XIX, 108-14). .
[20] Jefferson to Nicholas, 22 Nov. 1794 (ibid., IX, 291); Jefferson to J. Bannister, Jr., 15 Oct. 1785 (ibid., V, 185).
[21] Jefferson to Mr. McAlister, 22 Dec. 1791 (ibid., VIII, 274-75).

plish by indirection what a recalcitrant legislature and the binding charter of William and Mary had made impossible—a first-rate institution of higher learning for the state.

Another factor made D'Ivernois's proposal all the more appealing. Within the organization outlined by D'Ivernois was a "college of languages, preparatory to the principal one of sciences" as well as a third school for the "gratuitous teaching of . . . reading and writing" to the poor. In sum, D'Ivernois offered an imported system incorporating a free elementary school, a secondary level, and a university, all of which followed the drift of Jefferson's abortive education bills of 1779. The Geneva transplant seemed a ready-made solution to Virginia's education problems, as the frustrated reformer perceived them.

Jefferson realized that the Geneva project was an expensive one, which could only be attempted with public support. Accordingly, on 22 November 1794 he wrote Wilson Cary Nicholas, his neighbor and a delegate to the Virginia General Assembly, requesting that he make discreet inquiry among his colleagues regarding their interest in funding such a venture. In this letter Jefferson played up the Geneva faculty as one of the "two eyes of Europe." Curiously, however, he seems to have rejected D'Ivernois's claim that most of the faculty were proficient in English, anticipating instead the cost and difficulty of instruction offered in French and Latin.[22]

Nicholas, after consulting with fellow lawmakers in Richmond, reported back that the consensus was discouraging. A Geneva institution in Virginia was judged impractical for three reasons. First, D'Ivernois's assurances notwithstanding, the delegates shared Jefferson's assumption that instruction would be in a foreign language for which American students were not prepared. The secondary level of teaching designed to develop proficiency in European languages would apparently be unequal to the task. At the very least, the secondary school would have had to function for several years before a corps of French-trained American scholars capable of benefiting from the Geneva faculty's instruction could have been produced.

Second, the cost was considered prohibitive. This reaction was predictable, essentially the same resistance to expenditure of public funds for education that had helped seal the fate of Jefferson's early reform bills.

Finally, key legislators simply could not seriously contemplate importing the foreign faculty of one of the foremost universities in the world to serve the limited educational needs of a small population lacking both private and

---

[22] Jefferson to Washington, 23 Feb. 1795 (ibid., XIX, 111); Jefferson to Nicholas, 22 Nov. 1794 (ibid., IX, 291-92).

public means to support it.²³ The response from Richmond was that it would be a dangerous exercise in educational overkill. Then, too, the irony of a state that had only recently overcome its political subservience to England inviting the academic domination of European thought must have been noted.

With Geneva's political cauldron bubbling and its faculty at odds with the aristocratic regime in power, Jefferson owed that group a prompt reply, which would permit them to explore other avenues for exodus. On 6 February 1795 Jefferson reluctantly shared the legislators' reaction with a restless D'Ivernois.²⁴ On the same day, he wrote Vice-President Adams, who had also received an exploratory letter from D'Ivernois. In his letter to Adams, Jefferson explained how his fascination with the Geneva scheme had robbed him of the solitude of a premature retirement to Monticello:

> I have found so much tranquillity of mind in a total abstraction from everything political, that it was with some difficulty I could resolve to meddle even in the splendid project of transplanting the academy of Geneva, *en masse*, to Virginia; and I did it under the usual reserve of *sans tirer en conséquence*.²⁵

Interrupted solitude or not, Jefferson was not about to abandon the Geneva project so easily. An unfavorable reaction from the legislature boded ill for state funding, so Jefferson turned for support to Virginia's favorite son and his former superior, President George Washington.

Jefferson knew that Washington not only valued the importance of education in a republic but also had the financial means to endow an institution of higher learning. Nor had Jefferson been reluctant to tap those resources in the past. In 1785 Gov. Patrick Henry and the Virginia legislature had awarded Washington fifty shares in the Potomac River Canal Company in recognition of his service to his state and country during the Revolution.²⁶ Washington was always somewhat embarrassed by the gift, asking Benjamin Harrison, "How would this matter be viewed then by the eye of the world... when it comes to be related that G W——n... has received 20,000 Dollars and £5,000 Sterling of the public money as an interest therein?" ²⁷ Wash-

---

²³ Jefferson to D'Ivernois, 6 Feb. 1795 (Paul Leicester Ford, ed., *The Writings of Thomas Jefferson* [10 vols.; New York and London, 1892-99], VII, 2-6).
²⁴ Ibid.
²⁵ Jefferson to Adams, 6 Feb. 1795 (Honeywell, *Educational Work*, p. 59).
²⁶ William Waller Hening, ed., *The Statutes at Large...of Virginia*, XI (Richmond, 1823), 525-26. See also Herbert B. Adams, *The College of William and Mary: A Contribution to the History of Higher Education...* (Washington, D.C., 1887), p. 33. Many years later, a reconstituted James River Canal Company became the major project of Joseph C. Cabell, Jefferson's lieutenant in the campaign to found the University of Virginia.
²⁷ Washington to Harrison, 22 Jan. 1785 (John C. Fitzpatrick, ed., *The Writings of George Washington,...1745-1799* [39 vols.; Washington, D.C., 1931-44], XXVIII, 35).

ington's solution to this awkward problem was to donate the shares toward some worthwhile educational project. In 1785 he wrote the trustees of Alexandria Academy of his intention to fund their program for orphans, the poor, and children whose fathers had fallen in the war.[28] But the opportunistic Jefferson placed an alternative proposal before the general. On 4 January 1786 Jefferson tried to persuade Washington to steer his funds and support to the 1779 education reform bills, passage of which he claimed would "supersede the use and obscure the existence of the charity schools you have thought of." [29] But the old warrior demurred. Nine years later, as the "splendid" Geneva notion fired Jefferson's imagination, Washington had still not decided how best to dispose of his canal shares.

Jefferson's 1795 communication sought to convince the president that the Geneva plan was the perfect object for his financial and personal interests. The bulk of the letter attempted to dazzle Washington with the brilliance of the Geneva faculty. Jefferson wrote of Mouchon, its distinguished president; of the brothers Pictet in natural philosophy; of Bertrand and L'Huillier in mathematics; of the geologist De Saussure; and of Senebier, noted translator of Greek tragedies—names which he claimed were "well known . . . as standing foremost among the literati of Europe." He even held out hope that the French mathematician La Grange might be induced to join the exodus of Swiss scholars. What Jefferson did not mention was that only three of the entire faculty had indicated to D'Ivernois their interest in coming to the United States.

Inserted deftly between this professorial window dressing and a detailed discussion of his contact with D'Ivernois was consideration of the location for the new Swiss university. D'Ivernois had avoided this question, although his correspondence with Adams and Jefferson, the two most distinguished scholars associated with the Washington administration, suggests that he contemplated some sort of national establishment in the federal city. Jefferson, however, could not resist targeting the mobile university for Virginia, whose limited commitment to higher education had frustrated him to that time. Jefferson knew, however, the specifics of Washington's 8 January 1790 message to Congress, recommending the establishment of a national university. His letter to Washington anticipated presidential preference for a federally supported institution at the new capital (the location of which along the Potomac River Washington himself had selected and the planning of which Jefferson himself had been intimately involved in). Jefferson wrote

[28] Washington to the Trustees of the Alexandria Academy, 17 Dec. 1785 (ibid., pp. 356-58).
[29] Jefferson to Washington, 4 Jan. 1786 (Lipscomb and Bergh, *Writings*, XIX, 23-25).

of the Geneva faculty becoming the very "national university" he knew Washington favored, "national" in the sense that its European-born prestige would cause "such an *éclat* and such solid advantages as would ensure a very general concourse to it of the youth from all our states and probably from the other parts of America which are free enough to adopt it." [30]

Jefferson did not propose that the school be placed in the capital city. Rather, he reasoned that the national university should be located "near enough to it to be viewed as an appendix," effectively restricting the site to Maryland or Virginia. He suggested further that the institution be placed "so far from the federal city as moral considerations would recommend," implying that an urban setting would tend to distract young learners from their scholarly pursuits and was therefore inferior to the built-in seclusion of the countryside. He proceeded to offer the innocent-sounding suggestion that the institution be located in whichever state contributed most generously to its support. Given the fact that the Virginia legislature had awarded the canal shares to Washington, Jefferson led the president toward the conclusion that the "national" university should be placed in Virginia. He reinforced this conclusion by reminding Washington of the educational wants of their native state and reveling in the possibility that the needs of the state and the nation might be met by a single, wisely situated, institution in which "the splendor of the two objects would reflect usefully on each other." [31]

Jefferson's proposal had yet another appeal. As Daniel Boorstin recalls, a federal university, where the intellectual resources of America could be concentrated and where local prejudices could be dissolved, had been discussed since the colonial period. At the Constitutional Convention an early draft proposal by Charles C. Pinckney would have gone so far as to give the federal legislature express powers to establish a national university. [32]

Clearly, the plan within the plan was a shrewd one. By capitalizing on the timely offer of the Geneva faculty and the president's publicized support of a national university, Jefferson tried to establish an institution which would meet the needs of Virginia. Moreover, the promise of national prestige was designed to lure federal funding, a critical element in view of the state legislature's niggardly response to the issue. Honeywell maintains that Jefferson could not have seriously expected to procure a national university for his own state, reasoning rather that the man's zeal for education was great enough to support both a national and a state university. [33] Even conceding

---

[30] Jefferson to Washington, 23 Feb. 1795 (ibid., pp. 109-10).
[31] Ibid., p. 113.
[32] Boorstin, *The Americans: The Colonial Experience* (New York, 1958), p. 183.
[33] Honeywell, *Educational Work*, p. 62.

that zeal, Jefferson's 23 February 1795 letter to Washington suggests that he had just such a compromise in mind. Significantly, Jefferson sought first the support of the state legislature, turning to Washington only when members of that body withheld support. The Geneva proposal, at least as Jefferson translated it to Washington, was nothing less than a stratagem by which the back door to a university in Virginia could be opened.

Unfortunately for Jefferson, Washington needed no one to interpret the proposal for him. Unbeknownst to Jefferson, the dutiful Vice-President Adams had already supplied Washington with his copy of D'Ivernois's original letter. Washington knew perfectly well what D'Ivernois had offered and what he had not. He must have dismissed the Geneva idea even before Jefferson's 23 February letter arrived, because he indicated in his 15 March 1795 reply that he had been in receipt of the D'Ivernois letter for months. Furthermore, while knowing about the Swiss scheme, Washington advised the commissioners of the federal city on 28 January of his intention to give his Potomac shares to a university to be founded at the capital. He also indicated on that date that he would have preferred to donate the James River canal shares to that same end. But recognizing their source, he had resolved to write Gov. Robert Brooke of Virginia suggesting that the General Assembly use those shares for the support of some existing institution within the state.[34] Having thus ruled out the Geneva proposal, Washington proceeded to dismiss Jefferson's version of that plan with characteristic sobriety and finality.

After observing first that the plan was entirely too tentative and that the federal government was no more in a position to make firm commitments to the Swiss professors than that faculty was to commit itself to America (Jefferson's enthusiasm notwithstanding), Washington reiterated to Jefferson the same reservations Nicholas had relayed from the legislature. He noted first the danger of accepting the entire group without considering the probity and English-speaking ability of each candidate. Related to this was his concern that by accepting the Geneva contingent in toto, the employment of other capable scholars both imported and domestic would be impossible. This was particularly serious because native English-speaking academicians would be turned away. The Geneva transplant, he felt, "might preclude some of the first Professors in other countries from a participation; among whom some of the most celebrated characters in Scotland, in this line, I am told might be obtained."

---

[34] Washington to Jefferson, 15 Mar. 1795 (Fitzpatrick, *Washington*, XXXIV, 146-49).

Washington also noted the political implications of such a move. Tapping a faculty embroiled in class-centered revolution in Geneva might suggest that an aristocratic intelligentsia was being foisted upon impressionable American youth, thus exciting those who were "continually sounding the alarm bell of aristocracy." Washington and his Federalist cabinet had heard enough cries of elitism without going all the way to Switzerland to provoke more. Unlike the state legislature, Washington did not dwell on the cost of the venture or the logistical problems it would have posed. His primary objection was couched in conceptual terms: He doubted the expediency of importing a body of foreign professors unfamiliar with the English language and at variance with "the levelling party in their own country." [35]

In his 15 March reply to Jefferson, Washington also considered the site. He did not accept Jefferson's contention that a national university located in Virginia was a reasonable response to the requirements of both his state and nation. He observed that the federal city was the permanent seat of government for the United States and the place where its laws and the machinery of self-government were better understood than anywhere else. He expected the national university to be a training ground for government leadership by inculcating principles and practices of federalism:

> As this Seminary is contemplated for the *completion* of education, and study of the sciences (not for boys in their rudiments) it will afford the Students an opportunity of attending the debates in Congress, and thereby becoming more liberally, and better acquainted with the principles of law, and government. [36]

Given Washington's concept, any location other than the nation's capital was glaringly inappropriate.

Washington's indifference to Jefferson's concept of a Virginia-based national university endured to his death. The day after his negative reply, on 16 March 1795, Washington duly wrote Governor Brooke of his plan to give the Potomac River shares to a national university and the James River shares to some preparatory school in Virginia. [37] This was Washington's compromise between his interest in a federally based institution and his recognition that the shares in question had come from Virginia. In December 1795 the General Assembly endorsed his action and recommended that the secondary school he selected in Virginia be "at such place in the upper country as he may deem most convenient to a majority of the in-

---

[35] Ibid., p. 148.
[36] Ibid., p. 147.
[37] Washington to Brooke, 16 Mar. 1795 (ibid., pp. 149-51).

habitants thereof." [38] Characteristically, Washington was as good as his promise. In his Farewell Address to Congress, Washington reaffirmed his early interest in a national school:

> I have heretofore proposed to the consideration of Congress the expediency of establishing a national university. . . .
> Amongst the motives to such an institution, the assimilation of the principles, opinions, and manners of our countrymen by the common education of a portion of our youth from every quarter well deserves attention. The more homogeneous our citizens can be made in these particulars the greater will be our prospect of permanent union; and a primary object of such a national institution should be the education of our youth in the science of *government*.[39]

Four years later the site of this university was dictated in his will:

> I give and bequeath in perpetuity the fifty shares which I hold in the Potomac Company . . . towards the endowment of a university, to be established within the limits of the District of Columbia, under the auspices of the General Government, if that government should incline to extend a fostering hand towards it.[40]

Interestingly, the "convenient," "upper country" Virginia school Washington selected to receive his James River shares was Lexington's Liberty Hall Academy, later to become Washington College and a serious rival to a later Jeffersonian scheme for locating a state university in Virginia.

The reasons Washington rejected the Geneva offer go beyond the obvious weakness inherent in importing a foreign-speaking faculty from a city in revolution to become the academic base of a newborn country with limited resources. Jefferson's plan for a central Virginia location was fundamentally at odds with a District of Columbia site on which Washington's whole concept of a national university depended.

---

[38] Samuel Shepherd, ed., *The Statutes at Large of Virginia . . . in Three Volumes*, new ser., I (Richmond, 1835), 434-35. See also Berkeley Minor and James F. Minor, comps., *Legislative History of the University of Virginia as Set Forth in the Acts of the General Assembly of Virginia, 1802-1927* ([Charlottesville], 1928), p. 3.

[39] James D. Richardson, ed., *A Compilation of the Messages and Papers of the Presidents, 1789-1897*, I (Washington, D.C., 1896), 202.

[40] "Last Will and Testament" (Fitzpatrick, *Washington*, XXXVII, 280-81). George Washington's Potomac shares are popularly believed to have gone into the endowment of George Washington University in Washington, D.C. Certainly, his support of a national university did lead indirectly to the founding of that private institution. Yet the Potomac shares he bequeathed actually went elsewhere. When the Potomac Canal Company merged with the Chesapeake and Ohio Canal Company, Washington's shares came to be held in trust by the latter company. The Chesapeake and Ohio venture later became linked with the Baltimore and Ohio Railroad, whose philanthropy formed the chief endowment of Johns Hopkins University. In a technical if not a spiritual sense, then, Washington was more directly involved with the founding of Johns Hopkins University than the institution which bears his name (Adams, *William and Mary*, pp. 44-45).

Washington had other ties that stood to be threatened by a Geneva faculty installed in Virginia. The old president had a lifelong loyalty to the recent object of Jefferson's frustration, William and Mary College. Washington owed his first public office as county surveyor in 1749 to selection by the college.[41] Moreover, from 1788 until his death in 1799 he served as its first nonecclesiastical chancellor. His letter to Samuel Griffin, rector of the institution, accepting the chancellorship reflected his determination that the school's preeminence in the state not be undermined:

> Influenced by a heart-felt desire to promote the cause of science in general and the prosperity of the College of William and Mary in particular, I accept the office of chancellor in the same.... I confide fully in their strenuous endeavors for placing the system of education on such a basis as will render it the most beneficial to the State and the republic of letters, as well as to the more extensive interests of humanity and religion.[42]

Perhaps, as Herbert B. Adams suggests, Washington's concept of what amounted to a graduate school of political science and public administration located at the nation's capital was inspired by the very role William and Mary College had played in colonial Virginia.[43] Three factors, then, influenced Washington in not only anticipating Jefferson's proposal but discounting it in no uncertain terms: the weaknesses in the Geneva idea, which the state legislature had also noted; the importance of a federal site to Washington's concept of a national university; and concern for the continued prestige of the Williamsburg school.

More remarkable than Washington's coolness to the Geneva scheme are the lengths to which Jefferson went to promote it. No doubt frustrated by the slow death of his earlier reform bills and by William and Mary's old charter, he saw the importation of a ready-made faculty of world renown, foreign or not, as the shortcut to a state university.

The critical question here, and one asked by Philip Alexander Bruce, is why Jefferson turned a deaf ear on the Richmond Academy proposal of Quesnay de Beaurepaire but waxed so enthusiastic over its approximate counterpart, the offer of D'Ivernois.[44] The two plans had, after all, a great deal in common. Both were ambitious. Both were extravagant, "too extensive for the poverty of the country." Both involved the introduction of French

---

[41] Adams, *William and Mary*, p. 30.
[42] Washington to Griffin, 30 Apr. 1788 (ibid., p. 35).
[43] Ibid., pp. 46-47.
[44] Bruce, *History of the University of Virginia*, I, 59-63; Adams, *Jefferson and the University*, p. 45.

culture and science into a rough-hewn country scarcely ready to appreciate it. Both promised instant renown, the academy through its association with leading circles of European science, the D'Ivernois scheme through the availability of a distinguished faculty. In both cases, éclat came at the expense of a French-English language barrier. One would think that the prestige, broad liberal scholarship, and an emphasis on science and research offered by the two would have attracted Jefferson to both. And both, in offering lower levels of training to prepare students for more sophisticated instruction, reflected the same thinking behind the educational system broached in the revisal bills. The fact that Pictet and L'Huillier of the Geneva faculty had also been associated with the academy project suggests another parallel between the two undertakings.[45]

True, the historical contexts in which Jefferson weighed the Quesnay and D'Ivernois proposals were different. Quesnay's came at a time when Virginia still lay prostrate from the Revolution. Malone observes that by the early 1790s both the country's economic outlook and Jefferson's own perspective had brightened considerably:

> The prosperity of the country under the new government was undeniable. Jefferson referred to it repeatedly in letters to Americans abroad, and it extended to the Southern agricultural states sufficiently to take the edge off the early opposition of Southern leaders to Hamilton's financial policies and make this seem rather academic.[46]

Further, when Jefferson reviewed the Quesnay venture he was an ocean removed from the scene in Virginia. By the time of D'Ivernois's letter he had retreated to the Virginia countryside and found the time to champion a "splendid project." Likewise, by 1794 he had become thoroughly frustrated by partisan bickering and the machinations of federal leadership and welcomed the diversion. Given Peterson's view that Jefferson's disillusionment with the Washington administration had sectional overtones,[47] a plan which stood to benefit his native state would have been all the more attractive. An effort to free Geneva's scholars from political turmoil (rather as Jefferson himself had escaped late in 1793), as Malone implies, may have appealed to Jefferson's association of knowledge with freedom, that " 'first-born daughter of science.' "[48]

---

[45] Adams, *William and Mary*, p. 40; Adams, *Jefferson and the University*, pp. 23, 27.
[46] Malone, *Jefferson and His Time*, II, 434.
[47] Merrill D. Peterson, *Thomas Jefferson and the New Nation: A Biography* (New York, 1970), p. 436.
[48] Malone, *Jefferson and His Time*, III, 191-92; ibid., VI, 233.

Still, the Quesnay venture could have been as enticing to Jefferson as the Geneva transplant. It had a sounder financial footing, based on the assurances of Virginian support and donations of 60,000 francs. The Geneva idea had no financial backing whatsoever. By the time the Paris minister was approached by Quesnay, the academy was much closer to implementation and had far greater prospects for success than the Swiss inquiry. With funds accumulating, Quesnay had a building and a faculty under construction. As Washington reminded Jefferson, the only real assets D'Ivernois could boast were twelve scholars who needed to get out of town and one man in Virginia who wanted the band to repair there.

Further, Jefferson could not have been pleased by the ardent Calvinism of the Swiss. His abortive reform bills, his reform of William and Mary College, and his early campaign for separation of church and state in Virginia all point to a crusade to eradicate sectarianism from public concerns. The stern piety of Geneva was a classic negation of that freedom of religion. Quesnay's academy, on the other hand, posed less of a threat to the man's convictions. While plans did call for a Roman Catholic church and token homage to religious faith, the scheme was very much the product of a Voltairean secularism, to which many leading European intellectuals and Jefferson subscribed.

Moreover, the Quesnay project admitted the possibility of local scholars becoming involved in instruction, potentially reducing the problems of language and foreign monopoly on scholarship for which Washington had criticized the Geneva plan. The established professorships of Geneva promised no such flexibility. If one concedes a basic similarity between the Quesnay plan and Jefferson's later university concept, regardless of whether one actually influenced the other,[49] it would have been natural for Jefferson to look with greater favor upon Quesnay than D'Ivernois. Nevertheless, Jefferson remained fascinated by the Geneva plan despite its obvious dangers and did not countenance the Richmond scheme for a moment.

What did the Geneva scheme have to offer which the Quesnay plan did not? The answer does not lie in Jefferson's 1788 rebuff of the French entrepreneur. As noted before, Jefferson's main objection to the academy was ostensibly a fear that European scholars would come over to America with unrealistic expectations, only to be disappointed in their new situation. He

---

[49] Many historians concede basic similarities between the Richmond Academy and the later university. The greater question is whether, given those similarities, a cause-and-effect relationship can be determined. The consensus seems to be that Jefferson was already familiar with the typically French approaches reflected in the academy through earlier residence in France and that he was therefore not influenced in his university plans by the Quesnay scheme per se.

claimed he could not let himself be made responsible for their encouragement and subsequent chagrin. When D'Ivernois wrote Jefferson of the
Geneva contingent's interest in coming to America, Jefferson voiced no such
concern. If Jefferson had been sincerely torn by the adjustment problems
of Quesnay's band of scholars, he would have displayed similar feelings to
D'Ivernois. The reasoning in Jefferson's reply to Quesnay was a subterfuge
to conceal other objections.

It could be argued that Jefferson's basic problem with the Quesnay plan
was a fear that the academy, with its branch campuses along the eastern
seaboard, would become a national system of education dominated by the
federal government. As noted earlier, such an establishment would have
run counter to the statesman's distrust of political centralization and to his
belief in popular education as a check against governmental encroachment
upon civil liberty. A national university under government control would
have jeopardized that educational purpose. When Jefferson wrote Washington about the Geneva proposal, though, he seemed perfectly willing to risk
a centralized institution in order to lure presidential support and federal
funding for a Virginia-based university.

Jefferson may have protested the plans for the Quesnay academy because
they were essentially a fait accompli by the time they reached him. He
would not have had the opportunity to mold the institution into the educational system he wanted for Virginia. As Quesnay sought his endorsement
rather than his counsel, Jefferson's lack of interest may have reflected
annoyance that he had not been consulted earlier. How much more of a
shaping role could Jefferson have played with the Geneva group? It is hard
to imagine scholars of the stature Jefferson promised Washington acceding to
Jefferson's curricular wishes, regardless of how desperately they wished to
vacate Geneva. The University of Geneva was an established institution
with a set curriculum guided by prominent scholars. However, if Jefferson
could have effected its relocation in America near him, he may have believed that he could influence the development of an American "University
of Geneva."

Jefferson's scorn for the Quesnay plan and affection for the Geneva offer
involved the proposed locations for the two schools. Jefferson had no control
over the site of the Richmond Academy or its national and international
affiliates. Whether in Paris or back at Monticello, Jefferson perceived that
he would not be in a position to give personal direction to Quesnay or the
academy. Bruce suggests that Jefferson's objection to the site of the academy
forced his veto of the measure:

Why was it that he failed to offer a single suggestion towards lopping off the worst of its [the Richmond Academy proposal's] faults in order to reduce it to a shape that might make it workable? It was very unlike him to look at such a scheme with coldness, if there was any room whatever for hope of success. Did he jump beyond its apparently bald infeasibility and disapprove of it because it locked horns with the plan of a university which he was undoubtedly pondering over at this time, and which he had already perhaps decided to build, if possible, in the shadow of Monticello? Was the choice of Richmond, an hundred miles away, as the site of the new Academy, the true reason for an indifference which he had never before shown, and was never again to show, about any university scheme brought to his attention?[50]

The site of the Geneva transplant was, however, a negotiable item. His Geneva contact had mentioned no preference of place in his correspondence. Exploiting this fact, Jefferson proposed the scheme first through Nicholas to the state legislature, then to Washington, with the obvious intention of securing a Virginia seat.

The location of the Swiss-styled university within Virginia was a critical concern. While Jefferson never did say in so many words where in Virginia the Geneva faculty and the national university it portended were to be situated, certain inferences can be drawn. The letter to Washington suggested that the school be near enough to the capital city to be associated with the seat of government, but far enough away to avoid the moral pitfalls Jefferson consistently associated with urban study: "I am not a friend to placing growing men in populous cities, because they acquire there habits & partialities which do not contribute to the happiness of their after life." [51] By Jefferson's own reckoning, the limitations offered in his letter excluded the Alexandria area as being too close to Washington while effectively eliminating all parts of Virginia not within a one or two-day ride (perhaps 120 miles) of the nation's capital.

A circle with a radius of 120 miles and its center at Washington included the budding town of Richmond. By the end of the eighteenth century, however, Jefferson may not have considered Richmond desirable for his university. First, Richmond by virtue of its being the state capital was bound to grow in size and to evince qualities that Jefferson maintained were not conducive to higher education. Second, by the end of the century Jefferson came to see Richmond as a veritable hotbed of Federalism.[52] A Swiss-staffed

---

[50] Bruce, *History of the University of Virginia*, I, 59.

[51] Jefferson to Dr. Caspar Wistar, 21 June 1807 (Ford, *Writings*, IX, 79).

[52] Jefferson must initially have looked with favor on the town of Richmond, as he proposed a state library there in 1779 and relocated the state capital there during the Revolution. Exactly when creeping Federalism tainted the new capital in Jefferson's eyes is difficult to determine. The

national institution there would have been doubly threatening, given his fear of political consolidation.

The passage by Bruce cited earlier suggests an alternate site Jefferson preferred but had not yet made public. As his concept of a university began to crystallize, Jefferson became convinced of the necessity of placing the institution so that it could be guided by his own hand. Accordingly, he wanted a site accessible to his Monticello home in Albemarle County. As Bruce continues:

> There is no reason to doubt that he expected this college to be re-established in visiting distance of his own home at least. If he was really influenced by personal reasons... it was due to his perfectly correct impression that, if a university was to be found in Virginia, it would have more chance of succeeding under his own direct patronage and supervision than if left to the inadvertence and inexperience of foreigners, settled an hundred miles from Monticello.[53]

It is entirely feasible that the main reason why Jefferson endorsed the Geneva scheme and rejected the Quesnay plan was that locating the former in his own Albemarle County was possible. Before Washington's dismissal of the Swiss idea early in 1795, Jefferson was careful not to disclose any preference for his own county or its county seat at the village of Charlottesville. But in his discouraging reply to D'Ivernois, made after the legislative reaction relayed by Nicholas and before his correspondence with the president, Jefferson did go this far:

> I should have seen with peculiar satisfaction the establishment of such a mass of science in my country, and should probably have been tempted to approach myself to it, by procuring a residence in it's neighborhood, at those seasons of the year at least when the operations of agriculture are less active and interesting.[54]

The convenience of the university being brought to him, rather than his having to journey to it, occurred to him more than once. Significantly, when Jefferson first sounded out the legislature about the Geneva scheme, he turned to Nicholas, the delegate from Albemarle.

Jefferson's enthusiasm for the Geneva importation appears to have been based in large measure upon his hope that an Albemarle site could be ob-

---

fact that his old Federalist adversary John Marshall made his home in Richmond may have had some bearing on this new attitude. If so, Marshall's 1790 court ruling reasserting the privacy of William and Mary and John Adams's "midnight" selection of Marshall as chief justice (a parting gift to the incoming Republican Jefferson) gain new relevance. Anti-Richmond sentiments run through his later correspondence, especially his letters to Joseph C. Cabell.

[53] Bruce, *History of the University of Virginia,* I, 59-60.
[54] Jefferson to D'Ivernois, 6 Feb. 1795 (Ford, *Writings,* VII, 3-4).

tained. In 1803, by which time Washington's death and the disposition of the coveted Potomac and James River canal shares made the Geneva proposal a past issue, Jefferson admitted to Professor Pictet of that faculty the method behind his Geneva madness:

> I hoped ... that some canal shares, which were at the disposal of General Washington, might have been applied towards the establishment of a good seminary of learning; but he [Washington] had already proceeded too far on another plan to change their direction.[55]

The strategy of accommodating Washington's interest in a national university as a means of securing a state university located in Albemarle County sheds light on Jefferson's later inconsistency as president over the question of such a national institution. Jefferson's two administrations (1801-5, 1805-9) were marked by extensive efforts on behalf of education, notably the signing into law of a bill establishing a United States Military Academy (1802) and the appropriation of federal lands toward the endowment of academies and colleges in several states. Illustrative of just how far his interest in education went is the fact that during his presidency he served briefly as chairman of the Board of Education of the District of Columbia.[56] John Sharp Williams's 1913 contention that "under no single administration of the Federal Government was there ever so much done by the Government, with a view to helping the States establish and maintain education, as under his [Jefferson's] administration" is persuasive.[57]

Yet James B. Conant, Richard Beale Davis, and other recent scholars have criticized Jefferson for not using presidential power to push for a national university.[58] Certainly, their criticism is valid. In his sixth annual message to Congress, Jefferson pressed for a constitutional amendment that would have enabled the federal government to play a more direct role in some national educational establishment:

> Education is here placed among the articles of public care, not that it would be proposed to take its ordinary branches out of the hands of private enterprise, which manages so much better all the concerns to which it is equal, but a public institution can alone supply those sciences which though rarely called

---

[55] Jefferson to Pictet, 5 Feb. 1803 (Lipscomb and Bergh, *Writings*, X, 355).

[56] John C. Henderson, *Thomas Jefferson's Views on Public Education* (New York, 1890), p. 185.

[57] John Sharp Williams, *Thomas Jefferson: His Permanent Influence on American Institutions* (New York, 1913), p. 305.

[58] Conant, *Thomas Jefferson and the Development of American Public Education* (Berkeley and Los Angeles, 1963), pp. 9-12; Davis, *Intellectual Life in Jefferson's Virginia, 1790-1830* (Chapel Hill, 1964), pp. 60-61.

for are.yet necessary to complete the circle, all the parts of which contribute to the improvement of the country and some of them to its preservation.... I suppose an amendment to the Constitution by consent of the States, necessary, because the objects now recommended are not among those enumerated in the Constitution, and to which it permits the public money to be applied.

The present consideration of a national establishment for education particularly is rendered proper by this circumstance also, that if Congress, approving the proposition, shall yet think it more eligible to found it on a donation of lands, they have it now in their power to endow it with those which will be among the earliest to produce the necessary income.[59]

This position is consistent with Jefferson's view of the general government as acting where local and state governments were incapable. Asserting central authority in such areas would cement the Union, cause lines of intranational separation to disappear, and raise levels of cultural and academic accomplishment in the eyes of the world's intellectual elite. But Jefferson's language in his message is unclear. His acknowledgment of the effectiveness of private educational enterprise, his use of the terms "donation" and "endow," and his administration's other efforts to promote educational activity by the states indicate he was endorsing something short of a Washington-styled national university in his 1806 address. A "national establishment for education" sounds more like federal subsidy to state education than a national university per se. At any rate, nothing immediate came of Jefferson's appeal. As his secretary of the treasury, Albert Gallatin, had foreseen, canals and roads proved more popular internal improvements, and the national education institution fell by the wayside.[60]

Jefferson was temporarily attracted to the concept of a national university only when it served other, private purposes. Yet, other theorists took his interest literally rather than as a product of a unique set of historical circumstances. When faced with specific proposals drafted by men who thought him receptive to a national university, Jefferson backed down.

One such proposal came from Pierre Samuel Du Pont de Nemours, another intellectual confrere from Jefferson's days in Paris. Du Pont, whom Jefferson lured first to Delaware, then to Monticello,[61] completed by June 1800 a lengthy treatise, *Sur l'Education Nationale dans les États-Unis.*[62]

---

[59] Richardson, *Messages and Papers*, I, 409-10.

[60] Peterson, *Jefferson and the New Nation*, pp. 855-59; Malone, *Jefferson and His Time*, V, 555.

[61] Edgar Finley Shannon, Jr., *The University of Virginia: A Century and a Half of Innovation* (New York, 1969), p. 8; Culbreth, *University of Virginia*, p. 82.

[62] Pierre Samuel Du Pont de Nemours, *National Education in the United States of America*, trans. Bessie Gardner Du Pont (Newark, Del., 1923). In her introduction Du Pont also indicates that Du Pont de Nemours mentioned a political economist named François Quesnay as one who

This work, written specifically "à la demande de M. Jefferson, alors vice-président et depuis président des Étas-Unis d'Amérique," should have pleased its instigator greatly. The report called for a national system of public instruction at all levels, culminating in a national university in the District of Columbia. Within that university, separate schools or "grandes écoles" were to offer instruction in medicine, mineralogy, social sciences and legislation, and higher mathematics. A national library and museum were also part of the plan.[63] The lower levels of instruction leading to university training recalled the earlier revisal bills, while Du Pont's emphasis on teaching the highest levels of science by means of separate subject-schools was distinctly Jeffersonian in concept. Had Jefferson been thoroughly committed to a national system of education crowned by a national university, he would have embraced Du Pont's scheme wholeheartedly.

Jefferson read the proposal with interest[64] but took no steps as president to make Du Pont's system a reality. He had written Du Pont in April 1800[65] (much as he had written Joseph Priestley in January of that year) asking for curricular recommendations concerning a university for the state of Virginia. A 159-page document proposing a national system capped by a university in Washington that threatened to force his hand on the issue of a federal establishment was considerably more than he bargained for. An April 1816 letter, which Du Pont received the year before his death, reflects a lingering dislike of paternalism. Jefferson also felt this was implicit in national delivery of mass education. He commented, "You [the French] love them [citizens] as infants whom you are afraid to trust without nurses; and I as adults whom I freely leave to self-government."[66] Jefferson feared a national university headquartered in Washington and placed in the hands of functionaries there as a threat to individual liberty.

A proposal by poet Joel Barlow for a national university met a similar fate. As follow-up to earlier correspondence with Jefferson, Barlow drafted in 1806 a *Prospectus of a National Institution to be Established in the United*

"for eleven years was my master, my instructor, my father" (p. vii). This suggests a possible relationship between Alexandre Marie Quesnay de Beaurepaire's Richmond Academy and the national education system for the United States advanced by Du Pont.

[63] For further discussion of Du Pont de Nemours's national system of education, see Adams, *Jefferson and the University*, pp. 49-51; Culbreth, *University of Virginia*, pp. 80-83; Bruce, *History of the University of Virginia*, I, 63-67; and his lengthy correspondence with Jefferson contained in Dumas Malone, ed., *Correspondence between Thomas Jefferson and Pierre Samuel du Pont de Nemours, 1798-1817*, trans. Linwood Lehman (Boston and New York, 1930).

[64] Jefferson to Du Pont de Nemours, 12 Apr. 1800, Jefferson Papers.

[65] Ibid.

[66] Jefferson to Du Pont de Nemours, 24 Apr. 1816 (Lipscomb and Bergh, *Writings*, XIV, 489-90).

States." The proposal called for a series of district colleges reminiscent of the district schools Jefferson wanted for Virginia in 1779, but to be spread throughout the country. A university situated in Washington was to offer higher levels of instruction through the French-styled subject-schools Jefferson favored.

Thanks to Barlow's congressional contacts, his proposal got further than Du Pont's. A bill incorporating the Barlow university was introduced into the Senate but died in committee. A letter from Jefferson to Barlow in February 1806 indicates that Jefferson had suggested only minor editorial changes in the bill." Peterson is satisfied that the Barlow proposal fell to concerns of public economy, states' rights, and Federalist fears of undue political influence." As in the case of Jefferson's 1806 endorsement of a national establishment for education, it is difficult to say whether more aggressive presidential patronage would have altered the outcome. Almost two years later, Jefferson commiserated with Barlow over Congress's failure to support his proposed amendment for national education, without ratification of which he felt plans such as the poet's could not even be considered. One suspects that Jefferson was lamenting one loss and Barlow quite another. Barlow's ardent Federalism gave Jefferson's gesture of condolence an even more hollow ring.

Jefferson's inaction on specific proposals by Du Pont and Barlow for a national university, as well as his ambiguous pronouncements on the subject as president, makes questionable his commitment to a national institution. He did mention to son-in-law John Eppes four years after his retirement that he had considered a national establishment for education "one of the ardent goals of [my] Presidency." [70] But his strict constructionism, distaste for consolidation of political power, and faith in public education as a check against governmental excess must have pulled him in the opposite direction and stopped him short of supporting a national university.

Shortly before and during his presidency, by which time Jefferson's statements and his treatment of the Du Pont and Barlow proposals reflect a loss of interest in the national university concept, successive governors of Virginia called attention to Virginia's "educational needs and referred specifically to a university." Malone suggests that this attention steered him away

---

[67] Joel Barlow, *Prospectus of a National Institution to be Established in the United States* (Washington, D.C., 1806).

[68] Jefferson to Barlow, 24 Feb. 1806 (Paul Leicester Ford, ed., *The Works of Thomas Jefferson*, X [New York and London, 1905], 232).

[69] Peterson, *Jefferson and the New Nation*, p. 859.

[70] Jefferson to Eppes, 11 Sept. 1813, Jefferson Papers.

from a federal enterprise and prompted him to write Joseph Priestley, Du Pont, and others about curricular plans for a university in Virginia and to solicit word from Littleton W. Tazewell on the latest rumblings of legislative interest in Richmond.[71] Jefferson's lack of interest in a national educational establishment after 1800 and renewed interest in higher education in his native state were hardly coincidental.

Following his return to Monticello in 1809, the retired Jefferson succeeded in giving life to the "child of his old age," the University of Virginia. Stumbling by "accident" (as popular accounts would have us believe) upon an 1814 meeting of the remaining board members of Albemarle Academy, a Charlottesville preparatory school chartered in 1803 but otherwise inoperative, the elder statesman soon came to dominate the group. Relying upon good fortune and a measure of deception, he first gained the nominal institution's titular promotion to Central College, thus placing the school squarely under the eye and aegis of the state legislature. He then launched a furious campaign to raise funds; to construct impressive buildings; to engage distinguished faculty; to design a modern, advanced curriculum; and otherwise to groom the college for its second quantum leap to a university. After several rounds of debate in Richmond, which featured the intense rivalry of other towns and schools proposed as sites for a university, Central College in Charlottesville was adopted as the University of Virginia in 1819.

The remarkable series of events leading to the founding of the university has been carefully chronicled elsewhere and is beyond the scope of this study. Notably, though, Jefferson was not above resorting to subterfuge in order to bring higher education to Albemarle County and Virginia. Once he trained his considerable energies upon fathering a university virtually in the shadow of Monticello, the idea of a national university occupied neither his correspondence nor, presumably, his thoughts.

Thomas Jefferson's lifelong interest in higher education consistently focused on the creation of a first-rate university in Virginia. Following his failure to reshape William and Mary College, this interest became inseparable in his mind from a location near Charlottesville. In this light his advocacy of a national university may be viewed as a clever tactic containing a hidden agenda of diverting the attention of Washington and others toward a state university of national stature located in central Virginia. Jefferson was intrigued by one French-laid scheme for a national university whose unspecified location could have been Charlottesville, but he would not countenance proposals for establishments fixed at the capital city or else-

71 Malone, *Jefferson and His Time*, V, 22; ibid., VI, 234.

where. When French doors to Virginia higher education closed and he found other, local means by which a nominal Albemarle school could be promoted into the University of Virginia, the national university concept borrowed from Washington no longer served his own purposes and was discarded. Thomas Jefferson's temporary advocacy of a national university, more flirtation than fact, is best understood as further evidence of his forty-year commitment to bring a new level of public higher education to the Old Dominion.

Amer. Stud. **2**, 2, 161–175 *Printed in Great Britain*

Humanitarianism in the Early Republic: The Moral Reformers of New York, 1776-1825

by M. J. HEALE
University of Lancaster

I

During the eighteenth century humanitarian sentiment grew in both Britain and Europe and by the end of the century, as Michael Kraus has shown, this benevolent spirit was crossing the Atlantic and was touching many Americans.[1] Humanitarian activities of many kinds were undertaken in the early republic, presaging the great reforming crusades of the mid-nineteenth century, and the centres of these experiments were the large commercial cities of New York, Philadelphia and Boston, which possessed the necessary conditions of a conscientious middle-class, an adequate supply of funds, and social evils in need of attention.

Humanitarian and charitable enterprises of the first half-century after Independence were probably at their most abundant in New York City, largely by virtue of its size and rapid growth. In addition to the better-known schemes to emancipate the slaves and to ameliorate the condition of the Negro, civic-minded New Yorkers also interested themselves in the sufferings of the sick and the poor, the criminal and the drunkard, the delinquent child and the neglected infant. Americans were becoming increasingly conscious of such problems as pauperism, drunkenness, disease and crime, which were accentuated by the process of urbanization, and even many city-dwellers seemed to share Jefferson's unease about the rapid growth of cities, which Mayor De Witt Clinton saw as 'nurseries and hot-beds of crime', the refuge of criminals and the home of luxury and corruption.[2] One way of quietening these fears was by humanitarian activity: anxious and benevolent citizens banded together in private societies to work to protect their cities from the dangers to which they were exposed

---

[1] M. Kraus, *The Atlantic Civilization: Eighteenth-Century Origins* (Ithaca, N.Y., 1949), ch. vi, pp. 123–58.
[2] Quoted in W. W. Campbell, *The Life and Writings of De Witt Clinton* (New York, 1849), p. 314. For a general discussion of reactions to urban growth in this period see C. N. Glaab and A. T. Brown, *A History of Urban America* (New York and London, 1967), ch. iii, pp. 53–81.

and to help those who had been afflicted by hardship or had succumbed to temptation.

Schemes to aid the poor and the sick were launched in large number. There was the New York Hospital, founded in 1771 by a private society but finally opened in 1791, which made special provision for the sick poor.[1] The New York Dispensary was established in 1791 to aid those not sick enough to go to hospital but sufficiently sick to be urgently in need of help.[2] The ailing poor were also the concern of the Assistance Societies 'for relieving and advising sick and poor persons' established in New York and Brooklyn in 1808 and 1813 respectively.[3] Some of the most unhappy sufferers were women who had lost their husbands, perhaps during one of the yellow-fever epidemics, and were left to bring up their families as best they could; in 1797 a group of benevolent women took pity on this class and provided for their aid through the establishment of the Society for the Relief of Poor Widows with Small Children.[4] Other products of middle-class concern for the urban poor in these years included a society for providing the destitute with soup during periods of hardship (which also acquired the function of resuscitating persons apparently dead from drowning), societies for providing poor persons with employment, a Magdalen Society to rescue wayward girls from their unhappy fate, and an Association for the Relief of Respectable, Aged, Indigent Females.[5] After the War of 1812 some citizens became concerned lest the multiplicity of relief-giving organizations was actually encouraging pauperism, and the Society for the Prevention of Pauperism was founded in 1817 to investigate social problems anew. Among its recommendations were an overhaul of the public relief system, more effective preventive measures such as better educational facilities, and self-help in the form of savings-banks.[6]

[1] 'Condensed history of the Society of the New York Hospital, compiled from its records, 1769–1921' (anon. typescript in New York Public Library, dated 1921), pp. 2, 6.

[2] *Charter and Ordinances of the New-York Dispensary* (New York, 1797), pp. 12–18, 30.

[3] *Constitution of the Assistance Society, for Relieving and Advising Sick and Poor Persons in the City of New-York* (New York, 1809); *Constitution of the Brooklyn Assistant Society, for Relieving and Advising Sick and Poor Persons* (Brooklyn, 1813).

[4] *Constitution of the Ladies Society, Established in New-York, for the Relief of Poor Widows with Small Children* (2nd edn., New York, 1800), p. 11.

[5] *A Sketch of the Origin and Progress of the Humane Society of the City of New-York...* (New York, 1814); 'Constitution and Minutes of the New-York Manufacturing Society, 1789–1792' (New York Historical Society, MS.); *Plan of the Society for the Promotion of Industry; with the First Report of the Board of Managers* (New York, 1816); *Constitution and By-Laws of the Magdalen Society of New-York* (New York, 1812); *The Constitution, and First and Second Annual Reports of the Proceedings of the Association for the Relief of Respectable, Aged, Indigent Females* (New York, 1815). The Humane Society acquired its interest in the drowned in following the example of its namesake, the British Royal Humane Society; see Kraus, *op. cit.* pp. 138–9.

[6] Society for the Prevention of Pauperism in the City of New-York (hereafter cited as the S.P.P.), *Second Annual Report, 1819*, pp. 14–16, 38–9; *Fifth Annual Report. 1821*, pp. 29–31.

The attempts to reform the penal system were less directly related to the problems of urbanization, but reformers were none the less concerned about the growing crime rate in the city, which was not diminished by the practice of releasing criminals after some form of corporal punishment. The penal system inherited from the British prescribed capital or corporal punishment for most offences and in the 1790s Thomas Eddy and others succeeded in abolishing this rather savage code and in replacing it with a prison system, in which, it was hoped, criminals would be reformed as well as punished.[1] The one class for which the old code normally did prescribe imprisonment were the unfortunate debtors who could not meet their obligations, and a Society for the Relief of Distressed Debtors was founded to provide them with aid and to work for an amendment to the law.[2] The penal reformers began their experiments with high hopes, but after the War of 1812, when prisons were becoming overcrowded and when it was clear that prisoners were more likely to be further corrupted by one another than to be reformed, there were fresh demands for improvements in the prisons and for a system of solitary confinement.[3]

Neglected children also received their share of attention. One group of reformers observed that it was 'in vain that laws are made for the punishment of crimes, or that good men attempt to stem the torrent of irreligion and vice, if the evil is not checked at its source'.[4] The children of the poor needed to be properly trained. The New York Society for Promoting the Manumission of Slaves established a free school for coloured children in 1787.[5] A more important institution was the New York Free School Society, established in 1805 to provide schools for 'the education of such poor children as do not belong to, or are not provided for, by any religious society'.[6] Another unfortunate class of children were provided for when the New York Orphan Asylum Society was founded in 1806.[7] In the 1820s it was found that these institutions were inadequate to reach all the children in need. Many were escaping the benign influences of education and were

---

[1] For Eddy's own account see his *An Account of the State Prison or Penitentiary House, in the City of New-York*, 'By One of the Inspectors of the Prison' (New York, 1801), a much wider-ranging work than its title suggests.

[2] *Sketch...of the Humane Society*, pp. 3–4.

[3] E.g. see *Report on the Penitentiary System in the United States, Prepared under a Resolution of the Society for the Prevention of Pauperism in the City of New-York* (New York, 1822), pp. 19, 49–56. A recent study of penal developments is W. D. Lewis, *From Newgate to Dannemora: The Rise of the Penitentiary in New York, 1796–1848* (Ithaca, N.Y., 1965).

[4] New York Free School Society, Address of the Trustees 'To the Public', 18 May 1805, in W. O. Bourne, *History of the Public School Society of the City of New York* (New York, 1870), p. 7.

[5] C. C. Andrews, *The History of the New-York African Free-Schools...* (New York, 1830), p. 7.

[6] Bourne, *op. cit.* p. 6.

[7] *The Constitution and Laws of the Orphan Asylum of the City of New-York* (New York, 1808), p. 4.

ending in prison, a circumstance which led to the formation of the Society
for the Reformation of Juvenile Delinquents, which founded the House of
Refuge to which delinquent and vagrant children were sent for care.[1] Others
were apparently being led into bad habits even before they reached school
age, and infant schools were established by private societies to provide
education for the very young.[2]

II

These, then, were the principal developments in New York humanitarianism between the 1770s and the 1820s. Much of the credit for these
accomplishments was owed to a relatively small number of individuals who
played prominent parts in undertakings of all kinds. John Pintard complained that New York lacked a wealthy leisured class with the inclination
'to attend to the multiplied demands on humanity & benevolence...Here,
these duties fall oppressively heavy on a few public spirited citizens, whose
necessities compel them...to *toil* for their support'. Pintard himself in one
week attended two meetings of the Society for the Prevention of Pauperism
and meetings of the Historical Society, the American Bible Society, the
Free School Society and American Academy of the Fine Arts.[3] Thomas
Eddy was also a man of many interests. In addition to his work as a prison
reformer, he was secretary of the Society of the New York Hospital, he
played an important part in establishing the Insane Asylum in 1815, and
he was a founder member of the Free School Society and of the Society for
the Prevention of Pauperism (among others). John Murray, Jr., was a
vice-president of both the Free School Society and the Society for the
Prevention of Pauperism, and was prominent in the affairs of the hospital
and in penal reform. The Society for the Prevention of Pauperism arose out
of some informal meetings at the home of John Griscom, the Quaker educa-
tionist who also helped to establish the House of Refuge and the first infant
schools. Mrs Isabella Graham and her son-in-law and daughter, Divie and
Joanna Bethune, were associated with several charitable ventures, notably
the Society for the Relief of Poor Widows with Small Children, the Orphan
Asylum Society, and the Society for the Promotion of Industry. Others
whose names were often found on the boards of managers of benevolent

[1] *Report of a Committee appointed by the Society for the Prevention of Pauperism...on the Expediency of Erecting an Institution for the Reformation of Juvenile Delinquents* (New York, 1824), p. 63; *Documents Relative to the House of Refuge* (New York, 1832), pp. 37–41.

[2] *The Constitution and By-Laws of the Infant School Society of the City of New-York* (New York, 1828); New York Public School Society, *Twenty-Ninth Annual Report* (1834), p. 5.

[3] Pintard to his daughter, 28 Nov. 1818, *Letters from John Pintard to his Daughter, Eliza Noel Pintard Davidson, 1816–1833*, ed. Dorothy C. Barck, vol. I, (New York 1940), pp. 155–6.

societies included Stephen Allen and General Matthew Clarkson.[1] While it would be dangerous to assume that the several benevolent enterprises of these years were managed by a closely knit series of 'interlocking directorates', it is hardly surprising that similar attitudes and ideas frequently recurred in the publications of the different bodies.[2]

Most of these enterprises were new: only rare instances of such activities can be found before the Revolution. The forces which produced this spate of benevolent undertakings were complex. Social problems were themselves growing larger and could not easily be ignored. In part the associated philanthropy of these years was a rationalization of older methods of charity. In rural areas the traditional methods of neighbourly help continued, but in the growing city, where the well-to-do had little personal knowledge of the poor and found it difficult to distinguish the 'deserving' from the 'undeserving', a new system had to be devised for channelling funds from those with means to those without.

The men and women who took part in these philanthropic endeavours were moved by a variety of impulses. Some possessed a genuinely humanitarian concern for others; the first efforts in associated philanthropy were directed towards helping special classes whose appeal to the emotions was great: widowed mothers, imprisoned debtors, neglected children. Many saw philanthropy as the hand-maiden of religion. This was a period when religious interest was growing, an age of Bible, tract and missionary societies, and pious-minded citizens were eager to prepare the poor and the criminal for salvation (and, indeed, to ensure their own). Others doubtless participated to prove to themselves and to others that they were worthy of admiration and respect, or to rub shoulders with such distinguished citizens as De Witt Clinton or Mrs Alexander Hamilton, both prominent in benevolent undertakings. Some wished to use philanthropy as a form of social control, vividly portraying the dangers to society of allowing pauper-

[1] It is not possible to provide a detailed analysis of the backgrounds of humanitarians in this article, which is addressed mainly to their ideas and methods. However, they had strong links with the commercial circles of New York (Bethune and Murray were merchants, Eddy had been an insurance broker, Pintard held a similar post, and Allen was a sail-maker) and there was a strong Quaker contingent among them (e.g. Murray, Eddy, Griscom). The reports of the various societies carry full lists of officers. For more information about these figures see the entries on Clarkson, Griscom, Eddy, Murray and Pintard in the *Dictionary of American Biography* and the following publications: [D. Bethune], *The Power of Faith: Exemplified in the Life and Writings of the Late Mrs Isabella Graham, of New York* (New York, 1816); G. W. Bethune, *Memoirs of Mrs Joanna Bethune* (New York, 1864); T. Eddy, *Memoir of the Late John Murray, Jun.* (New York, 1819); J. H. Griscom, *Memoir of John Griscom, LL.D. ...* (New York, 1859); S. L. Knapp, *The Life of Thomas Eddy...* (London, 1836); [J. A. Scoville], *The Old Merchants of New York City* (1st and 2nd series, New York, 1863).

[2] On the methodological difficulties in identifying 'interlocking directories', see C. S. Griffin, *Their Brothers' Keepers: Moral Stewardship in the United States, 1800–1865* (New Brunswick, N.J., 1960), pp. 275–6.

11   Am. Stud. 2

ism to grow or of permitting poor children to be reared by idle and vicious parents. Yet others wished to fulfil their dream of an enlightened republic, free from the evils which contaminated European society, and they worked for civic improvements of all kinds, showing as much interest in cultural, economic, and religious activities as in humanitarian.[1]

If the impulses which produced the benevolent measures of these years were varied, there was remarkable agreement among humanitarians about the causes of social evils and about the methods of overcoming them. Nine-tenths of the 'poverty and wretchedness' of the city, declared the Society for the Prevention of Pauperism, 'proceeds directly or indirectly from the want of correct moral principle...'[2] It followed that if the poor and the criminal could be imbued with 'correct moral principle' then social problems would largely disappear. Many reformers recognized that the lack of a virtuous morality was itself often the product of environmental factors, attributable perhaps to irresponsible parents or an inadequate schooling, but whatever the causes it was this moral weakness itself which produced paupers, drunkards and criminals, and reformers believed it their duty to remove it.

But how were men to be made moral? The early humanitarians developed a twofold answer: remove those sources of temptation, such as grog-shops and betting houses, which led men into bad ways, and provide benign and reformatory influences which would make men virtuous and industrious.

The efforts to suppress corrupting influences met with little success and were, indeed, conducted rather half-heartedly: it was easier to found schools than to prohibit alcohol. Reformers counted the number of grog-shops and liquor licences, deplored their rising numbers, and bewailed in dramatic terms the evil effects of intemperance, which the Society for the Prevention of Pauperism designated 'the *Cause of Causes*' of poverty and vice.[3] The New York Society for the Suppression of Vice and Immorality was founded about 1810, and its aim was to arouse public opinion against such practices as the sale of liquor on the sabbath and gambling in taverns and other places where it was prohibited by law, but its existence was ephemeral.[4] Thomas Eddy, the Humane Society and the Society for the Prevention of

---

[1] These motives can be discerned in the many reports and other publications of humanitarian bodies and in the memoirs of reformers previously cited. Among those wishing to improve every aspect of city life were De Witt Clinton and John Pintard. See Dorothie Bobbé, *De Witt Clinton* (New York, 1933), *passim*, and *Letters from John Pintard to his Daughter*, ed. Barck, 'Introduction' and *passim*. New York had its boosters like other cities.

[2] *First Annual Report, 1819*, p. 21.   [3] *Ibid.* p. 14.

[4] 'The New York Society for the Suppression of Vice and Immorality' (MS. in John Jay Papers, box 4, New York Historical Society).

Pauperism called for a stricter licensing system, and the last-named body introduced a number of bills in the state legislature to this end, but the temperance movement was still in its infancy and attempts at reform proved futile.[1] Some modest gains were made when humanitarians like Cadwallader D. Colden and Stephen Allen filled the office of mayor and were able to exert their own personal influence in attempting to tighten the system of liquor-licenses, but such accomplishments were short-lived or proved to little avail.[2] Reformers also urged that measures be taken to suppress gambling, lotteries and 'houses of ill-fame', and when he was mayor Stephen Allen sought a law providing for the taxation of 'haunts of vice, of profligacy, and luxury, such as the gambling houses, the theatres, shows of all kind..., taverns and grog shops...', but only the movement to bring lotteries under control had any success.[3] Lotteries tempted the poor to spend money they could not afford, according to the Society for the Prevention of Pauperism, and some of its recommendations for putting severe restrictions on private lotteries were accepted by the legislature in 1819.[4]

Most of the energy of reformers was devoted to providing institutions to counteract the demoralizing influences which the depressed classes were thought to be subject to. The relief societies, the hospitals, the free schools, the prisons and all the other agencies of these upright humanitarians were used to impress upon their charges a proper respect for morality. It would be overly cynical to suggest that all these beneficent institutions were founded primarily with the object of indoctrinating the poor and the wayward with a middle-class morality, but the fact remains that wherever the middle-class reformers came into contact with those in need of help they seized the opportunity to work for some kind of moral reformation.

In the minds of these early reformers morality and religion were inseparable, and one guarantee of moral character was a sincere faith in the Christian (and preferably Protestant) religion. Clergymen and pious-minded citizens worked energetically to spread the word of God among all classes, not least among the poor and the criminal. The first New York Bible Society was founded in 1810 and by 1819 there were some sixty Bible societies in New York City and State affiliated to the American Bible

[1] [Eddy], *Account of the State Prison*, pp. 59–60; *A Report of a Committee of the Humane Society, Appointed to Inquire into the Number of Tavern Licenses...* (New York, 1810), p. 10; S.P.P., *Second Annual Report, 1819*, pp. 9–11; *Fourth Annual Report, 1821*, p. 11; *Fifth Annual Report, 1821*, pp. 22, 35–6.
[2] S.P.P., *Second Annual Report, 1819*, pp. 7–8; 'The memoirs of Stephen Allen (1757–1852)', ed. J. C. Travis (typescript dated 1927 in New York Public Library), pp 91–2.
[3] [Eddy], *op. cit.* p. 61; 'Memoirs of Allen', ed. Travis, p. 103; S.P.P., *First Annual Report, 1818*, pp. 15–16; *Second Annual Report, 1819*, p. 12; *Fourth Annual Report, 1821*, pp. 23–4.
[4] S.P.P., *Second Annual Report, 1819*, p. 12.

11-2

Society.[1] Soon after followed the tract and missionary societies, and Sunday schools which provided poor children (and sometimes adults) with an elementary education as well as instruction in religious and moral doctrines. It was widely believed that there had been a decline in popular moral standards, a doctrine vigorously propounded by Lyman Beecher, who advocated the formation of moral societies to awaken the public to its danger and to spread moral instruction.[2] Moral societies as such were founded more often in rural villages than in the larger towns,[3] and only the Society for the Suppression of Vice and Immorality came close to the Beecher model in New York, but fears about a general moral decay helped to give strength to the religious awakening of these years.[4]

But the main aim of the religious societies was salvation. Many reformers preferred a more utilitarian approach to the problem of instilling into the minds of the degenerate a proper regard for morality. The many benevolent societies established between the Revolution and the War of 1812 paid most attention to the 'deserving' poor, but they were not unmindful of the need to reform individual character. These bodies invariably required those who sought aid to behave in a becoming manner before their application was granted. The methods of the New York Society for the Relief of Poor Widows with Small Children were typical. Relief was to be given in 'necessaries' and never in money, which might be spent unwisely, and was not to be granted until the applicants had been visited in their homes and 'particular enquiry' made into their characters and circumstances. 'Immorality' disqualified applicants, and widows found begging or selling spirituous liquors were automatically excluded from relief. Applicants were refused aid unless they sent their children to school and placed the older ones in trades or in service in 'sober virtuous families'.[5]

Other institutions adopted similar regulations designed to promote virtuous behaviour. Patients in the New York Hospital were told that they might be discharged if they were to 'swear, curse, get drunk, behave rudely or indecently', go out without leave, play cards or dice, or smoke. The Society for the Promotion of Industry, which gave employment to women

[1] New York Bible Society, *Annual Report* (1810); American Bible Society, *Third Report* (1819), pp. 31–2.
[2] L. Beecher, *A Reformation of Morals Practicable and Indispensable* (2nd edn., Utica, N.Y., 1813), p. 17.
[3] For examples of Moral Societies see H. E. Abt, *Ithaca* (Ithaca, N.Y., 1926), pp. 47–8; B. F. Thompson, *History of Long Island from its Discovery and Settlement to the Present Time* (3rd edn., Port Washington, L.I., 1962), vol. II, 25–6.
[4] A recent discussion on the connexions between the revivals and fears of a decline in religion and morality is found in Perry Miller, *The Life of the Mind in America: From the Revolution to the Civil War* (London, 1966), pp. 3–9.
[5] *Constitution of the Ladies Society*, pp. 7–9; *The By-Laws and Regulations of the Society...* (New York, 1813), pp. 6–8.

in a house provided for the purpose, admitted applicants only after a careful examination of their characters and strictly prohibited the wearing of jewellery and ornaments and talking, laughing and singing during working hours. The regulations of both institutions required that chapters of the Bible be read aloud regularly.[1]

Only so much, however, could be achieved by seeking to influence the moral conduct of the adult poor, whose characters had already been formed. The children of the poor were thought to be more impressionable. 'The early cultivation of the tender mind', said John Vanderbilt, Jun., 'so open to impression from precept and example, will afford the strongest antidote to every deception, passion, vice, or depravity of morals.'[2] The Free School Society argued that where parents neglected their children's education, it became the duty of the public and of private individuals to 'assist them in the discharge of this important obligation'.[3] The society was confident that it could do good by the 'personal attention to be bestowed on these children for the improvement of their morals', assistance for their parents in providing situations for them, 'where industry will be inculcated and good habits formed', as well, it added almost as an afterthought, providing them with 'the learning requisite for the proper discharge of the duties of life...'[4]

But what kind of educational system could provide such 'moral' instruction? The reformers hit on an idea that delighted them—the Lancasterian system, the invention of the English Quaker Joseph Lancaster. This system had two great attractions: it was cheap and it was 'moral'. In each Lancasterian school there was one teacher, who trained a number of senior pupils to act as monitors, or, in effect, assistant teachers. In this way one teacher could preside over a very large school. The cheapness of the Lancasterian system made it practicable; its provision for moral training endeared it to reformers. The monitors were graded in terms of seniority, and the privileges enjoyed by them were an inducement to junior children to compete for promotion. An elaborate system of rewards and punishments was worked out. It was believed that this system, rewarding as it did those exhibiting industry, good behaviour and responsibility, and penalizing those guilty of sloth, bad habits and insolence would infuse pupils with a strong sense of the correct virtues. Within two years of its foundation the society was able to claim that children 'who before knew little other ambition than to surpass in the practice of those vices, to which idleness, and

---

[1] *A Brief Account of the New-York Hospital* (New York, 1804), pp. 26, 35; *Plan of the Society for the Promotion of Industry*, pp. 5–6, 8.
[2] J. Vanderbilt, Jun., *An Address Delivered in the New-York Free School, on the 27th day of December, 1809* (New York, 1810), p. 8.
[3] Address of the Trustees 'To the Public', 18 May 1805, in Bourne, *op. cit.* p. 7.
[4] Memorial to Legislature, 25 Feb. 1805, in *ibid.* p. 4.

their peculiar situations in life exposed them, are here engaged in the *new* scene of striving to excell [sic] in the performance of their tasks, and thereby secure the *honours* and *rewards* which their master confers upon them'.[1] Other Lancasterian schools were quickly established and for many years they continued to claim great success in their task of moral education.[2]

If reformers failed to mould the children of the poor as successfully as they wished, and if poor adults scorned the attentions of the philanthropic, there was still the hope that the work of reformation might be accomplished when the degenerate fell foul of the law. A principal reason for replacing the harsh colonial penal code with a prison system was that the latter provided the opportunity for reformation; indeed, the enthusiasm with which the moral reformers greeted the new system suggests that in their eyes one of its greatest virtues was that it provided them with a captive audience. Thomas Eddy, when in charge of the Newgate prison at Greenwich Village, introduced various measures designed to reform the criminal. As in the Lancasterian schools, the better-behaved reaped the most rewards. Inmates were provided with religious and moral instruction and the more meritorious were taught to read and write. Prisoners were allowed to see their wives every three months as a reward for good conduct. Eddy recommended that pardons normally be granted only to prisoners showing 'unequivocal evidence of reformation'. The best method of reforming the criminal, he thought, was imprisonment with hard labour, for this instilled habits of industry and sobriety, and also, if applied with sufficient rigour, acted as a deterrent, and Eddy did his best to put prisoners to work in suitable trades. Eddy's great hope, which he failed to see properly fulfilled in New York, was for a system of solitary confinement, where the prisoner never set eyes on a fellow-inmate. He saw this essentially as a reformatory device, where the prisoner was 'left in solitude to ruminate at leisure...In this situation, with his thoughts continually directed to his present condition and past conduct, he may sooner or later perceive the wickedness and folly of his former course of life, feel the bitter pangs of remorse, and be disposed to future amendment.'[3]

One technique which both the prison reformers and several benevolent societies made much use of was friendly visiting. The longing to capture

---

[1] 'A sketch of the New York Free School', printed as preface to J. Lancaster, *Improvements in Education, As It Respects the Industrious Classes of the Community...* (3rd edn., New York, 1807), p. xxx. See also *Manual of the Lancasterian System, of Teaching, Writing, Arithmetic, and Needle-work, as Practised in the Schools of the Free School Society, of New-York* (New York 1820).

[2] New York Free School Society, *Tenth Annual Report of the Trustees* (1815), pp. 1–2; *Eighteenth Annual Report of the Trustees* (1823), pp. 1–2.

[3] [Eddy], *Account of the State Prison*, p. 32. For his work in the prison see *ibid.* pp. 31–5 53–4, 65–7.

the poor and the criminal for morality and religion when they were at their most vulnerable was felt by many, and this delicate task was entrusted to the visitor. The visitor had two main functions. One was to infuse his or her charges with the proper moral values; the other was to ensure that aid was properly dispensed and to supervise the workings of the relevant institution. The visitors of the New York Assistance Society were 'strictly [to] recommend to the poor attendance on divine worship, industry, economy, cleanliness, whitewashing the walls of their houses and fresh air; and that whenever they discover any one whom they relieve, wilfully neglecting these, they shall in no wise spare suitable reproof'.[1] For convicts the prison inspectors were to act as visitors, seeing that they were fairly treated, admonishing bad conduct and applauding good, and 'to give them such advice as may awaken virtuous sensibility, and promote their moral and religious improvement'.[2]

These early reformers clearly had a remarkable faith in the ameliorative powers of visitors. This faith rested on the same optimistic belief which underlay the argument for solitary confinement in prisons: that if malign influences could be eliminated and benevolent ones substituted, then the better nature of the misguided individual would reassert itself. Eddy believed that criminals were once innocent but had 'mistaken their true interest' through passion and temptation.[3] Thus it was the task of visitors to help the degenerate to see their 'true interest', which once perceived, through the aid of education and religion, they would never again wish to forsake. This was an optimistic view of human nature, but optimism was a source of strength to reformers.[4]

III

For the most part the humanitarian and reformatory agencies established between the Revolution and the War of 1812 had placed greatest weight on providing benign influences, on rewarding good behaviour more than in punishing bad. After the War of 1812, when it became clear that social problems were still growing, reformers became more cautious and their attitude towards the less fortunate classes hardened. The newly formed Society for the Prevention of Pauperism drew attention to the growing number of paupers, criticized the rather indiscriminate dispensation of relief by the public authorities, blamed the 'numerous charitable institu-

[1] *Constitution of the Assistance Society*, p. 15.
[2] [Eddy], *op. cit.* p. 20.   [3] *Ibid.* p. 51.
[4] This view of the fundamental innocence of man reflects the influence of the eighteenth-century Enlightenment and of the new liberal developments in American Protestantism. Not everyone shared it. Lyman Beecher, for example, believed that man was by nature wicked, but could be improved through the 'influence of moral restraint' (Beecher, *op. cit.* pp. 15–16). Both attitudes provided a justification for reforming measures.

tions of the city' as one source of pauperism, and called for the abolition of the system of public outdoor relief and its replacement by a harsh work-house system, on the utilitarian principle of less-eligibility.[1] Prison reformers were unhappy about the overcrowded state of the prisons, where inmates were patently failing to be reformed, and accused the early penologists of excessive benevolence. The prison reformers of the 1820s wanted either a more severe discipline or the establishment of an austere system of solitary confinement, which was now praised for its deterrent rather than its re-formatory effects.[2] Thus reformers were finding that the application of beneficent influences and the tendency to reward good behaviour had their limitations: the former did not suffice to produce a genuine reformation and the latter proved more an incentive to rely on public or private bounty than an incentive to reform. The answer was to make pauperism and crime distinctly uncomfortable ways of life. In fact these harsher doctrines were only partially implemented: provision for a workhouse system in the state was made in 1824, but New York City was excluded from this; Elam Lynds pioneered the austere 'silent' system at Auburn, but a brief experiment with solitary confinement was soon abandoned.[3]

In essence these new measures did not differ greatly from the old: the aim remained that of moral reformation, mainly by the application of incentives to behave properly, but there was now greater emphasis on coercion than on persuasion. Many of the old techniques continued, although some refinements were made. Educationists found that many children were not attending school because their parents relied on their help at home or sent them out to work. But infant children were of little use in the home, so infant schools were established where they could be taught the obligations of morality at as early an age as possible and pro-tected from 'the contaminating influence to which, in a large city, they are so greatly exposed'.[4] Children who none the less found their way into

[1] S.P.P., *First Annual Report, 1818*, pp. 12, 16–17; *Fifth Annual Report, 1821*, pp. 29–33.
[2] *Report on the Penitentiary System in the U.S.*, pp. 36, 50–6; *Report from the Committee appointed to visit the State Prisons* [Albany, 1825], *passim* but especially pp. 14–15, 34–46.
[3] D. M. Schneider, *The History of Public Welfare in New York State, 1609–1866* (Chicago, 1938), pp. 227–9, 246; G. Powers, *A Brief Account of the Construction, Management, and Discipline Etc. etc., of the New York State Prison at Auburn* (Auburn, N.Y., 1826), pp. 4–38. David Owen, *English Philanthropy, 1660–1960* (Cambridge, Mass., 1965), pp. 97–9, finds that English humanitarians became increasingly austere in the late eighteenth century; demands for reform in the English poor laws of course mounted in the 1820s. The Americans were undoubtedly influenced by British ideas: the humanitarian cross-currents between the two were considerable, as has been shown by Kraus, *op. cit.*, ch. vi, and F. Thistlethwaite, *The Anglo-American Connection in the Early Nineteenth Century* (Philadelphia, 1959), chs. iii–v.
[4] 'Memorial of the Female Association of New-York, praying for pecuniary aid', *Documents of the Assembly of the State of New York*, vol. III (1830), no. 266, p. 2. See also *The Constitution and By-Laws of the Infant School Society of the City of New-York* (New York, 1828), *passim*.

prison became the concern of the Society for the Reformation of Juvenile Delinquents (founded in 1823 through a reconstitution of the Society for the Prevention of Pauperism), which established a House of Refuge for the accommodation of delinquent and vagrant children, offering them a moral and industrial training. Reformation was encouraged by a complex system of rewards and punishments, whereby the children were divided into four classes 'according to their moral conduct', and could be promoted to a higher class or demoted to a lower for good or bad behaviour. Membership of the highest class carried with it certain privileges, such as that allowing 'occasionally...on Saturday at dinner, a pudding or pie, fruit, etc. in addition to the usual fare', and punishments ranged from privation of play and exercise, through gruel without salt for all meals, to fetters and handcuffs 'only in *extreme cases*'.[1] The most important innovation in this period to aid the adult poor was the savings bank, introduced in New York in 1819 amid great hopes. Its advantages were thought to be that the poor would have their savings kept secure from theft and sudden temptation, and that they would have a fund (appreciated by the interest rate) to draw on in times of crisis or need. 'Perhaps no single plan of policy', said the institution's sponsors, 'could prove so important and effectual in undermining the foundation of pauperism...It is founded on principles calculated to inspire economy, produce reform, and inculcate a spirit of enterprise and industry, and self-respect, among the laboring classes of the community...' When saving was begun, they argued, a desire was created 'to see the progressive increase of the little capital'.[2] Thus the traditional virtues of thrift, industry and sobriety were to be promoted by harnessing the acquisitive instinct.

There was no radical change in the approach of humanitarians towards those they sought to help between the 1770s and the 1820s. Their agencies became more specialized and gaps in the empire of benevolence were gradually filled, while their earlier relatively sentimental approach was replaced by a more hard-headed attitude. But throughout the aim was the moral reformation of the distressed individual, an end towards which virtually every humanitarian endeavour of these years appeared to be directed; each seemed to have its place in an all-embracing (if rather unconsciously elaborated) plan for the moral conversion of the lower classes. The reformation of the individual was to be accomplished by persuading him that it was in his own best interest to behave well and by attempting to make it his interest to behave well. The middle-class reformers failed to

[1] *Rules and Regulations for the Government of the House of Refuge* (New York, 1825), *passim*, but especially pp. 3, 12–13, 16–17, 19.
[2] S.P.P., *Second Annual Report, 1819*, pp. 14–15; see also the society's *Documents Relative to Savings Banks, Intemperance, and Lotteries* (New York, 1819), pp. 3–16.

distinguish clearly between the two. 'By a just and inflexible law of Providence', said a committee of the Humane Society, 'misery is ordained to be the companion and the punishment of vice;...'[1] If the vicious failed to realize that they were miserable, then the reformers were but acting in accordance with the law of Providence when they sought to make them see this by heightening their misery. It was natural that virtue should be rewarded and vice punished, and all the reformers sought to do was to ensure that this was so.

Basically their methods were utilitarian. Reformers spoke eloquently about the need to awaken the moral sense of the individual, but they sought to do this primarily by appealing to his self-interest. The many relief-giving societies, the prisons, the schools, all gave rewards for good behaviour and penalties for bad. The savings-bank was also intended to appeal to the self-interest of the poor in rather a different way. The reformers had great confidence in these techniques; to them human beings reacted in rather a mechanical and predetermined way to a given stimulus (an assumption reflecting the influence of eighteenth century and Benthamite thought).[2] They seemed to take it for granted that the systems of rewards and punishments adopted in the Lancasterian schools or in the House of Refuge would produce a virtuous and well-trained mind, or that once a poor man had placed a deposit in a savings-bank the desired moral and social virtues would follow accordingly. As well as trying to force a code of behaviour on the poor, the reformers also sought to teach their charges by example. In the free schools and the House of Refuge they seemed to be trying to create small models of their ideal society, in which those in the lower classes would raise themselves to the higher by industry, self-help and good behaviour; the inmates of these institutions were presumably expected to draw the appropriate moral for their conduct in the outside world. Thus religious moralism and utilitarianism were fused together in the thought of these reformers: utilitarian techniques were used to teach a moral code which owed much to evangelical religion and the Protestant tradition. There was relatively little reliance on moral preaching; even the friendly visitor, despite the miracles that his advice and example were expected to accomplish, was armed with the power of withholding aid if his pious exhortations proved to no avail.

The achievements of these humanitarians were by no means negligible.

---

[1] *A Report of a Committee of the Humane Society...*, p. 5.

[2] The reformers were certainly familiar with the works of their British predecessors and contemporaries. The library of the Society for the Prevention of Pauperism contained many books and tracts of British origin, including publications by John Howard, Jeremy Bentham, Patrick Colquhoun and Adam Smith: S.P.P., *Second Annual Report, 1819*, appendix, pp. 83–91.

They certainly failed to fulfil their most optimistic expectations—the moral reformation of the degenerate and the elimination of social evils, and their preoccupation with morality doubtless blinded them to some of the causes of these evils. But their interest in moral character also turned their attention to environmental influences, and they accepted that the degenerate individual often owed his plight to a careless or faulty upbringing or to the existence of numerous temptations. They therefore sought to improve the environment, and whatever the moral overtones their practical reforms were valuable. They pioneered a prison system and a school system, they provided hospitals, dispensaries and a juvenile reformatory, and they began to deal with the problem of pauperism in a more systematic way than previously.[1] Had they not been so anxious about the moral condition of the lower-classes would they have accomplished so much? And perhaps their moral teaching did have some effect. In the 1820s and 1830s social reformers succeeded in launching mass movements: the moral exhortations of the temperance and antislavery men touched a responsive chord in many ordinary Americans.

[1] The public authorities, of course, were also very much involved in several of these developments. Often a private society founded and managed an institution, such as the House of Refuge or the New York Hospital, and persuaded the state and city governments to help finance it. Public bodies rarely initiated reform: the voluntary efforts of the humanitarians described here were more important in this respect. For the role of the city and state authorities in welfare services see D. M. Schneider, *The History of Public Welfare in New York State, 1609–1866* (Chicago, 1938), *passim*.

SHANE WHITE

A Question of Style
Blacks in and around New York City in the Late 18th Century

Scholars who have written about New York blacks in the late 18th and early 19th centuries have assumed that blacks were subsumed quickly within the dominant culture. Yet an examination of the "style" of black New Yorkers reveals that there was a significant difference from the whites, a sense of cultural distinctiveness that both reinforced continuities with their African past and demonstrated a creative adaptation to the often hostile world of the rapidly changing metropolis.

As ELIHU SMITH, a young physician, and William Dunlap, his dramatist friend, strolled through the streets of New York on an October day in 1795, their attention was attracted to the appearance of a black passerby. The man, Smith recorded that evening in his diary, had been "very flippantly drest . . . with legs like two semi-circles." The fellow was, Dunlap had quipped, "a very great beau *(bow)—about the legs*" (Cronin 1973:73; emphasis in original). Smith's description and Dunlap's pun suggest that the black's appearance was alien and comic. Something—not just the shape of the man's legs, but his clothes, their colors, or the two in combination—was not right. Neither of the two friends would have considered venturing abroad in such attire.

Over the last two decades historians have revolutionized our understanding of black culture, but they have generally concentrated on the rural areas of the South. Here blacks, when they were not a majority of the total population, were at least a sizable minority. Most were slaves, living and working on plantations, and separated from the whites by a physical and cultural gulf. Such factors have been emphasized by historians who have examined aspects of black culture that were strongly influenced by an African past. Black cultural distinctiveness has been seen largely as a function of demography, the high black-to-white ratios in the plantation South allowing sufficient social space for African patterns to be important in shaping the day-to-day life of blacks. Under these circumstances the cultural gap between the races was wide and the process of acculturation a matter not of years but of generations.[1]

Shane White *is a Lecturer in the Department of History,*
University of Sydney, N.S.W., 2006, Australia

The situation in and around the city of New York provides a strikingly different ground on which to investigate the creation of black culture, offering a new perspective that can contribute to an overall understanding of the complex process of acculturation. Although in 1800 New York's black population of 5,865 was second in size only to Charleston's, the more significant point is that free blacks and slaves made up only about 10% of the city's inhabitants. New York's black population was being further distinguished from that of the South at this time by changes in the balance between its free and slave components. In the colonial period virtually all of the blacks in the city had been slaves, but in the quarter-century after the Revolution the migration into the city of free blacks from the countryside and the West Indies, and the passage of the gradual abolition measure in 1799, reversed this situation. By 1810 only 16.2% of a much larger black population of 8,918 were still enslaved, and New York had become the largest center of free blacks in America.

Economic changes, too, helped to bring the races together. The gradual demise of slavery was part of a larger shift from bound labor to wage labor that was transforming the city and, in the process, incorporating blacks into the emerging working class. By 1810 quite a few of New York's free blacks were artisans, some were in domestic service, and others pieced together a livelihood by alternating between laboring around the docks or the city and working as sailors. But neither in employment nor in residence were these blacks and the dwindling number of slaves segregated. They often labored alongside working-class whites and occupied similar types of housing in the same areas of the city (White 1988a). On the face of it, the vast majority of New York blacks seem to have been incorporated successfully into the dominant culture.

Yet, as is suggested by the reaction of Elihu Smith and William Dunlap to the "flippantly" dressed black, the relationship between whites and blacks in New York was not so simple. In part because of an African influence often conveyed by African-born West Indian migrants, the process of acculturation did not create an exact replica of the dominant culture. Smith and Dunlap were certainly well aware that more than skin color distinguished the two races. Even where blacks wore the same clothes or spoke the same language as other inhabitants of the city, they did so in ways that were distinctive. A sense of the difference that I have in mind is best conveyed through the concept of "style," particularly as it has been developed in England in studies focusing on youth subcultures such as those of the teddy boys, mods, and punks. Here style means the process by which objects, such as the Edwardian suit of the teddy boy or the safety pin of the punk, are taken from the dominant culture and given a new meaning in the context of the subculture (see Hall and Jefferson 1976; Hebdige 1979). In this article I intend to examine the way New York blacks used style—through the language they spoke, the clothes they wore, and through gesture and bodily movements—to construct their own subculture.

At first glance this task appears daunting not only because New York blacks were a relatively small minority of the total population but because they were

also for the most part illiterate, leaving only faint traces on the historical record. Yet the situation is far from hopeless. By piecing together these traces,
often little more than one-line references gleaned from an immense amount of
material, one can reconstruct, if only in a limited fashion, the world these
blacks fashioned for themselves.

A major source of such evidence, a rich and largely untapped one, is contemporary newspapers, and especially the runaway notices contained in
them.[2] These notices can be found scattered through the 18th-century equivalent of the classified columns, where they lie buried between advertisements
for the sale of dry goods and the shipping news. The sample of such advertisements on which I shall base this analysis of black style was collected from
in excess of 12,000 issues of New York and New Jersey newspapers printed
between 1771 and 1805.[3] These advertisements provide descriptions of 1,232
runaway slaves from New York City and the surrounding countryside.[4] The
entire slave population of this region was only about 25,000 in 1790, but over
this 35-year period there was an average of 35 runaways a year, a figure larger
in relative terms than those for the southern states. Gerald Mullin's research
on Virginia for the period 1736 to 1801 uncovered 1,280 runaways, or an average of 19.7 a year (Mullin 1972:40), and Philip Morgan, in his analysis of
South Carolina from 1732 to 1782, collected advertisements describing 3,558
slaves, that is, 69.8 per year (Morgan 1985:57–78). Not only did these historians use *all* extant newspapers but the slave populations of Virginia (188,000
in 1770) and South Carolina (57,000 in 1760) were, of course, considerably
larger (Mullin 1972:16; Morgan 1983:89).[5] Although the New York advertisements provide a relatively larger sample of the slave population than comparable bodies of data from other states, that sample is still distorted.[6] Runaways
were, by definition, a select group and, consequently, certain segments of the
black population—in particular the young, males, mulattoes and the African-
and the West Indian–born—are overrepresented.[7] Possibly as a result of these
biases the runaway sample will tend to magnify and to exaggerate the cultural
traits that I intend to argue are the constituent elements of the New York black
style. But as we are unlikely to come up with sources that are any more revealing, historians must either attempt, however tentatively, to piece such
fragmentary and difficult material together or write these blacks even further
out of American history. At the very least, a close analysis of the runaway
advertisements, buttressed by insights from other sources, should reveal one
end of the spectrum of black stylistic behavior in and around New York City
at the end of the 18th century and help us to understand that New York blacks
did not enter their freedom in a vacuum but as people with a cultural life-style
that made them distinct.[8]

Black Language

Runaway advertisements, for example, provide much specific evidence
about the language of individual blacks. One in four of the descriptions of runaways in the sample (316 out of 1,232) mentioned the ability of the slaves to

speak English. Slaveowners, anxious to identify and reclaim their runaways, tried to categorize them succinctly by references to their "good English" or "broken English," terms that became accepted codes signifying the level of acculturation of the slaves.[9] Of these 316 slaves 229 or nearly three in four spoke English well or fluently. In 1804, for example, Silas Condit's slave Sharp spoke "good English" (*Centinel of Freedom*, 27 November 1804) and a few years earlier, in 1788, Lewis Mulford's runaway, Jacob, could, rather unusually for a slave, both "read and speak English remarkably well" (*Daily Advertiser*, 2 September 1788). Though such statements were almost certainly qualified by an implicit rider that the English that those being described spoke was good for a black, the language of these slaves was probably close to standard English. Occasionally blacks even incorporated some of the regional dialects into their language: Grotis, who had been brought up on Long Island, was, according to his owner John Brazier, "yankeyfied in his speech, and likewise slow in his motion" (*Daily Advertiser*, 25 June 1802). On the other hand, more than one in four of the blacks (87 out of 316) were described as using "bad" or "broken" English, or even as being incapable of uttering a single word in the language of their owner. The wording of some of the more detailed advertisements suggests that more was involved than an inability to master the language. Telemaque, for example, spoke "broken English with fluency" (*Daily Advertiser*, 14 April 1795), and other runaways were characterized as using a "negro English." It is likely that these blacks spoke a creole language.

Runaway advertisements are particularly effective in drawing attention to the unusually complex linguistic and cultural interaction that occurred in New York. On the mainland, African- and American-born blacks generally came in contact only with a relatively homogeneous English-speaking population. The state of New York, however, was noted for its ethnic diversity and particularly for the large Dutch component in its population. The Dutch in New York City had long been anglicized, but there was a large Dutch-speaking population in the surrounding area, on the western end of Long Island and in New Jersey, who made a living supplying the metropolis with food. These farmers were heavily involved in slavery: in some areas of Kings County more than 60% of households owned slaves, a rate that would not have been out of place in the South. Slaves from these areas were influenced by Dutch culture and many were brought up speaking a version of this language. At the very least, 75 out of the 1,232 runaways were fluent in Dutch.[10]

Not surprisingly, the presence of a Dutch-derived language in the New York area sometimes made communication between blacks difficult. In 1744 Alexander Hamilton, a Maryland doctor traveling for his health, made one of the earliest known attempts to record a conversation between two blacks (Needler 1967:211–218). As Hamilton approached New York, Dromo, his slave, went on ahead to ask the way. Hamilton rode up and

found him discoursing a negroe girl, who spoke Dutch to him. "Dis de way to York?" says Dromo. "Yaw, dat is Yarikee," said the wench, pointing to the steeples. "What devil you say?"

replies Dromo. "Yaw, mynheer," said the wench. "Damne you, what you say?" said Dromo again. "Yaw, yaw," said the girl. "You a damn black bitch," said Dromo, and so rid on. [Bridenbaugh 1973:40–41]

Fifty years later similar problems existed. Although the evidence is not conclusive, it seems that the three-way cultural interaction that occurred in New York created a situation analogous to 20th-century Louisiana. Throughout the 18th century the Dutch influence probably played a similar role to that of French Creole in Louisiana, complicating and reinforcing the patterns of "negro English," and delaying the decreolization process (Dillard 1972:223–224). In 1792 John De Wint's runaway Maria spoke "very broken English and good Negro Dutch" (*Daily Advertiser*, 21 July 1792), and there were many other blacks who, like Maria, were more fluent in Dutch than English. Cuff, who ran away from his owner Abraham Allen of Hackensack in 1789, spoke "broken English as he was brought up in a Dutch family" (*New Jersey Journal*, 16 December 1789), while 13 years later a black named Will, the slave of David Banks of Newark, spoke "Low Dutch and middling good English, although he frequently gives his words the Dutch accent" (*Centinel of Freedom*, 9 February 1802). This Dutch influence was particularly important in New York City in the quarter-century after the Revolution. There had always been a movement of blacks between the rural and urban areas, with slaves often traveling to the city to sell their owners' produce; and runaway advertisements provide abundant evidence that many such slaves expected to find refuge there. In the 1790s and early 1800s, however, freed rural blacks from the countryside where Dutch culture continued to be significant moved permanently into the city in large numbers and became an important part of the rapidly growing urban free black population (see White 1988a).

This pattern was further reinforced by an influx of blacks from the Caribbean, particularly from Saint Domingue, that occurred at the same time. Many of these blacks, brought in as slaves by émigrés fleeing the great rebellion in the French colony, had only recently been enslaved. In 1802 Nassau, a 16-year-old slave belonging to D. C. Dinnies, was described as speaking very broken English as he was "but 18 months from the coast of Africa" (*New York Evening Post*, 20 July 1802). The language of such blacks was more African, and possibly some spoke what the linguists have called West African Pidgin English (Stewart 1975:226–229). In 1800 a runaway named Beliour was said to speak a "little in African dialect" (*Daily Advertiser*, 4 September 1800), and in the same year Henry Spingler advertised that his slave Phillis, who was 45 years old, African-born, and scarred by "country marks" (or ritual scarifications), spoke with a "mixture of her natural dialect" (*Daily Advertiser*, 27 November 1800). Quite a few of these blacks, however, had spent enough time in the West Indies to have picked up a European language, usually French. Over the whole period from 1771 to 1805 56 of the runaways were described as speaking French; 47 of these slaves, however, absconded between 1791 and 1805. It is therefore not surprising that the surviving records from the New

York District Court in the 1790s and early 1800s show that at times an inter-preter was needed to translate the testimony of blacks (see St. Domingo 1801). Some blacks had a smattering of both languages. A Guinea-born black, who ran away in 1794, spoke "a little English and a little French" (*Daily Advertiser*, 30 August 1794). These languages were rather different from the ones spoken by Europeans, as John Lavallier acknowledged in 1805 when he described Jo-seph, who had originally come from Louisiana, as able to speak both "negro English and negro French" (*New York Evening Post*, 1 July 1805). Many other miscreants were bi- and some were even trilingual. In 1789 Lindor, who called himself a native of the West Indies, was able to speak "pretty good English, French and creole" (*Daily Advertiser*, 19 May 1789).

The evidence that we possess concerning the language of New York blacks is far from perfect: not only are we forced to rely on runaway advertisements, but the majority of slaveowners were regrettably silent on the abilities of their runaways to speak English. Nevertheless the evidence can still support the conclusion that there was a variety of black language styles in and around New York City, ranging along a continuum from those who spoke a language close to that of standard English, through creole-speaking blacks, to, at the other end, a few speakers of African languages. The majority of New York blacks were probably clustered near the former, or more acculturated, end of the spectrum, a conclusion that is supported by the evidence from one special use of language, the naming of free blacks and slaves (see Gutman 1977; Inscoe 1983; Nash 1983:20–27).

Under slavery, New York blacks were often named by their masters and frequently, though not always, were given only one name. Some masters in-dulged themselves, displaying their classical knowledge in names such as Cato or Caesar, or their sense of humor in names such as Romeo or Pleasant Queen Anne (*Royal Gazette*, 3 March 1781). Black reaction to such thoughtless or calculated humiliation surfaces in the runaway advertisements, which make it clear that many masters expected their slaves to use alternative names when they absconded. Charles Arding, for example, anticipated that his runaway would quickly abandon the appellation Flummary (*Daily Advertiser*, 4 August 1786). Such name-changing was more than just a matter of disguise as quite often the master could specify the name likely to be assumed by the slave. Some advertisements even imply that there was tacit acceptance by slaveown-ers of a dual system of nomenclature, with one name used by the master and the other by the blacks. One runaway, for example, was a "man named Cato but calls himself Curtis Johnson" (*The Federalist: New Jersey Gazette*, 8 July 1799); another, "named York, calls himself Jacob" (*Daily Advertiser*, 15 June 1790). The formulaic wording of these notices, with the passive "named" fol-lowed by the active "calls himself," underlines the fact that the name bestowed by the master was not necessarily the one used by the blacks.[11]

The preferred names of the runaways provide an interesting guide to the values of the slaves. Generally, the classical and the shortened given names associated with slavery were shunned. Joseph Blackwell's slave Caesar chose "William" and not the diminutive "Will" or "Billy" (*Daily Advertiser*, 26 May 1801). Similarly, a few advertisements indicate that the desire to assume a surname was a source of tension between slave and master. Theo. Fowler knew his slave as Scip, but "[a]mongst the black people he goes by the name Scipeo Bailey" (*Daily Advertiser*, 20 September 1793). Surnames were a sign of freedom. Not only did they give slaves a sense of dignity inappropriate to their servile status but, in America's patrilineal culture, surnames also flowed from paternity and so from exclusive marriage (both formally denied to slaves).

It was in this period near the turn of the century that many of the ex-slaves swelling New York's free black population first acquired a surname, a process that can be studied systematically by using the census records. In the first census in 1790 only the given names of most free blacks were included, with less than 15% of the small number of the listed free black heads of household having a surname. But by the time of the 1800 census the position had changed. Although there were over four times as many free black heads of household, 94% were recorded as having a surname.[12]

What sort of surnames did these blacks choose? A few took the family names of former slaveowners but the vast majority followed the more normal pattern of the runaways and eliminated all possible connection with slavery. The Dutch were heavily involved in slaveholding in east New Jersey and New York, yet Dutch surnames were rare, a Mingo Roosevelt being a conspicuous exception. A few blacks—New Year Evans, Royal Cromwell, and Hudson Rivers are examples—celebrated their freedom with what Gary Nash has aptly called an "etymological flourish" (Nash 1983:20–27). Some, like the rather more threatening Thomas Paine, took the names of the famous. Overwhelmingly, however, the blacks chose very common and neutral surnames. In 1800 the three most common surnames—Johnson, Williams, and Thomas—accounted for 8.1% of the names of all free blacks. In 1810 the top three—Johnson, Williams, and Smith—accounted for nearly 11% of all the black names listed in the census. In fact, in 1810 4.5%, or about 1 in 22, of all the heads of free black households had the surname Johnson. Such names were also common among the white population, but to nowhere near the same extent.[13] The use of such surnames probably reflected, in part, the desire for anonymity prevalent among many ex-slaves, a desire that had helped draw rural blacks to the metropolis. In their choice of names most New York blacks indicated, quite realistically, that their hopes and aspirations, and particularly their desire to be free, were conceived within the framework of a white world.

Much of the evidence about the language and naming patterns of New York blacks, then, points toward an overall process of acculturation and anglicization. But there is also enough material to suggest that in New York at the end of the 18th century the African past of these blacks was still of importance. Even the evidence from the nomenclature of the blacks is not totally one-sided: there were some African given names among the free blacks—the 1800 census included a few blacks, not mulattoes, such as Quaquo Minnisee and Cuffee McClair, with African day names—and there are more in the runaway advertisements.[14] Similarly, a significant minority of New York blacks spoke a language that was nearer the African end of the linguistic spectrum. In 1799 Augustus Griffin of Oysterponds, Long Island, commenting on the language of two elderly Africans, noted that John Tatoo "talked much plainer english than Jack, whose pronounciation was much broken." What is significant in this case is that Jack had been brought over from Africa 55 years previously (cited in Kruger 1985:87–88). In part because of the influx of African and West Indian blacks in the 1790s, but also because of the complicating influence of Dutch culture in the city's hinterland, New York continued to provide an environment where blacks such as Jack could use a variety of language styles.

Blacks' Presentation of Their Bodies

Linguistic diversity was only one aspect of black cultural distinctiveness. In 1794, an English traveler, William Strickland, noted that one of the few features that distinguished New York City from England was the number of blacks in the streets, blacks "who may be seen of all shades till the stain is entirely worne out" (Strickland 1971:63). Strickland's striking metaphor raises the important issue of the blacks' appearance. Historians who have touched on this subject have, like Strickland, generally confined themselves to the matter of color, over which blacks had no control. Yet in other areas blacks quite consciously shaped the visual impact of their bodies. They did so to a significant extent through the clothes that they wore, a matter that historians have usually examined in a different context—as an example of paternalism (Genovese 1976:550–561), or as some sort of measure of the physical well-being of slaves (Fogel and Engerman 1974:116–118). Here, following the lead of historians such as Stuart Cosgrove (1984) and Steve Chibnall (1985), I would like to try and examine the cultural meaning of the appearance of New York blacks.

For the most part free blacks and slaves wore garments similar to those of the rest of the working population of New York. The clothing free blacks were able to afford, and that given to slaves by their masters, was usually made of cheap homespun material. Typically, males wore either overalls or a pair of trousers, a shirt, often a waistcoat, and a jacket. Females usually wore a petticoat and a dress or gown (Olson 1941). Yet in spite of the limitations imposed by their position at the bottom of society many blacks took a great deal of care of, and pride in, their attire. Some slaveowners made precisely this point in their runaway notices. A 24-year-old runaway named Cuff, for example, "took with him a great variety of good cloaths is fond of dress and always appears very clean and smart" (*Daily Advertiser*, 8 October 1793). Other advertisements, such as that for Isaac Varian's slave Molly, who was "very fond of dress," help to suggest the important role clothing played in the lives of some blacks (*Daily Advertiser*, 14 September 1795).

Clothing helped to distinguish the hours of work from the hours of leisure and, in the case of those still enslaved, the master's time from the slave's. Many New York blacks, such as the West Indian runaway Lindor who was "very fond of dressing well on some occasions" (*Daily Advertiser*, 19 May 1789), took the utmost pains with their appearance before going out, often to the dancing cellars uptown in and around Bancker Street. In 1802 Isabella Thomas, a free black woman living in James Street, asked her servant girl-friend Elizabeth Mumford "to lend her a handkerchief to wear to a dance" (Thomas 1802). Similarly, important occasions like funerals and weddings required a certain standard of dress. When Frank Pero, the slave of David Dixon, was about to be married, he borrowed some 30 dollars from his friend John Jackson, who was also a slave. Having paid the minister a dollar for the marriage ceremony, he spent the rest of the money on a blue coat, a pair of blue pantaloons, a waistcoat, a pair of shoes, and a hat from a shop at the corner of Ann Street and Broadway (Pero 1802).

Evidence concerning New York blacks is scarce and hard to come by, but, quite strikingly, surviving fragments are commonly centered around clothing, further suggesting the importance of apparel to the blacks. Extra money that slaves occasionally received from their masters, earned by doing odd jobs in their free time, or stole, was often spent on clothes. In 1798, when Samuel Robertson was convicted of stealing 12 dollars from Elizabeth Graham, his mistress, he confessed that he had used the money to buy a jacket, a hat, and a pair of shoes from a black woman who lived in Cliff Street (Robertson 1798). Although most of our knowledge of this facet of black life stems, as in this case, from court records, such behavior illustrates a broader pattern.

As the last example shows, blacks did not have to spend the money in white-owned stores. A thriving market in secondhand clothes operated in New York. In 1804, for instance, a free black named John Young bought a pair of corduroy pantaloons from James Anderson, a black seaman, for two dollars (Young 1804). Not surprisingly, the original source of some of the merchandise could not bear too close a scrutiny; judging from the surviving court records, the crime of which both free blacks and slaves were most commonly accused was the theft of either clothing or material. In another incident in 1804, a free black named John Thomas stole a blue coat from the door of John Sickles' tailor shop on the corner of Nassau Street and Maiden Lane (Sickles 1804). Many cases brought before the courts involved servants, either free or slave, taking advantage of their position to steal goods from their masters. Sally Smith, a young indentured black girl, confessed to taking numerous items of clothing from John O'Brien while she was living in his house as a menial or house servant (Smith 1805). Sometimes blacks stole the garments for their own use, but generally items of clothing were quickly resold, being only marginally less negotiable than currency. In 1804 Nancy, a recently freed black, took a striped cotton apron from a line in the yard of a house in Bedlow Street and exchanged it for some food in a cook shop in East George Street (Nancy 1804).

If many New York blacks wore the same items of clothing as whites, the overall effect was often distinctive. Just as with the creole language, the vocabulary, or individual piece of clothing, may have been similar but the grammar was different. Of course, such nuances are extremely hard to pick up nearly 200 years later, but occasional reactions such as those of Dunlap and Smith to the "flippantly" dressed black have survived. In 1796, when Ned Cornell, an indentured black of about 16, absconded from the Alms House, the advertisement placed in the *Argus* on 27 April 1796 included the comment that he "also took with him a long fine coat and a pair of boots which he usually wears together and makes a fairly grotesque appearance." In this case, as in the Dunlap and Smith episode, the combination of clothes obviously offended white sensibilities.

West Indian blacks, who were either African-born or had lived in a culture heavily influenced by African patterns, were often noted for their distinctive appearance. A 37-year-old runaway, Peggy, who was born on St. Eustatia, was described as dressing "in the style of the West Indian wenches" (*Daily Advertiser*, 22 December 1794). This West Indian "style" may well have incorporated combinations of clothes and colors considered unusual within Euro-American culture, but the feature that attracted particular comment was the use of a handkerchief as a head covering. To extend the analogy with language, this was a case where blacks broadened the vocabulary of clothing. Charles Joyner, in his study of South Carolina, concluded that the white bandanna handkerchiefs commonly worn by women reflected continuity with African tradition and demonstrated a high degree of personal pride (Joyner 1984:113; see also Genovese 1976:558–559). Undoubtedly, they fulfilled a similar function in New York. There, however, colors other than white were used: Suke generally wore a black handkerchief (*Daily Advertiser*, 23 June 1801); Isabella wore a striped one on her head and another on her neck (*New York Evening Post*, 20 December 1804). Handkerchiefs were often part of male attire also. Lindor, a West Indian born runaway, "commonly wears an handkerchief on his head, according to the West India fashion" (*Daily Advertiser*, 19 May 1789). Another characteristic associated with black Caribbean males was the use of one or two earrings. Wanno, a 22-year-old runaway, had a ring in one of his ears and, according to his owner John Taylor, "looks and talks like a West India negro" (*Centinel of Freedom*, 10 August 1802).

The most important factor contributing to the distinctive appearance of the blacks was their hair. In descriptions of runaways slaveowners often emphasized the physical difference between white and black by using terms like "wool" or "negro hair." Orlando Patterson has recently argued in *Slavery and Social Death* that, contrary to the common view, it was not so much color but hair type that became critical as a mark of servility in the Americas (Patterson 1982:61). If this was the case in New York, it makes the distinctive way in which blacks styled their hair all the more significant. Mingo, who ran away in 1801, wore his hair either "tied or friz'd below his hat" (*Daily Advertiser*, 24

June 1801). A 24-year-old runaway named Jim had "a very bushy woolly head, and often plats and ties his hair" (*Daily Advertiser*, 23 November 1798). Henry Rogers' opinion that Abraham, his 28-year-old slave, was a "surly looking fellow" was probably due, at least in part, to the way the runaway wore his hair "much bushed out" (*Daily Advertiser*, 24 May 1793).

Blacks living in and around New York styled their hair in a variety of ways. Some wore it tied in a queue. Abraham Polhemus's runaway, a mulatto named Jack, gathered his hair behind (*Daily Advertiser*, 6 September 1792), and Daniel, who absconded from a ship in 1804, wore "his hair tied in a short tight queue" (*New York Evening Post*, 11 May 1804). A few had almost all of their hair in plaits. An 18-year-old runaway named Morris wore "his hair about 4 inches long, which is usually plaited and turned up" (*Minerva*, 15 March 1797). Others, like Calvin Woodruff's Jack, wore their earlocks braided (*Centinel of Freedom*, 14 July 1807). According to Thomas De Voe, the New York antiquarian, there was a pattern to these different styles. In his description of the breakdown contests (dancing performed on a plank and the forebear of break dancing) in Catharine Slip, De Voe stated that the New Jersey blacks, mostly from Tappan, wore their forelocks plaited with tea leads, while the Long Island blacks had their hair in a queue tied with a dried eelskin (De Voe 1862:345). The evidence from the runaway advertisements is, however, rather more confused and does not support such a neat geographic division.

In the case of black females, it is clear that these hairstyles reflected continuity with an African past. Styles like that of Mary, who wore her hair "braided in several parts of her head" (*Daily Advertiser*, 26 July 1799), or Caty, who had short hair but wore "a braid of long hair tied to her head" (*Daily Advertiser*, 3 March 1800), were common in West Africa. The situation with black males is more complex. According to Herskovits, black males in West Africa and the New World cut their hair close and wore it unparted. The sole exception that Herskovits noted was what he termed the "local elaboration" in Dutch Guiana, where males also braided their hair (Herskovits 1958:148–149). It may be little more than coincidence but it is interesting to note that such styles in New York were generally associated not with the Africans and West Indians, but with American-born blacks, particularly those brought up in the Dutch areas.

There are indications that the cultural meaning of some black male hairstyles was, in fact, ambiguous, paradoxically hinting on the one hand at both difference from whites and an African past, and, on the other, at similarity and acculturation. Again, it is the language used to describe hair arrangement that provides the clue. The hair of some blacks, often derogatorily termed "wool" to emphasize its difference from that of whites, appears to have been styled to resemble the appearance of the fashionable wigs worn by the New York elite. Jim, a 25-year-old runaway who lived near the Hoboken ferry opposite New York and could speak both Dutch and English fluently, tied "his hair in a cue, with an eel skin, but sometimes combs it about his head and shoulders in the form of a whig" (*Greenleaf's New York Journal,* 19 December 1795). De Voe used the same language when he noted that the Long Island blacks sometimes combed their hair "about their head and shoulders, in the form of a wig, then all the fashion" (De Voe 1862:345). Even the word "queue," which was frequently used to describe the plaited hair of blacks, was closely associated with wigs. Of course there was one crucial difference—the color of the blacks' hair was the reverse of the light-colored wigs. That being so, the effect must, at times, have been dangerously close to parody. Consider for example the appearance of Jack Jackson, who ran away in 1794. Like many other blacks, Jackson was fond of clothes and often dressed in a "rather beauish" fashion, wearing his "wool turn'd up and a comb behind." According to a postscript to the runaway advertisement, he had been seen on the Kingsbridge Road resplendent in a "dark blue coat, with a velvet collar and his *wool powdered*" (*Daily Advertiser,* 30 July 1794; emphasis added).

New York blacks functioned as *bricoleurs,* to borrow Lévi-Strauss' term, drawing from both their African past and the dominant Euro-American culture to create an appearance that, considered as a whole, was new (Lévi-Strauss 1966; see also Clarke 1976:175–191; Hawkes 1977:49–58; Hebdige 1979:102–106; Lears 1985:590–591). If, as in the case of hairstyles, individual components of this style revealed an ambiguity of meaning, the effect was magnified in the overall visual impact of the blacks. In part this originated from the juxtaposition and contrast between a coiffured head of hair or a bandanna handkerchief and clothes worn by whites. But it also derived from context. Blacks who wore expensive clothing or fashioned their hair to resemble a wig gave a fresh meaning to these items. This was particularly so when they dared to take on the trappings of the elite. The effect cannot have been too dissimilar from that of the mods in the 1960s, whose smart dress, according to one commentator, was all the more disturbing because of the impression they gave of "actors who are not quite in their places" (quoted in Hebdige 1976:88), a perception that, in the case of New York blacks, was heightened by their color. In spite of, or because of, the talk of manumission and the eventual passage of the Gradual Manumission Act, well dressed, and especially expensively dressed blacks caused considerable unease in the white population.

In part such unease resulted from white suspicions of the means blacks had employed to obtain the clothes. In the wake of the widespread yellow fever epidemics in the 1790s many whites believed that blacks had taken advantage of their supposed immunity to the disease to pillage the partly evacuated cities. John Bernard, an actor, recorded that it was a common remark in Philadelphia that "you might know where the fever had been raging by the Sunday dress of the black women" (Bernard 1887:195–196). Undoubtedly, similar comments circulated in New York. The assumed link between crime and smartly dressed blacks has been a constant theme in Afro-American history, and in this period, as we have seen, there was at least some justification for these views. But more was involved. Consider for example the language used to describe the free wife of one runaway slave: she had "lately been detected thieving—is noted for gay and fanatical dressing—and is particularly fond of wearing feathers in her hat" (*Greenleaf's New York Journal*, 23 September 1797). Similar behavior in a white woman could hardly have drawn such a reaction. Free blacks, such as this woman, or slaves, such as the runaway described as "genteely dressed" (*American Minerva*, 3 September 1797), represented an inversion of the natural order, with all the attendant dire consequences. Even in pre-Freudian times the black, apprehended on Long Island after assaulting a white woman, can hardly have allayed such fears by claiming that his name was Handsome Dick (*New Jersey Journal*, 14 August 1793).

Black Kinesics

Nearly half a century ago Melville Herskovits pointed out that such routine activities as walking, sitting, talking, laughing, singing, and dancing presented a very promising field for the study of African retentions in the New World. Referring to a film he had taken of an Ashanti ceremony in the village of Asokore, Herskovits pointed out that the dance he recorded was virtually identical to the Charleston (Herskovits 1958:145–146). Long before Herskovits made his suggestion some slaveowners were well aware of the nature of the distinctive motor behavior of blacks. Nowhere is this more obvious than in descriptions in runaway advertisements of the way blacks walked. In 1785, for example, Sam, according to his owner James Hepburn of New Windsor, Middlesex County, had "a very wide remarkable walk" (*New Jersey Gazette*, 29 August 1785). Will, another Jersey runaway, "throws out his feet and toes in a singular manner walking very wide" (*Centinel of Freedom*, 9 February 1802). At times it is possible to see white New Yorkers grappling with the language as they try to capture the alien movement of their slaves: Tom "spraddled" (*Daily Advertiser*, 13 December 1798); another black named Tom walked "loggy leaning forward" (*New York Journal*, 10 October 1792); and Nat had a "remarkable waddle in his walk, which makes him appear as if he was wounded in the hips" (*New Jersey Gazette*, 31 October 1785). Other phrases such as "a kind of rocking in his walk" (*American Minerva*, 29 August 1796) or a "peculiar swing in his gait" (*Argus*, 24 October 1795) suggest the rhythmic harmony that Kenneth Johnson would later characterize as one of the most important elements in the walk of blacks in the ghettos (Johnson 1975:301). However, it is probably descriptions such as "an awkward swaggering walk" (*Daily Advertiser*, 25 June 1801) or "walks with a strut" (*Daily Advertiser*, 20 September 1793) that resonate most strongly with 20th-century readers.

Other body movements and mannerisms are also described in the advertisements, often in terms that reflect quite acute observation of the ways in which blacks conducted themselves in conversation. This was the context with which slaveowners were most familiar, and within which readers of their advertisements would most likely come across the runaways. For some slaves, obviously adept at managing encounters with whites, descriptions took the form of a warning. Cudjo was "a fellow of great cunning and may forge a very plausible story on the road, as he is much addicted to lying" (*Daily Advertiser*, 3 September 1787). A few blacks were noted for their aggressive demeanor. Hannah had a "loud voice and saucy tongue" (*Daily Advertiser*, 1 February 1787). Scip, whose attitude toward his master was obviously disdainful, spoke "with a great deal of boldness and impertinence and walks with a strut" (*Daily Advertiser*, 20 September 1793).

Other blacks had similar attitudes but exhibited them in a more subtle fashion. Movements of the body, in particular the eyes, gave slaves and free blacks an opportunity to release their hostility nonverbally, and thus to avoid retribution. By their very nature such strategies only rarely enter what, for the 18th century anyway, is predominantly a white historical record. But with the aid of some studies of black behavior in 20th-century ghettos, it is possible to detect an occasional example of nonverbal hostility. Such studies make clear that one of the better known ways of expressing impudence and disapproval of an authority figure is "rolling the eyes." This movement is usually preceded by a stare, but not one in which there is eye contact. After the stare the eyes are moved from one side of the socket to the other, the eyelids being lowered, and the movement being always away from the other person. Sometimes the eye movement is accompanied by a slight lifting of the head or a twitching of the nose (Johnson 1975:298–299). Consider, then, the case of Bill who ran away in 1804. He "casts his eyes to the ground and raises them when spoken to, at which time he has a habit of inclining his head rather one side" (*New York Evening Post*, 10 August 1804). Although these descriptions are not identical there is at least the possibility that Bill may have been engaged in something rather akin to "rolling the eyes." This movement may or may not have had its origins in West Africa, but it is generally recognized as being distinctively black. Kenneth Johnson has pointed out that nonblacks often fail to recognize it and see its significance (Johnson 1975:299).

If some blacks, on occasion, were able to handle whites with ease, others had difficulty. Cuff, who spoke both Dutch and broken English, was likely if "cross examined" to stutter considerably (*New Jersey Journal*, 16 December 1789), and Han had a "remarkable impediment in her speech so as to be scarcely understood when answering questions" (*New York Evening Post*, 6 July 1803). The most common mannerism attributed to the runaways in their confrontations with whites was a "down look." Pompy used "plain English but when spoken to has a down look" (*Daily Advertiser*, 8 November 1793), and Aaron was "a remarkable man having a down look scarce to be equalled, and always appears as if his eyes were half shut" (*Daily Advertiser*, 2 June 1801). The "down look" of these blacks contrasts markedly with the behavior of white convicts as described in runaway advertisements. Roger Ekirch in his discussion of convict runaways in the Chesapeake cites examples all of which

emphasize eye contact—"bold staring," "hard looking man," and "very remarkable way of staring any body in the face" (Ekirch 1987:197). Although
this is hardly conclusive it does tend to suggest that the black "down look"
has cultural origins and is not just an example of lower class behavior. This
refusal, or inability, of many slaves to look their masters or other whites in the
eye during verbal encounters reinforced prejudices about the unreliability and
shiftiness of the blacks, an attitude that was conveyed in one owner's observation that his slave, Charles, had a "down sultry look" (*Centinel of Freedom,*
13 February 1810).

But slaveowners may well have been misinterpreting the behavior of their
slaves. For blacks in both West Africa and 20th-century America, avoiding eye
contact with people is a nonverbal way of acknowledging their power and authority. Herskovits pointed out that averting the eyes, and even the face, when
speaking to elders or other respected persons was an element of African etiquette (Herskovits 1958:150–152). Historians are by now very familiar with
the important role African-derived traditions played in resistance to slavery,
but it is just as likely that patterns of accommodation were influenced by similar factors. Slaves like Nero, who was "very obliging, stammers a little when
he speaks, [and] has rather a down look" in the presence of his owner (*New
York Evening Post,* 16 December 1802), may well have been drawing on an
African-derived gestural vocabulary to acknowledge their subordinate position.[15]

The relationship between white and black in New York was never one of
complete subservience. The above mentioned Nero may well have been ac-
quiescent, as his owner suggested, in his day-to-day dealings with whites, but
the master's opinion survives only through the agency of, ironically, a runaway advertisement. Nor, it should be added, was the relationship one of continuing antagonism. Black behavior was far too complex to be neatly bundled
into categories labeled "accommodation" or "resistance." The style constructed, both consciously and subconsciously, by New York blacks fully
demonstrates these complexities.

"A Short History of Sambo's Manuvers"

The ambiguities of this black style are well illustrated in the following example. Among the Forman papers in the New York Historical Society is a
small notebook kept by an unknown white woman (it is simply filed under
the title "Bound Volume") living near Mt. Pleasant in Westchester County.
The notebook is part diary and part letter and appears to have been designed
to inform a friend of the details of local life. From November 1798 to August
1799 there are regular, but very brief, entries mostly about the weather. Occasionally there are more detailed references to local elections or a funeral. But
in 1799 there is a change: "As there is nothing extroriadary throug [the] present
month September," the author writes, "I shall omit & fill up [the] remainder

with a short History of Sambo's manuvers through [the] Winter." What follows is a ten-page attempt by a white to understand the behavior of her slave
named, ironically enough, Sambo.

Until New Year's Eve Sambo had been a "fine boy" who stayed close at
home and was "very Submissive." This behavior induced his owners to allow
him, like other blacks in the country, to have a little liberty. Just before the
holidays they had "new sized him from stem to stern (as the Old man said he
did by Harriet when he left her in Ireland)." Fitting out Sambo with new
clothes reinforced the slaveowners' paternalistic self-image. In fact, the treatment of the occasion by the author, particularly the bracketed reference to the
family's history, was designed both to show that Sambo was treated like a
member of the family and to allow the narrator to organize, and to try to comprehend, Sambo's later actions within the framework of the parable of the
prodigal son. Sambo was given permission to go out in his new clothes but
was "beged & requested" to behave himself and return "according to orders."
But Sambo did not come home until daylight the next morning. Further, his
owners later found out, he had not only stolen two geese but he had also tried
to incriminate Old Cato, a free black living in the vicinity, by leaving the severed heads on his doorstep. The miscreant was taken to court and received a
hundred lashes the same day.

Sambo had been earning some extra money by going every morning and
evening to a Mr. OBrion's where he cut firewood and foddered the cattle. One
Sunday he "mounted his new Cloathes," collected the 12 shillings OBrion
owed him for four weeks' work, which, combined with two dollars he had
won at a "husslin frollick," gave him more than enough money for a "bout."
Sambo was not sighted until the next evening when the "Doctor," who appears to have been the writer's husband, was "lucky enough to nab him" in
Mt. Pleasant and took him home.

the Doctr. then reversed [the] Parable in Scripture & Strip'd him of his new Apperral put on his
rags & shaved his head which he had for some time before taken much pains in plaiting & tyeing
his wool in which he had a considerable cue.

Although some of the document appears to be missing at this point, it seems
that Sambo had also stolen something on this latest expedition. He was taken
to court again and sentenced to 70 lashes "well laid on." Soon afterwards he
was caught breaking into Josiah West's mill in search of cider. The court was
"collected" by a little after sunrise and "Sixty lashes was his Doom." Sambo
then ran away for a time but eventually returned. He remained at home for a
few weeks but was "unsetled & good for little." This period of relative quiet
ended when Sambo was caught breaking into Conover's store looking for liquor. He was sent to the courthouse and put in the dungeon for a month. On
each of the following three Saturdays Sambo was given a hundred lashes.
After the last of these whippings he was taken home where, according to the
writer,

Sambo with his sore back was that evening as happy as a lord, has ever since been contented at home & more faithfull than he ever was before, has played no tricks since. So far we flatter ourselves a reformation has taken place at length. God grant it may continue for I am sure we have beene well worne out with trouble with him.

What is striking about this case is the extent to which the writer, in an attempt to understand the slave's behavior, centers the narrative around Sambo's appearance and in particular his clothes. In fact, the struggle for control of Sambo took place quite literally over his body. To Sambo's owners the clothes represented their benevolence and paternalism. It is clear, though we are viewing the incident through the eyes not of Sambo but of his owner, that his garments meant something different to Sambo. The slave's new clothes and carefully styled hair had become closely associated in his mind with good times, drinking and gambling. It is significant that, in an effort to control his recalcitrant behavior, Sambo's body was scarred by the whip. When that failed the Doctor not only took back the clothes, but went to the extraordinary length of shaving Sambo's head, a symbolic castration that also had biblical antecedents (see Firth 1973:287–291; Patterson 1982:60–62).

Finally, after receiving a fearful number of lashes, Sambo returned, like the prodigal son, to the fold, "more faithful" than before. But his return was as abrupt and unexplained as his departure. In the last sentence in the notebook the writer attributes Sambo's deleterious behavior to his thirst for rum and surmises that, "if he should drink too deep he dont care what he does & may play his old pranks over again." However, as the opaque penultimate sentence—"It is true when the Holy Days come on the White Folks are right down mad as the Negro song says"—and, indeed, the perceived need to record the episode on paper suggest, the writer found Sambo's love of drink an unsatisfactory, or at least incomplete, explanation. Though removed by 200 years from "Sambo's manuvers," and compelled to view them through the eyes of an anonymous white woman, we may at least speculate that the symbolic importance of clothing and appearance was something that, if whites and blacks did not fully articulate, they nevertheless understood.

Conclusion

The material collected and analyzed in this article clearly demonstrates the existence of a style among *some* New York blacks. But the often fragmentary and difficult nature of such material requires that more general conclusions must be cautiously and tentatively worded. On any particular facet of black behavior—language, clothing, hairstyles, or bodily movements, for example—most owners of runaways made no comment at all. Only a minority, for example, described the way in which their runaways walked. But silence concerning the walking styles of other blacks does not mean that those styles were identical to those of whites. Undoubtedly, there existed a range of walking styles among the blacks, with some being merely less extravagant or exaggerated than others. They are not to be ignored on that account. The hallmarks of any style are variation and change and it is hardly surprising that uniformity in walking, or in any other facet of black behavior, did not exist.

What, then, was the importance of the black style detected here? Unlike most blacks in the South, New York blacks were not sheltered from the full impact of white culture by the existence of a plantation community. By the early years of the 19th century they were being drawn inexorably into the emerging working class of the city. As evidenced by the increasingly violent tenor of race relations and particularly the riots of the 1830s, whites were scarcely enamored of this prospect. Although their reaction was less aggressive, New York blacks, through the way they spoke, the manner in which they dressed, and through their bodily movements and gestures, made it clear that they viewed this process, if not with hostility, then at least with ambivalence. Not only did the style of New York blacks reinforce, albeit in a less dramatic form than in the South, continuities with their African past and differentiate black from white in the rapidly changing metropolis, but, as we have seen in this article, it was also of considerable importance in the day-to-day lives of black New Yorkers attempting to live in a white world. The piecing together of fragmentary and often neglected evidence and the patient teasing out of its significance reveals that the story of New York blacks was not simply one of rapid and wholesale assimilation, but more one of creative adaptation to an often hostile world. For black communities of the South, where sources are both more abundant and more easily deciphered, the possibilities for further research into black style, an elusive but important aspect of the black past, would appear to be bright.

Notes

The research for this article was funded by the complex juggling of the limits on a number of credit cards, but as these institutions have already received their dues in other ways they will not be mentioned by name here. My debts to people are rather more substantial. An early version of this article was given to the May 1986 conference of the Australian and New Zealand American Studies Association in Auckland, New Zealand. I would like to thank Richard Bosworth, Barbara Carson, Cary Carson, Thomas J. Davis, Roger Ekirch, Graham Hodges, Donna Merwick, Ian Mylchreest, Jonathan Prude, Daniel Walkowitz and particularly Stanley Engerman, Jim Gilbert, Philip Morgan and Gary Nash for helpful comments on various versions of this piece. My largest debts, however, are due to Rhys Isaac, Charles Joyner, Lawrence Levine, Richard Waterhouse and Graham White (no relation), both for their critical readings of this article and for the splendid support they have given my work.

[1] Berlin (1980) provides a very good discussion of much of the innovative work published in the 1970s. Recently, however, a few of the southern urban centers have received some attention (see Lebsock 1984; Morgan 1984). Most of the well-known studies of the antebellum South such as Levine (1977) or Genovese (1976) also concentrate on the rural areas.

[2] Runaway advertisements are the main, but certainly not the only, source used here. The District Attorney's Indictment Papers are also a rich source for the study of New York City that are just beginning to be exploited (see Gilfoyle 1987; Stansell 1986). Other sources yielded, as a glance at the references cited in this article suggests, very little information. These sources included virtually every published diary or traveler's account (and many unpublished ones too) mentioning New York and all extant issues of magazines published

north of the Mason and Dixon Line before 1800. Further, I looked at every item published in New York, New Jersey, and Pennsylvania between 1770 and 1800 reproduced in the microprint series of *Early American Imprints.*

³The following newspapers were used: *American Minerva* (1793–1796); *Argus* (1795–1797); *New York Evening Post* (1801–1805); *New York Gazette and Weekly Mercury* (1771–1783); *New York Journal* (1786–1794); *Greenleaf's New York Journal* (1794–1800); *Minerva* (1796–1797); *Rivington's New York Gazette* (varying titles—1773–1783); *Long Island Courier* (1799–1803); *New Jersey Gazette* (1777–1786); *New Jersey Journal* (1789–1793); *Centinel of Freedom* (1796–1805); *The Federalist: New Jersey Gazette* (1798–1800). An enormous number of newspapers were published in New Jersey and New York in this period and those listed above only represent a fraction of the total. Further, the holdings in the various institutions in which I read some of these newspapers (including the New York State Library, the New York Historical Society, and the Library of Congress) were incomplete. Even the microfilm and microcard copies I used were not always complete.

⁴The figure of 1,232 represents the total number of runaways who left of their own volition and excludes 47 children who ran away with a parent. Thus, eight-year-olds absconding by themselves have been counted but when they fled in company with a parent they have been left out. Only a fool would claim that this figure represents all the runaways in the newspapers read. Microfilm is difficult enough, but many of these newspapers were read on microcard, a medium seemingly designed to send readers both blind and to sleep and, undoubtedly, I have missed some. The figure of 1,232 excludes all runaways from the area of New York State which was to the north and west of Ulster and Dutchess counties. As well, all advertisements describing slaves who had decamped from their owners in Connecticut, Pennsylvania, and the southern states were discarded. In fact, most of the runaways came from New York City and the surrounding counties of Kings, Queens, Westchester, and Richmond and from Bergen and Somerset in New Jersey. The few runaways from further afield in New Jersey and from Ulster and Orange counties that were advertised in these newspapers have, however, been included.

⁵The runaway advertisements used here were collected from more newspapers than in the other two studies. According to Morgan there are, for the colonial period, approximately 1,750 issues surviving for Virginia and 3,500 for South Carolina (Morgan 1985:75). Here I have not used all surviving New York and New Jersey newspapers but have still read in excess of 12,000 issues.

⁶Morgan argues, I believe mistakenly, that the South Carolinian runaway sample was "representative" of the slave population as a whole. Although he does demonstrate correlations in the area of skill and in the number of Africans in the population, there certainly was no correlation in the sex ratio and there probably was not one in terms of age structure (see Morgan 1985:57–66).

⁷74.2% of the runaways were under the age of 26 and 78.3% were male. In 28.9% of cases the place of origin was specified; of these 32.3% came from either the West Indies or Africa and 47.2% were mulattoes. This is dealt with at considerably greater length in my more traditional analysis of these runaways (see White 1988b:135–176).

⁸As the text is meant to suggest, I am skeptical as to the existence of any precise correlation between running away and the cultural traits described in this article. Arguments that the "resistance" demonstrated by running away would flow through into such areas as clothing or hairstyles are based on misapprehensions about what running away meant (see Morgan 1985:57). Nevertheless, in an attempt to forestall such criticism, I have placed my findings within this more tentative framework.

⁹A useful analogy is the personal notices in the back pages of the *New York Review of Books*. To the *cognoscenti,* "WWF" or "SJM" has an immediate and obvious meaning but the rest of us have to grope around trying to work it out. Further, such words as "divorced" or "non-smoking" appear to have connotations about lifestyles that extend well beyond the literal meaning of the words. Extracting all of the information contained in both the personal notices and the runaway advertisements requires a careful analysis of the language used.

¹⁰This figure considerably understates the influence of the Dutch language. Dutch-speaking slaveowners probably did not advertise in the press. Most of the owners of Dutch-speaking slaves in fact had non-Dutch names and had presumably purchased these slaves from owners of Dutch origin. In 1772, for example, Sambo spoke good English but his owner, Caleb Morgan, also believed he spoke Dutch as he "was brought up among the Dutch on the west side of the [Hudson] river" (*New York Gazette and Weekly Mercury,* 2 November 1772). In 1796 there appears to have been a flurry of slave runaway activity in the Dutch stronghold of Ulster

County as a result of the legislative debates over the abolition of slavery. In Shawangunk, a society, a majority of whose members appear to have had Dutch names, was formed to "detect and apprehend" runaway slaves (Constitution and Minutes of the Slave Apprehending Society of Shawangunk 1796). There is no indication of the existence of this flurry in the newspaper advertisements for runaway slaves.

[11]The runaway advertisements overwhelmingly describe men, but a few of those for women indicate that the same pattern may have occurred with females as well. In 1792, for example, a 16-year-old was named Jane "but sometimes calls herself Sarah" (*Daily Advertiser*, 12 January 1792).

[12]There were 157 free black households in New York City in the 1790 census, 676 in 1800 and 1,228 in 1810 (White 1988a).

[13]Although the census is the most satisfactory means of examining black names, it is not without problems. Blacks dealing with whites (the census takers were white) assumed new names with great ease. Perhaps one can detect a slight note of frustration in one slaveowner's description of his 19-year-old slave, "named Peter, Victor, Le Sauce or any of these names" (*Daily Advertiser*, 14 September 1799). Even a cursory look at the court records demonstrates that many blacks used more than one surname when dealing with whites. However, as a case such as *People v. John Smith alias David Brown and John Scott alias Stephen Williams* illustrates, they were still very common names. Herskovits has also commented on this ease of changing names (Herskovits 1958:193–194).

[14]Unfortunately the material from New York is nowhere near detailed enough to allow a generational study of black names through time and within families (see, for example, Cody 1982, 1987). If suitable data can ever be found for New York an analysis of this sort may well detect distinctively black patterns in naming.

[15]Mullin developed an elaborate theory about the "stuttering" of the runaways in Virginia demonstrating the "assimilated's divided self and cultural marginality" (Mullin 1972:98–103). Herskovits, however, makes an intriguing comment in *The Myth of the Negro Past* that in Dutch Guiana young men speaking to elders had to use a "low voice" and introduce a "conventionalised stammer into his speech" (Herskovits 1958:152). It remains little more than speculation but possibly the stammer of some blacks has been misinterpreted by slaveowners and historians.

References Cited

Berlin, Ira. 1980. Time, Space, and the Evolution of Afro-American Society on British Mainland North America. *American Historical Review* 85:44–78.

Bernard, John. 1887. *Retrospections of America, 1797–1811*. New York.

Bridenbaugh, Carl, ed. 1973. *Gentleman's Progress: The Itinerarium of Dr Alexander Hamilton 1744*. Westport: Greenwood.

Chibnall, Steve. 1985. Whistle and Zoot: The Changing Meaning of a Suit of Clothes. *History Workshop* 20:56–81.

Clarke, John. 1976. Style. In *Resistance Through Rituals: Youth Subcultures in Post-War Britain*, eds. Stuart Hall and Tony Jefferson, pp. 175–191. London: Hutchinson.

Cody, Cheryll Ann. 1982. Naming, Kinship, and Estate Dispersal: Notes on Slave Family Life on a South Carolina Plantation, 1786 to 1833. *William and Mary Quarterly* 39:192–211.

——— . 1987. There Was No "Absalom" on the Ball Plantations: Slave-Naming Practices in the South Carolina Low Country, 1720–1865. *American Historical Review* 92:563–596.

Constitution and Minutes of the Slave Apprehending Society of Shawangunk. 1796. 21 May. New York State Library.

Cosgrove, Stuart. 1984. The Zoot Suit and Style Warfare. *History Workshop* 18:77–91.

Cronin, James E., ed. 1973. *The Diary of Elihu Hubbard Smith (1771–1798)*. Philadelphia: American Philosophical Society.

De Voe, Thomas F. 1862. *The Market Book: A History of the Public Markets of the City of New York*. New York.

Dillard, J. L. 1972. *Black English: Its History and Usage in the United States*. New York: Random House.

Ekirch, A. Roger. 1987. *Bound for America: The Transportation of British Convicts to the Colonies, 1718–1775*. Oxford: Clarendon Press.

Firth, Raymond. 1973. *Symbols: Public and Private*. Ithaca: Cornell University Press.

Fogel, Robert William, and Stanley L. Engerman. 1974. *Time on the Cross: The Economics of American Negro Slavery*. Boston: Little, Brown.

Genovese, Eugene D. 1976. *Roll, Jordan, Roll: The World the Slaves Made*. New York: Pantheon Books.

Gilfoyle, Timothy J. 1987. Strumpets and Misogynists: Brothel "Riots" and the Transformation of Prostitution in Antebellum New York City. *New York History* 68:45–65.

Gutman, Herbert G. 1977. *The Black Family in Slavery and Freedom, 1750–1925*. New York: Pantheon Books.

Hall, Stuart, and Tony Jefferson, eds. 1976. *Resistance Through Rituals: Youth Subcultures in Post-War Britain*. London: Hutchinson.

Hawkes, Terence. 1977. *Structuralism and Semiotics*. London: Methuen.

Hebdige, Dick. 1976. The Meaning of Mod. In *Resistance Through Rituals: Youth Subcultures in Post-War Britain*, eds. Stuart Hall and Tony Jefferson, pp. 87–96. London: Hutchinson.

————. 1979. *Subculture: The Meaning of Style*. London: Methuen.

Herskovits, Melville J. 1958. *The Myth of the Negro Past*. Boston: Beacon Press.

Inscoe, John C. 1983. Carolina Slave Names: An Index to Acculturation. *Journal of Southern History* 49:527–554.

Johnson, Kenneth R. 1975. Black Kinesics—Some Non-Verbal Communication Patterns in Black Culture. In *Perspectives on Black English*, ed. J. L. Dillard, pp. 296–306. The Hague: Mouton.

Joyner, Charles. 1984. *Down By the Riverside: A South Carolina Slave Community*. Urbana: University of Illinois Press.

Kruger, Vivienne L. 1985. Born to Run: The Slave Family in Early New York, 1626 to 1827. Ph.D. dissertation. History Department, Columbia University.

Lears, T. J. Jackson. 1985. The Concept of Cultural Hegemony: Problems and Possibilities. *American Historical Review* 90:567–593.

Lebsock, Suzanne. 1984. *The Free Women of Petersburg: Status and Culture in a Southern Town*. New York: Norton.

Levine, Lawrence W. 1977. *Black Culture and Black Consciousness: Afro-American Folk Thought From Slavery to Freedom*. New York: Oxford University Press.

Lévi-Strauss, Claude. 1966. *The Savage Mind*. London: Weidenfeld and Nicholson.

Morgan, Philip D. 1983. Black Society in the Lowcountry, 1760–1810. In *Slavery and Freedom in the Age of the American Revolution*, eds. Ira Berlin and Ronald Hoffman, pp. 83–141. Charlottesville: University of Virginia Press.

————. 1984. Black Life in Eighteenth-Century Charleston. *Perspectives in American History*, New Series 1:187–232.

————. 1985. Colonial South Carolina Runaways: Their Significance for Slave Culture. *Slavery and Abolition* 6:57–78.

Mullin, Gerald W. 1972. *Flight and Rebellion: Slave Resistance in Eighteenth-Century Virginia*. New York: Oxford University Press.

Nancy. 1804. Statement of Nancy. *People v. Nancy (a Black)*, filed 5 June 1804, Box 17, District Attorney's Indictment Papers, Municipal Archives, New York, N.Y.

Nash, Gary B. 1983. Forging Freedom: The Emancipation Experience in the Northern Seaport Cities, 1775–1820. In *Slavery and Freedom in the Age of the American Revolution*, eds. Ira Berlin and Ronald Hoffman, pp. 3–48. Charlottesville: University of Virginia Press.

Needler, Geoffrey D. 1967. Linguistic Evidence from Alexander Hamilton's Itinerarium. *American Speech* 42:211–218.

Olson, Edwin. 1941. Social Aspects of Slave Life in New York. *Journal of Negro History* 26:66–77.

Patterson, Orlando. 1982. *Slavery and Social Death: A Comparative Study.* Cambridge: Harvard University Press.

Pero, Frank. 1802. Statement of Frank Pero. *People v. John Jackson & Frank Pero,* filed 11 December 1802, Box 13, District Attorney's Indictment Papers, Municipal Archives, New York, N.Y.

Robertson, Samuel. 1798. Statement of Samuel Robertson. *People v. Samuel Robertson,* filed 4 January 1798, Box 2, District Attorney's Indictment Papers, Municipal Archives, New York, N.Y.

Sickles, John. 1804. Statement of John Sickles. *People v. John Thomas,* filed 4 April 1804, Box 16, District Attorney's Indictment Papers, Municipal Archives, New York, N.Y.

Smith, Sally. 1805. Statement of Sally Smith. *People v. Sally Smith,* filed 4 November 1805, Box 17, District Attorney's Indictment Papers, Municipal Archives, New York, N.Y.

Stansell, Christine. 1986. *City of Women: Sex and Class in New York, 1789–1860.* New York: Knopf.

St. Domingo, Jack. 1801. Statement of Jack St. Domingo. *People v. Jack St. Domingo,* filed 7 October 1801, Box 9, District Attorney's Indictment Papers, Municipal Archives, New York, N.Y.

Stewart, William A. 1975. Sociolinguistic Factors in the History of American Negro Dialects. In *Perspectives on Black English,* ed. J. L. Dillard, pp. 222–232. The Hague: Mouton.

Strickland, William. 1971. *Journal of a Tour in the United States of America 1794–1795,* ed. J. E. Strickland. New York: New York Historical Society.

Thomas, Isabella. 1802. Statement of Isabella Thomas. *People v. Isabella Thomas,* filed 4 June 1802, Box 12, District Attorney's Indictment Papers, Municipal Archives, New York, N.Y.

White, Shane. 1988a. "We Dwell in Safety and Pursue Our Honest Callings": Free Blacks in New York City, 1783–1810. *Journal of American History* 75:445–470.

————. 1988b. Somewhat More Independent: The End of Slavery in New York City, 1770–1810. Ph.D. dissertation. History Department, University of Sydney.

Young, John. 1804. Statement of John Young. *People v. Thomas Cooney and others,* filed 7 April 1804, Box 16, District Attorney's Indictment Papers, Municipal Archives, New York, N.Y.

The Christian Movement and the Demand for a Theology of the People

Nathan O. Hatch

In 1776, John Adams posed the question that would preoccupy his generation of American citizens and their children. "It is certain, in theory," he said, "that the only moral foundation of government is, the consent of the people. But to what extent shall we carry this principle?" The Revolution brought an accent of reality to a new self-evident truth, the sovereignty of the people, which Edmund Morgan has recently described as a "political fiction." For the founding fathers the fiction of popular sovereignty held some resemblance to the facts, but they fully expected the governed and the governors to "join in a benign conspiracy to suspend disbelief" in the new fiction, in other words, to believe it rhetorically rather than literally. The people were not so kind, however, and the shrill and unending debate that characterized American history from Adams to Andrew Jackson concerned how seriously this fiction should be taken.[1]

A number of scholars have recently explored the dimensions of this cultural ferment over the meaning of freedom. In the wake of their own and the French Revolution, Americans witnessed the rapid growth of voluntary organizations and popular newspapers, the formation of organized political parties amid heated and increasingly popular political debate, the armed protest of un-protected economic groups, sharp attacks upon elite professions and upon slavery, and new ideas of citizenship and representation, of old age and women's identity.[2] Eugene Genovese has even argued that a revolutionary

Nathan O. Hatch is assistant professor of history at University of Notre Dame. Research assistance was provided by the American Antiquarian Society and the Charles Warren Center for Studies in American History.

[1] Charles Francis Adams, ed., *The Works of John Adams, Second President of the United States* (10 vols., Boston, 1850-1856) IX, 375; Edmund S. Morgan, "The Great Political Fiction," *New York Review of Books*, XXV (March 9, 1978), 13-18.

[2] James A. Henretta, *The Evolution of American Society, 1700-1815* (Lexington, Mass., 1973); Richard D. Brown, *Modernization: The Transformation of American Life, 1600-1865* (New York, 1976); Richard D. Brown, "The Emergence of Voluntary Associations in Massachusetts, 1760-1830," *Journal of Voluntary Action Research*, II (April 1973), 64-73; Jackson Turner Main, "Government by the People: The American Revolution and the Democratization of the

ideology of liberty and equality transformed the character of slave resistance in North America and in the Caribbean.[3] Lamenting the awakening to political consciousness of the common man, Harrison Gray Otis gave to a Harvard audience in 1836 his view of what had happened since the Revolution: "Everywhere the disposition is found among those who live in the valleys, to ask those who live on the hills, 'How came we here and you there?' accompanied with intelligible demonstrations of a purpose in the former, to partake of the benefits of the mountain air."[4]

What became of American religion in these years—roughly 1780 to 1820— when traditional values were being turned upside down by what Gordon S. Wood has called a "democratization of mind"?[5] Despite a wealth of recent scholarship on the role of religion in the coming of the American Revolution, surprisingly little work has been done on the changing nature of popular religion after the Revolution. This imbalance stems in part from the conventional division between the era of the republic's founding and that of the middle period, but it also reflects the simple fact that a quickened interest in religion as a cultural force has emerged within a broader historiographical tendency to downplay the social impact of the Revolution. The result has been that while historians have noted many links between the Great Awakening and the Revolution, they have not followed through to ask how rapid social change in the young republic affected structures of religious belief and organization.[6] What happened when people began to call for a strenuous ap-

Legislatures," *William and Mary Quarterly*, XXIII (July 1966), 391–407; Bernard Bailyn, *The Ideological Origins of the American Revolution* (Cambridge, 1967); Richard E. Ellis, *The Jeffersonian Crisis: Courts and Politics in the Young Republic* (New York, 1971); David Brion Davis, *The Problem of Slavery in the Age of Revolution, 1770–1823* (Ithaca, 1975); David Hackett Fischer, *Growing Old in America* (New York, 1977); Robert A. Gross, *The Minutemen and Their World* (New York, 1976); and Mary Beth Norton, *The Revolutionary Experience of American Women, 1750–1800* (Boston, 1980).

[3] Eugene D. Genovese, *From Rebellion to Revolution: Afro-American Slave Revolts in the Making of the Modern World* (Baton Rouge, 1979).

[4] Harrison Gray Otis, who had delivered the English oration at Harvard when he graduated in 1783, was asked to give the primary address at Harvard's bicentennial celebration in 1836. His speech is the lament of an old man who had witnessed the "fiery furnace of democracy" destroy much of what he held dear. While he had hoped that the Revolution had been "completed by the establishment of independence," he lived to see a "new school" take charge that "would identify revolution with perpetual motion. They would put all ancient institutions, laws, customs, courts, colleges, and schools upon wheels, and keep them whirling for ever with the steam of their own eloquence." Josiah Quincy, *The History of Harvard University* (2 vols., Cambridge, 1840), II, 662–70.

[5] Gordon S. Wood, "The Democratization of Mind in the American Revolution," *Leadership in the American Revolution* (Washington, 1974), 63–89; and Gordon S. Wood, "Social Radicalism and Equality in the American Revolution," *The B. K. Smith Lectures in History* (Houston, 1976), 5–14.

[6] On the new scholarly interest in religion, see Henry F. May, "The Recovery of American Religious History," *American Historical Review*, LXX (Oct. 1964), 79–92. The broader trend to dismiss the social repercussions of the Revolution is evident in Frederick B. Tolles, "The American Revolution Considered as a Social Movement: A Re-Evaluation," *American Historical Review*, LX (Oct. 1954), 1–12. Studies of the Second Great Awakening in New England and the Great Revival in the Southwest have generally not addressed the question of how cultural ferment might have altered religion; they have focused, rather, on how traditional religion championed the revival technique in order to impose social order upon a disordered and secularized society. See

plication of popular sovereignty to the church? What did Christian freedom come to mean for people ready to question any source of authority that did not begin with an act of individual choice?

To explore these questions, this essay will focus on the cultural roots of a movement that assumed the name "Christian" or "Disciples of Christ." Between 1790 and 1815 this loose network of religious radicals demanded, in light of the American and French revolutions, a new dispensation set free from the trammels of history, a new kind of institutional church premised on the self-evident principles of republicanism, and a new form of Biblical authority calling for the inalienable right of common people to interpret the New Testament for themselves. The central figures in the reform movement—Elias Smith in New England, James O'Kelly in Virginia, Barton Stone in Kentucky, and Alexander Campbell in Pennsylvania—were a motley crew with few common characteristics, but they all moved independently to similar conclusions within a fifteen-year span. A Calvinist Baptist, a Methodist, and two Presbyterians all found traditional sources of authority anachronistic and found themselves groping toward similar definitions of egalitarian religion.[7] In a culture that increasingly balked at vested interests, symbols of hierarchy, and timeless authorities, a remarkable number of people would wake up one morning to find it self-evident that the priesthood of all believers meant just that—religion of, by, and for the people.

At the dawn of the nineteenth century, the Federalist citadel of Essex County, Massachusetts, witnessed a major assault on its well-bred and high-toned culture. Religious enthusiasm had taken hold among common people and its rude challenge to authority dismayed even the tolerant Jeffersonian diarist William Bentley of Salem. As late as 1803, Bentley had confided smugly that Essex County remained virtually free of sects. During the next five years, he watched with dismay the lower orders of his community championing "religious convulsions," "domestic fanaticism," and "Meeting-Mania." In chronicling the parade of sects that won attention—Baptist, Freewill Baptist, Methodist, Universalist, and Christian—Bentley noted the first field meeting in the county since George Whitefield, preaching by blacks and illiterate

Perry Miller, "From Covenant to Revival," in *The Shaping of American Religion*, ed. J. W. Smith and A. L. Jamison (Princeton, 1961), 350; Lois W. Banner, "Religious Benevolence as Social Control: A Critique of an Interpretation," *Journal of American History*, LX (June 1973), 23–41; and John B. Boles, *The Great Revival, 1787–1805: The Origins of the Southern Evangelical Mind* (Lexington, Ky., 1972). More sensitive to the ongoing impact of the Revolution in religious affairs is Donald G. Mathews, "The Second Great Awakening as an Organizing Process, 1780–1830: An Hypothesis," *American Quarterly*, XXI (Spring 1969), 23–43.

[7] Luther P. Gerlach and Virginia H. Hine define a social "movement" as "a group of people who are organized for, ideologically motivated by, and committed to a purpose which implements some form of personal or social change; who are actively engaged in the recruitment of others; and whose influence is spreading in opposition to the established order within which it originated." Luther P. Gerlach and Virginia H. Hine, *People, Power, Change: Movements of Social Transformation* (Indianapolis, 1970), xvi. The Christians, like the movements of which Gerlach and Hine speak, were decentralized and segmented, their web-like structures without clear lines of authority and often dependent upon shared publications. Their unity stemmed from little more than common ideology and perceived opposition from religious and political elites.

sailors, and servants angering their employers by frequenting night lectures "as in Mother Hutchinson's time." What Bentley found most appalling was that "the rabble" not only noised abroad strange doctrine but actually went beyond what they were told, attempting "to explain, condemn and reveal" religious matters. The people, he groaned, were doing theology for themselves.[8]

Bentley saved his sharpest barbs for an itinerant preacher, the "notorious" Smith who regularly barnstormed through Essex County, preaching in the open air, singing in the streets, and accosting people to question their spiritual state. If this was not enough to discomfit the respectable citizens of Salem, Smith kept the pot boiling by leaving behind bundles of his tracts and pamphlets.[9]

For all its parallels with the dissent of a Whitefield or an Isaac Backus, Smith's gospel for the people did have one different twist. It was laced with the language of politics and reflected the experience of a man whose radical pilgrimage began with a political conversion. Until 1800 Smith filled the pulpit of the respectable Baptist Church in Woburn, Massachusetts, and gave little attention to political questions of the day. During the election of 1800, however, he fell under the influence of the radical Jeffersonian publicist Benjamin Austin, Jr., who wrote regularly for the *Boston Independent Chronicle*. Smith quickly imbibed Austin's heady wine, which made much of the right of common people to think and act for themselves. Resigning from his church—as a manifesto of his own liberty—and denouncing formal religion of every kind, Smith began to translate the sovereignty of the people to the sphere of religion.[10] "Let us be republicans indeed," he declared in 1809. "Many are *republicans* as to *government*, and yet are but half republicans, being in matters of religion still bound to a catechism, creed, covenant or a superstitious priest. Venture to be as independent in things of religion, as those which respect the government in which you live."[11] From Portsmouth, New Hampshire, Smith launched the first religious newspaper in the United States, a fortnightly *Herald of Gospel Liberty*, which he edited from 1808 to 1818. From that forum and in scores of pamphlets and sermons, he and a band

[8] William Bentley, *The Diary of William Bentley, D. D.* (4 vols., Salem, Mass., 1911), III, 65, 503, 515, 271.

[9] In May 1805 William Bentley commented about Elias Smith that "the press has lately vomited out many nauseaus things from this writer." *Ibid.*, 157, 370, 291.

[10] Elias Smith, *The Life, Conversion, Preaching, Travels and Sufferings of Elias Smith* (Portsmouth, N.H., 1816), 341–42.

[11] Elias Smith, *The Lovingkindness of God Displayed in the Triumph of Republicanism in America: Being a Discourse Delivered at Taunton (Mass.) July Fourth, 1809; at the Celebration of American Independence* (n.p., 1809), 32. Smith's colleague Abner Jones also experienced what he called a "disintegration" of his Calvinist beliefs and was quick to note the theological implications of demands for social equality. "In giving the reader an account of my birth and parentage," Jones wrote in 1807, "I shall not (like the celebrated Franklin and others,) strive to prove that I arose from a family of eminence; believing that all men are born equal, and that every man shall die for his own iniquity." Abner Jones, *Memoirs of the Life and Experience, Travels and Preaching of Abner Jones* (Exeter, N.H., 1807), 3.

of fifty or so itinerants, who called themselves merely Christians, carried on a blistering attack upon Baptists, Congregationalists, Methodists, and Federalists of any religious peisuasion. The *Herald of Gospel Liberty*, which by 1815 had fourteen hundred subscribers and over fifty agents around the country, became a vehicle of communication for other individuals who were moving independently to the same conclusions as Smith.[12]

From Virginia came word of O'Kelly's Republican Methodists, founded in 1794 to undo the "ecclesiastical monarchy" in the Methodist church. A prime mover among early Virginia Methodists, O'Kelly could not abide the bishopric of Francis Asbury and withdrew with over thirty ministers to form a connection which had as many as twenty thousand members when it merged with Smith's forces, under the name Christian, in 1809.[13] "Episcopacy makes a bad appearance in our republican world," O'Kelly argued in 1798. "Francis was born and nurtured in the land of Bishops and Kings and what is bred in the bone, is hard to get out of the flesh."[14] O'Kelly, who had taken up arms in the Revolution and served a brief stint as a British captive, argued that he was "too sensible of the sweets of liberty, to be content any longer under British chains. . . . As a son of America, and a Christian," he challenged Asbury, "I shall oppose your political measures and contend for the Saviour's government. I contend for Bible government, Christian equality, and the Christian name."[15]

Stone was an equally interesting figure who had ventured upon much the same pilgrimage prior to the appearance of the *Herald of Gospel Liberty*. In 1802, in the wake of the Cane Ridge Revival in Kentucky, Stone decided he could no longer live under Presbyterian doctrine or church organization. A year later, he and five other ministers pushed this idea to its logical extreme and proclaimed that it was not just the Presbyterians who were wrong: all church structures were suspect. Signing "The Last Will and Testament of Springfield

[12] For a brief sketch of Smith's life, see William G. McLoughlin, *New England Dissent, 1630-1883: The Baptists and the Separation of Church and State* (2 vols., Cambridge, 1971), II, 745-49. Otherwise, no one has undertaken a serious study of Smith, despite his prominence as a religious and political radical in New England from 1800 to 1820, his scores of publications addressed to a popular audience, his newspaper that ran for a decade, and his fascinating memoir. The number of his itinerant followers is taken from one of his Congregational assailants. Thomas Andros, *The Scriptures Liable to be Wrested to Men's Own Destruction, and an Instance of This Found, in the Writings of Elias Smith* (Taunton, Mass., 1817), 18. A list of agents for Smith's newspaper is found in *Herald of Gospel Liberty*, Aug. 18, 1809, p. 104. For the number of subscribers, see *ibid.*, Sept. 29, 1815, p. 720. On Smith's movement, which became known as the Christian Connection, see Thomas H. Olbricht, "Christian Connection and Unitarian Relations," *Restoration Quarterly*, IX (Sept. 1966), 160-86.

[13] The best treatment of James O'Kelly is Charles Franklin Kilgore, *The James O'Kelly Schism in the Methodist Episcopal Church* (Mexico City, 1963). See also Edward J. Drinkhouse, *History of Methodist Reform* (2 vols., Baltimore, 1899), I; and Milo T. Morrill, *A History of the Christian Denomination in America* (Dayton, 1912). O'Kelly's primary works are James O'Kelly, *The Author's Apology for Protesting against the Methodist Episcopal Government* (Richmond, 1798); and James O'Kelly, *A Vindication of the Author's Apology* (Raleigh, 1801).

[14] O'Kelly, *Author's Apology*, 4, 21.

[15] O'Kelly, *Vindication*, 60-61.

Presbytery," these men vowed to follow nothing but the Christian name and the New Testament.[16]

Scholars have generally viewed Stone's beliefs as the product of the rough-and-tumble context of the frontier and of the rampant emotionalism of the Great Revival.[17] Stone was a rawboned character, no doubt, but he also spent his formative years during the Revolution, and his theology of "gospel-liberty" reflected this early experience. "From my earliest recollection I drank deeply into the spirit of liberty," he confessed late in life, "and was so warmed by the soul-inspiring draughts, that I could not hear the name of British, or tories, without feeling a rush of blood through the whole system. . . . I confess their magic influence to this advanced day of my life." It was not without deep connotation that Stone characterized his break with the Presbyterians as the "declaration of our independence."[18]

The final member of the quartet whose democratic theology this essay analyzes is the Scottish immigrant Alexander Campbell—the only college graduate among the four and the only one not to participate in the American Revolution.[19] Whatever Alexander Campell may have brought to America of his Scottish and Presbyterian heritage, he found much of it convenient to discard for an explicitly American theology. Writing to his uncle back in Scotland in 1815, he described his seven years in the United States: "During this period of years my mind and circumstances have undergone many revolutions . . . I have . . . renounced much of the traditions and errors of my early education." He described the change elsewhere in these words: "My mind was, for a time, set loose from all its former moorings. It was not a simple change: but a new commencement. . . . the whole landscape of

[16] "The Last Will and Testament of Springfield Presbytery," in John Rogers, *The Biography of Elder B. Warren Stone* (New York, 1972), 51–53. For other primary accounts of this movement, see Barton W. Stone, *An Apology for Renouncing the Jurisdiction of the Synod of Kentucky* (Lexington, Ky., 1804); [Richard McNemar], *Observations on Church Government, by the Presbytery of Springfield* (Cincinnati, 1807); Robert Marshall and James Thompson, *A Brief Historical Account of Sundry Things in the Doctrines and State of the Christian, or, as It Is Commonly Called, the Newlight Church* (Cincinnati, 1811); Levi Purviance, *The Biography of Elder David Purviance* (Dayton, 1848); and Robert H. Bishop, *An Outline of the History of the Church in the State of Kentucky, during a Period of Forty Years: Containing the Memoirs of Rev. David Rice* (Lexington, Ky., 1824).

[17] There is a considerable body of uncritical denominational literature on Barton W. Stone by the Disciples of Christ. See William Garrett West, *Barton Warren Stone: Early American Advocate of Christian Unity* (Nashville, 1954). For emphasis on Stone's contribution to the revivalist heritage of the South, see Boles, *Great Revival*. For appreciation of Stone in his full cultural context, see Ralph Morrow, "The Great Revival, the West, and the Crisis of the Church," in *The Frontier Re-examined*, ed. John. F. McDermott (Urbana, 1967), 65–78.

[18] Rogers, *Biography of Elder B. Warren Stone*, 3, 47.

[19] For discussions of the origins of the Campbellites, see David Edwin Harrell, Jr., *Quest for a Christian America: The Disciples of Christ and American Society to 1866* (Nashville, 1966); Robert Frederick West, *Alexander Campbell and Natural Religion* (New Haven, 1948); Lester G. McAllister, *Thomas Campbell: Man of the Book* (St. Louis, 1954); and Errett Gates, *The Early Relation and Separation of Baptists and Disciples* (Chicago, 1904). In addition, see the extensive memoirs of father and son: Alexander Campbell, *Memoirs of Elder Thomas Campbell* (Cincinnati, 1861); and Robert Richardson, *Memoirs of Alexander Campbell* (2 vols., Cincinnati, 1913).

Christianity presented itself to my mind in a new attitude and position."[20] By 1830 Alexander Campbell's quest for primitive Christianity led his movement, the Disciples of Christ, into union with Stone's Christians. By 1860 their denomination claimed about 200,000 adherents, the fifth largest Protestant body in the United States.[21] More important, for our purposes, his theology fell into an unmistakable pattern that was emerging in the early republic. Smith, O'Kelly, and Stone all knew what Campbell meant when he proclaimed that July 4, 1776, was "a day to be remembered as was the Jewish Passover. . . . This revolution, taken in all its influences, will make men free indeed."[22]

In many ways the message of the Christians built upon the kind of radical piety that Americans had known since the Great Awakening of the 1740s. These new reformers hammered relentlessly at the simple themes of sin, grace, and conversion; they organized fellowships that resisted social distinctions and welcomed spontaneous experience; and they denounced any religion that smacked of being bookish, cold, and formal. What sets the Christians apart from earlier revivalists is the extent to which they wrestled self-consciously with the loss of traditional sources of authority and found in democratic political culture a cornerstone for new foundations. Taking seriously the mandate of liberty and equality, the Christians espoused reform in three areas. First, they called for a revolution within the church that would place laity and clergy on an equal footing and would exalt the conscience of the individual over the collective will of any congregation or church organization. Second, they rejected the traditions of learned theology altogether and called for a new view of history that welcomed inquiry and innovation. Finally, they called for a populist hermeneutic premised on the inalienable right of every person to understand the New Testament for themselves.

A zeal to dismantle mediating elites within the church, more than anything else, triggered the Christians' revolt against tradition. O'Kelly broke with Asbury when the Methodist bishop refused to put up with representative government in the church. Smith bade farewell to Backus and the Warren Association after influential colleagues criticized his plain dress and suggested that the respectable parishioners of Woburn, Massachusetts, deserved more decorum. Both Stone and Thomas Campbell—Alexander's father, who had preceded him to America—withdrew from the Presbyterians when their

---

[20] Richardson, *Memoirs of Alexander Campbell*, I, 465–66, 438. Many scholars have assumed that Thomas and Alexander Campbell applied to an American context beliefs that they had learned under the influence of Scottish reformers such as Robert Haldane and James Alexander Haldane. See, for example, Sydney E. Ahlstrom, *A Religious History of the American People* (New Haven, 1972), 448–49. The early documents of the Campbellite movement, however, manifest a keen awareness that the issues to be faced were, in their intensity at least, peculiarly American and demanded new solutions. See, for example, Thomas Campbell, *The Declaration and Address of the Christian Association of Washington* (Washington, Pa., 1809).

[21] Lester G. McAllister and William E. Tucker, *Journey in Faith: A History of the Christian Church (Disciples of Christ)* (St. Louis, 1975), 154–55.

[22] Alexander Campbell, "An Oration in Honor of the Fourth of July, 1830," *Popular Lectures and Addresses* (Philadelphia, 1863), 374–75.

orthodox colleagues began to clamp down on their freedom of inquiry concerning Presbyterian standards. Before their respective separations, each of these men in his own way had offered stern opposition to received tradition; yet their dissent was contained within taken-for-granted cultural boundaries. Once they had severed organizational ties, however, mild questions reappeared as seething hostility, and suggestions for reform turned to ecclesiastical defiance.

The Christians excelled at popular communication. They ferreted out converts with an unremitting itinerancy and cranked out an avalanche of pamphlet and newspaper copy, which, in its form and content, conspired against social distinction.[23] Smith was aware of his innovative role when he began the first religious newspaper in the United States; he confessed on its opening page that the utility of such a paper had been suggested to him by the explosion of popular print all around. "In a short and cheap way," he asserted, "a general knowledge of our affairs is diffused through the whole." While his paper did include accounts of revivals of religion throughout the world, its overall strategy showed little resemblance to previous revival periodicals such as the *Christian History* of the Great Awakening, largely an intramural communication among the clergy. By promoting in common language the idea that "*right is equal among all,*" Smith knew that he would incur the judgment that he was "stirring up the people to revolt" and "turning the world upside down."[24] Just as he expected, the established clergy found his "vulgar stories and malicious sarcasm" totally beneath them, but they could hardly ignore the popularity of his "poisoned arrows of ridicule and reproach."[25]

The style of Smith's communication is well illustrated in one of his early pamphlets, *The Clergyman's Looking-Glass*, a stinging attack on men of the cloth that went through at least a dozen printings. Smith juxtaposed passages of the New Testament with satirical jibes at the contemporary clergy in mock-scripture style. After quoting from I Peter the instructions that elders were to serve God's flock "not for filthy lucre . . . neither as being lords over God's heritage," Smith gave his Petrine rendition of the modern clergy:

The reverend clergy who are with me I advise, who am also a clergyman, and a D. D. a member of that respectable body, who are numerous, and 'who seek honor one of another;' and a partaker of the benefit of it; feed yourselves upon the church and parish, over which we have settled you for life, and who are obliged to support you, whether they like you or not; taking the command by constraint, for filthy lucre, not of a ready mind, as lords over men's souls, not as ensamples to them, and when commencement day shall appear, you shall receive some honorary title, which shall make you appear very respectable among the reverend clergy.[26]

[23] "Elias Smith was here last week, distributing his books & pamphlets, & preached a lecture last week without sparing any of the hirelings as he calls them." Bentley, *Diary*, III, 388.

[24] *Herald of Gospel Liberty*, Sept. 1, 1808, p. 1.

[25] Stephen Porter, a Presbyterian clergyman, attempted to ward off the influence of Smith and his lieutenants among his congregation. Stephen Porter, *A Discourse, in Two Parts, Addressed to the Presbyterian Congregation in Ballston* (Ballston Spa, N.Y., 1814), 42–44.

[26] Elias Smith, *The Clergyman's Looking-Glass: Being a History of the Birth, Life, and Death of Anti-Christ* (Portsmouth, N.H., 1803), 11. For examples of Smith's sensitivity to elitist codes of all sorts, even while he was still a Baptist, see Smith, *Life*, 279–80.

In a similar vein, Alexander Campbell used his first newspaper, the *Christian Baptist*, to mock the pretensions of the clergy. In a burlesque "Third Epistle of Peter," a document reportedly discovered by a monk, he instructed preachers to live well, wear the best clothes, adorn themselves with high-sounding titles, drink costly wine, and fleece the people.[27] Evangelicals in the past had often questioned the spiritual state of individual clergymen; the Christians now took the liberty to slander the entire profession as money-grubbing tyrants.

This kind of billingsgate journalism employed two very powerful appeals. In the first place, it portrayed society as horizontally polarized: the people were arrayed against elites of all kind, military, legal, civic, and religious. In an early edition of the *Herald of Gospel Liberty*, Smith sketched a most revealing dialogue between the people and the privileged class. "The picture, is this: two companies standing in sight of each other, one large, the other small. The large containing every profession useful to society, the other small, wearing marks of distinction, appearing as though they did no labour, yet in rich attire, glittering with gold and silver, while their plump and ruddy countenances, prove them persons of leisure and riches." Seething with resentment, the people of Smith's dialogue happened to overhear what the privileged were saying to each other: "To mix and place ourselves on a level with the *common people*, would be beyond all measure degrading and vilifying. What! are they not born to serve us? and are we not men of a totally distinct blood and superior pedigree?" In response, the people insisted that they were going "to take the management of our affairs into our own hands. . . . When the people declare themselves free, such *privileged classes* will be as useles[s] as candles at noonday."[28]

Abel M. Sargent, another radical figure associated with the Christians, used his paper, the *Halcyon Itinerary and True Millennium Messenger*, to present a virtual class analysis of society. Writing in 1807 to extol Thomas Jefferson as the forerunner of a new millennial age, Sargent demanded that life, liberty, and happiness be extended to "the oppressed who have been deprived of them." His images of society bristle with the ongoing conflict between the powerful and the oppressed: "How often do we see it the case in earthly courts, under the dominion of the beast, that the power and influence of money and false Agency over-balance equity and right; so that the poor have but a dull chance to obtain Justice in carnal courts; and again, how often is the poor industrious and honest labourer, reduced to the absolute necessity of yielding up his rights and falling a prey to cruelty and injustice, merely for want of money enough to discharge the fees of those whose interest and livings (like the wolf and raven) depend on the ruin and destruction of others."[29]

[27] *Christian Baptist*, July 4, 1823, p. 280.
[28] *Herald of Gospel Liberty*, Dec. 8, 1808, pp. 29–30.
[29] Abel M. Sargent founded a radical sect in Marietta, Ohio, where he published six issues of *Halcyon Itinerary and True Millennium Messenger*. The quotation is found in *Halcyon Itinerary and True Millennium Messenger* [Dec. 1807], 147–48. For a letter from Sargent to Smith, see *Herald of Gospel Liberty*, Aug. 16, 1811, p. 310. On Sargent, see John W. Simpson, *A Century of Church Life* [Marietta, 1896], 31.

For all its innovation, however, this bombast against the privileged also employed a second appeal. It appropriated the rhetoric of civil and religious liberty that the respectable clergy had made popular during the Revolution and marshaled it for an entirely new purpose, to topple its very architects. The Christians exploited to the hilt the potent themes of tyranny, slavery, and Antichrist; they delighted in regaling their audiences with the latest chapter in the saga of the beast and the whore of Babylon. Simply put, Antichrist now worked his evil machinations through elites of all kind, particularly the clergy. In a splended example of the multivalency of language, rhetoric that had seemed benign when used by respectable clergymen during the Revolution came to have radical connotations when abstracted from a restricted context and transferred to people who had reason to lash out at vested interests.[30]

But what end did the Christians have in view when decrying ecclesiastical authority? What positive implications did they wring out of the notion of religious liberty? Smith came right to the point in an early issue of the *Herald of Gospel Liberty* when he contrasted the mere separation of church and state with "being wholly free to examine for ourselves, what is truth." He argued that every last Christian had the "unalienable right" to follow "the scripture wherever it leads him, even an equal right with the Bishops and Pastors of the churches . . . even though his principles may, in many things, be contrary to what the Reverend D. D.'s call Orthodoxy."[31] Using the same language, Alexander Campbell pressed for "the inalienable right of all laymen to examine the sacred writings for themselves." Brimming with conspiratorial notions of how clergymen of every stripe had "hoodwinked" the people, this logic eventually led each of these Christian leaders to demand that the traditional distinction between clergy and laity be abolished and that any leadership in the local church function according to new rules: "liberty is no where safe in any hands excepting those of the people themselves."[32] With demands for this sort of liberation afoot, it is little wonder that Congregational and Presbyterian clergymen came to view the Christians as but another tentacle of the Bavarian Illuminati's conspiracy to overthrow authority in church and state.[33]

[30] Christians assailed the clergy as "tyrannical oppressors," "the mystery of iniquity," "friends of monarchy religion," "old tories," "an *aristocratical body of uniform nobility*," and "hireling priests"; people who would submit to such tyrants they labeled priest-ridden, slavishly dependent, passively obedient. See Smith, *Life*, 384, 402-03; *Herald of Gospel Liberty*, Oct. 13, 1809, p. 117; O'Kelly, *Vindication*, 47. In 1815 Smith claimed that most people in New England from forty to seventy years old could remember the respectable clergy emphasizing apocalyptic themes such as "Anti-Christ, mystery Babylon, the great whore that sitteth on many waters, the beast with seven heads and ten horns, the man of sin &c." *Herald of Gospel Liberty*, May 20, 1815, p. 685. On the multivalency of language, see J. G. A. Pocock, *Politics, Language and Time: Essays on Political Thought and History* (New York, 1971), 3-41; and Harry S. Stout, "Religion, Communications, and the Ideological Origins of the American Revolution," *William and Mary Quarterly*, XXXIV (Oct. 1977), 538.

[31] Smith, *Lovingkindness of God Displayed*, 26-27; Smith, *Life*, 352-53. See also *Herald of Gospel Liberty*, April 14, 1809, p. 67.

[32] *Christian Baptist*, Jan. 2, 1826, p. 209; Smith, *Life*, 402-03; *Herald of Gospel Liberty*, Sept. 15, 1808, p. 6. See also Richardson, *Memoirs of Alexander Campbell*, I, 382-83.

[33] See David Rice, *An Epistle to the Citizens of Kentucky, Professing Christianity* (Lexington, Ky., 1805), 11-12.

The Christian idea of religious liberty stands in marked contrast to the eighteenth-century notion that religious liberty meant the civil right to choose or not to choose affiliation with a church. The religious dissent that had come out of the Great Awakening, despite its popular sources, had never begun to suggest that power should be surrendered to the people in this fashion. The Baptists in Virginia set themselves off from the culture of gentlemen by striving for more order, more discipline, and more social control within the local congregation.[34] In New England, as well, Baptists and Separatists called for closed communion and a tighter discipline within the pure church. By the 1760s, they were educating their clergy, forming associations to regulate doctrine and local disputes, and, as their people began to drift away to other sects during the Revolution, actually imposing stiff creedal tests upon local churches. Backus did not long for some new order that leveled the clergy and exalted the laity; he reminisced, instead, about the pious fathers of early New England. He argued time and again that his Baptists agreed "with the most eminent fathers of New England, except in sprinkling infants upon the faith of their parents and calling it baptism."[35] The same point has been made about the Separatists of New England: "they were reformers, not rebels; . . . they wished to fulfill their history as Puritans, not repudiate it."[36]

In contrast, the Christians called for the abolition of organizational restraints of any kind. In the "Last Will and Testament of Springfield Presbytery," Stone and five colleagues dissolved their association, already a splinter group from the Presbyterian church. Only by renouncing all institutional forms could "the oppressed . . . go free, and taste the sweets of gospel liberty."[37] Alexander Campbell did not even want to hear the words church government: "We have no system of our own, or of others, to substitute in lieu of the reigning systems. We only aim at substituting the New Testament."[38] In a similar vein, Stone and his associates declared that the attempt "to impose any form of government upon the church . . . should be justly abandoned by every child of gospel liberty." They went on to say that any human form of government would be "like binding two or more dead bodies together" and coercing people "like parts of a machine."[39] The organization of Protestant churches, which in colonial culture had been seen

[34] Rhys Isaac, "Evangelical Revolt: The Nature of the Baptists' Challenge to the Traditional Order in Virginia, 1765 to 1775," William and Mary Quarterly, XXXI (July 1974), 345-68.

[35] Isaac Backus, A History of New England with Particular Reference to the Denomination of Christians Called Baptists (2 vols., Newton, Mass., 1871), II, 487. For evidence of the Baptist quest for respectability in the generation after the Great Awakening, see C. C. Goen, Revivalism and Separatism in New England, 1740-1800 (New Haven, Conn., 1962). For the reaction of Baptists to the dissent spawned by the Revolution, see McLoughlin, New England Dissent, II, 710.

[36] James Patrick Walsh, "The Pure Church in Eighteenth Century Connecticut" (Ph.D. diss., Columbia University, 1964), 143.

[37] Rogers, Biography of Elder B. Warren Stone, 51-53.

[38] Christian Baptist, Nov. 3, 1823, p. 25; Richardson, Memoirs of Alexander Campbell, II, 63-64.

[39] [McNemar], Observations on Church Government, 4, 9, 15. This pamphlet, the best-developed statement of Christian ecclesiology, rejects "external rules" and insists that all human organization spring from the deliberate and uncoerced choice of the individual.

as vibrant and alive—the very body of Christ—now smacked of being dead and mechanistic.

By their appeal to "Bible government," the Christians removed the issue of power and authority from any concrete application. They opposed all ecclesiastical names not found in the New Testament, advocated the right of the individual unilaterally to withdraw from church membership, and refused to adhere to creeds as tests of fellowship, to undergo theological examinations, or to offer a confession of faith upon joining a church. In short, no human organization could exist that did not spring from the uncoerced will of the individual. When pressed by Bishop Asbury to heed the scriptural injunction, "Obey them that have rule over you," O'Kelly responded: "Rule over, is no more than for the church to follow those guides who delivered unto them the Word of God." O'Kelly was suggesting that, by submitting to the New Testament, a Christian in 1800 never would have to doff his hat to any mere mortal.[40]

In a passing reference in *The American Revolution Considered as a Social Movement*, J. Franklin Jameson noted the growth in numbers and zeal of those religious bodies that were revolting against Calvinism—the Methodists, Universalists, Unitarians, and Freewill Baptists.[41] He might also have included the loose combination of mavericks who called themselves merely Christians. Except for O'Kelly, whose Methodist background made Calvinism a dead issue, the other primary figures in this movement—Smith, Stone, and Campbell—were all zealous Calvinists early in life and experienced a conversion to what they called gospel liberty.

On one level this revolt seems simple enough to understand. The heady concepts of liberty that had led to denunciations of institutional constraints also rendered meaningless such concepts as unconditional election and limited atonement. After great intellectual turmoil, each of these men came to the point of harmonizing theology with their social experience. As a Calvinist, Stone confessed that he was "embarrassed with many abstruse doctrines." "Scores of objections would continually roll across my mind." What he called the "labyrinth of Calvinism" left his mind "distressed," "perplexed," and "bewildered." He found relief from this dissonance of values only as he came to attack Calvinism as falsehood.[42]

The revolt against Calvinism, however, becomes somewhat harder to understand when placed in its full context. The Christians were venting their hostility not against Calvinism in some narrow sense, as if they might find their niche as Methodists or Freewill Baptists, but against an entire system. "We are not personally acquainted with the writings of John Calvin," wrote

---

[40] O'Kelly, *Vindication*, 49. For similar expressions of resistance to human mediation of divine authority by Alexander Campbell and Thomas Campbell, see *Christian Baptist*, April 3, 1826, p. 229, and Campbell, *Declaration and Address of the Christian Association*, 3. For the recurrence of this line of thought a generation later, see Lewis Perry, *Radical Abolitionism: Anarchy and the Government of God in Antislavery Thought* (Ithaca, 1973).

[41] J. Franklin Jameson, *The American Revolution Considered as a Social Movement* (Princeton, 1926), 157.

[42] Rogers, *Biography of Elder B. Warren Stone*, 14, 31, 33.

Robert Marshall and John Thompson, two of Stone's colleagues, "nor are we certain how nearly we agree with his views of divine truth; neither do we care."[43]

This was no mere revolt against Calvinism but against theology itself. What was going on that gave Stone the audacity not only to reject the doctrine of the Trinity—Unitarians right and left were doing that—but also to maintain, "I have not spent, perhaps, an hour in ten years in thinking about the Trinity"? What made it credible for Smith, after seriously debating whether he would be a Calvinist or a Universalist, to remove the dilemma altogether by dropping them both? "I was now without a system," he confessed with obvious relief, "and felt ready to search the scriptures."[44] How could these men convince themselves, not to mention their followers, that the stage was set for a church without organization and a theology without theory?

Whatever else the Christians demanded, the rallying cry of their theological revolution was a new view of history. They called for a new dispensation of gospel liberty, radically discontinuous with the past. They advocated new theological ground rules that dismissed everything since the New Testament as irrelevant, if not destructive. What led Americans in the finest evangelical tradition of Jonathan Edwards, John Witherspoon, Backus, and Asbury to repudiate their heritage? Furthermore, what gave credence to the idea that they were standing on the brink of a new age?

One cannot understand the Christians apart from their deep conviction that they had witnessed in the American and French revolutions the most momentous historical events in two millennia—a *novus ordo seclorum*. The opening line of the *Herald of Gospel Liberty* proclaimed that "the age in which we live may certainly be distinguished from others in the history of Man," and Smith was quick to point out that it was the struggle for liberty and the rights of mankind that set it apart. According to Smith, the foundations of Christ's millennial kingdom were laid in the American and French revolutions. "The time will come," he said, "when there will not be a *crowned head* on earth. Every attempt which is made to keep up a Kingly government, and to pull down a Republican one, will . . . serve to destroy monarchy. . . . Every small piece, or plan, of Monarchy which is a part of the *image* [of Antichrist] will be wholly dissolved, when *the people* are resolved to 'live free or die.' "[45]

The following year in Washington, Pennsylvania, Thomas Campbell published the first salvo of their movement and pointed to the same state of revolutionary and apocalyptic affairs: "Do ye not discern the signs of the times? Have not the two witnesses arisen from their state of political death,

---

[43] Marshall and Thompson, *Brief Historical Account*, 3-4.

[44] Elias Smith, *Sermons, Containing an Illustration of the Prophecies* (Exeter, N.H., 1808), vi.

[45] *Herald of Gospel Liberty*, Sept. 1, 1808, p. 1; Elias Smith, *A Discourse Delivered at Jefferson Hall, Thanksgiving Day, November 25, 1802; and Redelivered (by Request) the Wednesday Evening Following, at the Same Place: The Subject, Nebuchadnezzar's Dream* (Portsmouth, N.H., 1803), 30-32. The sociologist Guy E. Swanson has argued that the political forms under which a people live significantly color their theological perceptions, particularly in times of rapid change. See Guy E. Swanson, *Religion and Regime: A Sociological Account of the Reformation* (Ann Arbor, 1967), 231.

from under the long proscription of ages? . . . Who amongst us has not heard the report of these things—of these lightnings and thunderings, and voices, of this tremendous earthquake and great hail; of these awful convulsions and revolutions that have dashed and are dashing to pieces the nations like a potter's vessel?'' In their view, such political convulsions spoke as the voice of providence "loudly and expressly calling us to repentance and refor- mation. . . . Resume that precious, that dear bought liberty, wherewith Christ has made his people free; a liberty from subjection to any authority but his own, in matters of religion. Call no man father. . . .'' Alexander Campbell argued that the War for Independence unveiled a new epoch that would deliver men from "the melancholy thraldom of relentless systems.'' America's "political regeneration'' gave her the responsibility to lead a comparable "ecclesiastical renovation.''[46] An expectancy and overt respect for novelty characterized the Christians, as Stone's two associates confessed: "We con- fidently thought that the Millennium was just at hand, and that a glorious church would soon be formed; we thought, also, that we had found the very plan for its formation and growth.'' Opponents of these men agreed, moreover, that a sense of apocalyptic urgency had fueled the movement from the start.[47]

If the age of democratic revolutions gave the Christians good reason to sever ties with the past, it also suggested egalitarian models for a new age. In describing the true gospel that would revolutionize the world, Alexander Campbell called it "the declaration of independence of the kingdom of Jesus.'' Smith and Stone chose the same term to describe their withdrawal from the Baptists and Presbyterians, respectively. Similarly, O'Kelly claimed that he broke with the Methodists because they left him no option but "unlimited submission'' or separation.[48] The lengths to which they allowed political idioms to color their thinking are sometimes difficult to comprehend: for example, they referred to the early church as a republican society with a New Testament constitution. In 1807, however, one maverick Christian in Marietta, Ohio, outdid them all, claiming that "the great potentate of the world, in principle, is the most *genuine* REPUBLICAN that ever existed.''[49]

From a modern viewpoint, it may seem odd that men so committed to the separation of church and state held up a given political structure as a model for the church. They endowed the republic with the same divine authority as did defenders of the Standing Order such as Timothy Dwight and Noah Webster, but for opposite reasons. The republic became a new city on a hill not because it kept faith with Puritan tradition, but because it sounded the death knell for corporate and hierarchic conceptions of the social order. For these radical

[46] Campbell, *Declaration and Address of the Christian Association*, 14; Campbell, "Oration in Honor of the Fourth of July,'' 374; *Christian Baptist*, Feb. 6, 1826, p. 213.

[47] Marshall and Thompson, *Brief Historical Account*, 255. Presbyterian David Rice complained in 1805 about Stone and his followers: "Another thing that prepared the minds of many for the reception of error, was their high expectation of the speedy approach of the Millennium.'' Rice, *Epistle to the Citizens of Kentucky*, 13.

[48] Campbell, "Oration in Honor of the Fourth of July,'' 377; Smith, *Life*, 292; Rogers, *Biography of Elder B. Warren Stone*, 47; O'Kelly, *Author's Apology*, 52.

[49] Abel Sargent, *Halcyon Itinerary and True Millennium Messenger*, V (Dec. 1807), 146.

sectarians, the constitutional guarantees of separation of church and state laid the groundwork for a new age. In sum, a government so enlightened as to tell the churches to go their own way must have also had prophetic power to tell them which way to go.[50]

Millennialism, then, served different functions for the Christians from those that it had during the Great Awakening. Revivals of the 1740s drew upon millennial themes to challenge traditionalists in the name of a greater commitment to traditional values.[51] This sense of eschatological drama, furthermore, served to define an evangelical identity over against political culture. By contrast, the democratic ferment experienced by the Christians convinced them that, in thinking about the future, they should work to erase the memory of the past and should learn from political culture whatever they could about a gospel of equality.

The Christians expressed their revolt against history most clearly in the radical way they chose to read the Bible. Amid unraveling cultural norms, they clung tenaciously to one final, unassailable authority, the *ipse dixit* of the New Testament. The direct propositions of Scripture became the only ground of certainty. In a letter to the *Herald of Gospel Liberty* in 1809, seventeen Christian ministers spelled out this central plank of the Christian platform: "In consequence of your receiving Christ as only head, and ruler of his church, it necessarily follows, *that his law as contained in the New Testament*, should be received without any addition, abridgment, alterations, or embellishments, to the exclusion of all articles of religion, confessions of faith, creeds, &c. &c. &c. composed by men." "The New Testament has been as the law once was, *among the rubbish*," proclaimed Smith. "Now we have found it, let us read it to the people from morning till evening."[52] These were fighting words, no doubt, to the genteel clergy, men accustomed to covenants being the linchpin of society and to thinking of America as the new Israel. But even more radical than dismissing the Old Testament as a priestly rag used to hoodwink the people was the approach that Christians used to interpret Scripture. "I have endeavored to read the scriptures as though no one had read them before me," claimed Alexander Campbell, "and I am as much on my guard against reading them to-day, through the medium of my own views yesterday, or a week ago, as I am against being influenced by any foreign name, authority, or system whatever." Protestants had always argued for *sola scriptura*, but this kind of radical individualism set the Bible against the entire history of biblical inter-

[50] Smith devoted a sermon of over 120 pages to the subject of how republican values should be applied to the church. See Elias Smith, *The Whole World Governed by a Jew; or the Government of the Second Adam, as King and Priest* (Exeter, N.H., 1805). On the Standing Order's conservative use of millennial themes, see Nathan O. Hatch. *The Sacred Cause of Liberty: Republican Thought and the Millennium in Revolutionary New England* (New Haven, 1977), 97–138. See also Richard M. Rollins, *The Long Journey of Noah Webster* (Philadelphia, 1980).

[51] James West Davidson, *The Logic of Millennial Thought: Eighteenth-Century New England* (New Haven, 1977), 122–41.

[52] *Herald of Gospel Liberty*, June 23, 1809, p. 87, Feb. 2, 1809, p. 47. The Christians repeatedly suggested that Americans accord the New Testament the same kind of exclusive authority that they did constitutions in civil affairs. See Smith, *World Governed by a Jew*, 114; and Campbell, *Declaration and Address of the Christian Association*, 16.

pretation. In this hermeneutic, no human authority, contemporary or historical, had the right to advise the individual in his spiritual quest. In order to ward off any systematic theology, these men insisted that religious discussion be limited to Bible language, as Smith put it, "to prove every particular from plain declarations recorded in the Bible."[53]

This fresh hermeneutic had considerable appeal because it spoke to three pressing issues. First, it proclaimed a new ground of certainty for a generation perplexed that it could no longer hear the voice of God above the din of sectarian confusion. If people would only abandon the husks of theological abstraction, the truth would be plain for all to see. Second, this approach to Scripture dared the common man to open the Bible and think for himself. All theological abstractions—such as the trinity, foreordination, and original sin— were abandoned, and all that was necessary to establish a given point was to string together texts from the King James Bible. Any Christian using New Testament words could fend off the most brilliant theological argument by the simple retort that he was using God's word against human opinion. All the weight of church history could not begin to tip the scale against the Christian's simple declaration, say, that the New Testament did not contain the word *trinity*.

This approach had a third appeal—obvious success in befuddling the respectable clergy. Smith, O'Kelly, Stone, and Alexander Campbell were to a man brilliant theological debaters, but they refused to abide by the etiquette of the opposition. Their coarse language, earthy humor, biting sarcasm, and commonsense reasoning appealed to the uneducated but left the professional clergy without a ready defense. In a pamphlet written in 1817 to combat Smith's influence in Massachusetts, the Congregationalist Thomas Andros recognized the new tactics:

Ridicule, sneer, malignant sarcasm and reproach, are the armor in which he goes forth. On this ground, and not on sober argumentation, he knows the success of his cause depends. . . . If he knows the doctrine of original sin is not true, let him sit down and write a manly and candid answer to President Edward's great work on that subject. . . . Were he a dignified, candid, and intelligent controversialist, there would be enough to answer him, but who would wish to attack a windmill? Who can refute a sneer?

Andros also recognized that popularity rather than virtue was the clarion call of the movement: "They measure the progress of religion by the numbers, who flock to their standard; not by the prevalence of faith, and piety, justice and charity, and the public virtues in society in general."[54]

Other Congregationalists and Presbyterians, less sensitive to the new measures, continued to use the language of orthodoxy to lambaste the Christians as a new form of the threadbare heresies of Arius, Pelagius, and Socinius.[55] The Christians merely sidestepped these attacks by putting the disputed points before their followers and letting them choose between the language of Scripture and that of metaphysical subtlety. This democratic

[53] *Christian Baptist*, April 3, 1826, p. 229; Smith, *Life*, 292.
[54] Andros, *Scriptures Liable to be Wrested to Men's Own Destruction*, 21, 6.
[55] Porter, *Discourse in Two Parts*, 14; Rice, *Epistle to the Citizens of Kentucky*, 9-12.

revolution in theology wrenched the queen of the sciences from the learned speculations of Harvard, Yale, and Princeton men and encouraged the blacksmith, cooper, and tiller of the soil not only to experience salvation but also to explain the process. Its genius was to allow common people to feel, for a fleeting moment at least, that they were beholden to no one and masters of their own fate.

How does one explain the theology of the people that came to be championed between 1790 and 1815? What kind of cultural context gave rise to similar movements in New England, the South, and the Midwest? Many historians have imagined that these radical pietists simply continued a tradition of dissent that had rippled through American culture since the 1740s. Others have viewed the Christians as prophets of the American frontier, men who developed notions in keeping with the self-sufficient characters that pushed into the hill country of New England and made their way across the Appalachians. This was religion following the frontier par excellence. Still other scholars have linked the Christian movement to the general revolt against Calvinism that followed the American Revolution. Rigid notions of depravity and predestination simply could not stir a generation that had witnessed at home and abroad the electrifying effects of liberty and natural rights. All of these—the ongoing tradition of evangelical dissent, the surge westward after the Revolution, and the disdain for Calvinistic explanations of the world—figure importantly in any explanation of the Christian movement.[56]

Yet these points of reference fail to locate the most intimate link between the Christians and American culture at the turn of the eighteenth century: a pervasive collapse of certainty within popular culture. From the debate over the Constitution to the election of Jefferson, a new and explicitly democratic revolution united many who were suspicious of power and many who were powerless in a common effort to pull down the cultural hegemony of a gentlemanly few. In a complex cultural process that historians have just begun to unravel, people on a number of fronts began to speak, write, and organize against the authority of mediating elites, of social distinctions, and of any human tie that did not spring from volitional allegiance.[57]

This crisis of confidence in a hierarchical, ordered society led to demands for fundamental reform in politics, law, and religion. In each of these areas,

[56] William G. McLoughlin views the later wave of dissent as but an extension of the revivalism of the Great Awakening. McLoughlin, *New England Dissent*, II, 697-750. William Warren Sweet described the Christians as "a new denomination which arose directly out of the soil of the west." William Warren Sweet, *Religion in the Development of American Culture, 1765-1840* (New York, 1952), 221; and Winifred Ernest Garrison, *Religion Follows the Frontier: A History of the Disciples of Christ* (New York, 1931). Sweet also links the Christians to the broader revolt against Calvinism.

[57] For the importance of the idea of volitional allegiance in this period, see James H. Kettner, *The Development of American Citizenship, 1608-1870* (Chapel Hill, 1978), 173-209. See also Gordon S. Wood, *The Creation of the American Republic, 1776-1787* (Chapel Hill, 1969), 483-99; Alfred F. Young, *The Democratic Republicans of New York: The Origins, 1763-1797* (Chapel Hill, 1967); and Edmund S. Morgan, *The Challenge of the American Revolution* (New York, 1976), 211-18.

radical Jeffersonians, seizing upon issues close to the hearts of the people, resurrected "the spirit of 1776" to protest the control of elites and the force of tradition. Rhetoric that had once unified people across the social spectrum now drove a powerful wedge between rich and poor, elite and commoner, privileged classes and the people. Federalists, members of the bar, and the professional clergy heard the wisdom of the ages ridiculed as mere connivances of the powerful to maintain the status quo.

The violence of politics from 1780 to 1800, more than anything else, gave sharp definition to egalitarian impulses in American society. From the Revolution onwards, republican equality became a rallying cry for people seeking to challenge all sorts of political authority. Incidents in South Carolina, Massachusetts, and New York illustrate how thoroughly the "virtue" of subjection and deference was giving way to an itching, smarting, writhing awareness of inferiority. In 1784, the South Carolina legislature threatened William Thompson, a tavern keeper, with banishment from the state for insulting the eminent John Rutledge. Thompson responded with a newspaper article that blasted the claims of "self-exalted" characters like Rutledge who had "conceived me his inferior." Thompson refused to "comprehend the *inferiority*" and denied the right of a conspicuous few to speak for the people.[58] During the debate over the Constitution, Antifederalists turned repeatedly to such arguments. At the Masachusetts ratification convention, for example, the self-taught Worcester County farmer Amos Singletary denounced the Constitution as a plot to consolidate the influence of the great: "these lawyers and men of learning, and moneyed men . . . talk so finely, and gloss over matters so smoothly, to make us poor illiterate people swallow down the pill. . . . They expect to be the managers of this Constitution, and get all the power and all the money into their own hands. And then they will swallow up us little fellows, like the great Leviathan."[59]

A decade later the urban democratic leader William Keteltas was able to shake Federalist control of New York City by a shrewd media campaign depicting politics as a clash between rich and poor. Ketaltas made into a cause célèbre the case of two Irish-born ferrymen whom Federalist magistrates punished summarily for reportedly insulting one of their number. Ketaltas dramatized the issue in the popular press and eventually came to attack the New York assembly for not impeaching the responsible magistrates. This led to his own arrest by the Federalist legislature on a charge of breach of privilege. When Keteltas appeared before the assembly, a crowd of several thousand gatherered in protest. His release from a brief prison sentence prompted a grand celebration in which the people pulled Keteltas through the streets in a carriage decked with American and French flags, a cap of liberty, and a picture of a man being whipped with the inscription, "What you rascal, insult your

[58] Wood, *Creation of the American Republic*, 482–83.

[59] Jonathan Elliot, *The Debates, Resolutions, and Other Proceedings, in Convention on the Adoption of the Federal Constitution* (4 vols., Washington, D.C., 1827–1830), I, 112.

superiors?'' By championing the cause of the ferrymen—what Keteltas called
'' 'the most flagrant abuse of [the people's] rights' since Independence''—he
effectively mobilized the common people of New York to challenge Federalist
domination.[60]

Such repeated attacks on the capacity of a conspicuous few to speak for the
whole of society struck at the root of traditional conceptions of society.[61]
Extending the logic of Antifederalists, radical Jeffersonians came to ridicule
the assumption that society was an organic hierarchy of ranks and degrees;
they argued, rather, that it was a heterogeneous mixture of many different
classes, orders, interest groups, and occupations. In such a society the elites
could no longer claim to be adequate spokesmen for people in general. In this
climate, it took little creativity for some to begin to reexamine the social
function of the clergy and to question the right of any order of men to claim
authority to interpret God's Word. If opinions about politics and society were
no longer the monopoly of the few, why could not anyone and everyone begin
to think for themselves in matters of religion?

The 1790s also witnessed fundamental challenges to the legal profession and
the common law. Richard E. Ellis has documented the strident attacks against
the legal system that surfaced in the popular press and in serious political
movements to reform the law in Kentucky, Pennsylvania, and Massachusetts.[62] Radical republicans such as Boston's Austin denounced the legal
profession for needlessly confusing court cases in order to charge high fees, deliberately making the law inaccessible to laymen, bartering justice to those
who could afford to pay, and monopolizing legislative and judicial posts.

Those who called for radical legal reform addressed three primary issues.
First, they demanded a simplified and easily accessible legal process, ''a
system of laws of our own, dictated by the genuine principles of
Republicanism, and made easy to be understood to every individual in the
community.''[63] Second, they attempted to replace the common law—
authority by precedent—with fresh legal codes designed for the new republic.
For many of these radicals, the common law conjured up images of complexity, mystery, intolerance, and bias in favor of the elite: ''Shall we be
directed by reason, equity, and a few simple and plain laws, promptly
executed, or shall we be ruled by volumes of statutes and cases decided by the
ignorance and intolerance of former times?''[64] Third, having jettisoned the
''monkist priesthood'' of lawyers and the ''absurdity of the common law,''
those who sought root-and-branch reform exhibited great faith in the ability of

[60] Young, *Democratic Republicans of New York*, 468-95.
[61] Wood, *Creation of the American Republic*, 483-99. One of the clearest calls that common
people should resist the traditional distinction between gentlemen and commoners came from the
pen of the uneducated Massachusetts farmer William Manning in 1798. Samuel Eliot Morrison,
ed., "William Manning's *The Key of Libberty*," *William and Mary Quarterly*, XIII (April 1956),
202-54.
[62] Ellis, *Jeffersonian Crisis*.
[63] Benjamin Austin, Jr., "Observations on the Pernicious Practice of the Law" (1786), in
American Journal of Legal History, XIII (July 1969), 258.
[64] "Decius," *Independent Chronicle*, Jan. 30, 1804, p. 1.

ordinary citizens to ascertain and dispense justice before the law. "Any person of common abilities," said Austin, "can easily distinguish between right and wrong" and "more especially when the parties are admitted to give a plain story, without any puzzle from lawyers."[65]

In retrospect, this faith in democratic, personalized, and simplified law appears hopelessly naive and utopian. Yet it reflects a moment of historical optimism, a time when many in politics, law, and religion, flushed with the promise of the American Revolution, found it reasonable to take literally the meaning of *novus ordo seclorum* and to declare a decisive expatriation from the past.[66]

That Smith came to jettison orthodox Calvinism through reading Austin's articles in the *Independent Chronicle* in 1799 and 1800 underscores the correlation between the Christian movement and reform efforts in politics and law.[67] In method, substance, and style, Smith championed the cause to which radical Jeffersonians were committed: an appeal to class as the fundamental problem of society, a refusal to recognize the cultural authority of elites, a disdain for the supposed lessons of history and tradition, a call for reform using the rhetoric of the Revolution, a commitment to turn the press into a sword of democracy, and an ardent faith in the future of the American republic. Smith's primary interest, of course, was the spread of evangelical religion; yet he could never divorce that message from the egalitarian principles that the frantic pace of the 1790s had made self-evident.

That other individuals came to advocate virtually identical reform is further evidence that questions were raging in popular culture that popular religion simply could not avoid. While other claims to truth also flourished in this atmosphere, the Christian movement stands out as an attempt to bring some harmony between denominational traditions and egalitarian values. In lashing out at the tyranny of the clergy, the foolishness of abstract theology, and the bondage of church discipline, the Christians fulfilled a mandate for reform that was widespread in popular culture. In exalting the idea that every man was his own interpreter, they brought a measure of certainty to people committed to the principle that all values, rights, and duties originate in the individual—the principle that Alexis de Tocqueville later called individualism.[68]

The legacy of the Christian movement is riddled with irony. Instead of taking America by storm, the Christian Connection under Smith and O'Kelly vanished into insignificance, while the Disciples in the West grew into a major denomination only by practicing the kind of organization they had once hoped

[65] Ellis, *Jeffersonian Crisis*, 171, 177; Austin, "Observations on the Pernicious Practice of the Law," 264.

[66] For the importance in Thomas Jefferson's thought of breaking the grip of custom and precedent, see Edmund S. Morgan, *The Meaning of Independence: John Adams, George Washington, Thomas Jefferson* (Charlottesville, 1976), 71-79; and Daniel J. Boorstin, *The Lost World of Thomas Jefferson* (Boston, 1948).

[67] Smith, *Lovingkindness of God Displayed*, 32.

[68] Alexis de Tocqueville, *Democracy in America*, trans. Henry Reeve (2 vols., New York, 1959), I, 104-05.

to stamp out. Instead of calming sectarian strife and restoring edenic harmony, the Christians engendered controversy at every step and had to put up with chronic factionalism within their own ranks.[69] Instead of offering a new foundation for certainty, the Christian approach to knowledge, which made no man the judge of another's conscience, had little holding power and sent many early advocates scrambling for surer footing.[70] Instead of erecting a primitive church free from theological tradition and authoritarian control, the Christians came to advocate their own sectarian theology and to defer to the influence and persuasion of a dominant few. These ironies suggest that the real significance of the Christian movement is not to be found in its institutional development or in the direct influence of Smith, O'Kelly, Stone, and Alexander Campbell. What the movement does illustrate graphically is a moment of wrenching change in American culture that had great import for popular religion. Many followed the path even if they did not know its trailblazers.

The Christian movement illustrates, in the first place, the intensity of religious ferment at work in a period of chaos and originality unmatched, perhaps, since the religious turbulence of seventeenth-century England.[71] As in England a century and a half before, common folk in America at the dawn of the nineteenth century came to scorn tradition, relish novelty and experimentation, grope for fresh sources of authority, and champion an array of millennial schemes, each in its own way dethroning hierarchy and static religious forms.[72] The resulting popular culture pulsated with the claims of supremely heterodox religious groups, with people veering from one sect to another, with the unbridled wrangling of competitors in a "war of words."[73] Scholars have only begun to assess the fragmentation that beset American religion in the period generally referred to as the Second Great Awakening, which they have too often viewed as a conservative response to rapid social change. The Christian movement serves as a helpful corrective and invites

[69] For an excellent example of the potential for factionalism within a local Christian church, see Don Harrison Doyle, *The Social Order of a Frontier Community: Jacksonville, Illinois, 1825-70* (Urbana, 1978), 157-60.

[70] Smith himself left the Christian Connection in 1818 to join the Universalists, and two of his colleagues, Joshua V. Himes and Joseph Marsh, became early advocates of William Miller. David L. Rowe, "A New Perspective on the Burned-Over District: The Millerites in Upstate New York," *Church History*, XLVII (Dec. 1978), 408-20. Of five men who signed the "Last Will and Testament of Springfield Presbytery," two returned to the Presbyterians, two became Shakers, and only Stone retained his identity as a Christian. Alexander Campbell, similarly, saw his best preacher, Sidney Rigdon, defect to the Mormons. Mario S. De Pillis, "The Quest for Religious Authority and the Rise of Mormonism," *Dialogue: A Journal of Mormon Thought*, I (Spring 1966), 68-88.

[71] Christopher Hill, *The World Turned Upside Down: Radical Ideas during the English Revolution* (New York, 1972).

[72] J. F. C. Harrison, *The Second Coming: Popular Millenarianism, 1780-1850* (New Brunswick, 1979), 163-206.

[73] The phrase is that of Joseph Smith, who reacted strongly to the sectarian competition he knew as a young man. Joseph Smith, *The Pearl of Great Price* (Salt Lake City, 1891), 56-70. In this period evangelicals were preoccupied with a sense of the transforming power of the printed word. See Joan Jacobs Brumberg, *Mission For Life: The Story of the Family of Adoniram Judson* (New York, 1980), 44-78.

fresh appraisals of the popular culture that nourished people like William Miller, John Humphrey Noyes, and Joseph Smith. Theirs was a religious environment that brought into question traditional authorities and exalted the right of the people to think for themselves. The result, quite simply, was a bewildering world of clashing opinion—to the sympathetic Smith, an "age of inquiry," to the distraught David Rice, a "hot bed of every extravagance of opinion and practice." Another erstwhile pilgrim, the Presbyterian-turned-Christian-turned-Shaker Richard McNemar, took up verse to capture the spirit of his times:

> Ten thousand Reformers like so many moles
> Have plowed all the Bible and cut it [in] holes
> And each has his church at the end of his trace
> Built up as he thinks of the subjects of grace.[74]

The Christians also illustrate the exaltation of public opinion as a primary religious authority. They called for common folk to read the New Testament as if mortal man had never seen it before. People were expected to discover the self-evident message of the Bible without any mediation from creeds, theologians, or clergymen not of their own choosing. This explicit faith that biblical authority could emerge from below, from the will of the people, was the most enduring legacy of the Christian movement. By the 1840s one analyst of American Protestantism concluded, after surveying fifty-three American sects, that the principle "No creed but the Bible" was the distinctive feature of American religion. John W. Nevin surmised that this emphasis grew out of a popular demand for "private judgment" and was "tacitly if not openly conditioned always by the assumption that every man is authorized and bound to get at this authority in a direct way for himself, through the medium simply of his own single mind."[75] Many felt the exhilarating hope that democracy had opened an immediate access to biblical truth for all persons of good will. What was difficult for Americans to realize was that a commitment to private judgment could drive people apart even as it raised beyond measure their hopes for unity.

The Christian movement also demonstrates the process by which popular culture became christianized in the early republic. One reason that evangelical churches and sects grew so rapidly during these years was that they proclaimed value systems that endowed common people with dignity and responsibility. People gladly accepted a theology that addressed them without condescension, balked at vested interests, and reinforced ideas of volitional allegiance and self-reliance. While such egalitarian strains were deeply rooted in the Great

---

[74] Elias Smith, *The Age of Enquiry* (Exeter, N.H., 1807); David Rice, "A Second Epistle to the Citizens of Kentucky, Professing the Christian Religion," in *An Outline of the History of the Church in the State of Kentucky*, ed. Robert Bishop (Lexington, Ky., 1824), 354; Richard McNemar, "The Mole's Little Pathways" as quoted in De Pillis, "Quest for Religious Authority," 75.

[75] John Williamson Nevin, "Antichrist and the Sect," in *The Mercersburg Theology*, ed. James Hastings Nichols (New York, 1966), 93-119, 98-99.

Awakening and subsequent revivals, historians have failed to appreciate the ways in which the founding of the American republic wrought, in Devereux Jarratt's words, "a vast alteration" in American religion. A staunch evangelical minister in Virginia prior to the Revolution, Jarratt by the 1790s had come to fear the volatile mix of things evangelical and egalitarian. Bemoaning the "levelling" spirit in "our high republican times," Jarrett recoiled from a religion "under the supreme controul of tinkers and taylors, weavers, shoemakers, and country mechanics of all kinds."[76] The theology that emerged between 1790 and 1815 to empower just these kinds of people certainly helps to clarify a process by which an America that had been largely Presbyterian, Congregational, Anglican, and Calvinist Baptist became a cauldron of Methodists, Disciples, Freewill, Free-Communion, and Primitive Baptists, Universalists, Mormons, and Millerites—to name a few. This new religious culture, which sanctioned the right of the individual to go his own way, would have been unthinkable apart from the crisis of authority in popular culture that accompanied the birth of the American republic.

[76] Devereux Jarratt, *The Life of the Reverend Devereux Jarratt* (Baltimore, 1806), 14–15, 181.

ROBERT CARTER'S JOURNEY: FROM COLONIAL PATRIARCH TO NEW NATION MYSTIC

SHOMER S. ZWELLING

The Center for History Now
Williamsburg, Virginia

AS A YOUNG MAN IN HIS EARLY THIRTIES, ROBERT CARTER SEEMED DESTINED TO play a leading role in Virginia politics and society. When he died in his mid-seventies, in Baltimore, Maryland, he was an obscure figure living on the fringes of American culture. His life, rather than following a preordained route, was marked by false starts, radical oscillations, personal tragedies, and philanthropic ventures.

Born in 1728 to a prestigious Virginia family and appointed to the Governor's Council when he was thirty years old, Carter abruptly withdrew from political life in the early 1770s. A few years afterwards, when he was in his late forties, Carter suddenly embraced evangelical Christianity. He began manumitting his approximately five hundred slaves during the 1790s and soon after departed rural Virginia for a newly acquired residence in Maryland. When he died in 1804 he was a devout Christian mystic. Had he been a more self-collected person or had his times been less tumultuous, Carter may well have flourished as a moderately conservative statesman. But his constitution was fragile and his times were revolutionary. As a result he spent the better part of his adult life trying to forge a personality which was publicly viable and personally meaningful.[1]

Carter was certainly not a representative eighteenth-century Chesapeake planter. Of his friends and colleagues from the early part of his adult life, few became Baptists, only a handful freed their slaves, and hardly any turned to mysticism. Carter alone tried all three. Nevertheless, many other members of the old Virginia elite were feeling challenged, unnerved and inadequate during the second half of the eighteenth century. Though Carter's response to the press of circumstances was unusual—even eccentric—other male contemporaries from

I am thankful to John Hemphill II, Michael Zuckerman, Brent Tartar, Robert J. Brugger, Ronald Shectman, Joshua Rubenstein, William W. Abbot, Avi Decter, Reginald Butler, Diane Rodolitz, Judy Zwelling, John R. Barden and Nancy Carter Crump. The Colonial Williamsburg Foundation supported my research during its early phases. Critical comments at seminars sponsored by the Institute for Early American History and Culture and the National Museum of American History, Smithsonian Institution, helped clarify my thinking and approach.

main-line Virginia families were also struggling to find their place in a changing world.[2]

Our knowledge of Carter's early life is sketchy, but a few critical pieces of information stand out. He was the second child and only son of Robert Carter II. His grandfather was Robert "King" Carter, among the wealthiest and most powerful Virginians during the first part of the eighteenth century. When Robert Carter III was only four years old his father, age twenty-eight, died. Within a year his grandfather, King Carter, also passed away. Young Carter's mother married John Lewis shortly after her first husband died, and the family moved to the Lewis plantation in Gloucester County. Materially the boy's life remained substantially unchanged: his stepfather was a well-to-do planter who served on the Governor's Council, as King Carter had. The nature of their relation, whether Carter and Lewis were close or distant, is, however, obscure. We only know that at age nine Robert was sent to Williamsburg to study at the College of William and Mary. We next pick up his trail in 1749 when, at age twenty-one, he traveled to England where he lived for the next two years.[3]

During his mature years Carter was virtually silent about his childhood. On two occasions he jotted down the outline of a family history, but in neither instance did he provide much information about himself or his family prior to his marriage.[4] In his surviving correspondence, journals and memobooks, he rarely mentioned his mother, father or stepfather, and when he did it is usually in reference to a property settlement. The one incident preceding his marriage which he noted with some frequency is the trip to England. In 1785, for example, Carter wrote, "Col. Charles Carter . . . delivered to me all my estate in the month of February A. D. 1749, I then being 21 years old. . . . I Robert Carter went to England in the [year] 1749 and returned to Virginia in June 1751, Col. John Lewis of Gloucester County was agent for me during my absence."[5]

A more intriguing reference to the years in England is contained in a letter from Carter to Samuel Athawes, written in 1764 when Carter was living in Williamsburg, a councillor to the Governor. "The last evening I passed in London," he wrote, "your father & I kissed each other: at that parting the mild part of my composition [or temperament] was more dominant! Upon my honor I esteemed him & loved the family." In this same letter to Athawes, Carter conceded that he was something of a spendthrift while in England because, he recalled, "my gratifications exceeded my yearly income" at that time.[6] A portrait of Carter from his days in London shows the young Virginian opulently dressed and holding a mask in his hand (see figure 1).

Were Carter's adult years less tumultuous or were the records of his childhood and youth more numerous, perhaps the trip to England would not stand out quite so conspicuously. After all, an extended stay in London was not uncommon for wealthy young Virginians. Indeed, Carter's father had spent some time there. The timing and circumstances of young Carter's trip, however, are noteworthy. Virginians were usually sent by their parents to England for an education or business training before attaining their majority. Robert Carter went of his own accord after celebrating his twenty-first birthday. Moreover, Carter himself—

Robert Carter, circa 1750. Attributed to Thomas Hudson. Courtesy, Virginia Historical Society Collections.

generally quiet about his early years—repeatedly calls our attention to this episode in his life. What then are we to make of it?

A person of wealth from a prominent Chesapeake family, Robert Carter III departed for England at the very moment he was to assume the duties and obligations of adulthood. While staying in London he was unencumbered by the carefully prescribed social role he was to fulfill when residing in provincial Virginia. Abroad he could live carefreely, assume new roles, and just as easily cast them off. It was a time when he had virtually no responsibilities and during which the fatherless young man wholeheartedly embraced a male many years his senior. Indeed, in Carter's several volumes of letterbooks and journals, Athawes, a probable father figure, is the only person Carter ever mentioned kissing. The trip to England seems to reveal a moment of hesitation as well as a time of freedom and expressiveness. It also foreshadows some of the self-doubt and indecision which plagued Carter during the Revolutionary War era.[7]

Carter's reentry into Virginia society during the early 1750s was difficult. John Page III recalled Carter as being "inconceivably illiterate, and also corrupted and vicious" upon his return to the colony.[8] John Blair also disapproved of young Carter. On July 4, 1751, he noted in his diary, "I hear Mr. Robert Carter intends to build and live in Williamsburg and to persuade all the gentlemen he can to do so too." Carter's plan seems to have gone awry, however, and less than two weeks later Blair wrote, "Sad news of poor wretched Bob Carter. I hope he won't come to live in Williamsburg."[9] The particular occurrence which Blair had in mind remains a mystery, but evidently something about Carter's manner and actions resulted in a frosty homecoming.

Rather than build a home in Williamsburg, Carter decided to establish himself at Nomini Hall in Westmoreland County, where he had briefly lived as a small boy before his father's death. In April, 1754, at age twenty-six, he married Frances Ann Tasker, age sixteen, of Annapolis, Maryland. Socially and economically it was a good connection, for Frances was the youngest child of Benjamin and Ann Tasker. Frances' father, one of the richest men in the colony, had served for over three decades on the Maryland Council. Two years after they married, the Carters' first child, Benjamin, was born. Over the course of the next twenty-seven years Mrs. Carter gave birth to another sixteen children, of whom twelve would survive infancy.[10]

During the mid-century period Carter also tried his hand at electoral politics. In 1752 and again in 1754 he was a candidate in Westmoreland County for a seat in the House of Burgesses. In the first contest he received only thirty-four votes and in the second—held shortly after his marriage—he garnered a mere seven. All was not lost, however, because Carter was well connected. In 1758, when he was thirty years old, Robert Carter, with the help of his wife's family, was appointed to the Governor's Council of Virginia. Socially and politically this appointment placed him on a par with his grandfather and father-in-law. He was subsequently called Councillor Robert Carter, and his selection is one of the few public events he records in a sketchy chronological autobiography written sometime between 1785 and 1788. Three years after assuming office, the Councillor, his wife, two sons and associated servants moved to Palace Street in Williamsburg. A small triumph given his earlier fumblings, Carter also noted this change of residence in his autobiographical notes.[11]

The years in Williamsburg seem to have been busy and—from outward appearances—relatively happy. The correspondence which survives from this era contains the letters of a man actively engaged in governing, adjudicating, and money-making. During this phase of his life Carter was a man with cosmopolitan interests, expensive tastes, and worldly ambitions.[12] He struck up a number of close male relationships with George Wythe, Thomas Jefferson, Thomas Everard, and Governor Francis Fauquier. John Page subsequently conceded that Carter overcame many of his previous shortcomings during his Williamsburg tenure. The Councillor, he claimed, "conversed a great deal with our highly enlightened Governor, Fauquier, and Mr. Wm. Small, the Professor of Mathematics at the College of Wm. and Mary, from whom he derived great advantage."[13] The Carters and the Fauquiers were so close—they were literally next-door neighbors—that when Ann Tasker Carter was christened in 1762 the Councillor asked Mrs. Fauquier to perform the requisite religious honors.[14] In turn, when the Governor traveled to New York in the latter part of 1762 and to Charleston in 1763 he requested Carter's company. Both trips were recorded in Carter's chronological autobiography.[15]

Energetic, influential, and well-established, Carter had every reason to be pleased with himself and his prospects during his mid-thirties. The children were young, the Governor was enlightened, and the neighbors were men of substance and character. Little of the reluctance which troubled Carter when he turned twenty-one is evident in this period. Indeed, he might have wondered why he ever had hesitated to assume his rightful role as a Virginia patriarch. He played his part well, with skill, confidence, and authority.

Ironically, Carter had finally assumed the obligations of patriarchy when the old order was starting to change. In politics, society, and family life, traditions of deference and hierarchy were coming into conflict with a new style of assertiveness and autonomy.[16] Carter seems to have weathered the initial storms of revolutionary Virginia effectively. Although he opposed the Stamp Act, there is no indication that his relationship with Fauquier suffered, and when the law was repealed Carter's peers asked him to write a letter of conciliation to the Crown. Respected by both sides in the dispute, Carter was living up to his self-concept as a moderate man.[17] His relationship with Fauquier's successor, Lord Botetourt, was also close and affectionate.[18] Carter's dealings with the last royal governor, Lord Dunmore, were more ambiguous. John Page recalled Carter as being "a pure and steady patriot" during the early 1770s when Dunmore took office. Nevertheless, Carter's supposedly patriotic attitude did not prevent him from selling the governor a large parcel of choice land near Williamsburg.[19]

Whatever his assessment of the new Governor, in 1772 Carter, age forty-four, abruptly packed up his family and returned to Nomini Hall where he would live for the next twenty years. Carter recorded his departure in his autobiographical chronology and also in his memobook for 1776 where he noted, "In the first part of the year 1772 a new system of politics in British North America began to prevail generally and in the month of May of the same year myself and family removed from Williamsburg back to Nomony Hall, and then became inhabitants in Westmoreland County."[20] The entry begs the question: was Carter opposed to British actions or American reactions? To friends in Williamsburg he was vague and evasive. In early 1773 he wrote Peyton Randolph, "Mrs. Carter & I are very happy in finding our acquaintances wish to see us return to Palace Street Once Again—We think the House there, is not Sufficiently roomy for our family, and must remain, here, 'till an Addition to be Built to that house—"[21] Instead of making changes in the Williamsburg home, however, Carter had the work done on his Westmoreland County estate and put the Palace Street residence up for sale.

Two years later, soon after Dunmore's raid on the Williamsburg Powder Magazine in April, 1775, Carter returned briefly to the Virginia capital. His goal was to persuade his associates to accept Lord North's proposal of February, 1775, as the basis of a negotiated settlement. Carter, however, stood almost alone in believing the North plan offered a possibility of a rapprochement, and he returned to Nomini disabused of this notion.[22] Over the next six months the political situation continued to deteriorate. At the end of the year Carter wrote to William Taylor: "The resolutions of the continental Congress made in consequence of many late acts of Parliament tending to create a mighty difference between his majesty's subjects living in Great Britain & this Continent, the former to continue free-men, the latter to become slaves—has greatly reduced the yearly profits of my estate, and I expect they, the resolutions, will, introduce here, very different modes of management."[23] Carter, in short, perceived himself to be in a bad situation no matter who triumphed: the British threatened his freedom, while the patriots diminished his profits. Tendered a position on the Governor's Council in the new revolutionary government, Carter demurred, giving personal and family reasons as an explanation. "I have passed the zenith of life and now have a numerous family—which situation make the private station most elligible," he informed Richard Lee in June, 1776.[24]

A man who sought reconciliation in a time of polarization, Carter was neither a patriot nor a loyalist. Instead he was among the uncommitted, not because of indifference or apathy but because he was conflicted.[25] Disturbed by what he saw happening in both the colonies and England, Carter could not find a role for a moderately inclined colonial patriarch. To compound matters, the revolutionary fervor was gaining momentum at the very time when Carter was entering mid-life and his two oldest sons were becoming adolescents. As early as 1769, when he turned forty-one, signs of a more sober and reflective man had begun to emerge. In a letter written shortly after his friend Fauquier and his father-in-law Benjamin Tasker died, Carter categorically denied that he was "in quest of pleasure only."[26] Instead, he pointedly claimed, he was committed to "diligence, integrity & candor, and I heartily wish that every human mind participated of those virtues."[27] Powerless to shape the course of political affairs and increasingly conscious of his own standards and mortality, Carter began to look to his family for solace and comfort during his mid-forties. In the privacy of family life he sought a refuge from a combative, competitive, and often deceitful world.[28]

During this difficult period of transition, Philip Fithian, the young Presbyterian tutor from New Jersey, joined the Carter household. Fithian's diary provides an outsider's perspective on Carter and his kin. His journal does not record everyday life in a flourishing genteel family. Rather, it describes the daily activities of a household in which the middle-aged father is seeking both order and equanimity in private life after realizing he could not attain them in the public sphere.[29]

When he arrived at Nomini Hall during the fall of 1773, Fithian was initially impressed by the Carters. In those early days of his tenure the young tutor described Mr. Carter as generous, sensible, civil and judicious, a model Virginia gentleman. The tutor was also fond of Frances Carter, the Councillor's wife. She was, he believed, "prudent, always cheerful, never without something pleasant, a remarkable economist, [and] perfectly acquainted . . . with the good management of children." Fithian was also pleased with his young charges. Only Bob, the second child and his father's namesake, presented a problem: he possessed a volatile temper. Even though Bob recovered from these violent outbursts quickly, Fithian, together with the Councillor and his wife, was concerned. The boy's aberrant behavior notwithstanding, the Carter family was, in Fithian's words, "most agreeable" and "well regulated" (40, 47-50).[30]

Soon, however, the young tutor found himself ill at ease in this household. His subsequent decision to leave after only one year was in part a consequence of this discomfort. Carter, for all his civil behavior, was a withdrawn, brooding and uncommunicative person at this point in his life. Indeed, Colonel Carter—as he was sometimes called—rarely joined his family for supper. While the family ate, Carter usually retired to his study, where, in Fithian's words, he was "indefatigable in the Practice" of music (30, 41, 111).

The longer Fithian stayed with the family the more he came to view Carter as an enigmatic figure. On one occasion during the spring of 1774, when Fithian asked Carter if he intended to observe the day set aside in early June for fasting and prayer in support of the rebellious citizens of Massachusetts, the Colonel replied, "No one must go from hence to Church, or observe the Fast at all." From this Fithian concluded that Carter was a "courtier," but then he hastily added that "it is hard to know his opinion from anything he declares" (111). On another occasion, when the subject of death was broached in a family discussion, Carter announced that "he proposed to make his Coffin & use it for a Chest til

its proper use be required—That no stone or Inscription . . . be put over him—
And that he would choose to be laid under a shady Tree where he might be
undisturbed & sleep in peace and obscurity'' (61). Depressed, disconsolate and
contemplating his own demise, Carter's quest for peace and obscurity had
already begun. As Fithian observed, the Colonel "was given to retirement"
(48).

With the Councillor increasingly wrapped in thought, Mrs. Carter was living
at the mercy of powerful and disabling fears. Whenever there was a
thunderstorm—and sometimes when there was only a dark cloud on the
horizon—she hastily fled to her room. One night, during a storm, she went about
the house, moving the girls' beds away from the chimneys and placing lights in
the passageways. "I wandered through the house," she reported the next
morning, "silent & lonely like a disturbed ghost" (183).

Underlying Mrs. Carter's "cheerful, chatty and agreeable" demeanor was a
deeply frightened person (40). She was, in her own words, a woman who was
"always supposing the worst," who feared that she had a "cancer breeding" in
her breast, and who claimed, when thirty-five years old, that if left a widow she
would have trouble remarrying because she was too old (207, 40). Fithian, in
some respects a surrogate eldest son, felt the uneasiness of a young person
caught between two troubled parents. One day at the family dinner table when
the conversation turned to winning and congenial personality traits, both Frances
and the Councillor justified their own very different tendencies and implicitly
criticized each other:

> Mrs. Carter said she loved a sociable, open, chatty person; that She could not bear
> Sulleness, and stupidity—Mr. Carter, on the other hand, observed . . . that there is
> a "time for all things under the Sun"; that it discovers great Judgment to laugh in
> Season, and that on the whole, he was pleased with Taciturnity—pray which of
> these two [people] should I suit? (37)

Although Bob, the Carters' second child, was usually the focus of concern in the
family, other members were evidently struggling.

Intense involvement and radical withdrawal characterized family life in the
Carter household at this time. The parents invested themselves in the daily lives
of their children, but the relationship of husband and wife was remote and often
testy. Although they were married in an era when romantic love was taking root
in Chesapeake society, interaction between Robert Carter and his wife Frances
remained formal.[31] The very business of a large household with many children
can serve to bridge the gap in a strained and distant marriage. The ongoing needs
and demands of children—especially in families with a "problem child"—can
force otherwise discordant or remote mates to work together in apparent
harmony. In this respect we can observe Mr. and Mrs. Carter developing
intense, clinging relationships with their offspring while masking tensions in the
conjugal unit and burying disappointments with the world of public affairs.[32]

The pattern can be gleaned from a variety of incidents. With large landownings and profitable investments, Carter could not envision family members ever setting out on their own. One morning, for example, when contemplating his death the Councillor announced that "him of his sons whom he finds most capable of doing Business when he leaves the world . . . shall have management of the whole [estate] & support the rest [of the family]." Another time, when the same subject was under discussion, Carter declared that if he lived "to see his children grown, he will pay no regard to age, but give his wealth to Him who bids fairest to be useful to mankind . . ." (83, 182). With these guidelines the children would remain competitively joined, trying to curry favor with their father until he either died or made a decision.

Another revealing incident occurred when Ben asked his parents if he could go on a trip to Philadelphia with Fithian. Initially Colonel Carter consented, but as the day of Ben's departure approached Mrs. Carter became agitated. On April 8 she informed Ben he could not go. Then, on the ninth, she said he could, but only as far as Annapolis. On the next day Fithian recorded in his diary, "Mrs. Carter altered her mind concerning Ben many times and in several different manners: At first she agreed for him to go with me as far as Annapolis without a waiting man; than She concluded he was not well and had better decline going entirely; towards evening she gave him full liberty if he will take a waiting-man & not set away till Monday morning. . . ." Eventually Ben journeyed to Annapolis with Fithian, but when the tutor returned to Nomini, Mrs. Carter rebuked him for leaving without a waiting-man (85, 95-96, 118).

Naming patterns in this gentry family also help to elucidate the tangled nature of daily life. To begin with, Robert Carter III was named after his father and grandfather. To distinguish him he was often referred to as Councillor Carter, but more frequently he was called Colonel Robert Carter, just as his grandfather had been. Councillor Carter named his first son, Benjamin, after his wife's father, Benjamin Tasker. The second son was called Robert Bladen Carter but for short he was called Bob (as the Councillor had been when young) or Robin (as King Carter was). One daughter was named Priscilla after the Councillor's mother. Another was named Ann Tasker Carter after Mrs. Carter's mother. A third daughter was christened Frances Tasker Carter after Mrs. Carter III. Is it any wonder that one evening Mrs. Carter chose as her epitaph, "Here lies Ann Tasker Carter"—using the name of one of her daughters and her mother rather than her own, which was Frances Ann Tasker Carter (61)? These naming patterns, not entirely unusual for a gentry family, could blur the distinctiveness and individuality of the various family members and play havoc with everyday interactions. In the process the relationship of the Colonel and his wife becomes even more obscured. Given these circumstances the well-regulated gentry family—tenuous from the start—turned unmanageable under stress, and the reasons for the patriarch's retreat from the supper table are more readily apparent.[33]

Subsequent developments make sense when viewed in light of Carter's needs and the family's style of behavior. The formal break with England exacerbated a quandary which had troubled Carter since the early 1770s. Compelled to choose between the lesser of two evils, he eventually sold supplies to the revolutionaries and vowed allegiance to the new government, even though he believed all considerate men were struck by the "impropriety of hostilities."[34] A loyalty oath and an additional source of income, however, did not end his difficulties. In late 1777 a sergeant from the county militia tried to enlist Carter's sons Ben and Bob in the war effort. Carter attempted to dissuade them with arguments against killing. The boys apparently understood their father's message. Ben announced that he would not fight this or any other war because "killing a fellow creature, intentionally, was a violence to God." Bob—unusually compliant—agreed with his brother. The problem, however, lingered. Although Ben was excused from service because he was infirm, Bob was forced to choose between the militia and thirty days in jail. As in the case of his father, the Revolution presented Bob with a dilemma, a no-win proposition. He eventually joined the militia, probably with a measure of guilt and perhaps with the burden of his father's disapproval.[35]

Ineffective on the political front, Carter was also increasingly disturbed by a grave situation at home. In the spring of 1776 Ben's recurrent sickness took a marked turn for the worse, and in May he left home for a medicinal spring in Frederick County. Until his death in May, 1779, Ben's ill health was a matter of frequent concern in the family. Ben's condition distressed his father—and undoubtedly his mother—but here again the Councillor's feelings were tangled and confused. In the early days of Ben's decline, Carter tried to dismiss his son's complaints and saw in the boy something of a hypochondriac.[36] Only much later did he acknowledge the gravity of the situation. Another illness in the family was more short-lived and virtually impossible to deny. In September, 1775, Frances gave birth to a baby girl who died nine days later.[37]

The strain on Carter must have become immense. He was ill for several weeks during mid-1776, and in the autumn he relinquished his position on the parish vestry. In late October he mysteriously began renaming some of his plantations after the signs of the zodiac.[38] By early 1777 Carter was showing signs of emotional collapse. In April, while sitting alone in his parlor after dinner, he fainted. Found on the floor by his wife, he had dislocated one finger and seriously bruised his face, neck and knees. He believed he was unconscious for approximately four minutes, and when he revived he vomited.[39]

Shortly afterwards, on May 21, 1777, Carter and three of his children left for St. Mary's County, Maryland, where he intended to be inoculated for smallpox. There, on the night of June 12, 1777, Carter declared, "the Lord . . . wrought a mighty work on my soul. . . ." In a flash, he understood and—even more importantly—"experienced the truth contained in the following scripture where Paul declares—'That he, Paul, was alive without the Law once; but when the commandment came, Sin revived, and he died.'" It was, Carter believed, nothing short of a "most gracious illumination" and was, of course, another of those turning points which he recorded in his chronological autobiography.[40]

Returning to Westmoreland County on July 4, 1777, Carter sought out other persons who had comparable experiences. He read copiously about revealed religion and regularly attended prayer meetings.[41] Faith and religious worship, however, failed to provide a sense of well-being. Instead Carter's emotional condition worsened, and the fainting spells continued. He passed out in December, 1777, when his sons were being considered for military service. A few months later, after Bob had completed his tour of military duty and set out for the College of William and Mary in Williamsburg, the Colonel fainted again. Meanwhile Frances Carter began spitting up blood. A doctor was called to the house.[42]

With Bob absent, Ben's condition worsening, Frances unwell, and the Revolutionary War dragging on, Carter's interest in evangelical religion intensified. During a forty-one-day period (from March 24 through May 3, 1778) he attended twenty-one prayer meetings or religious services.[43] At this time he also wrote a poem, "The Assaulted Christian leaving Recourse to Divine Mercy," which reads in part:

> My soul is beclouded and heavy my heart
> When Jesus the Spring of my joys disappears,
> My weeping sad eyes will betray the deep smart,
> Which sin hath inflicted, the source of my tears.
>
> I once was exulting in thoughts of his love.
> I once could anticipate heavenly bliss.
> Yet improvident wretch never thought I should prove
> A meritted change so surprizing as this.
>
> Now a train of diseases I draw in my breath.
> My foes rise against me by night and by day!
> My blessed Redeemer! thine absence is death!
> Greatest perils await me when thou art away.
>
> Restore me to peace in thy favour again
> And conduct to thy Kingdom a wanderer home;
> Let me joine with my praises thy ransomed train!
> Give me earnest of peace; let thy comforter come![44]

In May, 1778, Carter traveled by himself to Buckingham County where he attended a conference of the Baptist Association. While on this pilgrimage the Colonel believed he was visited by Jesus Christ in the flesh. Three months later, back in Westmoreland County, a still distraught Robert Carter wrote in his daybook, "O that I may have a saving knowledge of sin & Christ; and that I may have assurance of God's love to my soul." Finally, on September 6, 1778, Robert Carter communicated his various religious experiences to an assembly of approximately two hundred people and was baptized by Reverend Lewis Lunsford of the Baptist Church.[45]

In the late 1770s, as Carter learned, being a Baptist in Virginia still entailed a certain amount of risk and occasionally social abuse. During August, 1778, Carter participated in at least two large evangelical meetings which were broken up by local marauders.[46] These incidents, which preceded his formal baptism, may well have appealed to Carter. As a member of the gentry elite he was accustomed to being a member of a distinctive minority which considered itself morally superior to the mass of society; now, as a solitary religious pilgrim who felt besieged, assaulted and forsaken the role of martyr may well have affirmed his sense of self. Indeed, during this period he engaged in a bit of proselytizing, a practice which can shore up a weakened faith and also provoke intense enmity.[47]

Within the family, Carter remained paradoxically isolated and entangled. Although initial College reports on his son Bob were positive, Carter was dissatisfied with the boy's progress and behavior. When Bob returned home for a visit, Carter claimed that he exhibited the "depravity of mankind." Shortly afterwards when Robin consulted a doctor, his father complained that the "robust & strong seldom apply to a physician." In turn, when the youth bought a horse, Carter insisted that he sell it. Overall, Carter characterized Robin's conduct as "highly blameable" and informed Rev. James Madison of the College that his son must be "restrained in every matter."[48]

Other relationships proved no more satisfying. Ben's condition continued to deteriorate, notwithstanding frequent visits to the medicinal springs.[49] At the same time, dealings with the females in the family also became troublesome. To David Rice, an evangelical minister, the Councillor wrote, "The females have the outward form of religion, but they are strangers yet to the vital part thereof."[50] In mid-1778, when his daughter Priscilla asked her parents for permission to marry Robert Mitchell, Carter apparently turned her down. Four years later she married Mitchell anyway.[51]

In short, Carter became insistent on retaining rigid control within the family at the very time when certain members were demonstrating signs of autonomy. Initially evangelical religion offered the hope of a life "without the Law," but it rapidly became a means of exerting patriarchal domination at home. To help achieve this end, the Colonel inaugurated regular family prayer sessions. These meetings, he wrote in a pamphlet entitled "An Exhortation to Family-Prayer," would not only unify the family but also would restrain members tending to sin and wickedness.[52]

Ben's death in May, 1779, grieved the Councillor deeply, but it did not temper his growing rigidity. Six weeks later he insisted that his daughters cease their dancing lessons. When Bob, alternately defiant and dependent by this time, enrolled in dance classes, the Councillor refused to pay the bill.[53] For Frances Carter, who did not share her husband's religious zeal, life at Nomini Hall became unbearable. Shortly after Ben died she took to bed. In October, 1779, her doctor insisted that she leave the house for a brief respite. The Colonel declared her fully recovered in 1781, and she gave birth to another child—her last—in 1783. During the middle of the same year, however, Carter informed Francis Fauquier, Jr., that his wife had become an invalid. Still, he assured young Fauquier, "her cheerfulness continue[s]" unabated.[54]

With former colleagues engaged in a fight for political freedom and family relations increasingly out of control, evangelical religion offered Carter a new set of friends and acquaintances. Baptist ministers and exhorters—John Sutton, Lewis Lunsford, and John Toler—replaced Wythe, Jefferson and Fauquier as a circle of confidants and business associates. With some of his new companions Carter was remarkably open and affectionate.[55] Also, Carter'a attitude towards his slaves began to change. Although Fithian claimed in the early 1770s that the Councillor was one of "the most humane" masters in the Northern Neck, Carter could be harsh and punitive when he thought his slaves had misbehaved (38).[56] During the Baptist years, however, Carter became steadily more concerned with the well-being of his slaves. Moreover, blacks who had undergone religious conversions (like his own), he considered brothers and sisters.[57]

Evangelical religion, in short, provided Carter with a social circle which was neither loyalist or revolutionary, but it could not allay his feelings of grief, loss and isolation. During his years on the Governor's Council Carter used to speak of a "scheme of life"; now he preferred a less certain view, conceiving of life as a hazardous pilgrimage.[58] Formerly he signed his letters with the modest and repectful phrase, "I am your humble servant"; now he ended his correspondence by writing, "I am your unworthy brother in Christ."[59] By the 1780s Carter was claiming that he lived "out of the way" and "detached from the world."[60] Caught up in a sea of simultaneous political, social and familial change, he looked to God and eternity for stability and perspective. In 1783, writing to Fauquier, Jr., he recalled a poem which read in part:

Ah! What is life? with ills encompassed round,
amidst our hopes, fate strikes the sudden wound;
To-day the statesman of new honour dreams,
To-morrow death destroys his airy schemes; . . .

The virtuous soul pursues a nobler aim,
and life regards but as a fleeting dream;
She longs to wake, and wishes to get free,
To launch from earth into eternity. . . . [61]

In the years immediately following the conclusion of the Revolutionary War, Carter's intense involvement in evangelical religion waned somewhat, but he was hardly more sanguine. Immersed in the work of a planter-investor-industrialist, there are no indications that his work provided him with either satisfaction or consolation. On the contrary, as the country's economic problems and his financial difficulties mounted during the mid-1780s, Carter initiated several court cases and considered others against relatives, in-laws, creditors, employees, and associates.[62] In 1784 he had a major falling out with Reverend Sutton, his close friend, spiritual confidant, and the superintendent of his plantations. Carter accused Sutton of stealing from him. Their relationship never recovered.[63]

The full force of Carter's dissatisfaction and resentment, however, fell on his second son and namesake, Robin. Since September, 1780, Robin had been managing Billingsgate, one of his father's plantations. Although Robin was offered the profits of the quarter, the Councillor was hesitant to give the young man—who by then had attained his majority—a deed of conveyance. As a result, any serious economic problems which Robin encountered would recoil on his father, and, like several other planters in the 1780s—the Councillor included—Robin experienced considerable difficulty meeting the demands of his creditors. Had Carter given Robin the land outright, the Councillor would not have been implicated in his son's eventual economic failure. Perhaps Carter was trying to protect Robin; perhaps he did not trust his son's judgment; perhaps the Colonel simply did not want to give the young man his independence. Whatever the precise motive, Carter's entangled relations with his second son again came back to haunt the family. In December, 1784, with Robin heavily in debt, the Councillor placed Billingsgate in a trusteeship and publicly sold the land, stock, and slaves in an effort to satisfy creditors.[64]

A few months later Robin ran off to England, but he could not keep away from his father any more than this aggrieved patriarch could separate from his son. Back in America by June, 1786, a contrite Robin asked his father for instruction and employment. Carter consented, informing the young man that he must "depart from every exercise you have uniformly . . . [practiced] heretofore."[65]

From this point and until Robin's untimely and somewhat mysterious death in London in 1793, the Councillor sought to keep his son on a remarkably short rope. When Robin wanted to buy a suit of clothes in 1787 (he was then twenty-eight years old and the Councillor was almost sixty), he needed his father's consent.[66] And when he sought the hand of a Mrs. Baylor, a widow, in marriage, the Councillor wrote Mann Page, who was apparently brokering the union, "such an alliance we do very much approve of, but at the same time I think advisable to inform you that Mr. Bladen's conduct has been very blamable therefore a caution is requisite."[67] With this recommendation, Robin never married Mrs. Baylor or anyone else. For the rest of his life, he alternated between being a good boy and running off to England.

The irony, of course, is that Robin seems to have been remarkably like his father. In fact, their similarity in temperament was probably part of the problem.

After all, Carter too had once run off to England, and he also tended to live beyond his means a a young man. In addition, Colonel Carter was himself very much in debt when Robin was going bankrupt. Finally, other persons apparently confused father and son for the Councillor occasionally received letters intended for himself (Robert Carter) with his son's name (Robert Bladen Carter) mistakenly written on the envelope. In the late 1780s such blunders irritated the Councillor.[68] Nevertheless, his attachment to Robin was lifelong, and on the day when the Colonel learned of his son's unexpected death in England, he wrote in his daybook, "I died at Mr. George Prestmans," rather than "I dined at Mr. George Prestmans."[69]

In rearing his younger two sons, Carter was determined not to make the same mistakes again. Instead, he swung to the opposite extreme. In 1786, when John Tasker Carter was fourteen and his brother George nine, the Councillor sent the boys to a college in Providence, Rhode Island. Asking the Reverend James Manning to be their foster father, Carter wrote that "the example and custom in this neighborhood I take to be very destructive to the morals and advancement of youth." Even after his wife Frances died in 1787 the Councillor did not allow his sons to return home. He next saw John Tasker in November, 1790. A year later George came back to Nomini Hall for a brief stay. In sending these adolescent boys away from home for extended periods the Colonel began the process of systematically dispersing his family.[70]

Meanwhile, Carter's relationship with his wife Frances remained elusive and enigmatic to the end. On May 23, 1786—eight years after her husband embraced the Baptist faith—Frances finally converted. One month later the Councillor began to exhibit interest in mysticism and the occult.[71] Within a year Frances became terminally ill, and in June, 1787, she left Nomini Hall for an extended visit with her sister in Bladensburg, Maryland. She returned home only seven weeks before she died. During her absence Carter sent her several letters, most of which were signed, "I am my dear, yours affectionately," but one closed with the phrase "I am my dear your unworthy brother in the Gospel." Grieved at her death (Carter in 1787 was 59 years old and the couple had been married for 33 years), the Councillor was increasingly a man alone.[72] In the autumn of 1788 he sent his three daughters—Sarah, age 15; Sophia, age 9; and Julia, age 5—to live in Baltimore.[73] With the exception of sundry household servants and periodic visits from his children, Carter was becoming a patriarch without a family. By dispersing his young sons and daughters, Carter was reenacting an awesome event from his own childhood, this time playing the role of the parent.

His own severe judgment of himself as a father is obliquely contained in a letter to a Mrs. Elizabeth Whiting, who, in 1797, had asked him a question about child-rearing. "The government of a family," the Councillor replied, "is an arduous attempt. Therefore persons who have not been successful therein, it is judged adviseable that such should give up their children to reputible industrious families, the relinquished children they to be taught to read, write, [and] cipher.

. . . ."[74] To his daughter Harriot, who sought her father's help when she was undergoing economic difficulties in 1803, he wrote, "Why do you call upon a person to give you council who never ceased to advise when it was part of his duty. . . ."[75] Between the intrusiveness of a dominating father and a pattern of near abandonment, Carter could find no alternative.

For the Councillor the late 1780s was a time of transition: he entered old age; his wife died; and he virtually disbanded his household. During this period Carter again felt himself to be painfully adrift. "I trust in God that his grace will enable me to persevere," he wrote a friend during his wife's final illness. To another he declared, "I am dear sir your weak brother in the gospel."[76] Shortly after his wife's death, Carter, if only for a few months, attempted to reinvolve himself in political life. In late 1787 he offered himself as a candidate for the state convention to ratify the Constitution. Running without much enthusiasm, he was not elected. In 1789 he qualified as a justice of the peace.[77]

These efforts to revive his long dormant political career were an outgrowth of changes in his personal life, developments in both the nation and the Commonwealth, and also a mounting disenchantment with evangelical religion. Carter's estrangement from the Baptists in the late 1780s had several sources. Theological controversy was renting the Baptist denomination, and conflict was a phenomenon with which Carter could not deal effectively. Previously he had hoped evangelical religion would "promote order and regularity in [both the] . . . visible church . . . [and] the world" but toward the end of the eighties the Baptists fell to bickering over Calvinism, Arminianism, justification, and grace. It was an old story, according to Carter. In studying history, he wrote a friend, "it may be found that there are Popes against Popes—councils against councils—a [group] of fathers of one age against a [group] of fathers of another age. . . . Men build upon any composition short of scriptures."[78]

Another source of dissatisfaction with the Baptists concerned slavery. During the 1780s Carter became increasingly mindful of the welfare of his slaves and even hostile to the institution itself. His decision in 1786 to send his two youngest sons to school in the North was related in part to his belief that the boys would be morally corrupted if they grew up in a slave state. By 1788 Carter was supporting political efforts to free Virginia slaves, and in 1790 he claimed that the "situation of the Blacks here [in Virginia] is my greatest difficulty." Meanwhile the Baptists, who initially had been critical of slavery, were moving in the opposite direction. As the denomination became more popular and respectable in the Commonwealth, its critique of slavery became less pronounced.[79]

The failure of evangelical religion to establish social order, take an unequivocal stand against slavery, and provide personal solace in a time of grief figured prominently in Carter's disillusionment. In addition, it is likely, given his tendency to gravitate toward select groups, that the very popularity of the Baptists in post-Revolutionary Virginia troubled him. Formerly a member of the colonial elite, Carter, in a more egalitarian society, preferred the fringe.

Finally in the spring of 1789, shortly after turning sixty-one, Carter succumbed to another period of self-assessment which came on the heels of severe conflict in his life. Confused, unwell, and distraught, he again withdrew into himself. An aging patriarch who could not have or find his way, Carter took inventory in isolation. When he reemerged, he was a member of the New Jerusalem Church, a mystical Christian sect which anticipated mid-nineteenth-century Transcendentalism and emphasized personal self-examination.[80]

For Carter the widower and loner, the New Jerusalem Church had much to offer. Its claim that people continue to live in a spiritual realm after death as well as the belief that Emanuel Swedenborg—the founder of the New Church—had communicated with these spirits helped assuage Carter's deep grief after the demise of his wife. Nevertheless, coming to terms with his wife's death, although a cause, is not a sufficent explanation for his conversion, because Carter had exhibited some interest in spiritual communication as early as June, 1786—sixteen months before Frances died.[81]

Swedenborgianism, in fact, spoke to several of Carter's lifelong struggles as well as the immediate needs of a widower who was confronting the spectre of his own death. At least five themes appear in Swedenborg's works and Carter's religious writings from this period which are relevant to the Colonel's recurrent problems.[82] First, Swedenborg declared that the world as men had known it ended in 1757 when he received his first mystical illumination. The Second Coming, according to Swedenborg, had commenced during the middle of the eighteenth century, but this new dispensation, unlike earlier ones, was strictly spiritual in nature. It had no material counterpart and therefore could not be seen. This viewpoint proved attractive to Carter. He began to think that he was living in an era when society and culture were undergoing a major transformation. Consequently, he now considered the personal struggles of the Baptist years as part of this larger drama. He became increasingly millenarian and apocalyptic in outlook, examining his own private quests in light of large-scale contemporary trends and occurrences.[83]

Another New Church doctrine which appealed to Carter concerned the issue of reconciliation. According to Swedenborg a grand rapprochement was taking place: within the Godhead, among the angels, on earth, and within the individual. In his treatise, *On the Nature of Influx*, Swedenborg maintained that each person must reconcile inner spiritual reality with everyday behavior and actions. To the degree that the outer person is not in accord with the inner, Swedenborg believed, each person lives in a condition of tormenting conflict. This doctrine proved to be attractive to the Councillor. For a brief period in his early twenties Carter entertained some of the alternatives available to him, but shortly after his return from England in 1751 he adopted the role he was expected to assume in colonial society. During the third quarter of the eighteenth century he had been a man of the material world, dressing according to his social station and fulfilling his inherited obligations. With his departure to Nomini Hall when he was forty-four years old and his subsequent conversion to the Baptist faith, Carter attempted to change his ways, but the pursuit of private family happiness as well as the turn to evangelical religion were abortive efforts. Now in his declining years, Carter tried again to free himself of remaining constraints. He became increasingly self-expressive and self-divulging. Claiming that candor and truth were cardinal graces, Carter declare, "I *now* see the beauty of the divine precept, 'Let your communication be yea or nay; for whatsoever is more than these cometh of evil.'"[84]

Other aspects of the Swedenborgian call for reconciliation appealed to Carter. Throughout his adult life the Colonel had alternately espoused rationality and knowledge on the one hand, passion and spontaneity on the other. During his Swedenborgian phase, Carter finally tried to harmonize these warring tendencies within himself. For Carter, Swedenborg's simultaneous emphasis on truth and love, wisdom and affection represented a temperamental as well as a philosophical integration of polar opposites. In his own life at least, Carter hoped to square the rationality of the Enlightenment with the heightened emotionalism of evangelical religion. His embrace of the New Church was an expression of this commitment.[85]

Swedenborg's vision of harmonious reconciliation also applied to marital relations. Carter's thirty-three-year marriage was marked by remoteness and devotion, formality and procreation. His wife's death, however, left him depressed and disconsolate. Swedenborg offered a solution. In his book, *Marital Love*, the Swedish mystic claimed married partners would meet after death. If they were suitable for each other their relationship would resume and develop; if irreconcilable, they would part forever and discover compatible mates.[86] Presumably, other relations—with family members, friends, business associates and political colleagues—could also be successfully terminated or joyously continued in the spiritual realm.

A third Swedenborgian doctrine which attracted Carter concerned original innocence. Although each person was born innocent according to Swedenborg, at various points in their lives individuals turned to wickedness. Repentance, therefore, was a critical undertaking according to Swedenborg, but it should never overshadow innate innocence. In fact, Swedenborg repeatedly advised his followers to dwell on good as a means of overcoming evil. These ideas were not entirely new to Carter. Evangelical religion had initially offered the promise of freedom from sin and guilt, but it quickly became a means for expressing feelings of unworthiness and abandonment. Carter's struggles with guilt, isolation and inadequacy were powerful and recurrent. They probably had several sources: suppressed rage at his wife, regret over not fulfilling his socially assigned role, vague feelings of responsibility for the death of his father when young Robert was only four years old. Whatever the precise causes, Carter, in his old age, rediscovered through Swedenborg long-absent feelings of innocence and affirmation after his wife died.[87]

Another aspect of Swedenborg's philosophy which impressed Carter centered around matters of power and domination. Throughout his life Carter—sometimes covertly and sometimes overtly—had struggled to dominate both himself and family members. Alternatively active and passive, intrusive and withholding, Carter's goals had always included domination. Swedenborg, however, argued that persons must be simultaneously receptive and assertive. For Swedenborg, faith must be accompanied by good works. As a manifestation of this disposition, Carter began to assert himself in ways which were not domineering.[88] For example, in 1792 he initiated a program of gradual manumission for his approximately five hundred slaves. Although Carter's decision to free these slaves came at a time when he was also divesting himself of other duties and obligations, his plan of gradual liberation took into account the needs of the slaves as well as the opposition of his neighbors. If he was not entirely successful in realizing his goal, neither was he again simply embarking on a course of abandonment and reproach.[89]

Carter also sought a new tact in his dealings with family members. For years the Colonel had held his estate over his children as powerful patriarchs sometimes tended to do. In 1795, however, Carter divided his property into ten equal portions and gave one to each of his surviving offspring.[90] With this act—together with his program of manumission and his insistence at approximately the same time that he no longer be called Honorable Robert Carter but simply Citizen Carter—Robert Carter III relinquished his last claims to patriarchy.[91]

Finally, Swedenborg's works are permeated with extended discussions on self-love, and this subject held particular meaning for Carter. Swedenborg believed that self-absorption was a primary source of sinfulness. Self-serving motivations, he maintained, often undermine good deeds. In the place of relentless self-preoccupation, Swedenborg stressed the importance of charity and mercy. Carter grasped the thrust of his message. Since retiring to Nomini Hall in 1772 the Councillor had been a man obsessed with himself. Even though generosity was one of his characteristics, Carter's benevolence was inseparable from his role as a patriarch. Not until the mid-1790s—too late for Robert Bladen—did Carter begin to appreciate the importance of compassion in human relations. He even wrote an essay on the subject.[92] Carter also began to demonstrate an unaccustomed sense of humor about himself during this final phase of his life. To one of his children he wrote in 1794, "No complaining in our family save myself—I remain as when you saw me."[93] As a manifestation of this more well-disposed and humanitarian attitude—in one letter written during this period Carter signed with the phrase "Friend to Man I am"—he departed Nomini Hall in 1793 to reside near religious soul mates in Baltimore for the rest of his life.[94]

As much as Carter changed in his final years, some patterns of behavior remained. The New Jerusalem Church, like other groups with which he associated, was a small elitist body which believed it possessed a superior knowledge of truth. Also, in keeping with his previous ways, Carter assumed a position of leadership in the New Church. In this capacity he administered the sacrament, conducted public services, and gave sermons.[95] Finally, there is a striking resemblance between the New Church's emphasis on a multilevel reconciliation and Carter's earlier commitment to political moderation. In both instances, Carter sought to bring into harmony tendencies and polarities which were existing in conflict. In the first part of his adult life he generally saw these tendencies in society and politics; in the latter part he also saw them within himself.

Carter's embrace of the New Church philosophy could not entirely free him of old conflicts and struggles. Although he attained a degree of redemption, reconciliation and self-transcendence before he died in 1804, Carter's problems with intimacy—in an era which came to prize it—were lifelong. There were subsequent quarrels, lost friendships, and serious family difficulties.[96] Moreover, in turning to mysticism while others looked to love, sentimentality and evangelical fervor, Carter ended his life far removed from mainstream American society and culture. When writing to his daughter Harriot, a year before his death, he acknowledged his position. "My plans and advice," he wrote, "have never been pleasing to the world."[97]

Carter trod an unusual path. Still, he was not entirely divorced from his society or era. Although Carter often gravitated to the margins of his culture, he was responding not only to his own inner needs and convictions but also to broad-based trends, occurrences, and concerns.[98] In all his struggles, we can observe the efforts of a man trying to come to terms with both himself and a changing world. Carter's proposals and solutions were not common. His feelings of disquiet, however, were widespread among contemporaries from old-line Virginia families, and his sense of both doom and transcendental hope anticipated a later generation of nineteenth-century Americans.[99]

NOTES

[1]There is only one full-scale biography of Carter: Louis Morton, *Robert Carter of Nomini Hall, a Virginia Tobacco Planter of the Eighteenth Century* (Williamsburg: Colonial Williamsburg, Inc., 1945). On the theme of change in Virginia during this era see Rhys Isaac, *The Transformation of Virginia, 1740-1790* (Chapel Hill: Univ. of North Carolina Press, and The Institute of Early American History and Culture, 1982). On the North see Robert Gross, *The Minute Men and Their World* (New York: Hill and Wang, 1976).

[2]T. H. Breen, *Tobacco Culture: The Mentality of the Great Tidewater Planters on the Eve of Revolution* (Princeton: Princeton Univ. Press, 1985); Emory G. Evans, "Virginia's Old Political Elite, 1700-1783: What Happened To Them?" (unpublished ms.); James LaVerne Anderson, "The Virginia Councillors and the American Revolution: The Demise of an Aristocratic Clique," *Virginia Magazine of History and Biography*, 82 (January 1974), 56-74. In general see Richard Sennett, *The Fall of Public Man: On the Social Psychology of Capitalism* (New York: Vintage Books, 1976).

[3]Morton, *Robert Carter*, ch. 2.

[4]Robert Carter (hereafter RC), Daybook 16:161-64, Carter Papers, Duke University (hereafter DU); RC, Daybook 17:1-2, ibid.

[5]RC, Letterbook/Daybook 15, 4, 9 Nov. 1778, ibid.; idem, Letterbook 6 (1784-85): 219, ibid.

⁶RC to Samuel Athawes, 17 Feb. 1764, Carter Papers, Colonial Williamsburg Foundation (hereafter CWF).

⁷Erik H. Erikson, *Childhood and Society*, 2nd ed. (New York: W. W. Norton & Sons, 1963); idem, *Young Man Luther: A Study in Psychoanalysis and History* (New York: W. W. Norton & Co., 1958). On the role of England in the life of another Virginian see Michael Zuckerman, "William Byrd's Family," *Perspectives in American History*, 12 (1979), 253-311.

⁸"Governor Page," *Virginia Historical Register*, 3 (July 1850), 146-47.

⁹"Diary of John Blair," *William and Mary Quarterly*, 1st ser., 8 (July 1899), 8-9.

¹⁰RC, Daybook 16:161-64, DU.

¹¹RC, Daybook 17:1-2, ibid.; RC, Memobook 13:203, Oct. 1776, ibid., Morton, *Robert Carter*, 41-43.

¹²RC to John Morton Jordan, 16 Feb. 1762, CWF; RC to Thomas Bladen, 26 March [?] 1762, ibid.; RC to Messrs. Hyndman and Lancaster, Oct. 1769, ibid.

¹³"Governor Page," 146-47.

¹⁴RC to Thomas Bladen, 26 March [?] 1762, CWF.

¹⁵RC, Daybook 17: 1, DU.

¹⁶Daniel Blake Smith, *Inside the Great House: Planter Family Life in Eighteenth Century Chesapeake Society* (Ithaca: Cornell Univ. Press, 1980); Jan Lewis, *The Pursuit of Happiness: Family and Values in Jefferson's Virginia* (Cambridge, Eng.: Cambridge Univ. Press, 1983); Edwin G. Burrows and Michael Wallace, "The American Revolution: The Ideology and Psychology of National Liberation," *Perspectives in American History*, 6 (1972), 167-306; Isaac, *Transformation of Virginia*.

¹⁷Morton, *Robert Carter*, 50-51. On Carter's sense of himself as a moderate man see RC to John Tazewell, 9 Jan. 1773, DU; RC to Thomas and Roland Hunt, 24 July 1774, ibid.; RC to Wm. Taylor, 12 Aug. 1774, ibid.

¹⁸Robert Shosteck, "Notes on an Early Virginia Physician," *American Jewish Archives*, 23 (November 1971), 12-13.

¹⁹"Governor Page," 146-47; RC to Thomas Simpson, 1 April 1790, DU.

²⁰RC, Memobook 13: 203, Oct. 1776, DU.

²¹RC to Peyton Randolph, 23 Jan. 1773, ibid.

²²RC, Address, June 1775, Robert Carter Miscellaneous Papers, New York Public Library; Weldon A. Brown, *Empire or Independence: A Study of the Failure of Reconciliation, 1774-1783* (Louisiana: Louisiana State Univ. Press, 1941), chs. 2-3.

²³RC to William Taylor, 30 Dec. 1775, DU.

²⁴RC to Col. Richard Lee, 14 June 1776, ibid.

²⁵In general see Keith Bennett Berwick, "Loyalties in Crisis: A Study of the Attitudes of Virginians in the Revolution," Diss. Univ. of Chicago 1959.

²⁶RC to Mrs. Ann Ogle, 1 Feb. 1769, CWF.

²⁷RC to Ed Hunt & Son, 20 May 1769, ibid.

²⁸Lewis, *The Pursuit of Happiness*, esp. ch. 6; Daniel J. Levinson et al., *The Seasons of A Man's Life* (New York: Ballantine Books, 1978); Michael P. Farrell and Stanley D. Rosenberg, *Men at Midlife* (Boston: Auburn House Publishing Company, 1981); Elliott Jaques, "Death and the Mid-Life Crisis," *International Journal of Psychoanalysis*, 40 (1965), 502-14; C. G. Jung, "The Stages of Life," in Joseph Campbell, ed., *The Portable Jung* (New York: The Viking Press, 1971).

²⁹Hunter Dickinson Farish, ed., *Journal and Letters of Philip Vickers Fithian, 1773-1774: A Plantation Tutor of the Old Dominion* (Williamsburg, Va.: Colonial Williamsburg, Inc., 1957). Hereafter page numbers cited in text.

³⁰"Poor unhappy youth," wrote Fithian of Bob, "I fear he will come to an unhappy end." Ibid., 116.

³¹In general see Jan Lewis, "Domestic Tranquillity and the Management of Emotion among the Gentry of Pre-Revolutionary Virginia," *William and Mary Quarterly*, 3rd ser., 39 (January 1982), 135-49; Zuckerman, "William Byrd's Family"; Smith, *Inside the Great House*.

³²My understanding of family dynamics is informed by Lynn Hoffman, *Foundations of Family Therapy: A Conceptual Framework for Systems Change* (New York: Basic Books, Inc., 1981); Murray Bowen, *Family Therapy in Clinical Practice* (New York: Jason Aronson, 1978); Joseph Barnett, "Narcissism and Dependency in the Obsessional-Hysteric Marriage," *Family Process*, 10 (March 1971), 75-83; Salvador Minuchin, *Family Kaleidoscope* (Cambridge: Harvard Univ. Press, 1984). See also Farrell and Rosenberg, *Men at Midlife*; Levinson et al., *Seasons of a Man's Life*.

³³In general see Lewis, "Domestic Tranquillity."

³⁴RC to Capt. Burges Ball, 5 March 1776, DU; RC, Memobook 14:74-75, 29 July 1777, ibid.; RC to Messrs. Gildart and Busigny, 17 March 1777, ibid.

³⁵RC, Memobook 14:134, 3, 9 Dec. 1777, ibid.

³⁶See, for example, RC to John Hough, 15 May 1776, ibid.; RC, Memobook 14: 9, 16 Nov. 1776, ibid.

³⁷RC, Daybook 16: 161-64, ibid.; RC, Memobook 13:125-26, ibid.

³⁸RC to Capt. Jos. Lane, 23 Oct. 1776, RC, Letterbook 4:63, ibid.; RC, Memobook 13:215, ibid.

³⁹RC, Memobook 14: 46, 3 April 1777, ibid.

⁴⁰Robert Mitchell to Clemont Brooke, 22 May 1777, ibid.; RC, Letterbook/Journal 15:31-32, 18 May 1778, ibid.; Robert Carter, Daybook 17: 1-2, ibid.

⁴¹RC, Memobook 12: 1, 12 July 1777, 18 May 1778, ibid.; RC, Memobook 14: 140, 20 Dec. 1777, ibid.

⁴²RC, Memobook 14:134-35, 3, 9 Dec. 1777 and 14: 163, 18 Feb. 1778, ibid.; RC to Dr. Jones, 28 Feb. 1778, ibid.; RC, Letterbook/Daybook 15, 14, 15 March 1778, ibid.

⁴³RC, Letterbook/Journal 15, 24, 25, 28, 29 March, 4, 5, 9, 11, 15, 16, 17, 20, 21, 23, 25, 26, 29 April, 1, 2,3 May 1778, ibid.

⁴⁴RC, Journal/Memobook 15: 11-12, ibid.

⁴⁵RC, Letterbook/Daybook 15, 5, 16, 18 May, 30 Aug., 6 Sept. 1778, ibid.

⁴⁶RC, Letterbook/Daybook 15, 9, 15 Aug. 1778, ibid.

⁴⁷RC to Thomas Everard, 1 June 1778, ibid.; RC to Thomas Jefferson, 27 July 1778, ibid.

⁴⁸RC to Rev. Mr. Madison, 30 May 1778, ibid.; RC to Rev. Mr. Madison, 27 June 1778, ibid.; RC to Rev. Mr. Madison, 21 Jan. 1779, ibid.; RC to Robert Bladen Carter, 22 Nov. 1778, ibid.

⁴⁹See, for example, RC, Daybook 15:52, 91, 24 June, 28 Aug. 1778, ibid.

⁵⁰RC to Rev. David Rice, 15 Jan. 1779, ibid.

⁵¹RC, Daybook 15:85, 12 Aug. 1778, ibid.; Robert Carter, Daybook 16:161-64, ibid.

⁵²RC, "An Exhortation to Family-Prayer," Carter Papers, Virginia Historical Society (hereafter VHS); RC, Memobook 14:116, 119, 15, 23 Oct. 1777, DU.

⁵³RC to Mr. Francis Christian, 23 June, 22 Sept. 1779, DU.

⁵⁴RC to Doctor Todd, 30 Aug. 1779, ibid.; Robert Carter to Thomas Everard, 3 Nov. 1779, ibid.; RC to Doctor Jones, 18 April 1780, ibid.; RC to Dr. H. Todd, 24 Feb. 1781, ibid.; RC to Francis Fauquier, 5 July 1783, ibid.; RC, Daybook 16:161-64, ibid.

⁵⁵Carter helped support both Lunsford and Toler for a period and employed Sutton for several years. RC to John Toler, 20 Nov. 1778, ibid.; RC to Henry Toler, 3 Jan. 1782, ibid.; RC to Alex Hunton, 12 Dec. 1778, ibid.; RC to Rev. Lunsford, Letterbook 4:149-54, n.d., ibid.; RC to Rev. John Sutton, 29 April 1779, 21 Dec. 1781, ibid.

⁵⁶RC to Scott Pringle, Cheap & Co., 29 April 1767, CWF; RC to Jacob Bruce, 27 July 1772, DU.

⁵⁷See, for example, RC to John Pound, 16 March 1779, DU; RC to John Sutton, 9 June 1779, 19 Nov. 1781, ibid.; RC to Sam'l Carter, 10 March 1781, ibid.; Robert Carter to John Turner, 8 April 1782, ibid.; RC to Charles Haynic, 21 April 1784, ibid.

⁵⁸RC to Thomas J. Rowland and Hunt, 5 Aug. 1772, ibid.; RC to John Tazewell, 9 Jan. 1773, ibid.; RC to John Sutton, 9 June, 25 Oct. 1779, ibid.

⁵⁹See, for example, RC to John Sutton, 9 June 1779, 19 Nov. 1781, ibid.; RC to John Turner, 8 April 1782, ibid.

⁶⁰RC to Messrs. Thomas and Rowlands, July 1783, RC Letterbook 3:143, ibid.; RC to John Peck, Sept. 1785, RC, Letterbook 6: 214, ibid.

⁶¹RC to Francis Fauquier, 5 July 1783, ibid.

⁶²Evidence of Carter's economic difficulties and some of the court cases he was involved in can be found in RC to Richard Lemon, 7 May, 14 June 1784, ibid.; RC to William Carr, 11 Jan. 1785, ibid.; RC to Phillip Lee, 8 Feb. 1785, ibid.; RC to John Rose, 10 Feb. 1785, ibid.; RC to Robert Beverly, 10 Feb. 1785, ibid.; RC to John Hyndman, 25 Feb. 1785, ibid.

⁶³RC to George Newman, 8 June 1784, ibid.; RC to Ludwell Lee, 21 July 1784, ibid.; RC to William Carr, 3 Jan., 12 July, 30 Nov., 1785, ibid.; RC to John Sutton, 30 Aug. 1785, ibid.

⁶⁴RC to Ben Branum, Sept. 1780, RC, Letterbook 4:14, ibid.; RC to Richard Lemon, 29 July 1782, ibid.; RC to Robert Bladen Carter, 23 April 1783, ibid.; RC to Thomas Beale, 4 July 1783, ibid.; RC to J. Bailey, 15 April 1784, ibid.; RC, Advertisement, Letterbook 3:204, 226-27, ibid.; RC to John Hyndman, 4 March 1785, ibid.

⁴⁵Robert Bladen Carter to RC, 9 June 1786, VHS; RC to Robert Bladen Carter, 10 June 1786, DU.

⁴⁶RC to James Cramp, 10 Oct. 1787, DU; RC to Robert Bladen Carter, 27 Aug. 1789, ibid.

⁴⁷RC to Mann Page, 27 Oct. 1787, ibid.

⁴⁸RC to John and George Carter, 12 Feb., 9 April 1787, ibid.

⁴⁹RC, Journal, 15, 16 May 1793, ibid.

⁷⁰RC to Benjamin Ellerwood, 9 Feb. 1786, ibid.; RC to James Manning, 9 Feb., 8 May, 1786, 24 Sept. 1787, ibid.; RC to Robert Rogers, 7 Dec. 1787, ibid.; RC to Benjamin Wood, 7 Dec. 1787, ibid.; RC to Dr. Samuel Jones, 24 Nov. 1790, ibid.; RC, Daybook, 4 Nov. 1791, Carter Papers, Library of Congress (hereafter LC).

⁷¹RC, Daybook, 23 May, June 1786, DU.

⁷²RC to John Merryman, 3 March 1787, ibid.; RC to Robert Lemmon, 18 June, 12 Sept. 1787, ibid.; RC to John Peck, 19 June 1787, ibid.; RC to Francis Carter, 10, 17, 26 July, 14 Aug. 1787, ibid.; RC to Henry Toller, 1 Nov. 1787, ibid.; RC to James Manning, 9 Nov. 1787, ibid.; RC, Daybook, 31 Oct. 1787, ibid.; RC, Journal, 19 June, 31 Oct. 1787, LC.

⁷³RC to Revd. James Manning, 17 Nov. 1788, 4 Dec. 1789, DU.

⁷⁴RC to Mrs. Elizabeth Whiting, 28 Oct. 1797, LC.

⁷⁵RC to Harriot L. Maund, 30 May 1803, ibid.

⁷⁶RC to Elder William Wood, 6 Aug. 1787, DU; RC to Robert Lemmon, 12 Sept. 1787, ibid.

⁷⁷RC to [?], 27 Nov. 1787, ibid.; RC to Resident and non-Resident Electors, 6 Feb. 1788, ibid.; RC to Joseph Pierce, 6 Feb. 1788, ibid.; RC to Doctor Walter Jones, 12 Dec. 1788, ibid.; RC to John Dixon, 16 Feb. 1790, ibid.; RC, Daybook, July 1789, LC.

⁷⁸RC to Elder Lewis Lunsford, 8 May 1783, DU; RC to Elder Hunt, 26 Dec. 1787, ibid.; RC to John Rippon, 8 May 1790, ibid.

⁷⁹RC to James Manning, 9 Feb. 1786, ibid.; RC to Wm. Dawson, 6 Feb. 1788, ibid.; RC to John Rippon, 27 Aug. 1788, ibid.; RC to Samuel Jones, 24 Nov. 1790, ibid.; James David Essig, "A Very Wintry Season: Virginia Baptists and Slavery, 1785-1797," *Virginia Magazine of History and Biography*, 88 (April 1980), 170-86.

⁸⁰On Carter's illness see RC to Henry Tazewell, 11 April 1789, ibid.; RC to Cornelius Calvert, 19 Dec. 1789, ibid.; RC to Spencer Ball, 22 Dec. 1789, ibid.; RC to George Prestman, 9 Jan. 1790, ibid.; RC to William Hammond, 15 Nov. 1790, ibid. Carter first mentions Swedenborg on 25 Jan. 1788—three months after his wife's death. RC, Journal, 25 Jan. 1788, LC. Carter's growing interest in Swedenborg can be seen in RC to Robert Hindmarsh, 8 Sept. 1790, Carter Papers, Swedenborg School of Religion (hereafter SSR); RC to [Francis Bailey], 20 Sept. 1790, ibid.; RC to D. Bowley, 13 Nov. 1790, ibid.; RC to John Cooper, 15 Nov. 1790, ibid.; RC to Philip Merry, 30 March 1793, ibid.

⁸¹RC, Daybook, June 1786, DU.

⁸²Of Swedenborg's writings the following were particularly important to Carter: Emanuel Swedenborg, *A Summary Exposition of the Doctrine of the New Church* in idem, *Miscellaneous Theological Works* (Boston: Massachusetts New-Church Union, 1908); idem, *Soul-Body Interaction in Studia Swedenborg*, 2 (January, June 1976, January 1977). For a contemporary interpretation of Swedenborgianism see Wilson Van Dusen, *The Presence of Other Worlds: The Psychological/Spiritual Findings of Emanuel Swedenborg* (New York: Perennial Library, Harper & Row, 1974). For perspectives on this phase of Carter's life see Levinson et al., *Seasons of a Man's Life*; Erikson, *Childhood and Society*; C. G. Jung, *Collected Works of C. G. Jung*, 2nd ed., 20 vols. (Princeton: Princeton Univ. Press, 1953-79), vol. 9, pt. 1: *Archetypes of the Collective Unconscious*; C. G. Jung, "The Stages of Life."

⁸³RC to James Wilmer, 12 March 1792, SSR; RC to John Cooper et al., 10 May 1792, ibid.; RC to Revd. Mr. Bryan Fairfax, 12 July 1792, ibid.; RC to Samuel Jones and George Carter, 29 Oct. 1792, ibid.; RC, Religious Writings, 2, ibid.; RC, Wastebook, 17 March, 27 April 1794, LC.

⁸⁴RC to Ralph Mather, 24 Nov. 1795, LC; RC to General Lee, 30 March 1796, ibid.; RC to Robert Smith, 26 Jan. 1798, ibid. For some parallels see Lewis, *The Pursuit of Happiness*.

⁸⁵RC, Religious Writings, 9, 10, 21, 35, SSR; Swedenborg, *A Summary Exposition*; Emanuel Swedenborg, *Heaven and Its Wonders and Hell*, trans John G. Ager (New York: The Citadel Press, 1965).

⁸⁶Emanuel Swedenborg, *Marital Love, Its Wise Delights*, trans. William Frederic Wunsch (New York: Swedenborg Publishing Association, 1938). Interestingly Carter and his wife were supposed to be buried in separate burial grounds—she at Nomini Hall and he in Baltimore.

⁸⁷On Carter's concern with innocence, see RC to John Maund, 18 May 1795, SSR; RC to [?], n.d. [1795], ibid., RC to William Hill, 28 July 1794, ibid. On the effects of death on young children see John Bowlby, *Loss, Sadness and Depression* (New York: Basic Books, 1980). For a broader view see Ernest Becker, *The Denial of Death* (New York: The Free Press, 1973).

⁸⁸"Power and Dominion [are] . . . Enemies to Christ's Kingdom. . . . do not seek after Power in the natural world." RC, "A Plan to Unite an Independent Congregation," *The New-Church Messenger*, 62 (22 June 1982), 404. See also Swedenborg, *A Summary Exposition* and idem, *Heaven and its Wonders and Hell*.

⁸⁹Morton, *Robert Carter*, ch. 9. For Carter's attempt to help his freed slaves see RC to Elder Dawson, Nov. 1793, DU; RC to Elder Dawson, 22 Feb. 1794, LC; RC to Mordecai Miller, 7 Dec. 1803, ibid.

⁹⁰RC to Mrs. Spencer Ball, 13, May, 11 Aug. 1795, LC; RC to Elder Benjamin Dawson, 9, 16 Aug. 1796, ibid.

⁹¹RC to John T. Carter, 21 May 1795, ibid.; RC to George Carter, 25 Feb. 1795, ibid.; RC to John James Maund, 28 Feb. 1795, ibid.

⁹²RC, Religious Writings, 11-15, SSR.

⁹³RC to John Tasker Carter, 21 April 1794, LC.

⁹⁴RC to Francis Bailey, 28 Feb. 1791, SSR; RC to John Maund, 18 May 1795, ibid.

⁹⁵RC to Ralph Mather, 5 Aug. 1793, ibid.; RC, Wastebook, 12, 26 Jan., 2, 9 Feb., 15, 29 June, 13 July, 3, 10 Aug. 1794, 5 July 1795, LC; RC, Invoice Book, 16, 23 June, 1, 25 Sept., 3, 10 Nov. 1793, DU. Carter's commitment to Swedenborgianism was firm but not rigid. As early as 1792, when he was actively proselytizing on behalf of the New Jerusalem Church, Carter wrote "I apprehend in all cases where the sense, in the writings of the inspired E[manuel] S[wedenborg], is plain, that Jerusalemites should adopt & maintain the information therein—but not otherwise." Although he occasionally attended Quaker meetings in 1793 and 1795, there is no indication that he died "disillusioned" with Swedenborgianism and as late as 1802 he was still collecting the writings of Swedenborg. See RC to John Cooper et al., 10 May 1792, SSR; RC, Invoice Book, 17 Oct., 1 Dec. 1793, ibid.; RC, Daybook 16: 119, ibid.; RC, Wastebook, 30 Oct. 1795, LC. For another perspective see Marguerite Beck Block, *The New Church in the New World: A Study of Swedenborgianism in America* (New York: Octagon Books, Inc., 1968), 83-90.

⁹⁶See RC to J. T. Carter, Geo. Carter and J. J. Maund, 10 June 1798, LC; RC to John Purviance, 30 Oct. 1801, SSR; RC to Thomas Swan, 13 Oct. 1801, LC; RC to John James Maund, 17 March 1800, ibid.; RC to George Carter, 7 June 1800, ibid.

⁹⁷RC to Harriot Maund, 30 May 1803, LC.

⁹⁸On the relationship of "insiders" to "outsiders" in American life see R. Laurence Moore, "Insiders and Outsiders in American Historical Narrative and American History," *American Historical Review*, 87 (April 1982), 390-423.

⁹⁹In general see Breen, *Tobacco Culture*; Robert P. Sutton, "Nostalgia, Pessimism, and Malaise, the Doomed Aristocrat in Late-Jeffersonian Virginia," *Virginia Magazine of History and Biography*, 76 (January 1968), 41-55; Charles Royster, *Light-Horse Harry Lee and the Legacy of the American Revolution* (New York: Alfred A. Knopf, 1981), esp. 80-81; Emory Evans, "Virginia's Old Political Elite"; Daniel P. Jordan, *Political Leadership in Jefferson's Virginia* (Charlottesville: Univ. of Virginia Press, 1983); William Taylor, *Cavalier and Yankee: The Old South and American National Character* (New York: Braziller, 1961).

*AUTHOR'S NOTE

I WANT TO ALERT THE AMERICAN QUARTERLY'S READERS THAT MY SPRING 1986 (38:1) article, "The Early Republic's Supernatural Economy in the American Northeast, 1780-1830," quoted two documents that have since been proved forgeries made by Mark W. Hoffman, a Salt Lake City documents dealer. On January 23, 1987, Hoffman pled guilty to two counts of murder and confessed to forging a series of documents relating to Joseph Smith, Jr., the Mormon prophet. Hoffman killed two people with pipe bombs to prevent discovery of his profitable forgeries (Robert Lindsey, "Mormon Document Dealer Pleads Guilty to Murdering Two in 1985," The New York Times 24 Jan. 1987: 1, 8). Hoffman sold the forged documents to the Church of Jesus Christ of Latter-day Saints. Convinced of their authenticity, the Church made public two of those documents in the spring of 1985: (1) Martin Harris to William W. Phelps, 23 Oct. 1830 (published in The Church of Jesus Christ of Latter-day Saints, Church News 28 April 1985: 6), and (2) Joseph Smith, Jr., to Josiah Stowell, 18 June 1825 (in ibid., 12 May 1985: 10).

I also believed the documents authentic. My article quotes the Smith letter at the top of page 11 and the Harris letter near the top of page 14. My article was written and accepted for publication before the Church released the two documents; I added quotations from the letters to my final draft to illustrate points already documented from other sources. Therefore, to my mind, the article's interpretation of treasure seeking stands independently of the two quotations. I wish I could excise the two quotations but I would not alter my argument. In particular, I think that there remains abundant, strong evidence that Joseph Smith, Jr. engaged in treasure seeking. This evidence was essential to Mark W. Hoffman's ability to craft such clever forgeries.

Alan Taylor
Institute of Early American History and Culture
Williamsburg, Virginia

THE EARLY REPUBLIC'S SUPERNATURAL ECONOMY: TREASURE SEEKING IN THE AMERICAN NORTHEAST, 1780-1830

ALAN TAYLOR

Institute of Early American History and Culture

IN 1804 DANIEL LAMBERT'S NEIGHBORS IN THE RURAL TOWN OF CANAAN. MAINE of the upper Kennebec River Valley were impressed by his apparent new wealth. According to the traveler Edward Augustus Kendall, Lambert, like most of his

John Quidor, *Money Diggers* (1832), Courtesy, The Brooklyn Museum.

I appreciate the generous and invaluable research assistance provided by Rita M. Breton, Edward D. Ives, Danny D. Smith, Ronald W. Walker, and David Watters. I am also grateful to John L. Brooke, Richard L. Bushman, Robert A. Gross, David Hall, James A. Henretta, David Kaplan, Marvin Meyers, Richard "Pete" Moss, and Laurel Thatcher Ulrich for improving this essay with their helpful criticism. Karen Bowden and Julia Walkling of the Maine Humanities Council provided the encouragement, moral and financial, that got the essay started.

neighbors, had been a poor farmer and logger "in a very abject condition of life." So it attracted intense and widespread interest when Lambert and his two grown sons suddenly appeared in public mounted on good horses and wearing expensive clothes: twin marks of successful gentlemen. They ceased working on their homestead and idled their days away in the taverns of Canaan and adjoining Norridgewock. Daniel Lambert added immeasurably to his local popularity by buying round after round for his neighbors who gathered there to drink and gape at his fine appearance. He increased their consternation by ostentatiously lighting his pipe with burning bank-notes.[1]

Lacking any other apparent explanation, his neighbors attributed Daniel Lambert's sudden wealth to the discovery of buried pirate treasure. Despite Canaan's location dozens of miles from navigation, the inhabitants readily believed that Lambert had found a treasure chest because, as Kendall explained, "The settlers of Maine, like all the other settlers in New England indulge an unconquerable expectation of finding money buried in the earth." Indeed, backcountry folk insisted that troves of pirate treasure guarded by evil spirits pockmarked the New England countryside even in locales far from the coast. Daniel Lambert's reputed occult skills in handling divining rods further encouraged his neighbors' suspicions. Initially, the Lamberts remained guardedly mum, but in time hints of discovered treasure escaped from Daniel's lips. He needed to say no more, for rapid word-of-mouth fleshed out the remaining details. "Lambert was pronounced to be one of those fortunate persons who, born under a certain planetary aspect, are endowed with various and extraordinary powers: and he was soon found to possess enchanted mineral rods, which had been grown in the mystic form, and been cut at the proper age of the moon," Kendall recorded. Soon "nothing was talked of but Lambert and his gold; and every day gave birth to new histories of the chest that had been found, and of its immeasurable contents." Lambert confirmed the reports by publicly demonstrating his divining ability to locate a gold coin buried, as a test, in a field.[2]

Lambert's apparent good fortune inspired his neighbors' fervent hopes of discovering, and intense efforts to secure, their own treasure chests. Kendall quoted an eyewitness to the intense excitement: "All hands are digging in search of money, to the neglect of tilling their lands, and securing their crops. Days and nights are spent by many person, in digging up old swamps and deserts, sixty, seventy and eighty miles from *navigation*." Lambert encouraged this emulation by assisting several digging parties. In 1851 John W. Hanson recalled, "Gradually, he inoculated the entire population of the Kennebec valley with a treasure-seeking mania, and people in all conditions of life, were found digging from Anson to Seguin, and all along the coast, even to Rhode Island." Hanson concluded, "The excitement so universal and intense, can hardly be realized at the present day." It ended in June, 1804, when Lambert's sudden disappearance revealed that he had discovered no chest, but had led his neighbors on in order to obtain their livestock on undeserved credit.[3]

The outbreak of mass treasure seeking in the Kennebec Valley in 1804 raises two questions. First, was this a unique episode, or evidence of a widespread and systematic set of beliefs? In other words, how accurate was Kendall's assessment that many rural Yankees believed in the widespread existence of treasure chests and in the possibility of employing occult techniques to discover and recover them? If Kendall was essentially correct, a second question follows: why did this particular and peculiar set of beliefs thrive in the rural Northeast during the late eighteenth and early nineteenth centuries, and what do these treasure beliefs tell us about the concerns and aspirations of these rural folk? Travelers' accounts from this period stress just what a sharp dealer the rural Yankee was. Similarly, recent investigations of rural transactions and economic relationships reveal shrewd complexity and precise calculations. Why did such astute people cherish incredible fantasies of finding buried treasure? The persistence of this complex of implausible beliefs in the face of repeated frustration argues that they were important to sustaining the rural Yankee's self-image and way of life. Treasure seeking offers valuable insight into the world-view of rural Americans prior to the industrial revolution—a subject of great current interest to early American historians.[4]

Treasure seeking's proliferation was symptomatic of the early Republic's rapid population growth, geographic expansion, cultural volatility, and economic transition to capitalism in the hinterlands. Treasure seeking lay at the murky intersection of material aspiration and religious desire; it possessed a dual nature: functioning at once as a supernatural economy (an alternative to a disappointing natural economy) and as a materialistic faith (an alternative to unsatisfactory abstract religion). Treasure seeking met the needs of some people who felt troubled by their culture's increasing premium on possessive individualism and religious voluntarism, by promising both quick wealth and a sense of power over the supernatural world.[5]

TREASURE

Because few treasure seekers left any documents, and because no institution recorded their activities, no precise calculation of treasure-hunting episodes is possible. Yet a canvas of travelers' accounts, town histories, and other antiquarian sources for the American Northeast documents over forty incidents where groups of rural folk employed occult techniques to seek buried treasure, generally in very unlikely inland locales, and usually during the fifty years between 1780 and 1830 (see Table 1). Most episodes involved small parties, handfuls of men bound to share equally in any discoveries. Tradition held that a minimum of three (a particularly magical number that occurs repeatedly in treasure lore) seekers was essential for a successful dig. In 1831 the Palmyra, New York newspaper described the previous decade's widespread treasure seeking:

The MANIA of money-digging soon began rapidly to diffuse itself through many parts of the country; men and women without distinction of age or sex became marvelous wise in the occult sciences, many dreamed, and others saw visions disclosing to them deep in the bowels of the earth, rich and shining treasures, and to facilitate those *mighty* mining operations . . . divers devices and implements were invented, and although the SPIRIT was always able to retain his precious charge, these discomfited as well as deluded beings would on a succeeding night return to their toil, not in the least doubting that success would eventually attend their labors.

In 1825 a Windsor, Vermont newspaper observed, "We could name, if we pleased, at least five hundred respectable men who do in the simplicity and sincerity of their hearts believe that immense treasures lie concealed upon our Green Mountains, many of whom have been for a number of years industriously and perseveringly engaged in digging it up."[6]

Treasure seekers left behind considerable monuments attesting to their fervor, industry, and numbers. Writing in 1729 from Philadelphia, Benjamin Franklin and Joseph Breitnal noted, "You can hardly walk half a mile out of Town on any side, without observing several Pits dug with that Design, and perhaps some lately opened." In Pittston, Maine's "Pebble Hills" diggers excavated pits eighty feet deep. In Frankfort, Maine, a century of treasure seeking leveled a hundred-foot gravel mound named "Codlead"; observers estimated that the diggers removed enough soil to lay a twenty-mile railroad bed. A mid-nineteenth-century writer noted that rural New England abounded "in excavations, like those of the gold regions of California." Seekers dug dozens of tunnels into the solid rock face of a Bristol, Vermont cliff in futile search for a lost Spanish mine. In the later nineteenth century a visitor to the town found the surface of Bristol Notch "literally honeycombed with holes a few feet in depth, where generation after generation of money-diggers have worked their superstitious energies. . . . " William Little of Weare, New Hampshire noted, "Great holes, found in many wild, out-of-the-way places, made nobody knows by whom, show how many silent parties have dug in the night of [Captain] Kidd's gold."[7]

The varied accounts of rural treasure seeking describe a remarkably similar phenomenon throughout the American Northeast. The presumed identity of the treasure buriers was the only significant variation between regions. In New Jersey, southeastern Pennsylvania, eastern New York, and all of New England except Vermont tradition attributed the treasures to seventeenth-century pirates and especially to Captain Kidd. In Vermont this tradition overlapped with rumors that early Spanish explorers had opened, abandoned, and sealed mines filled with valuable ores and coins. The Yankee settlers in western New York and northern Pennsylvania could search for Captain Kidd's treasures, Spanish mines and coin caches, robbers' plunder, lost Revolutionary War payrolls, and the antediluvian hoards left behind by America's presumed original, ancient inhabitants. The eclecticism resembled the area's religious diversity. Further west, in the upper Ohio Valley, the Kidd tradition dissipated and a mixture of lost Spanish mines and ancient Indian treasures lured the treasure seekers.[8]

Seekers preferred to dig during the summer because, as Joseph Smith, Sr., of Palmyra, New York explained, "the heat of the sun caused the chests of money to rise near the top of the ground." Almost all seekers insisted that digging could only succeed at night, particularly between midnight and dawn. They also thought that the phase of the moon affected their chances of success, but disagreed over whether a new moon or a full moon drew treasure chests closer to the surface.[9]

Dreams, especially if thrice repeated, guided seekers to a suspected treasure. For example, after an angel appeared three times in a dream to Joseph Smith, Jr., the Mormon prophet, he hurried to the indicated spot near Palmyra, New York and discovered his "Golden Bible." Apparently the rural Yankee's subconscious was peculiarly concerned with finding money. In the 1780s Silas Hamilton of Whitingham, Vermont kept an elaborate journal of every treasure rumor he could collect. His journal records forty-four informants' information about thirty-two treasures located in twenty-two different communities from the Hudson Valley to Maine's Seguin Island and reaching into inland Vermont and New Hampshire. Dreams revealed the location of nineteen of those treasures.[10]

In the early nineteenth century, treasure seekers turned increasingly to "seer-stones" or "peep-stones" as a more ready and reliable alternative to dreams. To obtain visions revealing a treasure's location, a "glass-looker" or "seer" placed his stone in a hat and stuck his face in so as to exclude all light, sometimes staring for hours at a stretch. The seer-stone of an eighteen-year-old Rochester, New York boy named Smith (apparently no relation to Joseph Smith, Jr.) was described as "a round stone the size of a man's fist" that on one side displayed "all the dazzling splendor of the sun in full blaze—and on the other, the clearness of the moon." A seer needed to find the particular stone that was right for him. At age fourteen, Joseph Smith, Jr., of Palmyra, New York looked into a hat at the stone belonging to another seer; according to Smith's father, "It proved not to be the right stone for him; but he could see some things, and, among them, he saw the stone, and where it was, in which he could see whatever he wished to see." Digging at that spot uncovered the stone that enabled the future Mormon prophet to begin his career as a seer.[11]

To ascertain the precise spot to dig, the seekers employed a divining rod: a freshly-cut, forked witch hazel (or, sometimes a peach) branch with one eighteen- to twenty-four inch prong held in each fist and the third, center prong pointing directly away from the "conductor," who addressed his rod in a soft whisper, "work to the money." Then he advanced "with a slow and creeping step" over the suspected spot until a strong downward jerk indicated the proper

* spot. In a June 18, 1825 letter Joseph Smith, Jr. described an alternative method to divine treasure with a rod:

you Should not dig more untill you first discover if any valluables remain you know the treasure must be guarded by some clever spirit and if such is discovered so also is the treasure so do this take a hasel stick one yard long being new Cut and cleave it Just in the middle and lay it asunder on the mine so that both inner parts of the stick may look one right against the other one inch distant and if there is treasure after a while you shall see them draw and Join together again of themselves let me know how it is.[12]

As Smith's letter indicates, locating a treasure was but the early and relatively easy stage in the long, complex process of recovery; it was merely the preliminary to the real challenge of wresting the treasure away from its fierce guardian spirits, the ghosts of men sacrificed by the treasure buriers. Spirits did their job well, staging terrifying spectacles and frightening noises to scare off the treasure seekers. In Palmyra and Manchester, New York during the 1820s the seekers fled, once, when a nearby log schoolhouse "was suddenly lighted up," again when "a large man who appeared to be eight or nine feet high came and sat on the ridge of the [nearby] barn, and motioned to them that they must leave," and, a third time, when a spectral company of horsemen charged their hole.[13]

To fend off the guardian spirits, the seekers laid out protective magic circles, or, better still, three concentric circles, around the digging ground. For some seekers a surrounding groove scooped out with a silver spoon or incised with a sword blade sufficed. The failure of these relatively simple circles encouraged experimentation with evermore elaborate designs. In 1833 William Stafford of Manchester, New York described one of Joseph Smith, Sr.'s magic circles:

> Joseph, Sen. first made a circle twelve or fourteen feet in diameter. This circle, said he, contains the treasure. He then stuck in the ground a row of witch hazel sticks, around the said circle, for the purpose of keeping off the evil spirits. Within this circle he made another, of about eight or ten feet in diameter. He walked around three times on the periphery of the last circle, muttering to himself something which I could not understand. He next stuck a steel rod in the centre of the circles, and then enjoined profound silence upon us lest we should arouse the evil spirit who had charge of these treasures.

A party led by his son, Joseph Smith, Jr., drove stakes around their circle and one man with a drawn and brightly polished sword orbited the digging site while the rest shoveled. Ritual readings from astrological tracts and religious books frequently figured in the more complex circles. During the 1820s in the upper Ohio Valley diggers broke the enchantment, known there as "the single and double Spanish cross," placed by departing Spaniards over their mines, by laying out a circle large enough to enclose all their tailings; then they dropped nine new nails around the circle at equal distances; during the digging the conductor walked the circle "with the course of the sun" while reading a chapter in the "Apocrypha" where the angel Raphael exorcises the devil.[14]

Because the buriers had spilled blood to fix guardian spirits over their treasure, seekers often spilled animal's blood around or in their circles to help break the protective enchantment. In 1807, as a ten-year-old boy in Catskill, New York, the future publisher and Republican politician Thurlow Weed participated in a party of seekers who brought along a black cat and cut its throat over the digging ground, "and the precise spot was indicated by the direction the blood spurted." Joseph Smith, Jr., reputedly sacrificed either pure white or jet black sheep or dogs to lay out magic circles of blood. In the 1780s Silas Hamilton, Whitingham, Vermont's most enterprising treasure seeker, recorded in his journal a particularly elaborate design for a magic circle:

> tak nine Steel Rods about ten or twelve inches in Length Sharp or Piked to Perce into the Erth, and let them be Besmeared with fresh blood from a hen mixed with hogdung. Then mak two surkels round the hid Treasure one of Sd surkles a Little Larger in Surcumference than the hid Treasure lays in the Erth the other Surkel Sum Larger still, and as the hid treasure is wont to move to the North of South, East or West Place your Rods as is Discribed on the other Sid of this leaf.

A diagram on the reverse side of the journal page showed the rods placed between the two circles with their heads alternately on the inner and outer circle, totally surrounding the treasure.[15]

To preserve their magic circle's efficacy, seekers strictly adhered to "the rule of silence," for any spoken word would, at least, cause the treasure to settle beyond their reach into the bowels of the earth or, at worst, imperil their lives by unleashing enraged spirits. By creating some frightening spectacle, spirits often provoked the seekers into involuntary cries of alarm. Sometimes a mishap caused them to cry out. When one member of a Middletown, Vermont digging party stepped on the foot of another, he bellowed, "Get off from my toes." The conductor sprang out of the hole, yelling, "The money is gone, flee for your lives" and all followed him in terrified flight. More often some digger exclaimed with joy when he struck a suspected treasure chest, only to lapse into dismay, if not terror, as his hasty words caused the chest to plunge out of reach. In 1814 a party of Rochester, New York treasure seekers barely escaped with their lives when the conducter exclaimed, "Damn me, I've found it!" With that, a local newspaper recorded, "The charm was broken!—the scream of demons—the chattering of spirits—and hissing of serpents rent the air, and the treasure moved." No doubt the rule of silence helped put a lid on expressions of doubt and futility, and thereby kept a party at their task. If some disgruntled member did give vent to his frustration he became, for the others, the scapegoat for failure.[16]

Yet even if the diggers located a treasure, carefully laid out their circles, and proceeded in perfect silence, success usually eluded them, for, upon striking a suspected treasure chest the seekers confronted their final challenge: to break the enchantment. If they failed to do so, when they reached for the chest the spiteful spirits would violently attack, or simply wrest the chest away at the last minute. In 1804 an eyewitness reported the Kennebec Valley seekers' repeated frustrations, "Doleful sighs and dismal noises are heard; the chest moves in the earth, almost out of their very hands!" In 1826 Jonathan Thompson, one of Joseph Smith, Jr.'s compatriots, testified in court that "on account of enchantment, the trunk kept settling away from under them while digging; that notwithstanding they continued constantly removing the dirt, yet the trunk kept about the same distance from them." Most chests moved down deeper into the earth but one avidly sought pot of money in Braintree, Vermont moved horizontally; when diggers neared "the pot moved, the ground being seen to rise and fall in the direction in which the treasure took its departure." At one point the persistent seekers trapped the elusive pot by surrounding it with a magic circle of "old scythes stuck upright in the ground to prevent its escape." Unfortunately, a jealous onlooker pulled up one of the scythes and allowed the pot to flee.[17]

Occasional accidental discoveries of small coin caches along the New England coast encouraged the seekers, but few, if any, of the purposeful parties ever bested the guardian spirits (with the possible exception of Joseph Smith, Jr., and his "Golden Bible"). Nonetheless, seekers persisted year after year, decade after decade, even generation after generation. John W. Hanson noted that in Pittston, Maine despite unceasing failure, "there has hardly been a single summer which has not found men, wasting their time, and presenting a spectacle of folly, as they sifted and examined the locality for gold. As late as last year, 1851, there were several who were thus at work." Similarly, treasure diggers continued to excavate nocturnally in the hills of Pennsylvania's Susquehanna County and Vermont's Green Mountains into the 1870s.[18]

These treasure tales' fantastic details suggest that they were nothing more than folklore, elaborate fictions bearing little or no resemblance to actual events. Some may have been tall tales woven to explain away failures, a way of turning personal humiliations into public entertainment for the treasure seeker, to escape public ridicule by emerging as a locally celebrated storyteller with a good tale to tell. At other times fraudulent conductors enlisted assistants or the power of suggestion to shape the impressions of their jumpy and credulous followers. Yet some evidence does not fit these simple explanations of defensive or calculated deceit: contemporary letters, affidavits, and court depositions in which treasure seekers soberly described their confrontations with spirits. And seekers usually impressed contemporary observers with an utter conviction that their supernatural encounters had been real. Waitsfield, Vermont's nineteenth-century chronicler wrote of a local treasure seeker, "The most ridiculous part of the matter, is the fact well attested, that Mr. Savage believed all this, as long as he lived, and was never ridiculed out of it." Similarly, Martin Harris of Palmyra, New York believed his treasure-seeking neighbors' tales of spectral

appearances because different participants on separate occasions related the
* same details "and they seemed in earnest—I knew they were in earnest." In an
October 23, 1830 letter describing his confidence in Joseph Smith, Jr.'s
supernatural powers, Harris matter-of-factly recounted:

> Joseph Smith Jr first come to my notice in the year 1824. In the summer of that
> year I contracted with his father to build a fence on my property. In the course of
> that work I aproach Joseph & ask how it is in a half day you put up what requires
> your father & 2 brothers a full day working together? He says I have not been with
> out assistance but can not say more only you better find out. The next day I take the
> older Smith by the arm & he says Joseph can see any thing he wishes by looking at a
> stone. Joseph often sees Spirits here with great kettles of coin money. It was spirits
> who brought up rock because Joseph made no attempt on their money. I latter dream
> I converse with spirits which let me count their money. When I awake I have in my
> hand a dollar coin which I take for a sign. Joseph describes what I seen in every
> particular. Says he, the spirits are greived, so I through back the dollar.

Harris felt no need to explain to his correspondent, William W. Phelps of
Canandagua, New York what strikes a modern eye as inexplicable. Writing in
1826, a skeptical but fair-minded observer provided the soundest assessment:
"If there be a fraud, the diviners themselves are the first deceived, and the
greatest dupes."[19]

These supernatural encounters were very "real" to those who experienced
them. Childhood exposure to treasure tales and their careful performance of
elaborate ceremonies at the digging site created a nervous expectation to see the
extraordinary. Long hours of strenuous, nighttime digging by flickering lanterns
in dark, remote, and cold locales engendered exhaustion. Adherence to strict
procedures, especially the rule of silence, produced sustained tension. Finally,
seekers tended to bring along a generous supply of alcohol and drank freely to
fortify their nerves and warm their bodies. These circumstances developed their
anxiously expectant frame of mind to the point that one participant's suggestion,
or any unexpected sight or sound, could trigger a group hallucination.
Subsequent, repeated narration to others rapidly confirmed, refined, and
elaborated the experience.

TRANSITION

The American treasure seekers' beliefs were neither indigenous nor new. In
the sixteenth and seventeenth centuries their English and German forbears avidly
employed divining rods, magic circles, astrological books, and religious rituals
to wrest supposedly abundant buried treasures from evil guardian spirits. Until
the mid-eighteenth century any New England treasure seekers kept a very low
profile because of Puritanism's rigorous hostility to magic. But Pennsylvania's
religious tolerance promoted an ethnic and religious diversity that allowed magic

to prosper, particularly in association with German pietism and Quaker mysticism. In 1729 a Philadelphia newspaper essay by Benjamin Franklin and Joseph Breitnal described local treasure seeking's extent:

> There are amongst us great numbers of honest Artificers and labouring People, who fed with a Vain Hope of growing suddenly rich, neglect their Business, almost to the ruining of themselves and Families, and voluntarily endure abundance of fatigue in a fruitless search after imaginary treasures. They wander thro' the Woods and Bushes by Day to discover the Marks and Signs; at Midnight they repair to the hopeful spot with Spades and Pickaxes; full of Expectation they labour violently, trembling at the same time in every Joint, thro fear of certain malicious Demons who are said to haunt and guard such Places.[20]

Apparently, it was not until the late eighteenth century that treasure seeking proliferated in the Yankees' new backcountry settlements in northern New England and western New York. Settling there created both the opportunity and the desire to practice treasure seeking. Migration to the frontier removed settlers from the chilling influence of "enlightened" gentlemen and learned clergy equally hostile to occult beliefs as "irrational superstition," and as proof that rural folk were all too ready to forsake the disciplined labor that was their proper duty. Kendall quoted a gentleman who insisted, "[treasure seekers] become insolent and saucy, neglect economy and industry, and every benefit to society; and moral habits decay, wherever these ideas prevail." By the late eighteenth century rural Yankees were not immune to their wider culture's increasing emphasis on measuring a man's worth by his ability to accumulate wealth. However, they settled in backcountry district where poor soil, a harsh climate, and relative isolation from markets impeded their acquisition of prosperity from the natural economy. None of these circumstances "determined" that the hill folk would seek treasure. A multitude of religious sects and voluntary societies offered their adherents a variety of formulas for greater order and security in an increasingly fluid and disconcerting world. Treasure hunting with occult methods was but another response to the same social flux.[21]

For lack of quantifiable sources, the economic and social status of those who employed occult techniques to dig for buried treasure cannot be ascertained with precision. Literary sources indicate that in the early eighteenth century treasure seeking was not unknown among men of property and extensive education. But, as with witchcraft beliefs in the previous century, treasure beliefs lost their elite adherents to the Enlightenment's secular rationality. Thomas Forrest's satirical 1767 play on treasure seekers, *The Disappointment: or the Force of Credulity* suggested that the emerging cultural division over magic emerged along the lines of social class. The plot revolved around "four humorous gentlemen" making dupes out of four treasure-seeking tradesmen; a paternalistic desire to disabuse their humbler neighbors and restore them to "honesty and industry" and to a resigned contentment "with their respective stations" motivated the four gentlemen.[22]

This contempt for treasure seeking became universal among the genteel by the early nineteenth as part of their wider criticism of the common folk for inadequate ambition, lackluster work discipline, labor, and attachment to tradition. These critics saw treasure seeking as one more irrational obstacle to the necessary reeducation of rural folk to perform properly in a more enlightened, more commercial world. In 1826 an astute observer noted that "from north to south, from east to west" many "respectable" men "of large information, and of the most exemplary lives" continued to believe that divining rods could detect underground water; but "in all parts of the land, if the diviner hunts for metals, he becomes distrusted by the better sort of men." In 1842 the young Boston Brahmin and future historian Francis Parkman visited the ruins of Fort William Henry on the banks of Lake George, New York. He found "that some fools had come up the lake with a wizard and a divining rod to dig for money in the ruins. They went at midnight for many successive nights and dug till daylight." This contributed to Parkman's sour conclusion: "There would be no finer place of gentlemen's seats than this, but now, for the most part, it is occupied by a race of boors about as uncouth, mean, and stupid as the hogs they seem chiefly to delight in."²³

This attitude appears in James Fenimore Cooper's 1823 novel *The Pioneers*, a fictional account of the settlement of Cooperstown, his childhood village in western New York. Marmaduke Temple (the novelist's scarcely disguised father, the wealthy land-speculator Judge William Cooper) denounces a treasure seeker named Jotham Riddle as "that dissatisfied, shiftless, lazy, speculating fellow! He who changes his county every three years, his farm every six months, and his occupation every season." Riddle is fatally burned in a forest fire while pursuing his folly. On his deathbed he explained that "his reasons for believing in a mine were extracted from the lips of a sibyl, who, by looking in a magic glass, was enabled to discover the hidden treasures of the earth. Such superstition was frequent in the new settlements; and after the first surprise was over, the better part of the community forgot the subject."²⁴

Treasure beliefs persisted among rural folk with locally defined intellectual horizons. An observer considered seekers as "the simple-hearted people in the agricultural districts of the country." Another writer described Morris County's seekers as "aged, abstemious, honest, judicious, simple church members." The extensive treasure seeking inspired by Daniel Lambert captured the interest of virtually everyone, male and female, prosperous and poor, in the Kennebec Valley, with the noteworthy exception of the merchants—those with the widest knowledge of, and most regular ties with, the outside world of commerce and ideas. Schooled in oral traditions and the Bible, rural folk clung to their belief in the direct intervention of spiritual beings in their daily lives. In Morris County, New Jersey during the 1780s "the generality were apprehensive of witches riding them" inflicting illnesses on their families, disturbing their livestock, and interfering with the churning of butter. Consequently the inhabitants were ready to "spend much time in investigating curiosities." In a letter written from Thomaston, Maine in 1805 William Scales observed, "The belief of witches, pharies, apparitions, hobgobblings, and all manner of ridiculous fables prevail in these parts." Given such beliefs it was not unreasonable to identify spirits as the obstacle separating rural folk from the riches they needed to prove their worth in an increasingly competitive society.[25]

Yet while traditional folk beliefs provided the raw intellectual materials from which these rural folk constructed their treasure seeking, this was a process of creative reconstitution. The treasure seeking practiced in the American Northeast during the early Republic was something more than a timeless survivor; it was an attempt to sustain a folk tradition by adapting it to the demands of a new era. Rural folk had not fully left behind the traditional world of spirit beings and enchantments but they were not unaware of the claims made by rational scientific enquiry. Like the nineteenth century's spiritualists the treasure seekers were engaged in a quasi-science that through empirical experimentation sought to perfect practical techniques for understanding and exploiting the spirit world. These seekers sought to bring their spiritual beliefs into conformity with their notions of rational inquiry and logical proof. They meant to prove to themselves that they were canny investigators rather than credulous fools. As the historian Klaus Hansen notes, treasure seeking "frequently derived from logically consistent connections between religious belief, a specific need, and an empirical attitude toward nature." Similarly, folklorist Gerald T. Hurley observes that in treasure tales the spirits behave "according to a simple common-sense logic once the premise of the supernatural is accepted." A rather naive empiricism characterized the treasure seekers' world-view; for example, one seeker became, characteristically, a thorough Universalist, "believing that all mankind would finally be saved, and however vile, made pure and holy," as a result of his observation of a puddle of putrid water that upon evaporation formed clouds of pure moisture. The historian Whitney R. Cross nicely captures the rural Yankee's personality: "they were credulous in a particular way: they believed only upon evidence. Their observation, to be sure, was often inaccurate and usually incomplete, but when they arrived at a conclusion by presumably foolproof processes their adherence to it was positively fanatic." A 1791 account of the treasure seekers in New Jersey's Morris County said as much: "when any curiosities are presented to them, they are zealous in the pursuit of knowledge, and anxious to know their termination."[26]

Persistent failure and insistent belief progressively promoted evermore complex techniques and tools in the search for treasure. Unwilling to surrender their treasure beliefs, seekers concluded that they needed more sophisticated methods. They remained confident that, by trial and error, they would ultimately obtain the right combination of conductor, equipment, time, magic circle, silence, and ritual. As a result, the precise performance of complicated procedures increasingly characterized treasure seeking. In 1823 Joseph Smith, Jr. dreamed that a guardian spirit/angel pointed out a treasure that the young man could recover on an appointed day "if he would strictly follow his directions." These including dressing in "an old-fashioned suit of clothes of the same [black] color," bringing "a napkin to put the treasure in," riding to the spot on "a black horse with a switch tail," demanding the golden book "in a certain name, and after obtaining it he must go directly away, and neither lay it down nor look behind him." But, because of the imprecision in Smith's performance, the spirit snatched away the treasure on the appointed day for three successive years, before grudgingly giving it up on the fourth. Metal divining rods and mineral balls began to supplant mere witch hazel or peach rods, and seer-stones gradually eclipsed dreams as finding aids. These more complex tools and techniques increased the importance of pretended experts in the occult. As an expression of economic fantasy, perhaps treasure seeking was peculiarly sensitive to observed changes in the natural economy, and mirrored the increasing importance of substantial capital and expert knowledge.[27]

The Morris County seekers attributed their repeated frustration by hostile "hobgoblins . . . to the mismanagement of their conducter, as not having sufficient knowledge to dispel those apparitions." Seeking "a person whose knowledge descended into the bowels of the earth, and could reveal the secret things of darkness," they recruited Connecticut-born Ransom Rogers to lead their operations because of "his extensive knowledge of every art and science." Because of his "pretended copious knowledge in chemistry" Ransom could readily "raise or dispel good or evil spirits." He began by conducting a seance where a helpful spirit told the company of forty seekers that they would never recover the treasure they sought "unless they proceeded regular and without variance" in performing Rogers' complicated ceremonies over the next several months. In subsequent seances the seekers began with prayer on bended knees before parading around the room in an order "according to their age," that circuited "as many times as there were persons in number." They then cast blank sheets of paper into the center of their circle, "fell with their faces to the earth" and prayed with their eyes closed for the spirits to enter and inscribe directions for them.[28]

Treasure tales are often found in peasant cultures. In his work on the treasure tales of rural Mexico in this century, the anthropologist George M. Foster argues that a world-view of "limited good" characterizes peasant societies; that, given their almost static available technology and their persistent scarcity of land, peasants conceive of resources as finite and see economic life as a sort of zero-sum game where it is rare for anyone to advance except at someone else's expense. To explain sudden good fortune, peasants insist that the newly rich must have made a pact with the devil to recover a treasure. A different emphasis—on active, avid participation in treasure seeking—characterizes the treasure tales in the early American Republic. This suggests that treasure seekers were in the midst of a transition from the world-view of limited good characteristic of peasant societies to the unlimited good promised by capitalism. They sensed scientific inquiry's potential but they had not fully forgotten their heritage of supernatural beliefs. They were beginning to feel capitalism's imperatives but still thought that sudden wealth could only be had from outside the natural economy. Consequently, they eagerly sought riches but clung to the notion that spiritual beings could assist or retard that acquisition. Rural folk located at that point in the evolution of popular economic attitudes were prepared to act the part of capitalists *as they understood it*: to employ the latest occult technology to manipulate the supernatural in order to tap the presumed abundance of treasure chests. This transition was particularly prolonged in rural regions where poorer folk predominated, in areas where economic growth lagged behind aspirations, and where religious beliefs were most heterogeneous.[29]

THE SUPERNATURAL ECONOMY

As a supernatural economy treasure seeking appealed to the relatively poor men and women dwelling in rural areas where commercial prosperity was little known, where economic growth did not keep pace with enhanced post-Revolutionary aspirations. Seekers were men whose minds accepted the notion of unlimited good but whose bodies dwelled in locales offering only limited opportunity. Their belief in an alternative, supernatural economy helped psychologically to bridge the gap between their real conditions and what their competitive society taught them to aspire to; recovering a treasure would redress the unjust variance between the seeker's condition and his self-image. When he heard a (false) report that his son had recovered a treasure, a Rutland, Vermont blacksmith rejoiced; "he declared he would never shoe another horse for a living, that he always thought he was born to a better destiny." Joseph Smith, Sr. was a failed petty capitalist whose attempt to export Vermont ginseng to the Orient had plunged his family into deprivation; in 1827 he declared that as a result of his son's discovery of the golden bible, "my family will be placed on a level above the generality of mankind." Kendall quoted a settler in Maine's Sandy River Valley in 1804: "We go on toiling like fools; digging the ground for the sake of a few potatoes, and neglecting the treasures that have been left by those that have been before us! For myself, I confess it, to my mortification, that I have been toiling all my life, to make a paltry living, and neglecting all the while, the means that have been long been in my hands of making a sudden and boundless fortune." Treasure chests symbolized the long-promised prosperity still awaiting marginal farmers; they wanted to believe that their fortunes lay all about them beneath the stony ground that so slowed their material advance. Peter Ingersoll of Palmyra, New York recalled a conversation with Joseph Smith, Sr. that perfectly illustrates this theme: "You notice, said he, the large stones on the top of the ground—we call them rocks, and they truly appear to be so, but they are in fact, most of them, chests of money raised by the heat of the sun."[30]

Substantial farmers who shared their humbler neighbors' localist perspective and traditional culture often patronized treasure seeking, providing tools, food, drink, sacrificial animals, and, sometimes, wages. Two prosperous Susquehanna Valley farmers, Oliver Harper of Harpersville, New York, and Josiah Stowell of South Bainbridge (now Afton), New York, supported many of Joseph Smith, Jr.'s treasure-seeking forays. One of the most zealous treasure seekers, Silas Hamilton of Whitingham, Vermont was his small community's principal landowner, frequent selectman, and first legislative representative; but he apparently disliked commercial men and their lawyers for he participated in Shays's Rebellion and received a display in the pillory for his pains. As eager seekers, the same members of the Wood family who acted as Middletown, Vermont's selectman, town clerk, and legislative representative lent their name to the local treasure-seeking outburst: the "Wood scrape."[31]

Yet treasure seeking pivoted around seers rather than patrons. Many episodes occurred without a prosperous patron but none without a charismatic seer who could inspire confidence in his peculiar occult talents. Seers invariably began in poverty. An account of Morris County's treasure seekers described seers as "some illiterate persons" with "a genius adequate to prepossess themselves in favor with many." Western New York's preeminent treasure seekers, the Palmyra Smiths, were conspicuously poor. Daniel Lambert was also a poor man whose small farm and winter logging promised no better future.[32]

A black skin, female gender, and adolescent age were all marks of powerlessness in the early Republic and one or some combination of the three often characterized seers. Joseph Smith, Jr. and the Rochester Smith were both adolescents. Women seemed particularly prone to treasure dreams and particularly skilled at using seer-stones. Eleven of the nineteen dreamers cited in Silas Hamilton's notebook were female. Prior to her death in 1838, Dinah Rollins, a poor widowed black woman, who dwelled in a leaky shack on the edge of town, conducted the treasure seekers in York, Maine. About 1815 a black adolescent known only as "Mike" parlayed his skill with a seer-stone into the leadership of the diggers in Pittston, Maine. In the late eighteenth century, James Marks, an aged black man from Warren, Massachusetts, convinced many of his neighbors that he had, as a boy, sailed with Kidd and could successfully conduct their treasure seeking.[33]

Because treasure seeking thrived in the backcountry where few men were prosperous, most of the men who followed seers were in tight economic straits. The 1791 account of Morris County, New Jersey's treasure seekers ascribed their "turn of mind" to their "indigence." Because so many could not pay Ransom Rogers' £12 assessment for gifts to the spirits, collection dragged on for months and eventually forced him to reduce the levy to £4-6. Thurlow Weed described the treasure hunting companions of his youth as "poor but credulous people." It seems likely that his father, a poor farmer and cart-man, participated; his father's life reiterates the persistent themes of restless migration and recurrent economic disappointment despite hard work, themes that run through the lives of so many of the known treasure hunters, including the Palmyra Smiths. Thurlow Weed remembered, "everything went wrong with him. Constant and hard labor failed to better his condition. . . . The consequence was that we were always poor, sometimes very poor." In July 1807 the traveler Christian Schultz visited Rome, New York and found a connection between the economic decay of a once-promising frontier community, and avid treasure seeking. "This village consists at present of about eighty houses; but it seems quite destitute of every kind of trade, and rather upon the decline. The only spirit which I perceived stirring among them was that of *money digging*; and the old fort betrayed evident signs of the prevalence of this mania, as it had literally been turned inside out for the purpose of discovering concealed treasure."[34]

Canaan and her sister town, Norridgewock, spawned the most extensive treasure-seeking episode. Possessed of an unproductive and stony soil, afflicted by the insistent demands of absentee land speculators for burdensome land payments, condemned by latitude to five-month-long winters, and located seventy miles by bad roads from tidewater market, the two towns could promise most of their inhabitants little more than a hard-earned subsistence. According to Canaan's mid-nineteenth-century historian, the settlers "were very poor and much addicted to intemperance." The town's name "became a byword and synonym for poverty and drunkenness." Similarly, in 1807 Kendall described, "Norridgewoc is not a paradise;—it is not a paradise, at least if vice, ignorance or poverty is incompatible with the definition! . . . Nothing, as I am assured, is more common, than for families to live for three months in the year without animal food, even that of salt-fish, and with no other resources than milk, potatoes and rum." According to Massachusetts state valuation returns, Canaan and Norridgewock possessed less than half as much property per taxpayer as the average for the Commonwealth as a whole. Originally settled in the 1770s, by 1804 the two communities were classic examples of aging frontier towns which had yet to fulfill their settlers' expectations.[35]

In a postscript to their 1801 tax return Canaan's appraisers went to unusual lengths to persuade the legislature that local poverty exceeded even the miserable statistical appearance. They insisted that "a considerable number" of the inhabitants were "very poor & their whole taxes abated." Only 48 of the 144 taxpayers owned frame houses and most of those were "of little value, without windows or chimneys, there being not more than 10 or 12 houses of the 48 of much value & the residue consist of log huts." The local saw and grist mills were "of an ordinary quality indeed & will scarce pay the annual repairs." Only half the taxpayers possessed barns and most of those were "destitute of doors & underpinning & rapidly decaying." The inhabitants' horses, oxen, steers, cows, and swine were all "of a small size" and "of a mean & ordinary quality." Men did not become rich in Canaan or Norridgewock by any ordinary chain of events. In an era that insisted that all worthy men would prosper, the inhabitants of these districts desperately needed some alternative path to riches.[36]

MATERIALISTIC FAITH

For many rural folk, treasure seeking was a materialistic extension of their Christian faith as well as a supernatural economy. For them the actual contest with the supernatural assumed an importance equal to recovering a treasure. The early Republic knew a fierce competition between rival religious denominations that cast doubt on the true path to salvation. Anxious for palpable reassurance that they had found the true path to salvation, religious seekers wanted direct contact with divinity; they yearned for a religion that they could experience physically. For some, no experience with the supernatural seemed more tangible than the pull of a divining rod or the precise creation of a magic circle. And to the seeker, successfully besting an evil spirit connoted a share of divine power, a reassuring sense of confidence that he shared in divine grace. Like the subsequent spiritualists, the treasure seekers regarded their activities as part of their "experimental" Christianity; treasure seeking was *not* anti-Christian.[37]

Seekers considered adherence to a strict moral code and unqualified faith as indispensable to success. Many rural folk reached the hopeful conclusion that God would signify His favor by bestowing material good fortune on the deserving. In 1844 Joseph Smith, Jr. explained to Brigham Young that "every man who lived on earth is entitled to a seer stone, and should have one, but they are kept from them in consequence of their wickedness." Ransom Rogers recruited "only those of a truly moral character, either belonging to the church or abstaining from profane company, and walking circumspectly." He told his seekers that the spirits insisted they "pray without ceasing for they were just spirits sent unto them to inform them, that they should have great possessions if they should persevere in the faith." Rogers told his followers that "as the apparitions knew all things, they must be careful to walk circumspectly, and refrain from all immorality, or they would stimulate the spirits to withhold from them the treasures." Prayers and religious books figured in most attempts to break an enchantment. When a party struck a suspected chest they generally paused to pray, for if anyone doubted that God would help them overcome the spirits, the treasure would escape. Inevitable frustration led to recriminations that some member's weak faith had robbed the rest of their just reward.[38]

Joseph Smith, Jr.'s spiritual crisis and consequent first vision in 1820 at age fourteen exemplifies how religious concern could lead to treasure seeking. He was deeply troubled by sectarian conflict and "often" asked himself, "Who of all these parties are right; or, are they all wrong together? If any of them be right, which is it, and how shall I know it?" Thereafter, at first as a treasure seer and eventually as the Mormon prophet, Smith sought regular, direct contact with his God. Hostile preachers' skepticism only reinforced his psychological need to validate his powers regularly by consulting his seer-stone and grappling with demonic spirits. Smith was not unique among treasure seekers in discovering God's voice within. A spirit told the mid-nineteenth-century spiritualist treasure seeker, Hiram Marble of Lynn, Massachusetts, "What shall you do? Seems to be the question. Follow your own calculations or impressions for they are right." The spirit promised that Marble would recover a treasure, proving to a skeptical world that spiritualism was the way to divine knowledge.[39]

Treasure seeking closely paralleled, and occasionally intersected with, the evangelical proliferation in the rural Northeast. New evangelical sects enjoyed the same autonomy from orthodox authority that enabled treasure seeking to prosper in the backcountry. In a recent study Stephen Marini describes how evangelical sects emerged from dialogues between religious seekers collected into local prayer groups and charismatic preachers. He describes northern New England's evangelical seekers as marginal farmers discontented with their lot in the material world—the same sort of folk who sought treasure. The religious dynamic identified by Marini closely parallels Kendall's description of how treasure seers like Daniel Lambert gave "new food to the credulity of the multitude, and a fresh excitement to the inclination, constantly lurking in its mind, to depend for a living upon digging for money-chests, rather than upon daily and ordinary labour. The belief in the existence of thse buried money-chests, and the consequent inclination to search for them, is imbibed in infancy; and there wants nothing but the slightest occasion to awaken both."[40]

Backcountry treasure beliefs were widespread but ordinarily dormant. A charismatic seer encouraged men and women to act on their treasure beliefs: to become active seekers. When the young Smith of Rochester, New York began in 1814 to evince his skill with a seer-stone, "Numbers flocked to him to test his skill, and the first question among a certain class was, if there was any of Kidd's money hid in these parts in the earth." His confirmation that treasures abounded inspired numerous digging parties. According to the Palmyra *Reflector*, Joseph Smith, Sr.'s arrival in 1817 "revived . . . the vulgar yet popular belief" in abundant local treasure chests. The importance of a charismatic seer to the development of an extensive treasure-seeking episode helps to explain why treasure seeking was far from universal, even within the many towns that resembled Rome, Palmyra, Canaan, and Norridgewock in their stagnation. Many communities possessed the potential for such episodes but not all experienced the advent of a persuasive and charismatic treasure seer.[41]

Just as many treasure seekers found religious faith essential to their enterprise, some evangelical preachers found "rodomancy" a useful way to attract adherents who longed for tangible experience with the supernatural. In 1806 the first Universalist minister in western New York, M. T. Wooley of Hartwick, mixed avid treasure seeking with his preaching. Willard Chase, Palmyra's

Methodist preacher, avidly collaborated with the Smith family in their treasure seeking. The "New Israelites" of Middletown, Vermont also synthesized evangelical religion and treasure seeking. In 1789 Nathaniel Wood, Sr. and his extensive connections announced that they were the descendants of the ancient Jews and established their own separate church. In 1799 a seer named Wingate arrived in Middletown as a guest of the Woods and of William Cowdry in adjoining Wells, Vermont. The Woods began to feature divining rods in their rituals, insisting that the rods' jerks in answer to their questions represented divine messages. The town's historian recalled that "by the use of the rod many converts were added, and the zeal of all increased and continued to increase until it amounted to a distraction." Under Wingate's direction, for two years the New Israelites employed their rods to predict the future, seek lost property, detect valuable medicinal roots, search for buried treasures, and to order the construction, and then abandonment, of a "temple." They expected to find sufficient gold to pave the streets of the "New Jerusalem" that they planned to construct. In late 1800 Wingate and the Woods employed the rods to predict the end of the world on the night of January 14, 1801. When January 15 arrived on schedule, and shortly thereafter, when it was learned that Wingate had been a counterfeiter, the sect collapsed in local disgrace. Most of the members, including the Woods, migrated to western New York.[42]

A direct link can be drawn between the New Israelites and the Mormon church founded by Joseph Smith, Jr. in 1830. Both faiths stressed millenialism, confidence in their Jewish ancestry, insistence of recapturing Christian Primitivism, a separatist notion of building a New Jerusalem, and reliance on latter-day prophecies. There is also a genealogical connection. William Cowdry, the father of Oliver Cowdry who helped transcribe the *Book of Mormon* was a New Israelite. Some Middletowners who later moved to Palmyra claimed that they found Wingate there assisting the Smiths in their treasure seeking under an assumed name, perhaps the "magician Walters."[43]

No doubt the Smiths would have welcomed the discovery of a treasure chest to ease their material lot, and the pay young Joseph earned divining lost property, blessing neighbors' crops to preserve them from frost, or helping patrons search for buried treasure was a welcome supplement to the household income. But the Smiths sought far more than material rewards. Just as the New Israelites had used their divining rods, Joseph Smith, Jr. employed his seer-stone to communicate with God. The Smiths believed that young Joseph's talent indicated that God intended him for great things. At his 1826 trial before a justice of the peace in South Bainbridge, New York on the charge that his "glasslooking" disturbed the peace, Joseph Smith, Jr. testified that when he looked at his stone he "discovered that time, place and distance were annihilated; that all the intervening obstacles were removed, and that he possessed one of the attributes of Deity, an All-Seeing Eye." Indeed, the Smiths were not entirely comfortable with the patrons' materialistic employment of young Joseph's spiritual talents. At the trial Joseph Smith, Sr. testified that he was "mortified" that his son's "wonderful power which God had so miraculously given him should be used only in search of filthy lucre." He hoped that in time God would "illumine the heart of the boy, and enable him to see His will concerning Him."[44]

DECAY

Accumulated disappointments slowly took their toll of treasure seeking, as both a supernatural economy and a materialistic faith. Unless they continued their expansion, institutionalized their leadership and procedures, and harnessed their prophetic anarchy, evangelical sects enjoyed but a short and tumultous life. This was particularly true when they dabbled in treasure seeking, exposing their members to disillusionment by rashly promising material returns on their faith in the immediate future. The Wood family's failure to find treasure or to predict accurately the end of the world doomed the New Israelites. Hiram Marble's lifetime of fruitless quarrying in Lynn for a pirate's treasure discredited rather than supported his cherished spiritualism. Meanwhile itinerant preachers from the more institutionalized denominations gradually consolidated northern New England's groups of religious seekers. This reincorporation into the intellectual currents of the wider culture inhibited the earlier, localized spiritual spontaneity that had spilled over into treasure seeking. For example, the Universalist General Conference disowned and dismissed T. M. Wooley for his experimentation with "rodomancy." In developing the Mormon faith, Joseph Smith, Jr. avoided the New Israelites' fatal error of banking upon material rewards in this world. Early Mormonism graphically promised tangible riches, power, and glory to its believers but only after death. Consequently, Mormonism not only emerged from concerns with treasure seeking, it helped supplant the latter by recruiting its adherents and redirecting their efforts.[45]

Clever frauds discredited treasure seeking as a supernatural economy, disabusing many rural folk of their treasure beliefs. The early Republic was a golden age of imposters and counterfeiting because standards of trust in economic relationships lagged behind the escalating velocity of human movements and transactions. Because economic transformation was gradual and locally differential, opportunities developed for shrewd men to exploit the lax security of laggard districts. The treasure seekers in those areas were particularly ripe for exploitation because they wanted so badly for their beliefs to be true. In Morris County, Ransford Rogers proved an entrepreneurial-imposter who reportedly cleared £500 in gifts levied from his several dozen followers to mollify guardian spirits and persuade them to release their treasure. He fled the area to reenact similar scams in Adams County, Pennsylvania and Exeter, New Hampshire. Daniel Lambert banked on his reputed treasure to obtain livestock and produce in great quantities on credit from his neighbors. He set June 20,

1804 as the date of repayment in gold·and promised all takers free rum and a public dinner at Ware's store in Norridgewock. He resold the livestock and produce for cash and fled to Canada before the appointed day.[46]

Of course, the desire to find buried treasure outlasted faith in the efficacy of occult techniques to secure them. Although settlers carried their search for treasure westward to the Pacific, western treasure tales deemphasized spiritual obstacles in favor of natural obstructions: landslides, erosion, and collapsed tunnels. Finding a lost Spanish mine in the West became more a matter of reading the landscape correctly and obtaining a proper map, than of the use of seer-stones, divining rods, magic circles, and the rule of silence.[47]

TABLE 1:

Treasure-Seeking Episodes In The American Northeast

Location	Year	Buriers	Methods
1. Chichester, Pa.	1695-6	?	rods[48]
2. Philadelphia, Pa.	1729	Pirates	rods, astrology[49]
3. Lebanon, Ct.	1752	Pirates	?[50]
4. Middleboro, Ma.	1756	?	rods[51]
5. New Haven, Ct.	1785	Pirates	?[52]
6. Rutland, Vt.	1785	Settler	rods, conjurer[53]
7. Whitingham, Vt.	1786	Pirates	rods[54]
8. Morris County, N.J.	1788-9	Pirates	seances[55]
9. Adams County, Pa.	1797	?	seances[56]
10. Frankfort, Me.	1798	Pirates	rods[57]
11. Middletown, Poultney and Wells, Vt.	1799-1800	Pirates & Spanish	rods[58]
12. Exeter, N.H.	c. 1800	Pirates	rods[59]
13. Dalton, Ma.	c. 1800	Hessians	?[60]
14. Waitsfield, Vt.	1800	Pirates	dreams[61]
15. Kennebec Valley, Me.	1804	Pirates	dreams, rods[62]
16. Hartwick, N.Y.	1806	?	seer-stone[63]
17. Rome, N.Y.	1807	Soldiers	?[64]
18. Catskill, N.Y.	1807	Pirates	cat sacrifice[65]
19. Flushing, N.Y.	1807	?	?[66]
20. Georgetown, Me.	c. 1810	Pirates	rods[67]
21. Jewel's Island, Me.	c. 1810	Pirates	rods[68]
22. Little Falls, N.Y.	1810	?	?[69]
23. Rochester, N.Y.	1814	Pirates	seer-stone[70]
24. Pittston, Me.	1815-51	Pirates	seer-stone[71]
25. Marietta, Oh.	c. 1820	Spanish	rods[72]
26. Ogdensburgh, N.Y.	c. 1820	?	rods[73]
27. Ellisburgh, N.Y.	c. 1820	?	rods[74]
28. Groton, Ma.	c. 1821	Pirates	rods[75]

Location	Year	Buriers	Methods
29. Palmyra & Manchester, N.Y.	1817-27	Pirates & Indians	rods, dreams, & seer-stone[76]
30. Hancock & Antrim, N.H.	c. 1823	Pirates	rods[77]
31. Essex, Vt.	1824	Spanish	rods, seer-stone[78]
32. Tunbridge, Vt.	1825	?	rods, visions[79]
33. Afton, N.Y.	1825-6	Spanish	rods, seer-stone[80]
34. Harmony, Pa.	1825-6	Spanish	rods, seer-stone[81]
35. Middlesex, Vt.	1825-6	Pirates	seer-stone[82]
36. New London, Ct.	1827	Pirates	seer-stone[83]
37. Bristol, Vt.	1830-50	Spanish	?[84]
38. Lynn, Ma.	1834-86	Pirates	seances[85]
39. York, Me.	c. 1835	Pirates	rods, ball[86]
40. Lake George, N.Y.	1842	Soldiers	rods[87]
41. Crown Point, N.Y.	c. 1845	Soldiers	?[88]
42. Brandon, Vt.	c. 1860	Spanish	?[89]
43. Harmony, Pa.	c. 1870	Spanish	?[90]
44. Monmouth, Me.	?	Pirates	dreams[91]
45. Braintree, Vt.	?	?	dreams, rods[92]
46. Northfield, Ma.	?	Pirates	?[93]
47. Weare, N.H.	?	Pirates	rods[94]
48. Stockton Springs, Me.	?	Pirates	rods[95]

Possible Treasure-Seeking Episodes From
Folklore Sources[96]

49. Wernersville, Pa. (Tories)
50. Cold Spring Bay, N.Y. (Pirates)
51. Shark River, N.J. (Pirates)
52. Sale, Ma. (Pirates)
53. Dighton Rock, Ma. (Pirates)
54. Oneida Lake, N.Y. (Pirates)
55. Hell's Gate, N.Y. (Pirates)
56. Monhegan, Me. (Pirates)
57. Milford, Ct. (Pirates)
58. Ipswich, Ma. (Pirates)
59. Lyme, Ct. (Pirates)
60. Portsmouth, N.H. (Pirates)
61. Medford, Ma. (Pirates)
62. Martha's Vineyard, Ma. (Pirates)
63. Schoharie County, N.Y. (Pirates)

NOTES

[1]Edward Augustus Kendall, *Travels Through the Northern Parts of the United States in the Years 1807 and 1808* (New York, 1809), III:85; John W. Hanson, *History of the Old Towns, Norridgewock and Canaan* . . . (Boston, 1849), 148-50. Kendall, who visited Canaan and Norridgewock in 1807, dates the episode to 1804. At a much later date an eyewitness to the affair, William Allen, Jr., of Industry, Me., penned his reminiscences and dated the episode to 1801. Kendall must be correct because court records indicate Lambert's presence in Canaan until 1804. See William Allen, Jr., "Pittsfield, Maine," in William Allen, Jr., Papers, Maine Historical Society. No newspaper was published within forty miles of Canaan and Norridgewock to provide contemporary comment.

[2]Kendall, *Travels*, III:86; Hanson, *Norridgewock*, 148-50.

[3]Kendall, *Travels*, II:87-88; John W. Hanson, *History of Gardiner, Pittston, and West Gardiner* (Gardiner, Me., 1852), 168; Hanson, *Norridgewock*, 148-50. The fact that the English-born Kendall left the beaten path to travel to Canaan, Maine suggests that he was related to Abiatha Kendall, an English-born settler, who was probably his chief informant. For the Kendall family in Cannan see Clarence I. Chato, "History of Canaan," Maine State Library.

[4]In recent years there has been a spirited debate among historians over the "mentalité" of rural folk in pre-industrial New England. Some argue that rural folk tended to forsake individual economic advantage because familial and community ties were preeminent. Others insist upon the primacy of individual self-interest in rural economic behavior. The most pointed exchange in this debate occurs in James A. Henretta, "Families and Farms: Mentalité in Pre-Industrial America," *William and Mary Quarterly*, 3rd ser., 37 (1980), 688-700. For a recent summation of the abundant literature on this debate see Bettye Hobbs Pruitt, "Self-Sufficiency and the Agricultural Economy of Eighteenth-Century Massachusetts," ibid., 41 (1984), 334n.

[5]Klaus J. Hanson, *Mormonism and the American Experience* (Chicago: Univ. of Chicago Press, 1981), 90-91.

[6]"Golden Bible, No. 3," *The Reflector* (Palmyra, N.Y.), 1 Feb. 1831, reprinted in Francis W. Kirkham, *A New Witness For Christ in America: The Book of Mormon* (Salt Lake City: Utah Printing Co., 1967), II:69. The Windsor, Vermont newspaper is quoted in Fawn M. Brodie, *No Man Knows My History: The Life of Joseph Smith, the Mormon Prophet* (New York: A. A. Knopf, 1974), 18. For the three-man rule see J. H. Temple and George Sheldon, *History of the Town of Northfield, Massachusetts* (Albany, N.Y., 1875), 18-19.

[7]On Pittston, see Hanson, *Gardiner*, 185; on Frankfort see George J. Varney, *A Gazetteer of the State of Maine with Numerous Illustrations* (Boston, 1882), 471; and Henry Buxton, *Assignment Down East* (Brattleboro, Vt.: Stephen Daye Press, 1938), 173; Benjamin Franklin and Joseph Breitnal, "The Busy-Body, No. 8," in Franklin, *The Papers of Benjamin Franklin*, ed. Leonard W. Labaree (New Haven: Yale Univ. Press, 1959), I:136; on Bristol see Dorson, *Jonathan*, 185; for the traveler's quote see Curtis B. Norris, "The Ghost Shaft of Bristol Notch," in Austin N. Stevens, ed., *Mysterious New England* (Dublin, N.H.: Yankee, Inc., 1971), 318; William Little, *The History of Weare, New Hampshire* (Lowell, Mass., 1888), 589; L. C. Butler, "Essex," in Abby M. Hemenway, ed., *The Vermont Historical Gazetteer* (Burlington, Vt., 1867), I:785. For the mid-century writer see "The History of the Divining Rod: with the Adventures of an Old Rodsman," *The United States Magazine and Democratic Review*, 26 (1850), 218, 223.

[8]On the Kidd legends see Dorson, *Jonathan*, 174, on the Spanish see 185; and "History of the Divining Rod," 222, on Ohio see 224; Rev. W. R. Cochrane, *History of the Town of Antrim, New Hampshire* (Manchester, N.H., 1880), 317; and Caleb Butler, *History of the Town of Groton* (Boston, 1848), 256n; on the Spanish see Butler, "Essex," I:784-85; on New York see Donna Hill, *Joseph Smith, The First Mormon* (Garden City, N.Y.: Doubleday, 1977), 66-67; on New York and Ohio see Curtis Dahl, "Mound Builders, Mormons, and William Cullen Bryant," *New England Quarterly*, 34 (1961), 178-79. The component details of this treasure belief complex are frequently found in treasure tales from Europe and Asia. See Stith Thompson, *The Folktale* (New York: Dryden Press, 1946), 262-63; and Emelyn E. Gardner, *Folklore from the Schoharie Hills, New York* (Ann Arbor: Univ. of Michigan Press, 1937), 13n. Because treasure folklore is an American universal it is likely that treasure seeking was also an historical phenomenon in the South as well. For Louisiana see Lyle Saxon, *Gumbo Ya-Ya* (Boston: Houghton-Mifflin Co., 1945), 258-70; on North Carolina see the *Frank C. Brown Collection of North Carolina Folklore* (Durham, N.C.: Duke Univ. Press, 1952-64), I: 691-95; on the far West see Gerald T. Hurley, "Buried Treasure Tales in America," *Western Folklore*, 10 (1951), 197-216.

[9]"Imposition and Blasphemy!!—Money-diggers, Etc," *The Gem* (Rochester, N.Y.), 15 May 1830, reprinted in Kirkham, *A New Witness*, II:48; on the summer as best see Peter Ingersoll's

affidavit, 2 Dec. 1833, reprinted in ibid., II:135; Clark Jillson, *Green Leaves from Whitingham, Vermont* (Worcester, Mass., 1894), 121; Butler, "Essex," 785; *An Account of the Beginning, Transactions and Discovery of Ransford Rogers, Who Seduced Many By Pretended Hobgoblins and Apparitions, And Thereby Extorted Money From their Pockets* (Newark, N. J., 1792, Evans #24754), 12; for a new moon as best see William Stafford affidavit, 8 Dec. 1833 in E. D. Howe, *History of Mormonism: or a Faithful Account of That Singular Impositions and Delusion* (Painesville, Oh., 1840), 237-38; for a full moon as best see *Frank C. Brown Collection*, I:695.

¹⁰On dreams see Kendall, *Travels*, III:84-85; Dorson, *Jonathan*, 184; Charles M. Skinner, *Myths and Legends of Our Own Land* (Philadelphia: J. B. Lippincott Co., 1924), II:268; Gardner, *Folklore*, 14-15; Rev. P. B. Fisk, "Waitsfield," in Hemenway, *Vermont*, IV:776; *Frank C. Brown Collection*, I:693. On Smith's dress see *The Gem* (Rochester, N. Y.), 5 Sept. 1829, reprinted in Kirkham, *A New Witness*, I:151. Hamilton's journal is reprinted in Jillson, *Green Leaves*, 115-18. Evidence of the treasure seeking by Joseph Smith, Jr., and his father, Joseph Smith., Sr. prior to Joseph's recovery of the golden bible has engendered heated controversy. Beginning in the 1830s anti-Mormon writers zealously gathered testimony that they treated as proof that the Smiths were, first, unique in their activity, and, consequently, peculiarly indolent, deceitful, credulous, and greedy. In response to these attacks, Mormon writers have, until recently, felt compelled to dismiss all evidence that the Smiths engaged in treasure seeking as trumped-up by their enemies. This stand has perpetuated the anti-Mormons' erroneous presumption that treasure seeking was rare and symptomatic of moral bankruptcy. Fortunately, Mormon scholars have recently taken a sounder stand that much of the evidence of the Smiths' treasure seeking is credible, but that this in no way proves that Joseph Smith, Jr., was insincere in his religious faith then or subsequently. Indeed, treasure seeking represented a relatively immature but sincere manifestation of the religious concerns that he eventually refined into the Book of Mormon. For an example of the anti-Mormon interpretation see Pomeroy Rucker, *Origin, Rise, and Progress of Mormonism* (New York, 1867), 20-22. For a Mormon denial of the Smiths' treasure seeking see Hugh Nibley, *The Myth Makers* (Salt Lake City: Bookcraft, 1961), 182-89. For the more sophisticated recent work by Mormon scholars see D. Hill, *Joseph Smith*; Marvin S. Hill, "Joseph Smith and the 1826 Trial: New Evidence and New Difficulties," *Brigham Young University Studies*, 12 (1972), 231; Linda King Newell and Valeen Tippets Avery, *Mormon Enigma: Emma Hale Smith* (Garden City, N.Y.: Doubleday, 1984); and Richard L. Bushman, *Joseph Smith and the Beginnings of Mormonism* (Chicago and Urbana: Univ. of Chicago Press, 1984), 64-76. For the persistence of the anti-Mormon perspective see David Persuitte, *Joseph Smith and the Origins of the Book of Mormon* (Jefferson, N.C., 1985). In April and May 1985 The Church of Jesus Christ of Latter-day Saints * released two letters that document Joseph Smith, Jr.'s early career as a treasure-seer: Martin Harris to William W. Phelps, 23 Oct. 1830 in The Church of Jesus Christ of Latter-day Saints, *Church News*, 28 April 1985, 6; and Joseph Smith, Jr., to Josiah Stowell, 18 June 1825 in ibid., 12 May 1985, 10.

¹¹On young Smith of Rochester see "Impositions and Blasphemy . . . " *The Gem* (Rochester, N.Y.), 15 May 1830 reprinted in Kirkham, *A New Witness*, II:46; on Smith's seer-stone see Fayette Lapham, "Interview with the Father of Joseph Smith, the Mormon Prophet, Forty Years Ago," *The Historical Magazine*, 2nd ser., 7 (1970), reprinted in ibid., II:384; Brodie, *No Man*, 435-37; George W. Cowles, *Landmarks of Wayne County, New York* (Syracuse, N.Y., 1895), 80-81; Emily C. Blackman, *History of Susquehannah County, Pennsylvania* (Philadelphia, 1873), 580; and Pomeroy Tucker, *Origin, Rise and Progress of Mormonism* (New York, 1867), 19. Also see George Williamson to William D. Williamson, c. 1820, filed under "Pittston" in Maine Town File of the Willam D. Williamson Papers, Maine Historical Society, and Hanson, *Gardiner*, 169. See also Butler, "Essex," I:785.

¹²"History of the Divining Rod," 218-19, 319; Kendall, *Travels*, II:84-85, 101; Barnes Frisbie, *The History of Middletown, Vermont in Three Discourses* (Rutland, Vt., 1867), 47; and Robert Parks and Hiland Paul, *History of Wells, Vermont, For the First Century After Its Settlement*, 82; Herbert Leventhal, *In the Shadow of the Enlightenment: Occultism and Renaissance in Eighteenth-Century America* (New York: New York Univ. Press, 1976), 111; Temple and Sheldon, *Northfield*, 18-19; Buxton, *Assignment*, 169; Hanson, *Gardiner*, 168; on a soft whisper see Peter Ingersoll's affidavit, 2 Dec. 1833 in Kirkham, *A New Witness*, II:134-35; on a slow step see "The Divining Rod," *American Journal of Science*, 11 (1826), 203; on Smith's alternative see Joseph Smith, Jr. to Josiah * Stowell, 18 June 1825 reprinted in The Church of Jesus Christ of Latter-day Saints, *Church News*, 12 May 1985, 10.

¹³Gardner, *Folklore*, 13-15; Leventhal, *In the Shadow*, 113; Skinner, *Myths*, II:268-89; Kendall,

Travels, 84-85; Dorson. *Jonathan*, 174-76; *An Account*, 10; "History of the Divining Rod," 223; Benjamin A. Botkin, ed., *A Treasury of New England Folklore* (New York: Crown Publishers, 1947), 322; Parks and Paul, *Wells*, 80; on Palmyra see Martin Harris quoted in Kirkham, *A New Witness*, II:378.

¹⁴Jillson, *Green Leaves*, 121; Kendall, *Travels*, III:84-85; *An Account*, 12-13; Butler, *Groton*, 256n; Leventhal, *In the Shadow*, 107-11; Andrew Barton [Thomas Forrest], *The Disappointment: or the Force of Credulity* (Philadelphia, 1767, Evans #10554), 41; "Gold Bible, No. 5," *The Reflector* (Palmyra, N. Y.), 28 Feb. 1831, reprinted in Kirkham, *A New Witness*, II:73-74; on Joseph Smith, Jr.'s circle see Joseph Capron's affidavit, 8 Nov. 1833 in Howe, *History*, 259; on his father's circle see William Stafford's affidavit, 8 Dec. 1883, in ibid., 238; on breaking Spanish enchantments see "History of the Divining Rod," 224-25. On a magic triangle see Temple and Sheldon, *Northfield*, 18-19.

¹⁵"The Book of Pukei—Chapter 1," *The Reflector* (Palmyra, N. Y.), 22 June 1830, reprinted in Kirkham, *A New Witness*, II:51; Harriet A. Weed, ed., *Autobiography of Thurlow Weed* (Boston, 1884), I:7; on a similar black cat sacrifice see Gardner, *Folklore*, 13-15; on Smith's use of blood in his circles see Tucker, *Origin*, 24; Blackman, *Susquehannah*, 580; and William Stafford's affidavit, 8 Dec. 1833, in Howe, *History*, 239; on Hamilton's circle see Jillson, *Green Leaves*, 119. It is interesting that later in life Weed became a vigorous foe to Mormonism, the faith founded by another New York treasure seeker, Joseph Smith, Jr. See Weed's introduction to Mrs. Ellen Dickinson, *New Light on Mormonism* (New York, 1885).

¹⁶Gardner, *Folklore*, 13; Blackman, *Susquehannah*, 577; Jillson, *Green Leaves*, 121; Skinner, *Myths*, II:269; Dorson, *Jonathan*, 174; Parks and Paul, *Wells*, 80; "History of the Diving Rod," 320; Temple and Sheldon, *Northfield*, 181-19; Little, *Weare*, 589; L. C. Butler, "Essex," I:785; C. Butler, *Groton*, 256n; on stepped-on toes see Frisbie, *Middletown*, 48-49; on Rochester see "Imposition and Blasphemy . . ." *The Gem* (Rochester, N.Y.), 15 May 1930, reprinted in Kirkham, *A New Witness*, II:48; Tucker, *Origin*, 21.

¹⁷Parks and Paul, *Wells*, 80; Brodie, *No Man*, 428; Leventhal, *In the Shadow*, 113; Marvin S. Hill, "Joseph Smith and the 1826 Trial: New Evidence and New Difficulties," *Brigham Young University Studies*, 12 (1972), 230; Cowles, *Landmarks*, 81; Frisbie, *Middletown*, 48, 51; the eyewitness is quoted by Kendall, *Travels*, III:89; Thompson quoted in Brodie, *No Man*, 429; on Rutland see "Rutland," in Hemenway, *The Vermont Historical Gazetteer* (Claremont, N.H., 1877), III:1090; on the Braintree money pot see Bass, *Braintree*, 46.

¹⁸On small accidental discoveries see Dorson, *Jonathan*, 179; D. Hill, *Joseph Smith*, 68; and Buxton, *Assignment*, 179. Some Rochester diggers insisted that they found a chest but the local editor was suspicious of their claim. See "Imposition and Blasphemy . . ." in *The Gem* (Rochester, N.Y.), 15 May 1830, reprinted in Kirkham, *A New Witness*, II:48. Rumors "of the private success of some people" sustained dickers around Philadelphia according to Benjamin Franklin and Joseph Breitnal, "The Busy-Body, No. 8," in *Franklin Papers*, I:137. On Gardiner see Hanson, *Gardiner*, 169; on the Commodore see "History of the Divining Rod"; on Pennsylvania see Blackman, *Susquehannah County*, 580; on Vermont see "Rutland," 1090.

¹⁹The folklorist Gerald T. Hurley treats treasure tales as exclusively fictions with standard conventions: "The treasure tale is presented as fact and told with the same sense of literal truth that marks newspaper accounts of actual rediscovered gold." See Hurley, "Buried Treasure Tales," 197-98n. On Savage see Fisk, "Waitsfield," 776; the Martin Harris interview is reprinted from
* *Tiffany's Magazine*, May 1859 in Kirkham, *A New Witness*, II:378; Martin Harris to William Phelps, 23 Oct. 1830, reprinted in The Church of Jesus Christ of Latter-day Saints, *Church News*, 28 April 1985, 6. (Harris's letter is one, long, unpunctuated "sentence"; for easier reading I have inserted the necessary punctuation and capitalization; otherwise the letter is verbatim.) The 1826 assessment is in "The Divining Rod," 203.

²⁰On the early presence of treasure beliefs in and around early eighteenth-century Philadelphia see Leventhal, *In the Shadow*, 107-18; for treasure seeking in sixteenth- and seventeenth-century England see Keith Thomas, *Religion and the Decline of Magic* (New York: Scribner's, 1971), 234-37; John Brand, *Observations on the Popular Antiquities of Great Britain* (London, 1849), III:332-33; and Jonathan Swift, *The Virtues of Sid Hamet the Magician's Rod* (London, 1710); the quote is from "The Busy-Body, No. 8," *Franklin Papers*, I:136.

²¹Gordon S. Wood, "Evangelical America and Early Mormonism," *New York History*, 61 (1980), 363-70; Hansen, *Mormonism*, 73-77. The gentleman's quote appears in Kendall, *Travels*,

III:96. For the social function of volunteer societies and religious sects in America's fluid society see Don Harrison Doyle, *The Social Order of a Frontier Community: Jacksonville, Illinois, 1825-1870* (Urbana: Univ. of Illinois Press, 1978), 156-93. For an example of an orthodox Congregational minister who exercised his influence over a Massachusetts town against conjuring see Francis G. Walett, ed., *The Diary of Ebenezer Parkman, 1703-1782; Part I: 1719-1755* (Worcester, Mass.: American Antiquarian Society, 1974), 288.

[22]On the early eighteenth-century adherence to treasure beliefs of some well-educated men see Leventhal, *In the Shadow*, 107-15; on the similar decay of witchcraft beliefs occurring first among the elite, and only later among the common folk see John Putnam Demos, *Entertaining Satan: Witchcraft and the Culture of Early New England* (New York: Oxford Univ. Press, 1982), 393; on the discontinuity of elite and lower-class supernatural beliefs in England see Thomas, *Religion and the Decline of Magic*, 666. Thomas Forrest was probably the author of Barton, *The Disappointment*, see especially iv, 7, 55.

[23]"The Divining Rod," 202-03; Mason Wade, ed., *The Journals of Francis Parkman* (New York: Harper, 1947), I:47, 53. On criticism of rural folk see Robert A. Gross, "Culture and Cultivation: Agriculture and Society in Thoreau's Concord," *Journal of American History*, 69 (1982), 42-61.

[24]James Fenimore Cooper, *The Pioneers; or the Sources of the Susquehanna* (New York: G. P. Putnam's Sons, 1851), 327, 467.

[25]For the first observer see "History of the Divining Rod," 218; for Morris County see *An Account*, 7-8, 20; for Lambert see Kendall, *Travels*, III:90-92; William Scales to Henry Knox, Thomaston, 29 July 1805, Henry Knox Papers, vol. 46, item #67, Massachusetts Historical Society. See also Wood, "Evangelical America," 369-70; David D. Hall, "A World of Wonders: The Mentality of the Supernatural in Seventeenth-Century New England," in *Seventeenth-Century New England* (Boston: Colonial Society of Massachusetts, 1985), 239-73; and Demos, *Entertaining Satan*, 387-93.

[26]Hansen, *Mormonism*, 42; Hurley, "Buried Treasure Tales," 199; on the Universalist see "History of the Divining Rod," 327; Whitney R. Cross, *The Burned-Over District: The Social and Intellectual History of Enthusiastic Religion in Western New York, 1800-1850* (Ithaca: Cornell Univ. Press, 1950), 81; *An Account*, v. On American spiritualism see R. Laurence Moore, *In Search of White Crows: Spiritualism, Parapsychology, and American Culture* (New York: Oxford Univ. Press, 1977), 3-39; and Howard Kerr, *Mediums, and Spirit-Rappers, and Roaring Radicals: Spiritualism in American Literature, 1850-1900* (Urbana: Univ. of Illinois Press, 1972). On the pliancy of tradition to fit changing cultural needs see Alfred F. Young, "English Plebeian Culture and Eighteenth-Century American Radicalism," in Margaret and James Jacob, eds., *The Origins of Anglo-American Radicalism* (London, Allen & Unwin, 1984), 186-89. I would emphasize here the interaction of "popular" and "high" culture rather than their separation as seems to be argued in Jon Butler, "The Future of American Religious History: Prospectus, Agenda, Transatlantic Problematique," *William and Mary Quarterly*, 3rd ser., 42 (1985), 167-83.

[27]On persistent experimentation despite repeated discouragement see "Golden Bible, No. 3," *The Reflector* (Palmyra, N. Y.), 1 Feb. 1831, reprinted in Kirkham, *A New Witness*, II:69; and *An Account*, 9-10; and "Rutland," 1090; on Joseph Smith's dress see Lapham, "Interview," in Kirkham, *A New Witness*, II:385-87; Willard Chase's affidavit, 11 Dec. 1833, in Howe, *History of Mormonism*, 242; and Martin Harris to William W. Phelps, 23 Oct. 1830, reprinted in The Church of Jesus Christ of Latter-day Saints, *Church News*, 28 April 1985, 6.

[28]A decade later Rogers conducted a similar treasure search in Exeter, New Hampshire and demanded that the seekers wear white caps while digging. *An Account*, 9, 13-14, 19; Charles H. Bell, *History of Exeter, New Hampshire* (Boston, Mass., 1888), 412.

[29]George M. Foster, "Treasure Tales, and the Image of the Static Economy in a Mexican Peasant Community," *Journal of American Folklore*, 77 (1964), 39-40. Stith Thompson similarly argues that treasure tales express "the frustration that comes from thwarted ambition." See Thompson, *The Folktale*, 262.

[30]The blacksmith is quoted in "Rutland," 1087; Joseph Smith, Sr.'s aspirations are quoted in Joseph Capon's affidavit, 8 Nov. 1833 in Howe, *History of Mormonism*, 260; the Sandy River Valley settler is quoted in Kendall, *Travels*, III:96; Peter Ingersoll's affidavit, 2 Dec. 1833 in Kirkham, *A New Witness*, II:135; see also Rowell Nichols' affidavit, 1 Dec. 1833, in Howe, *History of Mormonism*, 257.

[31]On Stowell, see Kirkham, *A New Witness*, II:363-63; on Harper see Blackman, *Susquehannah*,

580; on Morris County see *An Account*, 9; on Hamilton see Clark Jillson, "Whitingham," in Hemenway, *The Vermont Historical Gazetteer* (Brandon, Vt., 1891); on the Woods see Frisbie, *Middletown*, 59, 109-10. See also Bell, *Exeter*, 412.

³²For the quote see *An Account*, vi. On the Smiths' poverty see Kirkham, *A New Witness*, I:32, 50; Cross, *Burned-Over District*, 138-40; Tucker, *Origin*, 11-16; Brodie, *No Man*, 10-18; and Bushman, *Joseph Smith*, 47-49. According the 1798 Federal Direct Tax Return for Canaan, Lambert owned 100 acres of barely developed land, and dwelled in a log cabin judged by the assessors to be of no real value. He ranked sixtieth out of that settlement's 106 taxpayers. Three years later, a state valuation return for Canaan showed a similar picture; Lambert still lived in a crude log cabin, possessed no barn, and owned 100 acres; only two of those acres were improved and forty-nine, or about half the homestead, were judged "unimprovable." He owned no horse, no oxen, but a single cow, and a lone pig. See the Canaan, Maine return, 1798 Direct Tax Returns for Massachusetts-Maine, I:351, New England Historic Genealogical Society Library; and the Canaan, Maine tax valuation, Maine valuation returns for 1801, reel 397, Massachusetts State Library.

³³On female seers see Skinner, *Myths*, II:282; M. S. Hill, "1826 Trial," 229; D. Hill, *Joseph Smith*, 68; Blackman, *Susquehannah*, 577; and Newell and Avery, *Mormon Enigma*, 22. On the dreams in Hamilton's journal see the excerpt in Jillson, *Green Leaves*, 115-18. On Marks see Botkin, *A Treasury*, 533-34. On "Mike" see Hanson, *Gardiner*, 169; and George Williamson to William D. Williamson, c. 1820, William D. Williamson Town Papers, filed under "Pittston." For Rollins see George A. Emery, *Ancient City of Gorgeana and Modern Town of York* (Boston, 1874), 203. On adolescence as a time of psychological unease over identity see Hansen, *Mormonism*, 21. For another black treasure seer see James Dow McCallum, *Eleazar Wheelock* (Hanover, N. H.: Dartmouth College Publications, 1939), 52.

³⁴*An Account*, 7; Weed, *Autobiography*, I:2, 7; Christian Schultz, *Travels on an Inland Voyage Through the States . . .* (New York, 1810), 16. On the occasional participation of prosperous farmers see Blackman, *Susquehannah*, 580; Frisbie, *Middletown*, 59, 109-11; and Bell, *Exeter*, 412.

³⁵Kendall, *Travels*, III:72; Hanson, *Norridgewock*, 150-51; *Report of the Committee of Valuation* (Boston, Mass., 1802, Shaw-Shoemaker #2625), 6-14.

³⁶Samuel Weston et al. to the General Court Committee on Valuation, 20 Oct. 1801, at the end of Canaan's Tax Valuation, 1801 Maine valuations, reel 397, Massachusetts State Library. The inhabitants of these rural backwaters have generally escaped the attention of historians preoccupied with commercial centers and boom towns.

³⁷Wood, "Evangelical America," 368, 375. Jon Butler in his "Magic, Astrology, and the Early American Religious Heritage, 1600-1760," *American Heritage Review*, 84 (1979), 317-46 insists on a stark line between allegedly pagan "magic" and orthodox Christian "religion." He is more sensitive to their interrelationship in popular religion in his subsequent "The Dark Ages of American Occultism, 1760-1848," in Howard Kerr and Charles L. Crow, eds., *The Occult in America: New Historical Perspectives* (Urbana: Univ. of Illinois Press, 1983), 58-78.

³⁸For Smith see D. Hill, *Joseph Smith*, 66. For Rogers see *An Account*, 12, 20. For praying see Kirkham, *A New Witness*, II:367; Gardner, *Folklore*, 14-15; and Frisbie, *Middletown*, 48.

³⁹Joseph Smith, Jr., to the editor of the *Chicago Democrat*, 1 March 1843, reprinted in Kirkham, *A New Witness*, I:46-48; Cross, *Burned-Over District*, 138-50; Hansen, *Mormonism*, 28. For the quoted spirit addressing Marble see Alonzo Lewis and James R. Newhall, *History of Lynn, Essex County, Massachusetts* (Boston, 1865), 247.

⁴⁰Stephen Marini, *Radical Sects of Revolutionary New England* (Cambridge: Harvard Univ. Press, 1982), 1-7, 28-31, 53-55; Kendall, *Travels*, III:87. On the importance of childhood stories in preparing treasure seekers see also Fayette Lapham, "Interview with the Father of Joseph Smith, the Mormon Prophet, Forty Years ago," Kirkham, *A New Witness*, II:384; and "Rutland," in Hemenway, *The Vermont Historical Gazetteer* (Claremont, N. H. 1877), III:1087.

⁴¹For Rochester see "Imposition and Blasphemy!!—Money diggers, etc.," from *The Gem* (Rochester, N. Y.), 15 May 1830, reprinted in Kirkham, *A New Witness*, I:46-48. On Joseph Smith, Sr., see "Golden Bible, No. 3," *Palmyra Reflector* (Palmyra, N.Y.), 1 Feb. 1831, reprinted in ibid., II:68-69.

⁴²For Wooley see Nathaniel Stacy, *Memoirs of the Life of Nathaniel Stacy* (Columbus, Penn., 1850), 172. For Willard Chase see Newell and Avery, *Mormon Enigma*, 16. The "Wood scrape" is thoroughly documented in Frisbie, *Middletown*, 43-65, quotation 59. Barnes Frisbie was a local clergyman who in the 1850s and 1860s interviewed several elderly eyewitnesses and participants.

Frisbie was the grandson of a Middletown resident in 1801. See also Marini, *Radical Sects*, 54-55; and Parks and Paul, *Wells*, 79-80. The Woods called their divining rods "St. John's rod." This probably reflects survival of a folk tradition originating in seventeenth-century Germany that rods had to be cut on St. John's Day. Many sixteenth-century magical writers deemed the presence of a cleric essential to a successful treasure search; see Thomas, *Religion and the Decline of Magic*, 274.

[43]For the link see Frisbie, *Middletown*, 57, 62; and Marini, *Radical Sects*, 55. A Mormon historian quotes Joseph Smith, Sr., as declaring in a High Council Meeting that "he knew more about money digging than any man alive, had been at it for 30 years." See D. Hill, *Joseph Smith*, 67.

[44]Brodie, *No Man*, 427-29; Blackman, *Susquehannah*, 579-80; Tucker, *Origins*, 20. For the quotes see W. D. Purple's transcription of the 1826 trial record in Kirkham, *A New Witness*, II:356-66. See also M. S. Hill, "1826 Trial," 229.

[45]For Wooley see Stacy, *Memoirs*, 172. For the materialism of early Mormonism see Hansen, *Mormonism*, 42, 71, 92; and Wood, "Evangelical America," 385. For Mormonism's appeal to marginal farmers of Yankee descent see Hansen, *Mormonism*, 41-42, 82, 122, 202, 208; Cross, *Burned-Over District*, 143-49; and Wood, "Evangelical America," 381, 383. For Marble's failure see Lewis, *Lynn*, 445-71.

[46]For Rogers see *An Account*, 14-28; and Bell, *Exeter*, 411-13. For Lambert see Kendall, *Travels*, III:86-89; and Allen, "Pittsfield," 17. For the corrosive impact of fraud see *An Account*, vol. 26; Bell, *Exeter*, 413; "Rutland," 1087; Barton, *The Disappointment*, iv, 53.

[47]For the persistence of treasure seeking until the early twentieth century in a few obscure corners of the Northeast see Emelyn E. Gardner, "Folklore from Schoharie County, N. Y.," *Journal of American Folklore*, 27 (1914), 304, 323. On western tales see Hurley, "Buried Treasure," 200.

[48]Leventhal, *In the Shadow*, 109.

[49]Franklin and Breitnal, "The Busy Body, No. 8," *Franklin Papers*, I:137.

[50]McCallum, *Eleazar Wheelock*, 52.

[51]Leventhal, *In the Shadow*, 114.

[52]Hemenway, "Rutland," 1087.

[53]Ibid., 1089.

[54]Jillson, *Green Leaves*, 113.

[55]*An Account.*

[56]Bell, *Exeter*, 411.

[57]Dorson, *Jonathan*, 176.

[58]Frisbie, *Middletown*, 57-61; Parks and Paul, *Wells*, 80.

[59]Bell, *Exeter*, 413.

[60]Skinner, *Myths*, II:280.

[61]Fisk, "Waitsfield," 776.

[62]Kendall, *Travels*, III:86; Hanson, *Norridgewock*, 148-50; William Allen, Jr., "Pittsfield."

[63]Stacy, *Memoirs*, 172.

[64]Schultz, *Inland Voyage*, I:46.

[65]Weed, *Autobiography*, I:7.

[66]John Harriott, *Struggles Through Life* . . . (New York, 1809, Shaw-Shoemaker #17708), II:168-70.

[67]"History of the Divining Rod," 222.

[68]Ibid., 223.

[69]William W. Campbell, ed., *The Life and Writings of De Witt Clinton* (New York, 1849), 47.

[70] "Impositions and Blasphemy . . . " in *The Gem* (Rochester, N. Y.), 5 May 1830, reprinted in Kirkham, *A New Witness*, II:48.

[71]Hanson, *Gardiner*, 169.

[72]"History of the Divining Rod," 224.

[73]Benjamin Franklin Hough, *A History of St. Lawrence and Franklin Counties, New York, From the Earliest Period to the Present Time* (Albany, N. Y., 1853), 108-09.

[74]Benjamin Franklin Hough, *A History of Jefferson County in the State of New York, From the Earliest Period to the Present Time* (Watertown, N. Y., 1854), 158.

[75]Butler, *Groton*, 256n.

[76]"Golden Bible, No. 3," *The Reflector* (Palmyra, N. Y.), 1 Feb. 1831, reprinted in Kirkham, *A New Witness*, II:69, Bushman, *Joseph Smith*, 69-76.

[77]Cochrane, *Antrim*, 317.

[78]Butler, "Essex," 785.
[79]D. Hill, *Joseph Smith*, 68.
[80]Brodie, *No Man*, 429; Bushman, *Joseph Smith*, 69.
[81]Blackman, *Susquehannah*, 578-80.
[82]Stephen Herrick, "Middlesex," in Hemenway, *The Vermont Historical Gazetteer* (Montpelier, Vt., 1882), IV:241.
[83]D. Hill, *Joseph Smith*, 68; Skinner, *Myths*, II:282.
[84]C. B. Norris, "The Ghost Shaft," 317-19.
[85]Lewis and Newhall, *History of Lynn*, 248-49.
[86]Emery, *Ancient City*, 203.
[87]Wade, *The Journals of Francis Parkman*, I:47.
[88]Skinner, *Myths*, II:283.
[89]"Rutland," 1087.
[90]Blackman, *Susquehannah*, 580.
[91]Harry Hayman Cochrane, *History of Monmouth and Wales* (East Winthrop, Maine, 1894), 312.
[92]Bass, *Braintree*, 46.
[93]Temple and Sheldon, *Northfield*, 18-19.
[94]Little, *Weare*, 589.
[95]Dorson, *Jonathan*, 176.
[96]Skinner, *Myths*, II:268-89; and Gardiner, *Schoharie*, 13-15.